This Is a Big Book, But It Is Very Easy to Use

How do you earn a paycheck? With your skills. An impressive degree, personal contacts, and the slickest resume in town can only *suggest* your skills. They may get you hired, but to keep a job you need to *own* the relevant skills. That's why, when you are making career plans, you should think in terms of the jobs that match your skills—the skills you already have or believe you can develop.

This book can help you identify your top skills and learn about jobs that use those skills. It guides you through an exercise that makes you think about your skills in greater depth than you may have ever done before. Then you can browse lists of jobs in which your top skills are used at a high level. The jobs on the lists are selected and ordered to emphasize those with the highest earnings and the highest demand for workers. Specialized lists arrange these jobs by the level of education or training required and by interest fields. You can also see lists of jobs that have high percentages of part-time or self-employed workers.

Every job is described in detail later in the book, so you can explore the jobs that interest you the most. You'll learn the major work tasks, all the important skills, educational programs, and many other informative facts.

Using this book, you'll be surprised how quickly you'll get new ideas for career goals that can use your top skills and can suit you in many other ways.

Some Things You Can Do with This Book

- Identify jobs for your skills that don't require you to get additional training or education.
- Develop long-term career plans that may require additional training, education, or experience.
- Explore and select a training or educational program that relates to a career objective suited to your skills.
- Find skill information to emphasize on your resume.
- Prepare for interviews by learning how to connect your skills to your career goal.

These are a few of the many ways you can use this book. We hope you find it as interesting to browse as we did to put together. We have tried to make it easy to use and as interesting as occupational information can be.

When you are done with this book, pass it along or tell someone else about it. We wish you well in your career and in your life.

(continued)

(continued)

Credits and Acknowledgments: While the authors created this book, it is based on the work of many others. The occupational information is based on data obtained from the U.S. Department of Labor and the U.S. Census Bureau. These sources provide the most authoritative occupational information available. The job titles and their related descriptions are from the O*NET database, which was developed by researchers and developers under the direction of the U.S. Department of Labor. They, in turn, were assisted by thousands of employers who provided details on the nature of work in the many thousands of job samplings used in the database's development. We used the most recent version of the O*NET database, release 10.0. We appreciate and thank the staff of the U.S. Department of Labor for their efforts and expertise in providing such a rich source of data.

Table of Contents

Summary of Major Sections

Introduction. A short overview to help you better understand and use the book. *Starts on page 1.*

Part I. Overview of Skills and Careers. Part I defines what a skill is and discusses various ways you can develop your skills. It clarifies the relationship between skills and career choice, as well as the role skills play in the hiring process. Finally, it explains which skills are included in this book and how this book can help you focus on your skills. *Starts on page 13.*

Part II. What Are Your Top Skills? Take an Assessment. This part helps you identify your strongest skills with an in-depth assessment. *Starts on page 21.*

Part III. The Best Jobs Lists: Jobs for Each of the 10 Skills. Very useful for exploring career options! Lists are arranged into easy-to-use groups based on skills. The first group of lists presents the 50 best jobs with a high level of each skill. These jobs are selected to be outstanding in terms of earnings, job growth, and job openings. Another series of lists gives the 20 best-paying jobs with a high level of each skill, the 20 fastest-growing jobs with a high level of each skill, and the 20 jobs with the most openings with a high level of each skill. More-specialized lists follow, presenting the best jobs with a high level of each skill with high percentages of part-time and self-employed workers, the best jobs by level of education or training (with their top skills identified), and the best jobs with a high level of each skill by interest area, as well as several bonus lists. The detailed table of contents starting at right presents all the list titles. *Starts on page 47.*

Part IV. Descriptions of the Best Jobs for Your Skills. Provides complete descriptions of the jobs that appear on the lists in Part III. Each description contains information on skills, education and training required, earnings, projected growth, job duties, related knowledge and courses, and many other details. *Starts on page 167.*

Appendix A. Resources for Further Exploration. Lists several helpful resources for researching the facts about jobs and for learning how to conduct a successful job hunt. *Starts on page 451.*

Appendix B. The GOE Interest Areas and Work Groups. This list of the 16 GOE Interest Areas and their related Work Groups can help you narrow down your career interests. *Starts on page 453.*

Detailed Table of Contents

Foreword

Today's workplace is one of rapid change, challenge, and opportunity. To survive and prosper nowadays, you need to keep up with changing job requirements and be able to bounce back from layoffs and move on to new opportunities. In a word, you need to be resilient. This is true whether you are just starting out or have many years of work experience.

Skills are at the heart of resilience in the workplace. Everybody has skills, but most people have a hard time talking about their skills. A prospective employer asks you to identify your top skills for a job and give examples of how you've used those skills in the past. You're looking for a new job and wondering which of your skills are transferable. You're trying to figure out what your best skills are. When it comes to skills, you probably have more questions than answers. Where to begin?

This book can help you find the answers to your questions about skills. It organizes the overwhelming array of transferable skills into 10 major types, gives you an exercise to clarify your strongest transferable skills, and helps you identify examples of how you used your skills effectively. It also provides lists and descriptions of the best jobs that require your key skills. When you understand your skills, you can target jobs that use them and you can make a powerful case in your resume, cover letter, and interview for why you're the person who should get hired. It's also important to know what skills are your weak spots so you can work on improving them or develop team strategies for getting help when necessary.

Ready to begin? Use this book as the launchpad for exploring your transferable skills and your career options. You'll find it's a handy guide throughout your career as you continue to face changes, meet challenges, and explore new work opportunities.

Linda Kobylarz
President, Kobylarz & Associates
Career Consultants

Introduction

Not everybody will want to read this introduction. You may want to skip this background information and go directly to Part I, which discusses what skills are, how to develop your skills and use them in choosing a career, and how this book can help you identify your top skills. If you're really impatient, you may want to jump directly to Part II and start assessing your skills.

But if you want to understand how (and why) we put this book together, where the information comes from, and what makes a job "best," this introduction can answer a lot of questions.

Why Skills Deserve Their Own Book

Ask employers what they look for when they hire, and they'll say, "Somebody with the right skills." A few of the skills they seek are technical skills that are uniquely related to the job at hand. For example, an all-around automobile mechanic must be able to change an oil filter, balance a tire, and adjust a timing belt. But employers mostly look for skills that are important on almost every job—for example, communication, problem-solving, and getting along with others. Automobile mechanics, accountants, and architects all need these skills, and somebody who moves from being an automobile mechanic to being an accountant can transfer many of these skills to the new job. For that reason, they are usually called *transferable* skills.

Not all transferable skills can transfer to *all* work settings. Some are much more important in certain jobs than in other jobs, and some combinations of skills—for example, the combination of managerial skills, math skills, and programming skills—are needed at a high level in only a limited selection of jobs. In fact, each occupation in the U.S. economy demands a particular mix of transferable skills. That's why this book can help you. It uses information from the U.S. Department of Labor on the skill requirements of 265 jobs to help you identify the jobs that are the best match for your transferable skills. It also uses information about the economic rewards of jobs so you can identify the *best* jobs that match your skills.

For a more complete discussion of skills, see Part I. The rest of this introduction focuses on the information in this book: where it came from, what it means, and how it is organized.

1

Where the Information Came From

The information we used in creating this book came mostly from databases created by the U.S. Department of Labor:

- We started with the jobs and skill information included in the Department of Labor's O*NET (Occupational Information Network) database, which is now the primary source of detailed information on occupations. The Labor Department updates the O*NET on a regular basis, and we used the most recent one available—O*NET release 10.

- We linked the information from O*NET to several other kinds of data that the U.S. Bureau of Labor Statistics collects: on earnings, projected growth, number of openings, part-time workers, and self-employed workers. For data on these topics, the BLS uses a slightly different set of job titles than the O*NET uses, so we had to match similar titles. In a few cases we could not obtain data about every one of these topics for every occupation. Nevertheless, the information we report here is the most reliable data we could obtain.

- We used the Classification of Instructional Programs, a system developed by the U.S. Department of Education, to cross-reference the education and training programs related to each job.

Of course, information in a database format can be boring and even confusing, so we did many things to help make the data useful and present it to you in a form that is easy to understand.

How the Best Jobs for Your Skills Were Selected

Here is the procedure we followed to select the 265 jobs we included in this book:

1. We began by analyzing the skills data in the O*NET database and simplified it so we could describe jobs using 10 skills instead of the 36 the O*NET uses. For a full explanation of our methods, see Part I. Of the 949 job titles in the O*NET, 796 have skills data.

2. For each of the 796 jobs, we determined the top three skills. The O*NET uses two scales to rate jobs on their skills: the level of skill and the importance of the skill. We based our ordering on the level of skill, but we eliminated skills that had very low importance ratings, and we based the ordering on the difference between the job's rating on each skill and the average rating for all occupations on that skill (a figure we call the skill's score).

3. We had to eliminate 132 jobs because for each of the 10 skills they had a score close to zero or lower—in other words, they had no skill with a rating that exceeded the average by a significant amount. It's not a coincidence that these low-skill jobs are not very

rewarding and therefore don't belong in a book about "best jobs." For each of the remaining 664 jobs, we ordered the 10 skills by their scores from highest to lowest. If the second-place skill for a job had a score less than 40 percent of the score of the first-place skill, of if the second-place skill had a score close to zero or lower, we identified only the single top skill for the job. If the score of the third-place skill was less than 40 percent of the score of the second-place skill or was close to zero or lower, we identified only the top two skills for the job. For most jobs, however, we identified three top skills.

4. We then linked the jobs to data we obtained from other sources at the Department of Labor. We had to eliminate 4 jobs because earnings figures were not available, and we eliminated another 11 jobs that are expected to employ fewer than 500 workers per year and to shrink rather than grow in workforce size. We also combined 36 very similar college teaching jobs into one job: Teachers, Postsecondary. This left 614 jobs.

5. For each of the 10 skills, we created a list of the jobs (from the remaining set of 614) for which the skill was among the top three. Because most jobs were assigned three top skills, most jobs appeared on three different lists. The sizes of the lists varied from 43 jobs (Computer Programming Skills) to 230 jobs (Equipment Use/Maintenance Skills).

6. On each list, we ranked the jobs three times, based on these major criteria: median annual earnings, projected growth through 2014, and number of job openings projected per year.

7. We then added the three numerical rankings for each job to calculate its overall score.

8. To emphasize jobs that tend to pay more, are likely to grow more rapidly, and have more job openings, we selected the 50 job titles from each list with the best numerical scores. For example, on the list of jobs linked to Communication Skills, the job with the best combined score for earnings, growth, and number of job openings is Teachers, Postsecondary, so this job is listed first among the "50 Best Jobs For Communication Skills" even though it is not the best-paying job (which is Surgeons), the fastest-growing job (which is Medical Assistants), or the job with the most openings (which is Customer Service Representatives). Because our list of jobs high in Computer Programming Skills numbered only 43 jobs, we selected the best 40 of these jobs.

In Part II of this book you'll determine your top three skills, and then in Part III you'll consult the list with the 50 best jobs for each skill. Because three times 50 equals 150, we call this book *150 Best Jobs for Your Skills*, but in fact when you look at the lists you'll notice that some jobs appear on multiple lists. The 10 lists of 50 jobs each actually contain 230 unique jobs. These jobs are the focus of this book and are described in full in Part IV. In Part IV we also provide full descriptions of all 36 of the postsecondary teaching jobs, so a total of 265 jobs are included there.

New Government Training Programs May Become Available

It is interesting to note that the federal government has made commitments to encourage people to prepare for the jobs included in this book. In 2003 the White House announced the President's High Growth Job Training Initiative and subsequently has launched a series of Community-Based Job Training Grants to fund community colleges and other training providers. In addition, Congress passed the Carl D. Perkins Career and Technical Education Improvement Act of 2006, which is intended to help states and localities fund training programs for "high skill, high wage, or high demand occupations in current or emerging professions."

Although the president's initiatives and the Perkins Act do not define *which* occupations are being targeted, the U.S. Department of Labor has identified jobs considered to be "high wage, high growth." Of the 196 such jobs for which there is O*NET information, 146 are included in this book. So it's possible that new government-funded training programs may become available in your community for some of the best jobs for your skills. When you find interesting jobs in this book, investigate local training opportunities. Don't assume because a job is unfamiliar to you that you can't find training for it. Ask at your local community college or career one-stop center.

Understand the Limits of the Data in This Book

In this book we use the most reliable and up-to-date information available on earnings, projected growth, number of openings, skills, and other topics. The earnings data came from the U.S. Department of Labor's Bureau of Labor Statistics. As you look at the figures, keep in mind that they are estimates. They give you a general idea about the number of workers employed, annual earnings, rate of job growth, and annual job openings.

Understand that a problem with such data is that it describes an average. Just as there is no precisely average person, there is no such thing as a statistically average example of a particular job. We say this because data, while helpful, can also be misleading.

Take, for example, the yearly earnings information in this book. This is highly reliable data obtained from a very large U.S. working population sample by the Bureau of Labor Statistics. It tells us the average annual pay received as of May 2005 by people in various job titles (actually, it is the median annual pay, which means that half earned more and half less).

This sounds great, except that half of all people in that occupation earned less than that amount. For example, people who are new to the occupation or with only a few years of work experience often earn much less than the average amount. People who live in rural areas or who work for smaller employers typically earn less than those who do similar work in cities (where the cost of living is higher) or for bigger employers. People in certain areas of the country earn less than those in others.

Also keep in mind that the figures for job growth and number of openings are projections by labor economists—their best guesses about what we can expect between now and 2014. They are not guarantees. A major economic downturn, war, or technological breakthrough could change the actual outcome.

Finally, don't forget that the job market consists of both job openings and job *seekers*. The figures on job growth and openings don't tell you how many people will be competing with you to be hired. The Department of Labor does not publish figures on the supply of job candidates, so we are unable to tell you about the level of competition you can expect. Competition is an important issue that you should research for any tentative career goal. In some cases, the *Occupational Outlook Handbook* provides informative statements. You should speak to people who educate or train tomorrow's workers; they probably have a good idea of how many graduates find rewarding employment and how quickly. People in the workforce also can provide insights into this issue. Use your critical thinking skills to evaluate what people tell you. For example, educators or trainers may be trying to recruit you, whereas people in the workforce may be trying to discourage you from competing. Get a variety of opinions to balance out possible biases.

So, in reviewing the information in this book, please understand the limitations of the data. You need to use common sense in career decision making as in most other things in life. We hope that, using that approach, you find the information helpful and interesting.

The Data Complexities

For those of you who like details, we present some of the complexities inherent in our sources of information and what we did to make sense of them here. You don't need to know this to use the book, so jump to the next section of the Introduction if you are bored with details.

Earnings, Growth, and Number of Openings

We include information on earnings, projected growth, and number of job openings for each job throughout this book.

Earnings

The employment security agency of each state gathers information on earnings for various jobs and forwards it to the U.S. Bureau of Labor Statistics. This information is organized in standardized ways by a BLS program called Occupational Employment Statistics, or OES. To keep the earnings for the various jobs and regions comparable, the OES screens out certain types of earnings and includes others, so the OES earnings we use in this book represent straight-time gross pay exclusive of premium pay. More specifically, the OES earnings include the job's base rate; cost-of-living allowances; guaranteed pay; hazardous-duty pay;

incentive pay, including commissions and production bonuses; on-call pay; and tips but do not include back pay, jury duty pay, overtime pay, severance pay, shift differentials, non-production bonuses, or tuition reimbursements. Also, self-employed workers are not included in the estimates, and they can be a significant segment in certain occupations. When data on earnings for an occupation is highly unreliable, OES does not report a figure, which meant that we reluctantly had to exclude from this book a few occupations such as Musicians and Singers. The median earnings for all workers in all occupations were $29,430 in May 2005.

The data from the OES survey is reported under a system of job titles called the Standard Occupational Classification system, or SOC. We cross-referenced these titles to the O*NET job titles we use in this book so we can rank the jobs by their earnings and include earnings information in the job descriptions. In some cases, an SOC title cross-references to more than one O*NET job title. For example, the O*NET has separate information for Accountants and Auditors, but the SOC reports earnings for a single occupation called Accountants and Auditors. Therefore you may notice that the salary we report for Accountants ($52,210) is identical to the salary we report for Auditors. In reality there probably is a difference, but this is the best information that is available.

Projected Growth and Number of Job Openings

This information comes from the Office of Occupational Statistics and Employment Projections, a program within the Bureau of Labor Statistics that develops information about projected trends in the nation's labor market for the next ten years. The most recent projections available cover the years from 2004 to 2014. The projections are based on information about people moving into and out of occupations. The BLS uses data from various sources in projecting the growth and number of openings for each job title—some data comes from the Census Bureau's Current Population Survey and some comes from an OES survey. The projections assume that there will be no major war, depression, or other economic upheaval.

Like the earnings figures, the figures on projected growth and job openings are reported according to the SOC classification, so again you will find that some of the SOC jobs cross-walk to more than one O*NET job. To continue the example we used earlier, SOC reports growth (22.4%) and openings (157,000) for one occupation called Accountants and Auditors, but in this book we report these figures separately for the occupation Accountants and for the occupation Auditors. When you see Accountants with 22.4% projected growth and 157,000 projected job openings and Auditors with the same two numbers, you should realize that the 22.4% rate of projected growth represents the *average* of these two occupations—one may actually experience higher growth than the other—and that these two occupations will *share* the 157,000 projected openings.

While salary figures are fairly straightforward, you may not know what to make of job-growth figures. For example, is projected growth of 15 percent good or bad? You should keep in mind that the average (mean) growth projected for all occupations by the Bureau of Labor Statistics is 13.0 percent. One-quarter of the SOC occupations have a growth projection of 3.2 percent or lower. Growth of 11.6 percent is the median, meaning that half of the occupations have more, half less. Only one-quarter of the occupations have growth projected at more than 17.4 percent.

Remember, however, that the jobs in this book were selected as "best" partly on the basis of high growth, so their mean growth is an impressive 21.0 percent. Among these 265 outstanding jobs, the job ranked 66th by projected growth has a figure of 29.4 percent, the jobs ranked 132nd and 133rd (the median) have a projected growth of 19.5 percent, and the job ranked 199th has a projected growth of 13.7 percent.

Perhaps you're wondering why we present figures on both job growth *and* number of openings. Aren't these two ways of saying the same thing? Actually, you need to know both. Consider the occupation Hydrologists, which is projected to grow at the outstanding rate of 31.6 percent. There should be lots of opportunities in such a fast-growing job, right? Not exactly. This is a tiny occupation, with only about 3,600 people currently employed, so even though it is growing rapidly, it will not create many new jobs (about 1,000 per year, to be exact). Now consider Team Assemblers. This occupation is growing at the anemic rate of 7.3 percent, largely because automation and foreign competition have eliminated the need for many of these workers. Nevertheless, this is a huge occupation that employs over 1.2 million workers, so even though its growth rate is unimpressive, it is expected to take on 262,000 new workers each year. That's why we base our selection of the best jobs on both of these economic indicators and why you should pay attention to both when you scan our lists of best jobs.

How This Book Is Organized

The information in this book about best jobs for your skills moves from the general to the highly specific.

Part I. Overview of Skills and Careers

Part I is an overview of what skills are, how to develop them, and how they relate to career choice. This chapter explains how we simplified the skills in the O*NET database to create a more manageable set for this book and how the assessment in Part II helps you to identify your outstanding skills.

Part II. What Are Your Top Skills? Take an Assessment

Part II is a self-assessment exercise that presents 10 major skills. It defines each skill, gives you a context for understanding how it is learned and used on the job, asks for your self-estimate of your level of skill, and challenges your self-estimate by asking you to provide examples from your own experiences of how you have demonstrated this skill. It takes about 45 minutes to complete—more or less, depending on how fast you work—and will help you understand which skills are your best.

As an extra benefit, the skill-related experiences that you jot down here can come in handy in the future when you are writing a resume or a cover letter for a job application.

Part III. The Best Jobs Lists: Jobs for Each of the 10 Skills

For many people, the 99 lists in Part III are the most interesting feature of the book. Here you can see titles of jobs that require a high level of one of your top skills and that have the best combination of high salaries, fast growth, and plentiful job openings. You can see which jobs are best in terms of each of these factors combined or considered separately. Each skill-oriented set of jobs is broken out further according to education levels and to highlight jobs with a high percentage of part-time and self-employed workers. Look in the Table of Contents for a complete list of lists. Although there are a lot of lists, they are not difficult to understand because they have clear titles and are organized into groupings of related lists.

We suggest that you use the lists that make the most sense for you. Following are the names of each group of lists along with short comments on each group. You will find additional information in a brief introduction provided at the beginning of each group of lists in Part III.

Best Jobs for Each Skill: Jobs with the Highest Pay, Fastest Growth, and Most Openings

These four sets of 10 lists (one for each skill) are the ones that you probably want to see first. The first set of lists presents, for each skill, the top 50 jobs that have that skill among their three most important skills. The second set presents the 20 best-paying jobs from the top 50 jobs for each skill. The third set presents the 20 fastest-growing jobs from the top 50 jobs for each skill. The fourth set presents the 20 jobs with the most openings from the top 50 jobs for each skill.

Best Jobs Lists by Work Arrangement

These two sets of 10 lists contain subsets of the top 50 jobs for each skill. The first set presents the jobs with a high percentage of part-time workers; the second set presents the jobs with a high percentage of self-employed workers.

Best Jobs Lists Based on Levels of Education, Training, and Experience

For each of the 10 skills, we created separate lists for each level of education and training as defined by the U.S. Department of Labor and assigned job titles to the lists based on the education, training, and experience usually required for entry. Jobs within these lists are presented in order of their total combined scores for earnings, growth, and number of openings. The lists include jobs in these groupings:

- Short-term on-the-job training
- Moderate-term on-the-job training

- Long-term on-the-job training
- Work experience in a related job
- Postsecondary vocational training
- Associate degree
- Bachelor's degree
- Work experience plus degree
- Master's degree
- Doctoral degree
- First professional degree

Best Jobs Lists Based on Interests

These lists organize the 230 best jobs into groups based on interests. Within each list, jobs are presented in order of their total scores for earnings, growth, and number of openings. Here are the 16 interest areas used in these lists: Agriculture and Natural Resources; Architecture and Construction; Arts and Communication; Business and Administration; Education and Training; Finance and Insurance; Government and Public Administration; Health Science; Hospitality, Tourism, and Recreation; Human Service; Information Technology; Law and Public Safety; Manufacturing; Retail and Wholesale Sales and Service; Scientific Research, Engineering, and Mathematics; and Transportation, Distribution, and Logistics.

Bonus Lists About Skills

Unlike the other lists, these are not based on the 50 best jobs. In fact, they don't contain jobs at all, but they do contain interesting information on the relationship between skills and work:

- One list orders the 10 skills by how closely they are associated with income. In other words, you can see which skills command the highest pay.
- A second list orders the 10 skills by how closely they are associated with job growth. This means you can see which skills are in greatest demand.
- A set of lists shows, for each of the 10 skills, the 10 industries where the skill is most concentrated in the workforce. Using this information, you can plan your career for a segment of the economy where demand for the skill is really hot.

Part IV: Descriptions of the Best Jobs for Your Skills

This part describes each of the best jobs for your skills, using a format that is informative yet compact and easy to read. The descriptions contain statistics such as earnings and projected percent of growth; lists such as major skills, work tasks, and related job titles; and key descriptors such as personality type and interest field. Because the jobs in this section are arranged in alphabetical order, you can easily find a job that you've identified from Part III and that you want to learn more about.

We used the most current information from a variety of government sources to create the descriptions. Although we've tried to make the descriptions easy to understand, the sample that follows—with an explanation of each of its parts—may help you better understand and use the descriptions.

Job Title →

Accountants

- Education/Training Required: Bachelor's degree
- Annual Earnings: $52,210
- Growth: 22.4%
- Annual Job Openings: 157,000
- Self-Employed: 10.9%
- Part-Time: 10.2%

Data Elements →

The job openings listed here are shared with Auditors.

Summary Description and Tasks →

Analyze financial information and prepare financial reports to determine or maintain record of assets, liabilities, profit and loss, tax liability, or other financial activities within an organization. Prepare, examine, or analyze accounting records, financial statements, or other financial reports to assess accuracy, completeness, and conformance to reporting and procedural standards. Compute taxes owed and prepare tax returns, ensuring compliance with payment, reporting, or other tax requirements. Analyze business operations, trends, costs, revenues, financial commitments, and obligations to project future revenues and expenses or to provide advice. Report to management regarding the finances of establishment. Establish tables of accounts and assign entries to proper accounts. Develop, maintain, and analyze budgets, preparing periodic reports that compare budgeted costs to actual costs. Develop, implement, modify, and document recordkeeping and accounting systems, making use of current computer technology. Prepare forms and manuals for accounting and bookkeeping personnel and direct their work activities. Survey operations to ascertain accounting needs and to recommend, develop, or maintain solutions to business and financial problems. Work as Internal Revenue Service (IRS) agents. Advise management about issues such as resource utilization, tax strategies, and the assumptions underlying budget forecasts. Provide internal and external auditing services for businesses or individuals. Advise clients in areas such as compensation, employee health-care benefits, the design of accounting or data processing systems, or long-range tax or estate plans. Investigate bankruptcies and other complex financial transactions and prepare reports summarizing the findings. Represent clients before taxing authorities and provide support during litigation involving finan-

cial issues. Appraise, evaluate, and inventory real property and equipment, recording information such as the description, value, and location of property. Maintain or examine the records of government agencies. Serve as bankruptcy trustees or business valuators.

SKILLS—Most Important: Computer Programming Skills; Mathematics Skills; Management Skills. **Other Above-Average Skills:** Thought-Processing Skills; Quality Control Skills; Equipment/Technology Analysis Skills. ← **Skills**

GOE—Interest Area: 04. Business and Administration. **Work Group:** 04.05. Accounting, Auditing, and Analytical Support. **Other Jobs in This Group:** Accountants and Auditors; Auditors; Budget Analysts; Industrial Engineering Technicians; Logisticians; Management Analysts; Operations Research Analysts. **PERSONALITY TYPE:** Conventional. Conventional occupations frequently involve following set procedures and routines. These occupations can include working with data and details more than with ideas. Usually there is a clear line of authority to follow. ← **GOE Information** / **Personality Type**

EDUCATION/TRAINING PROGRAM(S)— Accounting and Computer Science; Accounting; Accounting and Finance; Accounting and Business/Management. **RELATED KNOWLEDGE/ COURSES—Economics and Accounting:** Economic and accounting principles and practices, the financial markets, banking, and the analysis and reporting of financial data. **Clerical Practices:** Administrative and clerical procedures and systems such as word processing, managing files and records, stenography and transcription, designing forms, and other office procedures and terminology. **Mathematics:** Arithmetic, algebra, geometry, calculus, and statistics and their applications. **Law and Government:** Laws, legal codes, court procedures, precedents, government regulations, executive orders, agency rules, and the democratic political process. **Computers and Electronics:** Circuit boards; processors; chips; electronic equipment; and computer hardware and software, including applications and programming. **Personnel and Human Resources:** Principles and procedures for personnel recruitment, selection, training, compensation and benefits, labor relations and negotiation, and personnel information systems. ← **Education/Training Program(s)** / **Related Knowledge/ Courses**

Here are some details on each of the major parts of the job descriptions you will find in Part IV:

- ⚙ **Job Title:** This is the job title for the job as defined by the U.S. Department of Labor and used in its O*NET database.

- ⚙ **Data Elements:** The information comes from various U.S. Department of Labor and Census Bureau databases, as explained elsewhere in this Introduction.

- ⚙ **Summary Description and Tasks:** The bold sentence provides a summary description of the occupation. It is followed by a listing of tasks that are generally performed by people who work in this job. This information comes from the O*NET database but where necessary has been edited to avoid exceeding 2,200 characters.

- ⚙ **Skills:** The O*NET database provides data on 36 skills; we decided to collapse those into 10 skills, as explained in detail in Part II. First we list the three that are most important for each job. For each job, we identified any skill with a rating that was higher than the average rating for that skill for all jobs. If the score for a skill is less than 40 percent of the next-highest score, we do not list that score or any ranked lower. These outstanding skills are listed alphabetically. Following these skills are all the other skills that were significantly higher than the average rating for that skill for all jobs. These additional skills are ordered by descending level of mastery required.

- ⚙ **GOE Information:** This information cross-references the Guide for Occupational Exploration (or the GOE), a system developed by the U.S. Department of Labor that organizes jobs based on interests. We use the groups from the *New Guide for Occupational Exploration*, as published by JIST. This book uses a set of interest areas based on the 16 career clusters developed by the U.S. Department of Education and used in a variety of career information systems. The description includes the major Interest Area the job fits into, its more-specific Work Group, and a list of related O*NET job titles that are in this same GOE Work Group. This information will help you identify other job titles that have similar interests or require similar skills. You can find more information on the GOE and its Interest Areas in Appendix B.

- ⚙ **Personality Type:** The O*NET database assigns each job to its most closely related personality type. Our job descriptions include the name of the related personality type as well as a brief definition of this personality type.

- ⚙ **Education/Training Program(s):** This part of the job description provides the name of the educational or training program or programs for the job. It will help you identify sources of formal or informal training for a job that interests you. To get this information, we used a crosswalk created by the National Center for O*NET Development to connect information in the Classification of Instructional Programs (CIP) to the O*NET job titles we use in this book. We made various changes to connect the O*NET job titles to the education or training programs related to them and also modified the names of some education and training programs so they would be more easily understood.

◎ **Related Knowledge/Courses:** This entry can help you understand the most important knowledge areas that are required for a job and the types of courses or programs you will likely need to take to prepare for it. We used information in the Department of Labor's O*NET database for this entry. For each job, we identified any knowledge area with a rating that was higher than the average rating for that knowledge area for all jobs; then we listed them in descending order.

Getting all the information we used in the job descriptions was not a simple process, and it is not always perfect. Even so, we used the best and most recent sources of data we could find, and we think that our efforts will be helpful to many people.

Acknowledgments

We would like to thank Dave Anderson, Nancy Sosnowski, and Jason Thomas for their helpful feedback on the skills assessment in Part II.

PART I

Overview of Skills and Careers

What Exactly *Is* a Skill?

A skill is a learned capability to perform actions. Let's look at the parts of that definition.

A skill is a capability because it gives you the potential to do something competently. It's not a guarantee of success, but it means you are *able* to succeed. It's not a preference for doing something, although people tend to prefer doing what they're good at.

A skill is learned because it is not something you're born with, and it is not acquired through normal sensory development (as depth perception is) or through special physical conditioning (as the ability to bench-press 250 pounds would be). It is not a talent or aptitude, which means a capacity for learning something easily; it is the fruit of learning. Not all learning comes from books or formal instructional programs. In fact, you may learn a skill without conscious intent or even awareness of the learning process. For example, you may acquire certain social skills, such as getting along with diverse co-workers, through day-to-day experiences without realizing you are doing so.

A skill allows you to perform actions rather than just know or feel something, which is what makes it valuable to employers. It gets the job done. For example, some social skills may be referred to as "a positive attitude," but they require more than just a sunny feeling. They require such actions as seeing things from someone else's point of view, speaking in a cheerful tone of voice, or offering to help. Some skills are largely intellectual, but even these skills contribute to work tasks. For example, critical thinking skills would enable you to decide which supplier to buy from or where to drill for oil.

People sometimes don't realize all the skills they have. For example, they may think that a positive attitude on the job is just a feeling or that critical thinking is just a matter of raw intelligence. Part II of this book can help you take stock of your skills so you can aspire toward appropriate jobs and use effective wording on your resume, on job application letters, and in interviews.

How Can I Develop My Skills?

If you're presently in school (and paying attention), you're making progress on developing your skills. But skill-building is not just for young people. Because skills are learned, you can develop them throughout your lifetime. In fact, you'd better. If you're working now, your present job is going to undergo changes. What if part of your job is taken over by a computer? What if your employer wants to expand to a world market? Will you have the skills to adjust easily? And if you lose your job for whatever reason, if you decide to change your job, or if you're not yet in the workforce, will you have the skills that employers are looking for? Employers often complain that younger job applicants lack certain vital social skills (they're "slackers," they're "surly," or they "have an attitude problem") and that older job applicants lack emerging technology skills (they're "fuddy-duddies" or "dinosaurs"). Don't be one of those rejects! Develop the skills that employers want.

Informal Learning

The best way to learn work-related skills is on the job. Even for jobs that require certain educational credentials, most job-specific skills are learned after you're hired. When you see co-workers using skills that you don't have, watch what they do and ask them to show you how. When you feel you have mastered the skill, ask your supervisor for an assignment that uses the skill—perhaps not a high-stakes project, but something that will demonstrate your new skill. Then be sure to ask for feedback that specifically targets your use of the skill. What did you do right? How could you have done it better? Try not to be defensive in response to criticism; use this feedback as part of the learning process.

If you're not working now, you can get informal on-the-job training in specific skills by doing volunteer work in a relevant setting. For example, to improve your social skills, do volunteer work at a senior center, a charity fund-raising event, or some other setting where there's a lot of interaction with people. Some hobbies also provide opportunities for you to learn skills—for example, designing Web pages, customizing cars, or gardening. With hobbies, it helps to join a club so you can learn from more highly skilled hobbyists and get feedback on your accomplishments. Just keep in mind that your volunteer work can do more than just help others and your hobby can be more than just a self-indulgence. Use them as skill academies. Challenge yourself with new tasks; ask for feedback.

Sometimes you can create your own training program by studying a book or technical manual (maybe one aimed at "dummies"). In fact, if the skill you want to learn is very rare (for example, speaking Estonian) or on the cutting edge of technology (for example, using the very latest software program), you may have no choice but to design your own curriculum because you can't find anyone to teach you. If you're very lucky, you may be able to convince your employer to pay for the books or other learning aids and to give you time in the workday for upgrading your skills. But most workers find that they have to use lunch hours, evenings, and weekends for this self-training. Consider the time and expense of self-training as investments in your future employability. Try to find a study partner to learn with you; study partners help reinforce each other's learning and keep the learning program on track.

Formal Learning

Some skills can be learned only in formal settings. Doctors, for example, must go to medical school. Often a specific college degree or apprenticeship is the accepted way of preparing for a certain career. Accountants usually have a degree in accounting, or at least in business. Most electricians learn through a formal apprenticeship program.

But many other skills are taught in single classes rather than in long-term programs—and not because formal learning is required but because so many people want to learn these skills. Night schools and corporate training centers offer classes in technical skills, such as using spreadsheets or driving trucks, and in "soft" skills, such as conducting meetings or reading people's body language. Another setting for training is the annual conference of the professional association relevant to your career, where you can attend training workshops.

Because the need for these popular skills is so obvious, employers often are willing to cover the expenses and perhaps the time these classes require. Be sure to find out what classes your employer makes available and consider taking them if they are at all relevant to your work. Your employer will appreciate your desire to upgrade your skills.

Sometimes employers are not willing to set aside funding or time for classes that would add to your skills, especially if your workday is very busy or if the skills you are seeking are not obviously relevant to your job. In fact, your employer may fear that you would use your new skills to find work elsewhere—and, in fact, that is another good reason for upgrading your skills. If your employer is unwilling to help or you are not currently employed, you may need to find (and pay for) useful night classes at your local high school, vocational school, or community college. Alternatively, it may be worthwhile for you to invest your time and money in a very relevant night class at a proprietary technical school (or "institute"), but first be sure to get evidence that employers will value this credential.

If you are still in college, you should consider an internship as a way of acquiring skills that can't be learned in the classroom. Much of the learning on an internship is equivalent to informal on-the-job training, but internship programs often have formal requirements and procedures for recruitment, and sometimes they include some formal classes.

Just as you need nutritious food, exercise, and a good night's sleep to keep your body healthy, you need a regular program of upgrading your skills to keep your career healthy. It doesn't matter whether you learn formally or informally, from a book or by rolling up your sleeves, in cooperation with your employer or on your own. Just be sure you keep on learning.

How Are Skills and Career Choice Related?

A good career goal is one in which you will be successful and find satisfaction.

To be *successful* on the job, you need the specific skills that are relevant to the work tasks. For example, most health-care jobs involve tasks that require contact with patients, so the workers need social and communication skills, among others. Most teaching jobs involve tasks that require breaking ideas into bite-sized pieces, so the workers need thought-processing skills, among others.

Your *satisfaction* on the job also will depend on how well your skills match the job—because how happy can you be in a job where you constantly feel overwhelmed by the duties or where the work is so lacking in challenge that you are bored most of the time? In a recent poll, 54 percent of professionals stated that their current job does not utilize their skills and that they transfer jobs frequently. These workers need to find a better match between their skills and their work.

Therefore this book is designed to help you clarify your outstanding skills and identify good jobs that can use those skills.

You may not yet have *all* the skills needed for the job you choose as your goal. In fact, you may need to take classes, get on-the-job training, or get work experience to qualify for the job. But it makes sense for you to aim for a job where you already have *some* of the skills, because as you seek such a goal the learning curve will not be so steep, you will have a track record of relevant accomplishments, and you will have the self-confidence of already having tried and succeeded at some of the required tasks (or tasks similar to them).

That's why the next section of this book, Part II, helps you identify the skills you already have.

How Important Are Skills in the Hiring Process?

Whenever employers are looking at your resume, interviewing you, or talking to your references, the question that is uppermost in their minds is, "Does this job applicant have the skills needed to get the job done?"

As evidence, consider what the National Association of Manufacturers found in 2001 when they asked members why they reject job applicants. Of the 14 reasons most frequently cited, six were about skills deficiencies:

- Inadequate reading/writing skills
- Inadequate oral communication skills
- Inadequate math skills
- Inadequate technical/computer skills
- Inadequate problem-solving skills
- Inadequate basic employability skills (attendance, timeliness, work ethic, etc.)

A seventh reason, "inability to work in a team environment," may also be considered a skills deficiency.

Note that this research applies to only one industry: manufacturing. It is true that these same skills are vital in all industries and in almost all worksites. However, the particular blend of skills, the emphasis on some skills in the mix rather than on others, varies from industry to industry and from job to job. One of the goals of this book is to help you identify the jobs that emphasize your strongest skills.

What Do I Need Besides Skills?

You may have all the skills required for an occupation and still not get hired. That's because being hired often depends on many other factors. For example, the occupation may require a certain license or certification for workers. Having the necessary skills will probably help you qualify for the license or certification, but you may also have to overcome certain other hurdles, such as completing required classes or even a degree program at an accredited institution, passing a test, completing supervised work experience, paying a fee, and so forth.

In addition, there needs to be a job opening and you need to be aware of it. You may need to relocate. Alternatively, you may create a job opening for yourself by convincing an employer that your skills are just what the company needs or by starting your own business.

Finally, skills are not the same thing as motivation. To get and keep a job, you must want to do the work. As Muhammad Ali once remarked, "Champions...have to have the skill and the will. But the will must be stronger than the skill." This book is designed to help you find a job that appeals to you because it's a good match for your skills, pays well, and has lots of job openings. But be sure to read all the other details about the job in Part III—and then do additional career exploration—to make sure that the job is one you'll really enjoy.

What Skills Are Covered in This Book?

One of the best places to obtain information about the skill requirements of different jobs is the O*NET database created by the U.S. Department of Labor. Job analysts created detailed lists of the tasks of each occupation and then decided which skills were needed to perform these tasks. To be more precise, they considered each skill and gave a numerical rating for the *level* of mastery necessary for doing the work tasks and another numerical rating for the *importance* of the skill for doing the work tasks. Since the O*NET database was originally created, new skills ratings have been gathered from occupational experts and workers, and these have largely replaced the ratings made by job analysts, but the ratings are reported on the same two scales, level and importance.

The 46 skills that O*NET originally covered have been simplified somewhat, so the skill information in the database now covers 36 skills. But the O*NET skills information is still too detailed to be useful to most people. If you wanted to use O*NET to identify jobs for which you already have many of the skills, you'd have to consider your level of mastery of 36 skills—a tedious procedure.

So in this book we further simplified the O*NET taxonomy of skills. We collapsed the 36 skills down to 10 major skill types.

We did this by using a statistical analysis called correlation, which shows how well one variable can predict another. We applied it to the skill ratings (for level of mastery) in the O*NET database, and our thinking was that if the ratings for one skill can predict the ratings for another skill almost all the time, there's no need for two skills. Another way of saying this is that we don't need two skills if the two *don't say anything different about the jobs*. The two can be collapsed into one skill instead—provided we can devise a name and a definition that encompasses both of the component skills.

For example, consider the two O*NET skills Reading Comprehension and Writing. A perfect correlation of 1.0 between the ratings for these skills would mean that every occupation is rated exactly the same on both skills. In actuality, the correlation is 0.94, which is so close to perfect that there is no point in treating these as two separate skills. We also discovered very high correlations between these skills and the O*NET skills Active Listening and Speaking; no correlation between any two skills in this group was lower than 0.89. So we decided to roll all four skills into one that we call Communication Skills. (The "s" on the end of "Skills" is a reminder that this has several components.) We defined Communication Skills as "Exchanging information and feelings with others: understanding the words, ideas, and feelings of others through reading and attentive listening; effectively expressing ideas and feelings to others through writing, speaking, and body language." That's a bit of a mouthful, but we think it is easy enough to understand, and in the assessment in Part II you can respond much more quickly to this one skill than to the four that it replaces.

Here is a listing of the 36 O*NET skills that shows how we used them in creating our list of 10 skills. We used some of the O*NET skills without combining them with other skills because they had low correlations with other skills. For example, Science and Mathematics are often thought to go together, but they had a correlation of only 0.68, so we kept them as separate skills. We renamed two O*NET skills slightly to make them easier to understand. We also decided not to use three of the O*NET skills because they are difficult to explain to readers.

O*NET Skill	Skill Used in This Book
Reading Comprehension	Communication Skills
Active Listening	Communication Skills
Writing	Communication Skills
Speaking	Communication Skills
Programming	Computer Programming Skills
Mathematics	Mathematics Skills
Science	Science Skills
Critical Thinking	Thought-Processing Skills
Active Learning	Thought-Processing Skills
Learning Strategies	Thought-Processing Skills
Monitoring	Thought-Processing Skills
Complex Problem Solving	Thought-Processing Skills

O*NET Skill	Skill Used in This Book
Judgment and Decision Making	Thought-Processing Skills
Social Perceptiveness	Social Skills
Coordination	Social Skills
Persuasion	Social Skills
Negotiation	Social Skills
Instructing	Social Skills
Service Orientation	Social Skills
Operations Analysis	Technology Analysis Skills
Technology Design	Technology Analysis Skills
Equipment Selection	Technology Analysis Skills
Installation	Not used in this book
Operation Monitoring	Technology Use/Maintenance Skills
Operation and Control	Technology Use/Maintenance Skills
Equipment Maintenance	Technology Use/Maintenance Skills
Troubleshooting	Technology Use/Maintenance Skills
Repairing	Technology Use/Maintenance Skills
Quality Control Analysis Skills	Quality Control Skills
Systems Analysis	Not used in this book
Systems Evaluation	Not used in this book
Time Management	Management Skills
Management of Financial Resources	Management Skills
Management of Material Resources	Management Skills
Management of Personnel Resources	Management Skills

What Skills Are *Not* Covered in This Book?

Earlier in this chapter we referred to a survey in which manufacturers identified important skills they often find lacking in job applicants. Almost 70 percent of these employers said that they reject job applicants for production jobs because of "inadequate basic employability skills (attendance, timeliness, work ethic, etc.)." These basic employability skills are not included in this book because they underlie *all* jobs and therefore O*NET does not include them. In other words, they are so vital that it would not be meaningful to say they are more important for one job than for another.

Employers sometimes mention other personal qualities, such as self-esteem and honesty, that are essential in employees but arguably don't fit under the definition of skills. Because O*NET does not classify these under skills, we do not include them in this book. That does not mean, however, that you can neglect these personal qualities.

How Does This Book Help Me Identify My Outstanding Skills?

The best way to identify your outstanding skills would be to gather outside appraisals of *all* your previous experiences on the job, in school, and in leisure-time activities. This would require a huge effort. You'd need to get in touch with all your previous employers, co-workers, and customers; your teachers and trainers; and the people you spend time with on evenings and weekends. You'd need to remind them of all the tasks you performed in these settings and ask them for honest appraisals of your performance. Then you'd need to connect their responses to a consistent set of skill names and reconcile situations where one person thought you did well and another thought you did poorly. What a chore! But the results would be extremely well-informed and therefore extremely accurate.

At the other extreme, you could look at a listing of skills and check off the skills you think you have. This checklist approach often works very well for determining *interests*. But for a *skills* self-assessment to be accurate, it needs to give you some *contexts* for making decisions about which skills you have and which you lack. Specifically, you need a full understanding of what each skill is—a definition with examples, not just a name—and you need a way to connect the skill to your past experiences at work, in school, and elsewhere.

That's the kind of depth that you'll find in the assessment included in Part II of this book. For each of the 10 skills, it provides a definition, examples of high school courses that teach it, examples of leisure activities that use it, and examples of work tasks that use it—many of which are the same tasks considered as examples by the job analysts, experts, and workers who develop the O*NET skill ratings. It then asks you to give a preliminary self-estimate of your level of skill.

And it doesn't stop there. If you think you have more than a low level of skill, it asks you to jot down *examples* of how you have demonstrated the skill, drawn from your experience on the job, in school, or in leisure activities. This additional step gives you a way to provide a context for confirming your self-estimate. You may also find these examples useful in the future when you will need to provide evidence of your qualifications for a job, either in a resume, a cover letter, or an interview.

Finally, it asks you to review your responses and select the skills that have the highest self-estimates and the most examples of experiences. That means that your decisions about your skills are grounded in a context that allows you to make an informed judgment. If you are honest and thoughtful about your responses, you will gain a useful understanding of your top skills. Then you can use that understanding in Part III to identify good jobs that use your top skills.

So why not get started now? Find out the most important skills you already have by turning the page and doing the exercise in Part II.

PART II

What Are Your Top Skills? Take an Assessment

Before looking at the lists of best jobs, you need to determine which skills are your strongest. That's what you'll do in this chapter.

The exercise in this chapter takes about 45 minutes. It's time well spent, because the exercise can give you thoughtful insights into your skills, and it's linked to the U.S. Department of Labor's authoritative O*NET database of information about occupations. What you learn from this exercise can help you focus on one or more occupations as promising career goals.

This exercise will not *guarantee* you any particular job or *prove* that you're qualified for the job. However, what you say here about your experiences can provide useful material to include in resumes, cover letters, and interviews. This material, along with whatever formal credentials you possess (such as a certificate or a college degree), your natural abilities, the positive testimonials of your references, and your personal charm can prove that you're the candidate the employer should hire.

Keep in mind that this exercise focuses on *skills* but not on *abilities*, such as being able to carry 50 pounds—or a tune. It also does not emphasize interests. It focuses first on what you *can* do well, and only afterwards asks you to consider what you *like* to do. For most people these two are closely linked, but in some people there are differences.

Step 1: Rate Your Skills

Nobody is going to grade you on your answers to this exercise. The most important thing is to answer honestly. If someone else will be using this book, do the writing on a separate piece of paper.

For each skill, read the definition and examples and then estimate your level of mastery. If you believe you command the skill at a moderate or high level, you'll confirm that estimate by providing examples from your own experiences of using the skill. At the end of the exercise, you'll review your self-estimates and examples and decide which are your outstanding skills.

Communication Skills

Definition: Exchanging information and feelings with others: understanding the words, ideas, and feelings of others through reading and attentive listening; effectively expressing ideas and feelings to others through writing, speaking, and body language.

Examples of High School Subjects That Teach It:

- English
- Literature
- Public speaking

Examples of Leisure Activities That Use It:

- Announcing or emceeing a program
- Getting information through a phone call
- Listening to friends describe their personal problems
- Speaking at a meeting of a club, church, or other organization
- Reading magazines, newspapers, and books
- Writing articles, stories, or plays
- Writing letters and e-mails to friends and family
- Maintaining a Web log (blog)

Examples of Work Tasks That Use It:

- Taking a telephone message
- Reading step-by-step instructions for completing a form
- Taking a customer's order
- Greeting tourists and explaining tourist attractions
- Answering inquiries regarding credit references
- Explaining to a patient what cautions to use when taking a certain medication
- Writing a memo to staff outlining new directives
- Interviewing job applicants
- Initiating, facilitating, and moderating classroom discussions
- Reading a scientific journal article describing surgical procedures
- Interviewing radio show guests about their lives, their work, or topics of current interest
- Writing a short story for publication
- Arguing a legal case before a jury

Using the high school courses, leisure activities, work tasks, and your knowledge of yourself for guidance, circle a number to estimate your level of command of this skill.

Communication Skills Self-Estimate

Low Level			Moderate Level			High Level		
1	2	3	4	5	6	7	8	9

If your self-estimate is 3 or lower, move on to the next skill, **Computer Programming Skills**. Otherwise, continue.

Examples of How I Demonstrated Communication Skills

Think of examples of how you have demonstrated your command of this skill and write the examples in the following worksheet.

- ☺ Write as many as you can, but you don't have to fill all the blanks.
- ☺ If possible, base your examples on work you've done, following the style of the work examples listed earlier.
- ☺ If you have little or no relevant work experience, write examples from school or leisure activities.

Examples of How I Demonstrated Communication Skills

_____

_____

_____

_____

_____

_____

_____

Based on the examples, do you now want to change your self-estimate? Feel free to do so. Then go on to the next skill.

Computer Programming Skills

Definition: Writing computer programs for various purposes: structuring the algorithm for the task at hand; organizing data storage; determining methods of input and output; choosing the right commands and syntax; correcting errors.

Examples of High School Subjects That Teach It:

- Computer science

Examples of Leisure Activities That Use It:

- Creating and modifying a macro in a word-processing program to accomplish a complex task
- Programming computer games
- Writing computer programs to solve puzzles

Examples of Work Tasks That Use It:

- Writing a program to convert metric measurements to inches, pounds, and so forth
- Coding a BASIC program to sort objects in a database
- Writing a computer program to extract text from a Web page and reformat it for a book
- Coding a function to accomplish a common text-processing task
- Coding a statistical analysis program to analyze demographic data
- Writing a program to analyze coded messages by finding patterns of letters that resemble normal text
- Designing a program to search the Web, compare prices for similar items, and present them as a buying guide

Using the high school courses, leisure activities, work tasks, and your knowledge of yourself for guidance, circle a number to estimate your level of command of this skill.

Computer Programming Skills Self-Estimate

Low Level			Moderate Level			High Level		
1	2	3	4	5	6	7	8	9

If your self-estimate is 3 or lower, move on to the next skill, **Equipment Use/Maintenance Skills.** Otherwise, continue.

Examples of How I Demonstrated Computer Programming Skills

Think of examples of how you have demonstrated your command of this skill and write the examples in the following worksheet.

- ◎ Write as many as you can, but you don't have to fill all the blanks.
- ◎ If possible, base your examples on work you've done, following the style of the work examples listed earlier.
- ◎ If you have little or no relevant work experience, write examples from school or leisure activities.

Examples of How I Demonstrated Computer Programming Skills

_____

_____

_____

_____

_____

_____

_____

Based on the examples, do you now want to change your self-estimate? Feel free to do so. Then go on to the next skill.

Equipment Use/Maintenance Skills

Definition: Operating, maintaining, and repairing equipment: controlling the equipment; monitoring gauges, dials, or other indicators; performing routine maintenance; troubleshooting problems; making repairs as needed.

Examples of High School Subjects That Teach It:

- Computer science
- Driver education
- Technology education

Examples of Leisure Activities That Use It:

- Doing electrical wiring and repairs in the home
- Operating a model train layout
- Operating flight or driving simulators on the computer
- Repairing plumbing in the home
- Working on bicycles, minibikes, lawn mowers, or cars

Examples of Work Tasks That Use It:

- Identifying the source of a leak by looking under a machine
- Adding oil to an engine as indicated by a gauge or warning light
- Monitoring completion times while running a computer program
- Adjusting the settings on a copy machine to make reduced-size photocopies
- Tightening a screw to get a door to close properly
- Monitoring machine functions on an automated production line
- Adjusting the speed of assembly-line equipment based on the type of product being assembled
- Cleaning moving parts in production machinery
- Identifying the circuit causing an electrical system to fail
- Replacing a faulty hydraulic valve
- Checking and maintaining respiratory therapy equipment
- During earth-drilling operations, changing bits to match the rock layers
- Operating a master console to monitor the performance of a computer network
- Conducting maintenance checks on an aircraft
- Repairing structural damage to a building after an earthquake

Lowest

Level of Skill

Highest

Using the high school courses, leisure activities, work tasks, and your knowledge of yourself for guidance, circle a number to estimate your level of command of this skill.

Equipment Use/Maintenance Skills Self-Estimate

Low Level		Moderate Level			High Level		
1	2	3	4	5	6	7	8	9

If your self-estimate is 3 or lower, move on to the next skill, **Equipment/Technology Analysis Skills**. Otherwise, continue.

Examples of How I Demonstrated Equipment Use/Maintenance Skills

Think of examples of how you have demonstrated your command of this skill and write the examples in the following worksheet.

- Write as many as you can, but you don't have to fill all the blanks.
- If possible, base your examples on work you've done, following the style of the work examples listed earlier.
- If you have little or no relevant work experience, write examples from school or leisure activities.

Examples of How I Demonstrated Equipment Use/Maintenance Skills

_____

_____

_____

_____

_____

_____

_____

Based on the examples, do you now want to change your self-estimate? Feel free to do so. Then go on to the next skill.

Equipment/Technology Analysis Skills

Definition: Designing, adapting, or selecting equipment or technology that addresses a need.

Examples of High School Subjects That Teach It:

- Computer science
- Technology education

Examples of Leisure Activities That Use It:

- Building robots or electronic devices
- Creating Web pages
- Designing lighting or sound effects for school or other amateur plays
- Modifying a car to improve performance or fuel efficiency
- Upgrading hardware in personal computers

Examples of Work Tasks That Use It:

Lowest

Level of Skill

Highest

- Selecting a photocopy machine for an office
- Adjusting exercise equipment for use by a client
- Selecting a screwdriver to use in adjusting a vehicle's carburetor
- Suggesting changes in software to make a system more user-friendly
- Redesigning the handle of a tool for easier gripping
- Choosing a software application to use to complete a work assignment
- Adapting an assistive device to better meet the specific need of a disabled patient
- Designing structures for use on farms
- Evaluating technical specifications of medical equipment to identify the best choice for intended use

Using the high school courses, leisure activities, work tasks, and your knowledge of yourself for guidance, circle a number to estimate your level of command of this skill.

Equipment/Technology Analysis Skills Self-Estimate

Low Level			Moderate Level			High Level		
1	2	3	4	5	6	7	8	9

If your self-estimate is 3 or lower, move on to the next skill, **Management Skills**. Otherwise, continue.

Examples of How I Demonstrated Equipment/Technology Analysis Skills

Think of examples of how you have demonstrated your command of this skill and write the examples in the following worksheet.

- Write as many as you can, but you don't have to fill all the blanks.
- If possible, base your examples on work you've done, following the style of the work examples listed earlier.
- If you have little or no relevant work experience, write examples from school or leisure activities.

Examples of How I Demonstrated Equipment/Technology Analysis Skills

_____

_____

_____

_____

_____

_____

_____

Based on the examples, do you now want to change your self-estimate? Feel free to do so. Then go on to the next skill.

Management Skills

Definition: Allocating resources efficiently: time, money, materials, and personnel.

Examples of High School Subjects That Teach It:

- Any advanced course in which students have considerable freedom to budget their time on projects
- Accounting
- Business education

Examples of Leisure Activities That Use It:

- Directing school or other amateur plays or musicals
- Helping to organize and run school or community events
- Helping to organize things at home, such as shopping lists and budgets
- Serving as a leader of a scouting or other group
- Serving as president of a club or other organization

Examples of Work Tasks That Use It:

- Keeping a monthly calendar of appointments
- Taking money from petty cash to buy office supplies and recording the amount
- Renting a meeting room for a management meeting
- Encouraging a co-worker who is having difficulty finishing a project
- Allocating the time of subordinates to projects for the coming week
- Preparing and managing a budget for a short-term project
- Evaluating an annual uniform service contract for delivery drivers
- Directing the activities of a road repair crew with minimal disruption of traffic flow
- Budgeting the funds of a business for staff, supplies, materials, and equipment
- Directing recruitment, hiring, and training of personnel
- Establishing short- and long-term plans for management of natural resources
- Allocating the time of scientists to multiple research projects

Lowest

Level of Skill

Highest

Using the high school courses, leisure activities, work tasks, and your knowledge of yourself for guidance, circle a number to estimate your level of command of this skill.

Management Skills Self-Estimate

Low Level			Moderate Level			High Level		
1	2	3	4	5	6	7	8	9

If your self-estimate is 3 or lower, move on to the next skill, **Mathematics Skills**. Otherwise, continue.

Examples of How I Demonstrated Management Skills

Think of examples of how you have demonstrated your command of this skill and write the examples in the following worksheet.

- Write as many as you can, but you don't have to fill all the blanks.
- If possible, base your examples on work you've done, following the style of the work examples listed earlier.
- If you have little or no relevant work experience, write examples from school or leisure activities.

Examples of How I Demonstrated Management Skills

_____

_____

_____

_____

_____

_____

_____

Based on the examples, do you now want to change your self-estimate? Feel free to do so. Then go on to the next skill.

Mathematics Skills

Definition: Using mathematics to solve problems: calculating; estimating; constructing mathematical models.

Examples of High School Subjects That Teach It:

- Algebra
- Geometry
- Trigonometry
- Calculus
- Business/Applied Mathematics

Examples of Leisure Activities That Use It:

- Balancing checkbooks for family members
- Computing sports statistics
- Serving as treasurer of a club or other organization
- Preparing family income tax returns

Examples of Work Tasks That Use It:

- Computing totals of orders placed by clients
- Counting the amount of change to be given to a customer
- Computing total playing time of a CD containing twelve songs of varying length
- Calculating heights, depths, relative positions, and property lines on an area of terrain
- Estimating how many cans of paint are needed to cover a house with two coats
- Computing reduction of heat loss from a house after application of attic insulation
- Calculating the square footage of a new home under construction
- Applying a mathematical theory to develop a new way to encrypt data
- Developing a mathematical model of how a mutated gene spreads through a population

Level of Skill — Lowest / Highest

Using the high school courses, leisure activities, work tasks, and your knowledge of yourself for guidance, circle a number to estimate your level of command of this skill.

Mathematics Skills Self-Estimate

Low Level			Moderate Level			High Level		
1	2	3	4	5	6	7	8	9

If your self-estimate is 3 or lower, move on to the next skill, **Quality Control Skills.** Otherwise, continue.

Examples of How I Demonstrated Mathematics Skills

Think of examples of how you have demonstrated your command of this skill and write the examples in the following worksheet.

- Write as many as you can, but you don't have to fill all the blanks.
- If possible, base your examples on work you've done, following the style of the work examples listed earlier.
- If you have little or no relevant work experience, write examples from school or leisure activities.

Examples of How I Demonstrated Mathematics Skills

_____

_____

_____

_____

_____

_____

_____

Based on the examples, do you now want to change your self-estimate? Feel free to do so. Then go on to the next skill.

Quality Control Skills

Definition: Conducting tests and inspections of products, services, or processes to evaluate quality or performance.

Examples of High School Subjects That Teach It:

- Business education
- Computer science
- Home economics
- Technology education

Examples of Leisure Activities That Use It:

- Judging entries in a cooking or talent contest
- Running diagnostic tests on a home computer
- Selecting photographs or drawings to put into a portfolio
- Serving as a judge at an athletic competition

Examples of Work Tasks That Use It:

- Verifying that stair treads are horizontal, using a spirit level
- Inspecting a draft memo for clerical errors
- Examining budget estimates for completeness and accuracy
- Checking samples of animal feed under a microscope to measure the amount of contamination by insect parts
- Measuring newly machined parts to verify that they meet specifications
- Reviewing specifications for construction of industrial equipment to determine that all safety requirements have been met
- Developing procedures to test performance of a computer system

Lowest

Level of Skill

Highest

Using the high school courses, leisure activities, work tasks, and your knowledge of yourself for guidance, circle a number to estimate your level of command of this skill.

Quality Control Skills Self-Estimate

Low Level			Moderate Level			High Level		
1	2	3	4	5	6	7	8	9

If your self-estimate is 3 or lower, move on to the next skill, **Science Skills.** Otherwise, continue.

Examples of How I Demonstrated Quality Control Skills

Think of examples of how you have demonstrated your command of this skill and write the examples in the following worksheet.

- Write as many as you can, but you don't have to fill all the blanks.
- If possible, base your examples on work you've done, following the style of the work examples listed earlier.
- If you have little or no relevant work experience, write examples from school or leisure activities.

Examples of How I Demonstrated Quality Control Skills

_____

_____

_____

_____

_____

_____

Based on the examples, do you now want to change your self-estimate? Feel free to do so. Then go on to the next skill.

Science Skills

Definition: Using scientific rules and methods to solve problems: observing phenomena; proposing a hypothesis; making a prediction; designing and conducting experiments to test the prediction; constructing theories.

Examples of High School Subjects That Teach It:

- Biology
- Chemistry
- Earth science
- Physics

Examples of Leisure Activities That Use It:

- Collecting rocks or minerals
- Conducting experiments involving plants
- Experimenting with a chemistry set
- Observing and studying the moon and stars
- Performing experiments for a science fair
- Studying the habits of wildlife

Examples of Work Tasks That Use It:

- Collecting air samples to determine levels of radioactive contamination
- Conducting standard tests in a dairy to determine nutrient contents of milk
- Conducting chemical analysis of blood to detect the presence of toxins
- Designing an experiment to test a hypothesis about what causes a product to fail
- Creating a questionnaire to measure public opinion during a political campaign
- Analyzing the effect of forest conditions on tree growth rates and tree species prevalence
- Conducting a research study concerning important factors in animal nutrition

Lowest

Level of Skill

Highest

Using the high school courses, leisure activities, work tasks, and your knowledge of yourself for guidance, circle a number to estimate your level of command of this skill.

Science Skills Self-Estimate

Low Level		Moderate Level			High Level		
1	2	3	4	5	6	7	8	9

If your self-estimate is 3 or lower, move on to the next skill, **Social Skills**. Otherwise, continue.

Examples of How I Demonstrated Science Skills

Think of examples of how you have demonstrated your command of this skill and write the examples in the following worksheet.

- ⚙ Write as many as you can, but you don't have to fill all the blanks.
- ⚙ If possible, base your examples on work you've done, following the style of the work examples listed earlier.
- ⚙ If you have little or no relevant work experience, write examples from school or leisure activities.

Examples of How I Demonstrated Science Skills

_____

_____

_____

_____

_____

_____

_____

Based on the examples, do you now want to change your self-estimate? Feel free to do so. Then go on to the next skill.

Social Skills

Definition: Working with people to achieve goals: noticing others' reactions; understanding and adjusting to their reactions; persuading others to change their minds or behavior; bringing others together and trying to reconcile differences; teaching others how to do something; actively looking for ways to help people.

Examples of High School Subjects That Teach It:

- Any course in which students work in teams
- Family living

Examples of Leisure Activities That Use It:

- Coaching children or youth in sports activities
- Helping persuade people to sign petitions or support a cause
- Helping sick relatives, friends, and neighbors
- Recruiting members for a club or other organization
- Serving as a volunteer counselor at a youth camp or center
- Tutoring pupils in school subjects or adults in literacy

Examples of Work Tasks That Use It:

- Noticing that customers are angry because they have been waiting too long
- Scheduling appointments for a medical clinic
- Presenting justification to a manager for altering a work schedule
- Asking customers if they would like cups of coffee
- Instructing a new employee in the use of a time clock
- Being aware of how a co-worker's promotion will affect a work group
- Convincing a supervisor to purchase a new copy machine
- Contracting with a wholesaler to sell items at a given cost
- Instructing a co-worker in how to operate a software program
- Instructing through lectures, discussions, and demonstrations in one or more subjects, such as English, mathematics, or social studies
- Negotiating labor disputes
- Organizing, leading, and promoting interest in recreational activities such as arts, crafts, sports, games, camping, and hobbies
- Counseling depressive patients during a crisis period

Level of Skill (Lowest / Highest)

Using the high school courses, leisure activities, work tasks, and your knowledge of yourself for guidance, circle a number to estimate your level of command of this skill.

Social Skills Self-Estimate

Low Level			Moderate Level			High Level		
1	2	3	4	5	6	7	8	9

If your self-estimate is 3 or lower, move on to the next skill, **Thought-Processing Skills**. Otherwise, continue.

Examples of How I Demonstrated Social Skills

Think of examples of how you have demonstrated your command of this skill and write the examples in the following worksheet.

- ⊚ Write as many as you can, but you don't have to fill all the blanks.
- ⊚ If possible, base your examples on work you've done, following the style of the work examples listed earlier.
- ⊚ If you have little or no relevant work experience, write examples from school or leisure activities.

Examples of How I Demonstrated Social Skills

_____

_____

_____

_____

_____

_____

_____

Based on the examples, do you now want to change your self-estimate? Feel free to do so. Then go on to the next skill.

Thought-Processing Skills

Definition: Using information in original ways to solve problems and improve performance: identifying complex problems and reviewing related information to develop and evaluate options and implement solutions; deciding what new information still needs to be learned and how to learn it; monitoring your performance and that of others to make improvements or take corrective action.

Examples of High School Subjects That Teach It:

- Any advanced literature or social studies course that requires research and original thinking, perhaps for a term paper
- Science lab, especially in an advanced course

Examples of Leisure Activities That Use It:

- Campaigning for political candidates or issues
- Designing and building an addition or remodeling the interior of a home
- Doing crossword puzzles
- Playing strategy games such as bridge or chess
- Running a fantasy baseball team

Examples of Work Tasks That Use It:

- Determining whether a subordinate has a good excuse for being late
- Thinking about the implications of information in a news article
- Learning a different method of completing a task from a co-worker
- Deciding how scheduling a break will affect work flow
- Evaluating customer complaints and determining appropriate responses
- Monitoring a meeting's progress and revising the agenda to ensure that important topics are discussed
- Redesigning a floor layout to take advantage of new manufacturing techniques
- Evaluating a loan application for degree of risk
- Identifying an alternative approach that might help trainees who are having difficulties
- Evaluating a proposed marketing strategy, based on knowledge of company objectives, market characteristics, and cost and markup factors
- Analyzing evidence at the scene of a fire and determining the probable cause
- Applying principles of educational psychology to develop new a teaching strategy
- Developing and implementing a plan to provide emergency relief for a major metropolitan area

Lowest

Level of Skill

Highest

Using the high school courses, leisure activities, work tasks, and your knowledge of yourself for guidance, circle a number to estimate your level of command of this skill.

Thought-Processing Skills Self-Estimate

Low Level	Moderate Level	High Level
1 2 3	4 5 6	7 8 9

If your self-estimate is 3 or lower, move on to **Decide on Your Top Skills**. Otherwise, continue.

Examples of How I Demonstrated Thought-Processing Skills

Think of examples of how you have demonstrated your command of this skill and write the examples in the following worksheet.

- Write as many as you can, but you don't have to fill all the blanks.
- If possible, base your examples on work you've done, following the style of the work examples listed earlier.
- If you have little or no relevant work experience, write examples from school or leisure activities.

Examples of How I Demonstrated Thought-Processing Skills

_____

_____

_____

_____

_____

_____

_____

Based on the examples, do you now want to change your self-estimate? Feel free to do so. Then go on to **Decide on Your Top Skills**.

Step 2: Decide on Your Top Skills

Now that you have completed the skills exercise, it's time to draw some conclusions. Look back over your self-estimates and the examples you wrote on the worksheets.

- Which skills received your highest self-estimates?
- For which skills did you provide the most examples?

Identify the three skills that have **a combination of high self-estimates and lots of examples.** Write them in the spaces below. Don't agonize over the ordering; what matters most is which three you choose, not how you order them. And don't feel you have to choose three. If one or two skills stand out greatly from the others, choose fewer than three.

My Three Top Skills

1. _____

2. _____

3. _____

If you did not have trouble deciding on your three top skills, go on to Part III.

But maybe you're having trouble choosing your top skills for one of the following reasons.

One of the skills with lots of examples does not have a high self-estimate.

You may have had a good reason for this response. Perhaps you have used a certain skill many times but never at a high level. For example, with Mathematical Skills, maybe you have done a lot of adding and subtracting but rarely have done any more complicated math than that. If your situation is like this, stick with your self-estimate for this skill—it is not one of your top skills. Concentrate on the skills for which your self-estimates and the number of examples are most consistently high. Write these in the box for My Three Top Skills. Then go on to Part III.

The skills with the highest self-estimates do not have many examples.

This could happen if you feel you have excellent command of a skill but have had few opportunities to demonstrate it. However, you need to give some thought to *why* you believe you have a high level of this skill. Surely you must have had some occasions to show your high level of mastery. Did you excel in this skill when you were in school? (If you're a young person, perhaps you're *still* in school and are excelling at this skill.) Do you use a high level of this skill in a hobby? If so, write examples from school or from your leisure activities on the worksheet and reconsider including this among My Three Top Skills.

If you have had few or no opportunities to demonstrate one of your high-rated skills, even in school or in leisure activities, then maybe your self-estimate is too high. Keep in mind that even though you may be convinced you excel at this skill, you will have a hard time convincing employers because you have so little evidence. Therefore you should downgrade your self-estimate and maybe not include this skill among My Three Top Skills.

None of my self-estimates is particularly high.

Perhaps you're too modest. Look at the skills with lots of examples and reconsider your level of ability.

If you're a young person, don't forget to consider the skills you are demonstrating in school and in your leisure activities. Even without much work experience, you may have evidence that you command one or more of these skills at a moderate or high level.

It's possible that you really don't have any of these skills at a high level, especially if you don't have much work experience yet or a distinguished academic record. In that case, focus on your three highest-rated skills, even if the ratings are at the moderate level, and write them as My Three Top Skills. Then go on to Part III.

I have more than three skills with high self-estimates and lots of examples.

Perhaps you're overconfident. You may want to reconsider your self-estimates by comparing yourself with professionals. For example, if you said you have a high level of Communication Skills, think about how your skills stack up to those of people who communicate for a living: professional writers, radio announcers, clergy, or counseling psychologists.

If you really do have a high level of command of four or more skills, good for you. But you need to narrow down your options. A helpful strategy is to go back and ask yourself which three high-rated skills give you the most *satisfaction*. Which would you rather spend every workday using? Those belong on the list of My Three Top Skills. After you write them in, go on to Part III.

I have an outstanding skill that's not included here.

This assessment focuses on general skills that are transferable from one kind of job to another. As you may remember from Part I, a skill is a learned capability. Some highly specific capabilities that you may consider to be skills—for example, musical or athletic talent—are better classified as *abilities* because they are not learned, and therefore they are not included here. Anyway, if you have these abilities at an outstanding level, you probably know what careers make use of them.

A lot of people with special talents use them in hobbies rather than at work. For example, they may pursue a career in sales because of their strong Social and Communication Skills but use their evenings and weekends to play music in a band, play soccer for a team, or find some other outlet for their special talents. Others establish themselves in a career that is not directly related to their special ability but then carve out a niche where they can exploit their other talent. For example, they might go into sales and eventually focus on selling musical instruments, sports equipment, or some other product or service where their special ability gives them an instant bond with clients.

I command a skill at a high level, but I don't enjoy it.

Even though you are good at this skill, you probably should not include it among My Top Three Skills. The purpose of My Top Three Skills is to help you identify jobs (in Parts III and IV) that might suit you. Therefore, you probably should not seek jobs where this skill is important. Even though you may be capable of entering one of these jobs and performing the tasks, you are unlikely to be happy with the work.

Of course, millions of people are unhappy with their jobs, but often what irks them is not the skills and tasks involved, but rather the work conditions (for example, outdoor work exposed to the weather), low economic rewards, or the particular boss or co-workers they happen to be assigned to. These discontented workers may be able to move into a more satisfying job that requires similar skills.

However, if you are unhappy with the job's core skills and the related work tasks, it will be much more difficult for you to find work of a different nature. Employers look at your past work to judge what you are capable of, and they tend to hire people who have worked in a similar field or who have demonstrated the skill in their educational or training background.

For My Top Three Skills, list only the skills that you *enjoy* using, even if it means listing only one skill that may not be your strongest.

There's a skill that I enjoy using, but I'm not good at it.

If you enjoy using a skill, it's likely that you will try to use it constantly and therefore will improve your mastery of it over time. Particularly if you are a young person with much of your schooling and training ahead of you, you may not yet have developed a certain skill that attracts you.

Consider including this skill among My Top Three Skills if you understand that you have a long way to go until you may be ready to use this skill for your livelihood. But also be cautious about pinning all your career hopes on this skill. Try to construct a plan B that uses other skills in case you fail to master this one.

Step 3: Find Jobs That Match Your Top Skills

Now that you have decided on your top skills, it's time to identify jobs that use them. Part III of this book contains several sets of lists with the names of jobs and basic economic facts about them. Each list focuses on one of the ten skills and consists of jobs that use that skill at a high level.

Here are some pointers about identifying likely jobs:

◉ A good place to start is the set of lists called "The 50 Best Jobs for Each Skill." For example, if you have strong Communication Skills, you may want to start by looking at "The 50 Best Jobs with a High Level of Communication Skills."

◉ You will find other lists that identify jobs that use the skill and that also have some other features that may be important to you: for example, jobs that pay the best; jobs with lots of opportunities for part-time work; or jobs that require education or training at a certain level.

◉ Give some thought to your work-related interests. First, consider which one of My Top Three Skills you most *enjoy* using and note which jobs are linked to it. Secondly, look at the lists that are organized by interest areas. In the interest areas that appeal to you, find jobs that use your favorite skill.

◉ Look at the lists for *each* of the skills on My Top Three Skills. Compare the lists and try to find jobs that appear twice or even three times. These are the jobs that use a skill set close to your own and that therefore deserve particular attention.

◉ If a job looks promising or if you aren't sure what it is, turn to Part IV and read the description there. (The jobs are ordered alphabetically.) You'll see the detailed facts about the job, including major tasks, the most important skills, all other above-average skills, the educational or training program that prepares for it, and other important topics.

◉ Consider this effort the first step in a long process of career exploration. Although skills are very important for choosing a career goal, they are not the only issue you need to explore. Before you can decide whether the job really is a good choice for you, you need to read more about it, talk to people who do it, talk to students or trainees who are preparing for it, and perhaps get a taste of actual work experience by visiting a job site. Preparing for a career usually means a big investment—perhaps of money, perhaps of time, and certainly of hopes. Invest wisely.

PART III

The Best Jobs Lists: Jobs for Each of the 10 Skills

If you have completed the exercise in Part II, you now have an idea of which skills are your strongest. In this part of the book you can find jobs that use your top skills and that also have good rewards in terms of income and job opportunities. Browse the lists of jobs to get ideas about careers that might be good choices for you. Then turn to Part IV to read the job descriptions and get an overview of what the jobs are like.

Best Jobs Overall for Each Skill: Jobs with the Highest Pay, Fastest Growth, and Most Openings

The four sets of lists that follow are the most important lists in this book. The first set of lists presents, for each skill, the jobs with the highest combined scores for pay, growth, and number of openings. Note that a job appears in a list for a skill if that skill is one of its top three skills. Since most jobs have three top skills, most jobs appear on three of these lists. This also means that although there are nine lists of 50 jobs and one of 40 jobs, the total number of unique job titles is 230, rather than 490.

Look at the lists for *all three* of your top skills and try to find jobs that appear on two or three of these lists. These are the best match for your top skills. Or if your number-one skill greatly outweighs all other skills, focus on the list for that skill.

These are very appealing lists because they represent jobs with the very highest quantifiable measures from our labor market. The 230 jobs in these ten lists are the ones that are described in detail in Part IV.

The three additional sets of lists present, for each skill, 20 jobs with the highest scores in each of three measures: annual earnings, projected percentage growth, and largest number of openings.

The 50 Best Jobs for Each Skill

These are the lists that most people want to see first. For each skill, you can see the jobs that have the highest overall combined ratings for earnings, projected growth, and number of openings. (The section in the Introduction called "How the Best Jobs for Your Skills Were Selected" explains in detail how we rated jobs to assemble this list.)

Although each list covers one skill, you'll notice a wide variety of jobs on the list. For example, among the top 10 jobs with a high level of Communication Skills are some in the fields of business, higher education, and medicine. Among the top 10 jobs with a high level of Equipment Use/Maintenance Skills are some in the fields of high tech, health, construction, and transportation.

A look at one list will clarify how we ordered the jobs—take the Communication Skills list as an example. Teachers, Postsecondary, was the occupation with the best total score, and it is on the top of the list. The other occupations follow in descending order based on their total scores. Many jobs had tied scores and were simply listed one after another, so there are often only very small or even no differences between the scores of jobs that are near each other on the list. All other jobs lists in this book use these jobs as their source list. You can find descriptions for each of these jobs in Part IV, beginning on page 167. If a job appeals to you, or if you're not sure what it is, find it alphabetically in Part IV and read the description.

The 50 Best Jobs with a High Level of Communication Skills

Job	Annual Earnings	Percent Growth	Annual Openings
1. Teachers, Postsecondary	$53,590	32.2%	329,000
2. Surgeons	more than $145,600	24.0%	41,000
3. Dental Hygienists	$60,890	43.3%	17,000
4. Medical Scientists, Except Epidemiologists	$61,730	34.1%	15,000
5. Personal Financial Advisors	$63,500	25.9%	17,000
6. Physical Therapists	$63,080	36.7%	13,000
7. Physician Assistants	$72,030	49.6%	10,000
8. Pharmacists	$89,820	24.6%	16,000
9. Social and Community Service Managers	$49,500	25.5%	17,000
10. Market Research Analysts	$57,300	19.6%	20,000
11. Employment Interviewers	$41,780	30.5%	30,000
12. Lawyers	$98,930	15.0%	40,000
13. Public Relations Specialists	$45,020	22.9%	38,000
14. Computer Support Specialists	$40,610	23.0%	87,000
15. Occupational Therapists	$56,860	33.6%	7,000
16. Administrative Services Managers	$64,020	16.9%	25,000
17. Paralegals and Legal Assistants	$41,170	29.7%	28,000
18. Elementary School Teachers, Except Special Education	$44,040	18.2%	203,000

The 50 Best Jobs with a High Level of Communication Skills

Job	Annual Earnings	Percent Growth	Annual Openings
19. Training and Development Specialists	$45,870	20.8%	32,000
20. Radiologic Technicians	$45,950	23.2%	17,000
21. Radiologic Technologists	$45,950	23.2%	17,000
22. Diagnostic Medical Sonographers	$54,370	34.8%	5,000
23. Special Education Teachers, Preschool, Kindergarten, and Elementary School	$44,630	23.3%	18,000
24. Medical Assistants	$25,350	52.1%	93,000
25. Self-Enrichment Education Teachers	$32,360	25.3%	74,000
26. Clinical Psychologists	$57,170	19.1%	10,000
27. Counseling Psychologists	$57,170	19.1%	10,000
28. School Psychologists	$57,170	19.1%	10,000
29. Kindergarten Teachers, Except Special Education	$42,230	22.4%	28,000
30. Compensation, Benefits, and Job Analysis Specialists	$48,870	20.4%	15,000
31. Sales Agents, Financial Services	$67,130	11.5%	37,000
32. Police Patrol Officers	$46,290	15.5%	47,000
33. Sheriffs and Deputy Sheriffs	$46,290	15.5%	47,000
34. Public Relations Managers	$76,450	21.7%	5,000
35. Sales Representatives, Wholesale and Manufacturing, Except Technical and Scientific Products	$47,380	12.9%	169,000
36. Secondary School Teachers, Except Special and Vocational Education	$46,060	14.4%	107,000
37. Personal and Home Care Aides	$17,340	41.0%	230,000
38. Customer Service Representatives	$27,490	22.8%	510,000
39. Industrial Engineers	$66,670	16.0%	13,000
40. Technical Writers	$55,160	23.2%	5,000
41. Medical and Public Health Social Workers	$41,120	25.9%	14,000
42. Compensation and Benefits Managers	$69,130	21.5%	4,000
43. Preschool Teachers, Except Special Education	$21,990	33.1%	77,000
44. Social and Human Service Assistants	$25,030	29.7%	61,000
45. Educational, Vocational, and School Counselors	$46,440	14.8%	32,000
46. Licensed Practical and Licensed Vocational Nurses	$35,230	17.1%	84,000
47. Respiratory Therapists	$45,140	28.4%	7,000
48. Middle School Teachers, Except Special and Vocational Education	$44,640	13.7%	83,000
49. Bill and Account Collectors	$28,160	21.4%	85,000
50. Legal Secretaries	$37,750	17.4%	41,000

Job 2 shares 41,000 openings with six other jobs not included in this list. Job 11 shares 30,000 openings with another job not included in this list. Jobs 20 and 21 share 17,000 job openings. Jobs 26, 27, and 28 share 10,000 job openings. Job 31 shares 37,000 openings with another job not included in this list. Jobs 32 and 33 share 47,000 job openings. Job 42 shares 4,000 openings with another job not included in this list.

The 40 Best Jobs with a High Level of Computer Programming Skills

Job	Annual Earnings	Percent Growth	Annual Openings
1. Computer Software Engineers, Applications	$77,090	48.4%	54,000
2. Computer Software Engineers, Systems Software	$82,120	43.0%	37,000
3. Computer Systems Analysts	$68,300	31.4%	56,000
4. Computer and Information Systems Managers	$96,520	25.9%	25,000
5. Network Systems and Data Communications Analysts	$61,750	54.6%	43,000
6. Computer Security Specialists	$59,930	38.4%	34,000
7. Network and Computer Systems Administrators	$59,930	38.4%	34,000
8. Financial Analysts	$63,860	17.3%	28,000
9. Accountants	$52,210	22.4%	157,000
10. Actuaries	$81,640	23.2%	3,000
11. Administrative Services Managers	$64,020	16.9%	25,000
12. Database Administrators	$63,250	38.2%	9,000
13. Environmental Engineers	$68,090	30.0%	5,000
14. Sales Engineers	$74,200	14.0%	8,000
15. Electrical Engineers	$73,510	11.8%	12,000
16. Computer Hardware Engineers	$84,420	10.1%	5,000
17. Chemical Engineers	$77,140	10.6%	3,000
18. Atmospheric and Space Scientists	$73,940	16.5%	1,000
19. Hydrologists	$63,820	31.6%	1,000
20. Criminal Investigators and Special Agents	$55,790	16.3%	9,000
21. Astronomers	$104,670	10.4%	fewer than 500
22. Multi-Media Artists and Animators	$50,290	14.1%	14,000
23. Computer Programmers	$63,420	2.0%	28,000
24. Epidemiologists	$52,170	26.2%	1,000
25. Electronics Engineering Technicians	$48,040	9.8%	18,000
26. Operations Research Analysts	$62,180	8.4%	7,000
27. Agricultural Engineers	$64,890	12.0%	fewer than 500
28. Economists	$73,690	5.6%	1,000
29. Machinists	$34,350	4.3%	33,000
30. Materials Scientists	$71,450	8.0%	fewer than 500
31. Mapping Technicians	$31,290	9.6%	9,000
32. Statisticians	$62,450	4.6%	2,000
33. Archivists	$37,420	13.4%	1,000
34. Aerospace Engineering and Operations Technicians	$52,450	8.5%	1,000
35. Geographers	$63,550	6.8%	fewer than 500
36. Electrical and Electronic Equipment Assemblers	$25,130	–6.4%	33,000

The 40 Best Jobs with a High Level of Computer Programming Skills

Job	Annual Earnings	Percent Growth	Annual Openings
37. Foresters	$48,670	6.7%	1,000
38. Numerical Tool and Process Control Programmers	$41,830	–1.1%	2,000
39. Forging Machine Setters, Operators, and Tenders, Metal and Plastic	$28,970	–4.6%	4,000
40. Statistical Assistants	$28,950	5.7%	1,000

Jobs 6 and 7 share 34,000 job openings. Job 9 shares 157,000 openings with another job not included in this list. Job 20 shares 9,000 openings with three other jobs not included in this list. Job 25 shares 18,000 openings with another job not included in this list. Job 31 shares 9,000 openings with another job not included in this list.

The 50 Best Jobs with a High Level of Equipment Use/Maintenance Skills

Job	Annual Earnings	Percent Growth	Annual Openings
1. Network Systems and Data Communications Analysts	$61,750	54.6%	43,000
2. Anesthesiologists	more than $145,600	24.0%	41,000
3. Management Analysts	$66,380	20.1%	82,000
4. Network and Computer Systems Administrators	$59,930	38.4%	34,000
5. Computer Support Specialists	$40,610	23.0%	87,000
6. Pipe Fitters and Steamfitters	$42,160	15.7%	61,000
7. Plumbers	$42,160	15.7%	61,000
8. Medical and Clinical Laboratory Technologists	$47,710	20.5%	14,000
9. Airline Pilots, Copilots, and Flight Engineers	$138,170	17.2%	7,000
10. Forest Fire Fighters	$39,090	24.3%	21,000
11. Municipal Fire Fighters	$39,090	24.3%	21,000
12. First-Line Supervisors/Managers of Construction Trades and Extraction Workers	$51,970	10.9%	57,000
13. Construction Managers	$72,260	10.4%	28,000
14. First-Line Supervisors/Managers of Mechanics, Installers, and Repairers	$51,980	12.4%	33,000
15. Technical Directors/Managers	$53,860	16.6%	11,000
16. Heating and Air Conditioning Mechanics and Installers	$37,040	19.0%	33,000
17. Refrigeration Mechanics and Installers	$37,040	19.0%	33,000
18. Licensed Practical and Licensed Vocational Nurses	$35,230	17.1%	84,000
19. Electricians	$42,790	11.8%	68,000
20. Forest Fire Fighting and Prevention Supervisors	$60,840	21.1%	4,000
21. Municipal Fire Fighting and Prevention Supervisors	$60,840	21.1%	4,000

(continued)

(continued)

The 50 Best Jobs with a High Level of Equipment Use/Maintenance Skills

Job	Annual Earnings	Percent Growth	Annual Openings
22. Rough Carpenters	$35,580	13.8%	210,000
23. Automotive Master Mechanics	$33,050	15.7%	93,000
24. Automotive Specialty Technicians	$33,050	15.7%	93,000
25. Truck Drivers, Heavy and Tractor-Trailer	$34,280	12.9%	274,000
26. Dental Assistants	$29,520	42.7%	45,000
27. Cardiovascular Technologists and Technicians	$40,420	32.6%	5,000
28. Electrical Engineering Technicians	$48,040	9.8%	18,000
29. Electronics Engineering Technicians	$48,040	9.8%	18,000
30. Bus Drivers, Transit and Intercity	$31,010	21.7%	34,000
31. Bus and Truck Mechanics and Diesel Engine Specialists	$36,620	14.4%	32,000
32. Aircraft Mechanics and Service Technicians	$47,310	13.4%	11,000
33. Railroad Conductors and Yardmasters	$54,040	20.3%	3,000
34. Maintenance and Repair Workers, General	$31,210	15.2%	154,000
35. Telecommunications Line Installers and Repairers	$42,410	10.8%	23,000
36. Nuclear Medicine Technologists	$59,670	21.5%	2,000
37. Sheet Metal Workers	$36,390	12.2%	50,000
38. First-Line Supervisors/Managers of Production and Operating Workers	$46,140	2.7%	89,000
39. Medical and Clinical Laboratory Technicians	$31,700	25.0%	14,000
40. Operating Engineers and Other Construction Equipment Operators	$35,830	11.6%	37,000
41. Radiation Therapists	$62,340	26.3%	1,000
42. Highway Maintenance Workers	$30,250	23.3%	27,000
43. Commercial Pilots	$55,810	16.8%	2,000
44. Elevator Installers and Repairers	$59,190	14.8%	3,000
45. Film and Video Editors	$46,930	18.6%	3,000
46. Air Traffic Controllers	$107,590	14.3%	2,000
47. Industrial Engineering Technicians	$45,280	10.5%	7,000
48. First-Line Supervisors/Managers of Housekeeping and Janitorial Workers	$30,330	19.0%	21,000
49. Electrical and Electronics Repairers, Commercial and Industrial Equipment	$44,120	9.7%	8,000
50. Mobile Heavy Equipment Mechanics, Except Engines	$39,410	8.8%	14,000

Job 2 shares 41,000 openings with six other jobs not included in this list. Job 4 shares 34,000 openings with another job not included in this list. Jobs 6 and 7 share 61,000 job openings. Jobs 10 and 11 share 21,000 job openings. Job 14 shares 11,000 openings with four other jobs not included in this list. Jobs 16 and 17 share 33,000 job openings. Jobs 20 and 21 share 4,000 job openings. Job 22 shares 210,000 openings with another job not included in this list. Jobs 23 and 24 share 93,000 job openings. Jobs 28 and 29 share 18,000 job openings.

The 50 Best Jobs with a High Level of Equipment/Technology Analysis Skills

Job	Annual Earnings	Percent Growth	Annual Openings
1. Computer Software Engineers, Applications	$77,090	48.4%	54,000
2. Computer Software Engineers, Systems Software	$82,120	43.0%	37,000
3. Computer Systems Analysts	$68,300	31.4%	56,000
4. Network Systems and Data Communications Analysts	$61,750	54.6%	43,000
5. Computer Security Specialists	$59,930	38.4%	34,000
6. Network and Computer Systems Administrators	$59,930	38.4%	34,000
7. Civil Engineers	$66,190	16.5%	19,000
8. Database Administrators	$63,250	38.2%	9,000
9. Engineering Managers	$100,760	13.0%	15,000
10. Industrial Engineers	$66,670	16.0%	13,000
11. Cost Estimators	$52,020	18.2%	15,000
12. Pipe Fitters and Steamfitters	$42,160	15.7%	61,000
13. Plumbers	$42,160	15.7%	61,000
14. Directors—Stage, Motion Pictures, Television, and Radio	$53,860	16.6%	11,000
15. Technical Directors/Managers	$53,860	16.6%	11,000
16. Forest Fire Fighters	$39,090	24.3%	21,000
17. Municipal Fire Fighters	$39,090	24.3%	21,000
18. Storage and Distribution Managers	$69,120	12.7%	15,000
19. Copy Writers	$46,420	17.7%	14,000
20. Architects, Except Landscape and Naval	$62,850	17.3%	7,000
21. Criminal Investigators and Special Agents	$55,790	16.3%	9,000
22. Immigration and Customs Inspectors	$55,790	16.3%	9,000
23. Electrical Engineers	$73,510	11.8%	12,000
24. Refrigeration Mechanics and Installers	$37,040	19.0%	33,000
25. Technical Writers	$55,160	23.2%	5,000
26. Dental Assistants	$29,520	42.7%	45,000
27. Sales Engineers	$74,200	14.0%	8,000
28. First-Line Supervisors/Managers of Mechanics, Installers, and Repairers	$51,980	12.4%	33,000
29. Electronics Engineers, Except Computer	$78,030	9.7%	11,000
30. Multi-Media Artists and Animators	$50,290	14.1%	14,000
31. Mechanical Engineers	$67,590	11.1%	11,000
32. Electricians	$42,790	11.8%	68,000
33. Biomedical Engineers	$71,840	30.7%	1,000
34. Graphic Designers	$38,390	15.2%	35,000

(continued)

(continued)

The 50 Best Jobs with a High Level of Equipment/Technology Analysis Skills

Job	Annual Earnings	Percent Growth	Annual Openings
35. Fitness Trainers and Aerobics Instructors	$25,840	27.1%	50,000
36. Surgical Technologists	$34,830	29.5%	12,000
37. Automotive Specialty Technicians	$33,050	15.7%	93,000
38. Art Directors	$63,950	11.5%	10,000
39. Rough Carpenters	$35,580	13.8%	210,000
40. Radiation Therapists	$62,340	26.3%	1,000
41. Computer Hardware Engineers	$84,420	10.1%	5,000
42. Tile and Marble Setters	$36,530	22.9%	9,000
43. Computer Programmers	$63,420	2.0%	28,000
44. Film and Video Editors	$46,930	18.6%	3,000
45. Aerospace Engineers	$84,090	8.3%	6,000
46. Interior Designers	$41,350	15.5%	10,000
47. Industrial Production Managers	$75,580	0.8%	13,000
48. Landscape Architects	$54,220	19.4%	1,000
49. Chemical Engineers	$77,140	10.6%	3,000
50. Occupational Therapist Assistants	$39,750	34.1%	2,000

Jobs 5 and 6 share 34,000 job openings. Jobs 12 and 13 share 61,000 job openings. Jobs 14 and 15 share 11,000 openings with each other and with three other jobs not included in this list. Jobs 16 and 17 share 21,000 job openings. Job 18 shares 15,000 openings with another job not included in this list. Job 19 shares 14,000 openings with another job not included in this list. Job 21 and 22 share 9,000 openings with each other and with two other jobs not included in this list. Job 24 shares 33,000 openings with another job not included in this list. Job 37 shares 93,000 openings with another job not included in this list. Job 39 shares 210,000 openings with another job not included in this list.

The 50 Best Jobs with a High Level of Management Skills

Job	Annual Earnings	Percent Growth	Annual Openings
1. Computer and Information Systems Managers	$96,520	25.9%	25,000
2. General and Operations Managers	$81,480	17.0%	208,000
3. Computer Security Specialists	$59,930	38.4%	34,000
4. Medical and Health Services Managers	$69,700	22.8%	33,000
5. Sales Managers	$87,580	19.7%	40,000
6. Management Analysts	$66,380	20.1%	82,000
7. Marketing Managers	$92,680	20.8%	23,000
8. Accountants	$52,210	22.4%	157,000
9. Auditors	$52,210	22.4%	157,000

The 50 Best Jobs with a High Level of Management Skills

Job	Annual Earnings	Percent Growth	Annual Openings
10. Medical Scientists, Except Epidemiologists	$61,730	34.1%	15,000
11. Financial Managers, Branch or Department	$86,280	14.8%	63,000
12. Treasurers and Controllers	$86,280	14.8%	63,000
13. Education Administrators, Postsecondary	$70,350	21.3%	18,000
14. Chief Executives	$142,440	14.9%	38,000
15. Financial Analysts	$63,860	17.3%	28,000
16. Employment Interviewers	$41,780	30.5%	30,000
17. Personnel Recruiters	$41,780	30.5%	30,000
18. Administrative Services Managers	$64,020	16.9%	25,000
19. Instructional Coordinators	$50,430	27.5%	15,000
20. Social and Community Service Managers	$49,500	25.5%	17,000
21. Training and Development Managers	$74,180	25.9%	3,000
22. Public Relations Managers	$76,450	21.7%	5,000
23. Advertising and Promotions Managers	$68,860	20.3%	9,000
24. Forest Fire Fighters	$39,090	24.3%	21,000
25. Compensation and Benefits Managers	$69,130	21.5%	4,000
26. Chiropractors	$67,200	22.4%	4,000
27. Education Administrators, Elementary and Secondary School	$75,400	10.4%	27,000
28. Social and Human Service Assistants	$25,030	29.7%	61,000
29. Cost Estimators	$52,020	18.2%	15,000
30. Veterinarians	$68,910	17.4%	8,000
31. Optometrists	$88,040	19.7%	2,000
32. Sales Representatives, Wholesale and Manufacturing, Except Technical and Scientific Products	$47,380	12.9%	169,000
33. Bill and Account Collectors	$28,160	21.4%	85,000
34. Nursing Aides, Orderlies, and Attendants	$21,440	22.3%	307,000
35. Storage and Distribution Managers	$69,120	12.7%	15,000
36. Transportation Managers	$69,120	12.7%	15,000
37. Forest Fire Fighting and Prevention Supervisors	$60,840	21.1%	4,000
38. Municipal Fire Fighting and Prevention Supervisors	$60,840	21.1%	4,000
39. Directors—Stage, Motion Pictures, Television, and Radio	$53,860	16.6%	11,000
40. Producers	$53,860	16.6%	11,000
41. Program Directors	$53,860	16.6%	11,000
42. Technical Directors/Managers	$53,860	16.6%	11,000
43. Architects, Except Landscape and Naval	$62,850	17.3%	7,000
44. Property, Real Estate, and Community Association Managers	$41,900	15.3%	58,000

(continued)

(continued)

The 50 Best Jobs with a High Level of Management Skills

Job	Annual Earnings	Percent Growth	Annual Openings
45. Dentists, General	$125,300	13.5%	7,000
46. Coaches and Scouts	$25,990	20.4%	63,000
47. First-Line Supervisors/Managers of Construction Trades and Extraction Workers	$51,970	10.9%	57,000
48. First-Line Supervisors/Managers of Mechanics, Installers, and Repairers	$51,980	12.4%	33,000
49. First-Line Supervisors/Managers of Police and Detectives	$65,570	15.5%	9,000
50. First-Line Supervisors/Managers of Transportation and Material-Moving Machine and Vehicle Operators	$47,530	15.3%	22,000

Job 3 shares 34,000 openings with another job not included in this list. Jobs 8 and 9 share 157,000 job openings. Jobs 11 and 12 share 63,000 job openings. Jobs 16 and 17 share 30,000 job openings. Job 24 shares 21,000 openings with another job not included in this list. Job 25 shares 4,000 openings with another job not included in this list. Jobs 35 and 36 share 15,000 job openings. Jobs 37 and 38 share 4,000 job openings. Jobs 39, 40, 41, and 42 share 11,000 openings with each other and with another job not included in this list.

The 50 Best Jobs with a High Level of Mathematics Skills

Job	Annual Earnings	Percent Growth	Annual Openings
1. Pharmacists	$89,820	24.6%	16,000
2. Treasurers and Controllers	$86,280	14.8%	63,000
3. Accountants	$52,210	22.4%	157,000
4. Auditors	$52,210	22.4%	157,000
5. Personal Financial Advisors	$63,500	25.9%	17,000
6. Financial Analysts	$63,860	17.3%	28,000
7. Civil Engineers	$66,190	16.5%	19,000
8. Environmental Engineers	$68,090	30.0%	5,000
9. Industrial Engineers	$66,670	16.0%	13,000
10. Engineering Managers	$100,760	13.0%	15,000
11. Sales Agents, Financial Services	$67,130	11.5%	37,000
12. Sales Agents, Securities and Commodities	$67,130	11.5%	37,000
13. Actuaries	$81,640	23.2%	3,000
14. Cost Estimators	$52,020	18.2%	15,000
15. Construction Managers	$72,260	10.4%	28,000
16. Transportation Managers	$69,120	12.7%	15,000
17. Heating and Air Conditioning Mechanics and Installers	$37,040	19.0%	33,000

The 50 Best Jobs with a High Level of Mathematics Skills

Job	Annual Earnings	Percent Growth	Annual Openings
18. Property, Real Estate, and Community Association Managers	$41,900	15.3%	58,000
19. Environmental Scientists and Specialists, Including Health	$52,630	17.1%	8,000
20. Respiratory Therapists	$45,140	28.4%	7,000
21. Appraisers, Real Estate	$43,440	22.8%	9,000
22. Assessors	$43,440	22.8%	9,000
23. Medical Assistants	$25,350	52.1%	93,000
24. Natural Sciences Managers	$93,090	13.6%	5,000
25. Hydrologists	$63,820	31.6%	1,000
26. Mechanical Engineers	$67,590	11.1%	11,000
27. Real Estate Sales Agents	$39,240	14.7%	41,000
28. Construction Carpenters	$35,580	13.8%	210,000
29. Rough Carpenters	$35,580	13.8%	210,000
30. Payroll and Timekeeping Clerks	$31,360	17.3%	36,000
31. Tile and Marble Setters	$36,530	22.9%	9,000
32. Construction and Building Inspectors	$44,720	22.3%	6,000
33. Pharmacy Technicians	$24,390	28.6%	35,000
34. Electricians	$42,790	11.8%	68,000
35. Human Resources Assistants, Except Payroll and Timekeeping	$32,730	16.7%	28,000
36. Gaming Managers	$59,940	22.6%	1,000
37. Commercial Pilots	$55,810	16.8%	2,000
38. Budget Analysts	$58,910	13.5%	6,000
39. Epidemiologists	$52,170	26.2%	1,000
40. Cement Masons and Concrete Finishers	$32,030	15.9%	32,000
41. Interior Designers	$41,350	15.5%	10,000
42. Landscape Architects	$54,220	19.4%	1,000
43. Purchasing Managers	$76,270	7.0%	8,000
44. Electrical Engineering Technicians	$48,040	9.8%	18,000
45. Sheet Metal Workers	$36,390	12.2%	50,000
46. Real Estate Brokers	$57,190	7.8%	12,000
47. Fire-Prevention and Protection Engineers	$65,210	13.4%	2,000
48. Product Safety Engineers	$65,210	13.4%	2,000
49. Gaming Supervisors	$40,300	16.3%	8,000
50. Purchasing Agents, Except Wholesale, Retail, and Farm Products	$49,030	8.1%	19,000

Job 2 shares 63,000 openings with another job not included in this list. Jobs 3 and 4 share 157,000 job openings. Jobs 11 and 12 share 37,000 job openings. Job 16 shares 15,000 openings with another job not included in this list. Job 17 shares 33,000 openings with another job not included in this list. Jobs 21 and 22 share 9,000 job openings. Jobs 28 and 29 share 210,000 job openings. Job 44 shares 18,000 openings with another job not included in this list. Jobs 47 and 48 share 2,000 job openings.

The 50 Best Jobs with a High Level of Quality Control Skills

Job	Annual Earnings	Percent Growth	Annual Openings
1. Computer Software Engineers, Applications	$77,090	48.4%	54,000
2. Computer and Information Systems Managers	$96,520	25.9%	25,000
3. Computer Systems Analysts	$68,300	31.4%	56,000
4. Management Analysts	$66,380	20.1%	82,000
5. Medical and Health Services Managers	$69,700	22.8%	33,000
6. Database Administrators	$63,250	38.2%	9,000
7. Medical and Clinical Laboratory Technologists	$47,710	20.5%	14,000
8. First-Line Supervisors/Managers of Construction Trades and Extraction Workers	$51,970	10.9%	57,000
9. First-Line Supervisors/Managers of Transportation and Material-Moving Machine and Vehicle Operators	$47,530	15.3%	22,000
10. Pipe Fitters and Steamfitters	$42,160	15.7%	61,000
11. Copy Writers	$46,420	17.7%	14,000
12. Electronics Engineers, Except Computer	$78,030	9.7%	11,000
13. Diagnostic Medical Sonographers	$54,370	34.8%	5,000
14. Technical Writers	$55,160	23.2%	5,000
15. Graphic Designers	$38,390	15.2%	35,000
16. Construction Carpenters	$35,580	13.8%	210,000
17. Food Service Managers	$41,340	11.5%	61,000
18. Aircraft Mechanics and Service Technicians	$47,310	13.4%	11,000
19. Budget Analysts	$58,910	13.5%	6,000
20. Construction and Building Inspectors	$44,720	22.3%	6,000
21. Aerospace Engineers	$84,090	8.3%	6,000
22. Computer Hardware Engineers	$84,420	10.1%	5,000
23. Nuclear Medicine Technologists	$59,670	21.5%	2,000
24. Commercial and Industrial Designers	$52,200	10.8%	7,000
25. Medical and Clinical Laboratory Technicians	$31,700	25.0%	14,000
26. Biomedical Engineers	$71,840	30.7%	1,000
27. Elevator Installers and Repairers	$59,190	14.8%	3,000
28. Wholesale and Retail Buyers, Except Farm Products	$42,870	8.4%	20,000
29. Cardiovascular Technologists and Technicians	$40,420	32.6%	5,000
30. First-Line Supervisors/Managers of Production and Operating Workers	$46,140	2.7%	89,000
31. Industrial Production Managers	$75,580	0.8%	13,000
32. Product Safety Engineers	$65,210	13.4%	2,000
33. Biological Technicians	$34,270	17.2%	8,000

The 50 Best Jobs with a High Level of Quality Control Skills

Job	Annual Earnings	Percent Growth	Annual Openings
34. Forensic Science Technicians	$44,590	36.4%	2,000
35. Materials Engineers	$69,660	12.2%	2,000
36. Industrial Engineering Technicians	$45,280	10.5%	7,000
37. Atmospheric and Space Scientists	$73,940	16.5%	1,000
38. First-Line Supervisors/Managers of Helpers, Laborers, and Material Movers, Hand	$39,000	8.1%	15,000
39. Environmental Science and Protection Technicians, Including Health	$36,260	16.3%	6,000
40. Financial Examiners	$63,090	9.5%	3,000
41. Microbiologists	$56,870	17.2%	1,000
42. Chemists	$57,890	7.3%	5,000
43. Motorboat Mechanics	$32,780	15.1%	7,000
44. Aviation Inspectors	$49,490	11.4%	2,000
45. Transportation Vehicle, Equipment, and Systems Inspectors, Except Aviation	$49,490	11.4%	2,000
46. Medical Equipment Repairers	$39,570	14.8%	4,000
47. Machinists	$34,350	4.3%	33,000
48. Telecommunications Equipment Installers and Repairers, Except Line Installers	$50,620	–4.9%	21,000
49. Computer, Automated Teller, and Office Machine Repairers	$36,060	3.8%	31,000
50. Sound Engineering Technicians	$38,390	18.4%	2,000

Job 10 shares 61,000 openings with another job not included in this list. Job 11 shares 14,000 openings with another job not included in this list. Job 16 shares 210,000 openings with another job not included in this list. Job 32 shares 2,000 openings with two other jobs not included in this list. Jobs 44 and 45 share 2,000 openings with each other and with another job not included in this list.

The 50 Best Jobs with a High Level of Science Skills

Job	Annual Earnings	Percent Growth	Annual Openings
1. Anesthesiologists	more than $145,600	24.0%	41,000
2. Internists, General	more than $145,600	24.0%	41,000
3. Obstetricians and Gynecologists	more than $145,600	24.0%	41,000
4. Psychiatrists	more than $145,600	24.0%	41,000
5. Surgeons	more than $145,600	24.0%	41,000
6. Family and General Practitioners	$140,400	24.0%	41,000
7. Computer Software Engineers, Systems Software	$82,120	43.0%	37,000

(continued)

(continued)

The 50 Best Jobs with a High Level of Science Skills

Job	Annual Earnings	Percent Growth	Annual Openings
8. Pediatricians, General	$136,600	24.0%	41,000
9. Pharmacists	$89,820	24.6%	16,000
10. Teachers, Postsecondary	$53,590	32.2%	329,000
11. Marketing Managers	$92,680	20.8%	23,000
12. Physician Assistants	$72,030	49.6%	10,000
13. Registered Nurses	$54,670	29.4%	229,000
14. Dental Hygienists	$60,890	43.3%	17,000
15. Physical Therapists	$63,080	36.7%	13,000
16. Medical Scientists, Except Epidemiologists	$61,730	34.1%	15,000
17. Airline Pilots, Copilots, and Flight Engineers	$138,170	17.2%	7,000
18. Civil Engineers	$66,190	16.5%	19,000
19. Occupational Therapists	$56,860	33.6%	7,000
20. Environmental Engineers	$68,090	30.0%	5,000
21. Engineering Managers	$100,760	13.0%	15,000
22. Veterinarians	$68,910	17.4%	8,000
23. Diagnostic Medical Sonographers	$54,370	34.8%	5,000
24. Radiologic Technicians	$45,950	23.2%	17,000
25. Radiologic Technologists	$45,950	23.2%	17,000
26. Dentists, General	$125,300	13.5%	7,000
27. Sales Engineers	$74,200	14.0%	8,000
28. Chiropractors	$67,200	22.4%	4,000
29. Optometrists	$88,040	19.7%	2,000
30. Municipal Fire Fighters	$39,090	24.3%	21,000
31. Biomedical Engineers	$71,840	30.7%	1,000
32. Medical and Clinical Laboratory Technologists	$47,710	20.5%	14,000
33. Electrical Engineers	$73,510	11.8%	12,000
34. Physical Therapist Assistants	$39,490	44.2%	7,000
35. Respiratory Therapists	$45,140	28.4%	7,000
36. Natural Sciences Managers	$93,090	13.6%	5,000
37. Plumbers	$42,160	15.7%	61,000
38. Forest Fire Fighting and Prevention Supervisors	$60,840	21.1%	4,000
39. Electronics Engineers, Except Computer	$78,030	9.7%	11,000
40. Environmental Scientists and Specialists, Including Health	$52,630	17.1%	8,000
41. Hydrologists	$63,820	31.6%	1,000
42. Fitness Trainers and Aerobics Instructors	$25,840	27.1%	50,000

The 50 Best Jobs with a High Level of Science Skills

Job	Annual Earnings	Percent Growth	Annual Openings
43. Heating and Air Conditioning Mechanics and Installers	$37,040	19.0%	33,000
44. Refrigeration Mechanics and Installers	$37,040	19.0%	33,000
45. Mechanical Engineers	$67,590	11.1%	11,000
46. Licensed Practical and Licensed Vocational Nurses	$35,230	17.1%	84,000
47. Nuclear Medicine Technologists	$59,670	21.5%	2,000
48. Multi-Media Artists and Animators	$50,290	14.1%	14,000
49. Radiation Therapists	$62,340	26.3%	1,000
50. Surgical Technologists	$34,830	29.5%	12,000

Jobs 1, 2, 3, 4, 5, 6, and 8 share 41,000 job openings. Jobs 24 and 25 share 17,000 job openings. Job 30 shares 21,000 openings with another job not included in this list. Job 37 shares 61,000 openings with another job not included in this list. Job 38 shares 4,000 openings with another job not included in this list. Jobs 43 and 44 share 33,000 job openings.

The 50 Best Jobs with a High Level of Social Skills

Job	Annual Earnings	Percent Growth	Annual Openings
1. Internists, General	more than $145,600	24.0%	41,000
2. Obstetricians and Gynecologists	more than $145,600	24.0%	41,000
3. Psychiatrists	more than $145,600	24.0%	41,000
4. Registered Nurses	$54,670	29.4%	229,000
5. Family and General Practitioners	$140,400	24.0%	41,000
6. Pediatricians, General	$136,600	24.0%	41,000
7. General and Operations Managers	$81,480	17.0%	208,000
8. Dental Hygienists	$60,890	43.3%	17,000
9. Auditors	$52,210	22.4%	157,000
10. Medical and Health Services Managers	$69,700	22.8%	33,000
11. Sales Managers	$87,580	19.7%	40,000
12. Physical Therapists	$63,080	36.7%	13,000
13. Marketing Managers	$92,680	20.8%	23,000
14. Education Administrators, Postsecondary	$70,350	21.3%	18,000
15. Financial Managers, Branch or Department	$86,280	14.8%	63,000
16. Instructional Coordinators	$50,430	27.5%	15,000
17. Computer Support Specialists	$40,610	23.0%	87,000
18. Social and Community Service Managers	$49,500	25.5%	17,000
19. Employment Interviewers	$41,780	30.5%	30,000

(continued)

(continued)

The 50 Best Jobs with a High Level of Social Skills

Job	Annual Earnings	Percent Growth	Annual Openings
20. Personnel Recruiters	$41,780	30.5%	30,000
21. Chief Executives	$142,440	14.9%	38,000
22. Lawyers	$98,930	15.0%	40,000
23. Public Relations Specialists	$45,020	22.9%	38,000
24. Elementary School Teachers, Except Special Education	$44,040	18.2%	203,000
25. Market Research Analysts	$57,300	19.6%	20,000
26. Medical Assistants	$25,350	52.1%	93,000
27. Dental Assistants	$29,520	42.7%	45,000
28. Occupational Therapists	$56,860	33.6%	7,000
29. Self-Enrichment Education Teachers	$32,360	25.3%	74,000
30. Training and Development Specialists	$45,870	20.8%	32,000
31. Customer Service Representatives	$27,490	22.8%	510,000
32. Radiologic Technicians	$45,950	23.2%	17,000
33. Radiologic Technologists	$45,950	23.2%	17,000
34. Personal and Home Care Aides	$17,340	41.0%	230,000
35. Training and Development Managers	$74,180	25.9%	3,000
36. Special Education Teachers, Preschool, Kindergarten, and Elementary School	$44,630	23.3%	18,000
37. Preschool Teachers, Except Special Education	$21,990	33.1%	77,000
38. Social and Human Service Assistants	$25,030	29.7%	61,000
39. Advertising and Promotions Managers	$68,860	20.3%	9,000
40. Kindergarten Teachers, Except Special Education	$42,230	22.4%	28,000
41. Compensation, Benefits, and Job Analysis Specialists	$48,870	20.4%	15,000
42. Public Relations Managers	$76,450	21.7%	5,000
43. Sales Representatives, Wholesale and Manufacturing, Except Technical and Scientific Products	$47,380	12.9%	169,000
44. Clinical Psychologists	$57,170	19.1%	10,000
45. Counseling Psychologists	$57,170	19.1%	10,000
46. School Psychologists	$57,170	19.1%	10,000
47. Fitness Trainers and Aerobics Instructors	$25,840	27.1%	50,000
48. Police Patrol Officers	$46,290	15.5%	47,000
49. Sheriffs and Deputy Sheriffs	$46,290	15.5%	47,000
50. Secondary School Teachers, Except Special and Vocational Education	$46,060	14.4%	107,000

Jobs 1, 2, 3, 5, and 6 share 41,000 openings with each other and with two other jobs not included in this list. Job 9 shares 157,000 openings with another job not included in this list. Job 15 shares 63,000 openings with another job not included in this list. Jobs 19 and 20 share 30,000 job openings. Jobs 32 and 33 share 17,000 job openings. Jobs 44, 45, and 46 share 10,000 job openings. Jobs 48 and 49 share 47,000 job openings.

The 50 Best Jobs with a High Level of Thought-Processing Skills

Job	Annual Earnings	Percent Growth	Annual Openings
1. Anesthesiologists	more than $145,600	24.0%	41,000
2. Internists, General	more than $145,600	24.0%	41,000
3. Obstetricians and Gynecologists	more than $145,600	24.0%	41,000
4. Psychiatrists	more than $145,600	24.0%	41,000
5. Surgeons	more than $145,600	24.0%	41,000
6. Family and General Practitioners	$140,400	24.0%	41,000
7. Pediatricians, General	$136,600	24.0%	41,000
8. Teachers, Postsecondary	$53,590	32.2%	329,000
9. Registered Nurses	$54,670	29.4%	229,000
10. Sales Managers	$87,580	19.7%	40,000
11. General and Operations Managers	$81,480	17.0%	208,000
12. Physician Assistants	$72,030	49.6%	10,000
13. Financial Managers, Branch or Department	$86,280	14.8%	63,000
14. Treasurers and Controllers	$86,280	14.8%	63,000
15. Education Administrators, Postsecondary	$70,350	21.3%	18,000
16. Instructional Coordinators	$50,430	27.5%	15,000
17. Chief Executives	$142,440	14.9%	38,000
18. Lawyers	$98,930	15.0%	40,000
19. Personnel Recruiters	$41,780	30.5%	30,000
20. Personal and Home Care Aides	$17,340	41.0%	230,000
21. Public Relations Specialists	$45,020	22.9%	38,000
22. Market Research Analysts	$57,300	19.6%	20,000
23. Self-Enrichment Education Teachers	$32,360	25.3%	74,000
24. Elementary School Teachers, Except Special Education	$44,040	18.2%	203,000
25. Training and Development Managers	$74,180	25.9%	3,000
26. Customer Service Representatives	$27,490	22.8%	510,000
27. Training and Development Specialists	$45,870	20.8%	32,000
28. Advertising and Promotions Managers	$68,860	20.3%	9,000
29. Actuaries	$81,640	23.2%	3,000
30. Compensation, Benefits, and Job Analysis Specialists	$48,870	20.4%	15,000
31. Clinical Psychologists	$57,170	19.1%	10,000
32. Counseling Psychologists	$57,170	19.1%	10,000
33. School Psychologists	$57,170	19.1%	10,000
34. Police Patrol Officers	$46,290	15.5%	47,000
35. Sheriffs and Deputy Sheriffs	$46,290	15.5%	47,000

(continued)

(continued)

The 50 Best Jobs with a High Level of Thought-Processing Skills

Job	Annual Earnings	Percent Growth	Annual Openings
36. Special Education Teachers, Preschool, Kindergarten, and Elementary School	$44,630	23.3%	18,000
37. Airline Pilots, Copilots, and Flight Engineers	$138,170	17.2%	7,000
38. Medical and Public Health Social Workers	$41,120	25.9%	14,000
39. Kindergarten Teachers, Except Special Education	$42,230	22.4%	28,000
40. Sales Agents, Securities and Commodities	$67,130	11.5%	37,000
41. Optometrists	$88,040	19.7%	2,000
42. Secondary School Teachers, Except Special and Vocational Education	$46,060	14.4%	107,000
43. Coaches and Scouts	$25,990	20.4%	63,000
44. Mental Health and Substance Abuse Social Workers	$34,410	26.7%	15,000
45. Legal Secretaries	$37,750	17.4%	41,000
46. Education Administrators, Elementary and Secondary School	$75,400	10.4%	27,000
47. Mental Health Counselors	$34,010	27.2%	14,000
48. Veterinarians	$68,910	17.4%	8,000
49. Emergency Medical Technicians and Paramedics	$26,080	27.3%	21,000
50. Industrial-Organizational Psychologists	$84,690	20.4%	fewer than 500

Jobs 1, 2, 3, 4, 5, 6, and 7 share 41,000 job openings. Jobs 13 and 14 share 63,000 job openings. Job 19 shares 30,000 openings with another job not included in this list. Jobs 31, 32, and 33 share 10,000 job openings. Jobs 34 and 35 share 47,000 job openings. Job 40 shares 37,000 openings with another job not included in this list.

The 20 Best-Paying Jobs for Each Skill

In the following 10 lists you'll find the 20 best-paying jobs using each skill that met our criteria for this book. This is a popular set of lists, for obvious reasons.

If you compare these 10 lists, you may notice that some skills have better income possibilities than others. For example, the best-paying jobs with a high level of social skills and thought-processing skills command much higher incomes than the best-paying jobs with a high level of quality control skills. To see which skills pay the best and worst on average, look at the list called "Skills Used by the Best-Paid Jobs, Ordered from Highest to Lowest."

Keep in mind that the earnings figures are only averages. Also remember what we said earlier about how earnings can vary by region of the country, by amount of experience, and because of many other factors.

The 20 Best-Paying Jobs with a High Level of Communication Skills

Job	Annual Earnings
1. Surgeons	more than $145,600
2. Lawyers	$98,930
3. Pharmacists	$89,820
4. Public Relations Managers	$76,450
5. Physician Assistants	$72,030
6. Compensation and Benefits Managers	$69,130
7. Sales Agents, Financial Services	$67,130
8. Industrial Engineers	$66,670
9. Administrative Services Managers	$64,020
10. Personal Financial Advisors	$63,500
11. Physical Therapists	$63,080
12. Medical Scientists, Except Epidemiologists	$61,730
13. Dental Hygienists	$60,890
14. Market Research Analysts	$57,300
15. Clinical Psychologists	$57,170
16. Counseling Psychologists	$57,170
17. School Psychologists	$57,170
18. Occupational Therapists	$56,860
19. Technical Writers	$55,160
20. Diagnostic Medical Sonographers	$54,370

The 20 Best-Paying Jobs with a High Level of Computer Programming Skills

Job	Annual Earnings
1. Astronomers	$104,670
2. Computer and Information Systems Managers	$96,520
3. Computer Hardware Engineers	$84,420
4. Computer Software Engineers, Systems Software	$82,120
5. Actuaries	$81,640
6. Chemical Engineers	$77,140
7. Computer Software Engineers, Applications	$77,090
8. Sales Engineers	$74,200
9. Atmospheric and Space Scientists	$73,940
10. Economists	$73,690

(continued)

(continued)

The 20 Best-Paying Jobs with a High Level of Computer Programming Skills

Job	Annual Earnings
11. Electrical Engineers	$73,510
12. Materials Scientists	$71,450
13. Computer Systems Analysts	$68,300
14. Environmental Engineers	$68,090
15. Agricultural Engineers	$64,890
16. Administrative Services Managers	$64,020
17. Financial Analysts	$63,860
18. Hydrologists	$63,820
19. Geographers	$63,550
20. Computer Programmers	$63,420

The 20 Best-Paying Jobs with a High Level of Equipment Use/Maintenance Skills

Job	Annual Earnings
1. Anesthesiologists	more than $145,600
2. Airline Pilots, Copilots, and Flight Engineers	$138,170
3. Air Traffic Controllers	$107,590
4. Construction Managers	$72,260
5. Management Analysts	$66,380
6. Radiation Therapists	$62,340
7. Network Systems and Data Communications Analysts	$61,750
8. Forest Fire Fighting and Prevention Supervisors	$60,840
9. Municipal Fire Fighting and Prevention Supervisors	$60,840
10. Network and Computer Systems Administrators	$59,930
11. Nuclear Medicine Technologists	$59,670
12. Elevator Installers and Repairers	$59,190
13. Commercial Pilots	$55,810
14. Railroad Conductors and Yardmasters	$54,040
15. Technical Directors/Managers	$53,860
16. First-Line Supervisors/Managers of Mechanics, Installers, and Repairers	$51,980
17. First-Line Supervisors/Managers of Construction Trades and Extraction Workers	$51,970

The 20 Best-Paying Jobs with a High Level of Equipment Use/Maintenance Skills

Job	Annual Earnings
18. Electrical Engineering Technicians	$48,040
19. Electronics Engineering Technicians	$48,040
20. Medical and Clinical Laboratory Technologists	$47,710

The 20 Best-Paying Jobs with a High Level of Equipment/Technology Analysis Skills

Job	Annual Earnings
1. Engineering Managers	$100,760
2. Computer Hardware Engineers	$84,420
3. Aerospace Engineers	$84,090
4. Computer Software Engineers, Systems Software	$82,120
5. Electronics Engineers, Except Computer	$78,030
6. Chemical Engineers	$77,140
7. Computer Software Engineers, Applications	$77,090
8. Industrial Production Managers	$75,580
9. Sales Engineers	$74,200
10. Electrical Engineers	$73,510
11. Biomedical Engineers	$71,840
12. Storage and Distribution Managers	$69,120
13. Computer Systems Analysts	$68,300
14. Mechanical Engineers	$67,590
15. Industrial Engineers	$66,670
16. Civil Engineers	$66,190
17. Art Directors	$63,950
18. Computer Programmers	$63,420
19. Database Administrators	$63,250
20. Architects, Except Landscape and Naval	$62,850

(continued)

The 20 Best-Paying Jobs with a High Level of Management Skills

Job	Annual Earnings
1. Chief Executives	$142,440
2. Dentists, General	$125,300
3. Computer and Information Systems Managers	$96,520
4. Marketing Managers	$92,680
5. Optometrists	$88,040
6. Sales Managers	$87,580
7. Financial Managers, Branch or Department	$86,280
8. Treasurers and Controllers	$86,280
9. General and Operations Managers	$81,480
10. Public Relations Managers	$76,450
11. Education Administrators, Elementary and Secondary School	$75,400
12. Training and Development Managers	$74,180
13. Education Administrators, Postsecondary	$70,350
14. Medical and Health Services Managers	$69,700
15. Compensation and Benefits Managers	$69,130
16. Storage and Distribution Managers	$69,120
17. Transportation Managers	$69,120
18. Veterinarians	$68,910
19. Advertising and Promotions Managers	$68,860
20. Chiropractors	$67,200

The 20 Best-Paying Jobs with a High Level of Mathematics Skills

Job	Annual Earnings
1. Engineering Managers	$100,760
2. Natural Sciences Managers	$93,090
3. Pharmacists	$89,820
4. Treasurers and Controllers	$86,280
5. Actuaries	$81,640
6. Purchasing Managers	$76,270
7. Construction Managers	$72,260
8. Transportation Managers	$69,120
9. Environmental Engineers	$68,090
10. Mechanical Engineers	$67,590
11. Sales Agents, Financial Services	$67,130

The 20 Best-Paying Jobs with a High Level of Mathematics Skills

Job	Annual Earnings
12. Sales Agents, Securities and Commodities	$67,130
13. Industrial Engineers	$66,670
14. Civil Engineers	$66,190
15. Fire-Prevention and Protection Engineers	$65,210
16. Product Safety Engineers	$65,210
17. Financial Analysts	$63,860
18. Hydrologists	$63,820
19. Personal Financial Advisors	$63,500
20. Gaming Managers	$59,940

The 20 Best-Paying Jobs with a High Level of Quality Control Skills

Job	Annual Earnings
1. Computer and Information Systems Managers	$96,520
2. Computer Hardware Engineers	$84,420
3. Aerospace Engineers	$84,090
4. Electronics Engineers, Except Computer	$78,030
5. Computer Software Engineers, Applications	$77,090
6. Industrial Production Managers	$75,580
7. Atmospheric and Space Scientists	$73,940
8. Biomedical Engineers	$71,840
9. Medical and Health Services Managers	$69,700
10. Materials Engineers	$69,660
11. Computer Systems Analysts	$68,300
12. Management Analysts	$66,380
13. Product Safety Engineers	$65,210
14. Database Administrators	$63,250
15. Financial Examiners	$63,090
16. Nuclear Medicine Technologists	$59,670
17. Elevator Installers and Repairers	$59,190
18. Budget Analysts	$58,910
19. Chemists	$57,890
20. Microbiologists	$56,870

The 20 Best-Paying Jobs with a High Level of Science Skills

Job	Annual Earnings
1. Anesthesiologists	more than $145,600
2. Internists, General	more than $145,600
3. Obstetricians and Gynecologists	more than $145,600
4. Psychiatrists	more than $145,600
5. Surgeons	more than $145,600
6. Family and General Practitioners	$140,400
7. Airline Pilots, Copilots, and Flight Engineers	$138,170
8. Pediatricians, General	$136,600
9. Dentists, General	$125,300
10. Engineering Managers	$100,760
11. Natural Sciences Managers	$93,090
12. Marketing Managers	$92,680
13. Pharmacists	$89,820
14. Optometrists	$88,040
15. Computer Software Engineers, Systems Software	$82,120
16. Electronics Engineers, Except Computer	$78,030
17. Sales Engineers	$74,200
18. Electrical Engineers	$73,510
19. Physician Assistants	$72,030
20. Biomedical Engineers	$71,840

The 20 Best-Paying Jobs with a High Level of Social Skills

Job	Annual Earnings
1. Internists, General	more than $145,600
2. Obstetricians and Gynecologists	more than $145,600
3. Psychiatrists	more than $145,600
4. Chief Executives	$142,440
5. Family and General Practitioners	$140,400
6. Pediatricians, General	$136,600
7. Lawyers	$98,930
8. Marketing Managers	$92,680
9. Sales Managers	$87,580
10. Financial Managers, Branch or Department	$86,280
11. General and Operations Managers	$81,480
12. Public Relations Managers	$76,450

The 20 Best-Paying Jobs with a High Level of Social Skills

Job	Annual Earnings
13. Training and Development Managers	$74,180
14. Education Administrators, Postsecondary	$70,350
15. Medical and Health Services Managers	$69,700
16. Advertising and Promotions Managers	$68,860
17. Physical Therapists	$63,080
18. Dental Hygienists	$60,890
19. Market Research Analysts	$57,300
20. Clinical Psychologists	$57,170

The 20 Best-Paying Jobs with a High Level of Thought-Processing Skills

Job	Annual Earnings
1. Anesthesiologists	more than $145,600
2. Internists, General	more than $145,600
3. Obstetricians and Gynecologists	more than $145,600
4. Psychiatrists	more than $145,600
5. Surgeons	more than $145,600
6. Chief Executives	$142,440
7. Family and General Practitioners	$140,400
8. Airline Pilots, Copilots, and Flight Engineers	$138,170
9. Pediatricians, General	$136,600
10. Lawyers	$98,930
11. Optometrists	$88,040
12. Sales Managers	$87,580
13. Financial Managers, Branch or Department	$86,280
14. Treasurers and Controllers	$86,280
15. Industrial-Organizational Psychologists	$84,690
16. Actuaries	$81,640
17. General and Operations Managers	$81,480
18. Education Administrators, Elementary and Secondary School	$75,400
19. Training and Development Managers	$74,180
20. Physician Assistants	$72,030

The 20 Fastest-Growing Jobs for Each Skill

From the 10 lists of best jobs using each skill, these 10 lists show the 20 jobs using each skill that are projected to have the highest percentage increase in the numbers of people employed through 2014.

You will notice that just as income levels vary among the lists, rates of job growth vary, although not as greatly. The top 50 jobs with a high level of science skills and social skills have somewhat better opportunities (an average of about 23% growth) than do the top jobs in the other groups (an average of about 20% growth). This is partly because the jobs that require science skills and social skills tend to be in the booming health-care field. The jobs requiring communication skills are also growing rapidly; many of them are in the health-care field, too, and because communication works best in face-to-face exchanges between people, these jobs cannot easily be automated or outsourced to overseas workers. Although the exporting of technology jobs has received much press coverage, jobs requiring computer programming skills are also among those growing fastest.

For another way of looking at the relationship between skills and job growth, see the list titled "Skills Used by the Fastest-Growing Jobs, Ordered from Highest to Lowest."

The 20 Fastest-Growing Jobs with a High Level of Communication Skills

Job	Percent Growth
1. Medical Assistants	52.1%
2. Physician Assistants	49.6%
3. Dental Hygienists	43.3%
4. Personal and Home Care Aides	41.0%
5. Physical Therapists	36.7%
6. Diagnostic Medical Sonographers	34.8%
7. Medical Scientists, Except Epidemiologists	34.1%
8. Occupational Therapists	33.6%
9. Preschool Teachers, Except Special Education	33.1%
10. Teachers, Postsecondary	32.2%
11. Employment Interviewers	30.5%
12. Paralegals and Legal Assistants	29.7%
13. Social and Human Service Assistants	29.7%
14. Respiratory Therapists	28.4%
15. Medical and Public Health Social Workers	25.9%
16. Personal Financial Advisors	25.9%
17. Social and Community Service Managers	25.5%
18. Self-Enrichment Education Teachers	25.3%
19. Pharmacists	24.6%
20. Surgeons	24.0%

The 20 Fastest-Growing Jobs with a High Level of Computer Programming Skills

Job	Percent Growth
1. Network Systems and Data Communications Analysts	54.6%
2. Computer Software Engineers, Applications	48.4%
3. Computer Software Engineers, Systems Software	43.0%
4. Computer Security Specialists	38.4%
5. Network and Computer Systems Administrators	38.4%
6. Database Administrators	38.2%
7. Hydrologists	31.6%
8. Computer Systems Analysts	31.4%
9. Environmental Engineers	30.0%
10. Epidemiologists	26.2%
11. Computer and Information Systems Managers	25.9%
12. Actuaries	23.2%
13. Accountants	22.4%
14. Financial Analysts	17.3%
15. Administrative Services Managers	16.9%
16. Atmospheric and Space Scientists	16.5%
17. Criminal Investigators and Special Agents	16.3%
18. Multi-Media Artists and Animators	14.1%
19. Sales Engineers	14.0%
20. Archivists	13.4%

The 20 Fastest-Growing Jobs with a High Level of Equipment Use/Maintenance Skills

Job	Percent Growth
1. Network Systems and Data Communications Analysts	54.6%
2. Dental Assistants	42.7%
3. Network and Computer Systems Administrators	38.4%
4. Cardiovascular Technologists and Technicians	32.6%
5. Radiation Therapists	26.3%
6. Medical and Clinical Laboratory Technicians	25.0%
7. Forest Fire Fighters	24.3%
8. Municipal Fire Fighters	24.3%
9. Anesthesiologists	24.0%

(continued)

(continued)

The 20 Fastest-Growing Jobs with a High Level of Equipment Use/Maintenance Skills

Job	Percent Growth
10. Highway Maintenance Workers	23.3%
11. Computer Support Specialists	23.0%
12. Bus Drivers, Transit and Intercity	21.7%
13. Nuclear Medicine Technologists	21.5%
14. Forest Fire Fighting and Prevention Supervisors	21.1%
15. Municipal Fire Fighting and Prevention Supervisors	21.1%
16. Medical and Clinical Laboratory Technologists	20.5%
17. Railroad Conductors and Yardmasters	20.3%
18. Management Analysts	20.1%
19. Heating and Air Conditioning Mechanics and Installers	19.0%
20. Refrigeration Mechanics and Installers	19.0%

The 20 Fastest-Growing Jobs with a High Level of Equipment/Technology Analysis Skills

Job	Percent Growth
1. Network Systems and Data Communications Analysts	54.6%
2. Computer Software Engineers, Applications	48.4%
3. Computer Software Engineers, Systems Software	43.0%
4. Dental Assistants	42.7%
5. Computer Security Specialists	38.4%
6. Network and Computer Systems Administrators	38.4%
7. Database Administrators	38.2%
8. Occupational Therapist Assistants	34.1%
9. Computer Systems Analysts	31.4%
10. Biomedical Engineers	30.7%
11. Surgical Technologists	29.5%
12. Fitness Trainers and Aerobics Instructors	27.1%
13. Radiation Therapists	26.3%
14. Forest Fire Fighters	24.3%
15. Municipal Fire Fighters	24.3%
16. Technical Writers	23.2%
17. Tile and Marble Setters	22.9%

The 20 Fastest-Growing Jobs with a High Level of Equipment/Technology Analysis Skills

Job	Percent Growth
18. Landscape Architects	19.4%
19. Refrigeration Mechanics and Installers	19.0%
20. Film and Video Editors	18.6%

The 20 Fastest-Growing Jobs with a High Level of Management Skills

Job	Percent Growth
1. Computer Security Specialists	38.4%
2. Medical Scientists, Except Epidemiologists	34.1%
3. Employment Interviewers	30.5%
4. Personnel Recruiters	30.5%
5. Social and Human Service Assistants	29.7%
6. Instructional Coordinators	27.5%
7. Computer and Information Systems Managers	25.9%
8. Training and Development Managers	25.9%
9. Social and Community Service Managers	25.5%
10. Forest Fire Fighters	24.3%
11. Medical and Health Services Managers	22.8%
12. Accountants	22.4%
13. Auditors	22.4%
14. Chiropractors	22.4%
15. Nursing Aides, Orderlies, and Attendants	22.3%
16. Public Relations Managers	21.7%
17. Compensation and Benefits Managers	21.5%
18. Bill and Account Collectors	21.4%
19. Education Administrators, Postsecondary	21.3%
20. Forest Fire Fighting and Prevention Supervisors	21.1%

The 20 Fastest-Growing Jobs with a High Level of Mathematics Skills

Job	Percent Growth
1. Medical Assistants	52.1%
2. Hydrologists	31.6%
3. Environmental Engineers	30.0%
4. Pharmacy Technicians	28.6%
5. Respiratory Therapists	28.4%
6. Epidemiologists	26.2%
7. Personal Financial Advisors	25.9%
8. Pharmacists	24.6%
9. Actuaries	23.2%
10. Tile and Marble Setters	22.9%
11. Appraisers, Real Estate	22.8%
12. Assessors	22.8%
13. Gaming Managers	22.6%
14. Accountants	22.4%
15. Auditors	22.4%
16. Construction and Building Inspectors	22.3%
17. Landscape Architects	19.4%
18. Heating and Air Conditioning Mechanics and Installers	19.0%
19. Cost Estimators	18.2%
20. Financial Analysts	17.3%

The 20 Fastest-Growing Jobs with a High Level of Quality Control Skills

Job	Percent Growth
1. Computer Software Engineers, Applications	48.4%
2. Database Administrators	38.2%
3. Forensic Science Technicians	36.4%
4. Diagnostic Medical Sonographers	34.8%
5. Cardiovascular Technologists and Technicians	32.6%
6. Computer Systems Analysts	31.4%
7. Biomedical Engineers	30.7%
8. Computer and Information Systems Managers	25.9%
9. Medical and Clinical Laboratory Technicians	25.0%
10. Technical Writers	23.2%
11. Medical and Health Services Managers	22.8%
12. Construction and Building Inspectors	22.3%

The 20 Fastest-Growing Jobs with a High Level of Quality Control Skills

Job	Percent Growth
13. Nuclear Medicine Technologists	21.5%
14. Medical and Clinical Laboratory Technologists	20.5%
15. Management Analysts	20.1%
16. Sound Engineering Technicians	18.4%
17. Copy Writers	17.7%
18. Biological Technicians	17.2%
19. Microbiologists	17.2%
20. Atmospheric and Space Scientists	16.5%

The 20 Fastest-Growing Jobs with a High Level of Science Skills

Job	Percent Growth
1. Physician Assistants	49.6%
2. Physical Therapist Assistants	44.2%
3. Dental Hygienists	43.3%
4. Computer Software Engineers, Systems Software	43.0%
5. Physical Therapists	36.7%
6. Diagnostic Medical Sonographers	34.8%
7. Medical Scientists, Except Epidemiologists	34.1%
8. Occupational Therapists	33.6%
9. Teachers, Postsecondary	32.2%
10. Hydrologists	31.6%
11. Biomedical Engineers	30.7%
12. Environmental Engineers	30.0%
13. Surgical Technologists	29.5%
14. Registered Nurses	29.4%
15. Respiratory Therapists	28.4%
16. Fitness Trainers and Aerobics Instructors	27.1%
17. Radiation Therapists	26.3%
18. Pharmacists	24.6%
19. Municipal Fire Fighters	24.3%
20. Internists, General	24.0%

The 20 Fastest-Growing Jobs with a High Level of Social Skills

Job	Percent Growth
1. Medical Assistants	52.1%
2. Dental Hygienists	43.3%
3. Dental Assistants	42.7%
4. Personal and Home Care Aides	41.0%
5. Physical Therapists	36.7%
6. Occupational Therapists	33.6%
7. Preschool Teachers, Except Special Education	33.1%
8. Employment Interviewers	30.5%
9. Personnel Recruiters	30.5%
10. Social and Human Service Assistants	29.7%
11. Registered Nurses	29.4%
12. Instructional Coordinators	27.5%
13. Fitness Trainers and Aerobics Instructors	27.1%
14. Training and Development Managers	25.9%
15. Social and Community Service Managers	25.5%
16. Self-Enrichment Education Teachers	25.3%
17. Family and General Practitioners	24.0%
18. Internists, General	24.0%
19. Obstetricians and Gynecologists	24.0%
20. Psychiatrists	24.0%

The 20 Fastest-Growing Jobs with a High Level of Thought-Processing Skills

Job	Percent Growth
1. Physician Assistants	49.6%
2. Personal and Home Care Aides	41.0%
3. Teachers, Postsecondary	32.2%
4. Personnel Recruiters	30.5%
5. Registered Nurses	29.4%
6. Instructional Coordinators	27.5%
7. Emergency Medical Technicians and Paramedics	27.3%
8. Mental Health Counselors	27.2%
9. Mental Health and Substance Abuse Social Workers	26.7%
10. Medical and Public Health Social Workers	25.9%
11. Training and Development Managers	25.9%

The 20 Fastest-Growing Jobs with a High Level of Thought-Processing Skills	
Job	Percent Growth
12. Self-Enrichment Education Teachers 25.3%	
13. Anesthesiologists 24.0%	
14. Family and General Practitioners 24.0%	
15. Internists, General 24.0%	
16. Obstetricians and Gynecologists 24.0%	
17. Pediatricians, General 24.0%	
18. Psychiatrists 24.0%	
19. Surgeons 24.0%	
20. Special Education Teachers, Preschool, Kindergarten, and Elementary School 23.3%	

The 20 Jobs for Each Skill with the Most Openings

From the 10 lists of best jobs using each skill, this list shows the 20 jobs using each skill that are projected to have the largest number of job openings per year through 2014.

Jobs with many openings present several advantages that may be attractive to you. Because there are many openings, these jobs can be easier to obtain, particularly for those just entering the job market. These jobs may also offer more opportunities to move from one employer to another with relative ease. Though some of these jobs have average or below-average pay, some also pay quite well and can provide good long-term career opportunities or the ability to move up to more responsible roles.

Jobs high in communication skills, social skills, and thought-processing skills have the largest number of openings (an average of about 56,000 openings). Most of them require face-to-face interactions and on-site decisions, so the tasks are not likely to be taken over by computers or offshore workers. Jobs high in quality control skills, on the other hand, are more vulnerable to such competition and therefore promise far fewer openings. It is interesting that the 40 jobs high in computer programming skills are the group with the lowest average number of openings (an average of about 17,000), even though these occupations are among those growing fastest. The reason for this discrepancy is that these high-tech occupations also have a relatively small number of workers, so even though they are growing rapidly, they will not provide as many job openings as the other groups.

The 20 Jobs with a High Level of Communication Skills with the Most Openings

Job	Annual Openings
1. Customer Service Representatives	510,000
2. Teachers, Postsecondary	329,000
3. Personal and Home Care Aides	230,000
4. Elementary School Teachers, Except Special Education	203,000
5. Sales Representatives, Wholesale and Manufacturing, Except Technical and Scientific Products	169,000
6. Secondary School Teachers, Except Special and Vocational Education	107,000
7. Medical Assistants	93,000
8. Computer Support Specialists	87,000
9. Bill and Account Collectors	85,000
10. Licensed Practical and Licensed Vocational Nurses	84,000
11. Middle School Teachers, Except Special and Vocational Education	83,000
12. Preschool Teachers, Except Special Education	77,000
13. Self-Enrichment Education Teachers	74,000
14. Social and Human Service Assistants	61,000
15. Police Patrol Officers	47,000
16. Sheriffs and Deputy Sheriffs	47,000
17. Legal Secretaries	41,000
18. Surgeons	41,000
19. Lawyers	40,000
20. Public Relations Specialists	38,000

Jobs 15 and 16 share 47,000 job openings. Job 18 shares 41,000 openings with six other jobs not included in this list.

The 20 Jobs with a High Level of Computer Programming Skills with the Most Openings

Job	Annual Openings
1. Accountants	157,000
2. Computer Systems Analysts	56,000
3. Computer Software Engineers, Applications	54,000
4. Network Systems and Data Communications Analysts	43,000
5. Computer Software Engineers, Systems Software	37,000
6. Computer Security Specialists	34,000
7. Network and Computer Systems Administrators	34,000

The 20 Jobs with a High Level of Computer Programming Skills with the Most Openings

Job	Annual Openings
8. Electrical and Electronic Equipment Assemblers	33,000
9. Machinists	33,000
10. Computer Programmers	28,000
11. Financial Analysts	28,000
12. Administrative Services Managers	25,000
13. Computer and Information Systems Managers	25,000
14. Electronics Engineering Technicians	18,000
15. Multi-Media Artists and Animators	14,000
16. Electrical Engineers	12,000
17. Criminal Investigators and Special Agents	9,000
18. Database Administrators	9,000
19. Mapping Technicians	9,000
20. Sales Engineers	8,000

Job 1 shares 157,000 openings with another job not included in this list. Jobs 6 and 7 share 34,000 job openings. Job 14 shares 18,000 openings with another job not included in this list. Job 17 shares 9,000 openings with three other jobs not included in this list. Job 19 shares 9,000 openings with another job not included in this list.

The 20 Jobs with a High Level of Equipment Use/Maintenance Skills with the Most Openings

Job	Annual Openings
1. Truck Drivers, Heavy and Tractor-Trailer	274,000
2. Rough Carpenters	210,000
3. Maintenance and Repair Workers, General	154,000
4. Automotive Master Mechanics	93,000
5. Automotive Specialty Technicians	93,000
6. First-Line Supervisors/Managers of Production and Operating Workers	89,000
7. Computer Support Specialists	87,000
8. Licensed Practical and Licensed Vocational Nurses	84,000
9. Management Analysts	82,000
10. Electricians	68,000
11. Pipe Fitters and Steamfitters	61,000
12. Plumbers	61,000

(continued)

(continued)

The 20 Jobs with a High Level of Equipment Use/Maintenance Skills with the Most Openings

Job	Annual Openings
13. First-Line Supervisors/Managers of Construction Trades and Extraction Workers	57,000
14. Sheet Metal Workers	50,000
15. Dental Assistants	45,000
16. Network Systems and Data Communications Analysts	43,000
17. Anesthesiologists	41,000
18. Operating Engineers and Other Construction Equipment Operators	37,000
19. Bus Drivers, Transit and Intercity	34,000
20. Network and Computer Systems Administrators	34,000

Job 2 shares 210,000 openings with another job not included in this list. Jobs 4 and 5 share 93,000 job openings. Jobs 11 and 12 share 61,000 job openings. Job 17 shares 41,000 openings with six other jobs not included in this list. Job 20 shares 34,000 openings with another job not included in this list.

The 20 Jobs with a High Level of Equipment/Technology Analysis Skills with the Most Openings

Job	Annual Openings
1. Rough Carpenters	210,000
2. Automotive Specialty Technicians	93,000
3. Electricians	68,000
4. Pipe Fitters and Steamfitters	61,000
5. Plumbers	61,000
6. Computer Systems Analysts	56,000
7. Computer Software Engineers, Applications	54,000
8. Fitness Trainers and Aerobics Instructors	50,000
9. Dental Assistants	45,000
10. Network Systems and Data Communications Analysts	43,000
11. Computer Software Engineers, Systems Software	37,000
12. Graphic Designers	35,000
13. Computer Security Specialists	34,000
14. Network and Computer Systems Administrators	34,000
15. First-Line Supervisors/Managers of Mechanics, Installers, and Repairers	33,000
16. Refrigeration Mechanics and Installers	33,000
17. Computer Programmers	28,000

The 20 Jobs with a High Level of Equipment/Technology Analysis Skills with the Most Openings

Job	Annual Openings
18. Forest Fire Fighters	21,000
19. Municipal Fire Fighters	21,000
20. Civil Engineers	19,000

Job 1 shares 210,000 openings with another job not included in this list. Job 2 shares 93,000 openings with another job not included in this list. Jobs 4 and 5 share 61,000 job openings. Jobs 13 and 14 share 34,000 job openings. Job 16 shares 33,000 openings with another job not included in this list. Jobs 18 and 19 share 21,000 job openings.

The 20 Jobs with a High Level of Management Skills with the Most Openings

Job	Annual Openings
1. Nursing Aides, Orderlies, and Attendants	307,000
2. General and Operations Managers	208,000
3. Sales Representatives, Wholesale and Manufacturing, Except Technical and Scientific Products	169,000
4. Accountants	157,000
5. Auditors	157,000
6. Bill and Account Collectors	85,000
7. Management Analysts	82,000
8. Coaches and Scouts	63,000
9. Financial Managers, Branch or Department	63,000
10. Treasurers and Controllers	63,000
11. Social and Human Service Assistants	61,000
12. Property, Real Estate, and Community Association Managers	58,000
13. First-Line Supervisors/Managers of Construction Trades and Extraction Workers	57,000
14. Sales Managers	40,000
15. Chief Executives	38,000
16. Computer Security Specialists	34,000
17. First-Line Supervisors/Managers of Mechanics, Installers, and Repairers	33,000
18. Medical and Health Services Managers	33,000
19. Employment Interviewers	30,000
20. Personnel Recruiters	30,000

Jobs 4 and 5 share 157,000 job openings. Jobs 9 and 10 share 63,000 job openings. Job 16 shares 34,000 openings with another job not included in this list. Jobs 19 and 20 share 30,000 job openings.

The 20 Jobs with a High Level of Mathematics Skills with the Most Openings

Job	Annual Openings
1. Construction Carpenters	210,000
2. Rough Carpenters	210,000
3. Accountants	157,000
4. Auditors	157,000
5. Medical Assistants	93,000
6. Electricians	68,000
7. Treasurers and Controllers	63,000
8. Property, Real Estate, and Community Association Managers	58,000
9. Sheet Metal Workers	50,000
10. Real Estate Sales Agents	41,000
11. Sales Agents, Financial Services	37,000
12. Sales Agents, Securities and Commodities	37,000
13. Payroll and Timekeeping Clerks	36,000
14. Pharmacy Technicians	35,000
15. Heating and Air Conditioning Mechanics and Installers	33,000
16. Cement Masons and Concrete Finishers	32,000
17. Construction Managers	28,000
18. Financial Analysts	28,000
19. Human Resources Assistants, Except Payroll and Timekeeping	28,000
20. Civil Engineers	19,000

Jobs 1 and 2 share 210,000 job openings. Jobs 3 and 4 share 157,000 job openings. Job 7 shares 63,000 openings with another job not included in this list. Jobs 11 and 12 share 37,000 job openings. Job 15 shares 33,000 openings with another job not included in this list.

The 20 Jobs with a High Level of Quality Control Skills with the Most Openings

Job	Annual Openings
1. Construction Carpenters	210,000
2. First-Line Supervisors/Managers of Production and Operating Workers	89,000
3. Management Analysts	82,000
4. Food Service Managers	61,000
5. Pipe Fitters and Steamfitters	61,000
6. First-Line Supervisors/Managers of Construction Trades and Extraction Workers	57,000

The 20 Jobs with a High Level of Quality Control Skills with the Most Openings

Job	Annual Openings
7. Computer Systems Analysts	56,000
8. Computer Software Engineers, Applications	54,000
9. Graphic Designers	35,000
10. Machinists	33,000
11. Medical and Health Services Managers	33,000
12. Computer, Automated Teller, and Office Machine Repairers	31,000
13. Computer and Information Systems Managers	25,000
14. First-Line Supervisors/Managers of Transportation and Material-Moving Machine and Vehicle Operators	22,000
15. Telecommunications Equipment Installers and Repairers, Except Line Installers	21,000
16. Wholesale and Retail Buyers, Except Farm Products	20,000
17. First-Line Supervisors/Managers of Helpers, Laborers, and Material Movers, Hand	15,000
18. Copy Writers	14,000
19. Medical and Clinical Laboratory Technicians	14,000
20. Medical and Clinical Laboratory Technologists	14,000

Job 1 shares 210,000 openings with another job not included in this list. Job 5 shares 61,000 openings with another job not included in this list. Job 18 shares 14,000 openings with another job not included in this list.

The 20 Jobs with a High Level of Science Skills with the Most Openings

Job	Annual Openings
1. Teachers, Postsecondary	329,000
2. Registered Nurses	229,000
3. Licensed Practical and Licensed Vocational Nurses	84,000
4. Plumbers	61,000
5. Fitness Trainers and Aerobics Instructors	50,000
6. Anesthesiologists	41,000
7. Family and General Practitioners	41,000
8. Internists, General	41,000
9. Obstetricians and Gynecologists	41,000
10. Pediatricians, General	41,000
11. Psychiatrists	41,000

(continued)

(continued)

The 20 Jobs with a High Level of Science Skills with the Most Openings

Job	Annual Openings
12. Surgeons	41,000
13. Computer Software Engineers, Systems Software	37,000
14. Heating and Air Conditioning Mechanics and Installers	33,000
15. Refrigeration Mechanics and Installers	33,000
16. Marketing Managers	23,000
17. Municipal Fire Fighters	21,000
18. Civil Engineers	19,000
19. Dental Hygienists	17,000
20. Radiologic Technicians	17,000

Job 4 shares 61,000 openings with another job not included in this list. Jobs 6, 7, 8, 9, 10, 11, and 12 share 41,000 job openings. Jobs 14 and 15 share 33,000 job openings. Job 17 shares 21,000 openings with another job not included in this list. Job 20 shares 17,000 openings with another job not included in this list.

The 20 Jobs with a High Level of Social Skills with the Most Openings

Job	Annual Openings
1. Customer Service Representatives	510,000
2. Personal and Home Care Aides	230,000
3. Registered Nurses	229,000
4. General and Operations Managers	208,000
5. Elementary School Teachers, Except Special Education	203,000
6. Sales Representatives, Wholesale and Manufacturing, Except Technical and Scientific Products	169,000
7. Auditors	157,000
8. Secondary School Teachers, Except Special and Vocational Education	107,000
9. Medical Assistants	93,000
10. Computer Support Specialists	87,000
11. Preschool Teachers, Except Special Education	77,000
12. Self-Enrichment Education Teachers	74,000
13. Financial Managers, Branch or Department	63,000
14. Social and Human Service Assistants	61,000
15. Fitness Trainers and Aerobics Instructors	50,000
16. Police Patrol Officers	47,000
17. Sheriffs and Deputy Sheriffs	47,000

The 20 Jobs with a High Level of Social Skills with the Most Openings

Job	Annual Openings
18. Dental Assistants	45,000
19. Family and General Practitioners	41,000
20. Internists, General	41,000

Job 7 shares 157,000 openings with another job not included in this list. Job 13 shares 63,000 openings with another job not included in this list. Jobs 16 and 17 share 47,000 job openings. Jobs 19 and 20 share 41,000 openings with each other and with five other jobs not included in this list.

The 20 Jobs with a High Level of Thought-Processing Skills with the Most Openings

Job	Annual Openings
1. Customer Service Representatives	510,000
2. Teachers, Postsecondary	329,000
3. Personal and Home Care Aides	230,000
4. Registered Nurses	229,000
5. General and Operations Managers	208,000
6. Elementary School Teachers, Except Special Education	203,000
7. Secondary School Teachers, Except Special and Vocational Education	107,000
8. Self-Enrichment Education Teachers	74,000
9. Coaches and Scouts	63,000
10. Financial Managers, Branch or Department	63,000
11. Treasurers and Controllers	63,000
12. Police Patrol Officers	47,000
13. Sheriffs and Deputy Sheriffs	47,000
14. Anesthesiologists	41,000
15. Family and General Practitioners	41,000
16. Internists, General	41,000
17. Obstetricians and Gynecologists	41,000
18. Pediatricians, General	41,000
19. Psychiatrists	41,000
20. Surgeons	41,000

Jobs 10 and 11 share 63,000 job openings. Jobs 12 and 13 share 47,000 job openings. Jobs 14, 15, 16, 17, 18, 19, and 20 share 41,000 job openings.

Best Jobs Lists by Work Arrangement

Not everybody wants to work a 40-hour week under the eye of a supervisor. Many people are able to arrange part-time work or self-employment. Looking at alternate work arrangements can provide some useful insights into the jobs in this book, so we provided lists of jobs with high percentages of part-time or self-employed workers.

The Best Jobs for Each Skill with a High Percentage of Part-Time Workers

Starting with the 50 best jobs with a high level of each skill, we created lists that include those with a relatively large proportion of part-time workers. Among all employed people, about 22 percent work part-time, but among the best jobs the percentage tends to be much lower, so we set our cutoff at 10 percent. We ordered the lists by the same three economic factors (earnings, job growth, and job openings) that we used on many other lists. Finally, we limited each list to the 20 jobs that were ranked best according to those three factors. (For some skills there were fewer than 20 jobs that could be ranked, so those lists are smaller.)

If you want to work part time, these lists will be helpful in identifying where most others are finding opportunities for the kinds of work that use your top skills. Many people prefer to work less than full time. For example, people who are attending school or who have young children may prefer the flexibility of part-time work. People also work part time for money-related reasons, such as supplementing income from a full-time job or working two or more part-time jobs because one desirable full-time job is not available.

If you are interested in jobs with a high level of computer programming skills, you will note that you have very limited opportunities for part-time employment. Nevertheless, keep in mind that it may be possible for you to carve out a position for yourself that does not require a 40-hour work week even in occupations where few people work part time.

Many of these jobs can be learned quickly, offer flexible work schedules, are easy to obtain, and offer other desirable advantages. Although many people think of part-time jobs as requiring low skills and providing low pay, this is not always the case. Some of these jobs pay quite well, require substantial training or experience, or are growing rapidly. In fact, the average growth rate for the jobs in the following set of lists is 25.0%, almost double the average growth for all jobs.

Availability of part-time work varies greatly by geographic location. If you are interested in part-time work and have a particular job in mind, investigate the opportunities in your area to get a realistic sense of how easy or hard it will be to find part-time work.

Best Jobs with a High Level of Communication Skills with a High Percentage of Part-Time Workers

Job	Percent Part-Time Workers	Annual Earnings	Percent Growth	Annual Openings
1. Teachers, Postsecondary	27.3%	$53,590	32.2%	329,000
2. Dental Hygienists	56.0%	$60,890	43.3%	17,000
3. Physician Assistants	16.7%	$72,030	49.6%	10,000
4. Physical Therapists	24.7%	$63,080	36.7%	13,000
5. Medical Assistants	27.5%	$25,350	52.1%	93,000
6. Personal and Home Care Aides	36.6%	$17,340	41.0%	230,000
7. Pharmacists	21.1%	$89,820	24.6%	16,000
8. Social and Community Service Managers	12.5%	$49,500	25.5%	17,000
9. Market Research Analysts	13.8%	$57,300	19.6%	20,000
10. Occupational Therapists	29.4%	$56,860	33.6%	7,000
11. Paralegals and Legal Assistants	11.1%	$41,170	29.7%	28,000
12. Diagnostic Medical Sonographers	17.2%	$54,370	34.8%	5,000
13. Preschool Teachers, Except Special Education	25.1%	$21,990	33.1%	77,000
14. Customer Service Representatives	17.6%	$27,490	22.8%	510,000
15. Public Relations Specialists	11.8%	$45,020	22.9%	38,000
16. Radiologic Technicians	17.2%	$45,950	23.2%	17,000
17. Radiologic Technologists	17.2%	$45,950	23.2%	17,000
18. Self-Enrichment Education Teachers	45.6%	$32,360	25.3%	74,000
19. Elementary School Teachers, Except Special Education	12.6%	$44,040	18.2%	203,000
20. Social and Human Service Assistants	16.0%	$25,030	29.7%	61,000

Jobs 16 and 17 share 17,000 job openings.

Best Jobs with a High Level of Computer Programming Skills with a High Percentage of Part-Time Workers

Job	Percent Part-Time Workers	Annual Earnings	Percent Growth	Annual Openings
1. Network Systems and Data Communications Analysts	10.0%	$61,750	54.6%	43,000
2. Accountants	10.2%	$52,210	22.4%	157,000
3. Multi-Media Artists and Animators	30.9%	$50,290	14.1%	14,000
4. Geographers	14.8%	$63,550	6.8%	fewer than 500

(continued)

(continued)

Best Jobs with a High Level of Computer Programming Skills with a High Percentage of Part-Time Workers

Job	Percent Part-Time Workers	Annual Earnings	Percent Growth	Annual Openings
5. Statisticians	10.9%	$62,450	4.6%	2,000
6. Archivists	23.4%	$37,420	13.4%	1,000
7. Statistical Assistants	11.8%	$28,950	5.7%	1,000

Job 2 shares 157,000 openings with another job not included in this list.

Best Jobs with a High Level of Equipment Use/Maintenance Skills with a High Percentage of Part-Time Workers

Job	Percent Part-Time Workers	Annual Earnings	Percent Growth	Annual Openings
1. Network Systems and Data Communications Analysts	10.0%	$61,750	54.6%	43,000
2. Management Analysts	18.4%	$66,380	20.1%	82,000
3. Dental Assistants	38.9%	$29,520	42.7%	45,000
4. Medical and Clinical Laboratory Technologists	17.3%	$47,710	20.5%	14,000
5. Airline Pilots, Copilots, and Flight Engineers	14.8%	$138,170	17.2%	7,000
6. Bus Drivers, Transit and Intercity	38.4%	$31,010	21.7%	34,000
7. Cardiovascular Technologists and Technicians	17.2%	$40,420	32.6%	5,000
8. Medical and Clinical Laboratory Technicians	17.3%	$31,700	25.0%	14,000
9. Licensed Practical and Licensed Vocational Nurses	21.9%	$35,230	17.1%	84,000
10. Nuclear Medicine Technologists	17.2%	$59,670	21.5%	2,000
11. First-Line Supervisors/Managers of Housekeeping and Janitorial Workers	14.9%	$30,330	19.0%	21,000
12. Film and Video Editors	27.6%	$46,930	18.6%	3,000
13. Commercial Pilots	14.8%	$55,810	16.8%	2,000

Best Jobs with a High Level of Equipment/Technology Analysis Skills with a High Percentage of Part-Time Workers

Job	Percent Part-Time Workers	Annual Earnings	Percent Growth	Annual Openings
1. Network Systems and Data Communications Analysts	10.0%	$61,750	54.6%	43,000
2. Dental Assistants	38.9%	$29,520	42.7%	45,000
3. Copy Writers	30.7%	$46,420	17.7%	14,000
4. Fitness Trainers and Aerobics Instructors	41.3%	$25,840	27.1%	50,000
5. Multi-Media Artists and Animators	30.9%	$50,290	14.1%	14,000
6. Art Directors	30.9%	$63,950	11.5%	10,000
7. Surgical Technologists	23.2%	$34,830	29.5%	12,000
8. Film and Video Editors	27.6%	$46,930	18.6%	3,000
9. Graphic Designers	21.3%	$38,390	15.2%	35,000
10. Occupational Therapist Assistants	18.6%	$39,750	34.1%	2,000
11. Interior Designers	21.3%	$41,350	15.5%	10,000
12. Tile and Marble Setters	12.3%	$36,530	22.9%	9,000

Job 3 shares 14,000 openings with another job not included in this list.

Best Jobs with a High Level of Management Skills with a High Percentage of Part-Time Workers

Job	Percent Part-Time Workers	Annual Earnings	Percent Growth	Annual Openings
1. Accountants	10.2%	$52,210	22.4%	157,000
2. Auditors	10.2%	$52,210	22.4%	157,000
3. Instructional Coordinators	23.4%	$50,430	27.5%	15,000
4. Management Analysts	18.4%	$66,380	20.1%	82,000
5. Social and Community Service Managers	12.5%	$49,500	25.5%	17,000
6. Social and Human Service Assistants	16.0%	$25,030	29.7%	61,000
7. Nursing Aides, Orderlies, and Attendants	28.0%	$21,440	22.3%	307,000
8. Bill and Account Collectors	13.1%	$28,160	21.4%	85,000
9. Chiropractors	20.7%	$67,200	22.4%	4,000
10. Veterinarians	10.8%	$68,910	17.4%	8,000
11. Coaches and Scouts	47.6%	$25,990	20.4%	63,000
12. Dentists, General	22.4%	$125,300	13.5%	7,000

(continued)

(continued)

Best Jobs with a High Level of Management Skills with a High Percentage of Part-Time Workers

Job	Percent Part-Time Workers	Annual Earnings	Percent Growth	Annual Openings
13. Optometrists	16.5%	$88,040	19.7%	2,000
14. Property, Real Estate, and Community Association Managers	21.9%	$41,900	15.3%	58,000

Jobs 1 and 2 share 157,000 job openings.

Best Jobs with a High Level of Mathematics Skills with a High Percentage of Part-Time Workers

Job	Percent Part-Time Workers	Annual Earnings	Percent Growth	Annual Openings
1. Accountants	10.2%	$52,210	22.4%	157,000
2. Auditors	10.2%	$52,210	22.4%	157,000
3. Pharmacists	21.1%	$89,820	24.6%	16,000
4. Medical Assistants	27.5%	$25,350	52.1%	93,000
5. Appraisers, Real Estate	10.9%	$43,440	22.8%	9,000
6. Assessors	10.9%	$43,440	22.8%	9,000
7. Respiratory Therapists	15.9%	$45,140	28.4%	7,000
8. Pharmacy Technicians	23.2%	$24,390	28.6%	35,000
9. Property, Real Estate, and Community Association Managers	21.9%	$41,900	15.3%	58,000
10. Real Estate Brokers	18.6%	$57,190	7.8%	12,000
11. Tile and Marble Setters	12.3%	$36,530	22.9%	9,000
12. Commercial Pilots	14.8%	$55,810	16.8%	2,000
13. Payroll and Timekeeping Clerks	14.7%	$31,360	17.3%	36,000
14. Real Estate Sales Agents	18.6%	$39,240	14.7%	41,000
15. Interior Designers	21.3%	$41,350	15.5%	10,000
16. Gaming Supervisors	15.0%	$40,300	16.3%	8,000

Jobs 1 and 2 share 157,000 job openings. Jobs 5 and 6 share 9,000 job openings.

Best Jobs with a High Level of Quality Control Skills with a High Percentage of Part-Time Workers

Job	Percent Part-Time Workers	Annual Earnings	Percent Growth	Annual Openings
1. Management Analysts	18.4%	$66,380	20.1%	82,000
2. Diagnostic Medical Sonographers	17.2%	$54,370	34.8%	5,000
3. Medical and Clinical Laboratory Technologists	17.3%	$47,710	20.5%	14,000
4. Copy Writers	30.7%	$46,420	17.7%	14,000
5. Nuclear Medicine Technologists	17.2%	$59,670	21.5%	2,000
6. Forensic Science Technicians	22.7%	$44,590	36.4%	2,000
7. Cardiovascular Technologists and Technicians	17.2%	$40,420	32.6%	5,000
8. Medical and Clinical Laboratory Technicians	17.3%	$31,700	25.0%	14,000
9. Graphic Designers	21.3%	$38,390	15.2%	35,000
10. Commercial and Industrial Designers	21.3%	$52,200	10.8%	7,000
11. Wholesale and Retail Buyers, Except Farm Products	18.4%	$42,870	8.4%	20,000
12. Environmental Science and Protection Technicians, Including Health	22.7%	$36,260	16.3%	6,000
13. Sound Engineering Technicians	18.3%	$38,390	18.4%	2,000
14. Motorboat Mechanics	13.2%	$32,780	15.1%	7,000
15. Medical Equipment Repairers	12.1%	$39,570	14.8%	4,000

Job 4 shares 14,000 openings with another job not included in this list.

Best Jobs with a High Level of Science Skills with a High Percentage of Part-Time Workers

Job	Percent Part-Time Workers	Annual Earnings	Percent Growth	Annual Openings
1. Dental Hygienists	56.0%	$60,890	43.3%	17,000
2. Physician Assistants	16.7%	$72,030	49.6%	10,000
3. Teachers, Postsecondary	27.3%	$53,590	32.2%	329,000
4. Pharmacists	21.1%	$89,820	24.6%	16,000
5. Physical Therapists	24.7%	$63,080	36.7%	13,000
6. Registered Nurses	24.1%	$54,670	29.4%	229,000
7. Occupational Therapists	29.4%	$56,860	33.6%	7,000
8. Radiologic Technicians	17.2%	$45,950	23.2%	17,000

(continued)

(continued)

Best Jobs with a High Level of Science Skills with a High Percentage of Part-Time Workers

Job	Percent Part-Time Workers	Annual Earnings	Percent Growth	Annual Openings
9. Radiologic Technologists	17.2%	$45,950	23.2%	17,000
10. Airline Pilots, Copilots, and Flight Engineers	14.8%	$138,170	17.2%	7,000
11. Physical Therapist Assistants	28.6%	$39,490	44.2%	7,000
12. Diagnostic Medical Sonographers	17.2%	$54,370	34.8%	5,000
13. Fitness Trainers and Aerobics Instructors	41.3%	$25,840	27.1%	50,000
14. Veterinarians	10.8%	$68,910	17.4%	8,000
15. Dentists, General	22.4%	$125,300	13.5%	7,000
16. Medical and Clinical Laboratory Technologists	17.3%	$47,710	20.5%	14,000
17. Surgical Technologists	23.2%	$34,830	29.5%	12,000
18. Chiropractors	20.7%	$67,200	22.4%	4,000
19. Optometrists	16.5%	$88,040	19.7%	2,000
20. Licensed Practical and Licensed Vocational Nurses	21.9%	$35,230	17.1%	84,000

Jobs 8 and 9 share 17,000 job openings.

Best Jobs with a High Level of Social Skills with a High Percentage of Part-Time Workers

Job	Percent Part-Time Workers	Annual Earnings	Percent Growth	Annual Openings
1. Dental Hygienists	56.0%	$60,890	43.3%	17,000
2. Registered Nurses	24.1%	$54,670	29.4%	229,000
3. Physical Therapists	24.7%	$63,080	36.7%	13,000
4. Medical Assistants	27.5%	$25,350	52.1%	93,000
5. Personal and Home Care Aides	36.6%	$17,340	41.0%	230,000
6. Dental Assistants	38.9%	$29,520	42.7%	45,000
7. Auditors	10.2%	$52,210	22.4%	157,000
8. Market Research Analysts	13.8%	$57,300	19.6%	20,000
9. Occupational Therapists	29.4%	$56,860	33.6%	7,000
10. Preschool Teachers, Except Special Education	25.1%	$21,990	33.1%	77,000
11. Customer Service Representatives	17.6%	$27,490	22.8%	510,000
12. Self-Enrichment Education Teachers	45.6%	$32,360	25.3%	74,000

Best Jobs with a High Level of Social Skills with a High Percentage of Part-Time Workers

Job	Percent Part-Time Workers	Annual Earnings	Percent Growth	Annual Openings
13. Social and Community Service Managers	12.5%	$49,500	25.5%	17,000
14. Instructional Coordinators	23.4%	$50,430	27.5%	15,000
15. Social and Human Service Assistants	16.0%	$25,030	29.7%	61,000
16. Fitness Trainers and Aerobics Instructors	41.3%	$25,840	27.1%	50,000
17. Public Relations Specialists	11.8%	$45,020	22.9%	38,000
18. Radiologic Technicians	17.2%	$45,950	23.2%	17,000
19. Radiologic Technologists	17.2%	$45,950	23.2%	17,000
20. Special Education Teachers, Preschool, Kindergarten, and Elementary School	10.5%	$44,630	23.3%	18,000

Job 7 shares 157,000 openings with another job not included in this list. Jobs 18 and 19 share 17,000 job openings.

Best Jobs with a High Level of Thought-Processing Skills with a High Percentage of Part-Time Workers

Job	Percent Part-Time Workers	Annual Earnings	Percent Growth	Annual Openings
1. Teachers, Postsecondary	27.3%	$53,590	32.2%	329,000
2. Registered Nurses	24.1%	$54,670	29.4%	229,000
3. Physician Assistants	16.7%	$72,030	49.6%	10,000
4. Personal and Home Care Aides	36.6%	$17,340	41.0%	230,000
5. Instructional Coordinators	23.4%	$50,430	27.5%	15,000
6. Public Relations Specialists	11.8%	$45,020	22.9%	38,000
7. Customer Service Representatives	17.6%	$27,490	22.8%	510,000
8. Market Research Analysts	13.8%	$57,300	19.6%	20,000
9. Self-Enrichment Education Teachers	45.6%	$32,360	25.3%	74,000
10. Special Education Teachers, Preschool, Kindergarten, and Elementary School	10.5%	$44,630	23.3%	18,000
11. Emergency Medical Technicians and Paramedics	10.6%	$26,080	27.3%	21,000
12. Kindergarten Teachers, Except Special Education	25.1%	$42,230	22.4%	28,000
13. Mental Health and Substance Abuse Social Workers	11.5%	$34,410	26.7%	15,000
14. Elementary School Teachers, Except Special Education	12.6%	$44,040	18.2%	203,000

(continued)

(continued)

Best Jobs with a High Level of Thought-Processing Skills with a High Percentage of Part-Time Workers

Job	Percent Part-Time Workers	Annual Earnings	Percent Growth	Annual Openings
15. Medical and Public Health Social Workers	11.5%	$41,120	25.9%	14,000
16. Mental Health Counselors	16.7%	$34,010	27.2%	14,000
17. Optometrists	16.5%	$88,040	19.7%	2,000
18. Clinical Psychologists	22.8%	$57,170	19.1%	10,000
19. Counseling Psychologists	22.8%	$57,170	19.1%	10,000
20. School Psychologists	22.8%	$57,170	19.1%	10,000

Jobs 18, 19, and 20 share 10,000 job openings.

The Best Jobs for Each Skill with a High Percentage of Self-Employed Workers

About 8 percent of all working people are self-employed or own their own business. This substantial part of our workforce gets little mention in most career books.

The jobs in the lists in this section are selected from the 50 best jobs with a high level of each skill, and all have 5 percent or more self-employed workers. Like the part-time jobs, these jobs are ranked by earnings, job growth, and job openings. The lists are limited to the 20 top-ranked jobs with a high level of each skill, but for many skills we were able to rank only a smaller number of jobs.

Many jobs in these lists, such as the various types of designers, are held by people who operate one- or two-person businesses and who may also do this work part time. Those in other occupations, such as Rough Carpenters, often work on a per-job basis under the supervision of others.

As you will see from these lists, self-employed people hold a wide range of jobs at all levels of pay. Many of the jobs use management skills, equipment/technology analysis skills, or mathematics skills, but all 10 skills are represented here. While the lists do not include data on age and gender, you may be interested in the fact that older workers and women make up a rapidly growing part of the self-employed population. For example, some highly experienced older workers set up consulting and other small businesses following a layoff or as an alternative to full retirement. Large numbers of women are forming small businesses or creating self-employment opportunities as an alternative to traditional employment.

Best Jobs with a High Level of Communication Skills with a High Percentage of Self-Employed Workers

Job	Percent Self-Employed Workers	Annual Earnings	Percent Growth	Annual Openings
1. Surgeons	11.5% more than	$145,600	24.0%	41,000
2. Personal Financial Advisors	38.9%	$63,500	25.9%	17,000
3. Lawyers	24.1%	$98,930	15.0%	40,000
4. Self-Enrichment Education Teachers	31.1%	$32,360	25.3%	74,000
5. Market Research Analysts	7.2%	$57,300	19.6%	20,000
6. Sales Agents, Financial Services	12.5%	$67,130	11.5%	37,000
7. Clinical Psychologists	38.2%	$57,170	19.1%	10,000
8. Counseling Psychologists	38.2%	$57,170	19.1%	10,000
9. School Psychologists	38.2%	$57,170	19.1%	10,000
10. Occupational Therapists	6.0%	$56,860	33.6%	7,000
11. Educational, Vocational, and School Counselors	5.8%	$46,440	14.8%	32,000
12. Technical Writers	7.3%	$55,160	23.2%	5,000

Job 1 shares 41,000 openings with six other jobs not included in this list. Job 6 shares 37,000 openings with another job not included in this list. Jobs 7, 8, and 9 share 10,000 job openings.

Best Jobs with a High Level of Computer Programming Skills with a High Percentage of Self-Employed Workers

Job	Percent Self-Employed Workers	Annual Earnings	Percent Growth	Annual Openings
1. Network Systems and Data Communications Analysts	19.9%	$61,750	54.6%	43,000
2. Accountants	10.9%	$52,210	22.4%	157,000
3. Financial Analysts	6.7%	$63,860	17.3%	28,000
4. Multi-Media Artists and Animators	60.8%	$50,290	14.1%	14,000
5. Archivists	6.5%	$37,420	13.4%	1,000
6. Foresters	9.1%	$48,670	6.7%	1,000

Job 2 shares 157,000 openings with another job not included in this list.

Best Jobs with a High Level of Equipment Use/Maintenance Skills with a High Percentage of Self-Employed Workers

Job	Percent Self-Employed Workers	Annual Earnings	Percent Growth	Annual Openings
1. Management Analysts	24.7%	$66,380	20.1%	82,000
2. Anesthesiologists	11.5%	more than $145,600	24.0%	41,000
3. Network Systems and Data Communications Analysts	19.9%	$61,750	54.6%	43,000
4. Pipe Fitters and Steamfitters	13.3%	$42,160	15.7%	61,000
5. Plumbers	13.3%	$42,160	15.7%	61,000
6. Heating and Air Conditioning Mechanics and Installers	13.1%	$37,040	19.0%	33,000
7. Refrigeration Mechanics and Installers	13.1%	$37,040	19.0%	33,000
8. Automotive Master Mechanics	14.8%	$33,050	15.7%	93,000
9. Automotive Specialty Technicians	14.8%	$33,050	15.7%	93,000
10. Electricians	9.5%	$42,790	11.8%	68,000
11. Rough Carpenters	32.4%	$35,580	13.8%	210,000
12. Technical Directors/Managers	30.4%	$53,860	16.6%	11,000
13. Truck Drivers, Heavy and Tractor-Trailer	9.3%	$34,280	12.9%	274,000
14. Film and Video Editors	18.2%	$46,930	18.6%	3,000
15. First-Line Supervisors/Managers of Construction Trades and Extraction Workers	24.7%	$51,970	10.9%	57,000
16. Construction Managers	54.2%	$72,260	10.4%	28,000
17. Bus and Truck Mechanics and Diesel Engine Specialists	5.3%	$36,620	14.4%	32,000
18. First-Line Supervisors/Managers of Housekeeping and Janitorial Workers	8.9%	$30,330	19.0%	21,000
19. Operating Engineers and Other Construction Equipment Operators	5.4%	$35,830	11.6%	37,000

Job 2 shares 41,000 openings with six other jobs not included in this list. Jobs 4 and 5 share 61,000 job openings. Jobs 6 and 7 share 33,000 job openings. Jobs 8 and 9 share 93,000 job openings. Job 11 shares 210,000 openings with another job not included in this list. Job 12 shares 11,000 openings with four other jobs not included in this list.

Best Jobs with a High Level of Equipment/Technology Analysis Skills with a High Percentage of Self-Employed Workers

Job	Percent Self-Employed Workers	Annual Earnings	Percent Growth	Annual Openings
1. Network Systems and Data Communications Analysts	19.9%	$61,750	54.6%	43,000
2. Biomedical Engineers	7.2%	$71,840	30.7%	1,000

Best Jobs with a High Level of Equipment/Technology Analysis Skills with a High Percentage of Self-Employed Workers

Job	Percent Self-Employed Workers	Annual Earnings	Percent Growth	Annual Openings
3. Technical Writers	7.3%	$55,160	23.2%	5,000
4. Architects, Except Landscape and Naval	20.1%	$62,850	17.3%	7,000
5. Copy Writers	67.7%	$46,420	17.7%	14,000
6. Directors—Stage, Motion Pictures, Television, and Radio	30.4%	$53,860	16.6%	11,000
7. Technical Directors/Managers	30.4%	$53,860	16.6%	11,000
8. Fitness Trainers and Aerobics Instructors	6.6%	$25,840	27.1%	50,000
9. Pipe Fitters and Steamfitters	13.3%	$42,160	15.7%	61,000
10. Plumbers	13.3%	$42,160	15.7%	61,000
11. Landscape Architects	23.7%	$54,220	19.4%	1,000
12. Refrigeration Mechanics and Installers	13.1%	$37,040	19.0%	33,000
13. Automotive Specialty Technicians	14.8%	$33,050	15.7%	93,000
14. Electricians	9.5%	$42,790	11.8%	68,000
15. Art Directors	55.8%	$63,950	11.5%	10,000
16. Film and Video Editors	18.2%	$46,930	18.6%	3,000
17. Multi-Media Artists and Animators	60.8%	$50,290	14.1%	14,000
18. Rough Carpenters	32.4%	$35,580	13.8%	210,000
19. Tile and Marble Setters	24.4%	$36,530	22.9%	9,000
20. Graphic Designers	25.6%	$38,390	15.2%	35,000

Job 5 shares 14,000 openings with another job not included in this list. Jobs 6 and 7 share 11,000 openings with each other and with three other jobs not included in this list. Jobs 9 and 10 share 61,000 job openings. Job 12 shares 33,000 openings with another job not included in this list. Job 13 shares 93,000 openings with another job not included in this list. Job 18 shares 210,000 openings with another job not included in this list.

Best Jobs with a High Level of Management Skills with a High Percentage of Self-Employed Workers

Job	Percent Self-Employed Workers	Annual Earnings	Percent Growth	Annual Openings
1. Medical and Health Services Managers	5.7%	$69,700	22.8%	33,000
2. Accountants	10.9%	$52,210	22.4%	157,000
3. Auditors	10.9%	$52,210	22.4%	157,000

(continued)

(continued)

Best Jobs with a High Level of Management Skills with a High Percentage of Self-Employed Workers

Job	Percent Self-Employed Workers	Annual Earnings	Percent Growth	Annual Openings
4. Management Analysts	24.7%	$66,380	20.1%	82,000
5. Chief Executives	16.2%	$142,440	14.9%	38,000
6. Advertising and Promotions Managers	6.7%	$68,860	20.3%	9,000
7. Coaches and Scouts	21.5%	$25,990	20.4%	63,000
8. Financial Analysts	6.7%	$63,860	17.3%	28,000
9. Chiropractors	49.2%	$67,200	22.4%	4,000
10. Veterinarians	20.7%	$68,910	17.4%	8,000
11. Optometrists	27.4%	$88,040	19.7%	2,000
12. Directors—Stage, Motion Pictures, Television, and Radio	30.4%	$53,860	16.6%	11,000
13. Producers	30.4%	$53,860	16.6%	11,000
14. Program Directors	30.4%	$53,860	16.6%	11,000
15. Technical Directors/Managers	30.4%	$53,860	16.6%	11,000
16. Dentists, General	30.7%	$125,300	13.5%	7,000
17. Architects, Except Landscape and Naval	20.1%	$62,850	17.3%	7,000
18. Property, Real Estate, and Community Association Managers	48.2%	$41,900	15.3%	58,000
19. First-Line Supervisors/Managers of Construction Trades and Extraction Workers	24.7%	$51,970	10.9%	57,000

Jobs 2 and 3 share 157,000 job openings. Jobs 12, 13, 14, and 15 share 11,000 openings with each other and with another job not included in this list.

Best Jobs with a High Level of Mathematics Skills with a High Percentage of Self-Employed Workers

Job	Percent Self-Employed Workers	Annual Earnings	Percent Growth	Annual Openings
1. Accountants	10.9%	$52,210	22.4%	157,000
2. Auditors	10.9%	$52,210	22.4%	157,000
3. Personal Financial Advisors	38.9%	$63,500	25.9%	17,000
4. Financial Analysts	6.7%	$63,860	17.3%	28,000
5. Sales Agents, Financial Services	12.5%	$67,130	11.5%	37,000

Best Jobs with a High Level of Mathematics Skills with a High Percentage of Self-Employed Workers

Job	Percent Self-Employed Workers	Annual Earnings	Percent Growth	Annual Openings
6. Sales Agents, Securities and Commodities	12.5%	$67,130	11.5%	37,000
7. Appraisers, Real Estate	37.2%	$43,440	22.8%	9,000
8. Assessors	37.2%	$43,440	22.8%	9,000
9. Construction Managers	54.2%	$72,260	10.4%	28,000
10. Property, Real Estate, and Community Association Managers	48.2%	$41,900	15.3%	58,000
11. Electricians	9.5%	$42,790	11.8%	68,000
12. Construction Carpenters	32.4%	$35,580	13.8%	210,000
13. Rough Carpenters	32.4%	$35,580	13.8%	210,000
14. Landscape Architects	23.7%	$54,220	19.4%	1,000
15. Construction and Building Inspectors	10.2%	$44,720	22.3%	6,000
16. Heating and Air Conditioning Mechanics and Installers	13.1%	$37,040	19.0%	33,000
17. Tile and Marble Setters	24.4%	$36,530	22.9%	9,000
18. Real Estate Sales Agents	59.8%	$39,240	14.7%	41,000
19. Real Estate Brokers	59.9%	$57,190	7.8%	12,000
20. Interior Designers	25.3%	$41,350	15.5%	10,000

Jobs 1 and 2 share 157,000 job openings. Jobs 5 and 6 share 37,000 job openings. Jobs 7 and 8 share 9,000 job openings. Jobs 12 and 13 share 210,000 job openings. Job 16 shares 33,000 openings with another job not included in this list.

Best Jobs with a High Level of Quality Control Skills with a High Percentage of Self-Employed Workers

Job	Percent Self-Employed Workers	Annual Earnings	Percent Growth	Annual Openings
1. Management Analysts	24.7%	$66,380	20.1%	82,000
2. Medical and Health Services Managers	5.7%	$69,700	22.8%	33,000
3. Biomedical Engineers	7.2%	$71,840	30.7%	1,000
4. Technical Writers	7.3%	$55,160	23.2%	5,000
5. Pipe Fitters and Steamfitters	13.3%	$42,160	15.7%	61,000
6. First-Line Supervisors/Managers of Construction Trades and Extraction Workers	24.7%	$51,970	10.9%	57,000
7. Copy Writers	67.7%	$46,420	17.7%	14,000

(continued)

(continued)

Best Jobs with a High Level of Quality Control Skills with a High Percentage of Self-Employed Workers

Job	Percent Self-Employed Workers	Annual Earnings	Percent Growth	Annual Openings
8. Construction and Building Inspectors	10.2%	$44,720	22.3%	6,000
9. Food Service Managers	40.5%	$41,340	11.5%	61,000
10. Graphic Designers	25.6%	$38,390	15.2%	35,000
11. Construction Carpenters	32.4%	$35,580	13.8%	210,000
12. Commercial and Industrial Designers	30.1%	$52,200	10.8%	7,000
13. Telecommunications Equipment Installers and Repairers, Except Line Installers	6.6%	$50,620	−4.9%	21,000
14. Wholesale and Retail Buyers, Except Farm Products	10.9%	$42,870	8.4%	20,000
15. Sound Engineering Technicians	6.5%	$38,390	18.4%	2,000
16. Medical Equipment Repairers	16.2%	$39,570	14.8%	4,000
17. Motorboat Mechanics	18.9%	$32,780	15.1%	7,000
18. Computer, Automated Teller, and Office Machine Repairers	13.7%	$36,060	3.8%	31,000

Job 5 shares 61,000 openings with another job not included in this list. Job 7 shares 14,000 openings with another job not included in this list. Job 11 shares 210,000 openings with another job not included in this list.

Best Jobs with a High Level of Science Skills with a High Percentage of Self-Employed Workers

Job	Percent Self-Employed Workers	Annual Earnings	Percent Growth	Annual Openings
1. Anesthesiologists	11.5% more than	$145,600	24.0%	41,000
2. Internists, General	11.5% more than	$145,600	24.0%	41,000
3. Obstetricians and Gynecologists	11.5% more than	$145,600	24.0%	41,000
4. Psychiatrists	11.5% more than	$145,600	24.0%	41,000
5. Surgeons	11.5% more than	$145,600	24.0%	41,000
6. Family and General Practitioners	11.5%	$140,400	24.0%	41,000
7. Pediatricians, General	11.5%	$136,600	24.0%	41,000
8. Fitness Trainers and Aerobics Instructors	6.6%	$25,840	27.1%	50,000
9. Occupational Therapists	6.0%	$56,860	33.6%	7,000
10. Biomedical Engineers	7.2%	$71,840	30.7%	1,000
11. Plumbers	13.3%	$42,160	15.7%	61,000
12. Optometrists	27.4%	$88,040	19.7%	2,000

Best Jobs with a High Level of Science Skills with a High Percentage of Self-Employed Workers

Job	Percent Self-Employed Workers	Annual Earnings	Percent Growth	Annual Openings
13. Chiropractors	49.2%	$67,200	22.4%	4,000
14. Heating and Air Conditioning Mechanics and Installers	13.1%	$37,040	19.0%	33,000
15. Refrigeration Mechanics and Installers	13.1%	$37,040	19.0%	33,000
16. Veterinarians	20.7%	$68,910	17.4%	8,000
17. Dentists, General	30.7%	$125,300	13.5%	7,000
18. Multi-Media Artists and Animators	60.8%	$50,290	14.1%	14,000

Jobs 1, 2, 3, 4, 5, 6, and 7 share 41,000 job openings. Job 11 shares 210,000 openings with another job not included in this list. Jobs 14 and 15 share 33,000 job openings.

Best Jobs with a High Level of Social Skills with a High Percentage of Self-Employed Workers

Job	Percent Self-Employed Workers	Annual Earnings	Percent Growth	Annual Openings
1. Internists, General	11.5% more than	$145,600	24.0%	41,000
2. Obstetricians and Gynecologists	11.5% more than	$145,600	24.0%	41,000
3. Psychiatrists	11.5% more than	$145,600	24.0%	41,000
4. Family and General Practitioners	11.5%	$140,400	24.0%	41,000
5. Pediatricians, General	11.5%	$136,600	24.0%	41,000
6. Self-Enrichment Education Teachers	31.1%	$32,360	25.3%	74,000
7. Fitness Trainers and Aerobics Instructors	6.6%	$25,840	27.1%	50,000
8. Auditors	10.9%	$52,210	22.4%	157,000
9. Medical and Health Services Managers	5.7%	$69,700	22.8%	33,000
10. Chief Executives	16.2%	$142,440	14.9%	38,000
11. Lawyers	24.1%	$98,930	15.0%	40,000
12. Occupational Therapists	6.0%	$56,860	33.6%	7,000
13. Market Research Analysts	7.2%	$57,300	19.6%	20,000
14. Advertising and Promotions Managers	6.7%	$68,860	20.3%	9,000
15. Clinical Psychologists	38.2%	$57,170	19.1%	10,000
16. Counseling Psychologists	38.2%	$57,170	19.1%	10,000
17. School Psychologists	38.2%	$57,170	19.1%	10,000

Jobs 1, 2, 3, 4, and 5 share 41,000 job openings. Job 8 shares 157,000 openings with another job not included in this list. Jobs 15, 16, and 17 share 10,000 job openings.

Best Jobs with a High Level of Thought-Processing Skills with a High Percentage of Self-Employed Workers

Job	Percent Self-Employed Workers	Annual Earnings	Percent Growth	Annual Openings
1. Anesthesiologists	11.5% more than	$145,600	24.0%	41,000
2. Internists, General	11.5% more than	$145,600	24.0%	41,000
3. Obstetricians and Gynecologists	11.5% more than	$145,600	24.0%	41,000
4. Psychiatrists	11.5% more than	$145,600	24.0%	41,000
5. Surgeons	11.5% more than	$145,600	24.0%	41,000
6. Family and General Practitioners	11.5%	$140,400	24.0%	41,000
7. Pediatricians, General	11.5%	$136,600	24.0%	41,000
8. Self-Enrichment Education Teachers	31.1%	$32,360	25.3%	74,000
9. Coaches and Scouts	21.5%	$25,990	20.4%	63,000
10. Mental Health Counselors	5.0%	$34,010	27.2%	14,000
11. Chief Executives	16.2%	$142,440	14.9%	38,000
12. Lawyers	24.1%	$98,930	15.0%	40,000
13. Market Research Analysts	7.2%	$57,300	19.6%	20,000
14. Advertising and Promotions Managers	6.7%	$68,860	20.3%	9,000
15. Industrial-Organizational Psychologists	37.6%	$84,690	20.4%	fewer than 500
16. Optometrists	27.4%	$88,040	19.7%	2,000
17. Clinical Psychologists	38.2%	$57,170	19.1%	10,000
18. Counseling Psychologists	38.2%	$57,170	19.1%	10,000
19. School Psychologists	38.2%	$57,170	19.1%	10,000
20. Sales Agents, Securities and Commodities	12.5%	$67,130	11.5%	37,000

Jobs 1, 2, 3, 4, 5, 6, and 7 share 41,000 job openings. Jobs 17, 18, and 19 share 10,000 job openings. Job 20 shares 37,000 openings with another job not included in this list.

The Best Jobs for Your Skills Sorted by Education or Training Required

The lists that follow separate the 50 best jobs with a high level of each skill into lists based on the education or training typically required for entry. Next to each job title you'll find the job's top skills listed alphabetically. You'll also find the job's annual earnings, percent growth, and annual job openings, and these economic measures are used to order the jobs within each grouping. Thus you can easily find the best overall jobs for a given level of education or training and see what skills they are linked to.

You can use these lists in a variety of ways. For example, they can help you identify a job with higher potential than a job you now hold that requires a similar level of education.

You can also use these lists to figure out additional job possibilities that would open up if you were to get additional training, education, or work experience. For example, maybe you are a high school graduate working in a job associated with thought-processing skills. There are many jobs in this field at all levels of education, but especially at higher levels. You can identify the job you're interested in and the related training you need (you'll find more details in Part IV) so you can move ahead yet still be doing work that involves the same skill.

The lists of jobs by education should also help you when you're planning your education. For example, you might be thinking about a job that uses equipment use/maintenance skills and mathematics skills, but you aren't sure what kind of work you want to do. The lists show that Operating Engineers and Other Construction Equipment Operators need moderate-term on-the-job training and earn $35,830, while Rough Carpenters need long-term on-the-job training but earn an average of $35,580. If you want comparable (or sometimes even higher) earnings without lengthy training, this information might make a difference in your choice.

Descriptions of the Education Levels

Short-term on-the-job training. It is possible to work in these occupations and achieve an average level of performance within a few days or weeks through on-the-job training.

Moderate-term on-the-job training. Occupations that require this type of training can be performed adequately after a one- to 12-month period of combined on-the-job and informal training. Typically, untrained workers observe experienced workers performing tasks and are gradually moved into progressively more difficult assignments.

Long-term on-the-job training. This training requires more than 12 months of on-the-job training or combined work experience and formal classroom instruction. This includes occupations that use formal apprenticeships for training workers that may take up to four years. It also includes intensive occupation-specific, employer-sponsored training such as police academies. Furthermore, it includes occupations that require natural talent that must be developed over many years.

Work experience in a related occupation. This type of job requires experience in a related occupation. For example, police detectives are selected based on their experience as police patrol officers.

Postsecondary vocational training. This requirement can vary from training that involves a few months but is usually less than one year. In a few instances, there may be as many as four years of training.

Associate degree. This degree usually requires two years of full-time academic work beyond high school.

Bachelor's degree. This degree requires approximately four to five years of full-time academic work beyond high school.

Work experience plus degree. Jobs in this category are often management-related and require some experience in a related nonmanagerial position.

Master's degree. Completion of a master's degree usually requires one to two years of full-time study beyond the bachelor's degree.

Doctoral degree. This degree normally requires two or more years of full-time academic work beyond the bachelor's degree.

First professional degree. This type of degree normally requires a minimum of two years of education beyond the bachelor's degree and frequently requires three years.

Another Warning About the Data

We warned you in the introduction to use caution in interpreting the data we use, and we want to do it again here. The occupational data we use is the most accurate available anywhere, but it has its limitations. For example, the education or training requirements for entry into a job are those typically required as a minimum—but some people working in those jobs may have considerably more or different credentials. For example, most Registered Nurses now have a four-year bachelor's degree, although the two-year associate's degree is the minimum level of training the job requires.

In a similar way, people with jobs that require long-term on-the-job training typically earn more than people with jobs that require short-term on-the-job training. However, some people with short-term on-the-job training do earn more than the average for the highest-paying occupations listed in this book. On the other hand, some people with long-term on-the-job training earn much less than the average shown in this book—this is particularly true early in a person's career.

So as you browse the lists that follow, please use them as a way to be encouraged rather than discouraged. Education and training are very important for success in the labor market of the future, but so are ability, drive, initiative, and, yes, luck.

Having said this, we encourage you to get as much education and training as you can. See Part II for suggestions about how to improve your skills through either formal or informal learning.

An old saying goes, "The harder you work, the luckier you get." It is just as true now as it ever was.

Best Jobs Requiring Short-Term On-the-Job Training

Job	Top Skills	Annual Earnings	Percent Growth	Annual Openings
1. Bill and Account Collectors	Communication Skills; Management Skills; Social Skills	$28,160	21.4%	85,000
2. Personal and Home Care Aides	Communication Skills; Social Skills; Thought-Processing Skills	$17,340	41.0%	230,000
3. Human Resources Assistants, Except Payroll and Timekeeping	Communication Skills; Management Skills; Mathematics Skills	$32,730	16.7%	28,000
4. Electrical and Electronic Equipment Assemblers	Computer Programming Skills; Equipment Use/ Maintenance Skills; Quality Control Skills	$25,130	–6.4%	33,000

Best Jobs Requiring Moderate-Term On-the-Job Training

Job	Top Skills	Annual Earnings	Percent Growth	Annual Openings
1. Sales Representatives, Wholesale and Manufacturing, Except Technical and Scientific Products	Communication Skills; Management Skills; Social Skills	$47,380	12.9%	169,000
2. Truck Drivers, Heavy and Tractor-Trailer	Equipment Use/ Maintenance Skills	$34,280	12.9%	274,000
3. Dental Assistants	Equipment Use/ Maintenance Skills; Equipment/Technology Analysis Skills; Social Skills	$29,520	42.7%	45,000
4. Customer Service Representatives	Communication Skills; Social Skills; Thought-Processing Skills	$27,490	22.8%	510,000
5. Medical Assistants	Communication Skills; Mathematics Skills; Social Skills	$25,350	52.1%	93,000
6. Maintenance and Repair Workers, General	Equipment Use/ Maintenance Skills	$31,210	15.2%	154,000

(continued)

(continued)

Best Jobs Requiring Moderate-Term On-the-Job Training

Job	Top Skills	Annual Earnings	Percent Growth	Annual Openings
7. Payroll and Timekeeping Clerks	Communication Skills; Mathematics Skills; Thought-Processing Skills	$31,360	17.3%	36,000
8. Operating Engineers and Other Construction Equipment Operators	Equipment Use/ Maintenance Skills; Management Skills; Science Skills	$35,830	11.6%	37,000
9. Railroad Conductors and Yardmasters	Equipment Use/ Maintenance Skills	$54,040	20.3%	3,000
10. Social and Human Service Assistants	Communication Skills; Management Skills; Social Skills	$25,030	29.7%	61,000
11. Bus Drivers, Transit and Intercity	Equipment Use/ Maintenance Skills	$31,010	21.7%	34,000
12. Cement Masons and Concrete Finishers	Mathematics Skills	$32,030	15.9%	32,000
13. Highway Maintenance Workers	Equipment Use/ Maintenance Skills	$30,250	23.3%	27,000
14. Pharmacy Technicians	Communication Skills; Mathematics Skills	$24,390	28.6%	35,000
15. Mapping Technicians	Computer Programming Skills; Mathematics Skills; Quality Control Skills	$31,290	9.6%	9,000
16. Forging Machine Setters, Operators, and Tenders, Metal and Plastic	Computer Programming Skills; Equipment Use/ Maintenance Skills; Quality Control Skills	$28,970	–4.6%	4,000
17. Statistical Assistants	Computer Programming Skills; Mathematics Skills; Quality Control Skills	$28,950	5.7%	1,000

Job 15 shares 9,000 openings with another job not included in this list.

Best Jobs Requiring Long-Term On-the-Job Training

Job	Top Skills	Annual Earnings	Percent Growth	Annual Openings
1. Pipe Fitters and Steamfitters	Equipment Use/ Maintenance Skills; Equipment/Technology Analysis Skills; Quality Control Skills	$42,160	15.7%	61,000
2. Plumbers	Equipment Use/ Maintenance Skills; Equipment/Technology Analysis Skills; Science Skills	$42,160	15.7%	61,000
3. Police Patrol Officers	Communication Skills; Social Skills; Thought-Processing Skills	$46,290	15.5%	47,000
4. Sheriffs and Deputy Sheriffs	Communication Skills; Social Skills; Thought-Processing Skills	$46,290	15.5%	47,000
5. Forest Fire Fighters	Equipment Use/ Maintenance Skills; Equipment/Technology Analysis Skills; Management Skills	$39,090	24.3%	21,000
6. Municipal Fire Fighters	Equipment Use/ Maintenance Skills; Equipment/Technology Analysis Skills; Science Skills	$39,090	24.3%	21,000
7. Technical Directors/Managers	Equipment Use/ Maintenance Skills; Equipment/Technology Analysis Skills; Management Skills	$53,860	16.6%	11,000
8. Electricians	Equipment Use/ Maintenance Skills; Equipment/Technology Analysis Skills; Mathematics Skills	$42,790	11.8%	68,000

(continued)

(continued)

Best Jobs Requiring Long-Term On-the-Job Training

Job	Top Skills	Annual Earnings	Percent Growth	Annual Openings
9. Heating and Air Conditioning Mechanics and Installers	Equipment Use/ Maintenance Skills; Mathematics Skills; Science Skills	$37,040	19.0%	33,000
10. Refrigeration Mechanics and Installers	Equipment Use/ Maintenance Skills; Equipment/Technology Analysis Skills; Science Skills	$37,040	19.0%	33,000
11. Coaches and Scouts	Management Skills; Social Skills; Thought-Processing Skills	$25,990	20.4%	63,000
12. Construction Carpenters	Management Skills; Mathematics Skills; Quality Control Skills	$35,580	13.8%	210,000
13. Rough Carpenters	Equipment Use/ Maintenance Skills; Equipment/Technology Analysis Skills; Mathematics Skills	$35,580	13.8%	210,000
14. Elevator Installers and Repairers	Equipment Use/ Maintenance Skills; Quality Control Skills	$59,190	14.8%	3,000
15. Air Traffic Controllers	Equipment Use/ Maintenance Skills	$107,590	14.3%	2,000
16. Tile and Marble Setters	Equipment/Technology Analysis Skills; Management Skills; Mathematics Skills	$36,530	22.9%	9,000
17. Telecommunications Equipment Installers and Repairers, Except Line Installers	Equipment Use/ Maintenance Skills; Quality Control Skills	$50,620	–4.9%	21,000
18. Telecommunications Line Installers and Repairers	Equipment Use/ Maintenance Skills	$42,410	10.8%	23,000

Best Jobs Requiring Long-Term On-the-Job Training

Job	Top Skills	Annual Earnings	Percent Growth	Annual Openings
19. Sheet Metal Workers	Equipment Use/ Maintenance Skills; Mathematics Skills; Social Skills	$36,390	12.2%	50,000
20. Machinists	Computer Programming Skills; Equipment Use/ Maintenance Skills; Quality Control Skills	$34,350	4.3%	33,000
21. Motorboat Mechanics	Equipment Use/ Maintenance Skills; Quality Control Skills	$32,780	15.1%	7,000
22. Numerical Tool and Process Control Programmers	Computer Programming Skills; Mathematics Skills; Quality Control Skills	$41,830	−1.1%	2,000

Jobs 1 and 2 share 61,000 job openings. Jobs 3 and 4 share 47,000 job openings. Jobs 5 and 6 share 21,000 job openings. Job 7 shares 11,000 openings with four other jobs not included in this list. Jobs 9 and 10 share 33,000 job openings. Jobs 12 and 13 share 210,000 job openings.

Best Jobs Requiring Work Experience in a Related Occupation

Job	Top Skills	Annual Earnings	Percent Growth	Annual Openings
1. Storage and Distribution Managers	Equipment/Technology Analysis Skills; Management Skills; Social Skills	$69,120	12.7%	15,000
2. Transportation Managers	Management Skills; Mathematics Skills; Social Skills	$69,120	12.7%	15,000
3. Self-Enrichment Education Teachers	Communication Skills; Social Skills; Thought-Processing Skills	$32,360	25.3%	74,000
4. Cost Estimators	Equipment/Technology Analysis Skills; Management Skills; Mathematics Skills	$52,020	18.2%	15,000

(continued)

(continued)

Best Jobs Requiring Work Experience in a Related Occupation

Job	Top Skills	Annual Earnings	Percent Growth	Annual Openings
5. Forest Fire Fighting and Prevention Supervisors	Equipment Use/ Maintenance Skills; Management Skills; Science Skills	$60,840	21.1%	4,000
6. Municipal Fire Fighting and Prevention Supervisors	Equipment Use/ Maintenance Skills; Management Skills; Social Skills	$60,840	21.1%	4,000
7. First-Line Supervisors/ Managers of Police and Detectives	Management Skills; Social Skills; Thought-Processing Skills	$65,570	15.5%	9,000
8. First-Line Supervisors/ Managers of Mechanics, Installers, and Repairers	Equipment Use/ Maintenance Skills; Equipment/Technology Analysis Skills; Management Skills	$51,980	12.4%	33,000
9. Criminal Investigators and Special Agents	Computer Programming Skills; Equipment/ Technology Analysis Skills; Social Skills	$55,790	16.3%	9,000
10. Immigration and Customs Inspectors	Communication Skills; Equipment/Technology Analysis Skills; Social Skills	$55,790	16.3%	9,000
11. Gaming Managers	Management Skills; Mathematics Skills; Social Skills	$59,940	22.6%	1,000
12. First-Line Supervisors/ Managers of Transportation and Material-Moving Machine and Vehicle Operators	Management Skills; Quality Control Skills; Social Skills	$47,530	15.3%	22,000
13. First-Line Supervisors/ Managers of Construction Trades and Extraction Workers	Equipment Use/ Maintenance Skills; Management Skills; Quality Control Skills	$51,970	10.9%	57,000

Best Jobs Requiring Work Experience in a Related Occupation

Job	Top Skills	Annual Earnings	Percent Growth	Annual Openings
14. First-Line Supervisors/ Managers of Housekeeping and Janitorial Workers	Equipment Use/ Maintenance Skills; Management Skills; Social Skills	$30,330	19.0%	21,000
15. Food Service Managers	Management Skills; Quality Control Skills; Social Skills	$41,340	11.5%	61,000
16. Industrial Production Managers	Equipment/Technology Analysis Skills; Management Skills; Quality Control Skills	$75,580	0.8%	13,000
17. Construction and Building Inspectors	Mathematics Skills; Quality Control Skills; Social Skills	$44,720	22.3%	6,000
18. First-Line Supervisors/Managers of Production and Operating Workers	Equipment Use/ Maintenance Skills; Management Skills; Quality Control Skills	$46,140	2.7%	89,000
19. Purchasing Agents, Except Wholesale, Retail, and Farm Products	Communication Skills; Management Skills; Mathematics Skills	$49,030	8.1%	19,000
20. Real Estate Brokers	Management Skills; Mathematics Skills; Social Skills	$57,190	7.8%	12,000
21. Wholesale and Retail Buyers, Except Farm Products	Management Skills; Mathematics Skills; Quality Control Skills	$42,870	8.4%	20,000
22. Gaming Supervisors	Mathematics Skills; Social Skills; Thought-Processing Skills	$40,300	16.3%	8,000
23. Aviation Inspectors	Equipment Use/ Maintenance Skills; Quality Control Skills; Thought-Processing Skills	$49,490	11.4%	2,000
24. Transportation Vehicle, Equipment, and Systems Inspectors, Except Aviation	Equipment Use/ Maintenance Skills; Quality Control Skills	$49,490	11.4%	2,000

(continued)

(continued)

Best Jobs Requiring Work Experience in a Related Occupation

Job	Top Skills	Annual Earnings	Percent Growth	Annual Openings
25. First-Line Supervisors/ Managers of Helpers, Laborers, and Material Movers, Hand	Management Skills; Quality Control Skills; Social Skills	$39,000	8.1%	15,000

Jobs 1 and 2 share 15,000 job openings. Jobs 5 and 6 share 4,000 job openings. Jobs 9 and 10 share 9,000 openings with each other and with two other jobs not included in this list. Jobs 23 and 24 share 2,000 openings with another job not included in this list.

Best Jobs Requiring Postsecondary Vocational Training

Job	Top Skills	Annual Earnings	Percent Growth	Annual Openings
1. Appraisers, Real Estate	Communication Skills; Mathematics Skills; Thought-Processing Skills	$43,440	22.8%	9,000
2. Assessors	Communication Skills; Mathematics Skills; Social Skills	$43,440	22.8%	9,000
3. Preschool Teachers, Except Special Education	Communication Skills; Social Skills	$21,990	33.1%	77,000
4. Legal Secretaries	Communication Skills; Social Skills; Thought-Processing Skills	$37,750	17.4%	41,000
5. Licensed Practical and Licensed Vocational Nurses	Communication Skills; Equipment Use/ Maintenance Skills; Science Skills	$35,230	17.1%	84,000
6. Fitness Trainers and Aerobics Instructors	Equipment/Technology Analysis Skills; Science Skills; Social Skills	$25,840	27.1%	50,000
7. Nursing Aides, Orderlies, and Attendants	Management Skills; Science Skills; Social Skills	$21,440	22.3%	307,000
8. Automotive Master Mechanics	Equipment Use/ Maintenance Skills	$33,050	15.7%	93,000

Best Jobs Requiring Postsecondary Vocational Training

Job	Top Skills	Annual Earnings	Percent Growth	Annual Openings
9. Automotive Specialty Technicians	Equipment Use/ Maintenance Skills; Equipment/Technology Analysis Skills; Thought-Processing Skills	$33,050	15.7%	93,000
10. Real Estate Sales Agents	Communication Skills; Mathematics Skills; Social Skills	$39,240	14.7%	41,000
11. Surgical Technologists	Equipment/Technology Analysis Skills; Science Skills; Social Skills	$34,830	29.5%	12,000
12. Commercial Pilots	Equipment Use/ Maintenance Skills; Mathematics Skills; Thought-Processing Skills	$55,810	16.8%	2,000
13. Emergency Medical Technicians and Paramedics	Equipment Use/ Maintenance Skills; Social Skills; Thought-Processing Skills	$26,080	27.3%	21,000
14. Aircraft Mechanics and Service Technicians	Equipment Use/ Maintenance Skills; Quality Control Skills	$47,310	13.4%	11,000
15. Bus and Truck Mechanics and Diesel Engine Specialists	Equipment Use/ Maintenance Skills; Science Skills	$36,620	14.4%	32,000
16. Sound Engineering Technicians	Equipment Use/ Maintenance Skills; Equipment/Technology Analysis Skills; Quality Control Skills	$38,390	18.4%	2,000
17. Mobile Heavy Equipment Mechanics, Except Engines	Equipment Use/ Maintenance Skills	$39,410	8.8%	14,000

(continued)

(continued)

Best Jobs Requiring Postsecondary Vocational Training

Job	Top Skills	Annual Earnings	Percent Growth	Annual Openings
18. Electrical and Electronics Repairers, Commercial and Industrial Equipment	Equipment Use/ Maintenance Skills; Mathematics Skills; Science Skills	$44,120	9.7%	8,000
19. Computer, Automated Teller, and Office Machine Repairers	Equipment Use/ Maintenance Skills; Quality Control Skills; Science Skills	$36,060	3.8%	31,000

Jobs 1 and 2 share 9,000 job openings. Jobs 8 and 9 share 93,000 job openings.

Best Jobs Requiring an Associate Degree

Job	Top Skills	Annual Earnings	Percent Growth	Annual Openings
1. Dental Hygienists	Communication Skills; Science Skills; Social Skills	$60,890	43.3%	17,000
2. Registered Nurses	Science Skills; Social Skills; Thought-Processing Skills	$54,670	29.4%	229,000
3. Diagnostic Medical Sonographers	Communication Skills; Quality Control Skills; Science Skills	$54,370	34.8%	5,000
4. Paralegals and Legal Assistants	Communication Skills	$41,170	29.7%	28,000
5. Radiologic Technicians	Communication Skills; Science Skills; Social Skills	$45,950	23.2%	17,000
6. Radiologic Technologists	Communication Skills; Science Skills; Social Skills	$45,950	23.2%	17,000
7. Computer Support Specialists	Communication Skills; Equipment Use/ Maintenance Skills; Social Skills	$40,610	23.0%	87,000

150 Best Jobs for Your Skills © JIST Works

Best Jobs Requiring an Associate Degree

Job	Top Skills	Annual Earnings	Percent Growth	Annual Openings
8. Electrical Engineering Technicians	Equipment Use/ Maintenance Skills; Mathematics Skills; Science Skills	$48,040	9.8%	18,000
9. Electronics Engineering Technicians	Computer Programming Skills; Equipment Use/ Maintenance Skills; Science Skills	$48,040	9.8%	18,000
10. Physical Therapist Assistants	Communication Skills; Science Skills; Social Skills	$39,490	44.2%	7,000
11. Radiation Therapists	Equipment Use/ Maintenance Skills; Equipment/Technology Analysis Skills; Science Skills	$62,340	26.3%	1,000
12. Respiratory Therapists	Communication Skills; Mathematics Skills; Science Skills	$45,140	28.4%	7,000
13. Forensic Science Technicians	Communication Skills; Quality Control Skills; Science Skills	$44,590	36.4%	2,000
14. Nuclear Medicine Technologists	Equipment Use/ Maintenance Skills; Quality Control Skills; Science Skills	$59,670	21.5%	2,000
15. Cardiovascular Technologists and Technicians	Equipment Use/ Maintenance Skills; Quality Control Skills; Science Skills	$40,420	32.6%	5,000
16. Interior Designers	Equipment/Technology Analysis Skills; Mathematics Skills; Social Skills	$41,350	15.5%	10,000

(continued)

(continued)

Best Jobs Requiring an Associate Degree

Job	Top Skills	Annual Earnings	Percent Growth	Annual Openings
17. Occupational Therapist Assistants	Equipment/Technology Analysis Skills; Social Skills; Thought-Processing Skills	$39,750	34.1%	2,000
18. Industrial Engineering Technicians	Equipment Use/ Maintenance Skills; Equipment/Technology Analysis Skills; Quality Control Skills	$45,280	10.5%	7,000
19. Medical and Clinical Laboratory Technicians	Equipment Use/ Maintenance Skills; Quality Control Skills; Science Skills	$31,700	25.0%	14,000
20. Biological Technicians	Mathematics Skills; Quality Control Skills; Science Skills	$34,270	17.2%	8,000
21. Aerospace Engineering and Operations Technicians	Computer Programming Skills; Mathematics Skills; Science Skills	$52,450	8.5%	1,000
22. Environmental Science and Protection Technicians, Including Health	Mathematics Skills; Quality Control Skills; Science Skills	$36,260	16.3%	6,000
23. Medical Equipment Repairers	Equipment Use/ Maintenance Skills; Quality Control Skills; Science Skills	$39,570	14.8%	4,000

Jobs 5 and 6 share 17,000 job openings. Jobs 8 and 9 share 18,000 job openings.

Best Jobs Requiring a Bachelor's Degree

Job	Top Skills	Annual Earnings	Percent Growth	Annual Openings
1. Computer Software Engineers, Applications	Computer Programming Skills; Equipment/ Technology Analysis Skills; Quality Control Skills	$77,090	48.4%	54,000

Best Jobs Requiring a Bachelor's Degree

Job	Top Skills	Annual Earnings	Percent Growth	Annual Openings
2. Computer Software Engineers, Systems Software	Computer Programming Skills; Equipment/ Technology Analysis Skills; Science Skills	$82,120	43.0%	37,000
3. Computer Systems Analysts	Computer Programming Skills; Equipment/ Technology Analysis Skills; Quality Control Skills	$68,300	31.4%	56,000
4. Network Systems and Data Communications Analysts	Computer Programming Skills; Equipment Use/ Maintenance Skills; Equipment/Technology Analysis Skills	$61,750	54.6%	43,000
5. Physician Assistants	Communication Skills; Science Skills; Thought-Processing Skills	$72,030	49.6%	10,000
6. Computer Security Specialists	Computer Programming Skills; Equipment/ Technology Analysis Skills; Management Skills	$59,930	38.4%	34,000
7. Network and Computer Systems Administrators	Computer Programming Skills; Equipment Use/ Maintenance Skills; Equipment/Technology Analysis Skills	$59,930	38.4%	34,000
8. Accountants	Computer Programming Skills; Management Skills; Mathematics Skills	$52,210	22.4%	157,000
9. Auditors	Management Skills; Mathematics Skills; Social Skills	$52,210	22.4%	157,000
10. Personal Financial Advisors	Communication Skills; Mathematics Skills	$63,500	25.9%	17,000
11. Airline Pilots, Copilots, and Flight Engineers	Equipment Use/ Maintenance Skills; Science Skills; Thought-Processing Skills	$138,170	17.2%	7,000

(continued)

(continued)

Best Jobs Requiring a Bachelor's Degree

Job	Top Skills	Annual Earnings	Percent Growth	Annual Openings
12. Database Administrators	Computer Programming Skills; Equipment/ Technology Analysis Skills; Quality Control Skills	$63,250	38.2%	9,000
13. Environmental Engineers	Computer Programming Skills; Mathematics Skills; Science Skills	$68,090	30.0%	5,000
14. Financial Analysts	Computer Programming Skills; Management Skills; Mathematics Skills	$63,860	17.3%	28,000
15. Biomedical Engineers	Equipment/Technology Analysis Skills; Quality Control Skills; Science Skills	$71,840	30.7%	1,000
16. Sales Agents, Financial Services	Communication Skills; Mathematics Skills; Social Skills	$67,130	11.5%	37,000
17. Sales Agents, Securities and Commodities	Mathematics Skills; Social Skills; Thought-Processing Skills	$67,130	11.5%	37,000
18. Public Relations Specialists	Communication Skills; Social Skills; Thought-Processing Skills	$45,020	22.9%	38,000
19. Civil Engineers	Equipment/Technology Analysis Skills; Mathematics Skills; Science Skills	$66,190	16.5%	19,000
20. Construction Managers	Equipment Use/ Maintenance Skills; Mathematics Skills; Social Skills	$72,260	10.4%	28,000
21. Elementary School Teachers, Except Special Education	Communication Skills; Social Skills; Thought-Processing Skills	$44,040	18.2%	203,000

Best Jobs Requiring a Bachelor's Degree

Job	Top Skills	Annual Earnings	Percent Growth	Annual Openings
22. Employment Interviewers	Communication Skills; Management Skills; Social Skills	$41,780	30.5%	30,000
23. Personnel Recruiters	Management Skills; Social Skills; Thought-Processing Skills	$41,780	30.5%	30,000
24. Market Research Analysts	Communication Skills; Social Skills; Thought-Processing Skills	$57,300	19.6%	20,000
25. Social and Community Service Managers	Communication Skills; Management Skills; Social Skills	$49,500	25.5%	17,000
26. Sales Engineers	Computer Programming Skills; Equipment/ Technology Analysis Skills; Science Skills	$74,200	14.0%	8,000
27. Industrial Engineers	Communication Skills; Equipment/Technology Analysis Skills; Mathematics Skills	$66,670	16.0%	13,000
28. Training and Development Specialists	Communication Skills; Social Skills; Thought-Processing Skills	$45,870	20.8%	32,000
29. Electrical Engineers	Computer Programming Skills; Equipment/ Technology Analysis Skills; Science Skills	$73,510	11.8%	12,000
30. Secondary School Teachers, Except Special and Vocational Education	Communication Skills; Social Skills; Thought-Processing Skills	$46,060	14.4%	107,000
31. Kindergarten Teachers, Except Special Education	Communication Skills; Social Skills; Thought-Processing Skills	$42,230	22.4%	28,000
32. Electronics Engineers, Except Computer	Equipment/Technology Analysis Skills; Quality Control Skills; Science Skills	$78,030	9.7%	11,000

(continued)

(continued)

Best Jobs Requiring a Bachelor's Degree

Job	Top Skills	Annual Earnings	Percent Growth	Annual Openings
33. Special Education Teachers, Preschool, Kindergarten, and Elementary School	Communication Skills; Social Skills; Thought-Processing Skills	$44,630	23.3%	18,000
34. Atmospheric and Space Scientists	Computer Programming Skills; Quality Control Skills; Science Skills	$73,940	16.5%	1,000
35. Compensation, Benefits, and Job Analysis Specialists	Communication Skills; Social Skills; Thought-Processing Skills	$48,870	20.4%	15,000
36. Middle School Teachers, Except Special and Vocational Education	Communication Skills; Social Skills; Thought-Processing Skills	$44,640	13.7%	83,000
37. Property, Real Estate, and Community Association Managers	Management Skills; Mathematics Skills; Social Skills	$41,900	15.3%	58,000
38. Medical and Clinical Laboratory Technologists	Equipment Use/ Maintenance Skills; Quality Control Skills; Science Skills	$47,710	20.5%	14,000
39. Technical Writers	Communication Skills; Equipment/Technology Analysis Skills; Quality Control Skills	$55,160	23.2%	5,000
40. Computer Hardware Engineers	Computer Programming Skills; Equipment/ Technology Analysis Skills; Quality Control Skills	$84,420	10.1%	5,000
41. Architects, Except Landscape and Naval	Equipment/Technology Analysis Skills; Management Skills; Social Skills	$62,850	17.3%	7,000
42. Medical and Public Health Social Workers	Communication Skills; Social Skills; Thought-Processing Skills	$41,120	25.9%	14,000

Best Jobs Requiring a Bachelor's Degree

Job	Top Skills	Annual Earnings	Percent Growth	Annual Openings
43. Aerospace Engineers	Equipment/Technology Analysis Skills; Quality Control Skills; Science Skills	$84,090	8.3%	6,000
44. Mechanical Engineers	Equipment/Technology Analysis Skills; Mathematics Skills; Science Skills	$67,590	11.1%	11,000
45. Chemical Engineers	Computer Programming Skills; Equipment/ Technology Analysis Skills; Science Skills	$77,140	10.6%	3,000
46. Copy Writers	Equipment/Technology Analysis Skills; Quality Control Skills; Social Skills	$46,420	17.7%	14,000
47. Computer Programmers	Computer Programming Skills; Equipment/ Technology Analysis Skills; Thought-Processing Skills	$63,420	2.0%	28,000
48. Graphic Designers	Equipment/Technology Analysis Skills; Quality Control Skills; Social Skills	$38,390	15.2%	35,000
49. Multi-Media Artists and Animators	Computer Programming Skills; Equipment/ Technology Analysis Skills; Science Skills	$50,290	14.1%	14,000
50. Materials Engineers	Mathematics Skills; Quality Control Skills; Science Skills	$69,660	12.2%	2,000
51. Fire-Prevention and Protection Engineers	Management Skills; Mathematics Skills; Science Skills	$65,210	13.4%	2,000

(continued)

(continued)

Best Jobs Requiring a Bachelor's Degree

Job	Top Skills	Annual Earnings	Percent Growth	Annual Openings
52. Product Safety Engineers	Mathematics Skills; Quality Control Skills; Science Skills	$65,210	13.4%	2,000
53. Budget Analysts	Management Skills; Mathematics Skills; Quality Control Skills	$58,910	13.5%	6,000
54. Landscape Architects	Equipment/Technology Analysis Skills; Management Skills; Mathematics Skills	$54,220	19.4%	1,000
55. Film and Video Editors	Equipment Use/ Maintenance Skills; Equipment/Technology Analysis Skills	$46,930	18.6%	3,000
56. Agricultural Engineers	Computer Programming Skills; Equipment/ Technology Analysis Skills; Science Skills	$64,890	12.0%	fewer than 500
57. Materials Scientists	Computer Programming Skills; Quality Control Skills; Science Skills	$71,450	8.0%	fewer than 500
58. Commercial and Industrial Designers	Equipment/Technology Analysis Skills; Mathematics Skills; Quality Control Skills	$52,200	10.8%	7,000
59. Financial Examiners	Communication Skills; Quality Control Skills; Thought-Processing Skills	$63,090	9.5%	3,000
60. Chemists	Equipment/Technology Analysis Skills; Quality Control Skills; Science Skills	$57,890	7.3%	5,000
61. Foresters	Computer Programming Skills; Quality Control Skills; Science Skills	$48,670	6.7%	1,000

Jobs 6 and 7 share 34,000 job openings. Jobs 8 and 9 share 157,000 job openings. Jobs 16 and 17 share 37,000 job openings. Jobs 22 and 23 share 30,000 job openings. Job 46 shares 14,000 openings with another job not included in this list. Jobs 51 and 52 share 2,000 openings with each other and with another job not included in this list.

Best Jobs Requiring Work Experience Plus Degree

Job	Top Skills	Annual Earnings	Percent Growth	Annual Openings
1. Computer and Information Systems Managers	Computer Programming Skills; Management Skills; Quality Control Skills	$96,520	25.9%	25,000
2. Sales Managers	Management Skills; Social Skills; Thought-Processing Skills	$87,580	19.7%	40,000
3. General and Operations Managers	Management Skills; Social Skills; Thought-Processing Skills	$81,480	17.0%	208,000
4. Chief Executives	Management Skills; Social Skills; Thought-Processing Skills	$142,440	14.9%	38,000
5. Marketing Managers	Management Skills; Science Skills; Social Skills	$92,680	20.8%	23,000
6. Medical and Health Services Managers	Management Skills; Quality Control Skills; Social Skills	$69,700	22.8%	33,000
7. Financial Managers, Branch or Department	Management Skills; Social Skills; Thought-Processing Skills	$86,280	14.8%	63,000
8. Treasurers and Controllers	Management Skills; Mathematics Skills; Thought-Processing Skills	$86,280	14.8%	63,000
9. Management Analysts	Equipment Use/ Maintenance Skills; Management Skills; Quality Control Skills	$66,380	20.1%	82,000
10. Education Administrators, Postsecondary	Management Skills; Social Skills; Thought-Processing Skills	$70,350	21.3%	18,000
11. Actuaries	Computer Programming Skills; Mathematics Skills; Thought-Processing Skills	$81,640	23.2%	3,000

(continued)

(continued)

Best Jobs Requiring Work Experience Plus Degree

Job	Top Skills	Annual Earnings	Percent Growth	Annual Openings
12. Engineering Managers	Equipment/Technology Analysis Skills; Mathematics Skills; Science Skills	$100,760	13.0%	15,000
13. Public Relations Managers	Communication Skills; Management Skills; Social Skills	$76,450	21.7%	5,000
14. Training and Development Managers	Management Skills; Social Skills; Thought-Processing Skills	$74,180	25.9%	3,000
15. Administrative Services Managers	Communication Skills; Computer Programming Skills; Management Skills	$64,020	16.9%	25,000
16. Education Administrators, Elementary and Secondary School	Management Skills; Social Skills; Thought-Processing Skills	$75,400	10.4%	27,000
17. Natural Sciences Managers	Management Skills; Mathematics Skills; Science Skills	$93,090	13.6%	5,000
18. Advertising and Promotions Managers	Management Skills; Social Skills; Thought-Processing Skills	$68,860	20.3%	9,000
19. Compensation and Benefits Managers	Communication Skills; Management Skills; Social Skills	$69,130	21.5%	4,000
20. Directors—Stage, Motion Pictures, Television, and Radio	Communication Skills; Equipment/Technology Analysis Skills; Management Skills	$53,860	16.6%	11,000
21. Producers	Communication Skills; Management Skills; Social Skills	$53,860	16.6%	11,000
22. Program Directors	Management Skills; Social Skills; Thought-Processing Skills	$53,860	16.6%	11,000

Best Jobs Requiring Work Experience Plus Degree

Job	Top Skills	Annual Earnings	Percent Growth	Annual Openings
23. Purchasing Managers	Management Skills; Mathematics Skills; Social Skills	$76,270	7.0%	8,000
24. Art Directors	Equipment/Technology Analysis Skills; Management Skills; Social Skills	$63,950	11.5%	10,000

Jobs 7 and 8 share 63,000 job openings. Job 19 shares 4,000 openings with another job not included in this list. Jobs 20, 21, and 22 share 11,000 openings with each other and with two other jobs not included in this list.

Best Jobs Requiring a Master's Degree

Job	Top Skills	Annual Earnings	Percent Growth	Annual Openings
1. Physical Therapists	Communication Skills; Science Skills; Social Skills	$63,080	36.7%	13,000
2. Teachers, Postsecondary	Communication Skills; Science Skills; Thought-Processing Skills	$53,590	32.2%	329,000
3. Hydrologists	Computer Programming Skills; Mathematics Skills; Science Skills	$63,820	31.6%	1,000
4. Occupational Therapists	Communication Skills; Science Skills; Social Skills	$56,860	33.6%	7,000
5. Instructional Coordinators	Management Skills; Social Skills; Thought-Processing Skills	$50,430	27.5%	15,000
6. Industrial-Organizational Psychologists	Science Skills; Social Skills; Thought-Processing Skills	$84,690	20.4%	fewer than 500
7. Mental Health and Substance Abuse Social Workers	Communication Skills; Social Skills; Thought-Processing Skills	$34,410	26.7%	15,000

(continued)

(continued)

Best Jobs Requiring a Master's Degree

Job	Top Skills	Annual Earnings	Percent Growth	Annual Openings
8. Educational, Vocational, and School Counselors	Communication Skills; Social Skills; Thought-Processing Skills	$46,440	14.8%	32,000
9. Environmental Scientists and Specialists, Including Health	Mathematics Skills; Science Skills; Social Skills	$52,630	17.1%	8,000
10. Mental Health Counselors	Communication Skills; Social Skills; Thought-Processing Skills	$34,010	27.2%	14,000
11. Economists	Computer Programming Skills; Mathematics Skills; Thought-Processing Skills	$73,690	5.6%	1,000
12. Operations Research Analysts	Computer Programming Skills; Mathematics Skills; Science Skills	$62,180	8.4%	7,000
13. Epidemiologists	Computer Programming Skills; Mathematics Skills; Science Skills	$52,170	26.2%	1,000
14. Statisticians	Computer Programming Skills; Mathematics Skills; Science Skills	$62,450	4.6%	2,000
15. Geographers	Computer Programming Skills; Mathematics Skills; Science Skills	$63,550	6.8%	fewer than 500
16. Archivists	Communication Skills; Computer Programming Skills; Quality Control Skills	$37,420	13.4%	1,000

Best Jobs Requiring a Doctoral Degree

Job	Top Skills	Annual Earnings	Percent Growth	Annual Openings
1. Medical Scientists, Except Epidemiologists	Communication Skills; Management Skills; Science Skills	$61,730	34.1%	15,000
2. Clinical Psychologists	Communication Skills; Social Skills; Thought-Processing Skills	$57,170	19.1%	10,000
3. Counseling Psychologists	Communication Skills; Social Skills; Thought-Processing Skills	$57,170	19.1%	10,000
4. School Psychologists	Communication Skills; Social Skills; Thought-Processing Skills	$57,170	19.1%	10,000
5. Astronomers	Computer Programming Skills; Mathematics Skills; Science Skills	$104,670	10.4%	fewer than 500
6. Microbiologists	Equipment Use/ Maintenance Skills; Quality Control Skills; Science Skills	$56,870	17.2%	1,000

Jobs 2, 3, and 4 share 10,000 job openings.

Best Jobs Requiring a First Professional Degree

Job	Top Skills	Annual Earnings	Percent Growth	Annual Openings
1. Anesthesiologists	Equipment Use/ Maintenance Skills; Science Skills; Thought-Processing Skills	more than $145,600	24.0%	41,000
2. Internists, General	Science Skills; Social Skills; Thought-Processing Skills	more than $145,600	24.0%	41,000
3. Obstetricians and Gynecologists	Science Skills; Social Skills; Thought-Processing Skills	more than $145,600	24.0%	41,000

(continued)

(continued)

Best Jobs Requiring a First Professional Degree

Job	Top Skills	Annual Earnings	Percent Growth	Annual Openings
4. Psychiatrists	Science Skills; Social Skills; Thought-Processing Skills	more than $145,600	24.0%	41,000
5. Surgeons	Communication Skills; Science Skills; Thought-Processing Skills	more than $145,600	24.0%	41,000
6. Family and General Practitioners	Science Skills; Social Skills; Thought-Processing Skills	$140,400	24.0%	41,000
7. Pediatricians, General	Science Skills; Social Skills; Thought-Processing Skills	$136,600	24.0%	41,000
8. Pharmacists	Communication Skills; Mathematics Skills; Science Skills	$89,820	24.6%	16,000
9. Lawyers	Communication Skills; Social Skills; Thought-Processing Skills	$98,930	15.0%	40,000
10. Dentists, General	Management Skills; Science Skills; Thought-Processing Skills	$125,300	13.5%	7,000
11. Veterinarians	Management Skills; Science Skills; Thought-Processing Skills	$68,910	17.4%	8,000
12. Chiropractors	Management Skills; Science Skills; Social Skills	$67,200	22.4%	4,000
13. Optometrists	Management Skills; Science Skills; Thought-Processing Skills	$88,040	19.7%	2,000

Jobs 1, 2, 3, 4, 5, 6, and 7 share 41,000 job openings.

The Best Jobs for Your Skills Sorted by Interest

This group of lists organizes the 230 best jobs into 16 interest areas. You can use these lists to identify jobs quickly based on your interests.

Find the interest area or areas that appeal to you most. Then review the jobs in those areas and note what skills are listed for each job; they are presented in alphabetical order in the second column. When you find jobs you want to explore in more detail, especially those that have a skill set similar to your own, look up their descriptions in Part IV. You can also review interest areas where you have had past experience, education, or training to see whether other jobs in those areas would meet your current requirements.

Within each interest area, jobs are listed in order of their combined score on earnings, job growth, and job openings, from highest to lowest.

Note: The 16 interest areas used in these lists are those used in the *New Guide for Occupational Exploration,* Fourth Edition, published by JIST. The original GOE was developed by the U.S. Department of Labor as an intuitive way to assist in career exploration. The 16 interest areas used in the *New GOE* are based on the 16 career clusters that were developed by the U.S. Department of Education's Office of Vocational and Adult Education around 1999 and that presently are being used by many states to organize their career-oriented programs and career information.

Descriptions of the 16 Interest Areas

Brief descriptions of the 16 interest areas we use in the lists follow. The descriptions are from the *New Guide for Occupational Exploration,* Fourth Edition. Some of them refer to jobs (as examples) that aren't included in this book.

Also note that we put each of the 230 best jobs into only one interest area list, the one it fit into best. However, many jobs could be included in more than one list, so consider reviewing a variety of these interest areas to find jobs that you might otherwise overlook.

- Agriculture and Natural Resources: *An interest in working with plants, animals, forests, or mineral resources for agriculture, horticulture, conservation, extraction, and other purposes.* You can satisfy this interest by working in farming, landscaping, forestry, fishing, mining, and related fields. You may like doing physical work outdoors, such as on a farm or ranch, in a forest, or on a drilling rig. If you have scientific curiosity, you could study plants and animals or analyze biological or rock samples in a lab. If you have management ability, you could own, operate, or manage a fish hatchery, a landscaping business, or a greenhouse.

- Architecture and Construction: *An interest in designing, assembling, and maintaining components of buildings and other structures.* You may want to be part of the team of architects, drafters, and others who design buildings and render the plans. If construction interests you, you can find fulfillment in the many building projects that are being undertaken at all times. If you like to organize and plan, you can find careers in managing these projects. Or you can play a more direct role in putting up and finishing buildings by doing jobs such as plumbing, carpentry, masonry, painting, or roofing, either as a skilled craftsworker or as a helper. You can prepare the building site by operating heavy equipment or install, maintain, and repair vital building equipment and systems such as electricity and heating.

◎ Arts and Communication: *An interest in creatively expressing feelings or ideas, in communicating news or information, or in performing.* You can satisfy this interest in creative, verbal, or performing activities. For example, if you enjoy literature, perhaps writing or editing would appeal to you. Journalism and public relations are other fields for people who like to use their writing or speaking skills. Do you prefer to work in the performing arts? If so, you could direct or perform in drama, music, or dance. If you especially enjoy the visual arts, you could create paintings, sculpture, or ceramics or design products or visual displays. A flair for technology might lead you to specialize in photography, broadcast production, or dispatching.

◎ Business and Administration: *An interest in making a business organization or function run smoothly.* You can satisfy this interest by working in a position of leadership or by specializing in a function that contributes to the overall effort in a business, a nonprofit organization, or a government agency. If you especially enjoy working with people, you may find fulfillment from working in human resources. An interest in numbers may lead you to consider accounting, finance, budgeting, billing, or financial record-keeping. A job as an administrative assistant may interest you if you like a variety of work in a busy environment. If you are good with details and word processing, you may enjoy a job as a secretary or data entry keyer. Or perhaps you would do well as the manager of a business.

◎ Education and Training: *An interest in helping people learn.* You can satisfy this interest by teaching students, who may be preschoolers, retirees, or any age in between. You may specialize in a particular academic field or work with learners of a particular age, with a particular interest, or with a particular learning problem. Working in a library or museum may give you an opportunity to expand people's understanding of the world.

◎ Finance and Insurance: *An interest in helping businesses and people be assured of a financially secure future.* You can satisfy this interest by working in a financial or insurance business in a leadership or support role. If you like gathering and analyzing information, you may find fulfillment as an insurance adjuster or financial analyst. Or you may deal with information at the clerical level as a banking or insurance clerk or in person-to-person situations providing customer service. Another way to interact with people is to sell financial or insurance services that will meet their needs.

◎ Government and Public Administration: *An interest in helping a government agency serve the needs of the public.* You can satisfy this interest by working in a position of leadership or by specializing in a function that contributes to the role of government. You may help protect the public by working as an inspector or examiner to enforce standards. If you enjoy using clerical skills, you may work as a clerk in a law court or government office. Or perhaps you prefer the top-down perspective of a government executive or urban planner.

◎ Health Science: *An interest in helping people and animals be healthy.* You can satisfy this interest by working in a healthcare team as a doctor, therapist, or nurse. You might specialize in one of the many different parts of the body (such as the teeth or eyes) or in one of the many different types of care. Or you may want to be a generalist who deals with the whole patient. If you like technology, you might find satisfaction working with X rays or new methods of diagnosis. You might work with healthy people, helping them eat right. If you enjoy working with animals, you might care for them and keep them healthy.

◎ Hospitality, Tourism, and Recreation: *An interest in catering to the personal wishes and needs of others so that they may enjoy a clean environment, good food and drink, comfortable lodging away from home, and recreation.* You can satisfy this interest by providing services for the convenience, care, and pampering of others in hotels, restaurants, airplanes, beauty parlors, and so on. You may want to use your love of cooking as a chef. If you like working with people, you may want to provide personal services by being a travel guide, a flight attendant, a concierge, a hairdresser, or a waiter. You may want to work in cleaning and building services if you like a clean environment. If you enjoy sports or games, you may work for an athletic team or casino.

◎ Human Service: *An interest in improving people's social, mental, emotional, or spiritual well-being.* You can satisfy this interest as a counselor, social worker, or religious worker who helps people sort out their complicated lives or solve personal problems. You may work as a caretaker for very young people or the elderly. Or you may interview people to help identify the social services they need.

◎ Information Technology: *An interest in designing, developing, managing, and supporting information systems.* You can satisfy this interest by working with hardware, software, multimedia, or integrated systems. If you like to use your organizational skills, you might work as an administrator of a system or database. Or you can solve complex problems as a software engineer or systems analyst. If you enjoy getting your hands on the hardware, you might find work servicing computers, peripherals, and information-intense machines such as cash registers and ATMs.

◎ Law and Public Safety: *An interest in upholding people's rights or in protecting people and property by using authority, inspecting, or investigating.* You can satisfy this interest by working in law, law enforcement, fire fighting, the military, and related fields. For example, if you enjoy mental challenge and intrigue, you could investigate crimes or fires for a living. If you enjoy working with verbal skills and research skills, you may want to defend citizens in court or research deeds, wills, and other legal documents. If you want to help people in critical situations, you may want to fight fires, work as a police officer, or become a paramedic. Or, if you want more routine work in public safety, perhaps a job in guarding, patrolling, or inspecting would appeal to you. If you have management ability, you could seek a leadership position in law enforcement and the protective services. Work in the military gives you a chance to use technical and leadership skills while serving your country.

◎ Manufacturing: *An interest in processing materials into intermediate or final products or maintaining and repairing products by using machines or hand tools.* You can satisfy this interest by working in one of many industries that mass-produce goods or by working for a utility that distributes electric power or other resources. You may enjoy manual work, using your hands or hand tools in highly skilled jobs such as assembling engines or electronic equipment. If you enjoy making machines run efficiently or fixing them when they break down, you could seek a job installing or repairing such devices as copiers, aircraft engines, cars, or watches. Perhaps you prefer to set up or operate machines that are used to manufacture products made of food, glass, or paper. You may enjoy cutting and grinding metal and plastic parts to desired shapes and measurements. Or you may want to operate equipment in systems that provide water and process wastewater. You may like inspecting, sorting, counting, or weighing products. Another option is to work with your hands and machinery to move boxes and freight in a warehouse. If leadership appeals to you, you could manage people engaged in production and repair.

◎ Retail and Wholesale Sales and Service: *An interest in bringing others to a particular point of view by personal persuasion and by sales and promotional techniques.* You can satisfy this interest in a variety of jobs that involve persuasion and selling. If you like using knowledge of science, you may enjoy selling pharmaceutical, medical, or electronic products or services. Real estate offers several kinds of sales jobs as well. If you like speaking on the phone, you could work as a telemarketer. Or you may enjoy selling apparel and other merchandise in a retail setting. If you prefer to help people, you may want a job in customer service.

◎ Scientific Research, Engineering, and Mathematics: *An interest in discovering, collecting, and analyzing information about the natural world; in applying scientific research findings to problems in medicine, the life sciences, human behavior, and the natural sciences; in imagining and manipulating quantitative data; and in applying technology to manufacturing, transportation, and other economic activities.* You can satisfy this interest by working with the knowledge and processes of the sciences. You may enjoy researching and developing new knowledge in mathematics, or perhaps solving problems in the physical, life, or social sciences would appeal to you. You may want to study engineering and help create new machines, processes, and structures. If you want to work with scientific equipment and procedures, you could seek a job in a research or testing laboratory.

◎ Transportation, Distribution, and Logistics: *An interest in operations that move people or materials.* You can satisfy this interest by managing a transportation service, by helping vehicles keep on their assigned schedules and routes, or by driving or piloting a vehicle. If you enjoy taking responsibility, perhaps managing a rail line would appeal to you. If you work well with details and can take pressure on the job, you might consider being an air traffic controller. Or would you rather get out on the highway, on the water, or up in the air? If so, then you could drive a truck from state to state, be employed on a ship, or fly a crop duster over a cornfield. If you prefer to stay closer to home, you could drive a delivery van, taxi, or school bus. You can use your physical strength to load freight and arrange it so it gets to its destination in one piece.

Best Jobs for People Interested in Agriculture and Natural Resources

Job	Top Skills	Annual Earnings	Percent Growth	Annual Openings
1. Environmental Engineers	Computer Programming Skills; Mathematics Skills; Science Skills	$68,090	30.0%	5,000
2. First-Line Supervisors/ Managers of Construction Trades and Extraction Workers	Equipment Use/ Maintenance Skills; Management Skills; Quality Control Skills	$51,970	10.9%	57,000
3. Environmental Science and Protection Technicians, Including Health	Mathematics Skills; Quality Control Skills; Science Skills	$36,260	16.3%	6,000
4. Agricultural Engineers	Computer Programming Skills; Equipment/ Technology Analysis Skills; Science Skills	$64,890	12.0%	fewer than 500
5. Foresters	Computer Programming Skills; Quality Control Skills; Science Skills	$48,670	6.7%	1,000

Best Jobs for People Interested in Architecture and Construction

Job	Top Skills	Annual Earnings	Percent Growth	Annual Openings
1. Pipe Fitters and Steamfitters	Equipment Use/ Maintenance Skills; Equipment/Technology Analysis Skills; Quality Control Skills	$42,160	15.7%	61,000
2. Plumbers	Equipment Use/ Maintenance Skills; Equipment/Technology Analysis Skills; Science Skills	$42,160	15.7%	61,000
3. Heating and Air Conditioning Mechanics and Installers	Equipment Use/ Maintenance Skills; Mathematics Skills; Science Skills	$37,040	19.0%	33,000

(continued)

(continued)

Best Jobs for People Interested in Architecture and Construction

Job	Top Skills	Annual Earnings	Percent Growth	Annual Openings
4. Refrigeration Mechanics and Installers	Equipment Use/ Maintenance Skills; Equipment/Technology Analysis Skills; Science Skills	$37,040	19.0%	33,000
5. Architects, Except Landscape and Naval	Equipment/Technology Analysis Skills; Management Skills; Social Skills	$62,850	17.3%	7,000
6. Electricians	Equipment Use/ Maintenance Skills; Equipment/Technology Analysis Skills; Mathematics Skills	$42,790	11.8%	68,000
7. Landscape Architects	Equipment/Technology Analysis Skills; Management Skills; Mathematics Skills	$54,220	19.4%	1,000
8. Construction Carpenters	Management Skills; Mathematics Skills; Quality Control Skills	$35,580	13.8%	210,000
9. Rough Carpenters	Equipment Use/ Maintenance Skills; Equipment/Technology Analysis Skills; Mathematics Skills	$35,580	13.8%	210,000
10. Tile and Marble Setters	Equipment/Technology Analysis Skills; Management Skills; Mathematics Skills	$36,530	22.9%	9,000
11. Construction Managers	Equipment Use/ Maintenance Skills; Mathematics Skills; Social Skills	$72,260	10.4%	28,000
12. Maintenance and Repair Workers, General	Equipment Use/ Maintenance Skills	$31,210	15.2%	154,000

Best Jobs for People Interested in Architecture and Construction

Job	Top Skills	Annual Earnings	Percent Growth	Annual Openings
13. Elevator Installers and Repairers	Equipment Use/ Maintenance Skills; Quality Control Skills	$59,190	14.8%	3,000
14. Highway Maintenance Workers	Equipment Use/ Maintenance Skills	$30,250	23.3%	27,000
15. Sheet Metal Workers	Equipment Use/ Maintenance Skills; Mathematics Skills; Social Skills	$36,390	12.2%	50,000
16. Cement Masons and Concrete Finishers	Mathematics Skills	$32,030	15.9%	32,000
17. Operating Engineers and Other Construction Equipment Operators	Equipment Use/ Maintenance Skills; Management Skills; Science Skills	$35,830	11.6%	37,000
18. Telecommunications Line Installers and Repairers	Equipment Use/ Maintenance Skills	$42,410	10.8%	23,000
19. Telecommunications Equipment Installers and Repairers, Except Line Installers	Equipment Use/ Maintenance Skills; Quality Control Skills	$50,620	–4.9%	21,000

Jobs 1 and 2 share 61,000 job openings. Jobs 3 and 4 share 33,000 job openings. Jobs 8 and 9 share 210,000 job openings.

Best Jobs for People Interested in Arts and Communication

Job	Top Skills	Annual Earnings	Percent Growth	Annual Openings
1. Public Relations Specialists	Communication Skills; Social Skills; Thought-Processing Skills	$45,020	22.9%	38,000
2. Directors—Stage, Motion Pictures, Television, and Radio	Communication Skills; Equipment/Technology Analysis Skills; Management Skills	$53,860	16.6%	11,000

(continued)

(continued)

Best Jobs for People Interested in Arts and Communication

Job	Top Skills	Annual Earnings	Percent Growth	Annual Openings
3. Producers	Communication Skills; Management Skills; Social Skills	$53,860	16.6%	11,000
4. Program Directors	Management Skills; Social Skills; Thought-Processing Skills	$53,860	16.6%	11,000
5. Public Relations Managers	Communication Skills; Management Skills; Social Skills	$76,450	21.7%	5,000
6. Technical Directors/Managers	Equipment Use/ Maintenance Skills; Equipment/Technology Analysis Skills; Management Skills	$53,860	16.6%	11,000
7. Technical Writers	Communication Skills; Equipment/Technology Analysis Skills; Quality Control Skills	$55,160	23.2%	5,000
8. Copy Writers	Equipment/Technology Analysis Skills; Quality Control Skills; Social Skills	$46,420	17.7%	14,000
9. Art Directors	Equipment/Technology Analysis Skills; Management Skills; Social Skills	$63,950	11.5%	10,000
10. Multi-Media Artists and Animators	Computer Programming Skills; Equipment/ Technology Analysis Skills; Science Skills	$50,290	14.1%	14,000
11. Air Traffic Controllers	Equipment Use/ Maintenance Skills	$107,590	14.3%	2,000
12. Film and Video Editors	Equipment Use/ Maintenance Skills; Equipment/Technology Analysis Skills	$46,930	18.6%	3,000

Best Jobs for People Interested in Arts and Communication

Job	Top Skills	Annual Earnings	Percent Growth	Annual Openings
13. Graphic Designers	Equipment/Technology Analysis Skills; Quality Control Skills; Social Skills	$38,390	15.2%	35,000
14. Interior Designers	Equipment/Technology Analysis Skills; Mathematics Skills; Social Skills	$41,350	15.5%	10,000
15. Sound Engineering Technicians	Equipment Use/ Maintenance Skills; Equipment/Technology Analysis Skills; Quality Control Skills	$38,390	18.4%	2,000
16. Commercial and Industrial Designers	Equipment/Technology Analysis Skills; Mathematics Skills; Quality Control Skills	$52,200	10.8%	7,000

Jobs 2, 3, 4, and 5 share 11,000 jobs with each other and with another job not included in this list. Job 8 shares 14,000 jobs with another job not included in this list.

Best Jobs for People Interested in Business and Administration

Job	Top Skills	Annual Earnings	Percent Growth	Annual Openings
1. Accountants	Computer Programming Skills; Management Skills; Mathematics Skills	$52,210	22.4%	157,000
2. Auditors	Management Skills; Mathematics Skills; Social Skills	$52,210	22.4%	157,000
3. General and Operations Managers	Management Skills; Social Skills; Thought-Processing Skills	$81,480	17.0%	208,000

(continued)

(continued)

Best Jobs for People Interested in Business and Administration

Job	Top Skills	Annual Earnings	Percent Growth	Annual Openings
4. Management Analysts	Equipment Use/ Maintenance Skills; Management Skills; Quality Control Skills	$66,380	20.1%	82,000
5. Chief Executives	Management Skills; Social Skills; Thought-Processing Skills	$142,440	14.9%	38,000
6. Employment Interviewers	Communication Skills; Management Skills; Social Skills	$41,780	30.5%	30,000
7. Personnel Recruiters	Management Skills; Social Skills; Thought-Processing Skills	$41,780	30.5%	30,000
8. Training and Development Managers	Management Skills; Social Skills; Thought-Processing Skills	$74,180	25.9%	3,000
9. Training and Development Specialists	Communication Skills; Social Skills; Thought-Processing Skills	$45,870	20.8%	32,000
10. Compensation and Benefits Managers	Communication Skills; Management Skills; Social Skills	$69,130	21.5%	4,000
11. Administrative Services Managers	Communication Skills; Computer Programming Skills; Management Skills	$64,020	16.9%	25,000
12. Legal Secretaries	Communication Skills; Social Skills; Thought-Processing Skills	$37,750	17.4%	41,000
13. Compensation, Benefits, and Job Analysis Specialists	Communication Skills; Social Skills; Thought-Processing Skills	$48,870	20.4%	15,000
14. Payroll and Timekeeping Clerks	Communication Skills; Mathematics Skills; Thought-Processing Skills	$31,360	17.3%	36,000

Best Jobs for People Interested in Business and Administration

Job	Top Skills	Annual Earnings	Percent Growth	Annual Openings
15. Operations Research Analysts	Computer Programming Skills; Mathematics Skills; Science Skills	$62,180	8.4%	7,000
16. Budget Analysts	Management Skills; Mathematics Skills; Quality Control Skills	$58,910	13.5%	6,000
17. First-Line Supervisors/Managers of Housekeeping and Janitorial Workers	Equipment Use/ Maintenance Skills; Management Skills; Social Skills	$30,330	19.0%	21,000
18. Human Resources Assistants, Except Payroll and Timekeeping	Communication Skills; Management Skills; Mathematics Skills	$32,730	16.7%	28,000
19. Industrial Engineering Technicians	Equipment Use/ Maintenance Skills; Equipment/Technology Analysis Skills; Quality Control Skills	$45,280	10.5%	7,000

Jobs 1 and 2 share 157,000 job openings. Jobs 6 and 7 share 30,000 job openings. Job 10 shares 4,000 openings with another job not included in this list.

Best Jobs for People Interested in Education and Training

Job	Top Skills	Annual Earnings	Percent Growth	Annual Openings
1. Teachers, Postsecondary	Communication Skills; Science Skills; Thought-Processing Skills	$53,590	32.2%	329,000
2. Elementary School Teachers, Except Special Education	Communication Skills; Social Skills; Thought-Processing Skills	$44,040	18.2%	203,000
3. Instructional Coordinators	Management Skills; Social Skills; Thought-Processing Skills	$50,430	27.5%	15,000

(continued)

(continued)

Best Jobs for People Interested in Education and Training

Job	Top Skills	Annual Earnings	Percent Growth	Annual Openings
4. Preschool Teachers, Except Special Education	Communication Skills; Social Skills	$21,990	33.1%	77,000
5. Secondary School Teachers, Except Special and Vocational Education	Communication Skills; Social Skills; Thought-Processing Skills	$46,060	14.4%	107,000
6. Education Administrators, Postsecondary	Management Skills; Social Skills; Thought-Processing Skills	$70,350	21.3%	18,000
7. Educational, Vocational, and School Counselors	Communication Skills; Social Skills; Thought-Processing Skills	$46,440	14.8%	32,000
8. Middle School Teachers, Except Special and Vocational Education	Communication Skills; Social Skills; Thought-Processing Skills	$44,640	13.7%	83,000
9. Self-Enrichment Education Teachers	Communication Skills; Social Skills; Thought-Processing Skills	$32,360	25.3%	74,000
10. Fitness Trainers and Aerobics Instructors	Equipment/Technology Analysis Skills; Science Skills; Social Skills	$25,840	27.1%	50,000
11. Education Administrators, Elementary and Secondary School	Management Skills; Social Skills; Thought-Processing Skills	$75,400	10.4%	27,000
12. Special Education Teachers, Preschool, Kindergarten, and Elementary School	Communication Skills; Social Skills; Thought-Processing Skills	$44,630	23.3%	18,000
13. Kindergarten Teachers, Except Special Education	Communication Skills; Social Skills; Thought-Processing Skills	$42,230	22.4%	28,000
14. Archivists	Communication Skills; Computer Programming Skills; Quality Control Skills	$37,420	13.4%	1,000

Best Jobs for People Interested in Finance and Insurance

Job	Top Skills	Annual Earnings	Percent Growth	Annual Openings
1. Financial Managers, Branch or Department	Management Skills; Social Skills; Thought-Processing Skills	$86,280	14.8%	63,000
2. Treasurers and Controllers	Management Skills; Mathematics Skills; Thought-Processing Skills	$86,280	14.8%	63,000
3. Personal Financial Advisors	Communication Skills; Mathematics Skills	$63,500	25.9%	17,000
4. Bill and Account Collectors	Communication Skills; Management Skills; Social Skills	$28,160	21.4%	85,000
5. Sales Agents, Financial Services	Communication Skills; Mathematics Skills; Social Skills	$67,130	11.5%	37,000
6. Sales Agents, Securities and Commodities	Mathematics Skills; Social Skills; Thought-Processing Skills	$67,130	11.5%	37,000
7. Financial Analysts	Computer Programming Skills; Management Skills; Mathematics Skills	$63,860	17.3%	28,000
8. Market Research Analysts	Communication Skills; Social Skills; Thought-Processing Skills	$57,300	19.6%	20,000
9. Appraisers, Real Estate	Communication Skills; Mathematics Skills; Thought-Processing Skills	$43,440	22.8%	9,000
10. Assessors	Communication Skills; Mathematics Skills; Social Skills	$43,440	22.8%	9,000
11. Cost Estimators	Equipment/Technology Analysis Skills; Management Skills; Mathematics Skills	$52,020	18.2%	15,000

Jobs 1 and 2 share 63,000 job openings. Jobs 5 and 6 share 37,000 job openings. Jobs 9 and 10 share 9,000 job openings.

Best Jobs for People Interested in Government and Public Administration

Job	Top Skills	Annual Earnings	Percent Growth	Annual Openings
1. Social and Community Service Managers	Communication Skills; Management Skills; Social Skills	$49,500	25.5%	17,000
2. Immigration and Customs Inspectors	Communication Skills; Equipment/Technology Analysis Skills; Social Skills	$55,790	16.3%	9,000
3. Construction and Building Inspectors	Mathematics Skills; Quality Control Skills; Social Skills	$44,720	22.3%	6,000
4. Financial Examiners	Communication Skills; Quality Control Skills; Thought-Processing Skills	$63,090	9.5%	3,000
5. Aviation Inspectors	Equipment Use/ Maintenance Skills; Quality Control Skills; Thought-Processing Skills	$49,490	11.4%	2,000
6. Transportation Vehicle, Equipment, and Systems Inspectors, Except Aviation	Equipment Use/ Maintenance Skills; Quality Control Skills	$49,490	11.4%	2,000

Job 2 shares 9,000 openings with three other jobs not included in this list. Jobs 5 and 6 share 2,000 openings with each other and with another job not included in this list.

Best Jobs for People Interested in Health Science

Job	Top Skills	Annual Earnings	Percent Growth	Annual Openings
1. Anesthesiologists	Equipment Use/ Maintenance Skills; Science Skills; Thought-Processing Skills	more than $145,600	24.0%	41,000
2. Internists, General	Science Skills; Social Skills; Thought-Processing Skills	more than $145,600	24.0%	41,000
3. Obstetricians and Gynecologists	Science Skills; Social Skills; Thought-Processing Skills	more than $145,600	24.0%	41,000

Best Jobs for People Interested in Health Science

Job	Top Skills	Annual Earnings	Percent Growth	Annual Openings
4. Psychiatrists	Science Skills; Social Skills; Thought-Processing Skills	more than $145,600	24.0%	41,000
5. Surgeons	Communication Skills; Science Skills; Thought-Processing Skills	more than $145,600	24.0%	41,000
6. Family and General Practitioners	Science Skills; Social Skills; Thought-Processing Skills	$140,400	24.0%	41,000
7. Pediatricians, General	Science Skills; Social Skills; Thought-Processing Skills	$136,600	24.0%	41,000
8. Registered Nurses	Science Skills; Social Skills; Thought-Processing Skills	$54,670	29.4%	229,000
9. Dental Hygienists	Communication Skills; Science Skills; Social Skills	$60,890	43.3%	17,000
10. Physician Assistants	Communication Skills; Science Skills; Thought-Processing Skills	$72,030	49.6%	10,000
11. Medical Assistants	Communication Skills; Mathematics Skills; Social Skills	$25,350	52.1%	93,000
12. Physical Therapists	Communication Skills; Science Skills; Social Skills	$63,080	36.7%	13,000
13. Dental Assistants	Equipment Use/ Maintenance Skills; Equipment/ Technology Analysis Skills; Social Skills	$29,520	42.7%	45,000
14. Pharmacists	Communication Skills; Mathematics Skills; Science Skills	$89,820	24.6%	16,000
15. Medical and Health Services Managers	Management Skills; Quality Control Skills; Social Skills	$69,700	22.8%	33,000

(continued)

(continued)

Best Jobs for People Interested in Health Science

Job	Top Skills	Annual Earnings	Percent Growth	Annual Openings
16. Occupational Therapists	Communication Skills; Science Skills; Social Skills	$56,860	33.6%	7,000
17. Physical Therapist Assistants	Communication Skills; Science Skills; Social Skills	$39,490	44.2%	7,000
18. Diagnostic Medical Sonographers	Communication Skills; Quality Control Skills; Science Skills	$54,370	34.8%	5,000
19. Pharmacy Technicians	Communication Skills; Mathematics Skills	$24,390	28.6%	35,000
20. Radiologic Technicians	Communication Skills; Science Skills; Social Skills	$45,950	23.2%	17,000
21. Radiologic Technologists	Communication Skills; Science Skills; Social Skills	$45,950	23.2%	17,000
22. Surgical Technologists	Equipment/Technology Analysis Skills; Science Skills; Social Skills	$34,830	29.5%	12,000
23. Respiratory Therapists	Communication Skills; Mathematics Skills; Science Skills	$45,140	28.4%	7,000
24. Cardiovascular Technologists and Technicians	Equipment Use/ Maintenance Skills; Quality Control Skills; Science Skills	$40,420	32.6%	5,000
25. Nursing Aides, Orderlies, and Attendants	Management Skills; Science Skills; Social Skills	$21,440	22.3%	307,000
26. Medical and Clinical Laboratory Technicians	Equipment Use/ Maintenance Skills; Quality Control Skills; Science Skills	$31,700	25.0%	14,000

Best Jobs for People Interested in Health Science

Job	Top Skills	Annual Earnings	Percent Growth	Annual Openings
27. Radiation Therapists	Equipment Use/ Maintenance Skills; Equipment/Technology Analysis Skills; Science Skills	$62,340	26.3%	1,000
28. Licensed Practical and Licensed Vocational Nurses	Communication Skills; Equipment Use/ Maintenance Skills; Science Skills	$35,230	17.1%	84,000
29. Occupational Therapist Assistants	Equipment/Technology Analysis Skills; Social Skills; Thought-Processing Skills	$39,750	34.1%	2,000
30. Dentists, General	Management Skills; Science Skills; Thought-Processing Skills	$125,300	13.5%	7,000
31. Veterinarians	Management Skills; Science Skills; Thought-Processing Skills	$68,910	17.4%	8,000
32. Medical and Clinical Laboratory Technologists	Equipment Use/ Maintenance Skills; Quality Control Skills; Science Skills	$47,710	20.5%	14,000
33. Chiropractors	Management Skills; Science Skills; Social Skills	$67,200	22.4%	4,000
34. Optometrists	Management Skills; Science Skills; Thought-Processing Skills	$88,040	19.7%	2,000
35. Nuclear Medicine Technologists	Equipment Use/ Maintenance Skills; Quality Control Skills; Science Skills	$59,670	21.5%	2,000
36. Biological Technicians	Mathematics Skills; Quality Control Skills; Science Skills	$34,270	17.2%	8,000

Jobs 1, 2, 3, 4, 5, 6, and 7 share 41,000 job openings. Jobs 20 and 21 share 17,000 job openings.

Best Jobs for People Interested in Hospitality, Tourism, and Recreation

Job	Top Skills	Annual Earnings	Percent Growth	Annual Openings
1. Gaming Managers	Management Skills; Mathematics Skills; Social Skills	$59,940	22.6%	1,000
2. Coaches and Scouts	Management Skills; Social Skills; Thought-Processing Skills	$25,990	20.4%	63,000
3. Food Service Managers	Management Skills; Quality Control Skills; Social Skills	$41,340	11.5%	61,000
4. Gaming Supervisors	Mathematics Skills; Social Skills; Thought-Processing Skills	$40,300	16.3%	8,000

Best Jobs for People Interested in Human Service

Job	Top Skills	Annual Earnings	Percent Growth	Annual Openings
1. Personal and Home Care Aides	Communication Skills; Social Skills; Thought-Processing Skills	$17,340	41.0%	230,000
2. Social and Human Service Assistants	Communication Skills; Management Skills; Social Skills	$25,030	29.7%	61,000
3. Mental Health and Substance Abuse Social Workers	Communication Skills; Social Skills; Thought-Processing Skills	$34,410	26.7%	15,000
4. Medical and Public Health Social Workers	Communication Skills; Social Skills; Thought-Processing Skills	$41,120	25.9%	14,000
5. Mental Health Counselors	Communication Skills; Social Skills; Thought-Processing Skills	$34,010	27.2%	14,000

Best Jobs for People Interested in Human Service

Job	Top Skills	Annual Earnings	Percent Growth	Annual Openings
6. Clinical Psychologists	Communication Skills; Social Skills; Thought-Processing Skills	$57,170	19.1%	10,000
7. Counseling Psychologists	Communication Skills; Social Skills; Thought-Processing Skills	$57,170	19.1%	10,000

Jobs 6 and 7 share 10,000 openings with each other and with another job not included in this list.

Best Jobs for People Interested in Information Technology

Job	Top Skills	Annual Earnings	Percent Growth	Annual Openings
1. Computer Software Engineers, Applications	Computer Programming Skills; Equipment/ Technology Analysis Skills; Quality Control Skills	$77,090	48.4%	54,000
2. Computer Software Engineers, Systems Software	Computer Programming Skills; Equipment/ Technology Analysis Skills; Science Skills	$82,120	43.0%	37,000
3. Network Systems and Data Communications Analysts	Computer Programming Skills; Equipment Use/ Maintenance Skills; Equipment/Technology Analysis Skills	$61,750	54.6%	43,000
4. Computer Systems Analysts	Computer Programming Skills; Equipment/ Technology Analysis Skills; Quality Control Skills	$68,300	31.4%	56,000

(continued)

(continued)

Best Jobs for People Interested in Information Technology

Job	Top Skills	Annual Earnings	Percent Growth	Annual Openings
5. Computer Security Specialists	Computer Programming Skills; Equipment/ Technology Analysis Skills; Management Skills	$59,930	38.4%	34,000
6. Network and Computer Systems Administrators	Computer Programming Skills; Equipment Use/ Maintenance Skills; Equipment/Technology Analysis Skills	$59,930	38.4%	34,000
7. Computer and Information Systems Managers	Computer Programming Skills; Management Skills; Quality Control Skills	$96,520	25.9%	25,000
8. Computer Support Specialists	Communication Skills; Equipment Use/ Maintenance Skills; Social Skills	$40,610	23.0%	87,000
9. Database Administrators	Computer Programming Skills; Equipment/ Technology Analysis Skills; Quality Control Skills	$63,250	38.2%	9,000
10. Computer Programmers	Computer Programming Skills; Equipment/ Technology Analysis Skills; Thought-Processing Skills	$63,420	2.0%	28,000
11. Computer, Automated Teller, and Office Machine Repairers	Equipment Use/ Maintenance Skills; Quality Control Skills; Science Skills	$36,060	3.8%	31,000

Jobs 5 and 6 share 34,000 job openings.

Best Jobs for People Interested in Law and Public Safety

Job	Top Skills	Annual Earnings	Percent Growth	Annual Openings
1. Paralegals and Legal Assistants	Communication Skills	$41,170	29.7%	28,000
2. Lawyers	Communication Skills; Social Skills; Thought-Processing Skills	$98,930	15.0%	40,000
3. Police Patrol Officers	Communication Skills; Social Skills; Thought-Processing Skills	$46,290	15.5%	47,000
4. Sheriffs and Deputy Sheriffs	Communication Skills; Social Skills; Thought-Processing Skills	$46,290	15.5%	47,000
5. Forest Fire Fighters	Equipment Use/ Maintenance Skills; Equipment/Technology Analysis Skills; Management Skills	$39,090	24.3%	21,000
6. Forest Fire Fighting and Prevention Supervisors	Equipment Use/ Maintenance Skills; Management Skills; Science Skills	$60,840	21.1%	4,000
7. Municipal Fire Fighters	Equipment Use/ Maintenance Skills; Equipment/Technology Analysis Skills; Science Skills	$39,090	24.3%	21,000
8. Municipal Fire Fighting and Prevention Supervisors	Equipment Use/ Maintenance Skills; Management Skills; Social Skills	$60,840	21.1%	4,000
9. Emergency Medical Technicians and Paramedics	Equipment Use/ Maintenance Skills; Social Skills; Thought-Processing Skills	$26,080	27.3%	21,000
10. Criminal Investigators and Special Agents	Computer Programming Skills; Equipment/ Technology Analysis Skills; Social Skills	$55,790	16.3%	9,000

(continued)

(continued)

Best Jobs for People Interested in Law and Public Safety

Job	Top Skills	Annual Earnings	Percent Growth	Annual Openings
11. First-Line Supervisors/ Managers of Police and Detectives	Management Skills; Social Skills; Thought-Processing Skills	$65,570	15.5%	9,000
12. Forensic Science Technicians	Communication Skills; Quality Control Skills; Science Skills	$44,590	36.4%	2,000

Jobs 3 and 4 share 47,000 job openings. Jobs 6 and 7 share 21,000 job openings. Jobs 8 and 9 share 4,000 job openings. Job 11 shares 9,000 openings with four other jobs not included in this list.

Best Jobs for People Interested in Manufacturing

Job	Top Skills	Annual Earnings	Percent Growth	Annual Openings
1. First-Line Supervisors/Managers of Mechanics, Installers, and Repairers	Equipment Use/ Maintenance Skills; Equipment/Technology Analysis Skills; Management Skills	$51,980	12.4%	33,000
2. Automotive Master Mechanics	Equipment Use/ Maintenance Skills	$33,050	15.7%	93,000
3. Automotive Specialty Technicians	Equipment Use/ Maintenance Skills; Equipment/Technology Analysis Skills; Thought-Processing Skills	$33,050	15.7%	93,000
4. First-Line Supervisors/Managers of Production and Operating Workers	Equipment Use/ Maintenance Skills; Management Skills; Quality Control Skills	$46,140	2.7%	89,000
5. Aircraft Mechanics and Service Technicians	Equipment Use/ Maintenance Skills; Quality Control Skills	$47,310	13.4%	11,000
6. Bus and Truck Mechanics and Diesel Engine Specialists	Equipment Use/ Maintenance Skills; Science Skills	$36,620	14.4%	32,000

Best Jobs for People Interested in Manufacturing

Job	Top Skills	Annual Earnings	Percent Growth	Annual Openings
7. Industrial Production Managers	Equipment/Technology Analysis Skills; Management Skills; Quality Control Skills	$75,580	0.8%	13,000
8. Electrical and Electronics Repairers, Commercial and Industrial Equipment	Equipment Use/ Maintenance Skills; Mathematics Skills; Science Skills	$44,120	9.7%	8,000
9. Medical Equipment Repairers	Equipment Use/ Maintenance Skills; Quality Control Skills; Science Skills	$39,570	14.8%	4,000
10. Machinists	Computer Programming Skills; Equipment Use/ Maintenance Skills; Quality Control Skills	$34,350	4.3%	33,000
11. Mobile Heavy Equipment Mechanics, Except Engines	Equipment Use/ Maintenance Skills	$39,410	8.8%	14,000
12. First-Line Supervisors/ Managers of Helpers, Laborers, and Material Movers, Hand	Management Skills; Quality Control Skills; Social Skills	$39,000	8.1%	15,000
13. Motorboat Mechanics	Equipment Use/ Maintenance Skills; Quality Control Skills	$32,780	15.1%	7,000
14. Electrical and Electronic Equipment Assemblers	Computer Programming Skills; Equipment Use/ Maintenance Skills; Quality Control Skills	$25,130	–6.4%	33,000
15. Numerical Tool and Process Control Programmers	Computer Programming Skills; Mathematics Skills; Quality Control Skills	$41,830	–1.1%	2,000
16. Forging Machine Setters, Operators, and Tenders, Metal and Plastic	Computer Programming Skills; Equipment Use/ Maintenance Skills; Quality Control Skills	$28,970	–4.6%	4,000

Jobs 2 and 3 share 93,000 job openings.

Best Jobs for People Interested in Retail and Wholesale Sales and Service

Job	Top Skills	Annual Earnings	Percent Growth	Annual Openings
1. Marketing Managers	Management Skills; Science Skills; Social Skills	$92,680	20.8%	23,000
2. Sales Managers	Management Skills; Social Skills; Thought-Processing Skills	$87,580	19.7%	40,000
3. Customer Service Representatives	Communication Skills; Social Skills; Thought-Processing Skills	$27,490	22.8%	510,000
4. Advertising and Promotions Managers	Management Skills; Social Skills; Thought-Processing Skills	$68,860	20.3%	9,000
5. Property, Real Estate, and Community Association Managers	Management Skills; Mathematics Skills; Social Skills	$41,900	15.3%	58,000
6. Sales Representatives, Wholesale and Manufacturing, Except Technical and Scientific Products	Communication Skills; Management Skills; Social Skills	$47,380	12.9%	169,000
7. Real Estate Sales Agents	Communication Skills; Mathematics Skills; Social Skills	$39,240	14.7%	41,000
8. Sales Engineers	Computer Programming Skills; Equipment/ Technology Analysis Skills; Science Skills	$74,200	14.0%	8,000
9. Purchasing Agents, Except Wholesale, Retail, and Farm Products	Communication Skills; Management Skills; Mathematics Skills	$49,030	8.1%	19,000
10. Wholesale and Retail Buyers, Except Farm Products	Management Skills; Mathematics Skills; Quality Control Skills	$42,870	8.4%	20,000
11. Purchasing Managers	Management Skills; Mathematics Skills; Social Skills	$76,270	7.0%	8,000
12. Real Estate Brokers	Management Skills; Mathematics Skills; Social Skills	$57,190	7.8%	12,000

Best Jobs for People Interested in Scientific Research, Engineering, and Mathematics

Job	Top Skills	Annual Earnings	Percent Growth	Annual Openings
1. Engineering Managers	Equipment/Technology Analysis Skills; Mathematics Skills; Science Skills	$100,760	13.0%	15,000
2. Actuaries	Computer Programming Skills; Mathematics Skills; Thought-Processing Skills	$81,640	23.2%	3,000
3. Medical Scientists, Except Epidemiologists	Communication Skills; Management Skills; Science Skills	$61,730	34.1%	15,000
4. Civil Engineers	Equipment/Technology Analysis Skills; Mathematics Skills; Science Skills	$66,190	16.5%	19,000
5. Natural Sciences Managers	Management Skills; Mathematics Skills; Science Skills	$93,090	13.6%	5,000
6. Industrial Engineers	Communication Skills; Equipment/Technology Analysis Skills; Mathematics Skills	$66,670	16.0%	13,000
7. Electrical Engineers	Computer Programming Skills; Equipment/ Technology Analysis Skills; Science Skills	$73,510	11.8%	12,000
8. Biomedical Engineers	Equipment/Technology Analysis Skills; Quality Control Skills; Science Skills	$71,840	30.7%	1,000
9. Computer Hardware Engineers	Computer Programming Skills; Equipment/ Technology Analysis Skills; Quality Control Skills	$84,420	10.1%	5,000

(continued)

(continued)

Best Jobs for People Interested in
Scientific Research, Engineering, and Mathematics

Job	Top Skills	Annual Earnings	Percent Growth	Annual Openings
10. Electronics Engineers, Except Computer	Equipment/Technology Analysis Skills; Quality Control Skills; Science Skills	$78,030	9.7%	11,000
11. Industrial-Organizational Psychologists	Science Skills; Social Skills; Thought-Processing Skills	$84,690	20.4%	fewer than 500
12. Atmospheric and Space Scientists	Computer Programming Skills; Quality Control Skills; Science Skills	$73,940	16.5%	1,000
13. Mechanical Engineers	Equipment/Technology Analysis Skills; Mathematics Skills; Science Skills	$67,590	11.1%	11,000
14. School Psychologists	Communication Skills; Social Skills; Thought-Processing Skills	$57,170	19.1%	10,000
15. Chemical Engineers	Computer Programming Skills; Equipment/ Technology Analysis Skills; Science Skills	$77,140	10.6%	3,000
16. Hydrologists	Computer Programming Skills; Mathematics Skills; Science Skills	$63,820	31.6%	1,000
17. Aerospace Engineers	Equipment/Technology Analysis Skills; Quality Control Skills; Science Skills	$84,090	8.3%	6,000
18. Environmental Scientists and Specialists, Including Health	Mathematics Skills; Science Skills; Social Skills	$52,630	17.1%	8,000

Best Jobs for People Interested in
Scientific Research, Engineering, and Mathematics

Job	Top Skills	Annual Earnings	Percent Growth	Annual Openings
19. Materials Engineers	Mathematics Skills; Quality Control Skills; Science Skills	$69,660	12.2%	2,000
20. Fire-Prevention and Protection Engineers	Management Skills; Mathematics Skills; Science Skills	$65,210	13.4%	2,000
21. Product Safety Engineers	Mathematics Skills; Quality Control Skills; Science Skills	$65,210	13.4%	2,000
22. Astronomers	Computer Programming Skills; Mathematics Skills; Science Skills	$104,670	10.4%	fewer than 500
23. Electrical Engineering Technicians	Equipment Use/ Maintenance Skills; Mathematics Skills; Science Skills	$48,040	9.8%	18,000
24. Electronics Engineering Technicians	Computer Programming Skills; Equipment Use/ Maintenance Skills; Science Skills	$48,040	9.8%	18,000
25. Epidemiologists	Computer Programming Skills; Mathematics Skills; Science Skills	$52,170	26.2%	1,000
26. Microbiologists	Equipment Use/ Maintenance Skills; Quality Control Skills; Science Skills	$56,870	17.2%	1,000
27. Economists	Computer Programming Skills; Mathematics Skills; Thought-Processing Skills	$73,690	5.6%	1,000
28. Chemists	Equipment/Technology Analysis Skills; Quality Control Skills; Science Skills	$57,890	7.3%	5,000

(continued)

(continued)

Best Jobs for People Interested in Scientific Research, Engineering, and Mathematics

Job	Top Skills	Annual Earnings	Percent Growth	Annual Openings
29. Mapping Technicians	Computer Programming Skills; Mathematics Skills; Quality Control Skills	$31,290	9.6%	9,000
30. Materials Scientists	Computer Programming Skills; Quality Control Skills; Science Skills	$71,450	8.0%	fewer than 500
31. Statisticians	Computer Programming Skills; Mathematics Skills; Science Skills	$62,450	4.6%	2,000
32. Aerospace Engineering and Operations Technicians	Computer Programming Skills; Mathematics Skills; Science Skills	$52,450	8.5%	1,000
33. Geographers	Computer Programming Skills; Mathematics Skills; Science Skills	$63,550	6.8%	fewer than 500
34. Statistical Assistants	Computer Programming Skills; Mathematics Skills; Quality Control Skills	$28,950	5.7%	1,000

Job 14 shares 10,000 openings with two other jobs not included in this list. Jobs 20 and 21 share 2,000 openings with each other and with another job not included in this list. Jobs 23 and 24 share 18,000 job openings. Job 29 shares 9,000 openings with another job not included in this list.

Best Jobs for People Interested in Transportation, Distribution, and Logistics

Job	Top Skills	Annual Earnings	Percent Growth	Annual Openings
1. Airline Pilots, Copilots, and Flight Engineers	Equipment Use/Maintenance Skills; Science Skills; Thought-Processing Skills	$138,170	17.2%	7,000

Best Jobs for People Interested in Transportation, Distribution, and Logistics

Job	Top Skills	Annual Earnings	Percent Growth	Annual Openings
2. Bus Drivers, Transit and Intercity	Equipment Use/ Maintenance Skills	$31,010	21.7%	34,000
3. Storage and Distribution Managers	Equipment/Technology Analysis Skills; Management Skills; Social Skills	$69,120	12.7%	15,000
4. Transportation Managers	Management Skills; Mathematics Skills; Social Skills	$69,120	12.7%	15,000
5. First-Line Supervisors/Managers of Transportation and Material-Moving Machine and Vehicle Operators	Management Skills; Quality Control Skills; Social Skills	$47,530	15.3%	22,000
6. Railroad Conductors and Yardmasters	Equipment Use/ Maintenance Skills	$54,040	20.3%	3,000
7. Truck Drivers, Heavy and Tractor-Trailer	Equipment Use/ Maintenance Skills	$34,280	12.9%	274,000
8. Commercial Pilots	Equipment Use/ Maintenance Skills; Mathematics Skills; Thought-Processing Skills	$55,810	16.8%	2,000

Jobs 3 and 4 share 15,000 job openings.

Bonus Lists About Skills

The following lists do not contain jobs, but they are based on the relationships between skills and jobs. We think you'll find they add to your understanding of skills and career options.

These lists may also help with your long-range career planning. Over the course of your working lifetime, some new occupations will emerge and some existing occupations will go into decline. In addition, if you are diligent about acquiring new skills over the years, eventually you will be able to consider entering occupations that presently seem unreachable to you. That's why it's useful to step back from the 230 jobs included in this book and look at the larger issues of what skills tend to be high-paid, what skills are growing in demand, and which industries are in need of your strongest skills.

Skills Used by the Best-Paid Jobs

This list shows the relationship between skills and income. We used the statistical procedure called correlation to compare the skill requirements of occupations with their earnings. In other words, which skills tend to pay the best? Note that we based this calculation on *all* occupations in the workforce for which earnings figures are available, not just the 230 that are included in the lists. We also treated all occupations equally, regardless of how big or small their workforce might be.

The skills nearest the top of the list are associated with the highest incomes.

Skills Used by the Best-Paid Jobs, Ordered from Highest to Lowest

1. Thought-Processing Skills
2. Communication Skills
3. Mathematics Skills
4. Management Skills
5. Equipment/Technology Analysis Skills
6. Science Skills
7. Computer Programming Skills
8. Social Skills
9. Quality Control Skills
10. Equipment Use/Maintenance Skills

Skills Used by the Fastest-Growing Jobs

The next list shows the relationship between skills and job growth. It answers the question of which skills are associated with the fastest-growing jobs. Again, this is based on all occupations in the workforce, workforce size is not a factor, and the jobs nearest the top of the list are associated with the fastest growth.

Skills Used by the Fastest-Growing Jobs, Ordered from Highest to Lowest

1. Social Skills
2. Communication Skills
3. Thought-Processing Skills
4. Management Skills
5. Science Skills
6. Equipment/Technology Analysis Skills
7. Mathematics Skills
8. Computer Programming Skills
9. Quality Control Skills
10. Equipment Use/Maintenance Skills

Industries in Which the Skills Are Concentrated

Although most of the lists in this book are about jobs, another way of looking at the workforce is by industries. Industries are usually defined by their outputs. For example, the Aerospace Product and Parts Manufacturing industry produces airplanes and their parts, the Broadcasting industry produces radio and television broadcasts, and the Health Care industry produces healthy people.

Industries also require different *inputs*, and one of those inputs is skills. Each industry demands a different mix of skills from workers, so certain skills dominate in one industry more than in another. You may want to plan to pursue a career in an industry where your top skills are dominant because the jobs in that industry employ many workers with your skills. Of course, another important consideration is how fast an industry is growing.

So we created the next 10 lists to show, for each skill, the 10 industries in which the skill is most highly concentrated in the workforce, plus the projected growth rate for each industry between 2004 and 2014. To create these lists, we analyzed the 45 industries that are described in the US Department of Labor's *Career Guide to Industries* and that form the basis of *40 Best Fields for Your Career* (JIST Publishing). We then used a formula based on the representation of all significant occupations in each industry (according to the Bureau of Labor Statistics) and the skill requirements of each of these occupations (according to O*NET). The industries are listed in descending order by the level of skill required.

You'll note that several of the industries listed below have a negative rate of growth, which means they are shrinking. That does not mean you should not consider working in these industries. For certain occupations and in certain parts of the country the workforce in these industries may be growing, and even in a shrinking workforce there will be openings caused by job turnover.

The 10 Industries with the Highest Level of Communication Skills in Their Workforce

Industry	Growth Rate
1. Software Publishers	67.6%
2. Scientific Research and Development Services	11.9%
3. Computer Systems Design and Related Services	39.5%
4. Federal Government, Excluding the Postal Service	2.5%
5. Educational Services	16.6%
6. Management, Scientific, and Technical Consulting Services	60.5%
7. Health Care	27.3%
8. Broadcasting	10.7%
9. Securities, Commodities, and Other Investments	15.8%
10. Internet Service Providers, Web Search Portals, and Data Processing Services	27.8%

The 10 Industries with the Highest Level of Computer Programming Skills in Their Workforce

Industry	Growth Rate
1. Software Publishers	67.6%
2. Computer Systems Design and Related Services	39.5%
3. Internet Service Providers, Web Search Portals, and Data Processing Services	27.8%
4. Computer and Electronic Product Manufacturing	–7.1%
5. Scientific Research and Development Services	11.9%
6. Management, Scientific, and Technical Consulting Services	60.5%
7. Telecommunications	–6.5%
8. Aerospace Product and Parts Manufacturing	8.2%
9. Federal Government, Excluding the Postal Service	2.5%
10. Pharmaceutical and Medicine Manufacturing	26.1%

The 10 Industries with the Highest Level of Equipment Use/Maintenance Skills in Their Workforce

Industry	Growth Rate
1. Oil and Gas Extraction	–6.1%
2. Steel Manufacturing	–13.4%
3. Mining	–12.9%
4. Utilities	–1.3%
5. Chemical Manufacturing, Except Drugs	–14.4%
6. Computer and Electronic Product Manufacturing	–7.1%
7. Motor Vehicle and Parts Manufacturing	5.6%
8. Computer Systems Design and Related Services	39.5%
9. Printing	–9.8%
10. Machinery Manufacturing	–12.8%

The 10 Industries with the Highest Level of Equipment/Technology Analysis Skills in Their Workforce

Industry	Growth Rate
1. Software Publishers	67.6%
2. Computer Systems Design and Related Services	39.5%
3. Computer and Electronic Product Manufacturing	–7.1%
4. Scientific Research and Development Services	11.9%
5. Aerospace Product and Parts Manufacturing	8.2%
6. Internet Service Providers, Web Search Portals, and Data Processing Services	27.8%
7. Management, Scientific, and Technical Consulting Services	60.5%
8. Federal Government, Excluding the Postal Service	2.5%
9. Pharmaceutical and Medicine Manufacturing	26.1%
10. Oil and Gas Extraction	–6.1%

The 10 Industries with the Highest Level of Management Skills in Their Workforce

Industry	Growth Rate
1. Scientific Research and Development Services	11.9%
2. Management, Scientific, and Technical Consulting Services	60.5%
3. Computer Systems Design and Related Services	39.5%
4. Computer and Electronic Product Manufacturing	–7.1%
5. Federal Government, Excluding the Postal Service	2.5%
6. Software Publishers	67.6%
7. Aerospace Product and Parts Manufacturing	8.2%
8. Securities, Commodities, and Other Investments	15.8%
9. Pharmaceutical and Medicine Manufacturing	26.1%
10. Internet Service Providers, Web Search Portals, and Data Processing Services	27.8%

The 10 Industries with the Highest Level of Mathematics Skills in Their Workforce

Industry	Growth Rate
1. Scientific Research and Development Services	11.9%
2. Software Publishers	67.6%
3. Aerospace Product and Parts Manufacturing	8.2%
4. Computer Systems Design and Related Services	39.5%
5. Computer and Electronic Product Manufacturing	–7.1%
6. Federal Government, Excluding the Postal Service	2.5%
7. Securities, Commodities, and Other Investments	15.8%
8. Pharmaceutical and Medicine Manufacturing	26.1%
9. Internet Service Providers, Web Search Portals, and Data Processing Services	27.8%
10. Management, Scientific, and Technical Consulting Services	60.5%

The 10 Industries with the Highest Level of Quality Control Skills in Their Workforce

Industry	Growth Rate
1. Software Publishers	67.6%
2. Computer Systems Design and Related Services	39.5%
3. Aerospace Product and Parts Manufacturing	8.2%
4. Computer and Electronic Product Manufacturing	–7.1%
5. Scientific Research and Development Services	11.9%
6. Pharmaceutical and Medicine Manufacturing	26.1%
7. Motor Vehicle and Parts Manufacturing	5.6%
8. Machinery Manufacturing	–12.8%
9. Steel Manufacturing	–13.4%
10. Chemical Manufacturing, Except Drugs	–14.4%

The 10 Industries with the Highest Level of Science Skills in Their Workforce

Industry	Growth Rate
1. Scientific Research and Development Services	11.9%
2. Aerospace Product and Parts Manufacturing	8.2%
3. Pharmaceutical and Medicine Manufacturing	26.1%
4. Computer and Electronic Product Manufacturing	–7.1%
5. Federal Government, Excluding the Postal Service	2.5%
6. Health Care	27.3%
7. Software Publishers	67.6%
8. Computer Systems Design and Related Services	39.5%
9. Oil and Gas Extraction	–6.1%
10. Chemical Manufacturing, Except Drugs	–14.4%

The 10 Industries with the Highest Level of Social Skills in Their Workforce

Industry	Growth Rate
1. Educational Services	16.6%
2. Software Publishers	67.6%
3. Health Care	27.3%
4. Social Assistance, Except Child Day Care	32.6%
5. Management, Scientific, and Technical Consulting Services	60.5%
6. Computer Systems Design and Related Services	39.5%
7. Federal Government, Excluding the Postal Service	2.5%
8. Scientific Research and Development Services	11.9%
9. State and Local Government, Excluding Education and Hospitals	11.4%
10. Advertising and Public Relations Services	22.4%

The 10 Industries with the Highest Level
of Thought-Processing Skills in Their Workforce

Industry	Growth Rate
1. Software Publishers	67.6%
2. Computer Systems Design and Related Services	39.5%
3. Scientific Research and Development Services	11.9%
4. Federal Government, Excluding the Postal Service	2.5%
5. Management, Scientific, and Technical Consulting Services	60.5%
6. Internet Service Providers, Web Search Portals, and Data Processing Services	27.8%
7. Educational Services	16.6%
8. Aerospace Product and Parts Manufacturing	8.2%
9. Computer and Electronic Product Manufacturing	–7.1%
10. Securities, Commodities, and Other Investments	15.8%

PART IV

Descriptions of the Best Jobs for Your Skills

This part provides descriptions for all the jobs included in one or more of the lists in Part III. The Introduction gives more details on how to use and interpret the job descriptions, but here is some additional information:

- Job descriptions are arranged in alphabetical order by job title. This approach allows you to find a description quickly if you know its correct title from one of the lists in Part III.

- If you are using this section to browse for interesting options, we suggest you begin with the Table of Contents. Part III features many interesting lists that will help you identify job titles to explore in more detail. If you have not browsed the lists in Part III, consider spending some time there. The lists are interesting and will help you identify job titles you can find described in the material that follows. The job titles in Part IV are also listed in the Table of Contents.

- We include descriptions for the many specific jobs that we gathered under the single job title of Teachers, Postsecondary, in the lists in Part III. In Part III we assigned this combined job to skill-linked lists by computing the *average* skill requirements of the 36 component jobs. For this combined job, the top three skills are Communication Skills, Science Skills, and Thought-Processing Skills. In the descriptions here in Part IV, however, you can see the specific skills required by each of the specialized postsecondary teaching jobs: Agricultural Sciences Teachers, Postsecondary; Anthropology and Archeology Teachers, Postsecondary; Architecture Teachers, Postsecondary; Area, Ethnic, and Cultural Studies Teachers, Postsecondary; Art, Drama, and Music Teachers, Postsecondary; Atmospheric, Earth, Marine, and Space Sciences Teachers, Postsecondary; Biological Science Teachers, Postsecondary; Business Teachers, Postsecondary; Chemistry Teachers, Postsecondary; Communications Teachers, Postsecondary; Computer Science Teachers, Postsecondary; Criminal Justice and Law Enforcement Teachers, Postsecondary; Economics Teachers, Postsecondary; Education Teachers, Postsecondary; Engineering Teachers, Postsecondary; English Language and Literature Teachers, Postsecondary; Environmental Science Teachers, Postsecondary; Foreign Language and Literature Teachers, Postsecondary; Forestry and Conservation Science

Teachers, Postsecondary; Geography Teachers, Postsecondary; Graduate Teaching Assistants; Health Specialties Teachers, Postsecondary; History Teachers, Postsecondary; Home Economics Teachers, Postsecondary; Law Teachers, Postsecondary; Library Science Teachers, Postsecondary; Mathematical Science Teachers, Postsecondary; Nursing Instructors and Teachers, Postsecondary; Philosophy and Religion Teachers, Postsecondary; Physics Teachers, Postsecondary; Political Science Teachers, Postsecondary; Psychology Teachers, Postsecondary; Recreation and Fitness Studies Teachers, Postsecondary; Social Work Teachers, Postsecondary; Sociology Teachers, Postsecondary; and Vocational Education Teachers, Postsecondary.

Accountants

- Education/Training Required: Bachelor's degree
- Annual Earnings: $52,210
- Growth: 22.4%
- Annual Job Openings: 157,000
- Self-Employed: 10.9%
- Part-Time: 10.2%

The job openings listed here are shared with Auditors.

Analyze financial information and prepare financial reports to determine or maintain record of assets, liabilities, profit and loss, tax liability, or other financial activities within an organization. Prepare, examine, or analyze accounting records, financial statements, or other financial reports to assess accuracy, completeness, and conformance to reporting and procedural standards. Compute taxes owed and prepare tax returns, ensuring compliance with payment, reporting, or other tax requirements. Analyze business operations, trends, costs, revenues, financial commitments, and obligations to project future revenues and expenses or to provide advice. Report to management regarding the finances of establishment. Establish tables of accounts and assign entries to proper accounts. Develop, maintain, and analyze budgets, preparing periodic reports that compare budgeted costs to actual costs. Develop, implement, modify, and document recordkeeping and accounting systems, making use of current computer technology. Prepare forms and manuals for accounting and bookkeeping personnel and direct their work activities. Survey operations to ascertain accounting needs and to recommend, develop, or maintain solutions to business and financial problems. Work as Internal Revenue Service (IRS) agents. Advise management about issues such as resource utilization, tax strategies, and the assumptions underlying budget forecasts. Provide internal and external auditing services for businesses or individuals. Advise clients in areas such as compensation, employee health-care benefits, the design of accounting or data processing systems, or long-range tax or estate plans. Investigate bankruptcies and other complex financial transactions and prepare reports summarizing the findings. Represent clients before taxing authorities and provide support during litigation involving financial issues. Appraise, evaluate, and inventory real property and equipment, recording information such as the description, value, and location of property. Maintain or examine the records of government agencies. Serve as bankruptcy trustees or business valuators.

SKILLS—Most Important: Computer Programming Skills; Mathematics Skills; Management Skills. **Other Above-Average Skills:** Thought-Processing Skills; Quality Control Skills; Equipment/Technology Analysis Skills.

GOE—Interest Area: 04. Business and Administration. **Work Group:** 04.05. Accounting, Auditing, and Analytical Support. **Other Jobs in This Group:** Accountants and Auditors; Auditors; Budget Analysts; Industrial Engineering Technicians; Logisticians; Management Analysts; Operations Research Analysts. **PERSONALITY TYPE:** Conventional. Conventional occupations frequently involve following set procedures and routines. These occupations can include working with data and details more than with ideas. Usually there is a clear line of authority to follow.

EDUCATION/TRAINING PROGRAM(S)—Accounting and Computer Science; Accounting; Accounting and Finance; Accounting and Business/Management. **RELATED KNOWLEDGE/COURSES—Economics and Accounting:** Economic and accounting principles and practices, the financial markets, banking, and the analysis and reporting of financial data. **Clerical Practices:** Administrative and clerical procedures and systems such as word processing, managing files and records, stenography and transcription, designing forms, and other office procedures and terminology. **Mathematics:** Arithmetic, algebra, geometry, calculus, and statistics and their applications. **Law and Government:** Laws, legal codes, court procedures, precedents, government regulations, executive orders, agency rules, and the democratic political process. **Computers and Electronics:** Circuit boards; processors; chips; electronic equipment; and computer hardware and software, including applications and programming. **Personnel and Human Resources:** Principles and procedures for personnel recruitment, selection, training, compensation and benefits, labor relations and negotiation, and personnel information systems.

Actuaries

- Education/Training Required: Work experience plus degree
- Annual Earnings: $81,640
- Growth: 23.2%
- Annual Job Openings: 3,000
- Self-Employed: 0.0%
- Part-Time: 3.8%

Analyze statistical data, such as mortality, accident, sickness, disability, and retirement rates, and construct probability tables to forecast risk and liability for payment of future benefits. May ascertain premium rates required and cash reserves necessary to ensure payment of future benefits. Ascertain premium rates required and cash reserves and liabilities necessary to ensure payment of future benefits. Analyze statistical information to estimate mortality, accident, sickness, disability, and retirement rates. Design, review, and help administer insurance, annuity, and pension plans, determining financial soundness and calculating premiums. Collaborate with programmers, underwriters, accounts, claims experts, and senior management to help companies develop plans for new lines of business or improving existing business. Determine or help determine company policy and explain complex technical matters to company executives, government officials, shareholders, policyholders, or the public. Testify before public agencies on proposed legislation affecting businesses. Provide advice to clients on a contract basis, working as a consultant. Testify in court as expert witness or to provide legal evidence on matters such as the value of potential lifetime earnings of a person who is disabled or killed in an accident. Construct probability tables for events such as fires, natural disasters, and unemployment, based on analysis of statistical data and other pertinent information. Determine policy contract provisions for each type of insurance. Manage credit and help price corporate security offerings. Provide expertise to help financial institutions manage risks and maximize returns associated with investment products or credit offerings. Determine equitable basis for distributing surplus earnings under participating insurance and annuity contracts in mutual companies. Explain changes in contract provisions to customers.

SKILLS—Most Important: Computer Programming Skills; Mathematics Skills; Thought-Processing Skills. **Other Above-Average Skills:** Quality Control Skills; Equipment/Technology Analysis Skills; Science Skills; Management Skills.

GOE—Interest Area: 15. Scientific Research, Engineering, and Mathematics. **Work Group:** 15.06. Mathematics and Data Analysis. **Other Jobs in This Group:** Mathematical Technicians; Mathematicians; Social Science Research Assistants; Statistical Assistants; Statisticians. **PERSONALITY TYPE:** Conventional. Conventional occupations frequently involve following set procedures and routines. These occupations can include working with data and details more than with ideas. Usually there is a clear line of authority to follow.

EDUCATION/TRAINING PROGRAM(S)—Actuarial Science. **RELATED KNOWLEDGE/COURSES—Mathematics:** Arithmetic, algebra, geometry, calculus, and statistics and their applications. **Economics and Accounting:** Economic and accounting principles and practices, the financial markets, banking, and the analysis and reporting of financial data. **Sales and Marketing:** Principles and methods for showing, promoting, and selling products or services. This includes marketing strategy and tactics, product demonstration, sales techniques, and sales control systems. **Computers and Electronics:** Circuit boards; processors; chips; electronic equipment; and computer hardware and software, including applications and programming. **Personnel and Human Resources:** Principles and procedures for personnel recruitment, selection, training, compensation and benefits, labor relations and negotiation, and personnel information systems. **Administration and Management:** Business and management principles involved in strategic planning, resource allocation, human resources modeling, leadership technique, production methods, and coordination of people and resources.

Administrative Services Managers

- ◎ Education/Training Required: Work experience plus degree
- ◎ Annual Earnings: $64,020
- ◎ Growth: 16.9%
- ◎ Annual Job Openings: 25,000
- ◎ Self-Employed: 0.2%
- ◎ Part-Time: 4.9%

Plan, direct, or coordinate supportive services of an organization, such as recordkeeping, mail distribution, telephone operator/receptionist, and other office support services. May oversee facilities planning and maintenance and custodial operations. Monitor the facility to ensure that it remains safe, secure, and well-maintained. Direct or coordinate the supportive services department of a business, agency, or organization. Set goals and deadlines for the department. Prepare and review operational reports and schedules to ensure accuracy and efficiency. Analyze internal processes and recommend and implement procedural or policy changes to improve operations such as supply changes or the disposal of records. Acquire, distribute, and store supplies. Plan, administer, and control budgets for contracts, equipment, and supplies. Oversee construction and renovation projects to improve efficiency and to ensure that facilities meet environmental, health, and security standards and comply with government regulations. Hire and terminate clerical and administrative personnel. Oversee the maintenance and repair of machinery, equipment, and electrical and mechanical systems. Manage leasing of facility space. Participate in architectural and engineering planning and design, including space and installation management. Conduct classes to teach procedures to staff. Dispose of, or oversee the disposal of, surplus or unclaimed property.

SKILLS—Most Important: Computer Programming Skills; Management Skills; Communication Skills. **Other Above-Average Skills:** Social Skills; Mathematics Skills.

GOE—Interest Area: 04. Business and Administration. **Work Group:** 04.02. Managerial Work in Business Detail. **Other Jobs in This Group:** First-Line Supervisors/Managers of Housekeeping and Janitorial Workers; First-Line Supervisors/Managers of Office and Administrative Support Workers; Meeting and Convention Planners. **PERSONALITY TYPE:** Enterprising. Enterprising occupations frequently involve starting up and carrying out projects. These occupations can involve leading people and making many decisions. They sometimes require risk taking and often deal with business.

EDUCATION/TRAINING PROGRAM(S)—Public Administration; Medical/Health Management and Clinical Assistant/Specialist; Business/Commerce, General; Business Administration and Management, General; Purchasing, Procurement/Acquisitions, and Contracts Management; Transportation/Transportation Management. **RELATED KNOWLEDGE/COURSES—Personnel and Human Resources:** Principles and procedures for personnel recruitment, selection, training, compensation and benefits, labor relations and negotiation, and personnel information systems. **Clerical Practices:** Administrative and clerical procedures and systems such as word processing, managing files and records, stenography and transcription, designing forms, and other office procedures and terminology. **Economics and Accounting:** Economic and accounting principles and practices, the financial markets, banking, and the analysis and reporting of financial data. **Customer and Personal Service:** Principles and processes for providing customer and personal services. This includes customer needs assessment, meeting of quality standards for services, and evaluation of customer satisfaction. **Administration and Management:** Business and management principles involved in strategic planning, resource allocation, human resources modeling, leadership technique, production methods, and coordination of people and resources. **Public Safety and Security:** Relevant equipment, policies, procedures, and strategies to promote effective local, state, or national security operations for the protection of people, data, property, and institutions.

A

Advertising and Promotions Managers

- ◎ Education/Training Required: Work experience plus degree
- ◎ Annual Earnings: $68,860
- ◎ Growth: 20.3%
- ◎ Annual Job Openings: 9,000
- ◎ Self-Employed: 6.7%
- ◎ Part-Time: 4.0%

Plan and direct advertising policies and programs or produce collateral materials, such as posters, contests, coupons, or giveaways, to create extra interest in the purchase of a product or service for a department, for an entire organization, or on an account basis. Prepare budgets and submit estimates for program costs as part of campaign plan development. Plan and prepare advertising and promotional material to increase sales of products or services, working with customers, company officials, sales departments, and advertising agencies. Assist with annual budget development. Inspect layouts and advertising copy and edit scripts, audiotapes and videotapes, and other promotional material for adherence to specifications. Coordinate activities of departments, such as sales, graphic arts, media, finance, and research. Prepare and negotiate advertising and sales contracts. Identify and develop contacts for promotional campaigns and industry programs that meet identified buyer targets, such as dealers, distributors, or consumers. Gather and organize information to plan advertising campaigns. Confer with department heads or staff to discuss topics such as contracts, selection of advertising media, or product to be advertised. Confer with clients to provide marketing or technical advice. Monitor and analyze sales promotion results to determine cost-effectiveness of promotion campaigns. Read trade journals and professional literature to stay informed on trends, innovations, and changes that affect media planning. Formulate plans to extend business with established accounts and to transact business as agent for advertising accounts. Provide presentation and product demonstration support during the introduction of new products and services to field staff and customers. Direct, motivate, and monitor the mobilization of a campaign team to advance campaign goals.

Plan and execute advertising policies and strategies for organizations. Track program budgets and expenses and campaign response rates to evaluate each campaign based on program objectives and industry norms. Assemble and communicate with a strong, diverse coalition of organizations or public figures, securing their cooperation, support, and action to further campaign goals. Train and direct workers engaged in developing and producing advertisements. Coordinate with the media to disseminate advertising.

SKILLS—Most Important: Social Skills; Management Skills; Thought-Processing Skills. **Other Above-Average Skills:** Communication Skills; Mathematics Skills.

GOE—Interest Area: 14. Retail and Wholesale Sales and Service. **Work Group:** 14.01. Managerial Work in Retail/Wholesale Sales and Service. **Other Jobs in This Group:** First-Line Supervisors/Managers of Non-Retail Sales Workers; First-Line Supervisors/Managers of Retail Sales Workers; Funeral Directors; Marketing Managers; Property, Real Estate, and Community Association Managers; Purchasing Managers; Sales Managers. **PERSONALITY TYPE:** Artistic. Artistic occupations frequently involve working with forms, designs, and patterns. They often require self-expression, and the work can be done without following a clear set of rules.

EDUCATION/TRAINING PROGRAM(S)—Public Relations/Image Management; Advertising; Marketing/Marketing Management, General. **RELATED KNOWLEDGE/COURSES—Sales and Marketing:** Principles and methods for showing, promoting, and selling products or services. This includes marketing strategy and tactics, product demonstration, sales techniques, and sales control systems. **Fine Arts:** The theory and techniques required to compose, produce, and perform works of music, dance, visual arts, drama, and sculpture. **Design:** Design techniques, tools, and principles involved in production of precision technical plans, blueprints, drawings, and models. **Production and Processing:** Raw materials, production processes, quality control, costs, and other techniques for maximizing the effective manufacture and distribution of goods. **Communications and Media:** Media production, communication, and dissemination techniques and methods. This includes alternative ways to inform and entertain via written, oral, and visual media. **Customer and Personal Service:** Principles and processes for providing customer and personal services. This includes customer needs assessment, meeting of quality standards for services, and evaluation of customer satisfaction.

Aerospace Engineering and Operations Technicians

- Education/Training Required: Associate degree
- Annual Earnings: $52,450
- Growth: 8.5%
- Annual Job Openings: 1,000
- Self-Employed: 0.5%
- Part-Time: 6.7%

Operate, install, calibrate, and maintain integrated computer/communications systems consoles; simulators; and other data acquisition, test, and measurement instruments and equipment to launch, track, position, and evaluate air and space vehicles. May record and interpret test data. Inspect, diagnose, maintain, and operate test setups and equipment to detect malfunctions. Record and interpret test data on parts, assemblies, and mechanisms. Confer with engineering personnel regarding details and implications of test procedures and results. Adjust, repair, or replace faulty components of test setups and equipment. Identify required data, data acquisition plans, and test parameters, setting up equipment to conform to these specifications. Construct and maintain test facilities for aircraft parts and systems according to specifications. Operate and calibrate computer systems and devices to comply with test requirements and to perform data acquisition and analysis. Test aircraft systems under simulated operational conditions, performing systems readiness tests and pre- and post-operational checkouts, to establish design or fabrication parameters. Fabricate and install parts and systems to be tested in test equipment, using hand tools, power tools, and test instruments. Finish vehicle instrumentation and deinstrumentation. Exchange cooling system components in various vehicles.

SKILLS—Most Important: Science Skills; Computer Programming Skills; Mathematics Skills. **Other Above-Average Skills:** Quality Control Skills; Equipment Use/Maintenance Skills.

GOE—Interest Area: 15. Scientific Research, Engineering, and Mathematics. **Work Group:** 15.09. Engineering Technology. **Other Jobs in This Group:** Cartographers and Photogrammetrists; Civil Engineering Technicians; Electrical and Electronic Engineering Technicians; Electrical and Electronics Drafters; Electrical Drafters; Electrical Engineering Technicians; Electro-Mechanical Technicians; Electronic Drafters; Electronics Engineering Technicians; Environmental Engineering Technicians; Mapping Technicians; Mechanical Drafters; Mechanical Engineering Technicians; Surveying and Mapping Technicians; Surveying Technicians. **PERSONALITY TYPE:** Investigative. Investigative occupations frequently involve working with ideas and require an extensive amount of thinking. These occupations can involve searching for facts and figuring out problems mentally.

EDUCATION/TRAINING PROGRAM(S)—Aeronautical/Aerospace Engineering Technology/Technician. **RELATED KNOWLEDGE/COURSES—Engineering and Technology:** The practical application of engineering science and technology. This includes applying principles, techniques, procedures, and equipment to the design and production of various goods and services. **Computers and Electronics:** Circuit boards; processors; chips; electronic equipment; and computer hardware and software, including applications and programming. **Physics:** Physical principles and laws and their interrelationships and applications to understanding fluid, material, and atmospheric dynamics and mechanical, electrical, atomic, and subatomic structures and processes. **Mechanical Devices:** Machines and tools, including their designs, uses, repair, and maintenance. **Mathematics:** Arithmetic, algebra, geometry, calculus, and statistics and their applications.

Aerospace Engineers

- Education/Training Required: Bachelor's degree
- Annual Earnings: $84,090
- Growth: 8.3%
- Annual Job Openings: 6,000
- Self-Employed: 0.0%
- Part-Time: 2.4%

Perform a variety of engineering work in designing, constructing, and testing aircraft, missiles, and spacecraft. May conduct basic and applied research to evaluate adaptability of materials and equipment to aircraft design and manufacture. May recommend improvements in testing equipment and techniques. Formulate conceptual design of aeronautical or aerospace products or systems to meet customer requirements. Direct and coordinate activities of engineering or technical personnel designing, fabricating, modifying, or testing aircraft or aerospace products. Develop design criteria for aeronautical or aerospace products or systems, including testing methods, production costs, quality standards, and completion dates. Plan and conduct experimental, environmental, operational, and stress tests on models and prototypes of aircraft and aerospace systems and equipment. Evaluate product data and design from inspections and reports for conformance to engineering principles, customer requirements, and quality standards. Formulate mathematical models or other methods of computer analysis to develop, evaluate, or modify design according to customer engineering requirements. Write technical reports and other documentation, such as handbooks and bulletins, for use by engineering staff, management, and customers. Analyze project requests and proposals and engineering data to determine feasibility, productibility, cost, and production time of aerospace or aeronautical product. Review performance reports and documentation from customers and field engineers and inspect malfunctioning or damaged products to determine problem. Direct research and development programs. Evaluate and approve selection of vendors by study of past performance and new advertisements. Plan and coordinate activities concerned with investigating and resolving customers' reports of technical problems with aircraft or aerospace vehicles. Maintain records of performance reports for future reference.

SKILLS—Most Important: Science Skills; Equipment/Technology Analysis Skills; Quality Control Skills. **Other Above-Average Skills:** Management Skills; Thought-Processing Skills; Social Skills.

GOE—Interest Area: 15. Scientific Research, Engineering, and Mathematics. **Work Group:** 15.07. Research and Design Engineering. **Other Jobs in This Group:** Biomedical Engineers; Chemical Engineers; Civil Engineers; Computer Hardware Engineers; Electrical Engineers; Electronics Engineers, Except Computer; Marine Architects; Marine Engineers; Marine Engineers and Naval Architects; Materials Engineers; Mechanical Engineers; Nuclear Engineers. **PERSONALITY TYPE:** Investigative. Investigative occupations frequently involve working with ideas and require an extensive amount of thinking. These occupations can involve searching for facts and figuring out problems mentally.

EDUCATION/TRAINING PROGRAM(S)—Aerospace, Aeronautical, and Astronautical Engineering. **RELATED KNOWLEDGE/COURSES—Engineering and Technology:** The practical application of engineering science and technology. This includes applying principles, techniques, procedures, and equipment to the design and production of various goods and services. **Design:** Design techniques, tools, and principles involved in production of precision technical plans, blueprints, drawings, and models. **Physics:** Physical principles and laws and their interrelationships and applications to understanding fluid, material, and atmospheric dynamics and mechanical, electrical, atomic, and subatomic structures and processes. **Mechanical Devices:** Machines and tools, including their designs, uses, repair, and maintenance. **Production and Processing:** Raw materials, production processes, quality control, costs, and other techniques for maximizing the effective manufacture and distribution of goods. **Mathematics:** Arithmetic, algebra, geometry, calculus, and statistics and their applications.

Agricultural Engineers

- Education/Training Required: Bachelor's degree
- Annual Earnings: $64,890
- Growth: 12.0%
- Annual Job Openings: Fewer than 500
- Self-Employed: 0.0%
- Part-Time: No data available

Apply knowledge of engineering technology and biological science to agricultural problems concerned with power and machinery, electrification, structures, soil and water conservation, and processing of agricultural products. Visit sites to observe environmental problems, to consult with contractors, or to monitor construction activities. Design agricultural machinery components and equipment, using computer-aided design (CAD) technology. Test agricultural machinery and equipment to ensure adequate performance. Design structures for crop storage, animal shelter and loading, and animal and crop processing and supervise their construction. Provide advice on water quality and issues related to pollution management, river control, and ground and surface water resources. Conduct educational programs that provide farmers or farm cooperative members with information that can help them improve agricultural productivity. Discuss plans with clients, contractors, consultants, and other engineers so that they can be evaluated and necessary changes made. Supervise food processing or manufacturing plant operations. Design and supervise environmental and land reclamation projects in agriculture and related industries. Design food processing plants and related mechanical systems. Plan and direct construction of rural electric-power distribution systems and irrigation, drainage, and flood control systems for soil and water conservation. Prepare reports, sketches, working drawings, specifications, proposals, and budgets for proposed sites or systems. Meet with clients, such as district or regional councils, farmers, and developers, to discuss their needs. Design sensing, measuring, and recording devices and other instrumentation used to study plant or animal life.

SKILLS—Most Important: Computer Programming Skills; Science Skills; Equipment/Technology Analysis Skills. **Other Above-Average Skills:** Mathematics Skills; Management Skills; Thought-Processing Skills; Communication Skills; Social Skills.

GOE—Interest Area: 01. Agriculture and Natural Resources. **Work Group:** 01.02. Resource Science/Engineering for Plants, Animals, and the Environment. **Other Jobs in This Group:** Animal Scientists; Conservation Scientists; Environmental Engineers; Foresters; Mining and Geological Engineers, Including Mining Safety Engineers; Petroleum Engineers; Range Managers; Soil and Plant Scientists; Soil and Water Conservationists; Zoologists and Wildlife Biologists. **PERSONALITY TYPE:** Investigative. Investigative occupations frequently involve working with ideas and require an extensive amount of thinking. These occupations can involve searching for facts and figuring out problems mentally.

EDUCATION/TRAINING PROGRAM(S)—Agricultural/Biological Engineering and Bioengineering. **RELATED KNOWLEDGE/COURSES—Food Production:** Techniques and equipment for planting, growing, and harvesting food products (both plant and animal) for consumption, including storage/handling techniques. **Engineering and Technology:** The practical application of engineering science and technology. This includes applying principles, techniques, procedures, and equipment to the design and production of various goods and services. **Design:** Design techniques, tools, and principles involved in production of precision technical plans, blueprints, drawings, and models. **Physics:** Physical principles and laws and their interrelationships and applications to understanding fluid, material, and atmospheric dynamics and mechanical, electrical, atomic, and subatomic structures and processes. **Biology:** Plant and animal organisms and their tissues, cells, functions, interdependencies, and interactions with each other and the environment. **Building and Construction:** The materials, methods, and tools involved in the construction or repair of houses, buildings, or other structures such as highways and roads.

Agricultural Sciences Teachers, Postsecondary

- Education/Training Required: Master's degree
- Annual Earnings: $71,330
- Growth: 32.2%
- Annual Job Openings: 329,000
- Self-Employed: 0.4%
- Part-Time: 27.3%

The job openings listed here are shared with 35 other postsecondary teaching occupations. For a complete list, see the beginning of this section.

Teach courses in the agricultural sciences. Includes teachers of agronomy, dairy sciences, fisheries management, horticultural sciences, poultry sciences, range management, and agricultural soil conservation. Prepare course materials such as syllabi, homework assignments, and handouts. Evaluate and grade students' classwork, laboratory work, assignments, and papers. Keep abreast of developments in their field by reading current literature, talking with colleagues, and participating in professional conferences. Prepare and deliver lectures to undergraduate and/or graduate students on topics such as crop production, plant genetics, and soil chemistry. Initiate, facilitate, and moderate classroom discussions. Conduct research in a particular field of knowledge and publish findings in professional journals, books, and/or electronic media. Supervise laboratory sessions and fieldwork and coordinate laboratory operations. Supervise undergraduate and/or graduate teaching, internship, and research work. Compile, administer, and grade examinations or assign this work to others. Advise students on academic and vocational curricula and on career issues. Plan, evaluate, and revise curricula, course content, and course materials and methods of instruction. Maintain student attendance records, grades, and other required records. Write grant proposals to procure external research funding. Collaborate with colleagues to address teaching and research issues. Maintain regularly scheduled office hours in order to advise and assist students. Participate in student recruitment, registration, and placement activities. Select and obtain materials and supplies such as textbooks and laboratory equipment. Act as advisers to student organizations. Participate in campus and community events. Serve on academic or administrative committees that deal with institutional policies, departmental matters, and academic issues. Provide professional consulting services to government and/or industry. Perform administrative duties such as serving as department head. Compile bibliographies of specialized materials for outside reading assignments.

SKILLS—Most Important: Science Skills; Management Skills; Communication Skills. **Other Above-Average Skills:** Social Skills; Mathematics Skills; Quality Control Skills; Equipment Use/Maintenance Skills.

GOE—Interest Area: 05. Education and Training. **Work Group:** 05.03. Postsecondary and Adult Teaching and Instructing. **Other Jobs in This Group:** Adult Literacy, Remedial Education, and GED Teachers and Instructors; Anthropology and Archeology Teachers, Postsecondary; Architecture Teachers, Postsecondary; Area, Ethnic, and Cultural Studies Teachers, Postsecondary; Art, Drama, and Music Teachers, Postsecondary; Atmospheric, Earth, Marine, and Space Sciences Teachers, Postsecondary; Biological Science Teachers, Postsecondary; Business Teachers, Postsecondary; Chemistry Teachers, Postsecondary; Communications Teachers, Postsecondary; Computer Science Teachers, Postsecondary; Criminal Justice and Law Enforcement Teachers, Postsecondary; Economics Teachers, Postsecondary; Education Teachers, Postsecondary; Engineering Teachers, Postsecondary; English Language and Literature Teachers, Postsecondary; Environmental Science Teachers, Postsecondary; Farm and Home Management Advisors; Foreign Language and Literature Teachers, Postsecondary; Forestry and Conservation Science Teachers, Postsecondary; Geography Teachers, Postsecondary; Graduate Teaching Assistants; Health Specialties Teachers, Postsecondary; History Teachers, Postsecondary; Home Economics Teachers, Postsecondary; Law Teachers, Postsecondary; Library Science Teachers, Postsecondary; Mathematical Science Teachers, Postsecondary; Nursing Instructors and Teachers, Postsecondary; Philosophy and Religion Teachers, Postsecondary; Physics Teachers, Postsecondary; Political Science Teachers, Postsecondary; Psychology Teachers, Postsecondary; Recreation and Fitness Studies Teachers, Postsecondary; Self-Enrichment Education Teachers; Social Work Teachers, Postsecondary; Sociology Teachers, Postsecondary; Vocational Education Teachers, Postsecondary. **PERSONALITY TYPE:** Investigative. Investigative occupations frequently involve working with ideas and require an extensive amount of thinking. These occupations can involve searching for facts and figuring out problems mentally.

EDUCATION/TRAINING PROGRAM(S)—Agriculture, General; Agricultural Business and Management, General; Agribusiness/Agricultural Business Operations; Agricultural Economics; Farm/Farm and Ranch Management; Agricultural/Farm Supplies Retailing and Wholesaling; Agricultural Business and Management, Other; Agricultural Mechanization, General; Agricultural Power Machinery Operation; Agricultural Mechanization, Other; others. **RELATED KNOWLEDGE/COURSES—Biology:** Plant and animal organisms and their tissues, cells, functions, interdependencies, and interactions with each other and the environment. **Education and Training:** Principles and methods for curriculum and training design, teaching and instruction for individuals and groups, and the measurement of training effects. **Food Production:** Techniques and equipment for planting, growing, and harvesting food products (both plant and animal) for consumption, including storage/handling techniques. **Geography:** Principles and methods for describing the features of land, sea, and air masses, including their physical characteristics; locations; interrelationships; and distribution of plant, animal, and human life. **Chemistry:** The chemical composition, structure, and properties of substances and of the chemical processes and transformations that they undergo. This includes uses of chemicals and their danger signs, production techniques, and disposal methods. **English Language:** The structure and content of the English language, including the meaning and spelling of words, rules of composition, and grammar.

Air Traffic Controllers

- ◎ Education/Training Required: Long-term on-the-job training
- ◎ Annual Earnings: $107,590
- ◎ Growth: 14.3%
- ◎ Annual Job Openings: 2,000
- ◎ Self-Employed: 1.8%
- ◎ Part-Time: 1.4%

Control air traffic on and within vicinity of airport and movement of air traffic between altitude sectors and control centers according to established procedures and policies. Authorize, regulate, and control commercial airline flights according to government or company regulations to expedite and ensure flight safety. Issue landing and take-off authorizations and instructions. Monitor and direct the movement of aircraft within an assigned air space and on the ground at airports to minimize delays and maximize safety. Monitor aircraft within a specific airspace, using radar, computer equipment, and visual references. Inform pilots about nearby planes as well as potentially hazardous conditions such as weather, speed and direction of wind, and visibility problems. Provide flight path changes or directions to emergency landing fields for pilots traveling in bad weather or in emergency situations. Alert airport emergency services in cases of emergency and when aircraft are experiencing difficulties. Direct pilots to runways when space is available or direct them to maintain a traffic pattern until there is space for them to land. Transfer control of departing flights to traffic control centers and accept control of arriving flights. Direct ground traffic, including taxiing aircraft, maintenance and baggage vehicles, and airport workers. Determine the timing and procedures for flight vector changes. Maintain radio and telephone contact with adjacent control towers, terminal control units, and other area control centers to coordinate aircraft movement. Contact pilots by radio to provide meteorological, navigational, and other information. Initiate and coordinate searches for missing aircraft. Check conditions and traffic at different altitudes in response to pilots' requests for altitude changes. Relay to control centers such air traffic information as courses, altitudes, and expected arrival times. Compile information about flights from flight plans, pilot reports, radar, and observations. Inspect, adjust, and control radio equipment and airport lights. Conduct pre-flight briefings on weather conditions, suggested routes, altitudes, indications of turbulence, and other flight safety information. Analyze factors such as weather reports, fuel requirements, and maps to determine air routes. Organize flight plans and traffic management plans to prepare for planes about to enter assigned airspace.

SKILLS—Most Important: Equipment Use/Maintenance Skills. **Other Above-Average Skills:** None met the criteria.

GOE—**Interest Area:** 03. Arts and Communication. **Work Group:** 03.10. Communications Technology. **Other Jobs in This Group:** Airfield Operations Specialists; Dispatchers, Except Police, Fire, and Ambulance; Police, Fire, and Ambulance Dispatchers; Telephone Operators. **PERSONALITY TYPE:** Conventional. Conventional occupations frequently involve following set procedures and routines. These occupations can include working with data and details more than with ideas. Usually there is a clear line of authority to follow.

EDUCATION/TRAINING PROGRAM(S)—Air Traffic Controller. **RELATED KNOWLEDGE/COURSES**—**Transportation:** Principles and methods for moving people or goods by air, rail, sea, or road, including the relative costs and benefits. **Physics:** Physical principles and laws and their interrelationships and applications to understanding fluid, material, and atmospheric dynamics and mechanical, electrical, atomic, and subatomic structures and processes. **Telecommunications:** Transmission, broadcasting, switching, control, and operation of telecommunications systems. **Geography:** Principles and methods for describing the features of land, sea, and air masses, including their physical characteristics; locations; interrelationships; and distribution of plant, animal, and human life. **Computers and Electronics:** Circuit boards; processors; chips; electronic equipment; and computer hardware and software, including applications and programming. **Engineering and Technology:** The practical application of engineering science and technology. This includes applying principles, techniques, procedures, and equipment to the design and production of various goods and services.

Aircraft Mechanics and Service Technicians

- Education/Training Required: Postsecondary vocational training
- Annual Earnings: $47,310
- Growth: 13.4%
- Annual Job Openings: 11,000
- Self-Employed: 3.0%
- Part-Time: 1.8%

Diagnose, adjust, repair, or overhaul aircraft engines and assemblies, such as hydraulic and pneumatic systems. Read and interpret maintenance manuals, service bulletins, and other specifications to determine the feasibility and method of repairing or replacing malfunctioning or damaged components. Inspect completed work to certify that maintenance meets standards and that aircraft are ready for operation. Maintain repair logs, documenting all preventive and corrective aircraft maintenance. Conduct routine and special inspections as required by regulations. Examine and inspect aircraft components, including landing gear, hydraulic systems, and de-icers, to locate cracks, breaks, leaks, or other problem. Inspect airframes for wear or other defects. Maintain, repair, and rebuild aircraft structures; functional components; and parts such as wings and fuselage, rigging, hydraulic units, oxygen systems, fuel systems, electrical systems, gaskets, and seals. Measure the tension of control cables. Replace or repair worn, defective, or damaged components, using hand tools, gauges, and testing equipment. Measure parts for wear, using precision instruments. Assemble and install electrical, plumbing, mechanical, hydraulic, and structural components and accessories, using hand tools and power tools. Test operation of engines and other systems, using test equipment such as ignition analyzers, compression checkers, distributor timers, and ammeters. Obtain fuel and oil samples and check them for contamination. Reassemble engines following repair or inspection and re-install engines in aircraft. Read and interpret pilots' descriptions of problems to diagnose causes. Modify aircraft structures, space vehicles, systems, or components, following drawings, schematics, charts, engineering orders, and technical publications. Install and align repaired or replacement parts for subsequent riveting or welding, using clamps and wrenches. Locate and mark dimensions and reference lines on defective or replacement parts, using templates, scribes, compasses, and steel rules. Clean, strip, prime, and sand structural surfaces and materials to prepare them for bonding. Service and maintain aircraft and related apparatus by performing activities such as flushing crankcases, cleaning screens, and lubricating moving parts.

SKILLS—**Most Important:** Equipment Use/Maintenance Skills; Quality Control Skills. **Other Above-Average Skills:** Thought-Processing Skills; Communication Skills; Equipment/Technology Analysis Skills.

GOE—Interest Area: 13. Manufacturing. **Work Group:** 13.14. Vehicle and Facility Mechanical Work. **Other Jobs in This Group:** Aircraft Structure, Surfaces, Rigging, and Systems Assemblers; Automotive Body and Related Repairers; Automotive Glass Installers and Repairers; Automotive Master Mechanics; Automotive Service Technicians and Mechanics; Automotive Specialty Technicians; Bus and Truck Mechanics and Diesel Engine Specialists; Farm Equipment Mechanics; Fiberglass Laminators and Fabricators; Mobile Heavy Equipment Mechanics, Except Engines; Motorboat Mechanics; Motorcycle Mechanics; Outdoor Power Equipment and Other Small Engine Mechanics; Rail Car Repairers; Recreational Vehicle Service Technicians; Tire Repairers and Changers. **PERSONALITY TYPE:** Investigative. Investigative occupations frequently involve working with ideas and require an extensive amount of thinking. These occupations can involve searching for facts and figuring out problems mentally.

EDUCATION/TRAINING PROGRAM(S)—Agricultural Mechanics and Equipment/Machine Technology; Aircraft Powerplant Technology/Technician; Airframe Mechanics and Aircraft Maintenance Technology/Technician. **RELATED KNOWLEDGE/COURSES—Mechanical Devices:** Machines and tools, including their designs, uses, repair, and maintenance. **Design:** Design techniques, tools, and principles involved in production of precision technical plans, blueprints, drawings, and models. **Physics:** Physical principles and laws and their interrelationships and applications to understanding fluid, material, and atmospheric dynamics and mechanical, electrical, atomic, and subatomic structures and processes. **Chemistry:** The chemical composition, structure, and properties of substances and of the chemical processes and transformations that they undergo. This includes uses of chemicals and their danger signs, production techniques, and disposal methods. **Engineering and Technology:** The practical application of engineering science and technology. This includes applying principles, techniques, procedures, and equipment to the design and production of various goods and services. **Transportation:** Principles and methods for moving people or goods by air, rail, sea, or road, including the relative costs and benefits.

Airline Pilots, Copilots, and Flight Engineers

◎ Education/Training Required: Bachelor's degree
◎ Annual Earnings: $138,170
◎ Growth: 17.2%
◎ Annual Job Openings: 7,000
◎ Self-Employed: 2.4%
◎ Part-Time: 14.8%

Pilot and navigate the flight of multi-engine aircraft in regularly scheduled service for the transport of passengers and cargo. Requires Federal Air Transport rating and certification in specific aircraft type used. Use instrumentation to guide flights when visibility is poor. Respond to and report in-flight emergencies and malfunctions. Work as part of a flight team with other crew members, especially during takeoffs and landings. Contact control towers for takeoff clearances, arrival instructions, and other information, using radio equipment. Steer aircraft along planned routes with the assistance of autopilot and flight management computers. Monitor gauges, warning devices, and control panels to verify aircraft performance and to regulate engine speed. Start engines, operate controls, and pilot airplanes to transport passengers, mail, or freight while adhering to flight plans, regulations, and procedures. Inspect aircraft for defects and malfunctions according to pre-flight checklists. Check passenger and cargo distributions and fuel amounts to ensure that weight and balance specifications are met. Monitor engine operation, fuel consumption, and functioning of aircraft systems during flights. Confer with flight dispatchers and weather forecasters to keep abreast of flight conditions. Coordinate flight activities with ground crews and air-traffic control and inform crew members of flight and test procedures. Order changes in fuel supplies, loads, routes, or schedules to ensure safety of flights. Choose routes, altitudes, and speeds that will provide the fastest, safest, and smoothest flights. Direct activities of aircraft crews during flights. Brief crews about flight details such as destinations, duties, and responsibilities. Record in logbooks information such as flight times, distances flown, and fuel consumption. Make announcements regarding flights, using public address systems. File instrument flight plans with air traffic control to ensure that flights are coordinated with other air traffic. Perform minor maintenance work or arrange for major maintenance. Instruct other pilots and student pilots in aircraft operations and the principles of flight. Conduct in-flight tests and evaluations at specified altitudes and in all types of weather to determine the receptivity and other characteristics of equipment and systems.

SKILLS—Most Important: Equipment Use/Maintenance Skills; Science Skills; Thought-Processing Skills. **Other Above-Average Skills:** Social Skills; Communication Skills; Equipment/Technology Analysis Skills.

GOE—Interest Area: 16. Transportation, Distribution, and Logistics. **Work Group:** 16.02. Air Vehicle Operation. **Other Jobs in This Group:** Commercial Pilots. **PERSONALITY TYPE:** Realistic. Realistic occupations frequently involve work activities that include practical, hands-on problems and solutions. They often deal with plants, animals, and real-world materials like wood, tools, and machinery. Many of the occupations require working outside and do not involve a lot of paperwork or working closely with others.

EDUCATION/TRAINING PROGRAM(S)—Airline/Commercial/Professional Pilot and Flight Crew; Flight Instructor. **RELATED KNOWLEDGE/COURSES—Transportation:** Principles and methods for moving people or goods by air, rail, sea, or road, including the relative costs and benefits. **Geography:** Principles and methods for describing the features of land, sea, and air masses, including their physical characteristics; locations; interrelationships; and distribution of plant, animal, and human life. **Public Safety and Security:** Relevant equipment, policies, procedures, and strategies to promote effective local, state, or national security operations for the protection of people, data, property, and institutions. **Psychology:** Human behavior and performance; individual differences in ability, personality, and interests; learning and motivation; psychological research methods; and the assessment and treatment of behavioral and affective disorders. **Physics:** Physical principles and laws and their interrelationships and applications to understanding fluid, material, and atmospheric dynamics and mechanical, electrical, atomic, and subatomic structures and processes. **Law and Government:** Laws, legal codes, court procedures, precedents, government regulations, executive orders, agency rules, and the democratic political process.

Anesthesiologists

- Education/Training Required: First professional degree
- Annual Earnings: More than $145,600
- Growth: 24.0%
- Annual Job Openings: 41,000
- Self-Employed: 11.5%
- Part-Time: 9.6%

The job openings listed here are shared with Family and General Practitioners; Internists, General; Obstetricians and Gynecologists; Pediatricians, General; Psychiatrists; and Surgeons.

Administer anesthetics during surgery or other medical procedures. Administer anesthetic or sedation during medical procedures, using local, intravenous, spinal, or caudal methods. Monitor patient before, during, and after anesthesia and counteract adverse reactions or complications. Provide and maintain life support and airway management and help prepare patients for emergency surgery. Record type and amount of anesthesia and patient condition throughout procedure. Examine patient; obtain medical history; and use diagnostic tests to determine risk during surgical, obstetrical, and other medical procedures. Position patient on operating table to maximize patient comfort and surgical accessibility. Decide when patients have recovered or stabilized enough to be sent to another room or ward or to be sent home following outpatient surgery. Coordinate administration of anesthetics with surgeons during operation. Confer with other medical professionals to determine type and method of anesthetic or sedation to render patient insensible to pain. Coordinate and direct work of nurses, medical technicians, and other health-care providers. Order laboratory tests, X rays, and other diagnostic procedures. Diagnose illnesses, using examinations, tests, and reports. Manage anesthesiological services, coordinating them with other medical activities and formulating plans and procedures. Provide medical care and consultation in many settings, prescribing medication and treatment and referring patients for surgery. Inform students and staff of types and methods of anesthesia administration, signs of complications, and emergency methods to counteract reactions. Schedule and maintain use of surgical suite, including operating, wash-up, and waiting rooms and anesthetic and steriliz-ing equipment. Instruct individuals and groups on ways to preserve health and prevent disease. Conduct medical research to aid in controlling and curing disease, to investigate new medications, and to develop and test new medical techniques.

SKILLS—Most Important: Science Skills; Equipment Use/Maintenance Skills; Thought-Processing Skills. **Other Above-Average Skills:** Social Skills; Equipment/Technology Analysis Skills; Management Skills; Mathematics Skills.

GOE—Interest Area: 08. Health Science. **Work Group:** 08.02. Medicine and Surgery. **Other Jobs in This Group:** Family and General Practitioners; Internists, General; Medical Assistants; Medical Transcriptionists; Obstetricians and Gynecologists; Pediatricians, General; Pharmacists; Pharmacy Aides; Pharmacy Technicians; Physician Assistants; Psychiatrists; Registered Nurses; Surgeons; Surgical Technologists. **PERSONALITY TYPE:** Investigative. Investigative occupations frequently involve working with ideas and require an extensive amount of thinking. These occupations can involve searching for facts and figuring out problems mentally.

EDUCATION/TRAINING PROGRAM(S)—Anesthesiology; Critical Care Anesthesiology. **RELATED KNOWLEDGE/COURSES—Medicine and Dentistry:** The information and techniques needed to diagnose and treat human injuries, diseases, and deformities. This includes symptoms, treatment alternatives, drug properties and interactions, and preventive healthcare measures. **Biology:** Plant and animal organisms and their tissues, cells, functions, interdependencies, and interactions with each other and the environment. **Chemistry:** The chemical composition, structure, and properties of substances and of the chemical processes and transformations that they undergo. This includes uses of chemicals and their danger signs, production techniques, and disposal methods. **Psychology:** Human behavior and performance; individual differences in ability, personality, and interests; learning and motivation; psychological research methods; and the assessment and treatment of behavioral and affective disorders. **Physics:** Physical principles and laws and their interrelationships and applications to understanding fluid, material, and atmospheric dynamics and mechanical, electrical, atomic, and subatomic structures

and processes. **Customer and Personal Service:** Principles and processes for providing customer and personal services. This includes customer needs assessment, meeting of quality standards for services, and evaluation of customer satisfaction.

Anthropology and Archeology Teachers, Postsecondary

- Education/Training Required: Master's degree
- Annual Earnings: $60,710
- Growth: 32.2%
- Annual Job Openings: 329,000
- Self-Employed: 0.4%
- Part-Time: 27.3%

The job openings listed here are shared with 35 other postsecondary teaching occupations. For a complete list, see the beginning of this section.

Teach courses in anthropology or archeology. Conduct research in a particular field of knowledge and publish findings in professional journals, books, and electronic media. Keep abreast of developments in their field by reading current literature, talking with colleagues, and participating in professional conferences. Prepare and deliver lectures to undergraduate and graduate students on topics such as research methods, urban anthropology, and language and culture. Evaluate and grade students' classwork, assignments, and papers. Initiate, facilitate, and moderate classroom discussions. Write grant proposals to procure external research funding. Supervise undergraduate and/or graduate teaching, internship, and research work. Prepare course materials such as syllabi, homework assignments, and handouts. Compile, administer, and grade examinations or assign this work to others. Supervise students' laboratory work or fieldwork. Plan, evaluate, and revise curricula, course content, and course materials and methods of instruction. Advise students on academic and vocational curricula, career issues, and laboratory and field research. Maintain student attendance records, grades, and other required records. Maintain regularly scheduled office hours in order to advise and assist students. Collaborate with colleagues to address teaching and research issues. Compile bibliographies of specialized materials for outside reading assignments. Perform administrative duties such as serving as department head. Select and obtain materials and supplies such as textbooks and laboratory equipment. Serve on academic or administrative committees that deal with institutional policies, departmental matters, and academic issues. Participate in student recruitment, registration, and placement activities. Participate in campus and community events. Provide professional consulting services to government and industry. Act as advisers to student organizations.

SKILLS—Most Important: Science Skills; Communication Skills; Thought-Processing Skills. **Other Above-Average Skills:** Social Skills; Management Skills.

GOE—Interest Area: 05. Education and Training. **Work Group:** 05.03. Postsecondary and Adult Teaching and Instructing. **Other Jobs in This Group:** Adult Literacy, Remedial Education, and GED Teachers and Instructors; Agricultural Sciences Teachers, Postsecondary; Architecture Teachers, Postsecondary; Area, Ethnic, and Cultural Studies Teachers, Postsecondary; Art, Drama, and Music Teachers, Postsecondary; Atmospheric, Earth, Marine, and Space Sciences Teachers, Postsecondary; Biological Science Teachers, Postsecondary; Business Teachers, Postsecondary; Chemistry Teachers, Postsecondary; Communications Teachers, Postsecondary; Computer Science Teachers, Postsecondary; Criminal Justice and Law Enforcement Teachers, Postsecondary; Economics Teachers, Postsecondary; Education Teachers, Postsecondary; Engineering Teachers, Postsecondary; English Language and Literature Teachers, Postsecondary; Environmental Science Teachers, Postsecondary; Farm and Home Management Advisors; Foreign Language and Literature Teachers, Postsecondary; Forestry and Conservation Science Teachers, Postsecondary; Geography Teachers, Postsecondary; Graduate Teaching Assistants; Health Specialties Teachers, Postsecondary; History Teachers, Postsecondary; Home Economics Teachers, Postsecondary; Law Teachers, Postsecondary; Library Science Teachers, Postsecondary; Mathematical Science Teachers, Postsecondary; Nursing Instructors and Teachers, Postsecondary; Philosophy and Religion Teachers, Postsecondary; Physics Teachers, Postsecondary; Political Science Teachers, Postsecondary; Psychology Teachers, Postsecondary; Recreation and Fitness Studies

Teachers, Postsecondary; Self-Enrichment Education Teachers; Social Work Teachers, Postsecondary; Sociology Teachers, Postsecondary; Vocational Education Teachers, Postsecondary. **PERSONALITY TYPE:** Social. Social occupations frequently involve working with, communicating with, and teaching people. These occupations often involve helping or providing service to others.

EDUCATION/TRAINING PROGRAM(S)—Social Science Teacher Education; Anthropology; Physical Anthropology; Archeology. **RELATED KNOWLEDGE/COURSES—Sociology and Anthropology:** Group behavior and dynamics, societal trends and influences, human migrations, ethnicity, and cultures and their history and origins. **History and Archeology:** Historical events and their causes, indicators, and effects on civilizations and cultures. **Geography:** Principles and methods for describing the features of land, sea, and air masses, including their physical characteristics; locations; interrelationships; and distribution of plant, animal, and human life. **Foreign Language:** The structure and content of a foreign (non-English) language, including the meaning and spelling of words, rules of composition and grammar, and pronunciation. **Philosophy and Theology:** Different philosophical systems and religions. This includes their basic principles, values, ethics, ways of thinking, customs, practices, and impact on human culture. **Education and Training:** Principles and methods for curriculum and training design, teaching and instruction for individuals and groups, and the measurement of training effects.

Appraisers, Real Estate

- Education/Training Required: Postsecondary vocational training
- Annual Earnings: $43,440
- Growth: 22.8%
- Annual Job Openings: 9,000
- Self-Employed: 37.2%
- Part-Time: 10.9%

The job openings listed here are shared with Assessors.

Appraise real property to determine its value for purchase, sales, investment, mortgage, or loan purposes.

Prepare written reports that estimate property values, outline methods by which the estimations were made, and meet appraisal standards. Compute final estimation of property values, taking into account such factors as depreciation, replacement costs, value comparisons of similar properties, and income potential. Search public records for transactions such as sales, leases, and assessments. Inspect properties to evaluate construction, condition, special features, and functional design and to take property measurements. Photograph interiors and exteriors of properties in order to assist in estimating property value, substantiate findings, and complete appraisal reports. Evaluate land and neighborhoods where properties are situated, considering locations and trends or impending changes that could influence future values. Obtain county land values and sales information about nearby properties in order to aid in establishment of property values. Verify legal descriptions of properties by comparing them to county records. Check building codes and zoning bylaws in order to determine any effects on the properties being appraised. Estimate building replacement costs, using building valuation manuals and professional cost estimators. Examine income records and operating costs of income properties. Interview persons familiar with properties and immediate surroundings, such as contractors, homeowners, and realtors, in order to obtain pertinent information. Examine the type and location of nearby services such as shopping centers, schools, parks, and other neighborhood features in order to evaluate their impact on property values. Draw land diagrams that will be used in appraisal reports to support findings. Testify in court as to the value of a piece of real estate property.

SKILLS—Most Important: Mathematics Skills; Communication Skills; Thought-Processing Skills. **Other Above-Average Skills:** Equipment/Technology Analysis Skills; Management Skills.

GOE—Interest Area: 06. Finance and Insurance. **Work Group:** 06.02. Finance/Insurance Investigation and Analysis. **Other Jobs in This Group:** Appraisers and Assessors of Real Estate; Assessors; Claims Adjusters, Examiners, and Investigators; Claims Examiners, Property and Casualty Insurance; Cost Estimators; Credit Analysts; Financial Analysts; Insurance Adjusters, Examiners, and Investigators; Insurance Appraisers, Auto Damage; Insurance Underwriters; Loan Counselors; Loan Officers; Market Research Analysts;

Survey Researchers. **PERSONALITY TYPE:** Enterprising. Enterprising occupations frequently involve starting up and carrying out projects. These occupations can involve leading people and making many decisions. They sometimes require risk taking and often deal with business.

EDUCATION/TRAINING PROGRAM(S)—Real Estate. **RELATED KNOWLEDGE/COURSES— Building and Construction:** The materials, methods, and tools involved in the construction or repair of houses, buildings, or other structures such as highways and roads. **Economics and Accounting:** Economic and accounting principles and practices, the financial markets, banking, and the analysis and reporting of financial data. **Geography:** Principles and methods for describing the features of land, sea, and air masses, including their physical characteristics; locations; interrelationships; and distribution of plant, animal, and human life. **Clerical Practices:** Administrative and clerical procedures and systems such as word processing, managing files and records, stenography and transcription, designing forms, and other office procedures and terminology. **Customer and Personal Service:** Principles and processes for providing customer and personal services. This includes customer needs assessment, meeting of quality standards for services, and evaluation of customer satisfaction. **Law and Government:** Laws, legal codes, court procedures, precedents, government regulations, executive orders, agency rules, and the democratic political process.

Architects, Except Landscape and Naval

- Education/Training Required: Bachelor's degree
- Annual Earnings: $62,850
- Growth: 17.3%
- Annual Job Openings: 7,000
- Self-Employed: 20.1%
- Part-Time: 9.1%

Plan and design structures, such as private residences, office buildings, theaters, factories, and other structur-

al **property**. Prepare information regarding design, structure specifications, materials, color, equipment, estimated costs, or construction time. Consult with client to determine functional and spatial requirements of structure. Direct activities of workers engaged in preparing drawings and specification documents. Plan layout of project. Prepare contract documents for building contractors. Prepare scale drawings. Integrate engineering element into unified design. Conduct periodic on-site observation of work during construction to monitor compliance with plans. Administer construction contracts. Represent client in obtaining bids and awarding construction contracts. Prepare operating and maintenance manuals, studies, and reports.

SKILLS—Most Important: Management Skills; Equipment/Technology Analysis Skills; Social Skills. **Other Above-Average Skills:** Quality Control Skills; Thought-Processing Skills; Mathematics Skills.

GOE—Interest Area: 02. Architecture and Construction. **Work Group:** 02.02. Architectural Design. **Other Jobs in This Group:** Landscape Architects. **PERSONALITY TYPE:** Artistic. Artistic occupations frequently involve working with forms, designs, and patterns. They often require self-expression, and the work can be done without following a clear set of rules.

EDUCATION/TRAINING PROGRAM(S)—Architecture (BArch, BA/BS, MArch, MA/MS, PhD); Environmental Design/Architecture; Architectural History and Criticism, General; Architecture and Related Services, Other. **RELATED KNOWLEDGE/COURSES—Building and Construction:** The materials, methods, and tools involved in the construction or repair of houses, buildings, or other structures such as highways and roads. **Design:** Design techniques, tools, and principles involved in production of precision technical plans, blueprints, drawings, and models. **Engineering and Technology:** The practical application of engineering science and technology. This includes applying principles, techniques, procedures, and equipment to the design and production of various goods and services. **Fine Arts:** The theory and techniques required to compose, produce, and perform works of music, dance, visual arts, drama, and sculpture. **Law and Government:** Laws, legal codes, court procedures, precedents, government regulations, executive orders, agency rules, and the democratic political process. **Physics:** Physical principles and laws and their interrela-

tionships and applications to understanding fluid, material, and atmospheric dynamics and mechanical, electrical, atomic, and subatomic structures and processes.

Architecture Teachers, Postsecondary

- ◎ Education/Training Required: Master's degree
- ◎ Annual Earnings: $62,270
- ◎ Growth: 32.2%
- ◎ Annual Job Openings: 329,000
- ◎ Self-Employed: 0.4%
- ◎ Part-Time: 27.3%

The job openings listed here are shared with 35 other postsecondary teaching occupations. For a complete list, see the beginning of this section.

Teach courses in architecture and architectural design, such as architectural environmental design, interior architecture/design, and landscape architecture. Evaluate and grade students' work, including work performed in design studios. Prepare and deliver lectures to undergraduate and/or graduate students on topics such as architectural design methods, aesthetics and design, and structures and materials. Prepare course materials such as syllabi, homework assignments, and handouts. Initiate, facilitate, and moderate classroom discussions. Plan, evaluate, and revise curricula, course content, and course materials and methods of instruction. Keep abreast of developments in their field by reading current literature, talking with colleagues, and participating in professional conferences. Maintain student attendance records, grades, and other required records. Maintain regularly scheduled office hours to advise and assist students. Compile, administer, and grade examinations or assign this work to others. Conduct research in a particular field of knowledge and publish findings in professional journals, books, and/or electronic media. Supervise undergraduate and/or graduate teaching, internship, and research work. Advise students on academic and vocational curricula and on career issues. Collaborate with colleagues to address teaching and research issues. Compile bibliographies of specialized materials for outside reading assignments. Serve on academic or administrative committees that deal with institutional policies, departmental matters, and academic issues. Participate in student recruitment, registration, and placement activities. Select and obtain materials and supplies such as textbooks and laboratory equipment. Write grant proposals to procure external research funding. Provide professional consulting services to government and/or industry. Perform administrative duties such as serving as department head. Act as advisers to student organizations. Participate in campus and community events.

SKILLS—Most Important: Equipment/Technology Analysis Skills; Communication Skills; Social Skills. **Other Above-Average Skills:** Thought-Processing Skills; Science Skills; Quality Control Skills.

GOE—Interest Area: 05. Education and Training. **Work Group:** 05.03. Postsecondary and Adult Teaching and Instructing. **Other Jobs in This Group:** Adult Literacy, Remedial Education, and GED Teachers and Instructors; Agricultural Sciences Teachers, Postsecondary; Anthropology and Archeology Teachers, Postsecondary; Area, Ethnic, and Cultural Studies Teachers, Postsecondary; Art, Drama, and Music Teachers, Postsecondary; Atmospheric, Earth, Marine, and Space Sciences Teachers, Postsecondary; Biological Science Teachers, Postsecondary; Business Teachers, Postsecondary; Chemistry Teachers, Postsecondary; Communications Teachers, Postsecondary; Computer Science Teachers, Postsecondary; Criminal Justice and Law Enforcement Teachers, Postsecondary; Economics Teachers, Postsecondary; Education Teachers, Postsecondary; Engineering Teachers, Postsecondary; English Language and Literature Teachers, Postsecondary; Environmental Science Teachers, Postsecondary; Farm and Home Management Advisors; Foreign Language and Literature Teachers, Postsecondary; Forestry and Conservation Science Teachers, Postsecondary; Geography Teachers, Postsecondary; Graduate Teaching Assistants; Health Specialties Teachers, Postsecondary; History Teachers, Postsecondary; Home Economics Teachers, Postsecondary; Law Teachers, Postsecondary; Library Science Teachers, Postsecondary; Mathematical Science Teachers, Postsecondary; Nursing Instructors and Teachers, Postsecondary; Philosophy and Religion Teachers, Postsecondary; Physics Teachers, Postsecondary; Political Science Teachers, Postsecondary; Psychology Teachers, Postsecondary; Recreation and Fitness Studies Teachers, Postsecondary; Self-Enrichment Education Teachers; Social Work Teachers,

Postsecondary; Sociology Teachers, Postsecondary; Vocational Education Teachers, Postsecondary. **PERSONALITY TYPE:** No data available.

EDUCATION/TRAINING PROGRAM(S)—Architecture (BArch, BA/BS, MArch, MA/MS, PhD); City/Urban, Community, and Regional Planning; Environmental Design/Architecture; Interior Architecture; Landscape Architecture (BS, BSLA, BLA, MSLA, MLA, PhD); Teacher Education and Professional Development, Specific Subject Areas, Other; Architectural Engineering. **RELATED KNOWLEDGE/COURSES—Fine Arts:** The theory and techniques required to compose, produce, and perform works of music, dance, visual arts, drama, and sculpture. **Design:** Design techniques, tools, and principles involved in production of precision technical plans, blueprints, drawings, and models. **Building and Construction:** The materials, methods, and tools involved in the construction or repair of houses, buildings, or other structures such as highways and roads. **History and Archeology:** Historical events and their causes, indicators, and effects on civilizations and cultures. **Philosophy and Theology:** Different philosophical systems and religions. This includes their basic principles, values, ethics, ways of thinking, customs, practices, and impact on human culture. **Education and Training:** Principles and methods for curriculum and training design, teaching and instruction for individuals and groups, and the measurement of training effects.

Archivists

- Education/Training Required: Master's degree
- Annual Earnings: $37,420
- Growth: 13.4%
- Annual Job Openings: 1,000
- Self-Employed: 6.5%
- Part-Time: 23.4%

Appraise, edit, and direct safekeeping of permanent records and historically valuable documents. Participate in research activities based on archival materials. Create and maintain accessible, retrievable computer archives and databases, incorporating current advances in electric information storage technology.

Organize archival records and develop classification systems to facilitate access to archival materials. Authenticate and appraise historical documents and archival materials. Provide reference services and assistance for users needing archival materials. Direct activities of workers who assist in arranging, cataloguing, exhibiting, and maintaining collections of valuable materials. Prepare archival records, such as document descriptions, to allow easy access to information. Preserve records, documents, and objects, copying records to film, videotape, audiotape, disk, or computer formats as necessary. Establish and administer policy guidelines concerning public access and use of materials. Locate new materials and direct their acquisition and display. Research and record the origins and historical significance of archival materials. Specialize in an area of history or technology, researching topics or items relevant to collections to determine what should be retained or acquired. Coordinate educational and public outreach programs such as tours, workshops, lectures, and classes. Select and edit documents for publication and display, applying knowledge of subject, literary expression, and presentation techniques.

SKILLS—Most Important: Computer Programming Skills; Quality Control Skills; Communication Skills. **Other Above-Average Skills:** Management Skills; Thought-Processing Skills.

GOE—Interest Area: 05. Education and Training. **Work Group:** 05.05. Archival and Museum Services. **Other Jobs in This Group:** Audio-Visual Collections Specialists; Curators; Museum Technicians and Conservators. **PERSONALITY TYPE:** Investigative. Investigative occupations frequently involve working with ideas and require an extensive amount of thinking. These occupations can involve searching for facts and figuring out problems mentally.

EDUCATION/TRAINING PROGRAM(S)—Historic Preservation and Conservation; Cultural Resource Management and Policy Analysis; Historic Preservation and Conservation, Other; Museology/Museum Studies; Art History, Criticism, and Conservation; Public/Applied History and Archival Administration. **RELATED KNOWLEDGE/COURSES—Clerical Practices:** Administrative and clerical procedures and systems such as word processing, managing files and records, stenography and transcription, designing forms, and other office procedures and terminology. **History and**

Archeology: Historical events and their causes, indicators, and effects on civilizations and cultures. **Computers and Electronics:** Circuit boards; processors; chips; electronic equipment; and computer hardware and software, including applications and programming. **English Language:** The structure and content of the English language, including the meaning and spelling of words, rules of composition, and grammar. **Customer and Personal Service:** Principles and processes for providing customer and personal services. This includes customer needs assessment, meeting of quality standards for services, and evaluation of customer satisfaction. **Administration and Management:** Business and management principles involved in strategic planning, resource allocation, human resources modeling, leadership technique, production methods, and coordination of people and resources.

Area, Ethnic, and Cultural Studies Teachers, Postsecondary

- Education/Training Required: Master's degree
- Annual Earnings: $55,610
- Growth: 32.2%
- Annual Job Openings: 329,000
- Self-Employed: 0.4%
- Part-Time: 27.3%

The job openings listed here are shared with 35 other postsecondary teaching occupations. For a complete list, see the beginning of this section.

Teach courses pertaining to the culture and development of an area (e.g., Latin America), an ethnic group, or any other group (e.g., women's studies, urban affairs). Keep abreast of developments in their field by reading current literature, talking with colleagues, and participating in professional conferences. Conduct research in a particular field of knowledge and publish findings in professional journals, books, and/or electronic media. Evaluate and grade students' classwork, assignments, and papers. Prepare course materials such as syllabi, homework assignments, and handouts.

Prepare and deliver lectures to undergraduate and/or graduate students on topics such as race and ethnic relations, gender studies, and cross-cultural perspectives. Initiate, facilitate, and moderate classroom discussions. Compile, administer, and grade examinations or assign this work to others. Maintain regularly scheduled office hours in order to advise and assist students. Plan, evaluate, and revise curricula, course content, and course materials and methods of instruction. Maintain student attendance records, grades, and other required records. Advise students on academic and vocational curricula and on career issues. Supervise undergraduate and/or graduate teaching, internship, and research work. Select and obtain materials and supplies such as textbooks. Collaborate with colleagues to address teaching and research issues. Serve on academic or administrative committees that deal with institutional policies, departmental matters, and academic issues. Compile bibliographies of specialized materials for outside reading assignments. Write grant proposals to procure external research funding. Participate in campus and community events. Participate in student recruitment, registration, and placement activities. Act as advisers to student organizations. Incorporate experiential/site visit components into courses. Perform administrative duties such as serving as department head. Provide professional consulting services to government and/or industry.

SKILLS—Most Important: Communication Skills; Social Skills; Thought-Processing Skills. **Other Above-Average Skills:** Management Skills; Equipment/Technology Analysis Skills.

GOE—Interest Area: 05. Education and Training. **Work Group:** 05.03. Postsecondary and Adult Teaching and Instructing. **Other Jobs in This Group:** Adult Literacy, Remedial Education, and GED Teachers and Instructors; Agricultural Sciences Teachers, Postsecondary; Anthropology and Archeology Teachers, Postsecondary; Architecture Teachers, Postsecondary; Art, Drama, and Music Teachers, Postsecondary; Atmospheric, Earth, Marine, and Space Sciences Teachers, Postsecondary; Biological Science Teachers, Postsecondary; Business Teachers, Postsecondary; Chemistry Teachers, Postsecondary; Communications Teachers, Postsecondary; Computer Science Teachers, Postsecondary; Criminal Justice and Law Enforcement Teachers, Postsecondary; Economics Teachers, Postsecondary; Education Teachers, Postsecondary; Engineering Teachers, Postsecondary; English Language and Literature Teachers, Postsecondary; Environmental Science Teachers, Postsecondary; Farm and Home Management Advisors; Foreign Language and Literature Teachers, Postsecondary; Forestry and Conservation Science Teachers, Postsecondary; Geography Teachers, Postsecondary; Graduate Teaching Assistants; Health Specialties Teachers, Postsecondary; History Teachers, Postsecondary; Home Economics Teachers, Postsecondary; Law Teachers, Postsecondary; Library Science Teachers, Postsecondary; Mathematical Science Teachers, Postsecondary; Nursing Instructors and Teachers, Postsecondary; Philosophy and Religion Teachers, Postsecondary; Physics Teachers, Postsecondary; Political Science Teachers, Postsecondary; Psychology Teachers, Postsecondary; Recreation and Fitness Studies Teachers, Postsecondary; Self-Enrichment Education Teachers; Social Work Teachers, Postsecondary; Sociology Teachers, Postsecondary; Vocational Education Teachers, Postsecondary. **PERSONALITY TYPE:** Social. Social occupations frequently involve working with, communicating with, and teaching people. These occupations often involve helping or providing service to others.

EDUCATION/TRAINING PROGRAM(S)—African Studies; American/United States Studies/Civilization; Asian Studies/Civilization; East Asian Studies; Central/Middle and Eastern European Studies; European Studies/Civilization; Latin American Studies; Near and Middle Eastern Studies; Pacific Area/Pacific Rim Studies; Russian Studies; Scandinavian Studies; South Asian Studies; Southeast Asian Studies; Western European Studies; others. **RELATED KNOWLEDGE/COURSES—History and Archeology:** Historical events and their causes, indicators, and effects on civilizations and cultures. **Sociology and Anthropology:** Group behavior and dynamics, societal trends and influences, human migrations, ethnicity, and cultures and their history and origins. **Foreign Language:** The structure and content of a foreign (non-English) language, including the meaning and spelling of words, rules of composition and grammar, and pronunciation. **Philosophy and Theology:** Different philosophical systems and religions. This includes their basic principles, values, ethics, ways of thinking, customs, practices, and impact on human culture. **Education and Training:** Principles and methods for curriculum and training design, teaching and instruction for individuals and groups, and the measurement of training effects.

Geography: Principles and methods for describing the features of land, sea, and air masses, including their physical characteristics; locations; interrelationships; and distribution of plant, animal, and human life.

Art Directors

- ◎ Education/Training Required: Work experience plus degree
- ◎ Annual Earnings: $63,950
- ◎ Growth: 11.5%
- ◎ Annual Job Openings: 10,000
- ◎ Self-Employed: 55.8%
- ◎ Part-Time: 30.9%

Formulate design concepts and presentation approaches and direct workers engaged in art work, layout design, and copy writing for visual communications media, such as magazines, books, newspapers, and packaging. Formulate basic layout design or presentation approach and specify material details, such as style and size of type, photographs, graphics, animation, video, and sound. Review and approve proofs of printed copy and art and copy materials developed by staff members. Manage own accounts and projects, working within budget and scheduling requirements. Confer with creative, art, copy-writing, or production department heads to discuss client requirements and presentation concepts and to coordinate creative activities. Present final layouts to clients for approval. Confer with clients to determine objectives; budget; background information; and presentation approaches, styles, and techniques. Hire, train, and direct staff members who develop design concepts into art layouts or who prepare layouts for printing. Work with creative directors to develop design solutions. Review illustrative material to determine if it conforms to standards and specifications. Attend photo shoots and printing sessions to ensure that the products needed are obtained. Create custom illustrations or other graphic elements. Mark up, paste, and complete layouts and write typography instructions to prepare materials for typesetting or printing. Negotiate with printers and estimators to determine what services will be performed. Conceptualize and help design interfaces for multimedia games, products, and devices. Prepare detailed storyboards showing sequence and timing of story development for television production.

SKILLS—Most Important: Social Skills; Management Skills; Equipment/Technology Analysis Skills. **Other Above-Average Skills:** Communication Skills; Thought-Processing Skills.

GOE—Interest Area: 03. Arts and Communication. **Work Group:** 03.01. Managerial Work in Arts and Communication. **Other Jobs in This Group:** Agents and Business Managers of Artists, Performers, and Athletes; Producers; Producers and Directors; Program Directors; Public Relations Managers; Technical Directors/Managers. **PERSONALITY TYPE:** Artistic. Artistic occupations frequently involve working with forms, designs, and patterns. They often require self-expression, and the work can be done without following a clear set of rules.

EDUCATION/TRAINING PROGRAM(S)—Graphic Design; Intermedia/Multimedia. **RELATED KNOWLEDGE/COURSES—Design:** Design techniques, tools, and principles involved in production of precision technical plans, blueprints, drawings, and models. **Fine Arts:** The theory and techniques required to compose, produce, and perform works of music, dance, visual arts, drama, and sculpture. **Communications and Media:** Media production, communication, and dissemination techniques and methods. This includes alternative ways to inform and entertain via written, oral, and visual media. **Computers and Electronics:** Circuit boards; processors; chips; electronic equipment; and computer hardware and software, including applications and programming. **Production and Processing:** Raw materials, production processes, quality control, costs, and other techniques for maximizing the effective manufacture and distribution of goods. **Education and Training:** Principles and methods for curriculum and training design, teaching and instruction for individuals and groups, and the measurement of training effects.

Art, Drama, and Music Teachers, Postsecondary

- ◎ Education/Training Required: Master's degree
- ◎ Annual Earnings: $51,240
- ◎ Growth: 32.2%
- ◎ Annual Job Openings: 329,000
- ◎ Self-Employed: 0.4%
- ◎ Part-Time: 27.3%

The job openings listed here are shared with 35 other postsecondary teaching occupations. For a complete list, see the beginning of this section.

Teach courses in drama; music; and the arts, including fine and applied art, such as painting and sculpture, or design and crafts. Evaluate and grade students' class-work, performances, projects, assignments, and papers. Explain and demonstrate artistic techniques. Prepare students for performances, exams, or assessments. Prepare and deliver lectures to undergraduate or graduate students on topics such as acting techniques, fundamentals of music, and art history. Organize performance groups and direct their rehearsals. Prepare course materials such as syllabi, homework assignments, and handouts. Initiate, facilitate, and moderate classroom discussions. Keep abreast of developments in their field by reading current literature, talking with colleagues, and participating in professional conferences. Advise students on academic and vocational curricula and on career issues. Maintain student attendance records, grades, and other required records. Conduct research in a particular field of knowledge and publish findings in professional journals, books, or electronic media. Supervise undergraduate and/or graduate teaching, internship, and research work. Plan, evaluate, and revise curricula, course content, and course materials and methods of instruction. Maintain regularly scheduled office hours to advise and assist students. Compile, administer, and grade examinations or assign this work to others. Participate in student recruitment, registration, and placement activities. Select and obtain materials and supplies such as textbooks and performance pieces. Collaborate with colleagues to address teaching and research issues. Serve on academic or administrative committees that deal with institutional policies, departmental matters, and academic issues. Participate in cam-pus and community events. Keep students informed of community events such as plays and concerts. Compile bibliographies of specialized materials for outside reading assignments. Display students' work in schools, galleries, and exhibitions. Perform administrative duties such as serving as department head. Act as advisers to student organizations. Write grant proposals to procure external research funding. Provide professional consulting services to government or industry.

SKILLS—Most Important: Communication Skills; Social Skills; Thought-Processing Skills. **Other Above-Average Skills:** Management Skills.

GOE—Interest Area: 05. Education and Training. **Work Group:** 05.03. Postsecondary and Adult Teaching and Instructing. **Other Jobs in This Group:** Adult Literacy, Remedial Education, and GED Teachers and Instructors; Agricultural Sciences Teachers, Postsecondary; Anthropology and Archeology Teachers, Postsecondary; Architecture Teachers, Postsecondary; Area, Ethnic, and Cultural Studies Teachers, Postsecondary; Atmospheric, Earth, Marine, and Space Sciences Teachers, Postsecondary; Biological Science Teachers, Postsecondary; Business Teachers, Postsecondary; Chemistry Teachers, Postsecondary; Communications Teachers, Postsecondary; Computer Science Teachers, Postsecondary; Criminal Justice and Law Enforcement Teachers, Postsecondary; Economics Teachers, Postsecondary; Education Teachers, Postsecondary; Engineering Teachers, Postsecondary; English Language and Literature Teachers, Postsecondary; Environmental Science Teachers, Postsecondary; Farm and Home Management Advisors; Foreign Language and Literature Teachers, Postsecondary; Forestry and Conservation Science Teachers, Postsecondary; Geography Teachers, Postsecondary; Graduate Teaching Assistants; Health Specialties Teachers, Postsecondary; History Teachers, Postsecondary; Home Economics Teachers, Postsecondary; Law Teachers, Postsecondary; Library Science Teachers, Postsecondary; Mathematical Science Teachers, Postsecondary; Nursing Instructors and Teachers, Postsecondary; Philosophy and Religion Teachers, Postsecondary; Physics Teachers, Postsecondary; Political Science Teachers, Postsecondary; Psychology Teachers, Postsecondary; Recreation and Fitness Studies Teachers, Postsecondary; Self-Enrichment Education Teachers; Social Work Teachers, Postsecondary; Sociology Teachers, Postsecondary; Vocational Education Teachers, Postsecondary. **PERSONALITY TYPE:** Artistic. Artistic occupations frequently involve working with forms, designs, and patterns. They often require self-expression, and the work can be done without following a clear set of rules.

EDUCATION/TRAINING PROGRAM(S)—Visual and Performing Arts, General; Crafts/Craft Design, Folk Art, and Artisanry; Dance, General; Design and Visual Communications, General; Industrial Design; Commercial Photography; Fashion/Apparel Design; Interior Design; Graphic Design; Design and Applied Arts, Other; Drama and Dramatics/Theatre Arts, General; Technical Theatre/Theatre Design and Technology; Playwriting and Screenwriting; others. RELATED KNOWLEDGE/COURSES—Fine Arts: The theory and techniques required to compose, produce, and perform works of music, dance, visual arts, drama, and sculpture. History and Archeology: Historical events and their causes, indicators, and effects on civilizations and cultures. Philosophy and Theology: Different philosophical systems and religions. This includes their basic principles, values, ethics, ways of thinking, customs, practices, and impact on human culture. Education and Training: Principles and methods for curriculum and training design, teaching and instruction for individuals and groups, and the measurement of training effects. Communications and Media: Media production, communication, and dissemination techniques and methods. This includes alternative ways to inform and entertain via written, oral, and visual media. English Language: The structure and content of the English language, including the meaning and spelling of words, rules of composition, and grammar.

Assessors

- ⑤ Education/Training Required: Postsecondary vocational training
- ⑤ Annual Earnings: $43,440
- ⑤ Growth: 22.8%
- ⑤ Annual Job Openings: 9,000
- ⑤ Self-Employed: 37.2%
- ⑤ Part-Time: 10.9%

The job openings listed here are shared with Appraisers, Real Estate.

Appraise real and personal property to determine its fair value. May assess taxes in accordance with prescribed schedules. Determine taxability and value of properties, using methods such as field inspection, structural measurement, calculation, sales analysis, market trend studies, and income and expense analysis. Inspect new construction and major improvements to existing structures to determine values. Explain assessed values to property owners and defend appealed assessments at public hearings. Inspect properties, considering factors such as market value, location, and building or replacement costs to determine appraisal value. Prepare and maintain current data on each parcel assessed, including maps of boundaries, inventories of land and structures, property characteristics, and any applicable exemptions. Identify the ownership of each piece of taxable property. Conduct regular reviews of property within jurisdictions to determine changes in property due to construction or demolition. Complete and maintain assessment rolls that show the assessed values and status of all property in a municipality. Issue notices of assessments and taxes. Review information about transfers of property to ensure its accuracy, checking basic information on buyers, sellers, and sales prices and making corrections as necessary. Maintain familiarity with aspects of local real estate markets. Analyze trends in sales prices, construction costs, and rents to assess property values or determine the accuracy of assessments. Approve applications for property tax exemptions or deductions. Establish uniform and equitable systems for assessing all classes and kinds of property. Write and submit appraisal and tax reports for public record. Serve on assessment review boards. Hire staff members. Provide sales analyses to be used for equalization of school aid. Calculate tax bills for properties by multiplying assessed values by jurisdiction tax rates.

SKILLS—Most Important: Mathematics Skills; Communication Skills; Social Skills. Other Above-Average Skills: Management Skills; Thought-Processing Skills.

GOE—Interest Area: 06. Finance and Insurance. Work Group: 06.02. Finance/Insurance Investigation and Analysis. Other Jobs in This Group: Appraisers and Assessors of Real Estate; Appraisers, Real Estate; Claims Adjusters, Examiners, and Investigators; Claims Examiners, Property and Casualty Insurance; Cost Estimators; Credit Analysts; Financial Analysts;

Insurance Adjusters, Examiners, and Investigators; Insurance Appraisers, Auto Damage; Insurance Underwriters; Loan Counselors; Loan Officers; Market Research Analysts; Survey Researchers. **PERSONALITY TYPE:** Conventional. Conventional occupations frequently involve following set procedures and routines. These occupations can include working with data and details more than with ideas. Usually there is a clear line of authority to follow.

EDUCATION/TRAINING PROGRAM(S)—Real Estate. **RELATED KNOWLEDGE/COURSES—Building and Construction:** The materials, methods, and tools involved in the construction or repair of houses, buildings, or other structures such as highways and roads. **Clerical Practices:** Administrative and clerical procedures and systems such as word processing, managing files and records, stenography and transcription, designing forms, and other office procedures and terminology. **Law and Government:** Laws, legal codes, court procedures, precedents, government regulations, executive orders, agency rules, and the democratic political process. **Mathematics:** Arithmetic, algebra, geometry, calculus, and statistics and their applications. **Customer and Personal Service:** Principles and processes for providing customer and personal services. This includes customer needs assessment, meeting of quality standards for services, and evaluation of customer satisfaction. **Computers and Electronics:** Circuit boards; processors; chips; electronic equipment; and computer hardware and software, including applications and programming.

Astronomers

- ⊚ Education/Training Required: Doctoral degree
- ⊚ Annual Earnings: $104,670
- ⊚ Growth: 10.4%
- ⊚ Annual Job Openings: Fewer than 500
- ⊚ Self-Employed: 0.0%
- ⊚ Part-Time: 8.0%

Observe, research, and interpret celestial and astronomical phenomena to increase basic knowledge and apply such information to practical problems. Study celestial phenomena, using a variety of ground-based and space-borne telescopes and scientific instruments. Analyze research data to determine its significance, using computers. Present research findings at scientific conferences and in papers written for scientific journals. Measure radio, infrared, gamma, and X-ray emissions from extraterrestrial sources. Develop theories based on personal observations or on observations and theories of other astronomers. Raise funds for scientific research. Collaborate with other astronomers to carry out research projects. Develop instrumentation and software for astronomical observation and analysis. Teach astronomy or astrophysics. Develop and modify astronomy-related programs for public presentation. Calculate orbits and determine sizes, shapes, brightness, and motions of different celestial bodies. Direct the operations of a planetarium.

SKILLS—Most Important: Science Skills; Computer Programming Skills; Mathematics Skills. **Other Above-Average Skills:** Equipment/Technology Analysis Skills; Thought-Processing Skills; Management Skills; Equipment Use/Maintenance Skills; Social Skills.

GOE—Interest Area: 15. Scientific Research, Engineering, and Mathematics. **Work Group:** 15.02. Physical Sciences. **Other Jobs in This Group:** Atmospheric and Space Scientists; Chemists; Geographers; Geoscientists, Except Hydrologists and Geographers; Hydrologists; Materials Scientists; Physicists. **PERSONALITY TYPE:** Investigative. Investigative occupations frequently involve working with ideas and require an extensive amount of thinking. These occupations can involve searching for facts and figuring out problems mentally.

EDUCATION/TRAINING PROGRAM(S)—Astronomy; Astrophysics; Planetary Astronomy and Science; Astronomy and Astrophysics, Other. **RELATED KNOWLEDGE/COURSES—Physics:** Physical principles and laws and their interrelationships and applications to understanding fluid, material, and atmospheric dynamics and mechanical, electrical, atomic, and subatomic structures and processes. **Mathematics:** Arithmetic, algebra, geometry, calculus, and statistics and their applications. **Engineering and Technology:** The practical application of engineering science and technology. This includes applying principles, techniques, procedures, and equipment to the design and production of various goods and services. **Chemistry:** The chemical composition, structure, and properties of substances and of the chemical processes and transformations that they undergo. This includes uses of chemicals and their danger signs, production techniques, and disposal methods. **Computers and Electronics:** Circuit boards; processors; chips; electronic equipment; and computer hardware and software, including applications and programming. **Education and Training:** Principles and methods for curriculum and training design, teaching and instruction for individuals and groups, and the measurement of training effects.

Atmospheric and Space Scientists

- ◉ Education/Training Required: Bachelor's degree
- ◉ Annual Earnings: $73,940
- ◉ Growth: 16.5%
- ◉ Annual Job Openings: 1,000
- ◉ Self-Employed: 0.0%
- ◉ Part-Time: 4.3%

Investigate atmospheric phenomena and interpret meteorological data gathered by surface and air stations, satellites, and radar to prepare reports and forecasts for public and other uses. Study and interpret data, reports, maps, photographs, and charts to predict long- and short-range weather conditions, using computer models and knowledge of climate theory, physics, and mathematics. Broadcast weather conditions, forecasts, and severe weather warnings to the public via television, radio, and the Internet or provide this information to the news media. Gather data from sources such as surface and upper air stations, satellites, weather bureaus, and radar for use in meteorological reports and forecasts. Prepare forecasts and briefings to meet the needs of industry, business, government, and other groups. Apply meteorological knowledge to problems in areas including agriculture, pollution control, and water management and to issues such as global warming or ozone depletion. Conduct basic or applied meteorological research into the processes and determinants of atmospheric phenomena, weather, and climate. Operate computer graphic equipment to produce weather reports and maps for analysis, distribution, or use in weather broadcasts. Measure wind, temperature, and humidity in the upper atmosphere, using weather balloons. Develop and use weather forecasting tools such as mathematical and computer models. Direct forecasting services at weather stations or at radio or television broadcasting facilities. Research and analyze the impact of industrial projects and pollution on climate, air quality, and weather phenomena. Collect air samples from planes and ships over land and sea to study atmospheric composition. Conduct numerical simulations of climate conditions to understand and predict global and regional weather patterns. Collect and analyze historical climate information such as precipitation and temperature records help predict future weather and climate trends. Consult with agencies, professionals, or researchers regarding the use and interpretation of climatological information. Design and develop new equipment and methods for meteorological data collection, remote sensing, or related applications. Make scientific presentations and publish reports, articles, or texts.

SKILLS—Most Important: Science Skills; Computer Programming Skills; Quality Control Skills. **Other Above-Average Skills:** Equipment/Technology Analysis Skills; Thought-Processing Skills; Communication Skills; Equipment Use/Maintenance Skills; Management Skills.

GOE—Interest Area: 15. Scientific Research, Engineering, and Mathematics. **Work Group:** 15.02. Physical Sciences. **Other Jobs in This Group:** Astronomers; Chemists; Geographers; Geoscientists, Except Hydrologists and Geographers; Hydrologists; Materials Scientists; Physicists. **PERSONALITY TYPE:** Investigative. Investigative occupations frequently involve working with ideas and require an extensive amount of thinking. These occupations can involve searching for facts and figuring out problems mentally.

EDUCATION/TRAINING PROGRAM(S)—Atmospheric Sciences and Meteorology, General; Atmospheric Chemistry and Climatology; Atmospheric Physics and Dynamics; Meteorology; Atmospheric Sciences and Meteorology, Other. **RELATED KNOWLEDGE/ COURSES—Geography:** Principles and methods for describing the features of land, sea, and air masses, including their physical characteristics; locations; interrelationships; and distribution of plant, animal, and human life. **Physics:** Physical principles and laws and their interrelationships and applications to understanding fluid, material, and atmospheric dynamics and mechanical, electrical, atomic, and subatomic structures and processes. **Computers and Electronics:** Circuit boards; processors; chips; electronic equipment; and computer hardware and software, including applications and programming. **Mathematics:** Arithmetic, algebra, geometry, calculus, and statistics and their applications. **Customer and Personal Service:** Principles and processes for providing customer and personal services. This includes customer needs assessment, meeting of quality standards for services, and evaluation of customer satisfaction. **Communications and Media:** Media production, communication, and dissemination techniques and methods. This includes alternative ways to inform and entertain via written, oral, and visual media.

Atmospheric, Earth, Marine, and Space Sciences Teachers, Postsecondary

- Education/Training Required: Master's degree
- Annual Earnings: $65,720
- Growth: 32.2%
- Annual Job Openings: 329,000
- Self-Employed: 0.4%
- Part-Time: 27.3%

The job openings listed here are shared with 35 other postsecondary teaching occupations. For a complete list, see the beginning of this section.

Teach courses in the physical sciences, except chemistry and physics. Conduct research in a particular field of knowledge and publish findings in professional journals, books, and/or electronic media. Write grant proposals to procure external research funding. Keep abreast of developments in their field by reading current literature, talking with colleagues, and participating in professional conferences. Supervise undergraduate and/or graduate teaching, internship, and research work. Prepare and deliver lectures to undergraduate

and/or graduate students on topics such as structural geology, micrometeorology, and atmospheric thermodynamics. Supervise laboratory work and fieldwork. Evaluate and grade students' classwork, assignments, and papers. Prepare course materials such as syllabi, homework assignments, and handouts. Collaborate with colleagues to address teaching and research issues. Compile, administer, and grade examinations or assign this work to others. Plan, evaluate, and revise curricula, course content, and course materials and methods of instruction. Initiate, facilitate, and moderate classroom discussions. Maintain regularly scheduled office hours in order to advise and assist students. Advise students on academic and vocational curricula and on career issues. Maintain student attendance records, grades, and other required records. Participate in student recruitment, registration, and placement activities. Perform administrative duties such as serving as department head. Select and obtain materials and supplies such as textbooks and laboratory equipment. Serve on academic or administrative committees that deal with institutional policies, departmental matters, and academic issues. Compile bibliographies of specialized materials for outside reading assignments. Provide professional consulting services to government and/or industry. Act as advisers to student organizations. Participate in campus and community events.

SKILLS—Most Important: Science Skills; Computer Programming Skills; Mathematics Skills. **Other Above-Average Skills:** Communication Skills; Management Skills; Quality Control Skills; Social Skills.

GOE—Interest Area: 05. Education and Training. **Work Group:** 05.03. Postsecondary and Adult Teaching and Instructing. **Other Jobs in This Group:** Adult Literacy, Remedial Education, and GED Teachers and Instructors; Agricultural Sciences Teachers, Postsecondary; Anthropology and Archeology Teachers, Postsecondary; Architecture Teachers, Postsecondary; Area, Ethnic, and Cultural Studies Teachers, Postsecondary; Art, Drama, and Music Teachers, Postsecondary; Biological Science Teachers, Postsecondary; Business Teachers, Postsecondary; Chemistry Teachers, Postsecondary; Communications Teachers, Postsecondary; Computer Science Teachers, Postsecondary; Criminal Justice and Law Enforcement Teachers, Postsecondary; Economics Teachers, Postsecondary; Education Teachers, Postsecondary; Engineering Teachers, Postsecondary; English Language and Literature Teachers,

Postsecondary; Environmental Science Teachers, Postsecondary; Farm and Home Management Advisors; Foreign Language and Literature Teachers, Postsecondary; Forestry and Conservation Science Teachers, Postsecondary; Geography Teachers, Postsecondary; Graduate Teaching Assistants; Health Specialties Teachers, Postsecondary; History Teachers, Postsecondary; Home Economics Teachers, Postsecondary; Law Teachers, Postsecondary; Library Science Teachers, Postsecondary; Mathematical Science Teachers, Postsecondary; Nursing Instructors and Teachers, Postsecondary; Philosophy and Religion Teachers, Postsecondary; Physics Teachers, Postsecondary; Political Science Teachers, Postsecondary; Psychology Teachers, Postsecondary; Recreation and Fitness Studies Teachers, Postsecondary; Self-Enrichment Education Teachers; Social Work Teachers, Postsecondary; Sociology Teachers, Postsecondary; Vocational Education Teachers, Postsecondary. **PERSONALITY TYPE:** No data available.

EDUCATION/TRAINING PROGRAM(S)—Science Teacher Education/General Science Teacher Education; Physics Teacher Education; Astronomy; Astrophysics; Planetary Astronomy and Science; Atmospheric Sciences and Meteorology, General; Atmospheric Chemistry and Climatology; Atmospheric Physics and Dynamics; Meteorology; Atmospheric Sciences and Meteorology, Other; Geology/Earth Science, General; Geochemistry; Geophysics and Seismology; others. **RELATED KNOWLEDGE/COURSES—Physics:** Physical principles and laws and their interrelationships and applications to understanding fluid, material, and atmospheric dynamics and mechanical, electrical, atomic, and subatomic structures and processes. **Geography:** Principles and methods for describing the features of land, sea, and air masses, including their physical characteristics; locations; interrelationships; and distribution of plant, animal, and human life. **Education and Training:** Principles and methods for curriculum and training design, teaching and instruction for individuals and groups, and the measurement of training effects. **Chemistry:** The chemical composition, structure, and properties of substances and of the chemical processes and transformations that they undergo. This includes uses of chemicals and their danger signs, production techniques, and disposal methods. **Mathematics:** Arithmetic, algebra, geometry, calculus, and statistics and their applications. **Biology:** Plant and animal organisms and their tissues, cells, functions, interdependencies, and interactions with each other and the environment.

Auditors

- Education/Training Required: Bachelor's degree
- Annual Earnings: $52,210
- Growth: 22.4%
- Annual Job Openings: 157,000
- Self-Employed: 10.9%
- Part-Time: 10.2%

The job openings listed here are shared with Accountants.

Examine and analyze accounting records to determine financial status of establishment and prepare financial reports concerning operating procedures. Collect and analyze data to detect deficient controls; duplicated effort; extravagance; fraud; or non-compliance with laws, regulations, and management policies. Report to management about asset utilization and audit results and recommend changes in operations and financial activities. Prepare detailed reports on audit findings. Review data about material assets, net worth, liabilities, capital stock, surplus, income, and expenditures. Inspect account books and accounting systems for efficiency, effectiveness, and use of accepted accounting procedures to record transactions. Examine and evaluate financial and information systems, recommending controls to ensure system reliability and data integrity. Supervise auditing of establishments and determine scope of investigation required. Prepare, analyze, and verify annual reports, financial statements, and other records, using accepted accounting and statistical procedures to assess financial condition and facilitate financial planning. Confer with company officials about financial and regulatory matters. Inspect cash on hand, notes receivable and payable, negotiable securities, and canceled checks to confirm that records are accurate. Examine inventory to verify journal and ledger entries. Examine whether the organization's objectives are reflected in its management activities and whether employees understand the objectives. Examine records and interview workers to ensure recording of transactions and compliance with laws and regulations. Direct activities of personnel engaged in filing, recording, compiling, and transmitting financial records. Produce up-to-the-minute information, using internal computer systems, to allow management to base decisions on actual, not historical, data. Conduct pre-implementation audits to determine if systems and programs under development will work as planned. Review taxpayer accounts and conduct audits on site, by correspondence, or by summoning taxpayer to office. Evaluate taxpayer finances to determine tax liability, using knowledge of interest and discount rates, annuities, valuation of stocks and bonds, and amortization valuation of depletable assets.

SKILLS—Most Important: Mathematics Skills; Management Skills; Social Skills. **Other Above-Average Skills:** Communication Skills; Thought-Processing Skills.

GOE—Interest Area: 04. Business and Administration. **Work Group:** 04.05. Accounting, Auditing, and Analytical Support. **Other Jobs in This Group:** Accountants; Accountants and Auditors; Budget Analysts; Industrial Engineering Technicians; Logisticians; Management Analysts; Operations Research Analysts. **PERSONALITY TYPE:** Conventional. Conventional occupations frequently involve following set procedures and routines. These occupations can include working with data and details more than with ideas. Usually there is a clear line of authority to follow.

EDUCATION/TRAINING PROGRAM(S)—Accounting and Computer Science; Accounting; Auditing; Accounting and Finance; Accounting and Business/Management. **RELATED KNOWLEDGE/COURSES—Economics and Accounting:** Economic and accounting principles and practices, the financial markets, banking, and the analysis and reporting of financial data. **Sales and Marketing:** Principles and methods for showing, promoting, and selling products or services. This includes marketing strategy and tactics, product demonstration, sales techniques, and sales control systems. **Mathematics:** Arithmetic, algebra, geometry, calculus, and statistics and their applications. **Law and Government:** Laws, legal codes, court procedures, precedents, government regulations, executive orders, agency rules, and the democratic political process. **Customer and Personal Service:** Principles and processes for providing customer and personal services. This

includes customer needs assessment, meeting of quality standards for services, and evaluation of customer satisfaction. **Computers and Electronics:** Circuit boards; processors; chips; electronic equipment; and computer hardware and software, including applications and programming.

Automotive Master Mechanics

- ◎ Education/Training Required: Postsecondary vocational training
- ◎ Annual Earnings: $33,050
- ◎ Growth: 15.7%
- ◎ Annual Job Openings: 93,000
- ◎ Self-Employed: 14.8%
- ◎ Part-Time: 7.0%

The job openings listed here are shared with Automotive Specialty Technicians.

Repair automobiles, trucks, buses, and other vehicles. Master mechanics repair virtually any part on the vehicle or specialize in the transmission system. Examine vehicles to determine extent of damage or malfunctions. Test drive vehicles and test components and systems, using equipment such as infrared engine analyzers, compression gauges, and computerized diagnostic devices. Repair, reline, replace, and adjust brakes. Review work orders and discuss work with supervisors. Follow checklists to ensure all important parts are examined, including belts, hoses, steering systems, spark plugs, brake and fuel systems, wheel bearings, and other potentially troublesome areas. Plan work procedures, using charts, technical manuals, and experience. Test and adjust repaired systems to meet manufacturers' performance specifications. Confer with customers to obtain descriptions of vehicle problems and to discuss work to be performed and future repair requirements. Perform routine and scheduled maintenance services such as oil changes, lubrications, and tune-ups. Disassemble units and inspect parts for wear, using micrometers, calipers, and gauges. Overhaul or replace carburetors, blowers, generators, distributors, starters, and pumps. Repair and service air conditioning, heating, engine-cooling, and electrical systems. Repair or replace parts such as pistons, rods, gears, valves, and bearings. Tear down, repair, and rebuild faulty assemblies such as power systems, steering systems, and linkages. Rewire ignition systems, lights, and instrument panels. Repair radiator leaks. Install and repair accessories such as radios, heaters, mirrors, and windshield wipers. Repair manual and automatic transmissions. Repair or replace shock absorbers. Align vehicles' front ends. Rebuild parts such as crankshafts and cylinder blocks. Repair damaged automobile bodies. Replace and adjust headlights.

SKILLS—Most Important: Equipment Use/Maintenance Skills. **Other Above-Average Skills:** Equipment/ Technology Analysis Skills; Quality Control Skills; Thought-Processing Skills; Science Skills.

GOE—Interest Area: 13. Manufacturing. **Work Group:** 13.14. Vehicle and Facility Mechanical Work. **Other Jobs in This Group:** Aircraft Mechanics and Service Technicians; Aircraft Structure, Surfaces, Rigging, and Systems Assemblers; Automotive Body and Related Repairers; Automotive Glass Installers and Repairers; Automotive Service Technicians and Mechanics; Automotive Specialty Technicians; Bus and Truck Mechanics and Diesel Engine Specialists; Farm Equipment Mechanics; Fiberglass Laminators and Fabricators; Mobile Heavy Equipment Mechanics, Except Engines; Motorboat Mechanics; Motorcycle Mechanics; Outdoor Power Equipment and Other Small Engine Mechanics; Rail Car Repairers; Recreational Vehicle Service Technicians; Tire Repairers and Changers. **PERSONALITY TYPE:** Realistic. Realistic occupations frequently involve work activities that include practical, hands-on problems and solutions. They often deal with plants, animals, and real-world materials like wood, tools, and machinery. Many of the occupations require working outside and do not involve a lot of paperwork or working closely with others.

EDUCATION/TRAINING PROGRAM(S)—Automotive Engineering Technology/Technician; Automobile/Automotive Mechanics Technology/Technician; Medium/Heavy Vehicle and Truck Technology/ Technician. **RELATED KNOWLEDGE/COURSES—Mechanical Devices:** Machines and tools, including their designs, uses, repair, and maintenance. **Physics:** Physical principles and laws and their interrelationships and applications to understanding fluid, material, and atmospheric dynamics and mechanical, electrical, atomic, and subatomic structures and processes. **Computers and Electronics:** Circuit boards; proces-

sors; chips; electronic equipment; and computer hardware and software, including applications and programming. **Engineering and Technology:** The practical application of engineering science and technology. This includes applying principles, techniques, procedures, and equipment to the design and production of various goods and services. **Chemistry:** The chemical composition, structure, and properties of substances and of the chemical processes and transformations that they undergo. This includes uses of chemicals and their danger signs, production techniques, and disposal methods. **Education and Training:** Principles and methods for curriculum and training design, teaching and instruction for individuals and groups, and the measurement of training effects.

Automotive Specialty Technicians

- ◎ Education/Training Required: Postsecondary vocational training
- ◎ Annual Earnings: $33,050
- ◎ Growth: 15.7%
- ◎ Annual Job Openings: 93,000
- ◎ Self-Employed: 14.8%
- ◎ Part-Time: 7.0%

The job openings listed here are shared with Automotive Master Mechanics.

Repair only one system or component on a vehicle, such as brakes, suspension, or radiator. Examine vehicles, compile estimates of repair costs, and secure customers' approval to perform repairs. Repair, overhaul, and adjust automobile brake systems. Use electronic test equipment to locate and correct malfunctions in fuel, ignition, and emissions control systems. Repair and replace defective ball joint suspensions, brake shoes, and wheel bearings. Inspect and test new vehicles for damage; then record findings so that necessary repairs can be made. Test electronic computer components in automobiles to ensure that they are working properly. Tune automobile engines to ensure proper and efficient functioning. Install and repair air conditioners and service components such as compressors, condensers, and controls. Repair, replace, and adjust defective carburetor

A

parts and gasoline filters. Remove and replace defective mufflers and tailpipes. Repair and replace automobile leaf springs. Rebuild, repair, and test automotive fuel injection units. Align and repair wheels, axles, frames, torsion bars, and steering mechanisms of automobiles, using special alignment equipment and wheel-balancing machines. Repair, install, and adjust hydraulic and electromagnetic automatic lift mechanisms used to raise and lower automobile windows, seats, and tops. Repair and rebuild clutch systems. Convert vehicle fuel systems from gasoline to butane gas operations and repair and service operating butane fuel units.

SKILLS—Most Important: Equipment Use/Maintenance Skills; Equipment/Technology Analysis Skills; Thought-Processing Skills. **Other Above-Average Skills:** Computer Programming Skills; Social Skills.

GOE—Interest Area: 13. Manufacturing. **Work Group:** 13.14. Vehicle and Facility Mechanical Work. **Other Jobs in This Group:** Aircraft Mechanics and Service Technicians; Aircraft Structure, Surfaces, Rigging, and Systems Assemblers; Automotive Body and Related Repairers; Automotive Glass Installers and Repairers; Automotive Master Mechanics; Automotive Service Technicians and Mechanics; Bus and Truck Mechanics and Diesel Engine Specialists; Farm Equipment Mechanics; Fiberglass Laminators and Fabricators; Mobile Heavy Equipment Mechanics, Except Engines; Motorboat Mechanics; Motorcycle Mechanics; Outdoor Power Equipment and Other Small Engine Mechanics; Rail Car Repairers; Recreational Vehicle Service Technicians; Tire Repairers and Changers. **PERSONALITY TYPE:** Realistic. Realistic occupations frequently involve work activities that include practical, hands-on problems and solutions. They often deal with plants, animals, and real-world materials like wood, tools, and machinery. Many of the occupations require working outside and do not involve a lot of paperwork or working closely with others.

EDUCATION/TRAINING PROGRAM(S)—Automotive Engineering Technology/Technician; Vehicle Emissions Inspection and Maintenance Technology/Technician; Alternative Fuel Vehicle Technology/Technician. **RELATED KNOWLEDGE/COURSES—Mechanical Devices:** Machines and tools, including their designs, uses, repair, and maintenance. **Customer and Personal Service:** Principles and processes for providing customer and personal services. This includes customer needs assessment, meeting of quality standards for services, and evaluation of customer satisfaction. **Engineering and Technology:** The practical application of engineering science and technology. This includes applying principles, techniques, procedures, and equipment to the design and production of various goods and services. **Physics:** Physical principles and laws and their interrelationships and applications to understanding fluid, material, and atmospheric dynamics and mechanical, electrical, atomic, and subatomic structures and processes. **Administration and Management:** Business and management principles involved in strategic planning, resource allocation, human resources modeling, leadership technique, production methods, and coordination of people and resources. **Sales and Marketing:** Principles and methods for showing, promoting, and selling products or services. This includes marketing strategy and tactics, product demonstration, sales techniques, and sales control systems.

Aviation Inspectors

- Education/Training Required: Work experience in a related occupation
- Annual Earnings: $49,490
- Growth: 11.4%
- Annual Job Openings: 2,000
- Self-Employed: 1.9%
- Part-Time: 2.3%

The job openings listed here are shared with Freight and Cargo Inspectors and with Transportation Vehicle, Equipment, and Systems Inspectors, Except Aviation.

Inspect aircraft, maintenance procedures, air navigational aids, air traffic controls, and communications equipment to ensure conformance with federal safety regulations. Inspect work of aircraft mechanics performing maintenance, modification, or repair and overhaul of aircraft and aircraft mechanical systems to ensure adherence to standards and procedures. Start aircraft and observe gauges, meters, and other instruments to detect evidence of malfunctions. Examine aircraft access plates and doors for security. Examine landing gear, tires, and exteriors of fuselage, wings, and engines for evidence of damage or corrosion and to determine whether repairs are needed. Prepare and maintain detailed repair, inspection, investigation, and certification records and reports. Inspect new, repaired, or modified aircraft to identify damage or defects and to assess airworthiness and conformance to standards, using checklists, hand tools, and test instruments. Examine maintenance records and flight logs to determine if service and maintenance checks and overhauls were performed at prescribed intervals. Recommend replacement, repair, or modification of aircraft equipment. Recommend changes in rules, policies, standards, and regulations based on knowledge of operating conditions, aircraft improvements, and other factors. Issue pilots' licenses to individuals meeting standards. Investigate air accidents and complaints to determine causes. Observe flight activities of pilots to assess flying skills and to ensure conformance to flight and safety regulations. Conduct flight test programs to test equipment, instruments, and systems under a variety of conditions, using both manual and automatic controls. Approve or deny issuance of certificates of airworthiness. Analyze training programs and conduct oral and written examinations to ensure the competency of persons operating, installing, and repairing aircraft equipment. Schedule and coordinate in-flight testing programs with ground crews and air traffic control to ensure availability of ground tracking, equipment monitoring, and related services.

SKILLS—Most Important: Quality Control Skills; Equipment Use/Maintenance Skills; Thought-Processing Skills. **Other Above-Average Skills:** Communication Skills; Social Skills; Mathematics Skills; Science Skills.

GOE—Interest Area: 07. Government and Public Administration. **Work Group:** 07.03. Regulations Enforcement. **Other Jobs in This Group:** Agricultural Inspectors; Compliance Officers, Except Agriculture, Construction, Health and Safety, and Transportation; Construction and Building Inspectors; Environmental Compliance Inspectors; Equal Opportunity Representatives and Officers; Financial Examiners; Fire Inspectors; Fish and Game Wardens; Forest Fire Inspectors and Prevention Specialists; Freight and Cargo Inspectors; Government Property Inspectors and Investigators; Immigration and Customs Inspectors; Licensing Examiners and Inspectors; Nuclear Monitoring Technicians; Occupational Health and Safety Specialists; Occupational Health and Safety

Technicians; Tax Examiners, Collectors, and Revenue Agents; Transportation Vehicle, Equipment, and Systems Inspectors, Except Aviation. **PERSONALITY TYPE:** Realistic. Realistic occupations frequently involve work activities that include practical, hands-on problems and solutions. They often deal with plants, animals, and real-world materials like wood, tools, and machinery. Many of the occupations require working outside and do not involve a lot of paperwork or working closely with others.

EDUCATION/TRAINING PROGRAM(S)—Avionics Maintenance Technology/Technician. **RELATED KNOWLEDGE/COURSES—Mechanical Devices:** Machines and tools, including their designs, uses, repair, and maintenance. **Transportation:** Principles and methods for moving people or goods by air, rail, sea, or road, including the relative costs and benefits. **Physics:** Physical principles and laws and their interrelationships and applications to understanding fluid, material, and atmospheric dynamics and mechanical, electrical, atomic, and subatomic structures and processes. **Design:** Design techniques, tools, and principles involved in production of precision technical plans, blueprints, drawings, and models. **Chemistry:** The chemical composition, structure, and properties of substances and of the chemical processes and transformations that they undergo. This includes uses of chemicals and their danger signs, production techniques, and disposal methods. **Law and Government:** Laws, legal codes, court procedures, precedents, government regulations, executive orders, agency rules, and the democratic political process.

Bill and Account Collectors

- Education/Training Required: Short-term on-the-job training
- Annual Earnings: $28,160
- Growth: 21.4%
- Annual Job Openings: 85,000
- Self-Employed: 1.1%
- Part-Time: 13.1%

Locate and notify customers of delinquent accounts by mail, telephone, or personal visit to solicit payment. Duties include receiving payment and posting amount to customer's account, preparing statements to credit department if customer fails to respond, initiating repossession proceedings or service disconnection, and keeping records of collection and status of accounts. Receive payments and post amounts paid to customer accounts. Locate and monitor overdue accounts, using computers and a variety of automated systems. Record information about financial status of customers and status of collection efforts. Locate and notify customers of delinquent accounts by mail, telephone, or personal visits to solicit payment. Confer with customers by telephone or in person to determine reasons for overdue payments and to review the terms of sales, service, or credit contracts. Advise customers of necessary actions and strategies for debt repayment. Persuade customers to pay amounts due on credit accounts, damage claims, or nonpayable checks or to return merchandise. Sort and file correspondence and perform miscellaneous clerical duties such as answering correspondence and writing reports. Perform various administrative functions for assigned accounts, such as recording address changes and purging the records of deceased customers. Arrange for debt repayment or establish repayment schedules based on customers' financial situations. Negotiate credit extensions when necessary. Trace delinquent customers to new addresses by inquiring at post offices, telephone companies, or credit bureaus or through the questioning of neighbors. Notify credit departments, order merchandise repossession or service disconnection, and turn over account records to attorneys when customers fail to respond to collection attempts. Drive vehicles to visit customers, return merchandise to creditors, or deliver bills.

SKILLS—**Most Important:** Management Skills; Communication Skills; Social Skills. **Other Above-Average Skills:** Mathematics Skills; Thought-Processing Skills.

GOE—**Interest Area:** 06. Finance and Insurance. **Work Group:** 06.04. Finance/Insurance Customer Service. **Other Jobs in This Group:** Loan Interviewers and Clerks; New Accounts Clerks; Tellers. **PERSONALITY TYPE:** Conventional. Conventional occupations frequently involve following set procedures and routines. These occupations can include working with data and details more than with ideas. Usually there is a clear line of authority to follow.

EDUCATION/TRAINING PROGRAM(S)—Banking and Financial Support Services. **RELATED KNOWLEDGE/COURSES—Clerical Practices:** Administrative and clerical procedures and systems such as word processing, managing files and records, stenography and transcription, designing forms, and other office procedures and terminology. **Customer and Personal Service:** Principles and processes for providing customer and personal services. This includes customer needs assessment, meeting of quality standards for services, and evaluation of customer satisfaction. **Economics and Accounting:** Economic and accounting principles and practices, the financial markets, banking, and the analysis and reporting of financial data. **Law and Government:** Laws, legal codes, court procedures, precedents, government regulations, executive orders, agency rules, and the democratic political process. **Computers and Electronics:** Circuit boards; processors; chips; electronic equipment; and computer hardware and software, including applications and programming. **Personnel and Human Resources:** Principles and procedures for personnel recruitment, selection, training, compensation and benefits, labor relations and negotiation, and personnel information systems.

Biological Science Teachers, Postsecondary

- Education/Training Required: Master's degree
- Annual Earnings: $63,570
- Growth: 32.2%
- Annual Job Openings: 329,000
- Self-Employed: 0.4%
- Part-Time: 27.3%

The job openings listed here are shared with 35 other postsecondary teaching occupations. For a complete list, see the beginning of this section.

Teach courses in biological sciences. Prepare and deliver lectures to undergraduate and/or graduate students on topics such as molecular biology, marine biology, and botany. Evaluate and grade students' classwork, laboratory work, assignments, and papers. Prepare course materials such as syllabi, homework assignments, and handouts. Compile, administer, and grade examinations or assign this work to others. Supervise students' laboratory work. Keep abreast of developments in their field by reading current literature, talking with colleagues, and participating in professional conferences. Maintain student attendance records, grades, and other required records. Initiate, facilitate, and moderate classroom discussions. Plan, evaluate, and revise curricula, course content, and course materials and methods of instruction. Advise students on academic and vocational curricula and on career issues. Maintain regularly scheduled office hours to advise and assist students. Supervise undergraduate and/or graduate teaching, internship, and research work. Select and obtain materials and supplies such as textbooks and laboratory equipment. Collaborate with colleagues to address teaching and research issues. Conduct research in a particular field of knowledge and publish findings in professional journals, books, and/or electronic media. Serve on academic or administrative committees that deal with institutional policies, departmental matters, and academic issues. Participate in student recruitment, registration, and placement activities. Write grant proposals to procure external research funding. Perform administrative duties such as serving as department head. Act as advisers to student organizations. Compile bibliographies of specialized materials for outside reading assignments. Participate in campus and community events. Provide professional consulting services to government and/or industry.

SKILLS—Most Important: Science Skills; Communication Skills; Thought-Processing Skills. **Other Above-Average Skills:** Social Skills; Mathematics Skills; Quality Control Skills.

GOE—Interest Area: 05. Education and Training. **Work Group:** 05.03. Postsecondary and Adult Teaching and Instructing. **Other Jobs in This Group:** Adult Literacy, Remedial Education, and GED Teachers and Instructors; Agricultural Sciences Teachers, Postsecondary; Anthropology and Archeology Teachers, Postsecondary; Architecture Teachers, Postsecondary; Area, Ethnic, and Cultural Studies Teachers, Postsecondary; Art, Drama, and Music Teachers, Postsecondary; Atmospheric, Earth, Marine, and Space Sciences Teachers, Postsecondary; Business Teachers, Postsecondary; Chemistry Teachers, Postsecondary; Communications Teachers, Postsecondary; Computer Science Teachers, Postsecondary; Criminal Justice and Law Enforcement Teachers, Postsecondary; Economics

Teachers, Postsecondary; Education Teachers, Postsecondary; Engineering Teachers, Postsecondary; English Language and Literature Teachers, Postsecondary; Environmental Science Teachers, Postsecondary; Farm and Home Management Advisors; Foreign Language and Literature Teachers, Postsecondary; Forestry and Conservation Science Teachers, Postsecondary; Geography Teachers, Postsecondary; Graduate Teaching Assistants; Health Specialties Teachers, Postsecondary; History Teachers, Postsecondary; Home Economics Teachers, Postsecondary; Law Teachers, Postsecondary; Library Science Teachers, Postsecondary; Mathematical Science Teachers, Postsecondary; Nursing Instructors and Teachers, Postsecondary; Philosophy and Religion Teachers, Postsecondary; Physics Teachers, Postsecondary; Political Science Teachers, Postsecondary; Psychology Teachers, Postsecondary; Recreation and Fitness Studies Teachers, Postsecondary; Self-Enrichment Education Teachers; Social Work Teachers, Postsecondary; Sociology Teachers, Postsecondary; Vocational Education Teachers, Postsecondary. **PERSONALITY TYPE:** Investigative. Investigative occupations frequently involve working with ideas and require an extensive amount of thinking. These occupations can involve searching for facts and figuring out problems mentally.

EDUCATION/TRAINING PROGRAM(S)—Biology/Biological Sciences, General; Biochemistry; Biophysics; Molecular Biology; Radiation Biology/Radiobiology; Botany/Plant Biology; Plant Pathology/Phytopathology; Plant Physiology; Cell/Cellular Biology and Histology; Anatomy; Microbiology, General; Virology; Parasitology; Immunology; Zoology/Animal Biology; Entomology; Animal Physiology; others. **RELATED KNOWLEDGE/COURSES—Biology:** Plant and animal organisms and their tissues, cells, functions, interdependencies, and interactions with each other and the environment. **Chemistry:** The chemical composition, structure, and properties of substances and of the chemical processes and transformations that they undergo. This includes uses of chemicals and their danger signs, production techniques, and disposal methods. **Education and Training:** Principles and methods for curriculum and training design, teaching and instruction for individuals and groups, and the measurement of training effects. **Medicine and Dentistry:** The information and techniques needed to diagnose and treat human injuries, diseases, and deformities. This includes symptoms, treatment alternatives, drug properties and interactions, and preventive health-care measures. **English Language:** The structure and content of the English language, including the meaning and spelling of words, rules of composition, and grammar. **Physics:** Physical principles and laws and their interrelationships and applications to understanding fluid, material, and atmospheric dynamics and mechanical, electrical, atomic, and subatomic structures and processes.

Biological Technicians

- Education/Training Required: Associate degree
- Annual Earnings: $34,270
- Growth: 17.2%
- Annual Job Openings: 8,000
- Self-Employed: 0.0%
- Part-Time: 9.5%

Assist biological and medical scientists in laboratories. Set up, operate, and maintain laboratory instruments and equipment; monitor experiments; make observations; and calculate and record results. May analyze organic substances, such as blood, food, and drugs. Keep detailed logs of all work-related activities. Monitor laboratory work to ensure compliance with set standards. Isolate, identify, and prepare specimens for examination. Use computers, computer-interfaced equipment, robotics, or high-technology industrial applications to perform work duties. Conduct research or assist in the conduct of research, including the collection of information and samples such as blood, water, soil, plants, and animals. Set up, adjust, calibrate, clean, maintain, and troubleshoot laboratory and field equipment. Provide technical support and services for scientists and engineers working in fields such as agriculture, environmental science, resource management, biology, and health sciences. Clean, maintain, and prepare supplies and work areas. Participate in the research, development, or manufacturing of medicinal and pharmaceutical preparations. Conduct standardized biological, microbiological, or biochemical tests and laboratory analyses to evaluate the quantity or quality of physical or chemical substances in food or other prod-

ucts. Analyze experimental data and interpret results to write reports and summaries of findings. Measure or weigh compounds and solutions for use in testing or animal feed. Monitor and observe experiments, recording production and test data for evaluation by research personnel. Examine animals and specimens to detect the presence of disease or other problems. Conduct or supervise operational programs such as fish hatcheries, greenhouses, and livestock production programs. Feed livestock or laboratory animals.

SKILLS—Most Important: Science Skills; Quality Control Skills; Mathematics Skills. **Other Above-Average Skills:** Equipment Use/Maintenance Skills; Management Skills; Social Skills; Communication Skills.

GOE—Interest Area: 08. Health Science. **Work Group:** 08.06. Medical Technology. **Other Jobs in This Group:** Cardiovascular Technologists and Technicians; Diagnostic Medical Sonographers; Medical and Clinical Laboratory Technicians; Medical and Clinical Laboratory Technologists; Medical Equipment Preparers; Medical Records and Health Information Technicians; Nuclear Medicine Technologists; Opticians, Dispensing; Orthotists and Prosthetists; Radiologic Technicians; Radiologic Technologists; Radiologic Technologists and Technicians. **PERSONALITY TYPE:** Realistic. Realistic occupations frequently involve work activities that include practical, hands-on problems and solutions. They often deal with plants, animals, and real-world materials like wood, tools, and machinery. Many of the occupations require working outside and do not involve a lot of paperwork or working closely with others.

EDUCATION/TRAINING PROGRAM(S)—Biology Technician/Biotechnology Laboratory Technician. **RELATED KNOWLEDGE/COURSES—Chemistry:** The chemical composition, structure, and properties of substances and of the chemical processes and transformations that they undergo. This includes uses of chemicals and their danger signs, production techniques, and disposal methods. **Biology:** Plant and animal organisms and their tissues, cells, functions, interdependencies, and interactions with each other and the environment. **Mathematics:** Arithmetic, algebra, geometry, calculus, and statistics and their applications. **English Language:** The structure and content of the English language, including the meaning and spelling of words, rules of composition, and grammar.

Biomedical Engineers

- ◎ Education/Training Required: Bachelor's degree
- ◎ Annual Earnings: $71,840
- ◎ Growth: 30.7%
- ◎ Annual Job Openings: 1,000
- ◎ Self-Employed: 7.2%
- ◎ Part-Time: No data available

Apply knowledge of engineering, biology, and biomechanical principles to the design, development, and evaluation of biological and health systems and products, such as artificial organs, prostheses, instrumentation, medical information systems, and health management and care delivery systems. Evaluate the safety, efficiency, and effectiveness of biomedical equipment. Install, adjust, maintain, and/or repair biomedical equipment. Advise hospital administrators on the planning, acquisition, and use of medical equipment. Advise and assist in the application of instrumentation in clinical environments. Develop models or computer simulations of human bio-behavioral systems in order to obtain data for measuring or controlling life processes. Research new materials to be used for products such as implanted artificial organs. Design and develop medical diagnostic and clinical instrumentation, equipment, and procedures, utilizing the principles of engineering and bio-behavioral sciences. Conduct research, along with life scientists, chemists, and medical scientists, on the engineering aspects of the biological systems of humans and animals. Teach biomedical engineering or disseminate knowledge about field through writing or consulting. Design and deliver technology to assist people with disabilities. Diagnose and interpret bioelectric data, using signal-processing techniques. Adapt or design computer hardware or software for medical science uses. Analyze new medical procedures in order to forecast likely outcomes. Develop new applications for energy sources, such as using nuclear power for biomedical implants.

SKILLS—Most Important: Science Skills; Quality Control Skills; Equipment/Technology Analysis Skills. **Other Above-Average Skills:** Mathematics Skills; Management Skills; Equipment Use/Maintenance Skills; Social Skills.

GOE—Interest Area: 15. Scientific Research, Engineering, and Mathematics. **Work Group:** 15.07. Research and Design Engineering. **Other Jobs in This Group:** Aerospace Engineers; Chemical Engineers; Civil Engineers; Computer Hardware Engineers; Electrical Engineers; Electronics Engineers, Except Computer; Marine Architects; Marine Engineers; Marine Engineers and Naval Architects; Materials Engineers; Mechanical Engineers; Nuclear Engineers. **PERSONALITY TYPE:** No data available.

EDUCATION/TRAINING PROGRAM(S)—Biomedical/Medical Engineering. **RELATED KNOWLEDGE/COURSES—Engineering and Technology:** The practical application of engineering science and technology. This includes applying principles, techniques, procedures, and equipment to the design and production of various goods and services. **Computers and Electronics:** Circuit boards; processors; chips; electronic equipment; and computer hardware and software, including applications and programming. **Design:** Design techniques, tools, and principles involved in production of precision technical plans, blueprints, drawings, and models. **Physics:** Physical principles and laws and their interrelationships and applications to understanding fluid, material, and atmospheric dynamics and mechanical, electrical, atomic, and subatomic structures and processes. **Mechanical Devices:** Machines and tools, including their designs, uses, repair, and maintenance. **Chemistry:** The chemical composition, structure, and properties of substances and of the chemical processes and transformations that they undergo. This includes uses of chemicals and their danger signs, production techniques, and disposal methods.

Budget Analysts

- ◎ Education/Training Required: Bachelor's degree
- ◎ Annual Earnings: $58,910
- ◎ Growth: 13.5%
- ◎ Annual Job Openings: 6,000
- ◎ Self-Employed: 2.0%
- ◎ Part-Time: 3.9%

Examine budget estimates for completeness, accuracy, and conformance with procedures and regulations. Analyze budgeting and accounting reports for the purpose of maintaining expenditure controls. Direct the preparation of regular and special budget reports. Consult with managers to ensure that budget adjustments are made in accordance with program changes. Match appropriations for specific programs with appropriations for broader programs, including items for emergency funds. Provide advice and technical assistance with cost analysis, fiscal allocation, and budget preparation. Summarize budgets and submit recommendations for the approval or disapproval of funds requests. Seek new ways to improve efficiency and increase profits. Review operating budgets to analyze trends affecting budget needs. Perform cost-benefit analyses to compare operating programs, review financial requests, or explore alternative financing methods. Interpret budget directives and establish policies for carrying out directives. Compile and analyze accounting records and other data to determine the financial resources required to implement a program. Testify before examining and fund-granting authorities, clarifying and promoting the proposed budgets.

SKILLS—Most Important: Mathematics Skills; Quality Control Skills; Management Skills. Other Above-Average Skills: Thought-Processing Skills; Social Skills; Science Skills.

GOE—Interest Area: 04. Business and Administration. Work Group: 04.05. Accounting, Auditing, and Analytical Support. Other Jobs in This Group: Accountants; Accountants and Auditors; Auditors; Industrial Engineering Technicians; Logisticians; Management Analysts; Operations Research Analysts. PERSONALITY TYPE: Conventional. Conventional occupations frequently involve following set procedures and routines. These occupations can include working with data and details more than with ideas. Usually there is a clear line of authority to follow.

EDUCATION/TRAINING PROGRAM(S)—Accounting; Finance, General. RELATED KNOWLEDGE/COURSES—Economics and Accounting: Economic and accounting principles and practices, the financial markets, banking, and the analysis and reporting of financial data. Administration and Management: Business and management principles involved in strategic planning, resource allocation, human resources modeling, leadership technique, production methods, and coordination of people and resources. Computers and Electronics: Circuit boards; processors; chips; electronic equipment; and computer hardware and software, including applications and programming. Clerical Practices: Administrative and clerical procedures and systems such as word processing, managing files and records, stenography and transcription, designing forms, and other office procedures and terminology. Mathematics: Arithmetic, algebra, geometry, calculus, and statistics and their applications. Personnel and Human Resources: Principles and procedures for personnel recruitment, selection, training, compensation and benefits, labor relations and negotiation, and personnel information systems.

Bus and Truck Mechanics and Diesel Engine Specialists

- Education/Training Required: Postsecondary vocational training
- Annual Earnings: $36,620
- Growth: 14.4%
- Annual Job Openings: 32,000
- Self-Employed: 5.3%
- Part-Time: 2.8%

Diagnose, adjust, repair, or overhaul trucks, buses, and all types of diesel engines. Includes mechanics working primarily with automobile diesel engines. Use hand tools such as screwdrivers, pliers, wrenches, pressure gauges, and precision instruments, as well as power tools such as pneumatic wrenches, lathes, welding equipment, and jacks and hoists. Inspect brake systems, steering mechanisms, wheel bearings, and other important parts to ensure that they are in proper operating condition. Perform routine maintenance such as changing oil, checking batteries, and lubricating equipment and machinery. Adjust and reline brakes, align wheels, tighten bolts and screws, and reassemble equipment. Raise trucks, buses, and heavy parts or equipment, using hydraulic jacks or hoists. Test drive trucks and buses to diagnose malfunctions or to ensure that they are working properly. Inspect, test, and listen to defective equipment to diagnose malfunctions, using test instruments such as handheld computers, motor analyzers, chassis charts, and pressure gauges. Examine and adjust protective guards, loose bolts, and specified safety devices. Inspect and verify dimensions and clearances of parts to ensure conformance to factory specifications. Specialize in repairing and maintaining parts of the engine, such as fuel injection systems. Attach test instruments to equipment and read dials and gauges to diagnose malfunctions. Rewire ignition systems, lights, and instrument panels. Recondition and replace parts, pistons, bearings, gears, and valves. Repair and adjust seats, doors, and windows and install and repair accessories. Inspect, repair, and maintain automotive and mechanical equipment and machinery such as pumps and compressors. Disassemble and overhaul internal combustion engines, pumps, generators, transmissions, clutches, and differential units. Rebuild gas or diesel engines. Align front ends and suspension systems. Operate valve-grinding machines to grind and reset valves.

SKILLS—Most Important: Equipment Use/Maintenance Skills; Science Skills. **Other Above-Average Skills:** None met the criteria.

GOE—Interest Area: 13. Manufacturing. **Work Group:** 13.14. Vehicle and Facility Mechanical Work. **Other Jobs in This Group:** Aircraft Mechanics and Service Technicians; Aircraft Structure, Surfaces, Rigging, and Systems Assemblers; Automotive Body and Related Repairers; Automotive Glass Installers and Repairers; Automotive Master Mechanics; Automotive Service Technicians and Mechanics; Automotive Specialty Technicians; Farm Equipment Mechanics; Fiberglass Laminators and Fabricators; Mobile Heavy Equipment Mechanics, Except Engines; Motorboat Mechanics; Motorcycle Mechanics; Outdoor Power Equipment and Other Small Engine Mechanics; Rail Car Repairers; Recreational Vehicle Service Technicians; Tire Repairers and Changers. **PERSONALITY TYPE:** Realistic. Realistic occupations frequently involve work activities that include practical, hands-on problems and solutions. They often deal with plants, animals, and real-world materials like wood, tools, and machinery. Many of the occupations require working outside and do not involve a lot of paperwork or working closely with others.

EDUCATION/TRAINING PROGRAM(S)—Diesel Mechanics Technology/Technician; Medium/Heavy Vehicle and Truck Technology/Technician. **RELATED**

KNOWLEDGE/COURSES—Mechanical Devices: Machines and tools, including their designs, uses, repair, and maintenance. **Transportation:** Principles and methods for moving people or goods by air, rail, sea, or road, including the relative costs and benefits. **Public Safety and Security:** Relevant equipment, policies, procedures, and strategies to promote effective local, state, or national security operations for the protection of people, data, property, and institutions. **Physics:** Physical principles and laws and their interrelationships and applications to understanding fluid, material, and atmospheric dynamics and mechanical, electrical, atomic, and subatomic structures and processes. **Engineering and Technology:** The practical application of engineering science and technology. This includes applying principles, techniques, procedures, and equipment to the design and production of various goods and services. **Law and Government:** Laws, legal codes, court procedures, precedents, government regulations, executive orders, agency rules, and the democratic political process.

Bus Drivers, Transit and Intercity

- Education/Training Required: Moderate-term on-the-job training
- Annual Earnings: $31,010
- Growth: 21.7%
- Annual Job Openings: 34,000
- Self-Employed: 0.5%
- Part-Time: 38.4%

Drive bus or motor coach, including regular route operations, charters, and private carriage. May assist passengers with baggage. May collect fares or tickets. Inspect vehicles and check gas, oil, and water levels prior to departure. Drive vehicles over specified routes or to specified destinations according to time schedules to transport passengers, complying with traffic regulations. Park vehicles at loading areas so that passengers can board. Assist passengers with baggage and collect tickets or cash fares. Report delays or accidents. Advise passengers to be seated and orderly while on vehicles. Regulate heating, lighting, and ventilating systems for passenger comfort. Load and unload baggage in baggage compartments. Record cash receipts and ticket fares. Make minor repairs to vehicle and change tires.

SKILLS—Most Important: Equipment Use/Maintenance Skills. **Other Above-Average Skills:** None met the criteria.

GOE—Interest Area: 16. Transportation, Distribution, and Logistics. **Work Group:** 16.06. Other Services Requiring Driving. **Other Jobs in This Group:** Ambulance Drivers and Attendants, Except Emergency Medical Technicians; Bus Drivers, School; Couriers and Messengers; Driver/Sales Workers; Parking Lot Attendants; Postal Service Mail Carriers; Taxi Drivers and Chauffeurs. **PERSONALITY TYPE:** Realistic. Realistic occupations frequently involve work activities that include practical, hands-on problems and solutions. They often deal with plants, animals, and real-world materials like wood, tools, and machinery. Many of the occupations require working outside and do not involve a lot of paperwork or working closely with others.

EDUCATION/TRAINING PROGRAM(S)—Truck and Bus Driver/Commercial Vehicle Operation. **RELATED KNOWLEDGE/COURSES—Transportation:** Principles and methods for moving people or goods by air, rail, sea, or road, including the relative costs and benefits. **Geography:** Principles and methods for describing the features of land, sea, and air masses, including their physical characteristics; locations; interrelationships; and distribution of plant, animal, and human life. **Customer and Personal Service:** Principles and processes for providing customer and personal services. This includes customer needs assessment, meeting of quality standards for services, and evaluation of customer satisfaction. **Public Safety and Security:** Relevant equipment, policies, procedures, and strategies to promote effective local, state, or national security operations for the protection of people, data, property, and institutions. **Psychology:** Human behavior and performance; individual differences in ability, personality, and interests; learning and motivation; psychological research methods; and the assessment and treatment of behavioral and affective disorders. **Law and Government:** Laws, legal codes, court procedures, precedents, government regulations, executive orders, agency rules, and the democratic political process.

Business Teachers, Postsecondary

- Education/Training Required: Master's degree
- Annual Earnings: $59,210
- Growth: 32.2%
- Annual Job Openings: 329,000
- Self-Employed: 0.4%
- Part-Time: 27.3%

The job openings listed here are shared with 35 other postsecondary teaching occupations. For a complete list, see the beginning of this section.

Teach courses in business administration and management, such as accounting, finance, human resources, labor relations, marketing, and operations research. Prepare and deliver lectures to undergraduate and/or graduate students on topics such as financial accounting, principles of marketing, and operations management. Evaluate and grade students' classwork, assignments, and papers. Compile, administer, and grade examinations or assign this work to others. Prepare course materials such as syllabi, homework assignments, and handouts. Maintain student attendance records, grades, and other required records. Initiate, facilitate, and moderate classroom discussions. Plan, evaluate, and revise curricula, course content, and course materials and methods of instruction. Keep abreast of developments in their field by reading current literature, talking with colleagues, and participating in professional organizations and conferences. Maintain regularly scheduled office hours to advise and assist students. Advise students on academic and vocational curricula and on career issues. Select and obtain materials and supplies such as textbooks. Collaborate with colleagues to address teaching and research issues. Collaborate with members of the business community to improve programs, to develop new programs, and to provide student access to learning opportunities such as internships. Participate in student recruitment, registration, and placement activities. Serve on academic or administrative committees that deal with institutional policies, departmental matters, and academic issues. Participate in campus and community events. Compile bibliographies of specialized materials for outside reading assignments. Perform administrative duties such as serving as department head. Supervise undergraduate and/or graduate teaching, internship, and research work. Conduct research in a particular field of knowledge and publish findings in professional journals, books, and/or electronic media. Act as advisers to student organizations. Provide professional consulting services to government and/or industry. Write grant proposals to procure external research funding.

SKILLS—Most Important: Thought-Processing Skills; Communication Skills; Social Skills. **Other Above-Average Skills:** Mathematics Skills; Management Skills.

GOE—Interest Area: 05. Education and Training. **Work Group:** 05.03. Postsecondary and Adult Teaching and Instructing. **Other Jobs in This Group:** Adult Literacy, Remedial Education, and GED Teachers and Instructors; Agricultural Sciences Teachers, Postsecondary; Anthropology and Archeology Teachers, Postsecondary; Architecture Teachers, Postsecondary; Area, Ethnic, and Cultural Studies Teachers, Postsecondary; Art, Drama, and Music Teachers, Postsecondary; Atmospheric, Earth, Marine, and Space Sciences Teachers, Postsecondary; Biological Science Teachers, Postsecondary; Chemistry Teachers, Postsecondary; Communications Teachers, Postsecondary; Computer Science Teachers, Postsecondary; Criminal Justice and Law Enforcement Teachers, Postsecondary; Economics Teachers, Postsecondary; Education Teachers, Postsecondary; Engineering Teachers, Postsecondary; English Language and Literature Teachers, Postsecondary; Environmental Science Teachers, Postsecondary; Farm and Home Management Advisors; Foreign Language and Literature Teachers, Postsecondary; Forestry and Conservation Science Teachers, Postsecondary; Geography Teachers, Postsecondary; Graduate Teaching Assistants; Health Specialties Teachers, Postsecondary; History Teachers, Postsecondary; Home Economics Teachers, Postsecondary; Law Teachers, Postsecondary; Library Science Teachers, Postsecondary; Mathematical Science Teachers, Postsecondary; Nursing Instructors and Teachers, Postsecondary; Philosophy and Religion Teachers, Postsecondary; Physics Teachers, Postsecondary; Political Science Teachers, Postsecondary; Psychology Teachers, Postsecondary; Recreation and Fitness Studies Teachers, Postsecondary; Self-Enrichment Education Teachers; Social Work Teachers, Postsecondary; Sociology Teachers, Postsecondary; Vocational Education Teachers, Postsecondary. **PERSONALITY TYPE:** No data available.

EDUCATION/TRAINING PROGRAM(S)—Business Teacher Education; Business/Commerce, General; Business Administration and Management, General; Purchasing, Procurement/Acquisitions, and Contracts Management; Logistics and Materials Management; Operations Management and Supervision; Accounting; Business/Corporate Communications; Entrepreneurship/Entrepreneurial Studies; Franchising and Franchise Operations; Finance, General; others. **RELATED KNOWLEDGE/COURSES—Education and Training:** Principles and methods for curriculum and training design, teaching and instruction for individuals and groups, and the measurement of training effects. **Economics and Accounting:** Economic and accounting principles and practices, the financial markets, banking, and the analysis and reporting of financial data. **Sales and Marketing:** Principles and methods for showing, promoting, and selling products or services. This includes marketing strategy and tactics, product demonstration, sales techniques, and sales control systems. **English Language:** The structure and content of the English language, including the meaning and spelling of words, rules of composition, and grammar. **Sociology and Anthropology:** Group behavior and dynamics, societal trends and influences, human migrations, ethnicity, and cultures and their history and origins. **Personnel and Human Resources:** Principles and procedures for personnel recruitment, selection, training, compensation and benefits, labor relations and negotiation, and personnel information systems.

Cardiovascular Technologists and Technicians

- ◎ Education/Training Required: Associate degree
- ◎ Annual Earnings: $40,420
- ◎ Growth: 32.6%
- ◎ Annual Job Openings: 5,000
- ◎ Self-Employed: 0.4%
- ◎ Part-Time: 17.2%

Conduct tests on pulmonary or cardiovascular systems of patients for diagnostic purposes. May conduct or assist in electrocardiograms, cardiac catheterizations, pulmonary-functions, lung capacity, and similar tests. Monitor patients' blood pressure and heart rate, using electrocardiogram (EKG) equipment, during diagnostic and therapeutic procedures to notify the physician if something appears wrong. Monitor patients' comfort and safety during tests, alerting physicians to abnormalities or changes in patient responses. Explain testing procedures to patient to obtain cooperation and reduce anxiety. Prepare reports of diagnostic procedures for interpretation by physician. Observe gauges, recorder, and video screens of data analysis system during imaging of cardiovascular system. Conduct electrocardiogram (EKG), phonocardiogram, echocardiogram, stress testing, or other cardiovascular tests to record patients' cardiac activity, using specialized electronic test equipment, recording devices, and laboratory instruments. Obtain and record patient identification, medical history, or test results. Prepare and position patients for testing. Attach electrodes to the patients' chests, arms, and legs; connect electrodes to leads from the electrocardiogram (EKG) machine; and operate the EKG machine to obtain a reading. Adjust equipment and controls according to physicians' orders or established protocol. Check, test, and maintain cardiology equipment, making minor repairs when necessary, to ensure proper operation. Supervise and train other cardiology technologists and students. Assist physicians in diagnosis and treatment of cardiac and peripheral vascular treatments, for example, assisting with balloon angioplasties to treat blood vessel blockages. Operate diagnostic imaging equipment to produce contrast-enhanced radiographs of heart and cardiovascular system. Inject contrast medium into patients' blood vessels. Observe ultrasound display screen and listen to signals to record vascular information such as blood pressure, limb volume changes, oxygen saturation, and cerebral circulation. Assess cardiac physiology and calculate valve areas from blood flow velocity measurements. Compare measurements of heart wall thickness and chamber sizes to standard norms to identify abnormalities. Activate fluoroscope and camera to produce images used to guide catheter through cardiovascular system.

SKILLS—Most Important: Science Skills; Equipment Use/Maintenance Skills; Quality Control Skills. **Other Above-Average Skills:** Social Skills; Communication Skills; Management Skills; Mathematics Skills.

GOE—Interest Area: 08. Health Science. **Work Group:** 08.06. Medical Technology. **Other Jobs in This Group:** Biological Technicians; Diagnostic Medical Sonographers; Medical and Clinical Laboratory Technicians; Medical and Clinical Laboratory Technologists; Medical Equipment Preparers; Medical Records and Health Information Technicians; Nuclear Medicine Technologists; Opticians, Dispensing; Orthotists and Prosthetists; Radiologic Technicians; Radiologic Technologists; Radiologic Technologists and Technicians. **PERSONALITY TYPE:** Investigative. Investigative occupations frequently involve working with ideas and require an extensive amount of thinking. These occupations can involve searching for facts and figuring out problems mentally.

EDUCATION/TRAINING PROGRAM(S)—Cardiovascular Technology/Technologist; Electrocardiograph Technology/Technician; Perfusion Technology/Perfusionist; Cardiopulmonary Technology/Technologist. **RELATED KNOWLEDGE/COURSES—Medicine and Dentistry:** The information and techniques needed to diagnose and treat human injuries, diseases, and deformities. This includes symptoms, treatment alternatives, drug properties and interactions, and preventive healthcare measures. **Customer and Personal Service:** Principles and processes for providing customer and personal services. This includes customer needs assessment, meeting of quality standards for services, and evaluation of customer satisfaction. **Psychology:** Human behavior and performance; individual differences in ability, personality, and interests; learning and motivation; psychological research methods; and the assessment and treatment of behavioral and affective disorders. **Physics:** Physical principles and laws and their interrelationships and applications to understanding fluid, material, and atmospheric dynamics and mechanical, electrical, atomic, and subatomic structures and processes. **Biology:** Plant and animal organisms and their tissues, cells, functions, interdependencies, and interactions with each other and the environment. **Therapy and Counseling:** Principles, methods, and procedures for diagnosis, treatment, and rehabilitation of physical and mental dysfunctions and for career counseling and guidance.

Cement Masons and Concrete Finishers

- Education/Training Required: Moderate-term on-the-job training
- Annual Earnings: $32,030
- Growth: 15.9%
- Annual Job Openings: 32,000
- Self-Employed: 3.1%
- Part-Time: 8.5%

Smooth and finish surfaces of poured concrete, such as floors, walks, sidewalks, roads, or curbs, using a variety of hand and power tools. Align forms for sidewalks, curbs, or gutters; patch voids; and use saws to cut expansion joints. Check the forms that hold the concrete to see that they are properly constructed. Set the forms that hold concrete to the desired pitch and depth and align them. Spread, level, and smooth concrete, using rake, shovel, hand or power trowel, hand or power screed, and float. Mold expansion joints and edges, using edging tools, jointers, and straightedge. Monitor how the wind, heat, or cold affect the curing of the concrete throughout the entire process. Signal truck driver to position truck to facilitate pouring concrete and move chute to direct concrete on forms. Produce rough concrete surface, using broom. Operate power vibrator to compact concrete. Direct the casting of the concrete and supervise laborers who use shovels or special tools to spread it. Mix cement, sand, and water to produce concrete, grout, or slurry, using hoe, trowel, tamper, scraper, or concrete-mixing machine. Cut out damaged areas, drill holes for reinforcing rods, and position reinforcing rods to repair concrete, using power saw and drill. Wet surface to prepare for bonding, fill holes and cracks with grout or slurry, and smooth, using trowel. Wet concrete surface and rub with stone to smooth surface and obtain specified finish. Clean chipped area, using wire brush, and feel and observe surface to determine if it is rough or uneven. Apply hardening and sealing compounds to cure surface of concrete and waterproof or restore surface. Chip, scrape, and grind high spots, ridges, and rough projections to finish concrete, using pneumatic chisels, power grinders, or hand tools. Spread roofing paper on surface of foundation and spread concrete onto roofing paper with trowel to form terrazzo base.

Build wooden molds and clamp molds around area to be repaired, using hand tools. Sprinkle colored marble or stone chips, powdered steel, or coloring powder over surface to produce prescribed finish. Cut metal division strips and press them into terrazzo base so that top edges form desired design or pattern. Fabricate concrete beams, columns, and panels. Waterproof or restore concrete surfaces, using appropriate compounds.

SKILLS—Most Important: Mathematics Skills. **Other Above-Average Skills:** None met the criteria.

GOE—Interest Area: 02. Architecture and Construction. **Work Group:** 02.04. Construction Crafts. **Other Jobs in This Group:** Boilermakers; Brickmasons and Blockmasons; Carpet Installers; Commercial Divers; Construction Carpenters; Crane and Tower Operators; Drywall and Ceiling Tile Installers; Electricians; Fence Erectors; Floor Layers, Except Carpet, Wood, and Hard Tiles; Floor Sanders and Finishers; Glaziers; Hazardous Materials Removal Workers; Insulation Workers, Floor, Ceiling, and Wall; Insulation Workers, Mechanical; Manufactured Building and Mobile Home Installers; Operating Engineers and Other Construction Equipment Operators; Painters, Construction and Maintenance; Paperhangers; Paving, Surfacing, and Tamping Equipment Operators; Pile-Driver Operators; Pipe Fitters and Steamfitters; Pipelayers; Plasterers and Stucco Masons; Plumbers; Plumbers, Pipefitters, and Steamfitters; Rail-Track Laying and Maintenance Equipment Operators; Refractory Materials Repairers, Except Brickmasons; Reinforcing Iron and Rebar Workers; Riggers; Roofers; Rough Carpenters; Security and Fire Alarm Systems Installers; Segmental Pavers; Sheet Metal Workers; Stone Cutters and Carvers, Manufacturing; Stonemasons; Structural Iron and Steel Workers; Tapers; Terrazzo Workers and Finishers; Tile and Marble Setters. **PERSONALITY TYPE:** Realistic. Realistic occupations frequently involve work activities that include practical, hands-on problems and solutions. They often deal with plants, animals, and real-world materials like wood, tools, and machinery. Many of the occupations require working outside and do not involve a lot of paperwork or working closely with others.

EDUCATION/TRAINING PROGRAM(S)—Concrete Finishing/Concrete Finisher. **RELATED KNOWLEDGE/COURSES—Building and Construction:** The materials, methods, and tools involved in the construction or repair of houses, buildings, or other structures such as highways and roads. **Foreign Language:** The structure and content of a foreign (non-English) language, including the meaning and spelling of words, rules of composition and grammar, and pronunciation. **Mechanical Devices:** Machines and tools, including their designs, uses, repair, and maintenance. **Design:** Design techniques, tools, and principles involved in production of precision technical plans, blueprints, drawings, and models. **Administration and Management:** Business and management principles involved in strategic planning, resource allocation, human resources modeling, leadership technique, production methods, and coordination of people and resources. **Engineering and Technology:** The practical application of engineering science and technology. This includes applying principles, techniques, procedures, and equipment to the design and production of various goods and services.

Chemical Engineers

- ⚙ Education/Training Required: Bachelor's degree
- ⚙ Annual Earnings: $77,140
- ⚙ Growth: 10.6%
- ⚙ Annual Job Openings: 3,000
- ⚙ Self-Employed: 0.0%
- ⚙ Part-Time: 4.5%

Design chemical plant equipment and devise processes for manufacturing chemicals and products, such as gasoline, synthetic rubber, plastics, detergents, cement, paper, and pulp, by applying principles and technology of chemistry, physics, and engineering. Perform tests throughout stages of production to determine degree of control over variables, including temperature, density, specific gravity, and pressure. Develop safety procedures to be employed by workers operating equipment or working in close proximity to ongoing chemical reactions. Determine most effective arrangement of operations such as mixing, crushing, heat transfer, distillation, and drying. Prepare estimate of production costs and production progress reports for management. Direct activities of workers who operate or who are engaged in constructing and improving

absorption, evaporation, or electromagnetic equipment. Perform laboratory studies of steps in manufacture of new product and test proposed process in small-scale operation such as a pilot plant. Develop processes to separate components of liquids or gases or generate electrical currents by using controlled chemical processes. Conduct research to develop new and improved chemical manufacturing processes. Design measurement and control systems for chemical plants based on data collected in laboratory experiments and in pilot plant operations. Design and plan layout of equipment.

SKILLS—Most Important: Science Skills; Computer Programming Skills; Equipment/Technology Analysis Skills. **Other Above-Average Skills:** Mathematics Skills; Quality Control Skills; Management Skills; Communication Skills; Social Skills.

GOE—Interest Area: 15. Scientific Research, Engineering, and Mathematics. **Work Group:** 15.07. Research and Design Engineering. **Other Jobs in This Group:** Aerospace Engineers; Biomedical Engineers; Civil Engineers; Computer Hardware Engineers; Electrical Engineers; Electronics Engineers, Except Computer; Marine Architects; Marine Engineers; Marine Engineers and Naval Architects; Materials Engineers; Mechanical Engineers; Nuclear Engineers. **PERSONALITY TYPE:** Investigative. Investigative occupations frequently involve working with ideas and require an extensive amount of thinking. These occupations can involve searching for facts and figuring out problems mentally.

EDUCATION/TRAINING PROGRAM(S)—Chemical Engineering. **RELATED KNOWLEDGE/COURSES—Engineering and Technology:** The practical application of engineering science and technology. This includes applying principles, techniques, procedures, and equipment to the design and production of various goods and services. **Chemistry:** The chemical composition, structure, and properties of substances and of the chemical processes and transformations that they undergo. This includes uses of chemicals and their danger signs, production techniques, and disposal methods. **Physics:** Physical principles and laws and their interrelationships and applications to understanding fluid, material, and atmospheric dynamics and mechanical, electrical, atomic, and subatomic structures and processes. **Design:** Design techniques, tools, and principles involved in production of precision technical plans, blueprints, drawings, and models. **Production and Processing:** Raw materials, production processes, quality control, costs, and other techniques for maximizing the effective manufacture and distribution of goods. **Mathematics:** Arithmetic, algebra, geometry, calculus, and statistics and their applications.

Chemistry Teachers, Postsecondary

- Education/Training Required: Master's degree
- Annual Earnings: $58,060
- Growth: 32.2%
- Annual Job Openings: 329,000
- Self-Employed: 0.4%
- Part-Time: 27.3%

The job openings listed here are shared with 35 other postsecondary teaching occupations. For a complete list, see the beginning of this section.

Teach courses pertaining to the chemical and physical properties and compositional changes of substances. Work may include instruction in the methods of qualitative and quantitative chemical analysis. Includes both teachers primarily engaged in teaching and those who do a combination of both teaching and research. Prepare and deliver lectures to undergraduate and/or graduate students on topics such as organic chemistry, analytical chemistry, and chemical separation. Supervise students' laboratory work. Evaluate and grade students' classwork, laboratory performance, assignments, and papers. Compile, administer, and grade examinations or assign this work to others. Maintain student attendance records, grades, and other required records. Prepare course materials such as syllabi, homework assignments, and handouts. Maintain regularly scheduled office hours in order to advise and assist students. Plan, evaluate, and revise curricula, course content, and course materials and methods of instruction. Supervise undergraduate and/or graduate teaching, internship, and research work. Keep abreast of developments in their field by reading current literature, talking with colleagues, and participating in professional conferences.

Initiate, facilitate, and moderate classroom discussions. Select and obtain materials and supplies such as textbooks and laboratory equipment. Conduct research in a particular field of knowledge and publish findings in professional journals, books, and/or electronic media. Advise students on academic and vocational curricula and on career issues. Collaborate with colleagues to address teaching and research issues. Serve on academic or administrative committees that deal with institutional policies, departmental matters, and academic issues. Write grant proposals to procure external research funding. Participate in student recruitment, registration, and placement activities. Prepare and submit required reports related to instruction. Perform administrative duties such as serving as a department head. Act as advisers to student organizations. Compile bibliographies of specialized materials for outside reading assignments. Participate in campus and community events. Provide professional consulting services to government and/or industry.

SKILLS—Most Important: Science Skills; Mathematics Skills; Communication Skills. **Other Above-Average Skills:** Thought-Processing Skills; Equipment/Technology Analysis Skills; Equipment Use/Maintenance Skills; Quality Control Skills.

GOE—Interest Area: 05. Education and Training. **Work Group:** 05.03. Postsecondary and Adult Teaching and Instructing. **Other Jobs in This Group:** Adult Literacy, Remedial Education, and GED Teachers and Instructors; Agricultural Sciences Teachers, Postsecondary; Anthropology and Archeology Teachers, Postsecondary; Architecture Teachers, Postsecondary; Area, Ethnic, and Cultural Studies Teachers, Postsecondary; Art, Drama, and Music Teachers, Postsecondary; Atmospheric, Earth, Marine, and Space Sciences Teachers, Postsecondary; Biological Science Teachers, Postsecondary; Business Teachers, Postsecondary; Communications Teachers, Postsecondary; Computer Science Teachers, Postsecondary; Criminal Justice and Law Enforcement Teachers, Postsecondary; Economics Teachers, Postsecondary; Education Teachers, Postsecondary; Engineering Teachers, Postsecondary; English Language and Literature Teachers, Postsecondary; Environmental Science Teachers, Postsecondary; Farm and Home Management Advisors; Foreign Language and Literature Teachers, Postsecondary; Forestry and Conservation Science

Teachers, Postsecondary; Geography Teachers, Postsecondary; Graduate Teaching Assistants; Health Specialties Teachers, Postsecondary; History Teachers, Postsecondary; Home Economics Teachers, Postsecondary; Law Teachers, Postsecondary; Library Science Teachers, Postsecondary; Mathematical Science Teachers, Postsecondary; Nursing Instructors and Teachers, Postsecondary; Philosophy and Religion Teachers, Postsecondary; Physics Teachers, Postsecondary; Political Science Teachers, Postsecondary; Psychology Teachers, Postsecondary; Recreation and Fitness Studies Teachers, Postsecondary; Self-Enrichment Education Teachers; Social Work Teachers, Postsecondary; Sociology Teachers, Postsecondary; Vocational Education Teachers, Postsecondary. **PERSONALITY TYPE:** Investigative. Investigative occupations frequently involve working with ideas and require an extensive amount of thinking. These occupations can involve searching for facts and figuring out problems mentally.

EDUCATION/TRAINING PROGRAM(S)—Chemistry, General; Analytical Chemistry; Inorganic Chemistry; Organic Chemistry; Physical and Theoretical Chemistry; Polymer Chemistry; Chemical Physics; Chemistry, Other; Geochemistry. **RELATED KNOWLEDGE/COURSES—Chemistry:** The chemical composition, structure, and properties of substances and of the chemical processes and transformations that they undergo. This includes uses of chemicals and their danger signs, production techniques, and disposal methods. **Biology:** Plant and animal organisms and their tissues, cells, functions, interdependencies, and interactions with each other and the environment. **Physics:** Physical principles and laws and their interrelationships and applications to understanding fluid, material, and atmospheric dynamics and mechanical, electrical, atomic, and subatomic structures and processes. **Education and Training:** Principles and methods for curriculum and training design, teaching and instruction for individuals and groups, and the measurement of training effects. **Mathematics:** Arithmetic, algebra, geometry, calculus, and statistics and their applications. **English Language:** The structure and content of the English language, including the meaning and spelling of words, rules of composition, and grammar.

Chemists

◎ Education/Training Required: Bachelor's degree
◎ Annual Earnings: $57,890
◎ Growth: 7.3%
◎ Annual Job Openings: 5,000
◎ Self-Employed: 0.4%
◎ Part-Time: 6.6%

Conduct qualitative and quantitative chemical analyses or chemical experiments in laboratories for quality or process control or to develop new products or knowledge. Analyze organic and inorganic compounds to determine chemical and physical properties, composition, structure, relationships, and reactions, utilizing chromatography, spectroscopy, and spectrophotometry techniques. Develop, improve, and customize products, equipment, formulas, processes, and analytical methods. Compile and analyze test information to determine process or equipment operating efficiency and to diagnose malfunctions. Confer with scientists and engineers to conduct analyses of research projects, interpret test results, or develop nonstandard tests. Direct, coordinate, and advise personnel in test procedures for analyzing components and physical properties of materials. Induce changes in composition of substances by introducing heat, light, energy, and chemical catalysts for quantitative and qualitative analysis. Write technical papers and reports and prepare standards and specifications for processes, facilities, products, or tests. Study effects of various methods of processing, preserving, and packaging on composition and properties of foods. Prepare test solutions, compounds, and reagents for laboratory personnel to conduct test.

SKILLS—Most Important: Science Skills; Quality Control Skills; Equipment/Technology Analysis Skills. **Other Above-Average Skills:** Management Skills; Mathematics Skills; Equipment Use/Maintenance Skills; Communication Skills; Social Skills.

GOE—Interest Area: 15. Scientific Research, Engineering, and Mathematics. **Work Group:** 15.02. Physical Sciences. **Other Jobs in This Group:** Astronomers; Atmospheric and Space Scientists; Geographers; Geoscientists, Except Hydrologists and

Geographers; Hydrologists; Materials Scientists; Physicists. **PERSONALITY TYPE:** Investigative. Investigative occupations frequently involve working with ideas and require an extensive amount of thinking. These occupations can involve searching for facts and figuring out problems mentally.

EDUCATION/TRAINING PROGRAM(S)—Chemistry, General; Analytical Chemistry; Inorganic Chemistry; Organic Chemistry; Physical and Theoretical Chemistry; Polymer Chemistry; Chemical Physics; Chemistry, Other. **RELATED KNOWLEDGE/COURSES—Chemistry:** The chemical composition, structure, and properties of substances and of the chemical processes and transformations that they undergo. This includes uses of chemicals and their danger signs, production techniques, and disposal methods. **Mathematics:** Arithmetic, algebra, geometry, calculus, and statistics and their applications. **Engineering and Technology:** The practical application of engineering science and technology. This includes applying principles, techniques, procedures, and equipment to the design and production of various goods and services. **Production and Processing:** Raw materials, production processes, quality control, costs, and other techniques for maximizing the effective manufacture and distribution of goods. **Computers and Electronics:** Circuit boards; processors; chips; electronic equipment; and computer hardware and software, including applications and programming. **Education and Training:** Principles and methods for curriculum and training design, teaching and instruction for individuals and groups, and the measurement of training effects.

Chief Executives

- ◎ Education/Training Required: Work experience plus degree
- ◎ Annual Earnings: $142,440
- ◎ Growth: 14.9%
- ◎ Annual Job Openings: 38,000
- ◎ Self-Employed: 16.2%
- ◎ Part-Time: 6.8%

Determine and formulate policies and provide the overall direction of companies or private and public **sector organizations within the guidelines set up by a board of directors or similar governing body. Plan, direct, or coordinate operational activities at the highest level of management with the help of subordinate executives and staff managers.** Direct and coordinate an organization's financial and budget activities in order to fund operations, maximize investments, and increase efficiency. Confer with board members, organization officials, and staff members to discuss issues, coordinate activities, and resolve problems. Analyze operations to evaluate performance of a company and its staff in meeting objectives and to determine areas of potential cost reduction, program improvement, or policy change. Direct, plan, and implement policies, objectives, and activities of organizations or businesses in order to ensure continuing operations, to maximize returns on investments, and to increase productivity. Prepare budgets for approval, including those for funding and implementation of programs. Direct and coordinate activities of businesses or departments concerned with production, pricing, sales, and/or distribution of products. Negotiate or approve contracts and agreements with suppliers, distributors, federal and state agencies, and other organizational entities. Review reports submitted by staff members in order to recommend approval or to suggest changes. Appoint department heads or managers and assign or delegate responsibilities to them. Direct human resources activities, including the approval of human resource plans and activities, the selection of directors and other high-level staff, and establishment and organization of major departments. Preside over or serve on boards of directors, management committees, or other governing boards. Prepare and present reports concerning activities, expenses, budgets, government statutes and rulings, and other items affecting businesses or program services. Establish departmental responsibilities and coordinate functions among departments and sites. Implement corrective action plans to solve organizational or departmental problems. Coordinate the development and implementation of budgetary control systems, recordkeeping systems, and other administrative control processes. Direct non-merchandising departments such as advertising, purchasing, credit, and accounting. Deliver speeches, write articles, and present information at meetings or conventions in order to promote services, exchange ideas, and accomplish objectives.

SKILLS—**Most Important:** Management Skills; Social Skills; Thought-Processing Skills. **Other Above-Average Skills:** Equipment/Technology Analysis Skills; Communication Skills.

GOE—Interest Area: 04. Business and Administration. **Work Group:** 04.01. Managerial Work in General Business. **Other Jobs in This Group:** Compensation and Benefits Managers; General and Operations Managers; Human Resources Managers; Training and Development Managers. **PERSONALITY TYPE:** Enterprising. Enterprising occupations frequently involve starting up and carrying out projects. These occupations can involve leading people and making many decisions. They sometimes require risk taking and often deal with business.

EDUCATION/TRAINING PROGRAM(S)—Business Administration/Management; Business/Commerce, General; Entrepreneurship/Entrepreneurial Studies; International Business/Trade/Commerce; International Relations and Affairs; Public Administration; Public Administration and Services, Other; Public Policy Analysis; Transportation/Transportation Management. **RELATED KNOWLEDGE/COURSES**—**Administration and Management:** Business and management principles involved in strategic planning, resource allocation, human resources modeling, leadership technique, production methods, and coordination of people and resources. **Economics and Accounting:** Economic and accounting principles and practices, the financial markets, banking, and the analysis and reporting of financial data. **Sales and Marketing:** Principles and methods for showing, promoting, and selling products or services. This includes marketing strategy and tactics, product demonstration, sales techniques, and sales control systems. **Personnel and Human Resources:** Principles and procedures for personnel recruitment, selection, training, compensation and benefits, labor relations and negotiation, and personnel information systems. **Law and Government:** Laws, legal codes, court procedures, precedents, government regulations, executive orders, agency rules, and the democratic political process. **Customer and Personal Service:** Principles and processes for providing customer and personal services. This includes customer needs assessment, meeting of quality standards for services, and evaluation of customer satisfaction.

Chiropractors

- Education/Training Required: First professional degree
- Annual Earnings: $67,200
- Growth: 22.4%
- Annual Job Openings: 4,000
- Self-Employed: 49.2%
- Part-Time: 20.7%

Adjust spinal column and other articulations of the body to correct abnormalities of the human body believed to be caused by interference with the nervous system. Examine patient to determine nature and extent of disorder. Manipulate spine or other involved area. May utilize supplementary measures, such as exercise, rest, water, light, heat, and nutritional therapy. Perform a series of manual adjustments to the spine, or other articulations of the body, to correct the musculoskeletal system. Evaluate the functioning of the neuromuscularskeletal system and the spine, using systems of chiropractic diagnosis. Diagnose health problems by reviewing patients' health and medical histories; questioning, observing, and examining patients; and interpreting X rays. Maintain accurate case histories of patients. Advise patients about recommended courses of treatment. Obtain and record patients' medical histories. Analyze X rays to locate the sources of patients' difficulties and to rule out fractures or diseases as sources of problems. Counsel patients about nutrition, exercise, sleeping habits, stress management, and other matters. Arrange for diagnostic X rays to be taken. Consult with and refer patients to appropriate health practitioners when necessary. Suggest and apply the use of supports such as straps, tapes, bandages, and braces if necessary.

SKILLS—Most Important: Science Skills; Social Skills; Management Skills. **Other Above-Average Skills:** Communication Skills; Thought-Processing Skills; Equipment Use/Maintenance Skills.

GOE—Interest Area: 08. Health Science. **Work Group:** 08.04. Health Specialties. **Other Jobs in This Group:** Optometrists; Podiatrists. **PERSONALITY TYPE:** Investigative. Investigative occupations frequently involve working with ideas and require an extensive amount of thinking. These occupations can involve searching for facts and figuring out problems mentally.

EDUCATION/TRAINING PROGRAM(S)—Chiropractic (DC). **RELATED KNOWLEDGE/ COURSES—Medicine and Dentistry:** The information and techniques needed to diagnose and treat human injuries, diseases, and deformities. This includes symptoms, treatment alternatives, drug properties and interactions, and preventive healthcare measures. **Therapy and Counseling:** Principles, methods, and procedures for diagnosis, treatment, and rehabilitation of physical and mental dysfunctions and for career counseling and guidance. **Biology:** Plant and animal organisms and their tissues, cells, functions, interdependencies, and interactions with each other and the environment. **Psychology:** Human behavior and performance; individual differences in ability, personality, and interests; learning and motivation; psychological research methods; and the assessment and treatment of behavioral and affective disorders. **Sales and Marketing:** Principles and methods for showing, promoting, and selling products or services. This includes marketing strategy and tactics, product demonstration, sales techniques, and sales control systems. **Customer and Personal Service:** Principles and processes for providing customer and personal services. This includes customer needs assessment, meeting of quality standards for services, and evaluation of customer satisfaction.

Civil Engineers

- ◎ Education/Training Required: Bachelor's degree
- ◎ Annual Earnings: $66,190
- ◎ Growth: 16.5%
- ◎ Annual Job Openings: 19,000
- ◎ Self-Employed: 4.9%
- ◎ Part-Time: 3.4%

Perform engineering duties in planning, designing, and overseeing construction and maintenance of building structures and facilities, such as roads, railroads, airports, bridges, harbors, channels, dams, irrigation projects, pipelines, power plants, water and sewage systems, and waste disposal units. Includes architectural, structural, traffic, ocean, and geo-technical engineers. Analyze survey reports, maps, drawings, blueprints, aerial photography, and other topographical

or geologic data to plan projects. Plan and design transportation or hydraulic systems and structures, following construction and government standards and using design software and drawing tools. Compute load and grade requirements, water flow rates, and material stress factors to determine design specifications. Inspect project sites to monitor progress and ensure conformance to design specifications and safety or sanitation standards. Direct construction, operations, and maintenance activities at project site. Direct or participate in surveying to lay out installations and establish reference points, grades, and elevations to guide construction. Estimate quantities and cost of materials, equipment, or labor to determine project feasibility. Prepare or present public reports on topics such as bid proposals, deeds, environmental impact statements, or property and right-of-way descriptions. Test soils and materials to determine the adequacy and strength of foundations, concrete, asphalt, or steel. Provide technical advice regarding design, construction, or program modifications and structural repairs to industrial and managerial personnel. Conduct studies of traffic patterns or environmental conditions to identify engineering problems and assess the potential impact of projects.

SKILLS—Most Important: Science Skills; Mathematics Skills; Equipment/Technology Analysis Skills. **Other Above-Average Skills:** Social Skills; Computer Programming Skills; Communication Skills; Management Skills; Equipment Use/Maintenance Skills.

GOE—Interest Area: 15. Scientific Research, Engineering, and Mathematics. **Work Group:** 15.07. Research and Design Engineering. **Other Jobs in This Group:** Aerospace Engineers; Biomedical Engineers; Chemical Engineers; Computer Hardware Engineers; Electrical Engineers; Electronics Engineers, Except Computer; Marine Architects; Marine Engineers; Marine Engineers and Naval Architects; Materials Engineers; Mechanical Engineers; Nuclear Engineers. **PERSONALITY TYPE:** Realistic. Realistic occupations frequently involve work activities that include practical, hands-on problems and solutions. They often deal with plants, animals, and real-world materials like wood, tools, and machinery. Many of the occupations require working outside and do not involve a lot of paperwork or working closely with others.

EDUCATION/TRAINING PROGRAM(S)—Civil Engineering, General; Transportation and Highway

Engineering; Water Resources Engineering; Civil Engineering, Other. **RELATED KNOWLEDGE/ COURSES—Engineering and Technology:** The practical application of engineering science and technology. This includes applying principles, techniques, procedures, and equipment to the design and production of various goods and services. **Design:** Design techniques, tools, and principles involved in production of precision technical plans, blueprints, drawings, and models. **Building and Construction:** The materials, methods, and tools involved in the construction or repair of houses, buildings, or other structures such as highways and roads. **Physics:** Physical principles and laws and their interrelationships and applications to understanding fluid, material, and atmospheric dynamics and mechanical, electrical, atomic, and subatomic structures and processes. **Mathematics:** Arithmetic, algebra, geometry, calculus, and statistics and their applications. **Transportation:** Principles and methods for moving people or goods by air, rail, sea, or road, including the relative costs and benefits.

Clinical Psychologists

◎ Education/Training Required: Doctoral degree
◎ Annual Earnings: $57,170
◎ Growth: 19.1%
◎ Annual Job Openings: 10,000
◎ Self-Employed: 38.2%
◎ Part-Time: 22.8%

The job openings listed here are shared with Counseling Psychologists and School Psychologists.

Diagnose or evaluate mental and emotional disorders of individuals through observation, interview, and psychological tests and formulate and administer programs of treatment. Identify psychological, emotional, or behavioral issues and diagnose disorders, using information obtained from interviews, tests, records, and reference materials. Develop and implement individual treatment plans, specifying type, frequency, intensity, and duration of therapy. Interact with clients to assist them in gaining insight, defining goals, and planning action to achieve effective personal, social, educational, and vocational development and adjustment. Discuss the treatment of problems with clients. Utilize a variety of treatment methods such as psychotherapy, hypnosis, behavior modification, stress reduction therapy, psychodrama, and play therapy. Counsel individuals and groups regarding problems such as stress, substance abuse, and family situations to modify behavior or to improve personal, social, and vocational adjustment. Write reports on clients and maintain required paperwork. Evaluate the effectiveness of counseling or treatments and the accuracy and completeness of diagnoses; then modify plans and diagnoses as necessary. Obtain and study medical, psychological, social, and family histories by interviewing individuals, couples, or families and by reviewing records. Consult reference material such as textbooks, manuals, and journals to identify symptoms, make diagnoses, and develop approaches to treatment. Maintain current knowledge of relevant research. Observe individuals at play, in group interactions, or in other contexts to detect indications of mental deficiency, abnormal behavior, or maladjustment. Select, administer, score, and interpret psychological tests to obtain information on individuals' intelligence, achievements, interests, and personalities. Refer clients to other specialists, institutions, or support services as necessary. Develop, direct, and participate in training programs for staff and students. Provide psychological or administrative services and advice to private firms and community agencies regarding mental health programs or individual cases. Provide occupational, educational, and other information to individuals so that they can make educational and vocational plans.

SKILLS—Most Important: Social Skills; Thought-Processing Skills; Communication Skills. **Other Above-Average Skills:** Science Skills.

GOE—Interest Area: 10. Human Service. **Work Group:** 10.01. Counseling and Social Work. **Other Jobs in This Group:** Child, Family, and School Social Workers; Clinical, Counseling, and School Psychologists; Counseling Psychologists; Marriage and Family Therapists; Medical and Public Health Social Workers; Mental Health and Substance Abuse Social Workers; Mental Health Counselors; Probation Officers and Correctional Treatment Specialists; Rehabilitation Counselors; Residential Advisors; Social and Human Service Assistants; Substance Abuse and Behavioral Disorder Counselors. **PERSONALITY TYPE:** Investigative. Investigative occupations frequently involve working with ideas and require an extensive amount of thinking. These occupations can involve searching for facts and figuring out problems mentally.

EDUCATION/TRAINING PROGRAM(S)—Psychology, General; Clinical Psychology; Counseling Psychology; Developmental and Child Psychology; School Psychology; Clinical Child Psychology; Psychoanalysis and Psychotherapy. **RELATED KNOWLEDGE/COURSES—Therapy and Counseling:** Principles, methods, and procedures for diagnosis, treatment, and rehabilitation of physical and mental dysfunctions and for career counseling and guidance. **Psychology:** Human behavior and performance; individual differences in ability, personality, and interests; learning and motivation; psychological research methods; and the assessment and treatment of behavioral and affective disorders. **Sociology and Anthropology:** Group behavior and dynamics, societal trends and influences, human migrations, ethnicity, and cultures and their history and origins. **Philosophy and Theology:** Different philosophical systems and religions. This includes their basic principles, values, ethics, ways of thinking, customs, practices, and impact on human culture. **Customer and Personal Service:** Principles and processes for providing customer and personal services. This includes customer needs assessment, meeting of quality standards for services, and evaluation of customer satisfaction. **Medicine and Dentistry:** The information and techniques needed to diagnose and treat human injuries, diseases, and deformities. This includes symptoms, treatment alternatives, drug properties and interactions, and preventive healthcare measures.

Coaches and Scouts

- ⊚ Education/Training Required: Long-term on-the-job training
- ⊚ Annual Earnings: $25,990
- ⊚ Growth: 20.4%
- ⊚ Annual Job Openings: 63,000
- ⊚ Self-Employed: 21.5%
- ⊚ Part-Time: 47.6%

Instruct or coach groups or individuals in the fundamentals of sports. Demonstrate techniques and methods of participation. May evaluate athletes' strengths and weaknesses as possible recruits or to improve the athletes' technique to prepare them for competition. Plan, organize, and conduct practice sessions. Provide training direction, encouragement, and motivation to prepare athletes for games, competitive events, or tours. Identify and recruit potential athletes, arranging and offering incentives such as athletic scholarships. Plan strategies and choose team members for individual games or sports seasons. Plan and direct physical conditioning programs that will enable athletes to achieve maximum performance. Adjust coaching techniques based on the strengths and weaknesses of athletes. File scouting reports that detail player assessments, provide recommendations on athlete recruitment, and identify locations and individuals to be targeted for future recruitment efforts. Keep records of athlete, team, and opposing team performance. Instruct individuals or groups in sports rules, game strategies, and performance principles such as specific ways of moving the body, hands, and feet in order to achieve desired results. Analyze the strengths and weaknesses of opposing teams to develop game strategies. Evaluate athletes' skills and review performance records to determine their fitness and potential in a particular area of athletics. Keep abreast of changing rules, techniques, technologies, and philosophies relevant to their sport. Monitor athletes' use of equipment to ensure safe and proper use. Explain and enforce safety rules and regulations. Develop and arrange competition schedules and programs. Serve as organizer, leader, instructor, or referee for outdoor and indoor games such as volleyball, football, and soccer. Explain and demonstrate the use of sports and training equipment, such as trampolines or weights. Perform activities that support a team or a specific sport, such as meeting with media representatives and appearing at fundraising events. Arrange and conduct sports-related activities such as training camps, skill-improvement courses, clinics, or pre-season try-outs. Select, acquire, store, and issue equipment and other materials as necessary. Negotiate with professional athletes or their representatives to obtain services and arrange contracts.

SKILLS—Most Important: Social Skills; Management Skills; Thought-Processing Skills. **Other Above-Average Skills:** Communication Skills; Equipment/Technology Analysis Skills.

GOE—Interest Area: 09. Hospitality, Tourism, and Recreation. **Work Group:** 09.06. Sports. **Other Jobs in This Group:** Athletes and Sports Competitors;

Umpires, Referees, and Other Sports Officials. **PERSONALITY TYPE:** Enterprising. Enterprising occupations frequently involve starting up and carrying out projects. These occupations can involve leading people and making many decisions. They sometimes require risk taking and often deal with business.

EDUCATION/TRAINING PROGRAM(S)—Physical Education Teaching and Coaching; Health and Physical Education, General; Sport and Fitness Administration/Management. **RELATED KNOWLEDGE/COURSES**—**Psychology:** Human behavior and performance; individual differences in ability, personality, and interests; learning and motivation; psychological research methods; and the assessment and treatment of behavioral and affective disorders. **Education and Training:** Principles and methods for curriculum and training design, teaching and instruction for individuals and groups, and the measurement of training effects. **Sales and Marketing:** Principles and methods for showing, promoting, and selling products or services. This includes marketing strategy and tactics, product demonstration, sales techniques, and sales control systems. **Therapy and Counseling:** Principles, methods, and procedures for diagnosis, treatment, and rehabilitation of physical and mental dysfunctions and for career counseling and guidance. **Personnel and Human Resources:** Principles and procedures for personnel recruitment, selection, training, compensation and benefits, labor relations and negotiation, and personnel information systems. **Sociology and Anthropology:** Group behavior and dynamics, societal trends and influences, human migrations, ethnicity, and cultures and their history and origins.

Commercial and Industrial Designers

- Education/Training Required: Bachelor's degree
- Annual Earnings: $52,200
- Growth: 10.8%
- Annual Job Openings: 7,000
- Self-Employed: 30.1%
- Part-Time: 21.3%

Develop and design manufactured products, such as cars, home appliances, and children's toys. Combine artistic talent with research on product use, marketing, and materials to create the most functional and appealing product design. Prepare sketches of ideas, detailed drawings, illustrations, artwork, or blueprints, using drafting instruments, paints and brushes, or computer-aided design equipment. Direct and coordinate the fabrication of models or samples and the drafting of working drawings and specification sheets from sketches. Modify and refine designs, using working models, to conform with customer specifications, production limitations, or changes in design trends. Coordinate the look and function of product lines. Confer with engineering, marketing, production, or sales departments, or with customers, to establish and evaluate design concepts for manufactured products. Present designs and reports to customers or design committees for approval and discuss need for modification. Evaluate feasibility of design ideas based on factors such as appearance, safety, function, serviceability, budget, production costs/methods, and market characteristics. Read publications, attend showings, and study competing products and design styles and motifs to obtain perspective and generate design concepts. Research production specifications, costs, production materials, and manufacturing methods and provide cost estimates and itemized production requirements. Design graphic material for use as ornamentation, illustration, or advertising on manufactured materials and packaging or containers. Develop manufacturing procedures and monitor the manufacture of their designs in a factory to improve operations and product quality. Supervise assistants' work throughout the design process. Fabricate models or samples in paper, wood, glass, fabric, plastic, metal, or other materials, using hand or power tools. Investigate product characteristics such as the product's safety and handling qualities; its market appeal; how efficiently it can be produced; and ways of distributing, using, and maintaining it. Develop industrial standards and regulatory guidelines. Participate in new product planning or market research, including studying the potential need for new products. Advise corporations on issues involving corporate image projects or problems.

SKILLS—**Most Important:** Equipment/Technology Analysis Skills; Quality Control Skills; Mathematics Skills. **Other Above-Average Skills:** Thought-Processing Skills; Communication Skills.

GOE—Interest Area: 03. Arts and Communication. **Work Group:** 03.05. Design. **Other Jobs in This Group:** Fashion Designers; Floral Designers; Graphic Designers; Interior Designers; Merchandise Displayers and Window Trimmers; Set and Exhibit Designers. **PERSONALITY TYPE:** Artistic. Artistic occupations frequently involve working with forms, designs, and patterns. They often require self-expression, and the work can be done without following a clear set of rules.

EDUCATION/TRAINING PROGRAM(S)—Design and Visual Communications, General; Commercial and Advertising Art; Industrial Design; Design and Applied Arts, Other. **RELATED KNOWLEDGE/COURSES—Design:** Design techniques, tools, and principles involved in production of precision technical plans, blueprints, drawings, and models. **Engineering and Technology:** The practical application of engineering science and technology. This includes applying principles, techniques, procedures, and equipment to the design and production of various goods and services. **Mathematics:** Arithmetic, algebra, geometry, calculus, and statistics and their applications. **Production and Processing:** Raw materials, production processes, quality control, costs, and other techniques for maximizing the effective manufacture and distribution of goods. **Clerical Practices:** Administrative and clerical procedures and systems such as word processing, managing files and records, stenography and transcription, designing forms, and other office procedures and terminology. **Mechanical Devices:** Machines and tools, including their designs, uses, repair, and maintenance.

Commercial Pilots

- Education/Training Required: Postsecondary vocational training
- Annual Earnings: $55,810
- Growth: 16.8%
- Annual Job Openings: 2,000
- Self-Employed: 2.5%
- Part-Time: 14.8%

Pilot and navigate the flight of small fixed or rotary winged aircraft primarily for the transport of cargo and passengers. Requires Commercial Rating. Check aircraft prior to flights to ensure that the engines, controls, instruments, and other systems are functioning properly. Start engines, operate controls, and pilot airplanes to transport passengers, mail, or freight while adhering to flight plans, regulations, and procedures. Contact control towers for takeoff clearances, arrival instructions, and other information, using radio equipment. Monitor engine operation, fuel consumption, and functioning of aircraft systems during flights. Consider airport altitudes, outside temperatures, plane weights, and wind speeds and directions to calculate the speed needed to become airborne. Order changes in fuel supplies, loads, routes, or schedules to ensure safety of flights. Obtain and review data such as load weights, fuel supplies, weather conditions, and flight schedules to determine flight plans and to see if changes might be necessary. Plan flights, following government and company regulations, using aeronautical charts and navigation instruments. Use instrumentation to pilot aircraft when visibility is poor. Check baggage or cargo to ensure that it has been loaded correctly. Request changes in altitudes or routes as circumstances dictate. Choose routes, altitudes, and speeds that will provide the fastest, safest, and smoothest flights. Coordinate flight activities with ground crews and air-traffic control and inform crew members of flight and test procedures. Write specified information in flight records, such as flight times, altitudes flown, and fuel consumption. Teach company regulations and procedures to other pilots. Instruct other pilots and student pilots in aircraft operations. Co-pilot aircraft or perform captain's duties if required. File instrument flight plans with air traffic control so that flights can be coordinated with other air traffic. Conduct in-flight tests and evaluations at specified altitudes and in all types of weather to determine the receptivity and other characteristics of equipment and systems. Rescue and evacuate injured persons. Supervise other crew members. Perform minor aircraft maintenance and repair work or arrange for major maintenance.

SKILLS—Most Important: Equipment Use/Maintenance Skills; Mathematics Skills; Thought-Processing Skills. **Other Above-Average Skills:** Communication Skills; Science Skills.

GOE—Interest Area: 16. Transportation, Distribution, and Logistics. **Work Group:** 16.02. Air Vehicle Operation. **Other Jobs in This Group:** Airline Pilots, Copilots, and Flight Engineers. **PERSONALITY TYPE:** Realistic. Realistic occupations frequently involve work activities that include practical, hands-on problems and solutions. They often deal with plants, animals, and real-world materials like wood, tools, and machinery. Many of the occupations require working outside and do not involve a lot of paperwork or working closely with others.

EDUCATION/TRAINING PROGRAM(S)—Airline/Commercial/Professional Pilot and Flight Crew; Flight Instructor. **RELATED KNOWLEDGE/ COURSES—Transportation:** Principles and methods for moving people or goods by air, rail, sea, or road, including the relative costs and benefits. **Geography:** Principles and methods for describing the features of land, sea, and air masses, including their physical characteristics; locations; interrelationships; and distribution of plant, animal, and human life. **Mechanical Devices:** Machines and tools, including their designs, uses, repair, and maintenance. **Physics:** Physical principles and laws and their interrelationships and applications to understanding fluid, material, and atmospheric dynamics and mechanical, electrical, atomic, and subatomic structures and processes. **Customer and Personal Service:** Principles and processes for providing customer and personal services. This includes customer needs assessment, meeting of quality standards for services, and evaluation of customer satisfaction. **Psychology:** Human behavior and performance; individual differences in ability, personality, and interests; learning and motivation; psychological research methods; and the assessment and treatment of behavioral and affective disorders.

Communications Teachers, Postsecondary

- Education/Training Required: Master's degree
- Annual Earnings: $50,890
- Growth: 32.2%
- Annual Job Openings: 329,000
- Self-Employed: 0.4%
- Part-Time: 27.3%

The job openings listed here are shared with 35 other postsecondary teaching occupations. For a complete list, see the beginning of this section.

Teach courses in communications, such as organizational communications, public relations, radio/television broadcasting, and journalism. Evaluate and grade students' classwork, assignments, and papers. Prepare course materials such as syllabi, homework assignments, and handouts. Initiate, facilitate, and moderate classroom discussions. Prepare and deliver lectures to undergraduate or graduate students on topics such as public speaking, media criticism, and oral traditions. Compile, administer, and grade examinations or assign this work to others. Maintain student attendance records, grades, and other required records. Plan, evaluate, and revise curricula, course content, and course materials and methods of instruction. Maintain regularly scheduled office hours to advise and assist students. Keep abreast of developments in their field by reading current literature, talking with colleagues, and participating in professional conferences. Advise students on academic and vocational curricula and on career issues. Supervise undergraduate or graduate teaching, internship, and research work. Select and obtain materials and supplies such as textbooks. Collaborate with colleagues to address teaching and research issues. Conduct research in a particular field of knowledge and publish findings in professional journals, books, or electronic media. Participate in student recruitment, registration, and placement activities. Serve on academic or administrative committees that deal with institutional policies, departmental matters, and academic issues. Compile bibliographies of specialized materials for outside reading assignments. Act as advisers to student organizations. Participate in campus and community events. Perform administrative duties such as serving as department head. Write grant proposals to procure external research funding. Provide professional consulting services to government or industry.

SKILLS—**Most Important:** Social Skills; Communication Skills; Thought-Processing Skills. **Other Above-Average Skills:** Management Skills; Equipment/ Technology Analysis Skills; Mathematics Skills.

GOE—**Interest Area:** 05. Education and Training. **Work Group:** 05.03. Postsecondary and Adult Teaching and Instructing. **Other Jobs in This Group:** Adult Literacy, Remedial Education, and GED Teachers and Instructors; Agricultural Sciences Teachers, Postsecondary; Anthropology and Archeology Teachers, Postsecondary; Architecture Teachers, Postsecondary; Area, Ethnic, and Cultural Studies Teachers,

C

Postsecondary; Art, Drama, and Music Teachers, Postsecondary; Atmospheric, Earth, Marine, and Space Sciences Teachers, Postsecondary; Biological Science Teachers, Postsecondary; Business Teachers, Postsecondary; Chemistry Teachers, Postsecondary; Computer Science Teachers, Postsecondary; Criminal Justice and Law Enforcement Teachers, Postsecondary; Economics Teachers, Postsecondary; Education Teachers, Postsecondary; Engineering Teachers, Postsecondary; English Language and Literature Teachers, Postsecondary; Environmental Science Teachers, Postsecondary; Farm and Home Management Advisors; Foreign Language and Literature Teachers, Postsecondary; Forestry and Conservation Science Teachers, Postsecondary; Geography Teachers, Postsecondary; Graduate Teaching Assistants; Health Specialties Teachers, Postsecondary; History Teachers, Postsecondary; Home Economics Teachers, Postsecondary; Law Teachers, Postsecondary; Library Science Teachers, Postsecondary; Mathematical Science Teachers, Postsecondary; Nursing Instructors and Teachers, Postsecondary; Philosophy and Religion Teachers, Postsecondary; Physics Teachers, Postsecondary; Political Science Teachers, Postsecondary; Psychology Teachers, Postsecondary; Recreation and Fitness Studies Teachers, Postsecondary; Self-Enrichment Education Teachers; Social Work Teachers, Postsecondary; Sociology Teachers, Postsecondary; Vocational Education Teachers, Postsecondary. **PERSONALITY TYPE:** No data available.

EDUCATION/TRAINING PROGRAM(S)—Communication Studies/Speech Communication and Rhetoric; Mass Communication/Media Studies; Journalism; Broadcast Journalism; Journalism, Other; Radio and Television; Digital Communication and Media/Multimedia; Public Relations/Image Management; Advertising; Political Communication; Health Communication; Communication, Journalism, and Related Programs, Other. **RELATED KNOWLEDGE/COURSES—Communications and Media:** Media production, communication, and dissemination techniques and methods. This includes alternative ways to inform and entertain via written, oral, and visual media. **Education and Training:** Principles and methods for curriculum and training design, teaching and instruction for individuals and groups, and the measurement of training effects. **English Language:** The structure and content of the English language, including the meaning and spelling of words, rules of composition, and grammar. **Philosophy and Theology:** Different philosophical

systems and religions. This includes their basic principles, values, ethics, ways of thinking, customs, practices, and impact on human culture. **Sociology and Anthropology:** Group behavior and dynamics, societal trends and influences, human migrations, ethnicity, and cultures and their history and origins. **History and Archeology:** Historical events and their causes, indicators, and effects on civilizations and cultures.

Compensation and Benefits Managers

- Education/Training Required: Work experience plus degree
- Annual Earnings: $69,130
- Growth: 21.5%
- Annual Job Openings: 4,000
- Self-Employed: 1.2%
- Part-Time: 3.5%

The job openings listed here are shared with Human Resources Managers.

Plan, direct, or coordinate compensation and benefits activities and staff of an organization. Advise management on such matters as equal employment opportunity, sexual harassment, and discrimination. Direct preparation and distribution of written and verbal information to inform employees of benefits, compensation, and personnel policies. Administer, direct, and review employee benefit programs, including the integration of benefit programs following mergers and acquisitions. Plan and conduct new employee orientations to foster positive attitude toward organizational objectives. Plan, direct, supervise, and coordinate work activities of subordinates and staff relating to employment, compensation, labor relations, and employee relations. Identify and implement benefits to increase the quality of life for employees by working with brokers and researching benefits issues. Design, evaluate, and modify benefits policies to ensure that programs are current, competitive, and in compliance with legal requirements. Analyze compensation policies, government regulations, and prevailing wage rates to develop competitive compensation plan. Formulate policies, procedures, and programs for recruitment, testing, placement, classification, orientation, benefits and compensation, and labor and industrial relations. Mediate between benefits providers and employees, such as by assisting in handling employees' benefits-related questions or taking suggestions. Fulfill all reporting requirements of all relevant government rules and regulations, including the Employee Retirement Income Security Act (ERISA). Maintain records and compile statistical reports concerning personnel-related data such as hires, transfers, performance appraisals, and absenteeism rates. Analyze statistical data and reports to identify and determine causes of personnel problems and develop recommendations for improvement of organization's personnel policies and practices. Develop methods to improve employment policies, processes, and practices and recommend changes to management. Negotiate bargaining agreements. Investigate and report on industrial accidents for insurance carriers. Represent organization at personnel-related hearings and investigations.

SKILLS—Most Important: Management Skills; Social Skills; Communication Skills. **Other Above-Average Skills:** Thought-Processing Skills; Mathematics Skills.

GOE—Interest Area: 04. Business and Administration. **Work Group:** 04.01. Managerial Work in General Business. **Other Jobs in This Group:** Chief Executives; General and Operations Managers; Human Resources Managers; Training and Development Managers. **PERSONALITY TYPE:** Enterprising. Enterprising occupations frequently involve starting up and carrying out projects. These occupations can involve leading people and making many decisions. They sometimes require risk taking and often deal with business.

EDUCATION/TRAINING PROGRAM(S)—Human Resources Management/Personnel Administration, General; Labor and Industrial Relations. **RELATED KNOWLEDGE/COURSES—Personnel and Human Resources:** Principles and procedures for personnel recruitment, selection, training, compensation and benefits, labor relations and negotiation, and personnel information systems. **Economics and Accounting:** Economic and accounting principles and practices, the financial markets, banking, and the analysis and reporting of financial data. **Clerical Practices:** Administrative and clerical procedures and systems such as word processing, managing files and records, stenography and transcription, designing forms, and other office

procedures and terminology. **Administration and Management:** Business and management principles involved in strategic planning, resource allocation, human resources modeling, leadership technique, production methods, and coordination of people and resources. **Law and Government:** Laws, legal codes, court procedures, precedents, government regulations, executive orders, agency rules, and the democratic political process. **Education and Training:** Principles and methods for curriculum and training design, teaching and instruction for individuals and groups, and the measurement of training effects.

Compensation, Benefits, and Job Analysis Specialists

- Education/Training Required: Bachelor's degree
- Annual Earnings: $48,870
- Growth: 20.4%
- Annual Job Openings: 15,000
- Self-Employed: 2.7%
- Part-Time: 7.7%

Conduct programs of compensation and benefits and job analysis for employer. May specialize in specific areas, such as position classification and pension programs. Evaluate job positions, determining classification, exempt or non-exempt status, and salary. Ensure company compliance with federal and state laws, including reporting requirements. Advise managers and employees on state and federal employment regulations, collective agreements, benefit and compensation policies, personnel procedures, and classification programs. Plan, develop, evaluate, improve, and communicate methods and techniques for selecting, promoting, compensating, evaluating, and training workers. Provide advice on the resolution of classification and salary complaints. Prepare occupational classifications, job descriptions, and salary scales. Assist in preparing and maintaining personnel records and handbooks. Prepare reports such as organization and flow charts and career path reports to summarize job analysis and evaluation and compensation analysis information. Administer employee insurance, pension, and savings plans, working with insurance brokers and plan carriers. Negotiate collective agreements on behalf of employers or workers and mediate labor disputes and grievances. Develop, implement, administer, and evaluate personnel and labor relations programs, including performance appraisal, affirmative action, and employment equity programs. Perform multifactor data and cost analyses that may be used in areas such as support of collective bargaining agreements. Research employee benefit and health and safety practices and recommend changes or modifications to existing policies. Analyze organizational, occupational, and industrial data to facilitate organizational functions and provide technical information to business, industry, and government. Advise staff of individuals' qualifications. Assess need for and develop job analysis instruments and materials. Review occupational data on Alien Employment Certification Applications to determine the appropriate occupational title and code; provide local offices with information about immigration and occupations. Research job and worker requirements, structural and functional relationships among jobs and occupations, and occupational trends.

SKILLS—Most Important: Social Skills; Communication Skills; Thought-Processing Skills. **Other Above-Average Skills:** Mathematics Skills; Management Skills.

GOE—Interest Area: 04. Business and Administration. **Work Group:** 04.03. Human Resources Support. **Other Jobs in This Group:** Employment Interviewers; Employment, Recruitment, and Placement Specialists; Personnel Recruiters; Training and Development Specialists. **PERSONALITY TYPE:** Investigative. Investigative occupations frequently involve working with ideas and require an extensive amount of thinking. These occupations can involve searching for facts and figuring out problems mentally.

EDUCATION/TRAINING PROGRAM(S)—Human Resources Management/Personnel Administration, General; Labor and Industrial Relations. **RELATED KNOWLEDGE/COURSES—Personnel and Human Resources:** Principles and procedures for personnel recruitment, selection, training, compensation and benefits, labor relations and negotiation, and personnel information systems. **Clerical Practices:** Administrative and clerical procedures and systems such as word processing, managing files and records, stenography and transcription, designing forms, and other office procedures and terminology. **Customer and Personal Service:** Principles and processes for providing customer and personal services. This includes customer needs assessment, meeting of quality standards for services, and evaluation of customer satisfaction. **Administration and Management:** Business and management principles involved in strategic planning, resource allocation, human resources modeling, leadership technique, production methods, and coordination of people and resources. **English Language:** The structure and content of the English language, including the meaning and spelling of words, rules of composition, and grammar. **Education and Training:** Principles and methods for curriculum and training design, teaching and instruction for individuals and groups, and the measurement of training effects.

Computer and Information Systems Managers

- Education/Training Required: Work experience plus degree
- Annual Earnings: $96,520
- Growth: 25.9%
- Annual Job Openings: 25,000
- Self-Employed: 1.2%
- Part-Time: 3.2%

Plan, direct, or coordinate activities in such fields as electronic data processing, information systems, systems analysis, and computer programming. Manage backup, security, and user help systems. Consult with users, management, vendors, and technicians to assess computing needs and system requirements. Direct daily operations of department, analyzing workflow, establishing priorities, developing standards, and setting deadlines. Assign and review the work of systems analysts, programmers, and other computer-related workers. Stay abreast of advances in technology. Develop computer information resources, providing for data security and control, strategic computing, and disaster recovery. Review and approve all systems charts and programs prior to their implementation. Evaluate the organization's technology use and needs and recommend improvements, such as hardware and software upgrades. Control operational budget and expenditures. Meet with department heads, managers, supervisors, vendors, and others to solicit cooperation and resolve problems. Develop and interpret organizational goals, policies, and procedures. Recruit, hire, train, and supervise staff or participate in staffing decisions. Review project plans to plan and coordinate project activity. Evaluate data-processing proposals to assess project feasibility and requirements. Prepare and review operational reports or project progress reports. Purchase necessary equipment.

SKILLS—Most Important: Computer Programming Skills; Management Skills; Quality Control Skills. **Other Above-Average Skills:** Equipment/Technology Analysis Skills; Social Skills; Thought-Processing Skills; Equipment Use/Maintenance Skills; Communication Skills.

GOE—Interest Area: 11. Information Technology. **Work Group:** 11.01. Managerial Work in Information Technology. **Other Jobs in This Group:** Network and Computer Systems Administrators. **PERSONALITY TYPE:** Enterprising. Enterprising occupations frequently involve starting up and carrying out projects. These occupations can involve leading people and making many decisions. They sometimes require risk taking and often deal with business.

EDUCATION/TRAINING PROGRAM(S)—Computer and Information Sciences, General; Information Science/Studies; Computer Science; System Administration/Administrator; Operations Management and Supervision; Management Information Systems, General; Information Resources Management/CIO Training; Knowledge Management. **RELATED KNOWLEDGE/COURSES—Clerical Practices:** Administrative and clerical procedures and systems such as word processing, managing files and records, stenography and transcription, designing forms, and other office procedures and terminology. **Computers and Electronics:** Circuit boards; processors; chips; electronic equipment; and computer hardware and software, including applications and programming. **Economics and Accounting:** Economic and accounting principles and practices, the financial markets, banking, and the analysis and reporting of financial data. **Engineering and Technology:** The practical application of engineering science and technology. This includes applying principles, techniques, procedures, and equipment to the design and production of various goods and services.

Design: Design techniques, tools, and principles involved in production of precision technical plans, blueprints, drawings, and models. **Administration and Management:** Business and management principles involved in strategic planning, resource allocation, human resources modeling, leadership technique, production methods, and coordination of people and resources.

Computer Hardware Engineers

- Education/Training Required: Bachelor's degree
- Annual Earnings: $84,420
- Growth: 10.1%
- Annual Job Openings: 5,000
- Self-Employed: 0.8%
- Part-Time: 4.1%

Research, design, develop, and test computer or computer-related equipment for commercial, industrial, military, or scientific use. May supervise the manufacturing and installation of computer or computer-related equipment and components. Update knowledge and skills to keep up with rapid advancements in computer technology. Provide technical support to designers, marketing and sales departments, suppliers, engineers, and other team members throughout the product development and implementation process. Test and verify hardware and support peripherals to ensure that they meet specifications and requirements, analyzing and recording test data. Monitor functioning of equipment and make necessary modifications to ensure system operates in conformance with specifications. Analyze information to determine, recommend, and plan layout, including type of computers and peripheral equipment modifications. Build, test, and modify product prototypes, using working models or theoretical models constructed using computer simulation. Analyze user needs and recommend appropriate hardware. Direct technicians, engineering designers, or other technical support personnel as needed. Confer with engineering staff and consult specifications to evaluate interface between hardware and software and operational and performance requirements of overall system.

C

Select hardware and material, assuring compliance with specifications and product requirements. Store, retrieve, and manipulate data for analysis of system capabilities and requirements. Write detailed functional specifications that document the hardware development process and support hardware introduction. Specify power supply requirements and configuration, drawing on system performance expectations and design specifications. Provide training and support to system designers and users. Assemble and modify existing pieces of equipment to meet special needs. Evaluate factors such as reporting formats required, cost constraints, and need for security restrictions to determine hardware configuration. Design and develop computer hardware and support peripherals, including central processing units (CPUs), support logic, microprocessors, custom integrated circuits, and printers and disk drives. Recommend purchase of equipment to control dust, temperature, and humidity in area of system installation.

SKILLS—Most Important: Computer Programming Skills; Equipment/Technology Analysis Skills; Quality Control Skills. Other Above-Average Skills: Science Skills; Mathematics Skills; Communication Skills; Social Skills; Management Skills.

GOE—Interest Area: 15. Scientific Research, Engineering, and Mathematics. Work Group: 15.07. Research and Design Engineering. Other Jobs in This Group: Aerospace Engineers; Biomedical Engineers; Chemical Engineers; Civil Engineers; Electrical Engineers; Electronics Engineers, Except Computer; Marine Architects; Marine Engineers; Marine Engineers and Naval Architects; Materials Engineers; Mechanical Engineers; Nuclear Engineers. PERSONALITY TYPE: Investigative. Investigative occupations frequently involve working with ideas and require an extensive amount of thinking. These occupations can involve searching for facts and figuring out problems mentally.

EDUCATION/TRAINING PROGRAM(S)—Computer Engineering, General; Computer Hardware Engineering. RELATED KNOWLEDGE/COURSES—Computers and Electronics: Circuit boards; processors; chips; electronic equipment; and computer hardware and software, including applications and programming. Engineering and Technology: The practical application of engineering science and technology. This includes applying principles, techniques, procedures,

and equipment to the design and production of various goods and services. Design: Design techniques, tools, and principles involved in production of precision technical plans, blueprints, drawings, and models. Telecommunications: Transmission, broadcasting, switching, control, and operation of telecommunications systems. Education and Training: Principles and methods for curriculum and training design, teaching and instruction for individuals and groups, and the measurement of training effects. Physics: Physical principles and laws and their interrelationships and applications to understanding fluid, material, and atmospheric dynamics and mechanical, electrical, atomic, and subatomic structures and processes.

Computer Programmers

- Education/Training Required: Bachelor's degree
- Annual Earnings: $63,420
- Growth: 2.0%
- Annual Job Openings: 28,000
- Self-Employed: 4.5%
- Part-Time: 6.0%

Convert project specifications and statements of problems and procedures to detailed logical flow charts for coding into computer language. Develop and write computer programs to store, locate, and retrieve specific documents, data, and information. May program Web sites. Correct errors by making appropriate changes and rechecking the program to ensure that the desired results are produced. Conduct trial runs of programs and software applications to be sure that they will produce the desired information and that the instructions are correct. Compile and write documentation of program development and subsequent revisions, inserting comments in the coded instructions so others can understand the program. Write, update, and maintain computer programs or software packages to handle specific jobs such as tracking inventory, storing or retrieving data, or controlling other equipment. Consult with managerial, engineering, and technical personnel to clarify program intent, identify problems, and suggest changes. Perform or direct revision, repair, or expansion of existing programs to increase operating efficiency or adapt to new requirements. Write, analyze, review, and rewrite programs, using workflow chart and diagram and applying knowledge of computer capabilities, subject matter, and symbolic logic. Write or contribute to instructions or manuals to guide end users. Investigate whether networks, workstations, the central processing unit of the system, or peripheral equipment are responding to a program's instructions. Prepare detailed workflow charts and diagrams that describe input, output, and logical operation and convert them into a series of instructions coded in a computer language. Perform systems analysis and programming tasks to maintain and control the use of computer systems software as a systems programmer. Consult with and assist computer operators or system analysts to define and resolve problems in running computer programs. Assign, coordinate, and review work and activities of programming personnel. Collaborate with computer manufacturers and other users to develop new programming methods. Train subordinates in programming and program coding.

SKILLS—Most Important: Computer Programming Skills; Equipment/Technology Analysis Skills; Thought-Processing Skills. **Other Above-Average Skills:** Equipment Use/Maintenance Skills; Mathematics Skills; Social Skills.

GOE—Interest Area: 11. Information Technology. **Work Group:** 11.02. Information Technology Specialties. **Other Jobs in This Group:** Computer and Information Scientists, Research; Computer Operators; Computer Security Specialists; Computer Software Engineers, Applications; Computer Software Engineers, Systems Software; Computer Support Specialists; Computer Systems Analysts; Computer Systems Engineers/Architects; Database Administrators; Network Designers; Network Systems and Data Communications Analysts; Software Quality Assurance Engineers and Testers; Web Administrators; Web Developers. **PERSONALITY TYPE:** Investigative. Investigative occupations frequently involve working with ideas and require an extensive amount of thinking. These occupations can involve searching for facts and figuring out problems mentally.

EDUCATION/TRAINING PROGRAM(S)—Artificial Intelligence and Robotics; Computer Programming/Programmer, General; Computer Programming, Specific Applications; Computer Programming,

Vendor/Product Certification; Web Page, Digital/Multimedia, and Information Resources Design; Computer Graphics; Web/Multimedia Management and Webmaster; Bioinformatics; Medical Office Computer Specialist/Assistant; Medical Informatics; E-Commerce/Electronic Commerce; others. **RELATED KNOWLEDGE/COURSES—Computers and Electronics:** Circuit boards; processors; chips; electronic equipment; and computer hardware and software, including applications and programming. **Design:** Design techniques, tools, and principles involved in production of precision technical plans, blueprints, drawings, and models. **Mathematics:** Arithmetic, algebra, geometry, calculus, and statistics and their applications. **Economics and Accounting:** Economic and accounting principles and practices, the financial markets, banking, and the analysis and reporting of financial data. **Telecommunications:** Transmission, broadcasting, switching, control, and operation of telecommunications systems. **Engineering and Technology:** The practical application of engineering science and technology. This includes applying principles, techniques, procedures, and equipment to the design and production of various goods and services.

Computer Science Teachers, Postsecondary

- ◎ Education/Training Required: Master's degree
- ◎ Annual Earnings: $54,270
- ◎ Growth: 32.2%
- ◎ Annual Job Openings: 329,000
- ◎ Self-Employed: 0.4%
- ◎ Part-Time: 27.3%

The job openings listed here are shared with 35 other postsecondary teaching occupations. For a complete list, see the beginning of this section.

Teach courses in computer science. May specialize in a field of computer science, such as the design and function of computers or operations and research analysis. Evaluate and grade students' classwork, laboratory work, assignments, and papers. Maintain student attendance records, grades, and other required records. Prepare and deliver lectures to undergraduate and/or graduate students on topics such as programming, data structures, and software design. Prepare course materials such as syllabi, homework assignments, and handouts. Compile, administer, and grade examinations or assign this work to others. Keep abreast of developments in their field by reading current literature, talking with colleagues, and participating in professional conferences. Initiate, facilitate, and moderate classroom discussions. Plan, evaluate, and revise curricula, course content, and course materials and methods of instruction. Supervise students' laboratory work. Maintain regularly scheduled office hours to advise and assist students. Select and obtain materials and supplies such as textbooks and laboratory equipment. Advise students on academic and vocational curricula and on career issues. Participate in student recruitment, registration, and placement activities. Collaborate with colleagues to address teaching and research issues. Serve on academic or administrative committees that deal with institutional policies, departmental matters, and academic issues. Act as advisers to student organizations. Supervise undergraduate and/or graduate teaching, internship, and research work. Perform administrative duties such as serving as department head. Conduct research in a particular field of knowledge and publish findings in professional journals, books, and/or electronic media. Direct research of other teachers or of graduate students working for advanced academic degrees. Provide professional consulting services to government and/or industry. Participate in campus and community events. Compile bibliographies of specialized materials for outside reading assignments. Write grant proposals to procure external research funding.

SKILLS—Most Important: Computer Programming Skills; Mathematics Skills; Equipment/Technology Analysis Skills. **Other Above-Average Skills:** Science Skills; Thought-Processing Skills; Management Skills; Quality Control Skills; Equipment Use/Maintenance Skills.

GOE—Interest Area: 05. Education and Training. **Work Group:** 05.03. Postsecondary and Adult Teaching and Instructing. **Other Jobs in This Group:** Adult Literacy, Remedial Education, and GED Teachers and Instructors; Agricultural Sciences Teachers, Postsecondary; Anthropology and Archeology Teachers, Postsecondary; Architecture Teachers, Postsecondary;

Area, Ethnic, and Cultural Studies Teachers, Postsecondary; Art, Drama, and Music Teachers, Postsecondary; Atmospheric, Earth, Marine, and Space Sciences Teachers, Postsecondary; Biological Science Teachers, Postsecondary; Business Teachers, Postsecondary; Chemistry Teachers, Postsecondary; Communications Teachers, Postsecondary; Criminal Justice and Law Enforcement Teachers, Postsecondary; Economics Teachers, Postsecondary; Education Teachers, Postsecondary; Engineering Teachers, Postsecondary; English Language and Literature Teachers, Postsecondary; Environmental Science Teachers, Postsecondary; Farm and Home Management Advisors; Foreign Language and Literature Teachers, Postsecondary; Forestry and Conservation Science Teachers, Postsecondary; Geography Teachers, Postsecondary; Graduate Teaching Assistants; Health Specialties Teachers, Postsecondary; History Teachers, Postsecondary; Home Economics Teachers, Postsecondary; Law Teachers, Postsecondary; Library Science Teachers, Postsecondary; Mathematical Science Teachers, Postsecondary; Nursing Instructors and Teachers, Postsecondary; Philosophy and Religion Teachers, Postsecondary; Physics Teachers, Postsecondary; Political Science Teachers, Postsecondary; Psychology Teachers, Postsecondary; Recreation and Fitness Studies Teachers, Postsecondary; Self-Enrichment Education Teachers; Social Work Teachers, Postsecondary; Sociology Teachers, Postsecondary; Vocational Education Teachers, Postsecondary. **PERSONALITY TYPE:** Investigative. Investigative occupations frequently involve working with ideas and require an extensive amount of thinking. These occupations can involve searching for facts and figuring out problems mentally.

EDUCATION/TRAINING PROGRAM(S)—Computer and Information Sciences, General; Computer Programming/Programmer, General; Information Science/Studies; Computer Systems Analysis/Analyst; Computer Science. **RELATED KNOWLEDGE/ COURSES—Education and Training:** Principles and methods for curriculum and training design, teaching and instruction for individuals and groups, and the measurement of training effects. **Computers and Electronics:** Circuit boards; processors; chips; electronic equipment; and computer hardware and software, including applications and programming. **Telecommunications:** Transmission, broadcasting, switching, control, and operation of telecommunications systems.

Mathematics: Arithmetic, algebra, geometry, calculus, and statistics and their applications. **English Language:** The structure and content of the English language, including the meaning and spelling of words, rules of composition, and grammar. **Engineering and Technology:** The practical application of engineering science and technology. This includes applying principles, techniques, procedures, and equipment to the design and production of various goods and services.

Computer Security Specialists

- Education/Training Required: Bachelor's degree
- Annual Earnings: $59,930
- Growth: 38.4%
- Annual Job Openings: 34,000
- Self-Employed: 0.6%
- Part-Time: 4.2%

The job openings listed here are shared with Network and Computer Systems Administrators.

Plan, coordinate, and implement security measures for information systems to regulate access to computer data files and prevent unauthorized modification, destruction, or disclosure of information. Train users and promote security awareness to ensure system security and to improve server and network efficiency. Develop plans to safeguard computer files against accidental or unauthorized modification, destruction, or disclosure and to meet emergency data processing needs. Confer with users to discuss issues such as computer data access needs, security violations, and programming changes. Monitor current reports of computer viruses to determine when to update virus protection systems. Modify computer security files to incorporate new software, correct errors, or change individual access status. Coordinate implementation of computer system plan with establishment personnel and outside vendors. Monitor use of data files and regulate access to safeguard information in computer files. Perform risk assessments and execute tests of data-processing system to ensure functioning of data-processing activities and security

measures. Encrypt data transmissions and erect firewalls to conceal confidential information as it is being transmitted and to keep out tainted digital transfers. Document computer security and emergency measures policies, procedures, and tests. Review violations of computer security procedures and discuss procedures with violators to ensure violations are not repeated. Maintain permanent fleet cryptologic and carry-on direct support systems required in special land, sea surface, and subsurface operations.

SKILLS—Most Important: Computer Programming Skills; Management Skills; Equipment/Technology Analysis Skills. **Other Above-Average Skills:** Equipment Use/Maintenance Skills; Thought-Processing Skills; Social Skills; Science Skills; Mathematics Skills.

GOE—Interest Area: 11. Information Technology. **Work Group:** 11.02. Information Technology Specialties. **Other Jobs in This Group:** Computer and Information Scientists, Research; Computer Operators; Computer Programmers; Computer Software Engineers, Applications; Computer Software Engineers, Systems Software; Computer Support Specialists; Computer Systems Analysts; Computer Systems Engineers/Architects; Database Administrators; Network Designers; Network Systems and Data Communications Analysts; Software Quality Assurance Engineers and Testers; Web Administrators; Web Developers. **PERSONALITY TYPE:** Investigative. Investigative occupations frequently involve working with ideas and require an extensive amount of thinking. These occupations can involve searching for facts and figuring out problems mentally.

EDUCATION/TRAINING PROGRAM(S)—Computer and Information Sciences, General; Information Science/Studies; Computer Systems Analysis/Analyst; Computer Systems Networking and Telecommunications; System Administration/Administrator; System, Networking, and LAN/WAN Management/Manager; Computer and Information Systems Security; Computer and Information Sciences and Support Services, Other. **RELATED KNOWLEDGE/COURSES—Computers and Electronics:** Circuit boards; processors; chips; electronic equipment; and computer hardware and software, including applications and programming. **Telecommunications:** Transmission, broadcasting, switching, control, and operation of telecommunications systems. **Education and Training:**

Principles and methods for curriculum and training design, teaching and instruction for individuals and groups, and the measurement of training effects. **Design:** Design techniques, tools, and principles involved in production of precision technical plans, blueprints, drawings, and models. **Engineering and Technology:** The practical application of engineering science and technology. This includes applying principles, techniques, procedures, and equipment to the design and production of various goods and services. **Clerical Practices:** Administrative and clerical procedures and systems such as word processing, managing files and records, stenography and transcription, designing forms, and other office procedures and terminology.

Computer Software Engineers, Applications

- ◎ Education/Training Required: Bachelor's degree
- ◎ Annual Earnings: $77,090
- ◎ Growth: 48.4%
- ◎ Annual Job Openings: 54,000
- ◎ Self-Employed: 2.4%
- ◎ Part-Time: 2.5%

Develop, create, and modify general computer applications software or specialized utility programs. Analyze user needs and develop software solutions. Design software or customize software for client use with the aim of optimizing operational efficiency. May analyze and design databases within an application area, working individually or coordinating database development as part of a team. Confer with systems analysts, engineers, programmers, and others to design system and to obtain information on project limitations and capabilities, performance requirements, and interfaces. Modify existing software to correct errors, allow it to adapt to new hardware, or improve its performance. Analyze user needs and software requirements to determine feasibility of design within time and cost constraints. Consult with customers about software system design and maintenance. Coordinate software system installation and monitor equipment functioning to ensure specifications are met. Design, develop, and modify software systems, using scientific analysis and mathematical models to predict and measure outcome and consequences of design. Develop and direct software system testing and validation procedures, programming, and documentation. Analyze information to determine, recommend, and plan computer specifications and layouts and peripheral equipment modifications. Supervise the work of programmers, technologists, and technicians and other engineering and scientific personnel. Obtain and evaluate information on factors such as reporting formats required, costs, and security needs to determine hardware configuration. Determine system performance standards. Train users to use new or modified equipment. Store, retrieve, and manipulate data for analysis of system capabilities and requirements. Specify power supply requirements and configuration. Recommend purchase of equipment to control dust, temperature, and humidity in area of system installation.

SKILLS—Most Important: Computer Programming Skills; Quality Control Skills; Equipment/Technology Analysis Skills. **Other Above-Average Skills:** Thought-Processing Skills; Science Skills; Social Skills; Equipment Use/Maintenance Skills; Management Skills.

GOE—Interest Area: 11. Information Technology. **Work Group:** 11.02. Information Technology Specialties. **Other Jobs in This Group:** Computer and Information Scientists, Research; Computer Operators; Computer Programmers; Computer Security Specialists; Computer Software Engineers, Systems Software; Computer Support Specialists; Computer Systems Analysts; Computer Systems Engineers/Architects; Database Administrators; Network Designers; Network Systems and Data Communications Analysts; Software Quality Assurance Engineers and Testers; Web Administrators; Web Developers. **PERSONALITY TYPE:** Investigative. Investigative occupations frequently involve working with ideas and require an extensive amount of thinking. These occupations can involve searching for facts and figuring out problems mentally.

EDUCATION/TRAINING PROGRAM(S)—Artificial Intelligence and Robotics; Information Technology; Computer Science; Computer Engineering, General; Computer Software Engineering; Computer Engineering Technologies/Technicians, Other; Bioinformatics; Medical Informatics; Medical Illustration and Informatics, Other. **RELATED KNOWLEDGE/COURSES—Computers and Electronics:**

Circuit boards; processors; chips; electronic equipment; and computer hardware and software, including applications and programming. **Telecommunications:** Transmission, broadcasting, switching, control, and operation of telecommunications systems. **Engineering and Technology:** The practical application of engineering science and technology. This includes applying principles, techniques, procedures, and equipment to the design and production of various goods and services. **Design:** Design techniques, tools, and principles involved in production of precision technical plans, blueprints, drawings, and models. **Mathematics:** Arithmetic, algebra, geometry, calculus, and statistics and their applications. **Physics:** Physical principles and laws and their interrelationships and applications to understanding fluid, material, and atmospheric dynamics and mechanical, electrical, atomic, and subatomic structures and processes.

Computer Software Engineers, Systems Software

- Education/Training Required: Bachelor's degree
- Annual Earnings: $82,120
- Growth: 43.0%
- Annual Job Openings: 37,000
- Self-Employed: 2.4%
- Part-Time: 2.5%

Research, design, develop, and test operating systems-level software, compilers, and network distribution software for medical, industrial, military, communications, aerospace, business, scientific, and general computing applications. Set operational specifications and formulate and analyze software requirements. Apply principles and techniques of computer science, engineering, and mathematical analysis. Modify existing software to correct errors, to adapt it to new hardware, or to upgrade interfaces and improve performance. Design and develop software systems, using scientific analysis and mathematical models to predict and measure outcome and consequences of design. Consult with engineering staff to evaluate interface between hardware

and software, develop specifications and performance requirements, and resolve customer problems. Analyze information to determine, recommend, and plan installation of a new system or modification of an existing system. Develop and direct software system testing and validation procedures. Direct software programming and development of documentation. Consult with customers or other departments on project status, proposals, and technical issues such as software system design and maintenance. Advise customer about, or perform, maintenance of software system. Coordinate installation of software system. Monitor functioning of equipment to ensure system operates in conformance with specifications. Store, retrieve, and manipulate data for analysis of system capabilities and requirements. Confer with data processing and project managers to obtain information on limitations and capabilities for data-processing projects. Prepare reports and correspondence concerning project specifications, activities, and status. Evaluate factors such as reporting formats required, cost constraints, and need for security restrictions to determine hardware configuration. Supervise and assign work to programmers, designers, technologists and technicians, and other engineering and scientific personnel. Train users to use new or modified equipment. Utilize microcontrollers to develop control signals; implement control algorithms; and measure process variables such as temperatures, pressures, and positions. Recommend purchase of equipment to control dust, temperature, and humidity in area of system installation. Specify power supply requirements and configuration.

SKILLS—Most Important: Computer Programming Skills; Equipment/Technology Analysis Skills; Science Skills. **Other Above-Average Skills:** Mathematics Skills; Quality Control Skills; Communication Skills; Management Skills; Social Skills.

GOE—Interest Area: 11. Information Technology. **Work Group:** 11.02. Information Technology Specialties. **Other Jobs in This Group:** Computer and Information Scientists, Research; Computer Operators; Computer Programmers; Computer Security Specialists; Computer Software Engineers, Applications; Computer Support Specialists; Computer Systems Analysts; Computer Systems Engineers/Architects; Database Administrators; Network Designers; Network Systems and Data Communications Analysts; Software Quality Assurance Engineers and Testers; Web Administrators; Web Developers. **PERSONALITY**

TYPE: Investigative. Investigative occupations frequently involve working with ideas and require an extensive amount of thinking. These occupations can involve searching for facts and figuring out problems mentally.

EDUCATION/TRAINING PROGRAM(S)—Artificial Intelligence and Robotics; Information Technology; Information Science/Studies; Computer Science; System, Networking, and LAN/WAN Management/Manager; Computer Engineering, General; Computer Engineering Technologies/Technicians, Other. **RELATED KNOWLEDGE/COURSES**—**Computers and Electronics:** Circuit boards; processors; chips; electronic equipment; and computer hardware and software, including applications and programming. **Design:** Design techniques, tools, and principles involved in production of precision technical plans, blueprints, drawings, and models. **Engineering and Technology:** The practical application of engineering science and technology. This includes applying principles, techniques, procedures, and equipment to the design and production of various goods and services. **Telecommunications:** Transmission, broadcasting, switching, control, and operation of telecommunications systems. **Mathematics:** Arithmetic, algebra, geometry, calculus, and statistics and their applications. **Education and Training:** Principles and methods for curriculum and training design, teaching and instruction for individuals and groups, and the measurement of training effects.

Computer Support Specialists

- ◎ Education/Training Required: Associate degree
- ◎ Annual Earnings: $40,610
- ◎ Growth: 23.0%
- ◎ Annual Job Openings: 87,000
- ◎ Self-Employed: 0.9%
- ◎ Part-Time: 8.3%

Provide technical assistance to computer system users. Answer questions or resolve computer problems for clients in person, via telephone, or from remote location. May provide assistance concerning the use of computer hardware and software, including printing, installation, word processing, electronic mail, and operating systems. Answer user inquiries regarding computer software or hardware operation to resolve problems. Enter commands and observe system functioning to verify correct operations and detect errors. Install and perform minor repairs to hardware, software, or peripheral equipment, following design or installation specifications. Oversee the daily performance of computer systems. Set up equipment for employee use, performing or ensuring proper installation of cables, operating systems, or appropriate software. Maintain records of daily data communication transactions, problems and remedial actions taken, or installation activities. Read technical manuals, confer with users, or conduct computer diagnostics to investigate and resolve problems or to provide technical assistance and support. Confer with staff, users, and management to establish requirements for new systems or modifications. Develop training materials and procedures or train users in the proper use of hardware or software. Refer major hardware or software problems or defective products to vendors or technicians for service. Prepare evaluations of software or hardware and recommend improvements or upgrades. Read trade magazines and technical manuals or attend conferences and seminars to maintain knowledge of hardware and software. Supervise and coordinate workers engaged in problem-solving, monitoring, and installing data communication equipment and software. Inspect equipment and read order sheets to prepare for delivery to users. Modify and customize commercial programs for internal needs. Conduct office automation feasibility studies, including workflow analysis, space design, or cost comparison analysis.

SKILLS—**Most Important:** Equipment Use/Maintenance Skills; Social Skills; Communication Skills. **Other Above-Average Skills:** Equipment/Technology Analysis Skills; Thought-Processing Skills.

GOE—**Interest Area:** 11. Information Technology. **Work Group:** 11.02. Information Technology Specialties. **Other Jobs in This Group:** Computer and Information Scientists, Research; Computer Operators; Computer Programmers; Computer Security Specialists; Computer Software Engineers, Applications; Computer Software Engineers, Systems Software; Computer Systems Analysts; Computer Systems Engineers/Architects; Database Administrators; Network Designers; Network Systems and Data

Communications Analysts; Software Quality Assurance Engineers and Testers; Web Administrators; Web Developers. **PERSONALITY TYPE:** Investigative. Investigative occupations frequently involve working with ideas and require an extensive amount of thinking. These occupations can involve searching for facts and figuring out problems mentally.

EDUCATION/TRAINING PROGRAM(S)—Agricultural Business Technology; Data Processing and Data Processing Technology/Technician; Computer Hardware Technology/Technician; Computer Software Technology/Technician; Accounting and Computer Science; Medical Office Computer Specialist/Assistant. **RELATED KNOWLEDGE/COURSES—Computers and Electronics:** Circuit boards; processors; chips; electronic equipment; and computer hardware and software, including applications and programming. **Telecommunications:** Transmission, broadcasting, switching, control, and operation of telecommunications systems. **Engineering and Technology:** The practical application of engineering science and technology. This includes applying principles, techniques, procedures, and equipment to the design and production of various goods and services. **Customer and Personal Service:** Principles and processes for providing customer and personal services. This includes customer needs assessment, meeting of quality standards for services, and evaluation of customer satisfaction. **Production and Processing:** Raw materials, production processes, quality control, costs, and other techniques for maximizing the effective manufacture and distribution of goods. **Design:** Design techniques, tools, and principles involved in production of precision technical plans, blueprints, drawings, and models.

Computer Systems Analysts

- Education/Training Required: Bachelor's degree
- Annual Earnings: $68,300
- Growth: 31.4%
- Annual Job Openings: 56,000
- Self-Employed: 5.0%
- Part-Time: 6.2%

Analyze science, engineering, business, and all other data-processing problems for application to electronic data processing systems. Analyze user requirements, procedures, and problems to automate or improve existing systems and review computer system capabilities, workflow, and scheduling limitations. May analyze or recommend commercially available software. May supervise computer programmers. Provide staff and users with assistance solving computer-related problems, such as malfunctions and program problems. Test, maintain, and monitor computer programs and systems, including coordinating the installation of computer programs and systems. Use object-oriented programming languages as well as client and server applications development processes and multimedia and Internet technology. Confer with clients regarding the nature of the information processing or computation needs a computer program is to address. Coordinate and link the computer systems within an organization to increase compatibility and so information can be shared. Consult with management to ensure agreement on system principles. Expand or modify system to serve new purposes or improve workflow. Interview or survey workers, observe job performance, or perform the job to determine what information is processed and how it is processed. Determine computer software or hardware needed to set up or alter system. Train staff and users to work with computer systems and programs. Analyze information processing or computation needs and plan and design computer systems, using techniques such as structured analysis, data modeling, and information engineering. Assess the usefulness of pre-developed application packages and adapt them to a user environment. Define the goals of the system and devise flow charts and diagrams describing logical operational steps of programs. Develop, document, and revise system design procedures, test procedures, and quality standards. Review and analyze computer printouts and performance indicators to locate code problems; correct errors by correcting codes. Recommend new equipment or software packages. Read manuals, periodicals, and technical reports to learn how to develop programs that meet staff and user requirements. Supervise computer programmers or other systems analysts or serve as project leaders for particular systems projects. Utilize the computer in the analysis and solution of business problems such as development of integrated production and inventory control and cost analysis systems.

SKILLS—Most Important: Quality Control Skills; Computer Programming Skills; Equipment/Technology Analysis Skills. **Other Above-Average Skills:** Equipment Use/Maintenance Skills; Thought-Processing Skills; Mathematics Skills; Communication Skills.

GOE—Interest Area: 11. Information Technology. **Work Group:** 11.02. Information Technology Specialties. **Other Jobs in This Group:** Computer and Information Scientists, Research; Computer Operators; Computer Programmers; Computer Security Specialists; Computer Software Engineers, Applications; Computer Software Engineers, Systems Software; Computer Support Specialists; Computer Systems Engineers/Architects; Database Administrators; Network Designers; Network Systems and Data Communications Analysts; Software Quality Assurance Engineers and Testers; Web Administrators; Web Developers. **PERSONALITY TYPE:** Investigative. Investigative occupations frequently involve working with ideas and require an extensive amount of thinking. These occupations can involve searching for facts and figuring out problems mentally.

EDUCATION/TRAINING PROGRAM(S)—Computer and Information Sciences, General; Information Technology; Computer Systems Analysis/Analyst; Web/Multimedia Management and Webmaster. **RELATED KNOWLEDGE/COURSES—Computers and Electronics:** Circuit boards; processors; chips; electronic equipment; and computer hardware and software, including applications and programming. **Design:** Design techniques, tools, and principles involved in production of precision technical plans, blueprints, drawings, and models. **Telecommunications:** Transmission, broadcasting, switching, control, and operation of telecommunications systems. **Customer and Personal**

Service: Principles and processes for providing customer and personal services. This includes customer needs assessment, meeting of quality standards for services, and evaluation of customer satisfaction. **Education and Training:** Principles and methods for curriculum and training design, teaching and instruction for individuals and groups, and the measurement of training effects. **Law and Government:** Laws, legal codes, court procedures, precedents, government regulations, executive orders, agency rules, and the democratic political process.

Computer, Automated Teller, and Office Machine Repairers

- ◎ Education/Training Required: Postsecondary vocational training
- ◎ Annual Earnings: $36,060
- ◎ Growth: 3.8%
- ◎ Annual Job Openings: 31,000
- ◎ Self-Employed: 13.7%
- ◎ Part-Time: 9.9%

Repair, maintain, or install computers; word-processing systems; automated teller machines; and electronic office machines, such as duplicating and fax machines. Converse with customers to determine details of equipment problems. Reassemble machines after making repairs or replacing parts. Travel to customers' stores or offices to service machines or to provide emergency repair service. Reinstall software programs or adjust settings on existing software to fix machine malfunctions. Advise customers concerning equipment operation, maintenance, and programming. Assemble machines according to specifications, using hand tools, power tools, and measuring devices. Test new systems to ensure that they are in working order. Operate machines to test functioning of parts and mechanisms. Maintain records of equipment maintenance work and repairs. Install and configure new equipment, including operating software and peripheral equipment. Maintain parts inventories and order any additional parts needed for repairs. Update existing equipment, performing tasks such as installing updated circuit boards or additional memory.

Test components and circuits of faulty equipment to locate defects, using oscilloscopes, signal generators, ammeters, voltmeters, or special diagnostic software programs. Align, adjust, and calibrate equipment according to specifications. Repair, adjust, or replace electrical and mechanical components and parts, using hand tools, power tools, and soldering or welding equipment. Complete repair bills, shop records, time cards, and expense reports. Disassemble machine to examine parts such as wires, gears, and bearings for wear and defects, using hand tools, power tools, and measuring devices. Clean, oil, and adjust mechanical parts to maintain machines' operating efficiency and to prevent breakdowns. Enter information into computers to copy programs from one electronic component to another or to draw, modify, or store schematics. Read specifications such as blueprints, charts, and schematics to determine machine settings and adjustments. Lay cable and hook up electrical connections between machines, power sources, and phone lines. Analyze equipment performance records to assess equipment functioning.

SKILLS—Most Important: Equipment Use/Maintenance Skills; Science Skills; Quality Control Skills. **Other Above-Average Skills:** None met the criteria.

GOE—Interest Area: 11. Information Technology. **Work Group:** 11.03. Digital Equipment Repair. **Other Jobs in This Group:** Coin, Vending, and Amusement Machine Servicers and Repairers. **PERSONALITY TYPE:** Realistic. Realistic occupations frequently involve work activities that include practical, hands-on problems and solutions. They often deal with plants, animals, and real-world materials like wood, tools, and machinery. Many of the occupations require working outside and do not involve a lot of paperwork or working closely with others.

EDUCATION/TRAINING PROGRAM(S)—Business Machine Repair; Computer Installation and Repair Technology/Technician. **RELATED KNOWLEDGE/COURSES—Computers and Electronics:** Circuit boards; processors; chips; electronic equipment; and computer hardware and software, including applications and programming. **Telecommunications:** Transmission, broadcasting, switching, control, and operation of telecommunications systems. **Design:** Design techniques, tools, and principles involved in production of precision technical plans, blueprints, drawings, and models. **Mechanical Devices:** Machines and tools, including their designs, uses, repair, and maintenance.

Engineering and Technology: The practical application of engineering science and technology. This includes applying principles, techniques, procedures, and equipment to the design and production of various goods and services. **Physics:** Physical principles and laws and their interrelationships and applications to understanding fluid, material, and atmospheric dynamics and mechanical, electrical, atomic, and subatomic structures and processes.

Construction and Building Inspectors

- Education/Training Required: Work experience in a related occupation
- Annual Earnings: $44,720
- Growth: 22.3%
- Annual Job Openings: 6,000
- Self-Employed: 10.2%
- Part-Time: 7.8%

Inspect structures, using engineering skills to determine structural soundness and compliance with specifications, building codes, and other regulations. Inspections may be general in nature or may be limited to a specific area, such as electrical systems or plumbing. Use survey instruments; metering devices; tape measures; and test equipment, such as concrete strength measurers, to perform inspections. Inspect bridges, dams, highways, buildings, wiring, plumbing, electrical circuits, sewers, heating systems, and foundations during and after construction for structural quality, general safety, and conformance to specifications and codes. Maintain daily logs and supplement inspection records with photographs. Review and interpret plans, blueprints, site layouts, specifications, and construction methods to ensure compliance to legal requirements and safety regulations. Inspect and monitor construction sites to ensure adherence to safety standards, building codes, and specifications. Measure dimensions and verify level, alignment, and elevation of structures and fixtures to ensure compliance to building plans and codes. Issue violation notices and stop-work orders, conferring with owners, violators, and authorities to explain regulations and recommend rectifications. Issue permits for construction, relocation, demolition, and occupancy.

Approve and sign plans that meet required specifications. Compute estimates of work completed or of needed renovations or upgrades and approve payment for contractors. Monitor installation of plumbing, wiring, equipment, and appliances to ensure that installation is performed properly and is in compliance with applicable regulations. Examine lifting and conveying devices, such as elevators, escalators, moving sidewalks, lifts and hoists, inclined railways, ski lifts, and amusement rides, to ensure safety and proper functioning. Train, direct, and supervise other construction inspectors. Evaluate premises for cleanliness, including proper garbage disposal and lack of vermin infestation.

SKILLS—Most Important: Mathematics Skills; Quality Control Skills; Social Skills. **Other Above-Average Skills:** Science Skills; Communication Skills; Equipment Use/Maintenance Skills.

GOE—Interest Area: 07. Government and Public Administration. **Work Group:** 07.03. Regulations Enforcement. **Other Jobs in This Group:** Agricultural Inspectors; Aviation Inspectors; Compliance Officers, Except Agriculture, Construction, Health and Safety, and Transportation; Environmental Compliance Inspectors; Equal Opportunity Representatives and Officers; Financial Examiners; Fire Inspectors; Fish and Game Wardens; Forest Fire Inspectors and Prevention Specialists; Freight and Cargo Inspectors; Government Property Inspectors and Investigators; Immigration and Customs Inspectors; Licensing Examiners and Inspectors; Nuclear Monitoring Technicians; Occupational Health and Safety Specialists; Occupational Health and Safety Technicians; Tax Examiners, Collectors, and Revenue Agents; Transportation Vehicle, Equipment, and Systems Inspectors, Except Aviation. **PERSONALITY TYPE:** Conventional. Conventional occupations frequently involve following set procedures and routines. These occupations can include working with data and details more than with ideas. Usually there is a clear line of authority to follow.

EDUCATION/TRAINING PROGRAM(S)—Building/Home/Construction Inspection/Inspector. **RELATED KNOWLEDGE/COURSES—Building and Construction:** The materials, methods, and tools involved in the construction or repair of houses, buildings, or other structures such as highways and roads. **Design:** Design techniques, tools, and principles involved in production of precision technical plans, blueprints, drawings, and models. **Engineering and**

Technology: The practical application of engineering science and technology. This includes applying principles, techniques, procedures, and equipment to the design and production of various goods and services. **Public Safety and Security:** Relevant equipment, policies, procedures, and strategies to promote effective local, state, or national security operations for the protection of people, data, property, and institutions. **Mechanical Devices:** Machines and tools, including their designs, uses, repair, and maintenance. **Customer and Personal Service:** Principles and processes for providing customer and personal services. This includes customer needs assessment, meeting of quality standards for services, and evaluation of customer satisfaction.

Construction Carpenters

- Education/Training Required: Long-term on-the-job training
- Annual Earnings: $35,580
- Growth: 13.8%
- Annual Job Openings: 210,000
- Self-Employed: 32.4%
- Part-Time: 8.2%

The job openings listed here are shared with Rough Carpenters.

Construct, erect, install, and repair structures and fixtures of wood, plywood, and wallboard, using carpenter's hand tools and power tools. Measure and mark cutting lines on materials, using ruler, pencil, chalk, and marking gauge. Follow established safety rules and regulations and maintain a safe and clean environment. Verify trueness of structure, using plumb bob and level. Shape or cut materials to specified measurements, using hand tools, machines, or power saw. Study specifications in blueprints, sketches, or building plans to prepare project layout and determine dimensions and materials required. Assemble and fasten materials to make framework or props, using hand tools and wood screws, nails, dowel pins, or glue. Build or repair cabinets, doors, frameworks, floors, and other wooden fixtures used in buildings, using woodworking machines, carpenter's hand tools, and power tools. Erect scaffolding and ladders for assembling structures above ground level.

Remove damaged or defective parts or sections of structures and repair or replace, using hand tools. Install structures and fixtures, such as windows, frames, floorings, and trim, or hardware, using carpenter's hand and power tools. Select and order lumber and other required materials. Maintain records, document actions, and present written progress reports. Finish surfaces of woodwork or wallboard in houses and buildings, using paint, hand tools, and paneling. Prepare cost estimates for clients or employers. Arrange for subcontractors to deal with special areas such as heating and electrical wiring work. Inspect ceiling or floor tile, wall coverings, siding, glass, or woodwork to detect broken or damaged structures. Work with or remove hazardous material. Construct forms and chutes for pouring concrete. Cover subfloors with building paper to keep out moisture and lay hardwood, parquet, and wood-strip-block floors by nailing floors to subfloor or cementing them to mastic or asphalt base. Fill cracks and other defects in plaster or plasterboard and sand patch, using patching plaster, trowel, and sanding tool. Perform minor plumbing, welding, or concrete mixing work. Apply shock-absorbing, sound-deadening, and decorative paneling to ceilings and walls.

SKILLS—Most Important: Management Skills; Quality Control Skills; Mathematics Skills. **Other Above-Average Skills:** Science Skills; Equipment Use/Maintenance Skills; Social Skills; Computer Programming Skills; Communication Skills.

GOE—Interest Area: 02. Architecture and Construction. **Work Group:** 02.04. Construction Crafts. **Other Jobs in This Group:** Boilermakers; Brickmasons and Blockmasons; Carpet Installers; Cement Masons and Concrete Finishers; Commercial Divers; Crane and Tower Operators; Drywall and Ceiling Tile Installers; Electricians; Fence Erectors; Floor Layers, Except Carpet, Wood, and Hard Tiles; Floor Sanders and Finishers; Glaziers; Hazardous Materials Removal Workers; Insulation Workers, Floor, Ceiling, and Wall; Insulation Workers, Mechanical; Manufactured Building and Mobile Home Installers; Operating Engineers and Other Construction Equipment Operators; Painters, Construction and Maintenance; Paperhangers; Paving, Surfacing, and Tamping Equipment Operators; Pile-Driver Operators; Pipe Fitters and Steamfitters; Pipelayers; Plasterers and Stucco Masons; Plumbers; Plumbers, Pipefitters, and Steamfitters; Rail-Track Laying and Maintenance Equipment Operators; Refractory Materials Repairers, Except Brickmasons; Reinforcing Iron and Rebar Workers; Riggers; Roofers; Rough Carpenters; Security and Fire Alarm Systems Installers; Segmental Pavers; Sheet Metal Workers; Stone Cutters and Carvers, Manufacturing; Stonemasons; Structural Iron and Steel Workers; Tapers; Terrazzo Workers and Finishers; Tile and Marble Setters. **PERSONALITY TYPE:** Realistic. Realistic occupations frequently involve work activities that include practical, hands-on problems and solutions. They often deal with plants, animals, and real-world materials like wood, tools, and machinery. Many of the occupations require working outside and do not involve a lot of paperwork or working closely with others.

EDUCATION/TRAINING PROGRAM(S)—Carpentry/Carpenter. **RELATED KNOWLEDGE/ COURSES—Building and Construction:** The materials, methods, and tools involved in the construction or repair of houses, buildings, or other structures such as highways and roads. **Design:** Design techniques, tools, and principles involved in production of precision technical plans, blueprints, drawings, and models. **Production and Processing:** Raw materials, production processes, quality control, costs, and other techniques for maximizing the effective manufacture and distribution of goods. **Mechanical Devices:** Machines and tools, including their designs, uses, repair, and maintenance. **Engineering and Technology:** The practical application of engineering science and technology. This includes applying principles, techniques, procedures, and equipment to the design and production of various goods and services. **Public Safety and Security:** Relevant equipment, policies, procedures, and strategies to promote effective local, state, or national security operations for the protection of people, data, property, and institutions.

Construction Managers

- Education/Training Required: Bachelor's degree
- Annual Earnings: $72,260
- Growth: 10.4%
- Annual Job Openings: 28,000
- Self-Employed: 54.2%
- Part-Time: 5.4%

Plan, direct, coordinate, or budget, usually through subordinate supervisory personnel, activities concerned with the construction and maintenance of structures, facilities, and systems. Participate in the conceptual development of a construction project and oversee its organization, scheduling, and implementation. Confer with supervisory personnel, owners, contractors, and design professionals to discuss and resolve matters such as work procedures, complaints, and construction problems. Plan, organize, and direct activities concerned with the construction and maintenance of structures, facilities, and systems. Schedule the project in logical steps and budget time required to meet deadlines. Determine labor requirements and dispatch workers to construction sites. Inspect and review projects to monitor compliance with building and safety codes and other regulations. Prepare contracts and negotiate revisions, changes, and additions to contractual agreements with architects, consultants, clients, suppliers, and subcontractors. Interpret and explain plans and contract terms to administrative staff, workers, and clients, representing the owner or developer. Obtain all necessary permits and licenses. Direct and supervise workers. Study job specifications to determine appropriate construction methods. Select, contract, and oversee workers who complete specific pieces of the project, such as painting or plumbing. Requisition supplies and materials to complete construction projects. Prepare and submit budget estimates and progress and cost tracking reports. Take actions to deal with the results of delays, bad weather, or emergencies at construction site. Develop and implement quality control programs. Investigate damage, accidents, or delays at construction sites to ensure that proper procedures are being carried out. Evaluate construction methods and determine cost-effectiveness of plans, using computers. Direct acquisition of land for construction projects.

SKILLS—Most Important: Mathematics Skills; Equipment Use/Maintenance Skills; Social Skills. **Other Above-Average Skills:** Management Skills; Equipment/Technology Analysis Skills.

GOE—Interest Area: 02. Architecture and Construction. **Work Group:** 02.01. Managerial Work in Architecture and Construction. **Other Jobs in This Group:** No other jobs in this group. **PERSONALITY TYPE:** Enterprising. Enterprising occupations frequently involve starting up and carrying out projects. These occupations can involve leading people and making many decisions. They sometimes require risk taking and often deal with business.

EDUCATION/TRAINING PROGRAM(S)—Construction Engineering Technology/Technician; Business/Commerce, General; Business Administration and Management, General; Operations Management and Supervision; Construction Management. **RELATED KNOWLEDGE/COURSES—Building and Construction:** The materials, methods, and tools involved in the construction or repair of houses, buildings, or other structures such as highways and roads. **Design:** Design techniques, tools, and principles involved in production of precision technical plans, blueprints, drawings, and models. **Mechanical Devices:** Machines and tools, including their designs, uses, repair, and maintenance. **Administration and Management:** Business and management principles involved in strategic planning, resource allocation, human resources modeling, leadership technique, production methods, and coordination of people and resources. **Public Safety and Security:** Relevant equipment, policies, procedures, and strategies to promote effective local, state, or national security operations for the protection of people, data, property, and institutions. **Sales and Marketing:** Principles and methods for showing, promoting, and selling products or services. This includes marketing strategy and tactics, product demonstration, sales techniques, and sales control systems.

Copy Writers

- ◎ Education/Training Required: Bachelor's degree
- ◎ Annual Earnings: $46,420
- ◎ Growth: 17.7%
- ◎ Annual Job Openings: 14,000
- ◎ Self-Employed: 67.7%
- ◎ Part-Time: 30.7%

The job openings listed here are shared with Poets, Lyricists and Creative Writers.

Write advertising copy for use by publication or broadcast media to promote sale of goods and services. Write advertising copy for use by publication, broadcast, or Internet media to promote the sale of goods and services. Present drafts and ideas to clients. Discuss with the client the product, advertising themes and methods, and any changes that should be made in advertising copy. Consult with sales, media, and marketing representatives to obtain information on product or service and discuss style and length of advertising copy. Vary language and tone of messages based on product and medium. Edit or rewrite existing copy as necessary and submit copy for approval by supervisor. Write to customers in their terms and on their level so that the advertiser's sales message is more readily received. Write articles; bulletins; sales letters; speeches; and other related informative, marketing, and promotional material. Invent names for products and write the slogans that appear on packaging, brochures, and other promotional material. Review advertising trends, consumer surveys, and other data regarding marketing of goods and services to determine the best way to promote products. Develop advertising campaigns for a wide range of clients, working with an advertising agency's creative director and art director to determine the best way to present advertising information. Conduct research and interviews to determine which of a product's selling features should be promoted.

SKILLS—Most Important: Quality Control Skills; Equipment/Technology Analysis Skills; Social Skills. **Other Above-Average Skills:** Communication Skills; Thought-Processing Skills.

GOE—Interest Area: 03. Arts and Communication. **Work Group:** 03.02. Writing and Editing. **Other Jobs in This Group:** Editors; Poets, Lyricists and Creative Writers; Technical Writers; Writers and Authors. **PERSONALITY TYPE:** Artistic. Artistic occupations frequently involve working with forms, designs, and patterns. They often require self-expression, and the work can be done without following a clear set of rules.

EDUCATION/TRAINING PROGRAM(S)—Communication Studies/Speech Communication and Rhetoric; Mass Communication/Media Studies; Journalism; Broadcast Journalism; Communication, Journalism, and Related Programs, Other; English Composition. **RELATED KNOWLEDGE/COURSES—Sales and Marketing:** Principles and methods for showing, promoting, and selling products or services. This includes marketing strategy and tactics, product demonstration, sales techniques, and sales control systems. **Communications and Media:** Media production, communication, and dissemination techniques and methods. This includes alternative ways to inform and entertain via written, oral, and visual media. **Sociology and Anthropology:** Group behavior and dynamics, societal trends and influences, human migrations, ethnicity, and cultures and their history and origins. **English Language:** The structure and content of the English language, including the meaning and spelling of words, rules of composition, and grammar. **Computers and Electronics:** Circuit boards; processors; chips; electronic equipment; and computer hardware and software, including applications and programming. **Psychology:** Human behavior and performance; individual differences in ability, personality, and interests; learning and motivation; psychological research methods; and the assessment and treatment of behavioral and affective disorders.

C

Cost Estimators

- Education/Training Required: Work experience in a related occupation
- Annual Earnings: $52,020
- Growth: 18.2%
- Annual Job Openings: 15,000
- Self-Employed: 2.2%
- Part-Time: 5.9%

Prepare cost estimates for product manufacturing, construction projects, or services to aid management in bidding on or determining price of product or service. May specialize according to particular service performed or type of product manufactured. Analyze blueprints and other documentation to prepare time, cost, materials, and labor estimates. Assess cost-effectiveness of products, projects, or services, tracking actual costs relative to bids as the project develops. Consult with clients, vendors, personnel in other departments, or construction foremen to discuss and formulate estimates and resolve issues. Confer with engineers, architects, owners, contractors, and subcontractors on changes and adjustments to cost estimates. Prepare estimates used by management for purposes such as planning, organizing, and scheduling work. Prepare estimates for use in selecting vendors or subcontractors. Review material and labor requirements to decide whether it is more cost-effective to produce or purchase components. Prepare cost and expenditure statements and other necessary documentation at regular intervals for the duration of the project. Prepare and maintain a directory of suppliers, contractors, and subcontractors. Set up cost-monitoring and -reporting systems and procedures. Establish and maintain tendering process and conduct negotiations. Conduct special studies to develop and establish standard hour and related cost data or to effect cost reduction. Visit site and record information about access, drainage and topography, and availability of services such as water and electricity.

SKILLS—Most Important: Mathematics Skills; Management Skills; Equipment/Technology Analysis Skills. **Other Above-Average Skills:** Social Skills; Communication Skills; Science Skills.

GOE—Interest Area: 06. Finance and Insurance. **Work Group:** 06.02. Finance/Insurance Investigation and Analysis. **Other Jobs in This Group:** Appraisers and Assessors of Real Estate; Appraisers, Real Estate; Assessors; Claims Adjusters, Examiners, and Investigators; Claims Examiners, Property and Casualty Insurance; Credit Analysts; Financial Analysts; Insurance Adjusters, Examiners, and Investigators; Insurance Appraisers, Auto Damage; Insurance Underwriters; Loan Counselors; Loan Officers; Market Research Analysts; Survey Researchers. **PERSONALITY TYPE:** Conventional. Conventional occupations frequently involve following set procedures and routines. These occupations can include working with data and details more than with ideas. Usually there is a clear line of authority to follow.

EDUCATION/TRAINING PROGRAM(S)—Materials Engineering; Mechanical Engineering; Construction Engineering; Manufacturing Engineering; Construction Engineering Technology/Technician; Business/Commerce, General; Business Administration and Management, General. **RELATED KNOWLEDGE/COURSES—Economics and Accounting:** Economic and accounting principles and practices, the financial markets, banking, and the analysis and reporting of financial data. **Production and Processing:** Raw materials, production processes, quality control, costs, and other techniques for maximizing the effective manufacture and distribution of goods. **Administration and Management:** Business and management principles involved in strategic planning, resource allocation, human resources modeling, leadership technique, production methods, and coordination of people and resources. **Sales and Marketing:** Principles and methods for showing, promoting, and selling products or services. This includes marketing strategy and tactics, product demonstration, sales techniques, and sales control systems. **Clerical Practices:** Administrative and clerical procedures and systems such as word processing, managing files and records, stenography and transcription, designing forms, and other office procedures and terminology. **Personnel and Human Resources:** Principles and procedures for personnel recruitment, selection, training, compensation and benefits, labor relations and negotiation, and personnel information systems.

Counseling Psychologists

- Education/Training Required: Doctoral degree
- Annual Earnings: $57,170
- Growth: 19.1%
- Annual Job Openings: 10,000
- Self-Employed: 38.2%
- Part-Time: 22.8%

The job openings listed here are shared with Clinical Psychologists and School Psychologists.

Assess and evaluate individuals' problems through the use of case history, interview, and observation and provide individual or group counseling services to assist individuals in achieving more effective personal, social, educational, and vocational development and adjustment. Collect information about individuals or clients, using interviews, case histories, observational techniques, and other assessment methods. Counsel individuals, groups, or families to help them understand problems, define goals, and develop realistic action plans. Develop therapeutic and treatment plans based on clients' interests, abilities, and needs. Consult with other professionals to discuss therapies, treatments, counseling resources, or techniques and to share occupational information. Analyze data such as interview notes, test results, and reference manuals in order to identify symptoms and to diagnose the nature of clients' problems. Advise clients on how they could be helped by counseling. Evaluate the results of counseling methods to determine the reliability and validity of treatments. Provide consulting services to schools, social service agencies, and businesses. Refer clients to specialists or to other institutions for non-counseling treatment of problems. Select, administer, and interpret psychological tests to assess intelligence, aptitudes, abilities, or interests. Conduct research to develop or improve diagnostic or therapeutic counseling techniques.

SKILLS—Most Important: Social Skills; Communication Skills; Thought-Processing Skills. **Other Above-Average Skills:** Management Skills.

GOE—Interest Area: 10. Human Service. **Work Group:** 10.01. Counseling and Social Work. **Other Jobs in This Group:** Child, Family, and School Social Workers; Clinical Psychologists; Clinical, Counseling, and School Psychologists; Marriage and Family Therapists; Medical and Public Health Social Workers; Mental Health and Substance Abuse Social Workers; Mental Health Counselors; Probation Officers and Correctional Treatment Specialists; Rehabilitation Counselors; Residential Advisors; Social and Human Service Assistants; Substance Abuse and Behavioral Disorder Counselors. **PERSONALITY TYPE:** Social. Social occupations frequently involve working with, communicating with, and teaching people. These occupations often involve helping or providing service to others.

EDUCATION/TRAINING PROGRAM(S)—Psychology, General; Clinical Psychology; Counseling Psychology; Developmental and Child Psychology; School Psychology; Clinical Child Psychology; Psychoanalysis and Psychotherapy. **RELATED KNOWLEDGE/COURSES—Therapy and Counseling:** Principles, methods, and procedures for diagnosis, treatment, and rehabilitation of physical and mental dysfunctions and for career counseling and guidance. **Philosophy and Theology:** Different philosophical systems and religions. This includes their basic principles, values, ethics, ways of thinking, customs, practices, and impact on human culture. **Sociology and Anthropology:** Group behavior and dynamics, societal trends and influences, human migrations, ethnicity, and cultures and their history and origins. **Psychology:** Human behavior and performance; individual differences in ability, personality, and interests; learning and motivation; psychological research methods; and the assessment and treatment of behavioral and affective disorders. **English Language:** The structure and content of the English language, including the meaning and spelling of words, rules of composition, and grammar. **Customer and Personal Service:** Principles and processes for providing customer and personal services. This includes customer needs assessment, meeting of quality standards for services, and evaluation of customer satisfaction.

C

Criminal Investigators and Special Agents

- Education/Training Required: Work experience in a related occupation
- Annual Earnings: $55,790
- Growth: 16.3%
- Annual Job Openings: 9,000
- Self-Employed: 0.0%
- Part-Time: 2.5%

The job openings listed here are shared with Immigration and Customs Inspectors; Police Detectives; and Police Identification and Records Officers.

Investigate alleged or suspected criminal violations of federal, state, or local laws to determine if evidence is sufficient to recommend prosecution. Record evidence and documents, using equipment such as cameras and photocopy machines. Obtain and verify evidence by interviewing and observing suspects and witnesses or by analyzing records. Examine records to locate links in chains of evidence or information. Prepare reports that detail investigation findings. Determine scope, timing, and direction of investigations. Collaborate with other offices and agencies to exchange information and coordinate activities. Testify before grand juries concerning criminal activity investigations. Analyze evidence in laboratories or in the field. Investigate organized crime, public corruption, financial crime, copyright infringement, civil rights violations, bank robbery, extortion, kidnapping, and other violations of federal or state statutes. Identify case issues and evidence needed, based on analysis of charges, complaints, or allegations of law violations. Obtain and use search and arrest warrants. Serve subpoenas or other official papers. Collaborate with other authorities on activities such as surveillance, transcription, and research. Develop relationships with informants to obtain information related to cases. Search for and collect evidence such as fingerprints, using investigative equipment. Collect and record physical information about arrested suspects, including fingerprints, height and weight measurements, and photographs. Compare crime scene fingerprints with those from suspects or fingerprint files to identify perpetrators, using computers. Administer counter-terrorism and counter-narcotics reward programs. Provide protection for individuals such as government leaders, political candidates, and visiting foreign dignitaries. Perform undercover assignments and maintain surveillance, including monitoring authorized wiretaps. Manage security programs designed to protect personnel, facilities, and information. Issue security clearances.

SKILLS—Most Important: Computer Programming Skills; Social Skills; Equipment/Technology Analysis Skills. **Other Above-Average Skills:** Thought-Processing Skills; Equipment Use/Maintenance Skills; Mathematics Skills; Science Skills; Quality Control Skills.

GOE—Interest Area: 12. Law and Public Safety. **Work Group:** 12.04. Law Enforcement and Public Safety. **Other Jobs in This Group:** Bailiffs; Correctional Officers and Jailers; Detectives and Criminal Investigators; Fire Investigators; Forensic Science Technicians; Parking Enforcement Workers; Police and Sheriff's Patrol Officers; Police Detectives; Police Identification and Records Officers; Police Patrol Officers; Sheriffs and Deputy Sheriffs; Transit and Railroad Police. **PERSONALITY TYPE:** Enterprising. Enterprising occupations frequently involve starting up and carrying out projects. These occupations can involve leading people and making many decisions. They sometimes require risk taking and often deal with business.

EDUCATION/TRAINING PROGRAM(S)—Criminal Justice/Police Science; Criminalistics and Criminal Science. **RELATED KNOWLEDGE/COURSES—Law and Government:** Laws, legal codes, court procedures, precedents, government regulations, executive orders, agency rules, and the democratic political process. **Psychology:** Human behavior and performance; individual differences in ability, personality, and interests; learning and motivation; psychological research methods; and the assessment and treatment of behavioral and affective disorders. **Public Safety and Security:** Relevant equipment, policies, procedures, and strategies to promote effective local, state, or national security operations for the protection of people, data, property, and institutions. **Geography:** Principles and methods for describing the features of land, sea, and air masses, including their physical characteristics; locations; interrelationships; and distribution of plant, animal, and human life. **Clerical Practices:** Administrative and clerical procedures and systems such as word processing, managing files and records, stenography and transcription, designing forms, and other office procedures and terminology. **Sociology and Anthropology:** Group behavior and dynamics, societal trends and influences, human migrations, ethnicity, and cultures and their history and origins.

Criminal Justice and Law Enforcement Teachers, Postsecondary

- Education/Training Required: Master's degree
- Annual Earnings: $49,240
- Growth: 32.2%
- Annual Job Openings: 329,000
- Self-Employed: 0.4%
- Part-Time: 27.3%

The job openings listed here are shared with 35 other postsecondary teaching occupations. For a complete list, see the beginning of this section.

Teach courses in criminal justice, corrections, and law enforcement administration. Initiate, facilitate, and moderate classroom discussions. Keep abreast of developments in their field by reading current literature, talking with colleagues, and participating in professional conferences. Evaluate and grade students' classwork, assignments, and papers. Compile, administer, and grade examinations or assign this work to others. Prepare and deliver lectures to undergraduate or graduate students on topics such as criminal law, defensive policing, and investigation techniques. Prepare course materials such as syllabi, homework assignments, and handouts. Conduct research in a particular field of knowledge and publish findings in professional journals, books, and/or electronic media. Plan, evaluate, and revise curricula, course content, and course materials and methods of instruction. Supervise undergraduate and/or graduate teaching, internship, and research work. Maintain student attendance records, grades, and other required records. Select and obtain materials and supplies such as textbooks. Advise students on academic and vocational curricula and on career issues. Maintain regularly scheduled office hours to advise and

assist students. Collaborate with colleagues to address teaching and research issues. Write grant proposals to procure external research funding. Serve on academic or administrative committees that deal with institutional policies, departmental matters, and academic issues. Compile bibliographies of specialized materials for outside reading assignments. Participate in student recruitment, registration, and placement activities. Provide professional consulting services to government and/or industry. Perform administrative duties such as serving as department head. Participate in campus and community events. Act as advisers to student organizations.

SKILLS—Most Important: Communication Skills; Thought-Processing Skills; Social Skills. **Other Above-Average Skills:** Science Skills; Mathematics Skills.

GOE—Interest Area: 05. Education and Training. **Work Group:** 05.03. Postsecondary and Adult Teaching and Instructing. **Other Jobs in This Group:** Adult Literacy, Remedial Education, and GED Teachers and Instructors; Agricultural Sciences Teachers, Postsecondary; Anthropology and Archeology Teachers, Postsecondary; Architecture Teachers, Postsecondary; Area, Ethnic, and Cultural Studies Teachers, Postsecondary; Art, Drama, and Music Teachers, Postsecondary; Atmospheric, Earth, Marine, and Space Sciences Teachers, Postsecondary; Biological Science Teachers, Postsecondary; Business Teachers, Postsecondary; Chemistry Teachers, Postsecondary; Communications Teachers, Postsecondary; Computer Science Teachers, Postsecondary; Economics Teachers, Postsecondary; Education Teachers, Postsecondary; Engineering Teachers, Postsecondary; English Language and Literature Teachers, Postsecondary; Environmental Science Teachers, Postsecondary; Farm and Home Management Advisors; Foreign Language and Literature Teachers, Postsecondary; Forestry and Conservation Science Teachers, Postsecondary; Geography Teachers, Postsecondary; Graduate Teaching Assistants; Health Specialties Teachers, Postsecondary; History Teachers, Postsecondary; Home Economics Teachers, Postsecondary; Law Teachers, Postsecondary; Library Science Teachers, Postsecondary; Mathematical Science Teachers, Postsecondary; Nursing Instructors and Teachers, Postsecondary; Philosophy and Religion Teachers, Postsecondary; Physics Teachers, Postsecondary; Political Science Teachers, Postsecondary; Psychology Teachers, Postsecondary; Recreation and Fitness Studies Teachers, Postsecondary; Self-Enrichment Education Teachers; Social Work Teachers, Postsecondary; Sociology

Teachers, Postsecondary; Vocational Education Teachers, Postsecondary. **PERSONALITY TYPE:** No data available.

EDUCATION/TRAINING PROGRAM(S)—Teacher Education and Professional Development, Specific Subject Areas, Other; Corrections; Criminal Justice/Law Enforcement Administration; Criminal Justice/Safety Studies; Forensic Science and Technology; Criminal Justice/Police Science; Security and Loss Prevention Services; Juvenile Corrections; Criminalistics and Criminal Science; Corrections Administration; Corrections and Criminal Justice, Other. **RELATED KNOWLEDGE/COURSES—Sociology and Anthropology:** Group behavior and dynamics, societal trends and influences, human migrations, ethnicity, and cultures and their history and origins. **Philosophy and Theology:** Different philosophical systems and religions. This includes their basic principles, values, ethics, ways of thinking, customs, practices, and impact on human culture. **History and Archeology:** Historical events and their causes, indicators, and effects on civilizations and cultures. **Law and Government:** Laws, legal codes, court procedures, precedents, government regulations, executive orders, agency rules, and the democratic political process. **Education and Training:** Principles and methods for curriculum and training design, teaching and instruction for individuals and groups, and the measurement of training effects. **English Language:** The structure and content of the English language, including the meaning and spelling of words, rules of composition, and grammar.

Customer Service Representatives

- Education/Training Required: Moderate-term on-the-job training
- Annual Earnings: $27,490
- Growth: 22.8%
- Annual Job Openings: 510,000
- Self-Employed: 0.3%
- Part-Time: 17.6%

Interact with customers to provide information in response to inquiries about products and services and to handle and resolve complaints. Confer with customers by telephone or in person to provide information about products and services, to take orders or cancel accounts, or to obtain details of complaints. Keep records of customer interactions and transactions, recording details of inquiries, complaints, and comments, as well as actions taken. Resolve customers' service or billing complaints by performing activities such as exchanging merchandise, refunding money, and adjusting bills. Check to ensure that appropriate changes were made to resolve customers' problems. Contact customers to respond to inquiries or to notify them of claim investigation results and any planned adjustments. Refer unresolved customer grievances to designated departments for further investigation. Determine charges for services requested, collect deposits or payments, or arrange for billing. Complete contract forms, prepare change of address records, and issue service discontinuance orders, using computers. Obtain and examine all relevant information to assess validity of complaints and to determine possible causes, such as extreme weather conditions, that could increase utility bills. Solicit sale of new or additional services or products. Review insurance policy terms to determine whether a particular loss is covered by insurance. Review claims adjustments with dealers, examining parts claimed to be defective and approving or disapproving dealers' claims. Compare disputed merchandise with original requisitions and information from invoices and prepare invoices for returned goods. Order tests that could determine the causes of product malfunctions. Recommend improvements in products, packaging, shipping, service, or billing methods and procedures to prevent future problems.

SKILLS—Most Important: Social Skills; Communication Skills; Thought-Processing Skills. **Other Above-Average Skills:** None met the criteria.

GOE—Interest Area: 14. Retail and Wholesale Sales and Service. **Work Group:** 14.06. Customer Service. **Other Jobs in This Group:** Cashiers; Counter and Rental Clerks; Gaming Cage Workers; Gaming Change Persons and Booth Cashiers; Order Clerks; Receptionists and Information Clerks. **PERSONALITY TYPE:** Conventional. Conventional occupations frequently involve following set procedures and routines. These occupations can include working with data and details more than with ideas. Usually there is a clear line of authority to follow.

EDUCATION/TRAINING PROGRAM(S)—Customer Service Support/Call Center/Teleservice Operation; Receptionist. **RELATED KNOWLEDGE/ COURSES—Customer and Personal Service:** Principles and processes for providing customer and personal services. This includes customer needs assessment, meeting of quality standards for services, and evaluation of customer satisfaction. **Clerical Practices:** Administrative and clerical procedures and systems such as word processing, managing files and records, stenography and transcription, designing forms, and other office procedures and terminology. **Sales and Marketing:** Principles and methods for showing, promoting, and selling products or services. This includes marketing strategy and tactics, product demonstration, sales techniques, and sales control systems. **Administration and Management:** Business and management principles involved in strategic planning, resource allocation, human resources modeling, leadership technique, production methods, and coordination of people and resources. **Computers and Electronics:** Circuit boards; processors; chips; electronic equipment; and computer hardware and software, including applications and programming. **Mathematics:** Arithmetic, algebra, geometry, calculus, and statistics and their applications.

Database Administrators

- Education/Training Required: Bachelor's degree
- Annual Earnings: $63,250
- Growth: 38.2%
- Annual Job Openings: 9,000
- Self-Employed: 0.5%
- Part-Time: 5.0%

Coordinate changes to computer databases; test and implement the database, applying knowledge of database management systems. May plan, coordinate, and implement security measures to safeguard computer databases. Develop standards and guidelines to guide the use and acquisition of software and to protect vulnerable information. Modify existing databases and database management systems or direct programmers and analysts to make changes. Test programs or databases, correct errors, and make necessary modifications.

Plan, coordinate, and implement security measures to safeguard information in computer files against accidental or unauthorized damage, modification, or disclosure. Approve, schedule, plan, and supervise the installation and testing of new products and improvements to computer systems, such as the installation of new databases. Train users and answer questions. Establish and calculate optimum values for database parameters, using manuals and calculator. Specify users and user access levels for each segment of database. Develop data model describing data elements and how they are used, following procedures and using pen, template, or computer software. Develop methods for integrating different products so they work properly together, such as customizing commercial databases to fit specific needs. Review project requests describing database user needs to estimate time and cost required to accomplish project. Review procedures in database management system manuals for making changes to database. Work as part of a project team to coordinate database development and determine project scope and limitations. Select and enter codes to monitor database performance and to create production database. Identify and evaluate industry trends in database systems to serve as a source of information and advice for upper management. Write and code logical and physical database descriptions and specify identifiers of database to management system or direct others in coding descriptions. Review workflow charts developed by programmer analyst to understand tasks computer will perform, such as updating records. Revise company definition of data as defined in data dictionary.

SKILLS—Most Important: Computer Programming Skills; Equipment/Technology Analysis Skills; Quality Control Skills. **Other Above-Average Skills:** Social Skills; Management Skills; Communication Skills; Mathematics Skills.

GOE—Interest Area: 11. Information Technology. **Work Group:** 11.02. Information Technology Specialties. **Other Jobs in This Group:** Computer and Information Scientists, Research; Computer Operators; Computer Programmers; Computer Security Specialists; Computer Software Engineers, Applications; Computer Software Engineers, Systems Software; Computer Support Specialists; Computer Systems Analysts; Computer Systems Engineers/Architects; Network Designers; Network Systems and Data Communications Analysts; Software Quality Assurance Engineers and Testers; Web Administrators; Web

Developers. **PERSONALITY TYPE:** Investigative. Investigative occupations frequently involve working with ideas and require an extensive amount of thinking. These occupations can involve searching for facts and figuring out problems mentally.

EDUCATION/TRAINING PROGRAM(S)—Computer and Information Sciences, General; Computer Systems Analysis/Analyst; Data Modeling/Warehousing and Database Administration; Computer and Information Systems Security; Management Information Systems, General. **RELATED KNOWLEDGE/ COURSES—Computers and Electronics:** Circuit boards; processors; chips; electronic equipment; and computer hardware and software, including applications and programming. **Economics and Accounting:** Economic and accounting principles and practices, the financial markets, banking, and the analysis and reporting of financial data. **Clerical Practices:** Administrative and clerical procedures and systems such as word processing, managing files and records, stenography and transcription, designing forms, and other office procedures and terminology. **Administration and Management:** Business and management principles involved in strategic planning, resource allocation, human resources modeling, leadership technique, production methods, and coordination of people and resources. **Customer and Personal Service:** Principles and processes for providing customer and personal services. This includes customer needs assessment, meeting of quality standards for services, and evaluation of customer satisfaction. **Mathematics:** Arithmetic, algebra, geometry, calculus, and statistics and their applications.

Dental Assistants

- Education/Training Required: Moderate-term on-the-job training
- Annual Earnings: $29,520
- Growth: 42.7%
- Annual Job Openings: 45,000
- Self-Employed: 0.0%
- Part-Time: 38.9%

Assist dentist, set up patient and equipment, and keep records. Prepare patient, sterilize and disinfect instruments, set up instrument trays, prepare materials, and assist dentist during dental procedures. Expose dental diagnostic X rays. Record treatment information in patient records. Take and record medical and dental histories and vital signs of patients. Provide postoperative instructions prescribed by dentist. Assist dentist in management of medical and dental emergencies. Pour, trim, and polish study casts. Instruct patients in oral hygiene and plaque control programs. Make preliminary impressions for study casts and occlusal registrations for mounting study casts. Clean and polish removable appliances. Clean teeth, using dental instruments. Apply protective coating of fluoride to teeth. Fabricate temporary restorations and custom impressions from preliminary impressions. Schedule appointments, prepare bills, and receive payment for dental services; complete insurance forms; and maintain records, manually or using computer.

SKILLS—Most Important: Equipment Use/ Maintenance Skills; Social Skills; Equipment/ Technology Analysis Skills. **Other Above-Average Skills:** Communication Skills; Management Skills.

GOE—Interest Area: 08. Health Science. **Work Group:** 08.03. Dentistry. **Other Jobs in This Group:** Dental Hygienists; Dentists, General; Oral and Maxillofacial Surgeons; Orthodontists; Prosthodontists. **PERSONALITY TYPE:** Social. Social occupations frequently involve working with, communicating with, and teaching people. These occupations often involve helping or providing service to others.

EDUCATION/TRAINING PROGRAM(S)—Dental Assisting/Assistant. **RELATED KNOWLEDGE/ COURSES—Medicine and Dentistry:** The information and techniques needed to diagnose and treat human injuries, diseases, and deformities. This includes symptoms, treatment alternatives, drug properties and interactions, and preventive healthcare measures. **Chemistry:** The chemical composition, structure, and properties of substances and of the chemical processes and transformations that they undergo. This includes uses of chemicals and their danger signs, production techniques, and disposal methods. **Clerical Practices:** Administrative and clerical procedures and systems such as word processing, managing files and records, stenography and transcription, designing forms, and other office procedures and terminology. **Customer and Personal Service:** Principles and processes for providing customer and personal services. This includes customer needs assessment, meeting of quality standards for services, and evaluation of customer satisfaction. **Psychology:** Human behavior and performance; individual differences in ability, personality, and interests; learning and motivation; psychological research methods; and the assessment and treatment of behavioral and affective disorders. **Computers and Electronics:** Circuit boards; processors; chips; electronic equipment; and computer hardware and software, including applications and programming.

Dental Hygienists

- ◎ Education/Training Required: Associate degree
- ◎ Annual Earnings: $60,890
- ◎ Growth: 43.3%
- ◎ Annual Job Openings: 17,000
- ◎ Self-Employed: 0.3%
- ◎ Part-Time: 56.0%

Clean teeth and examine oral areas, head, and neck for signs of oral disease. May educate patients on oral hygiene, take and develop X rays, or apply fluoride or sealants. Clean calcareous deposits, accretions, and stains from teeth and beneath margins of gums, using dental instruments. Feel and visually examine gums for sores and signs of disease. Chart conditions of decay and disease for diagnosis and treatment by dentist. Feel lymph nodes under patient's chin to detect swelling or tenderness that could indicate presence of oral cancer. Apply fluorides and other cavity-preventing agents to arrest dental decay. Examine gums, using probes, to locate periodontal recessed gums and signs of gum disease. Expose and develop X-ray film. Provide clinical services and health education to improve and maintain oral health of schoolchildren. Remove excess cement from coronal surfaces of teeth. Make impressions for study casts. Place, carve, and finish amalgam restorations. Administer local anesthetic agents. Conduct dental health clinics for community groups to augment services of dentist. Remove sutures and dressings. Place and remove rubber dams, matrices, and temporary restorations.

SKILLS—Most Important: Science Skills; Communication Skills; Social Skills. **Other Above-Average Skills:** Thought-Processing Skills.

GOE—Interest Area: 08. Health Science. **Work Group:** 08.03. Dentistry. **Other Jobs in This Group:** Dental Assistants; Dentists, General; Oral and Maxillofacial Surgeons; Orthodontists; Prosthodontists. **PERSONALITY TYPE:** Social. Social occupations frequently involve working with, communicating with, and teaching people. These occupations often involve helping or providing service to others.

EDUCATION/TRAINING PROGRAM(S)—Dental Hygiene/Hygienist. **RELATED KNOWLEDGE/ COURSES—Biology:** Plant and animal organisms and their tissues, cells, functions, interdependencies, and interactions with each other and the environment. **Medicine and Dentistry:** The information and techniques needed to diagnose and treat human injuries, diseases, and deformities. This includes symptoms, treatment alternatives, drug properties and interactions, and preventive healthcare measures. **Chemistry:** The chemical composition, structure, and properties of substances and of the chemical processes and transformations that they undergo. This includes uses of chemicals and their danger signs, production techniques, and disposal methods. **Psychology:** Human behavior and performance; individual differences in ability, personality, and interests; learning and motivation; psychological research methods; and the assessment and treatment of behavioral and affective disorders. **Sales and Marketing:** Principles and methods for showing, promoting, and selling products or services. This includes marketing strategy and tactics, product demonstration, sales techniques, and sales control systems. **Customer and Personal Service:** Principles and processes for providing customer and personal services. This includes customer needs assessment, meeting of quality standards for services, and evaluation of customer satisfaction.

D

Dentists, General

- ◎ Education/Training Required: First professional degree
- ◎ Annual Earnings: $125,300
- ◎ Growth: 13.5%
- ◎ Annual Job Openings: 7,000
- ◎ Self-Employed: 30.7%
- ◎ Part-Time: 22.4%

Diagnose and treat diseases, injuries, and malformations of teeth and gums and related oral structures. May treat diseases of nerve, pulp, and other dental tissues affecting vitality of teeth. Use masks, gloves, and safety glasses to protect themselves and their patients from infectious diseases. Administer anesthetics to limit the amount of pain experienced by patients during procedures. Examine teeth, gums, and related tissues, using dental instruments, X rays, and other diagnostic equipment, to evaluate dental health, diagnose diseases or abnormalities, and plan appropriate treatments. Formulate plan of treatment for patient's teeth and mouth tissue. Use air turbine and hand instruments, dental appliances, and surgical implements. Advise and instruct patients regarding preventive dental care, the causes and treatment of dental problems, and oral health-care services. Design, make, and fit prosthodontic appliances such as space maintainers, bridges, and dentures or write fabrication instructions or prescriptions for denturists and dental technicians. Diagnose and treat diseases, injuries, and malformations of teeth, gums, and related oral structures and provide preventive and corrective services. Fill pulp chamber and canal with endodontic materials. Write prescriptions for antibiotics and other medications. Analyze and evaluate dental needs to determine changes and trends in patterns of dental disease. Treat exposure of pulp by pulp capping, removal of pulp from pulp chamber, or root canal, using dental instruments. Eliminate irritating margins of fillings and correct occlusions, using dental instruments. Perform oral and periodontal surgery on the jaw or mouth. Remove diseased tissue, using surgical instruments. Apply fluoride and sealants to teeth. Manage business, employing and supervising staff and handling paperwork and insurance claims. Bleach, clean, or polish teeth to restore natural color. Plan, organize, and maintain dental health programs. Produce and evaluate dental health educational materials.

SKILLS—Most Important: Science Skills; Management Skills; Thought-Processing Skills. **Other Above-Average Skills:** Social Skills; Equipment/Technology Analysis Skills; Equipment Use/Maintenance Skills; Mathematics Skills.

GOE—Interest Area: 08. Health Science. **Work Group:** 08.03. Dentistry. **Other Jobs in This Group:** Dental Assistants; Dental Hygienists; Oral and Maxillofacial Surgeons; Orthodontists; Prosthodontists. **PERSONALITY TYPE:** Investigative. Investigative occupations frequently involve working with ideas and require an extensive amount of thinking. These occupations can involve searching for facts and figuring out problems mentally.

EDUCATION/TRAINING PROGRAM(S)—Dentistry (DDS, DMD); Dental Clinical Sciences, General (MS, PhD); Advanced General Dentistry (Cert, MS, PhD); Oral Biology and Oral Pathology (MS, PhD); Dental Public Health and Education (Cert, MS/MPH, PhD/DPH); Dental Materials (MS, PhD); Pediatric Dentistry/Pedodontics (Cert, MS, PhD); Dental Public Health Specialty; Pedodontics Specialty. **RELATED KNOWLEDGE/COURSES—Medicine and Dentistry:** The information and techniques needed to diagnose and treat human injuries, diseases, and deformities. This includes symptoms, treatment alternatives, drug properties and interactions, and preventive health-care measures. **Biology:** Plant and animal organisms and their tissues, cells, functions, interdependencies, and interactions with each other and the environment. **Psychology:** Human behavior and performance; individual differences in ability, personality, and interests; learning and motivation; psychological research methods; and the assessment and treatment of behavioral and affective disorders. **Personnel and Human Resources:** Principles and procedures for personnel recruitment, selection, training, compensation and benefits, labor relations and negotiation, and personnel information systems. **Chemistry:** The chemical composition, structure, and properties of substances and of the chemical processes and transformations that they undergo. This includes uses of chemicals and their danger signs, production techniques, and disposal methods. **Sales and Marketing:** Principles and methods for showing, promoting, and selling products or services. This includes marketing strategy and tactics, product demonstration, sales techniques, and sales control systems.

Diagnostic Medical Sonographers

◎ Education/Training Required: Associate degree

◎ Annual Earnings: $54,370

◎ Growth: 34.8%

◎ Annual Job Openings: 5,000

◎ Self-Employed: 0.4%

◎ Part-Time: 17.2%

Produce ultrasonic recordings of internal organs for use by physicians. Decide which images to include, looking for differences between healthy and pathological areas. Observe screen during scan to ensure that image produced is satisfactory for diagnostic purposes, making adjustments to equipment as required. Observe and care for patients throughout examinations to ensure their safety and comfort. Provide sonogram and oral or written summary of technical findings to physician for use in medical diagnosis. Operate ultrasound equipment to produce and record images of the motion, shape, and composition of blood, organs, tissues, and bodily masses such as fluid accumulations. Select appropriate equipment settings and adjust patient positions to obtain the best sites and angles. Determine whether scope of exam should be extended based on findings. Process and code film from procedures and complete appropriate documentation. Obtain and record accurate patient history, including prior test results and information from physical examinations. Prepare patient for exam by explaining procedure, transferring them to ultrasound table, scrubbing skin and applying gel, and positioning them properly. Record and store suitable images, using camera unit connected to the ultrasound equipment. Coordinate work with physicians and other health-care team members, including providing assistance during invasive procedures. Maintain records that include patient information; sonographs and interpretations; files of correspondence, publications, and regulations; or quality assurance records such as pathology, biopsy, or post-operative reports. Perform legal and ethical duties, including preparing safety and accident reports, obtaining written consent from patient to perform invasive procedures, and reporting symptoms of abuse and neglect. Supervise and train students and other medical sonographers. Maintain stock and supplies, preparing supplies for special examinations and ordering supplies when necessary. Clean, check, and maintain sonographic equipment, submitting maintenance requests or performing minor repairs as necessary. Perform clerical duties such as scheduling exams and special procedures, keeping records, and archiving computerized images.

SKILLS—Most Important: Science Skills; Communication Skills; Quality Control Skills. **Other Above-Average Skills:** Thought-Processing Skills; Equipment Use/Maintenance Skills; Management Skills.

GOE—Interest Area: 08. Health Science. **Work Group:** 08.06. Medical Technology. **Other Jobs in This Group:** Biological Technicians; Cardiovascular Technologists and Technicians; Medical and Clinical Laboratory Technicians; Medical and Clinical Laboratory Technologists; Medical Equipment Preparers; Medical Records and Health Information Technicians; Nuclear Medicine Technologists; Opticians, Dispensing; Orthotists and Prosthetists; Radiologic Technicians; Radiologic Technologists; Radiologic Technologists and Technicians. **PERSONALITY TYPE:** No data available.

EDUCATION/TRAINING PROGRAM(S)—Diagnostic Medical Sonography/Sonographer and Ultrasound Technician; Allied Health Diagnostic, Intervention, and Treatment Professions, Other. **RELATED KNOWLEDGE/COURSES—Medicine and Dentistry:** The information and techniques needed to diagnose and treat human injuries, diseases, and deformities. This includes symptoms, treatment alternatives, drug properties and interactions, and preventive healthcare measures. **Biology:** Plant and animal organisms and their tissues, cells, functions, interdependencies, and interactions with each other and the environment. **Physics:** Physical principles and laws and their interrelationships and applications to understanding fluid, material, and atmospheric dynamics and mechanical, electrical, atomic, and subatomic structures and processes. **Therapy and Counseling:** Principles, methods, and procedures for diagnosis, treatment, and rehabilitation of physical and mental dysfunctions and for career counseling and guidance. **Education and Training:** Principles and methods for curriculum and training design, teaching and instruction for individuals and groups, and the measurement of training effects.

Customer and Personal Service: Principles and processes for providing customer and personal services. This includes customer needs assessment, meeting of quality standards for services, and evaluation of customer satisfaction.

Directors—Stage, Motion Pictures, Television, and Radio

- ◉ Education/Training Required: Work experience plus degree
- ◉ Annual Earnings: $53,860
- ◉ Growth: 16.6%
- ◉ Annual Job Openings: 11,000
- ◉ Self-Employed: 30.4%
- ◉ Part-Time: 8.1%

The job openings listed here are shared with Producers, Program Directors, Talent Directors, and Technical Directors/Managers.

Interpret script, conduct rehearsals, and direct activities of cast and technical crew for stage, motion pictures, television, or radio programs. Direct live broadcasts, films and recordings, or non-broadcast programming for public entertainment or education. Supervise and coordinate the work of camera, lighting, design, and sound crew members. Study and research scripts to determine how they should be directed. Cut and edit film or tape to integrate component parts into desired sequences. Collaborate with film and sound editors during the post-production process as films are edited and soundtracks are added. Confer with technical directors, managers, crew members, and writers to discuss details of production, such as photography, script, music, sets, and costumes. Plan details such as framing, composition, camera movement, sound, and actor movement for each shot or scene. Communicate to actors the approach, characterization, and movement needed for each scene in such a way that rehearsals and takes are minimized. Establish pace of programs and sequences of scenes according to time requirements and cast and set accessibility. Choose settings and locations for films and determine how scenes will be shot in these settings. Identify and approve equipment and elements required for productions, such as scenery, lights, props, costumes, choreography, and music. Compile scripts, program notes, and other material related to productions. Perform producers' duties such as securing financial backing, establishing and administering budgets, and recruiting cast and crew. Select plays or scripts for production and determine how material should be interpreted and performed. Compile cue words and phrases; cue announcers, cast members, and technicians during performances. Consult with writers, producers, or actors about script changes or "workshop" scripts, through rehearsal with writers and actors, to create final drafts. Collaborate with producers to hire crew members such as art directors, cinematographers, and costumer designers. Review film daily to check on work in progress and to plan for future filming. Interpret stage-set diagrams to determine stage layouts and supervise placement of equipment and scenery. Hold auditions for parts or negotiate contracts with actors determined suitable for specific roles, working in conjunction with producers.

SKILLS—Most Important: Management Skills; Communication Skills; Equipment/Technology Analysis Skills. **Other Above-Average Skills:** Thought-Processing Skills; Social Skills.

GOE—Interest Area: 03. Arts and Communication. **Work Group:** 03.06. Drama. **Other Jobs in This Group:** Actors; Costume Attendants; Makeup Artists, Theatrical and Performance; Public Address System and Other Announcers; Radio and Television Announcers. **PERSONALITY TYPE:** Artistic. Artistic occupations frequently involve working with forms, designs, and patterns. They often require self-expression, and the work can be done without following a clear set of rules.

EDUCATION/TRAINING PROGRAM(S)—Radio and Television; Drama and Dramatics/Theatre Arts, General; Directing and Theatrical Production; Theatre/Theatre Arts Management; Dramatic/Theatre Arts and Stagecraft, Other; Film/Cinema Studies; Cinematography and Film/Video Production. **RELATED KNOWLEDGE/COURSES—Communications and Media:** Media production, communication, and dissemination techniques and methods. This includes alternative ways to inform and entertain via written, oral, and visual media. **Telecommunications:** Transmission, broadcasting, switching, control, and operation of telecommunications systems. **Fine Arts:**

The theory and techniques required to compose, produce, and perform works of music, dance, visual arts, drama, and sculpture. **Geography:** Principles and methods for describing the features of land, sea, and air masses, including their physical characteristics; locations; interrelationships; and distribution of plant, animal, and human life. **Computers and Electronics:** Circuit boards; processors; chips; electronic equipment; and computer hardware and software, including applications and programming. **Education and Training:** Principles and methods for curriculum and training design, teaching and instruction for individuals and groups, and the measurement of training effects.

Economics Teachers, Postsecondary

- Education/Training Required: Master's degree
- Annual Earnings: $68,910
- Growth: 32.2%
- Annual Job Openings: 329,000
- Self-Employed: 0.4%
- Part-Time: 27.3%

The job openings listed here are shared with 35 other postsecondary teaching occupations. For a complete list, see the beginning of this section.

Teach courses in economics. Prepare and deliver lectures to undergraduate and/or graduate students on topics such as econometrics, price theory, and macroeconomics. Prepare course materials such as syllabi, homework assignments, and handouts. Evaluate and grade students' classwork, assignments, and papers. Compile, administer, and grade examinations or assign this work to others. Keep abreast of developments in their field by reading current literature, talking with colleagues, and participating in professional conferences. Maintain student attendance records, grades, and other required records. Initiate, facilitate, and moderate classroom discussions. Maintain regularly scheduled office hours in order to advise and assist students. Select and obtain materials and supplies such as textbooks. Plan, evaluate, and revise curricula, course content, and course materials and methods of instruction. Conduct research in a particular field of knowledge and publish findings in professional journals, books, and/or electronic media. Supervise undergraduate and/or graduate teaching, internship, and research work. Advise students on academic and vocational curricula and on career issues. Serve on academic or administrative committees that deal with institutional policies, departmental matters, and academic issues. Collaborate with colleagues to address teaching and research issues. Compile bibliographies of specialized materials for outside reading assignments. Participate in student recruitment, registration, and placement activities. Perform administrative duties such as serving as department head. Write grant proposals to procure external research funding. Participate in campus and community events. Provide professional consulting services to government and/or industry. Act as advisers to student organizations.

SKILLS—Most Important: Mathematics Skills; Communication Skills; Thought-Processing Skills. **Other Above-Average Skills:** Social Skills; Science Skills.

GOE—Interest Area: 05. Education and Training. **Work Group:** 05.03. Postsecondary and Adult Teaching and Instructing. **Other Jobs in This Group:** Adult Literacy, Remedial Education, and GED Teachers and Instructors; Agricultural Sciences Teachers, Postsecondary; Anthropology and Archeology Teachers, Postsecondary; Architecture Teachers, Postsecondary; Area, Ethnic, and Cultural Studies Teachers, Postsecondary; Art, Drama, and Music Teachers, Postsecondary; Atmospheric, Earth, Marine, and Space Sciences Teachers, Postsecondary; Biological Science Teachers, Postsecondary; Business Teachers, Postsecondary; Chemistry Teachers, Postsecondary; Communications Teachers, Postsecondary; Computer Science Teachers, Postsecondary; Criminal Justice and Law Enforcement Teachers, Postsecondary; Education Teachers, Postsecondary; Engineering Teachers, Postsecondary; English Language and Literature Teachers, Postsecondary; Environmental Science Teachers, Postsecondary; Farm and Home Management Advisors; Foreign Language and Literature Teachers, Postsecondary; Forestry and Conservation Science Teachers, Postsecondary; Geography Teachers, Postsecondary; Graduate Teaching Assistants; Health Specialties Teachers, Postsecondary; History Teachers, Postsecondary; Home Economics Teachers, Postsecondary; Law Teachers, Postsecondary; Library Science

E

Teachers, Postsecondary; Mathematical Science Teachers, Postsecondary; Nursing Instructors and Teachers, Postsecondary; Philosophy and Religion Teachers, Postsecondary; Physics Teachers, Postsecondary; Political Science Teachers, Postsecondary; Psychology Teachers, Postsecondary; Recreation and Fitness Studies Teachers, Postsecondary; Self-Enrichment Education Teachers; Social Work Teachers, Postsecondary; Sociology Teachers, Postsecondary; Vocational Education Teachers, Postsecondary. **PERSONALITY TYPE:** Social. Social occupations frequently involve working with, communicating with, and teaching people. These occupations often involve helping or providing service to others.

EDUCATION/TRAINING PROGRAM(S)—Social Science Teacher Education; Economics, General; Applied Economics; Econometrics and Quantitative Economics; Development Economics and International Development; International Economics; Economics, Other; Business/Managerial Economics. **RELATED KNOWLEDGE/COURSES—Economics and Accounting:** Economic and accounting principles and practices, the financial markets, banking, and the analysis and reporting of financial data. **History and Archeology:** Historical events and their causes, indicators, and effects on civilizations and cultures. **Mathematics:** Arithmetic, algebra, geometry, calculus, and statistics and their applications. **Education and Training:** Principles and methods for curriculum and training design, teaching and instruction for individuals and groups, and the measurement of training effects. **English Language:** The structure and content of the English language, including the meaning and spelling of words, rules of composition, and grammar. **Philosophy and Theology:** Different philosophical systems and religions. This includes their basic principles, values, ethics, ways of thinking, customs, practices, and impact on human culture.

Economists

- Education/Training Required: Master's degree
- Annual Earnings: $73,690
- Growth: 5.6%
- Annual Job Openings: 1,000
- Self-Employed: 0.0%
- Part-Time: 2.4%

Conduct research, prepare reports, or formulate plans to aid in solution of economic problems arising from production and distribution of goods and services. May collect and process economic and statistical data, using econometric and sampling techniques. Study economic and statistical data in area of specialization, such as finance, labor, or agriculture. Provide advice and consultation on economic relationships to businesses, public and private agencies, and other employers. Compile, analyze, and report data to explain economic phenomena and forecast market trends, applying mathematical models and statistical techniques. Formulate recommendations, policies, or plans to solve economic problems or to interpret markets. Develop economic guidelines and standards and prepare points of view used in forecasting trends and formulating economic policy. Testify at regulatory or legislative hearings concerning the estimated effects of changes in legislation or public policy and present recommendations based on cost-benefit analyses. Supervise research projects and students' study projects. Forecast production and consumption of renewable resources and supply, consumption, and depletion of non-renewable resources. Teach theories, principles, and methods of economics.

SKILLS—Most Important: Mathematics Skills; Computer Programming Skills; Thought-Processing Skills. **Other Above-Average Skills:** Communication Skills; Social Skills.

GOE—Interest Area: 15. Scientific Research, Engineering, and Mathematics. **Work Group:** 15.04. Social Sciences. **Other Jobs in This Group:** Anthropologists; Anthropologists and Archeologists; Archeologists; Historians; Industrial-Organizational Psychologists; Political Scientists; School Psychologists; Sociologists.

PERSONALITY TYPE: Investigative. Investigative occupations frequently involve working with ideas and require an extensive amount of thinking. These occupations can involve searching for facts and figuring out problems mentally.

EDUCATION/TRAINING PROGRAM(S)—Agricultural Economics; Economics, General; Applied Economics; Econometrics and Quantitative Economics; Development Economics and International Development; International Economics; Economics, Other; Business/Managerial Economics. **RELATED KNOWLEDGE/COURSES—Economics and Accounting:** Economic and accounting principles and practices, the financial markets, banking, and the analysis and reporting of financial data. **Mathematics:** Arithmetic, algebra, geometry, calculus, and statistics and their applications. **Sales and Marketing:** Principles and methods for showing, promoting, and selling products or services. This includes marketing strategy and tactics, product demonstration, sales techniques, and sales control systems. **Computers and Electronics:** Circuit boards; processors; chips; electronic equipment; and computer hardware and software, including applications and programming. **Geography:** Principles and methods for describing the features of land, sea, and air masses, including their physical characteristics; locations; interrelationships; and distribution of plant, animal, and human life. **English Language:** The structure and content of the English language, including the meaning and spelling of words, rules of composition, and grammar.

Education Administrators, Elementary and Secondary School

- ◎ Education/Training Required: Work experience plus degree
- ◎ Annual Earnings: $75,400
- ◎ Growth: 10.4%
- ◎ Annual Job Openings: 27,000
- ◎ Self-Employed: 3.6%
- ◎ Part-Time: 9.3%

Plan, direct, or coordinate the academic, clerical, or auxiliary activities of public or private elementary or secondary-level schools. Review and approve new programs or recommend modifications to existing programs, submitting program proposals for school board approval as necessary. Prepare, maintain, or oversee the preparation and maintenance of attendance, activity, planning, or personnel reports and records. Confer with parents and staff to discuss educational activities, policies, and student behavioral or learning problems. Prepare and submit budget requests and recommendations or grant proposals to solicit program funding. Direct and coordinate school maintenance services and the use of school facilities. Counsel and provide guidance to students regarding personal, academic, vocational, or behavioral issues. Organize and direct committees of specialists, volunteers, and staff to provide technical and advisory assistance for programs. Teach classes or courses to students. Advocate for new schools to be built or for existing facilities to be repaired or remodeled. Plan and develop instructional methods and content for educational, vocational, or student activity programs. Develop partnerships with businesses, communities, and other organizations to help meet identified educational needs and to provide school-to-work programs. Direct and coordinate activities of teachers, administrators, and support staff at schools, public agencies, and institutions. Evaluate curricula, teaching methods, and programs to determine their effectiveness, efficiency, and utilization and to ensure that school activities comply with federal, state, and local regulations. Set educational standards and goals and help establish policies and procedures to carry them out. Recruit, hire, train, and evaluate primary and supplemental staff. Enforce discipline and attendance rules. Observe teaching methods and examine learning materials to evaluate and standardize curricula and teaching techniques and to determine areas where improvement is needed. Establish, coordinate, and oversee particular programs across school districts, such as programs to evaluate student academic achievement. Review and interpret government codes and develop programs to ensure adherence to codes and facility safety, security, and maintenance.

SKILLS—Most Important: Management Skills; Social Skills; Thought-Processing Skills. **Other Above-Average Skills:** Communication Skills; Equipment/Technology Analysis Skills; Science Skills.

GOE—Interest Area: 05. Education and Training. **Work Group:** 05.01. Managerial Work in Education. **Other Jobs in This Group:** Education Administrators, Postsecondary; Education Administrators, Preschool and Child Care Center/Program; Instructional Coordinators. **PERSONALITY TYPE:** Social. Social occupations frequently involve working with, communicating with, and teaching people. These occupations often involve helping or providing service to others.

EDUCATION/TRAINING PROGRAM(S)—Educational Leadership and Administration, General; Educational, Instructional, and Curriculum Supervision; Elementary and Middle School Administration/Principalship; Secondary School Administration/Principalship; Educational Administration and Supervision, Other. **RELATED KNOWLEDGE/COURSES—Education and Training:** Principles and methods for curriculum and training design, teaching and instruction for individuals and groups, and the measurement of training effects. **Therapy and Counseling:** Principles, methods, and procedures for diagnosis, treatment, and rehabilitation of physical and mental dysfunctions and for career counseling and guidance. **Personnel and Human Resources:** Principles and procedures for personnel recruitment, selection, training, compensation and benefits, labor relations and negotiation, and personnel information systems. **Psychology:** Human behavior and performance; individual differences in ability, personality, and interests; learning and motivation; psychological research methods; and the assessment and treatment of behavioral and affective disorders. **Customer and Personal Service:** Principles and processes for providing customer and personal services. This includes customer needs assessment, meeting of quality standards for services, and evaluation of customer satisfaction. **Administration and Management:** Business and management principles involved in strategic planning, resource allocation, human resources modeling, leadership technique, production methods, and coordination of people and resources.

Education Administrators, Postsecondary

- Education/Training Required: Work experience plus degree
- Annual Earnings: $70,350
- Growth: 21.3%
- Annual Job Openings: 18,000
- Self-Employed: 3.3%
- Part-Time: 9.3%

Plan, direct, or coordinate research, instructional, student administration and services, and other educational activities at postsecondary institutions, including universities, colleges, and junior and community colleges. Recruit, hire, train, and terminate departmental personnel. Plan, administer, and control budgets; maintain financial records; and produce financial reports. Represent institutions at community and campus events, in meetings with other institution personnel, and during accreditation processes. Participate in faculty and college committee activities. Provide assistance to faculty and staff in duties such as teaching classes, conducting orientation programs, issuing transcripts, and scheduling events. Establish operational policies and procedures and make any necessary modifications, based on analysis of operations, demographics, and other research information. Confer with other academic staff to explain and formulate admission requirements and course credit policies. Appoint individuals to faculty positions and evaluate their performance. Direct activities of administrative departments such as admissions, registration, and career services. Develop curricula and recommend curricula revisions and additions. Determine course schedules and coordinate teaching assignments and room assignments to ensure optimum use of buildings and equipment. Consult with government regulatory and licensing agencies to ensure the institution's conformance with applicable standards. Direct, coordinate, and evaluate the activities of personnel engaged in administering academic institutions, departments, and/or alumni organizations. Teach courses within their department. Participate in student recruitment, selection, and admission, making admissions recommendations when required to do so. Review student misconduct reports requiring disciplinary action and counsel students regarding such reports. Supervise coaches. Assess and collect tuition and fees. Direct scholarship, fellowship, and loan programs, performing activities such as selecting recipients and distributing aid. Coordinate the production and dissemination of university publications such as course catalogs and class schedules. Review registration statistics and consult with faculty officials to develop registration policies. Audit the financial status of student organizations and facility accounts.

SKILLS—Most Important: Management Skills; Social Skills; Thought-Processing Skills. Other Above-Average Skills: Communication Skills; Equipment/Technology Analysis Skills.

GOE—Interest Area: 05. Education and Training. Work Group: 05.01. Managerial Work in Education. Other Jobs in This Group: Education Administrators, Elementary and Secondary School; Education Administrators, Preschool and Child Care Center/ Program; Instructional Coordinators. PERSONALITY TYPE: Enterprising. Enterprising occupations frequently involve starting up and carrying out projects. These occupations can involve leading people and making many decisions. They sometimes require risk taking and often deal with business.

EDUCATION/TRAINING PROGRAM(S)—Educational Leadership and Administration, General; Educational, Instructional, and Curriculum Supervision; Higher Education/Higher Education Administration; Community College Education; Educational Administration and Supervision, Other. RELATED KNOWLEDGE/COURSES—Education and Training: Principles and methods for curriculum and training design, teaching and instruction for individuals and groups, and the measurement of training effects. Personnel and Human Resources: Principles and procedures for personnel recruitment, selection, training, compensation and benefits, labor relations and negotiation, and personnel information systems. Sociology and Anthropology: Group behavior and dynamics, societal trends and influences, human migrations, ethnicity, and cultures and their history and origins. Administration and Management: Business and management principles involved in strategic planning, resource allocation, human resources modeling, leadership technique, production methods, and coordination of people and resources. Customer and Personal

Service: Principles and processes for providing customer and personal services. This includes customer needs assessment, meeting of quality standards for services, and evaluation of customer satisfaction. Sales and Marketing: Principles and methods for showing, promoting, and selling products or services. This includes marketing strategy and tactics, product demonstration, sales techniques, and sales control systems.

Education Teachers, Postsecondary

- Education/Training Required: Master's degree
- Annual Earnings: $50,380
- Growth: 32.2%
- Annual Job Openings: 329,000
- Self-Employed: 0.4%
- Part-Time: 27.3%

The job openings listed here are shared with 35 other postsecondary teaching occupations. For a complete list, see the beginning of this section.

Teach courses pertaining to education, such as counseling, curriculum, guidance, instruction, teacher education, and teaching English as a second language. Prepare course materials such as syllabi, homework assignments, and handouts. Prepare and deliver lectures to undergraduate and/or graduate students on topics such as children's literature, learning and development, and reading instruction. Initiate, facilitate, and moderate classroom discussions. Evaluate and grade students' classwork, assignments, and papers. Plan, evaluate, and revise curricula, course content, and course materials and methods of instruction. Supervise students' fieldwork, internship, and research work. Keep abreast of developments in their field by reading current literature, talking with colleagues, and participating in professional conferences. Advise students on academic and vocational curricula and on career issues. Maintain regularly scheduled office hours to advise and assist students. Maintain student attendance records, grades, and other required records. Collaborate with colleagues to address teaching and research issues. Compile, administer, and grade examinations or assign this work to others.

E

Conduct research in a particular field of knowledge and publish findings in professional journals, books, or electronic media. Select and obtain materials and supplies such as textbooks. Participate in student recruitment, registration, and placement activities. Advise and instruct teachers employed in school systems by providing activities such as in-service seminars. Serve on academic or administrative committees that deal with institutional policies, departmental matters, and academic issues. Compile bibliographies of specialized materials for outside reading assignments. Write grant proposals to procure external research funding. Participate in campus and community events. Perform administrative duties such as serving as department head. Act as advisers to student organizations. Provide professional consulting services to government and/or industry.

SKILLS—Most Important: Social Skills; Communication Skills; Thought-Processing Skills. **Other Above-Average Skills:** Science Skills; Mathematics Skills; Quality Control Skills.

GOE—Interest Area: 05. Education and Training. **Work Group:** 05.03. Postsecondary and Adult Teaching and Instructing. **Other Jobs in This Group:** Adult Literacy, Remedial Education, and GED Teachers and Instructors; Agricultural Sciences Teachers, Postsecondary; Anthropology and Archeology Teachers, Postsecondary; Architecture Teachers, Postsecondary; Area, Ethnic, and Cultural Studies Teachers, Postsecondary; Art, Drama, and Music Teachers, Postsecondary; Atmospheric, Earth, Marine, and Space Sciences Teachers, Postsecondary; Biological Science Teachers, Postsecondary; Business Teachers, Postsecondary; Chemistry Teachers, Postsecondary; Communications Teachers, Postsecondary; Computer Science Teachers, Postsecondary; Criminal Justice and Law Enforcement Teachers, Postsecondary; Economics Teachers, Postsecondary; Engineering Teachers, Postsecondary; English Language and Literature Teachers, Postsecondary; Environmental Science Teachers, Postsecondary; Farm and Home Management Advisors; Foreign Language and Literature Teachers, Postsecondary; Forestry and Conservation Science Teachers, Postsecondary; Geography Teachers, Postsecondary; Graduate Teaching Assistants; Health Specialties Teachers, Postsecondary; History Teachers, Postsecondary; Home Economics Teachers, Postsecondary; Law Teachers, Postsecondary; Library Science Teachers, Postsecondary; Mathematical Science Teachers, Postsecondary; Nursing Instructors and Teachers, Postsecondary; Philosophy and Religion Teachers, Postsecondary; Physics Teachers, Postsecondary; Political Science Teachers, Postsecondary; Psychology Teachers, Postsecondary; Recreation and Fitness Studies Teachers, Postsecondary; Self-Enrichment Education Teachers; Social Work Teachers, Postsecondary; Sociology Teachers, Postsecondary; Vocational Education Teachers, Postsecondary. **PERSONALITY TYPE:** No data available.

EDUCATION/TRAINING PROGRAM(S)—Education, General; Indian/Native American Education; Social and Philosophical Foundations of Education; Agricultural Teacher Education; Art Teacher Education; Business Teacher Education; Driver and Safety Teacher Education; English/Language Arts Teacher Education; Foreign Language Teacher Education; Health Teacher Education; Family and Consumer Sciences/Home Economics Teacher Education; others. **RELATED KNOWLEDGE/COURSES—Education and Training:** Principles and methods for curriculum and training design, teaching and instruction for individuals and groups, and the measurement of training effects. **Therapy and Counseling:** Principles, methods, and procedures for diagnosis, treatment, and rehabilitation of physical and mental dysfunctions and for career counseling and guidance. **Sociology and Anthropology:** Group behavior and dynamics, societal trends and influences, human migrations, ethnicity, and cultures and their history and origins. **Philosophy and Theology:** Different philosophical systems and religions. This includes their basic principles, values, ethics, ways of thinking, customs, practices, and impact on human culture. **Psychology:** Human behavior and performance; individual differences in ability, personality, and interests; learning and motivation; psychological research methods; and the assessment and treatment of behavioral and affective disorders. **English Language:** The structure and content of the English language, including the meaning and spelling of words, rules of composition, and grammar.

Educational, Vocational, and School Counselors

- Education/Training Required: Master's degree
- Annual Earnings: $46,440
- Growth: 14.8%
- Annual Job Openings: 32,000
- Self-Employed: 5.8%
- Part-Time: 16.7%

Counsel individuals and provide group educational and vocational guidance services. Counsel students regarding educational issues such as course and program selection, class scheduling, school adjustment, truancy, study habits, and career planning. Counsel individuals to help them understand and overcome personal, social, or behavioral problems affecting their educational or vocational situations. Maintain accurate and complete student records as required by laws, district policies, and administrative regulations. Confer with parents or guardians, teachers, other counselors, and administrators to resolve students' behavioral, academic, and other problems. Provide crisis intervention to students when difficult situations occur at schools. Identify cases involving domestic abuse or other family problems affecting students' development. Meet with parents and guardians to discuss their children's progress and to determine their priorities for their children and their resource needs. Prepare students for later educational experiences by encouraging them to explore learning opportunities and to persevere with challenging tasks. Encourage students and/or parents to seek additional assistance from mental health professionals when necessary. Observe and evaluate students' performance, behavior, social development, and physical health. Enforce all administration policies and rules governing students. Meet with other professionals to discuss individual students' needs and progress. Provide students with information on such topics as college degree programs and admission requirements, financial aid opportunities, trade and technical schools, and apprenticeship programs. Evaluate individuals' abilities, interests, and personality characteristics, using tests, records, interviews, and professional sources. Collaborate with teachers and administrators in the development, evaluation, and revision of school programs. Establish and enforce behavioral rules and procedures to maintain order among students. Teach classes and present self-help or information sessions on subjects related to education and career planning. Attend professional meetings, educational conferences, and teacher training workshops to maintain and improve professional competence.

SKILLS—Most Important: Social Skills; Communication Skills; Thought-Processing Skills. **Other Above-Average Skills:** Management Skills.

GOE—Interest Area: 05. Education and Training. **Work Group:** 05.06. Counseling, Health, and Fitness Education. **Other Jobs in This Group:** Fitness Trainers and Aerobics Instructors; Health Educators. **PERSONALITY TYPE:** Social. Social occupations frequently involve working with, communicating with, and teaching people. These occupations often involve helping or providing service to others.

EDUCATION/TRAINING PROGRAM(S)—Counselor Education/School Counseling and Guidance Services; College Student Counseling and Personnel Services. **RELATED KNOWLEDGE/COURSES—Therapy and Counseling:** Principles, methods, and procedures for diagnosis, treatment, and rehabilitation of physical and mental dysfunctions and for career counseling and guidance. **Psychology:** Human behavior and performance; individual differences in ability, personality, and interests; learning and motivation; psychological research methods; and the assessment and treatment of behavioral and affective disorders. **Education and Training:** Principles and methods for curriculum and training design, teaching and instruction for individuals and groups, and the measurement of training effects. **Sociology and Anthropology:** Group behavior and dynamics, societal trends and influences, human migrations, ethnicity, and cultures and their history and origins. **Philosophy and Theology:** Different philosophical systems and religions. This includes their basic principles, values, ethics, ways of thinking, customs, practices, and impact on human culture. **Customer and Personal Service:** Principles and processes for providing customer and personal services. This includes customer needs assessment, meeting of quality standards for services, and evaluation of customer satisfaction.

E

Electrical and Electronic Equipment Assemblers

- Education/Training Required: Short-term on-the-job training
- Annual Earnings: $25,130
- Growth: –6.4%
- Annual Job Openings: 33,000
- Self-Employed: 1.5%
- Part-Time: 4.1%

Assemble or modify electrical or electronic equipment, such as computers, test equipment telemetering systems, electric motors, and batteries. Inspect and test wiring installations, assemblies, and circuits for resistance factors and for operation and record results. Assemble electrical or electronic systems and support structures and install components, units, subassemblies, wiring, and assembly casings, using rivets, bolts, and soldering and micro-welding equipment. Adjust, repair, or replace electrical or electronic component parts to correct defects and to ensure conformance to specifications. Clean parts, using cleaning solutions, air hoses, and cloths. Read and interpret schematic drawings, diagrams, blueprints, specifications, work orders, and reports to determine materials requirements and assembly instructions. Mark and tag components so that stock inventory can be tracked and identified. Position, align, and adjust workpieces and electrical parts to facilitate wiring and assembly. Pack finished assemblies for shipment and transport them to storage areas, using hoists or handtrucks. Confer with supervisors or engineers to plan and review work activities and to resolve production problems. Explain assembly procedures or techniques to other workers. Measure and adjust voltages to specified values to determine operational accuracy of instruments. Fabricate and form parts, coils, and structures according to specifications, using drills, calipers, cutters, and saws. Drill and tap holes in specified equipment locations to mount control units and to provide openings for elements, wiring, and instruments. Complete, review, and maintain production, time, and component waste reports. Paint structures as specified, using paint sprayers. Instruct customers in the installation, repair, and maintenance of products. Distribute materials, supplies, and subassemblies to work areas.

SKILLS—Most Important: Quality Control Skills; Computer Programming Skills; Equipment Use/Maintenance Skills. **Other Above-Average Skills:** Equipment/Technology Analysis Skills; Management Skills; Social Skills.

GOE—Interest Area: 13. Manufacturing. **Work Group:** 13.06. Production Precision Work. **Other Jobs in This Group:** Bookbinders; Dental Laboratory Technicians; Electromechanical Equipment Assemblers; Engine and Other Machine Assemblers; Gem and Diamond Workers; Jewelers; Jewelers and Precious Stone and Metal Workers; Medical Appliance Technicians; Molding, Coremaking, and Casting Machine Setters, Operators, and Tenders, Metal and Plastic; Ophthalmic Laboratory Technicians; Precious Metal Workers; Semiconductor Processors; Timing Device Assemblers, Adjusters, and Calibrators. **PERSONALITY TYPE:** Realistic. Realistic occupations frequently involve work activities that include practical, hands-on problems and solutions. They often deal with plants, animals, and real-world materials like wood, tools, and machinery. Many of the occupations require working outside and do not involve a lot of paperwork or working closely with others.

EDUCATION/TRAINING PROGRAM(S)—Communications Systems Installation and Repair Technology; Industrial Electronics Technology/Technician. **RELATED KNOWLEDGE/COURSES—Sales and Marketing:** Principles and methods for showing, promoting, and selling products or services. This includes marketing strategy and tactics, product demonstration, sales techniques, and sales control systems. **Production and Processing:** Raw materials, production processes, quality control, costs, and other techniques for maximizing the effective manufacture and distribution of goods.

Electrical and Electronics Repairers, Commercial and Industrial Equipment

- Education/Training Required: Postsecondary vocational training
- Annual Earnings: $44,120
- Growth: 9.7%
- Annual Job Openings: 8,000
- Self-Employed: 0.0%
- Part-Time: 5.5%

Repair, test, adjust, or install electronic equipment, such as industrial controls, transmitters, and antennas. Perform scheduled preventive maintenance tasks, such as checking, cleaning, and repairing equipment, to detect and prevent problems. Examine work orders and converse with equipment operators to detect equipment problems and to ascertain whether mechanical or human errors contributed to the problems. Operate equipment to demonstrate proper use and to analyze malfunctions. Set up and test industrial equipment to ensure that it functions properly. Test faulty equipment to diagnose malfunctions, using test equipment and software and applying knowledge of the functional operation of electronic units and systems. Repair and adjust equipment, machines, and defective components, replacing worn parts such as gaskets and seals in watertight electrical equipment. Calibrate testing instruments and installed or repaired equipment to prescribed specifications. Advise management regarding customer satisfaction, product performance, and suggestions for product improvements. Study blueprints, schematics, manuals, and other specifications to determine installation procedures. Inspect components of industrial equipment for accurate assembly and installation and for defects such as loose connections and frayed wires. Maintain equipment logs that record performance problems, repairs, calibrations, and tests. Coordinate efforts with other workers involved in installing and maintaining equipment or components. Maintain inventory of spare parts. Consult with customers, supervisors, and engineers to plan layout of equipment and to resolve problems in system operation and maintenance. Install repaired equipment in various settings, such as industrial or military establishments. Send defective units to the manufacturer or to a specialized repair shop for repair. Determine feasibility of using standardized equipment and develop specifications for equipment required to perform additional functions. Enter information into computer to copy program or to draw, modify, or store schematics, applying knowledge of software package used. Sign overhaul documents for equipment replaced or repaired. Develop or modify industrial electronic devices, circuits, and equipment according to available specifications.

SKILLS—Most Important: Equipment Use/Maintenance Skills; Science Skills; Mathematics Skills. **Other Above-Average Skills:** Equipment/Technology Analysis Skills; Thought-Processing Skills.

GOE—Interest Area: 13. Manufacturing. **Work Group:** 13.12. Electrical and Electronic Repair. **Other Jobs in This Group:** Avionics Technicians; Electric Motor, Power Tool, and Related Repairers; Electrical and Electronics Installers and Repairers, Transportation Equipment; Electronic Equipment Installers and Repairers, Motor Vehicles; Electronic Home Entertainment Equipment Installers and Repairers; Radio Mechanics. **PERSONALITY TYPE:** Realistic. Realistic occupations frequently involve work activities that include practical, hands-on problems and solutions. They often deal with plants, animals, and real-world materials like wood, tools, and machinery. Many of the occupations require working outside and do not involve a lot of paperwork or working closely with others.

EDUCATION/TRAINING PROGRAM(S)—Computer Installation and Repair Technology/Technician; Industrial Electronics Technology/Technician. **RELATED KNOWLEDGE/COURSES—Mechanical Devices:** Machines and tools, including their designs, uses, repair, and maintenance. **Computers and Electronics:** Circuit boards; processors; chips; electronic equipment; and computer hardware and software, including applications and programming. **Telecommunications:** Transmission, broadcasting, switching, control, and operation of telecommunications systems. **Engineering and Technology:** The practical application of engineering science and technology. This includes applying principles, techniques, procedures, and equipment to the design and production of various goods and services.

E

Electrical Engineering Technicians

- ⊚ Education/Training Required: Associate degree
- ⊚ Annual Earnings: $48,040
- ⊚ Growth: 9.8%
- ⊚ Annual Job Openings: 18,000
- ⊚ Self-Employed: 0.4%
- ⊚ Part-Time: 6.7%

The job openings listed here are shared with Electronics Engineering Technicians.

Apply electrical theory and related knowledge to test and modify developmental or operational electrical machinery and electrical control equipment and circuitry in industrial or commercial plants and laboratories. Usually work under direction of engineering staff. Assemble electrical and electronic systems and prototypes according to engineering data and knowledge of electrical principles, using hand tools and measuring instruments. Provide technical assistance and resolution when electrical or engineering problems are encountered before, during, and after construction. Install and maintain electrical control systems and solid state equipment. Modify electrical prototypes, parts, assemblies, and systems to correct functional deviations. Set up and operate test equipment to evaluate performance of developmental parts, assemblies, or systems under simulated operating conditions and record results. Collaborate with electrical engineers and other personnel to identify, define, and solve developmental problems. Build, calibrate, maintain, troubleshoot, and repair electrical instruments or testing equipment. Analyze and interpret test information to resolve design-related problems. Write commissioning procedures for electrical installations. Prepare project cost and work-time estimates. Evaluate engineering proposals, shop drawings, and design comments for sound electrical engineering practice and conformance with established safety and design criteria and recommend approval or disapproval. Draw or modify diagrams and write engineering specifications to clarify design details and functional criteria of experimental electronics units. Conduct inspections for quality control and assurance programs, reporting findings and recommendations. Prepare contracts and initiate, review, and coordinate modifications to contract specifications and plans throughout the construction process. Plan, schedule, and monitor work of support personnel to assist supervisor. Review existing electrical engineering criteria to identify necessary revisions, deletions, or amendments to outdated material. Perform supervisory duties such as recommending work assignments, approving leaves, and completing performance evaluations. Plan method and sequence of operations for developing and testing experimental electronic and electrical equipment. Visit construction sites to observe conditions impacting design and to identify solutions to technical design problems involving electrical systems equipment that arise during construction.

SKILLS—Most Important: Science Skills; Mathematics Skills; Equipment Use/Maintenance Skills. **Other Above-Average Skills:** Equipment/Technology Analysis Skills; Quality Control Skills; Social Skills; Communication Skills; Management Skills.

GOE—Interest Area: 15. Scientific Research, Engineering, and Mathematics. **Work Group:** 15.09. Engineering Technology. **Other Jobs in This Group:** Aerospace Engineering and Operations Technicians; Cartographers and Photogrammetrists; Civil Engineering Technicians; Electrical and Electronic Engineering Technicians; Electrical and Electronics Drafters; Electrical Drafters; Electro-Mechanical Technicians; Electronic Drafters; Electronics Engineering Technicians; Environmental Engineering Technicians; Mapping Technicians; Mechanical Drafters; Mechanical Engineering Technicians; Surveying and Mapping Technicians; Surveying Technicians. **PERSONALITY TYPE:** Realistic. Realistic occupations frequently involve work activities that include practical, hands-on problems and solutions. They often deal with plants, animals, and real-world materials like wood, tools, and machinery. Many of the occupations require working outside and do not involve a lot of paperwork or working closely with others.

EDUCATION/TRAINING PROGRAM(S)—Electrical, Electronic, and Communications Engineering Technology/Technician; Telecommunications Technology/Technician; Electrical and Electronic Engineering Technologies/Technicians, Other; Computer Engineering Technology/Technician; Computer Technology/

Computer Systems Technology. **RELATED KNOWL-EDGE/COURSES—Engineering and Technology:** The practical application of engineering science and technology. This includes applying principles, techniques, procedures, and equipment to the design and production of various goods and services. **Design:** Design techniques, tools, and principles involved in production of precision technical plans, blueprints, drawings, and models. **Computers and Electronics:** Circuit boards; processors; chips; electronic equipment; and computer hardware and software, including applications and programming. **Physics:** Physical principles and laws and their interrelationships and applications to understanding fluid, material, and atmospheric dynamics and mechanical, electrical, atomic, and subatomic structures and processes. **Mechanical Devices:** Machines and tools, including their designs, uses, repair, and maintenance. **Telecommunications:** Transmission, broadcasting, switching, control, and operation of telecommunications systems.

Electrical Engineers

- Education/Training Required: Bachelor's degree
- Annual Earnings: $73,510
- Growth: 11.8%
- Annual Job Openings: 12,000
- Self-Employed: 3.3%
- Part-Time: 2.1%

Design, develop, test, or supervise the manufacturing and installation of electrical equipment, components, or systems for commercial, industrial, military, or scientific use. Confer with engineers, customers, and others to discuss existing or potential engineering projects and products. Design, implement, maintain, and improve electrical instruments, equipment, facilities, components, products, and systems for commercial, industrial, and domestic purposes. Operate computer-assisted engineering and design software and equipment to perform engineering tasks. Direct and coordinate manufacturing, construction, installation, maintenance, support, documentation, and testing activities to ensure compliance with specifications, codes, and customer requirements. Perform detailed calculations to compute

and establish manufacturing, construction, and installation standards and specifications. Inspect completed installations and observe operations to ensure conformance to design and equipment specifications and compliance with operational and safety standards. Plan and implement research methodology and procedures to apply principles of electrical theory to engineering projects. Prepare specifications for purchase of materials and equipment. Supervise and train project team members as necessary. Investigate and test vendors' and competitors' products. Oversee project production efforts to assure projects are completed satisfactorily, on time, and within budget. Prepare and study technical drawings, specifications of electrical systems, and topographical maps to ensure that installation and operations conform to standards and customer requirements. Investigate customer or public complaints, determine nature and extent of problem, and recommend remedial measures. Plan layout of electric-power-generating plants and distribution lines and stations. Assist in developing capital project programs for new equipment and major repairs. Develop budgets, estimating labor, material, and construction costs. Compile data and write reports regarding existing and potential engineering studies and projects. Collect data relating to commercial and residential development, population, and power system interconnection to determine operating efficiency of electrical systems. Conduct field surveys and study maps, graphs, diagrams, and other data to identify and correct power system problems.

SKILLS—Most Important: Science Skills; Equipment/Technology Analysis Skills; Computer Programming Skills. **Other Above-Average Skills:** Management Skills; Mathematics Skills; Quality Control Skills; Communication Skills; Social Skills.

GOE—Interest Area: 15. Scientific Research, Engineering, and Mathematics. **Work Group:** 15.07. Research and Design Engineering. **Other Jobs in This Group:** Aerospace Engineers; Biomedical Engineers; Chemical Engineers; Civil Engineers; Computer Hardware Engineers; Electronics Engineers, Except Computer; Marine Architects; Marine Engineers; Marine Engineers and Naval Architects; Materials Engineers; Mechanical Engineers; Nuclear Engineers. **PERSONALITY TYPE:** Investigative. Investigative occupations frequently involve working with ideas and require an extensive amount of thinking. These occupations can involve searching for facts and figuring out problems mentally.

EDUCATION/TRAINING PROGRAM(S)—Electrical, Electronics, and Communications Engineering. RELATED KNOWLEDGE/COURSES—**Engineering and Technology:** The practical application of engineering science and technology. This includes applying principles, techniques, procedures, and equipment to the design and production of various goods and services. **Design:** Design techniques, tools, and principles involved in production of precision technical plans, blueprints, drawings, and models. **Physics:** Physical principles and laws and their interrelationships and applications to understanding fluid, material, and atmospheric dynamics and mechanical, electrical, atomic, and subatomic structures and processes. **Computers and Electronics:** Circuit boards; processors; chips; electronic equipment; and computer hardware and software, including applications and programming. **Telecommunications:** Transmission, broadcasting, switching, control, and operation of telecommunications systems. **Mathematics:** Arithmetic, algebra, geometry, calculus, and statistics and their applications.

Electricians

- Education/Training Required: Long-term on-the-job training
- Annual Earnings: $42,790
- Growth: 11.8%
- Annual Job Openings: 68,000
- Self-Employed: 9.5%
- Part-Time: 3.3%

Install, maintain, and repair electrical wiring, equipment, and fixtures. Ensure that work is in accordance with relevant codes. May install or service street lights, intercom systems, or electrical control systems. Assemble, install, test, and maintain electrical or electronic wiring, equipment, appliances, apparatus, and fixtures, using hand tools and power tools. Diagnose malfunctioning systems, apparatus, and components, using test equipment and hand tools, to locate the cause of a breakdown and correct the problem. Connect wires to circuit breakers, transformers, or other components. Inspect electrical systems, equipment, and components to identify hazards, defects, and the need for adjustment or repair and to ensure compliance with codes. Advise

management on whether continued operation of equipment could be hazardous. Test electrical systems and continuity of circuits in electrical wiring, equipment, and fixtures, using testing devices such as ohmmeters, voltmeters, and oscilloscopes, to ensure compatibility and safety of system. Maintain current electrician's license or identification card to meet governmental regulations. Plan layout and installation of electrical wiring, equipment, and fixtures based on job specifications and local codes. Direct and train workers to install, maintain, or repair electrical wiring, equipment, and fixtures. Prepare sketches or follow blueprints to determine the location of wiring and equipment and to ensure conformance to building and safety codes. Use a variety of tools and equipment, such as power construction equipment; measuring devices; power tools; and testing equipment, including oscilloscopes, ammeters, and test lamps. Install ground leads and connect power cables to equipment such as motors. Perform business management duties such as maintaining records and files, preparing reports, and ordering supplies and equipment. Repair or replace wiring, equipment, and fixtures, using hand tools and power tools. Work from ladders, scaffolds, and roofs to install, maintain, or repair electrical wiring, equipment, and fixtures. Place conduit, pipes, or tubing inside designated partitions, walls, or other concealed areas and pull insulated wires or cables through the conduit to complete circuits between boxes. Construct and fabricate parts, using hand tools and specifications.

SKILLS—Most Important: Equipment Use/Maintenance Skills; Equipment/Technology Analysis Skills; Mathematics Skills. **Other Above-Average Skills:** Quality Control Skills; Science Skills.

GOE—Interest Area: 02. Architecture and Construction. **Work Group:** 02.04. Construction Crafts. **Other Jobs in This Group:** Boilermakers; Brickmasons and Blockmasons; Carpet Installers; Cement Masons and Concrete Finishers; Commercial Divers; Construction Carpenters; Crane and Tower Operators; Drywall and Ceiling Tile Installers; Fence Erectors; Floor Layers, Except Carpet, Wood, and Hard Tiles; Floor Sanders and Finishers; Glaziers; Hazardous Materials Removal Workers; Insulation Workers, Floor, Ceiling, and Wall; Insulation Workers, Mechanical; Manufactured Building and Mobile Home Installers; Operating Engineers and Other Construction Equipment Operators; Painters, Construction and

Maintenance; Paperhangers; Paving, Surfacing, and Tamping Equipment Operators; Pile-Driver Operators; Pipe Fitters and Steamfitters; Pipelayers; Plasterers and Stucco Masons; Plumbers; Plumbers, Pipefitters, and Steamfitters; Rail-Track Laying and Maintenance Equipment Operators; Refractory Materials Repairers, Except Brickmasons; Reinforcing Iron and Rebar Workers; Riggers; Roofers; Rough Carpenters; Security and Fire Alarm Systems Installers; Segmental Pavers; Sheet Metal Workers; Stone Cutters and Carvers, Manufacturing; Stonemasons; Structural Iron and Steel Workers; Tapers; Terrazzo Workers and Finishers; Tile and Marble Setters. **PERSONALITY TYPE:** Realistic. Realistic occupations frequently involve work activities that include practical, hands-on problems and solutions. They often deal with plants, animals, and real-world materials like wood, tools, and machinery. Many of the occupations require working outside and do not involve a lot of paperwork or working closely with others.

EDUCATION/TRAINING PROGRAM(S)—Electrician. **RELATED KNOWLEDGE/COURSES— Building and Construction:** The materials, methods, and tools involved in the construction or repair of houses, buildings, or other structures such as highways and roads. **Mechanical Devices:** Machines and tools, including their designs, uses, repair, and maintenance. **Design:** Design techniques, tools, and principles involved in production of precision technical plans, blueprints, drawings, and models. **Production and Processing:** Raw materials, production processes, quality control, costs, and other techniques for maximizing the effective manufacture and distribution of goods. **Physics:** Physical principles and laws and their interrelationships and applications to understanding fluid, material, and atmospheric dynamics and mechanical, electrical, atomic, and subatomic structures and processes. **Administration and Management:** Business and management principles involved in strategic planning, resource allocation, human resources modeling, leadership technique, production methods, and coordination of people and resources.

Electronics Engineering Technicians

- Education/Training Required: Associate degree
- Annual Earnings: $48,040
- Growth: 9.8%
- Annual Job Openings: 18,000
- Self-Employed: 0.4%
- Part-Time: 6.7%

The job openings listed here are shared with Electrical Engineering Technicians.

Lay out, build, test, troubleshoot, repair, and modify developmental and production electronic components, parts, equipment, and systems, such as computer equipment, missile control instrumentation, electron tubes, test equipment, and machine tool numerical controls, applying principles and theories of electronics, electrical circuitry, engineering mathematics, electronic and electrical testing, and physics. Usually work under direction of engineering staff. Test electronics units, using standard test equipment, and analyze results to evaluate performance and determine need for adjustment. Perform preventative maintenance and calibration of equipment and systems. Read blueprints, wiring diagrams, schematic drawings, and engineering instructions for assembling electronics units, applying knowledge of electronic theory and components. Identify and resolve equipment malfunctions, working with manufacturers and field representatives as necessary to procure replacement parts. Maintain system logs and manuals to document testing and operation of equipment. Assemble, test, and maintain circuitry or electronic components according to engineering instructions, technical manuals, and knowledge of electronics, using hand and power tools. Adjust and replace defective or improperly functioning circuitry and electronics components, using hand tools and soldering iron. Procure parts and maintain inventory and related documentation. Maintain working knowledge of state-of-the-art tools or software by reading or attending conferences, workshops, or other training. Provide user applications and engineering support and recommendations for new and existing equipment with regard to installation, upgrades, and enhancement. Write reports

E

and record data on testing techniques, laboratory equipment, and specifications to assist engineers. Provide customer support and education, working with users to identify needs, determine sources of problems, and provide information on product use. Design basic circuitry and draft sketches for clarification of details and design documentation under engineers' direction, using drafting instruments and computer-aided design (CAD) equipment. Build prototypes from rough sketches or plans. Develop and upgrade preventative maintenance procedures for components, equipment, parts, and systems. Fabricate parts, such as coils, terminal boards, and chassis, using bench lathes, drills, or other machine tools. Research equipment and component needs, sources, competitive prices, delivery times, and ongoing operational costs. Write computer or microprocessor software programs.

SKILLS—Most Important: Equipment Use/Maintenance Skills; Computer Programming Skills; Science Skills. **Other Above-Average Skills:** Equipment/Technology Analysis Skills; Quality Control Skills; Thought-Processing Skills; Social Skills; Communication Skills.

GOE—Interest Area: 15. Scientific Research, Engineering, and Mathematics. **Work Group:** 15.09. Engineering Technology. **Other Jobs in This Group:** Aerospace Engineering and Operations Technicians; Cartographers and Photogrammetrists; Civil Engineering Technicians; Electrical and Electronic Engineering Technicians; Electrical and Electronics Drafters; Electrical Drafters; Electrical Engineering Technicians; Electro-Mechanical Technicians; Electronic Drafters; Environmental Engineering Technicians; Mapping Technicians; Mechanical Drafters; Mechanical Engineering Technicians; Surveying and Mapping Technicians; Surveying Technicians. **PERSONALITY TYPE:** Realistic. Realistic occupations frequently involve work activities that include practical, hands-on problems and solutions. They often deal with plants, animals, and real-world materials like wood, tools, and machinery. Many of the occupations require working outside and do not involve a lot of paperwork or working closely with others.

EDUCATION/TRAINING PROGRAM(S)—Electrical, Electronic, and Communications Engineering Technology/Technician; Telecommunications Technology/Technician; Electrical and Electronic Engineering

Technologies/Technicians, Other; Computer Engineering Technology/Technician. **RELATED KNOWLEDGE/COURSES—Engineering and Technology:** The practical application of engineering science and technology. This includes applying principles, techniques, procedures, and equipment to the design and production of various goods and services. **Computers and Electronics:** Circuit boards; processors; chips; electronic equipment; and computer hardware and software, including applications and programming. **Mechanical Devices:** Machines and tools, including their designs, uses, repair, and maintenance. **Design:** Design techniques, tools, and principles involved in production of precision technical plans, blueprints, drawings, and models. **Telecommunications:** Transmission, broadcasting, switching, control, and operation of telecommunications systems. **Mathematics:** Arithmetic, algebra, geometry, calculus, and statistics and their applications.

Electronics Engineers, Except Computer

- Education/Training Required: Bachelor's degree
- Annual Earnings: $78,030
- Growth: 9.7%
- Annual Job Openings: 11,000
- Self-Employed: 3.2%
- Part-Time: 2.1%

Research, design, develop, and test electronic components and systems for commercial, industrial, military, or scientific use, utilizing knowledge of electronic theory and materials properties. Design electronic circuits and components for use in fields such as telecommunications, aerospace guidance and propulsion control, acoustics, or instruments and controls. Design electronic components, software, products, or systems for commercial, industrial, medical, military, or scientific applications. Provide technical support and instruction to staff or customers regarding equipment standards, assisting with specific, difficult in-service engineering. Operate computer-assisted engineering and design software and equipment to perform engineering tasks.

Analyze system requirements, capacity, cost, and customer needs to determine feasibility of project and develop system plan. Confer with engineers, customers, vendors, or others to discuss existing and potential engineering projects or products. Review and evaluate work of others inside and outside the organization to ensure effectiveness, technical adequacy, and compatibility in the resolution of complex engineering problems. Determine material and equipment needs and order supplies. Inspect electronic equipment, instruments, products, and systems to ensure conformance to specifications, safety standards, and applicable codes and regulations. Evaluate operational systems, prototypes, and proposals and recommend repair or design modifications based on factors such as environment, service, cost, and system capabilities. Prepare documentation containing information such as confidential descriptions and specifications of proprietary hardware and software, product development and introduction schedules, product costs, and information about product performance weaknesses. Direct and coordinate activities concerned with manufacture, construction, installation, maintenance, operation, and modification of electronic equipment, products, and systems. Develop and perform operational, maintenance, and testing procedures for electronic products, components, equipment, and systems. Plan and develop applications and modifications for electronic properties used in components, products, and systems to improve technical performance. Plan and implement research, methodology, and procedures to apply principles of electronic theory to engineering projects. Prepare engineering sketches and specifications for construction, relocation, and installation of equipment, facilities, products, and systems.

SKILLS—Most Important: Science Skills; Equipment/Technology Analysis Skills; Quality Control Skills. **Other Above-Average Skills:** Mathematics Skills; Computer Programming Skills; Thought-Processing Skills; Social Skills; Equipment Use/Maintenance Skills.

GOE—Interest Area: 15. Scientific Research, Engineering, and Mathematics. **Work Group:** 15.07. Research and Design Engineering. **Other Jobs in This Group:** Aerospace Engineers; Biomedical Engineers; Chemical Engineers; Civil Engineers; Computer Hardware Engineers; Electrical Engineers; Marine Architects; Marine Engineers; Marine Engineers and Naval Architects; Materials Engineers; Mechanical Engineers; Nuclear Engineers. **PERSONALITY TYPE:** Investi-

gative. Investigative occupations frequently involve working with ideas and require an extensive amount of thinking. These occupations can involve searching for facts and figuring out problems mentally.

EDUCATION/TRAINING PROGRAM(S)—Electrical, Electronics, and Communications Engineering. **RELATED KNOWLEDGE/COURSES—Engineering and Technology:** The practical application of engineering science and technology. This includes applying principles, techniques, procedures, and equipment to the design and production of various goods and services. **Design:** Design techniques, tools, and principles involved in production of precision technical plans, blueprints, drawings, and models. **Computers and Electronics:** Circuit boards; processors; chips; electronic equipment; and computer hardware and software, including applications and programming. **Physics:** Physical principles and laws and their interrelationships and applications to understanding fluid, material, and atmospheric dynamics and mechanical, electrical, atomic, and subatomic structures and processes. **Telecommunications:** Transmission, broadcasting, switching, control, and operation of telecommunications systems. **Production and Processing:** Raw materials, production processes, quality control, costs, and other techniques for maximizing the effective manufacture and distribution of goods.

Elementary School Teachers, Except Special Education

- Education/Training Required: Bachelor's degree
- Annual Earnings: $44,040
- Growth: 18.2%
- Annual Job Openings: 203,000
- Self-Employed: 0.0%
- Part-Time: 12.6%

Teach pupils in public or private schools at the elementary level basic academic, social, and other formative skills. Establish and enforce rules for behavior and procedures for maintaining order among the students for whom they are responsible. Observe and evaluate students' performance, behavior, social development, and physical health. Prepare materials and classrooms for class activities. Adapt teaching methods and instructional materials to meet students' varying needs and interests. Plan and conduct activities for a balanced program of instruction, demonstration, and work time that provides students with opportunities to observe, question, and investigate. Instruct students individually and in groups, using various teaching methods such as lectures, discussions, and demonstrations. Establish clear objectives for all lessons, units, and projects and communicate those objectives to students. Assign and grade classwork and homework. Read books to entire classes or small groups. Prepare, administer, and grade tests and assignments in order to evaluate students' progress. Confer with parents or guardians, teachers, counselors, and administrators to resolve students' behavioral and academic problems. Meet with parents and guardians to discuss their children's progress and to determine their priorities for their children and their resource needs. Prepare students for later grades by encouraging them to explore learning opportunities and to persevere with challenging tasks. Maintain accurate and complete student records as required by laws, district policies, and administrative regulations. Guide and counsel students with adjustment or academic problems or special academic interests. Prepare and implement remedial programs for students requiring extra help. Prepare objectives and outlines for courses of study, following curriculum guidelines or requirements of states and schools. Provide a variety of materials and resources for children to explore, manipulate, and use, both in learning activities and in imaginative play. Enforce administration policies and rules governing students. Confer with other staff members to plan and schedule lessons promoting learning, following approved curricula.

SKILLS—Most Important: Social Skills; Communication Skills; Thought-Processing Skills. **Other Above-Average Skills:** Mathematics Skills; Science Skills.

GOE—Interest Area: 05. Education and Training. **Work Group:** 05.02. Preschool, Elementary, and Secondary Teaching and Instructing. **Other Jobs in This Group:** Kindergarten Teachers, Except Special Education; Middle School Teachers, Except Special and Vocational Education; Preschool Teachers, Except Special Education; Secondary School Teachers, Except Special and Vocational Education; Special Education Teachers, Middle School; Special Education Teachers, Preschool, Kindergarten, and Elementary School; Special Education Teachers, Secondary School; Teacher Assistants; Vocational Education Teachers, Middle School; Vocational Education Teachers, Secondary School. **PERSONALITY TYPE:** Social. Social occupations frequently involve working with, communicating with, and teaching people. These occupations often involve helping or providing service to others.

EDUCATION/TRAINING PROGRAM(S)—Elementary Education and Teaching; Teacher Education, Multiple Levels; Montessori Teacher Education. **RELATED KNOWLEDGE/COURSES—Geography:** Principles and methods for describing the features of land, sea, and air masses, including their physical characteristics; locations; interrelationships; and distribution of plant, animal, and human life. **History and Archeology:** Historical events and their causes, indicators, and effects on civilizations and cultures. **Education and Training:** Principles and methods for curriculum and training design, teaching and instruction for individuals and groups, and the measurement of training effects. **Sociology and Anthropology:** Group behavior and dynamics, societal trends and influences, human migrations, ethnicity, and cultures and their history and origins. **Therapy and Counseling:** Principles, methods, and procedures for diagnosis, treatment, and rehabilitation of physical and mental dysfunctions and for career counseling and guidance. **Psychology:** Human behavior and performance; individual differences in ability, personality, and interests; learning and motivation; psychological research methods; and the assessment and treatment of behavioral and affective disorders.

Elevator Installers and Repairers

- Education/Training Required: Long-term on-the-job training
- Annual Earnings: $59,190
- Growth: 14.8%
- Annual Job Openings: 3,000
- Self-Employed: 0.4%
- Part-Time: No data available

Assemble, install, repair, or maintain electric or hydraulic freight or passenger elevators, escalators, or dumbwaiters. Assemble, install, repair, and maintain elevators, escalators, moving sidewalks, and dumbwaiters, using hand and power tools and testing devices such as test lamps, ammeters, and voltmeters. Test newly installed equipment to ensure that it meets specifications, such as stopping at floors for set amounts of time. Locate malfunctions in brakes, motors, switches, and signal and control systems, using test equipment. Check that safety regulations and building codes are met and complete service reports verifying conformance to standards. Connect electrical wiring to control panels and electric motors. Read and interpret blueprints to determine the layout of system components, frameworks, and foundations and to select installation equipment. Adjust safety controls; counterweights; door mechanisms; and components such as valves, ratchets, seals, and brake linings. Inspect wiring connections, control panel hookups, door installations, and alignments and clearances of cars and hoistways to ensure that equipment will operate properly. Disassemble defective units and repair or replace parts such as locks, gears, cables, and electric wiring. Maintain logbooks that detail all repairs and checks performed. Participate in additional training to keep skills up to date. Attach guide shoes and rollers to minimize the lateral motion of cars as they travel through shafts. Connect car frames to counterweights, using steel cables. Bolt or weld steel rails to the walls of shafts to guide elevators, working from scaffolding or platforms. Assemble elevator cars, installing each car's platform, walls, and doors. Install outer doors and door frames at elevator entrances on each floor of a structure. Install electrical wires and controls by attaching conduit along shaft walls from floor to floor and then pulling plastic-covered wires through the conduit. Cut prefabricated sections of framework, rails, and other components to specified dimensions. Operate elevators to determine power demands and test power consumption to detect overload factors. Assemble electrically powered stairs, steel frameworks, and tracks and install associated motors and electrical wiring.

SKILLS—Most Important: Equipment Use/Maintenance Skills; Quality Control Skills. **Other Above-Average Skills:** None met the criteria.

GOE—Interest Area: 02. Architecture and Construction. **Work Group:** 02.05. Systems and Equipment Installation, Maintenance, and Repair. **Other Jobs in This Group:** Electrical and Electronics Repairers, Powerhouse, Substation, and Relay; Electrical Power-Line Installers and Repairers; Heating and Air Conditioning Mechanics and Installers; Maintenance and Repair Workers, General; Refrigeration Mechanics and Installers; Telecommunications Equipment Installers and Repairers, Except Line Installers; Telecommunications Line Installers and Repairers. **PERSONALITY TYPE:** Realistic. Realistic occupations frequently involve work activities that include practical, hands-on problems and solutions. They often deal with plants, animals, and real-world materials like wood, tools, and machinery. Many of the occupations require working outside and do not involve a lot of paperwork or working closely with others.

EDUCATION/TRAINING PROGRAM(S)—Industrial Mechanics and Maintenance Technology. **RELATED KNOWLEDGE/COURSES—Building and Construction:** The materials, methods, and tools involved in the construction or repair of houses, buildings, or other structures such as highways and roads. **Mechanical Devices:** Machines and tools, including their designs, uses, repair, and maintenance. **Engineering and Technology:** The practical application of engineering science and technology. This includes applying principles, techniques, procedures, and equipment to the design and production of various goods and services. **Physics:** Physical principles and laws and their interrelationships and applications to understanding fluid, material, and atmospheric dynamics and mechanical, electrical, atomic, and subatomic structures and processes. **Public Safety and Security:** Relevant equipment, policies, procedures, and strategies to promote effective local, state, or national security operations for the protection of people, data, property, and institutions.

E

Emergency Medical Technicians and Paramedics

- Education/Training Required: Postsecondary vocational training
- Annual Earnings: $26,080
- Growth: 27.3%
- Annual Job Openings: 21,000
- Self-Employed: 0.1%
- Part-Time: 10.6%

Assess injuries, administer emergency medical care, and extricate trapped individuals. Transport injured or sick persons to medical facilities. Administer first-aid treatment and life-support care to sick or injured persons in prehospital setting. Operate equipment such as electrocardiograms (EKGs), external defibrillators, and bag-valve mask resuscitators in advanced life-support environments. Assess nature and extent of illness or injury to establish and prioritize medical procedures. Maintain vehicles and medical and communication equipment and replenish first-aid equipment and supplies. Observe, record, and report to physician the patient's condition or injury, the treatment provided, and reactions to drugs and treatment. Perform emergency diagnostic and treatment procedures, such as stomach suction, airway management, or heart monitoring, during ambulance ride. Administer drugs, orally or by injection, and perform intravenous procedures under a physician's direction. Comfort and reassure patients. Coordinate work with other emergency medical team members and police and fire department personnel. Communicate with dispatchers and treatment center personnel to provide information about situation, to arrange reception of victims, and to receive instructions for further treatment. Immobilize patient for placement on stretcher and ambulance transport, using backboard or other spinal immobilization device. Decontaminate ambulance interior following treatment of patient with infectious disease and report case to proper authorities. Drive mobile intensive care unit to specified location, following instructions from emergency medical dispatcher. Coordinate with treatment center personnel to obtain patients' vital statistics and medical history, to determine the circumstances of the emergency, and to administer emergency treatment.

SKILLS—Most Important: Equipment Use/Maintenance Skills; Social Skills; Thought-Processing Skills. **Other Above-Average Skills:** Quality Control Skills; Communication Skills; Management Skills; Mathematics Skills.

GOE—Interest Area: 12. Law and Public Safety. **Work Group:** 12.06. Emergency Responding. **Other Jobs in This Group:** Fire Fighters; Forest Fire Fighters; Municipal Fire Fighters. **PERSONALITY TYPE:** Social. Social occupations frequently involve working with, communicating with, and teaching people. These occupations often involve helping or providing service to others.

EDUCATION/TRAINING PROGRAM(S)— Emergency Care Attendant (EMT Ambulance); Emergency Medical Technology/Technician (EMT Paramedic). **RELATED KNOWLEDGE/COURSES—Medicine and Dentistry:** The information and techniques needed to diagnose and treat human injuries, diseases, and deformities. This includes symptoms, treatment alternatives, drug properties and interactions, and preventive healthcare measures. **Customer and Personal Service:** Principles and processes for providing customer and personal services. This includes customer needs assessment, meeting of quality standards for services, and evaluation of customer satisfaction. **Therapy and Counseling:** Principles, methods, and procedures for diagnosis, treatment, and rehabilitation of physical and mental dysfunctions and for career counseling and guidance. **Chemistry:** The chemical composition, structure, and properties of substances and of the chemical processes and transformations that they undergo. This includes uses of chemicals and their danger signs, production techniques, and disposal methods. **Psychology:** Human behavior and performance; individual differences in ability, personality, and interests; learning and motivation; psychological research methods; and the assessment and treatment of behavioral and affective disorders. **Biology:** Plant and animal organisms and their tissues, cells, functions, interdependencies, and interactions with each other and the environment.

Employment Interviewers

- ◎ Education/Training Required: Bachelor's degree
- ◎ Annual Earnings: $41,780
- ◎ Growth: 30.5%
- ◎ Annual Job Openings: 30,000
- ◎ Self-Employed: 2.5%
- ◎ Part-Time: 7.7%

The job openings listed here are shared with Personnel Recruiters.

Interview job applicants in employment office and refer them to prospective employers for consideration. Search application files, notify selected applicants of job openings, and refer qualified applicants to prospective employers. Contact employers to verify referral results. Record and evaluate various pertinent data. Inform applicants of job openings and details such as duties and responsibilities, compensation, benefits, schedules, working conditions, and promotion opportunities. Interview job applicants to match their qualifications with employers' needs, recording and evaluating applicant experience, education, training, and skills. Review employment applications and job orders to match applicants with job requirements, using manual or computerized file searches. Select qualified applicants or refer them to employers according to organization policy. Perform reference and background checks on applicants. Maintain records of applicants not selected for employment. Instruct job applicants in presenting a positive image by providing help with resume writing, personal appearance, and interview techniques. Refer applicants to services such as vocational counseling, literacy or language instruction, transportation assistance, vocational training, and child care. Contact employers to solicit orders for job vacancies, determining their requirements and recording relevant data such as job descriptions. Conduct workshops and demonstrate the use of job listings to assist applicants with skill building. Search for and recruit applicants for open positions through campus job fairs and advertisements. Provide background information on organizations with which interviews are scheduled. Administer assessment tests to identify skill-building needs. Conduct or arrange for skill, intelligence, or psychological testing of applicants

and current employees. Hire workers and place them with employers needing temporary help. Evaluate selection and testing techniques by conducting research or follow-up activities and conferring with management and supervisory personnel.

SKILLS—Most Important: Social Skills; Management Skills; Communication Skills. **Other Above-Average Skills:** Thought-Processing Skills; Equipment/Technology Analysis Skills.

GOE—Interest Area: 04. Business and Administration. **Work Group:** 04.03. Human Resources Support. **Other Jobs in This Group:** Compensation, Benefits, and Job Analysis Specialists; Employment, Recruitment, and Placement Specialists; Personnel Recruiters; Training and Development Specialists. **PERSONALITY TYPE:** Social. Social occupations frequently involve working with, communicating with, and teaching people. These occupations often involve helping or providing service to others.

EDUCATION/TRAINING PROGRAM(S)—Human Resources Management/Personnel Administration, General; Labor and Industrial Relations. **RELATED KNOWLEDGE/COURSES—Foreign Language:** The structure and content of a foreign (non-English) language, including the meaning and spelling of words, rules of composition and grammar, and pronunciation. **Clerical Practices:** Administrative and clerical procedures and systems such as word processing, managing files and records, stenography and transcription, designing forms, and other office procedures and terminology. **Customer and Personal Service:** Principles and processes for providing customer and personal services. This includes customer needs assessment, meeting of quality standards for services, and evaluation of customer satisfaction. **Personnel and Human Resources:** Principles and procedures for personnel recruitment, selection, training, compensation and benefits, labor relations and negotiation, and personnel information systems. **Sales and Marketing:** Principles and methods for showing, promoting, and selling products or services. This includes marketing strategy and tactics, product demonstration, sales techniques, and sales control systems. **Education and Training:** Principles and methods for curriculum and training design, teaching and instruction for individuals and groups, and the measurement of training effects.

E

Engineering Managers

- Education/Training Required: Work experience plus degree
- Annual Earnings: $100,760
- Growth: 13.0%
- Annual Job Openings: 15,000
- Self-Employed: 0.5%
- Part-Time: 1.2%

Plan, direct, or coordinate activities in such fields as architecture and engineering or research and development in these fields. Confer with management, production, and marketing staff to discuss project specifications and procedures. Coordinate and direct projects, making detailed plans to accomplish goals and directing the integration of technical activities. Analyze technology, resource needs, and market demand to plan and assess the feasibility of projects. Plan and direct the installation, testing, operation, maintenance, and repair of facilities and equipment. Direct, review, and approve product design and changes. Recruit employees; assign, direct, and evaluate their work; and oversee the development and maintenance of staff competence. Prepare budgets, bids, and contracts and direct the negotiation of research contracts. Develop and implement policies, standards, and procedures for the engineering and technical work performed in the department, service, laboratory, or firm. Review and recommend or approve contracts and cost estimates. Perform administrative functions such as reviewing and writing reports, approving expenditures, enforcing rules, and making decisions about the purchase of materials or services. Present and explain proposals, reports, and findings to clients. Consult or negotiate with clients to prepare project specifications. Set scientific and technical goals within broad outlines provided by top management. Administer highway planning, construction, and maintenance. Direct the engineering of water control, treatment, and distribution projects. Plan, direct, and coordinate survey work with other staff activities, certifying survey work and writing land legal descriptions. Confer with and report to officials and the public to provide information and solicit support for projects.

SKILLS—Most Important: Science Skills; Equipment/Technology Analysis Skills; Mathematics Skills. **Other Above-Average Skills:** Quality Control Skills; Management Skills; Communication Skills.

GOE—Interest Area: 15. Scientific Research, Engineering, and Mathematics. **Work Group:** 15.01. Managerial Work in Scientific Research, Engineering, and Mathematics. **Other Jobs in This Group:** Natural Sciences Managers. **PERSONALITY TYPE:** Enterprising. Enterprising occupations frequently involve starting up and carrying out projects. These occupations can involve leading people and making many decisions. They sometimes require risk taking and often deal with business.

EDUCATION/TRAINING PROGRAM(S)—Architecture (BArch, BA/BS, MArch, MA/MS, PhD); City/Urban, Community, and Regional Planning; Environmental Design/Architecture; Interior Architecture; Landscape Architecture (BS, BSLA, BLA, MSLA, MLA, PhD); Engineering, General; Aerospace, Aeronautical, and Astronautical Engineering; Agricultural/Biological Engineering and Bioengineering; Architectural Engineering; Biomedical/Medical Engineering; others. **RELATED KNOWLEDGE/ COURSES—Engineering and Technology:** The practical application of engineering science and technology. This includes applying principles, techniques, procedures, and equipment to the design and production of various goods and services. **Design:** Design techniques, tools, and principles involved in production of precision technical plans, blueprints, drawings, and models. **Physics:** Physical principles and laws and their interrelationships and applications to understanding fluid, material, and atmospheric dynamics and mechanical, electrical, atomic, and subatomic structures and processes. **Building and Construction:** The materials, methods, and tools involved in the construction or repair of houses, buildings, or other structures such as highways and roads. **Personnel and Human Resources:** Principles and procedures for personnel recruitment, selection, training, compensation and benefits, labor relations and negotiation, and personnel information systems. **Mathematics:** Arithmetic, algebra, geometry, calculus, and statistics and their applications.

Engineering Teachers, Postsecondary

- Education/Training Required: Master's degree
- Annual Earnings: $74,540
- Growth: 32.2%
- Annual Job Openings: 329,000
- Self-Employed: 0.4%
- Part-Time: 27.3%

The job openings listed here are shared with 35 other postsecondary teaching occupations. For a complete list, see the beginning of this section.

Teach courses pertaining to the application of physical laws and principles of engineering for the development of machines, materials, instruments, processes, and services. Includes teachers of subjects such as chemical, civil, electrical, industrial, mechanical, mineral, and petroleum engineering. Includes both teachers primarily engaged in teaching and those who do a combination of both teaching and research. Prepare and deliver lectures to undergraduate and/or graduate students on topics such as mechanics, hydraulics, and robotics. Keep abreast of developments in their field by reading current literature, talking with colleagues, and participating in professional conferences. Supervise undergraduate and/or graduate teaching, internship, and research work. Evaluate and grade students' classwork, laboratory work, assignments, and papers. Conduct research in a particular field of knowledge and publish findings in professional journals, books, and/or electronic media. Prepare course materials such as syllabi, homework assignments, and handouts. Compile, administer, and grade examinations or assign this work to others. Write grant proposals to procure external research funding. Supervise students' laboratory work. Initiate, facilitate, and moderate class discussions. Maintain regularly scheduled office hours to advise and assist students. Plan, evaluate, and revise curricula, course content, and course materials and methods of instruction. Advise students on academic and vocational curricula and on career issues. Maintain student attendance records, grades, and other required records. Collaborate with colleagues to address teaching and research issues. Select and obtain materials and supplies such as textbooks and laboratory equipment. Participate in student recruitment, registration, and placement activities. Serve on academic or administrative committees that deal with institutional policies, departmental matters, and academic issues. Perform administrative duties such as serving as department head. Provide professional consulting services to government and/or industry. Compile bibliographies of specialized materials for outside reading assignments. Act as advisers to student organizations. Participate in campus and community events.

SKILLS—Most Important: Science Skills; Computer Programming Skills; Mathematics Skills. **Other Above-Average Skills:** Equipment/Technology Analysis Skills; Thought-Processing Skills; Social Skills; Quality Control Skills.

GOE—Interest Area: 05. Education and Training. **Work Group:** 05.03. Postsecondary and Adult Teaching and Instructing. **Other Jobs in This Group:** Adult Literacy, Remedial Education, and GED Teachers and Instructors; Agricultural Sciences Teachers, Postsecondary; Anthropology and Archeology Teachers, Postsecondary; Architecture Teachers, Postsecondary; Area, Ethnic, and Cultural Studies Teachers, Postsecondary; Art, Drama, and Music Teachers, Postsecondary; Atmospheric, Earth, Marine, and Space Sciences Teachers, Postsecondary; Biological Science Teachers, Postsecondary; Business Teachers, Postsecondary; Chemistry Teachers, Postsecondary; Communications Teachers, Postsecondary; Computer Science Teachers, Postsecondary; Criminal Justice and Law Enforcement Teachers, Postsecondary; Economics Teachers, Postsecondary; Education Teachers, Postsecondary; English Language and Literature Teachers, Postsecondary; Environmental Science Teachers, Postsecondary; Farm and Home Management Advisors; Foreign Language and Literature Teachers, Postsecondary; Forestry and Conservation Science Teachers, Postsecondary; Geography Teachers, Postsecondary; Graduate Teaching Assistants; Health Specialties Teachers, Postsecondary; History Teachers, Postsecondary; Home Economics Teachers, Postsecondary; Law Teachers, Postsecondary; Library Science Teachers, Postsecondary; Mathematical Science Teachers, Postsecondary; Nursing Instructors and Teachers, Postsecondary; Philosophy and Religion

Teachers, Postsecondary; Physics Teachers, Postsecondary; Political Science Teachers, Postsecondary; Psychology Teachers, Postsecondary; Recreation and Fitness Studies Teachers, Postsecondary; Self-Enrichment Education Teachers; Social Work Teachers, Postsecondary; Sociology Teachers, Postsecondary; Vocational Education Teachers, Postsecondary. **PERSONALITY TYPE:** Investigative. Investigative occupations frequently involve working with ideas and require an extensive amount of thinking. These occupations can involve searching for facts and figuring out problems mentally.

EDUCATION/TRAINING PROGRAM(S)—Teacher Education and Professional Development, Specific Subject Areas, Other; Engineering, General; Aerospace, Aeronautical, and Astronautical Engineering; Agricultural/Biological Engineering and Bioengineering; Architectural Engineering; Biomedical/Medical Engineering; Ceramic Sciences and Engineering; Chemical Engineering; Civil Engineering, General; Geotechnical Engineering; Structural Engineering; others. **RELATED KNOWLEDGE/COURSES—Engineering and Technology:** The practical application of engineering science and technology. This includes applying principles, techniques, procedures, and equipment to the design and production of various goods and services. **Design:** Design techniques, tools, and principles involved in production of precision technical plans, blueprints, drawings, and models. **Physics:** Physical principles and laws and their interrelationships and applications to understanding fluid, material, and atmospheric dynamics and mechanical, electrical, atomic, and subatomic structures and processes. **Mathematics:** Arithmetic, algebra, geometry, calculus, and statistics and their applications. **Education and Training:** Principles and methods for curriculum and training design, teaching and instruction for individuals and groups, and the measurement of training effects. **Telecommunications:** Transmission, broadcasting, switching, control, and operation of telecommunications systems.

English Language and Literature Teachers, Postsecondary

- Education/Training Required: Master's degree
- Annual Earnings: $49,480
- Growth: 32.2%
- Annual Job Openings: 329,000
- Self-Employed: 0.4%
- Part-Time: 27.3%

The job openings listed here are shared with 35 other postsecondary teaching occupations. For a complete list, see the beginning of this section.

Teach courses in English language and literature, including linguistics and comparative literature. Initiate, facilitate, and moderate classroom discussions. Evaluate and grade students' classwork, assignments, and papers. Prepare course materials such as syllabi, homework assignments, and handouts. Prepare and deliver lectures to undergraduate and graduate students on topics such as poetry, novel structure, and translation and adaptation. Maintain student attendance records, grades, and other required records. Plan, evaluate, and revise curricula, course content, and course materials and methods of instruction. Compile, administer, and grade examinations or assign this work to others. Maintain regularly scheduled office hours in order to advise and assist students. Keep abreast of developments in their field by reading current literature, talking with colleagues, and participating in professional conferences. Select and obtain materials and supplies such as textbooks. Advise students on academic and vocational curricula and on career issues. Conduct research in a particular field of knowledge and publish findings in professional journals, books, or electronic media. Collaborate with colleagues to address teaching and research issues. Serve on academic or administrative committees that deal with institutional policies, departmental matters, and academic issues. Participate in campus and community events. Participate in student recruitment, registration, and placement activities. Compile bibliographies of specialized materials for outside reading assignments. Supervise undergraduate and/or graduate teaching, internship, and research work. Provide assistance to students in college writing centers. Perform administrative duties such as serving as department head. Recruit, train, and supervise student writing instructors. Act as advisers to student organizations. Write grant proposals to procure external research funding. Provide professional consulting services to government or industry.

SKILLS—Most Important: Communication Skills; Social Skills; Thought-Processing Skills. **Other Above-Average Skills:** Management Skills; Quality Control Skills.

GOE—Interest Area: 05. Education and Training. **Work Group:** 05.03. Postsecondary and Adult Teaching and Instructing. **Other Jobs in This Group:** Adult Literacy, Remedial Education, and GED Teachers and Instructors; Agricultural Sciences Teachers, Postsecondary; Anthropology and Archeology Teachers, Postsecondary; Architecture Teachers, Postsecondary; Area, Ethnic, and Cultural Studies Teachers, Postsecondary; Art, Drama, and Music Teachers, Postsecondary; Atmospheric, Earth, Marine, and Space Sciences Teachers, Postsecondary; Biological Science Teachers, Postsecondary; Business Teachers, Postsecondary; Chemistry Teachers, Postsecondary; Communications Teachers, Postsecondary; Computer Science Teachers, Postsecondary; Criminal Justice and Law Enforcement Teachers, Postsecondary; Economics Teachers, Postsecondary; Education Teachers, Postsecondary; Engineering Teachers, Postsecondary; Environmental Science Teachers, Postsecondary; Farm and Home Management Advisors; Foreign Language and Literature Teachers, Postsecondary; Forestry and Conservation Science Teachers, Postsecondary; Geography Teachers, Postsecondary; Graduate Teaching Assistants; Health Specialties Teachers, Postsecondary; History Teachers, Postsecondary; Home Economics Teachers, Postsecondary; Law Teachers, Postsecondary; Library Science Teachers, Postsecondary; Mathematical Science Teachers, Postsecondary; Nursing Instructors and Teachers, Postsecondary; Philosophy and Religion Teachers, Postsecondary; Physics Teachers, Postsecondary; Political Science Teachers, Postsecondary; Psychology Teachers, Postsecondary; Recreation and Fitness Studies Teachers,

Postsecondary; Self-Enrichment Education Teachers; Social Work Teachers, Postsecondary; Sociology Teachers, Postsecondary; Vocational Education Teachers, Postsecondary. **PERSONALITY TYPE:** Artistic. Artistic occupations frequently involve working with forms, designs, and patterns. They often require self-expression, and the work can be done without following a clear set of rules.

EDUCATION/TRAINING PROGRAM(S)—Comparative Literature; English Language and Literature, General; English Composition; Creative Writing; American Literature (United States); American Literature (Canadian); English Literature (British and Commonwealth); Technical and Business Writing; English Language and Literature/Letters, Other. **RELATED KNOWLEDGE/COURSES—Philosophy and Theology:** Different philosophical systems and religions. This includes their basic principles, values, ethics, ways of thinking, customs, practices, and impact on human culture. **English Language:** The structure and content of the English language, including the meaning and spelling of words, rules of composition, and grammar. **Education and Training:** Principles and methods for curriculum and training design, teaching and instruction for individuals and groups, and the measurement of training effects. **History and Archeology:** Historical events and their causes, indicators, and effects on civilizations and cultures. **Sociology and Anthropology:** Group behavior and dynamics, societal trends and influences, human migrations, ethnicity, and cultures and their history and origins. **Fine Arts:** The theory and techniques required to compose, produce, and perform works of music, dance, visual arts, drama, and sculpture.

Environmental Engineers

- Education/Training Required: Bachelor's degree
- Annual Earnings: $68,090
- Growth: 30.0%
- Annual Job Openings: 5,000
- Self-Employed: 0.3%
- Part-Time: 1.9%

Design, plan, or perform engineering duties in the prevention, control, and remediation of environmental

health hazards, utilizing various engineering disciplines. **Work may include waste treatment, site remediation, or pollution control technology.** Prepare, review, and update environmental investigation and recommendation reports. Collaborate with environmental scientists, planners, hazardous waste technicians, engineers, and other specialists and experts in law and business to address environmental problems. Obtain, update, and maintain plans, permits, and standard operating procedures. Provide technical-level support for environmental remediation and litigation projects, including remediation system design and determination of regulatory applicability. Monitor progress of environmental improvement programs. Inspect industrial and municipal facilities and programs to evaluate operational effectiveness and ensure compliance with environmental regulations. Provide administrative support for projects by collecting data, providing project documentation, training staff, and performing other general administrative duties. Develop proposed project objectives and targets and report to management on progress in attaining them. Advise corporations and government agencies of procedures to follow in cleaning up contaminated sites to protect people and the environment. Advise industries and government agencies about environmental policies and standards. Inform company employees and other interested parties of environmental issues. Assess the existing or potential environmental impact of land use projects on air, water, and land. Assist in budget implementation, forecasts, and administration. Develop site-specific health and safety protocols, such as spill contingency plans and methods for loading and transporting waste. Coordinate and manage environmental protection programs and projects, assigning and evaluating work. Serve as liaison with federal, state, and local agencies and officials on issues pertaining to solid and hazardous waste program requirements. Design systems, processes, and equipment for control, management, and remediation of water, air, and soil quality. Prepare hazardous waste manifests and land disposal restriction notifications. Serve on teams conducting multimedia inspections at complex facilities, providing assistance with planning, quality assurance, safety inspection protocols, and sampling.

SKILLS—Most Important: Science Skills; Mathematics Skills; Computer Programming Skills. **Other Above-Average Skills:** Communication Skills; Social Skills; Thought-Processing Skills; Quality Control Skills.

GOE—Interest Area: 01. Agriculture and Natural Resources. **Work Group:** 01.02. Resource Science/Engineering for Plants, Animals, and the Environment. **Other Jobs in This Group:** Agricultural Engineers; Animal Scientists; Conservation Scientists; Foresters; Mining and Geological Engineers, Including Mining Safety Engineers; Petroleum Engineers; Range Managers; Soil and Plant Scientists; Soil and Water Conservationists; Zoologists and Wildlife Biologists. **PERSONALITY TYPE:** No data available.

EDUCATION/TRAINING PROGRAM(S)—Environmental/Environmental Health Engineering. **RELATED KNOWLEDGE/COURSES—Education and Training:** Principles and methods for curriculum and training design, teaching and instruction for individuals and groups, and the measurement of training effects. **Chemistry:** The chemical composition, structure, and properties of substances and of the chemical processes and transformations that they undergo. This includes uses of chemicals and their danger signs, production techniques, and disposal methods. **Biology:** Plant and animal organisms and their tissues, cells, functions, interdependencies, and interactions with each other and the environment. **Law and Government:** Laws, legal codes, court procedures, precedents, government regulations, executive orders, agency rules, and the democratic political process. **Engineering and Technology:** The practical application of engineering science and technology. This includes applying principles, techniques, procedures, and equipment to the design and production of various goods and services. **Design:** Design techniques, tools, and principles involved in production of precision technical plans, blueprints, drawings, and models.

Environmental Science and Protection Technicians, Including Health

- ◎ Education/Training Required: Associate degree
- ◎ Annual Earnings: $36,260
- ◎ Growth: 16.3%
- ◎ Annual Job Openings: 6,000
- ◎ Self-Employed: 1.4%
- ◎ Part-Time: 22.7%

Perform laboratory and field tests to monitor the environment and investigate sources of pollution, including those that affect health. Under direction of an environmental scientist or specialist, may collect samples of gases, soil, water, and other materials for testing and take corrective actions as assigned. Record test data and prepare reports, summaries, and charts that interpret test results. Collect samples of gases, soils, water, industrial wastewater, and asbestos products to conduct tests on pollutant levels and identify sources of pollution. Respond to and investigate hazardous conditions or spills or outbreaks of disease or food poisoning, collecting samples for analysis. Provide information and technical and program assistance to government representatives, employers, and the general public on the issues of public health, environmental protection, or workplace safety. Calibrate microscopes and test instruments. Make recommendations to control or eliminate unsafe conditions at workplaces or public facilities. Inspect sanitary conditions at public facilities. Prepare samples or photomicrographs for testing and analysis. Calculate amount of pollutant in samples or compute air pollution or gas flow in industrial processes, using chemical and mathematical formulas. Initiate procedures to close down or fine establishments violating environmental or health regulations. Determine amounts and kinds of chemicals to use in destroying harmful organisms and removing impurities from purification systems. Discuss test results and analyses with customers. Maintain files such as hazardous waste databases, chemical usage data, personnel exposure information, and diagrams showing equipment loca-

tions. Perform statistical analysis of environmental data. Set up equipment or stations to monitor and collect pollutants from sites such as smokestacks, manufacturing plants, or mechanical equipment. Distribute permits, closure plans, and cleanup plans. Inspect workplaces to ensure the absence of health and safety hazards such as high noise levels, radiation, or potential lighting hazards. Weigh, analyze, and measure collected sample particles, such as lead, coal dust, or rock, to determine concentration of pollutants. Examine and analyze material for presence and concentration of contaminants such as asbestos, using variety of microscopes. Develop testing procedures or direct activities of workers in laboratory.

SKILLS—Most Important: Science Skills; Mathematics Skills; Quality Control Skills. **Other Above-Average Skills:** Thought-Processing Skills; Social Skills; Equipment Use/Maintenance Skills; Management Skills.

GOE—Interest Area: 01. Agriculture and Natural Resources. **Work Group:** 01.03. Resource Technologies for Plants, Animals, and the Environment. **Other Jobs in This Group:** Agricultural and Food Science Technicians; Agricultural Technicians; Food Science Technicians; Food Scientists and Technologists; Geological and Petroleum Technicians; Geological Sample Test Technicians; Geophysical Data Technicians. **PERSONALITY TYPE:** Investigative. Investigative occupations frequently involve working with ideas and require an extensive amount of thinking. These occupations can involve searching for facts and figuring out problems mentally.

EDUCATION/TRAINING PROGRAM(S)—Environmental Studies; Environmental Science; Physical Science Technologies/Technicians, Other; Science Technologies/Technicians, Other. **RELATED KNOWLEDGE/COURSES—Biology:** Plant and animal organisms and their tissues, cells, functions, interdependencies, and interactions with each other and the environment. **Engineering and Technology:** The practical application of engineering science and technology. This includes applying principles, techniques, procedures, and equipment to the design and production of various goods and services. **Chemistry:** The chemical composition, structure, and properties of substances and of the chemical processes and transformations that they undergo. This includes uses of chemicals and their danger signs, production techniques, and disposal methods.

Building and Construction: The materials, methods, and tools involved in the construction or repair of houses, buildings, or other structures such as highways and roads. **Physics:** Physical principles and laws and their interrelationships and applications to understanding fluid, material, and atmospheric dynamics and mechanical, electrical, atomic, and subatomic structures and processes. **Design:** Design techniques, tools, and principles involved in production of precision technical plans, blueprints, drawings, and models.

Environmental Science Teachers, Postsecondary

- Education/Training Required: Master's degree
- Annual Earnings: $60,880
- Growth: 32.2%
- Annual Job Openings: 329,000
- Self-Employed: 0.4%
- Part-Time: 27.3%

The job openings listed here are shared with 35 other postsecondary teaching occupations. For a complete list, see the beginning of this section.

Teach courses in environmental science. Supervise undergraduate and/or graduate teaching, internship, and research work. Conduct research in a particular field of knowledge and publish findings in professional journals, books, and/or electronic media. Keep abreast of developments in their field by reading current literature, talking with colleagues, and participating in professional conferences. Evaluate and grade students' classwork, laboratory work, assignments, and papers. Write grant proposals to procure external research funding. Supervise students' laboratory work and fieldwork. Prepare course materials such as syllabi, homework assignments, and handouts. Plan, evaluate, and revise curricula, course content, and course materials and methods of instruction. Compile, administer, and grade examinations or assign this work to others. Initiate, facilitate, and moderate classroom discussions. Advise students on academic and vocational curricula and on career issues. Prepare and deliver lectures to undergraduate and/or graduate students on topics such as hazardous waste management, industrial safety, and environmental toxicology. Maintain student attendance records, grades, and other required records. Select and obtain materials and supplies such as textbooks and laboratory equipment. Maintain regularly scheduled office hours in order to advise and assist students. Collaborate with colleagues to address teaching and research issues. Perform administrative duties such as serving as department head. Participate in student recruitment, registration, and placement activities. Provide professional consulting services to government and/or industry. Serve on academic or administrative committees that deal with institutional policies, departmental matters, and academic issues. Compile bibliographies of specialized materials for outside reading assignments. Participate in campus and community events. Act as advisers to student organizations.

SKILLS—Most Important: Science Skills; Computer Programming Skills; Mathematics Skills. **Other Above-Average Skills:** Communication Skills; Thought-Processing Skills; Equipment/Technology Analysis Skills; Quality Control Skills.

GOE—Interest Area: 05. Education and Training. **Work Group:** 05.03. Postsecondary and Adult Teaching and Instructing. **Other Jobs in This Group:** Adult Literacy, Remedial Education, and GED Teachers and Instructors; Agricultural Sciences Teachers, Postsecondary; Anthropology and Archeology Teachers, Postsecondary; Architecture Teachers, Postsecondary; Area, Ethnic, and Cultural Studies Teachers, Postsecondary; Art, Drama, and Music Teachers, Postsecondary; Atmospheric, Earth, Marine, and Space Sciences Teachers, Postsecondary; Biological Science Teachers, Postsecondary; Business Teachers, Postsecondary; Chemistry Teachers, Postsecondary; Communications Teachers, Postsecondary; Computer Science Teachers, Postsecondary; Criminal Justice and Law Enforcement Teachers, Postsecondary; Economics Teachers, Postsecondary; Education Teachers, Postsecondary; Engineering Teachers, Postsecondary; English Language and Literature Teachers, Postsecondary; Farm and Home Management Advisors; Foreign Language and Literature Teachers, Postsecondary; Forestry and Conservation Science Teachers, Postsecondary; Geography Teachers, Postsecondary; Graduate Teaching Assistants; Health Specialties Teachers, Postsecondary; History Teachers, Postsecondary; Home Economics Teachers, Postsecondary; Law Teachers, Postsecondary; Library Science Teachers, Postsecondary; Mathematical Science Teachers, Postsecondary; Nursing Instructors and Teachers, Postsecondary; Philosophy and Religion Teachers, Postsecondary; Physics Teachers, Postsecondary; Political Science Teachers, Postsecondary; Psychology Teachers, Postsecondary; Recreation and Fitness Studies Teachers, Postsecondary; Self-Enrichment Education Teachers; Social Work Teachers, Postsecondary; Sociology Teachers, Postsecondary; Vocational Education Teachers, Postsecondary. **PERSONALITY TYPE:** No data available.

EDUCATION/TRAINING PROGRAM(S)—Environmental Studies; Environmental Science; Science Teacher Education/General Science Teacher Education. **RELATED KNOWLEDGE/COURSES**—**Biology:** Plant and animal organisms and their tissues, cells, functions, interdependencies, and interactions with each other and the environment. **Geography:** Principles and methods for describing the features of land, sea, and air masses, including their physical characteristics; locations; interrelationships; and distribution of plant, animal, and human life. **Education and Training:** Principles and methods for curriculum and training design, teaching and instruction for individuals and groups, and the measurement of training effects. **Chemistry:** The chemical composition, structure, and properties of substances and of the chemical processes and transformations that they undergo. This includes uses of chemicals and their danger signs, production techniques, and disposal methods. **Physics:** Physical principles and laws and their interrelationships and applications to understanding fluid, material, and atmospheric dynamics and mechanical, electrical, atomic, and subatomic structures and processes. **History and Archeology:** Historical events and their causes, indicators, and effects on civilizations and cultures.

Environmental Scientists and Specialists, Including Health

- Education/Training Required: Master's degree
- Annual Earnings: $52,630
- Growth: 17.1%
- Annual Job Openings: 8,000
- Self-Employed: 4.2%
- Part-Time: 5.7%

Conduct research or perform investigation for the purpose of identifying, abating, or eliminating sources of pollutants or hazards that affect either the environment or the health of the population. Utilizing knowledge of various scientific disciplines, may collect, synthesize, study, report, and take action based on data derived from measurements or observations of air, food, soil, water, and other sources. Conduct environmental audits and inspections and investigations of violations. Evaluate violations or problems discovered during inspections to determine appropriate regulatory actions or to provide advice on the development and prosecution of regulatory cases. Communicate scientific and technical information through oral briefings, written documents, workshops, conferences, and public hearings. Review and implement environmental technical standards, guidelines, policies, and formal regulations that meet all appropriate requirements. Provide technical guidance, support, and oversight to environmental programs, industry, and the public. Provide advice on proper standards and regulations or the development of policies, strategies, and codes of practice for environmental management. Analyze data to determine validity, quality, and scientific significance and to interpret correlations between human activities and environmental effects. Collect, synthesize, and analyze data derived from pollution emission measurements, atmospheric monitoring, meteorological and mineralogical information, and soil or water samples. Determine data collection methods to be employed in research projects and surveys. Prepare charts or graphs from data samples, providing summary information on the environmental relevance of the data. Develop the technical portions of legal documents, administrative orders, or consent decrees. Investigate and report on accidents affecting the environment. Monitor environmental impacts of development activities. Supervise environmental technologists and technicians. Develop programs designed to obtain the most productive, non-damaging use of land. Research sources of pollution to determine their effects on the environment and to develop theories or methods of pollution abatement or control. Monitor effects of pollution and land degradation and recommend means of prevention or control. Design and direct studies to obtain technical environmental information about planned projects. Conduct applied research on topics such as waste control and treatment and pollution control methods.

SKILLS—Most Important: Science Skills; Social Skills; Mathematics Skills. **Other Above-Average Skills:** Thought-Processing Skills; Quality Control Skills; Management Skills.

GOE—Interest Area: 15. Scientific Research, Engineering, and Mathematics. **Work Group:** 15.03. Life Sciences. **Other Jobs in This Group:** Biochemists and Biophysicists; Biologists; Epidemiologists; Medical Scientists, Except Epidemiologists; Microbiologists. **PERSONALITY TYPE:** Investigative. Investigative occupations frequently involve working with ideas and require an extensive amount of thinking. These occupations can involve searching for facts and figuring out problems mentally.

EDUCATION/TRAINING PROGRAM(S)—Environmental Studies; Environmental Science. **RELATED KNOWLEDGE/COURSES—Biology:** Plant and animal organisms and their tissues, cells, functions, interdependencies, and interactions with each other and the environment. **Geography:** Principles and methods for describing the features of land, sea, and air masses, including their physical characteristics; locations; interrelationships; and distribution of plant, animal, and human life. **Chemistry:** The chemical composition, structure, and properties of substances and of the chemical processes and transformations that they undergo. This includes uses of chemicals and their danger signs, production techniques, and disposal methods. **Law and Government:** Laws, legal codes, court procedures, precedents, government regulations, executive orders, agency rules, and the democratic political process. **Engineering and Technology:** The practical application

of engineering science and technology. This includes applying principles, techniques, procedures, and equipment to the design and production of various goods and services. **Physics:** Physical principles and laws and their interrelationships and applications to understanding fluid, material, and atmospheric dynamics and mechanical, electrical, atomic, and subatomic structures and processes.

Epidemiologists

- Education/Training Required: Master's degree
- Annual Earnings: $52,170
- Growth: 26.2%
- Annual Job Openings: 1,000
- Self-Employed: 0.4%
- Part-Time: 5.5%

Investigate and describe the determinants and distribution of disease, disability, and other health outcomes and develop the means for prevention and control. Oversee public health programs, including statistical analysis, health-care planning, surveillance systems, and public health improvement. Investigate diseases or parasites to determine cause and risk factors, progress, life cycle, or mode of transmission. Plan and direct studies to investigate human or animal disease, preventive methods, and treatments for disease. Plan, administer, and evaluate health safety standards and programs to improve public health, conferring with health department, industry personnel, physicians, and others. Provide expertise in the design, management, and evaluation of study protocols and health status questionnaires, sample selection, and analysis. Conduct research to develop methodologies, instrumentation, and procedures for medical application, analyzing data and presenting findings. Consult with and advise physicians, educators, researchers, government health officials, and others regarding medical applications of sciences such as physics, biology, and chemistry. Supervise professional, technical, and clerical personnel. Identify and analyze public health issues related to foodborne parasitic diseases and their impact on public policies or scientific studies or surveys. Teach principles of medicine and medical and laboratory procedures to physicians, residents, students, and technicians. Standardize drug dosages, methods of immunization, and procedures for manufacture of drugs and medicinal compounds. Prepare and analyze samples to study effects of drugs, gases, pesticides, or microorganisms on cell structure and tissue.

SKILLS—Most Important: Science Skills; Computer Programming Skills; Mathematics Skills. **Other Above-Average Skills:** Communication Skills; Thought-Processing Skills; Equipment/Technology Analysis Skills; Management Skills.

GOE—Interest Area: 15. Scientific Research, Engineering, and Mathematics. **Work Group:** 15.03. Life Sciences. **Other Jobs in This Group:** Biochemists and Biophysicists; Biologists; Environmental Scientists and Specialists, Including Health; Medical Scientists, Except Epidemiologists; Microbiologists. **PERSONALITY TYPE:** Investigative. Investigative occupations frequently involve working with ideas and require an extensive amount of thinking. These occupations can involve searching for facts and figuring out problems mentally.

EDUCATION/TRAINING PROGRAM(S)—Biophysics; Cell/Cellular Biology and Histology; Epidemiology; Medical Scientist (MS, PhD). **RELATED KNOWLEDGE/COURSES—Biology:** Plant and animal organisms and their tissues, cells, functions, interdependencies, and interactions with each other and the environment. **Sociology and Anthropology:** Group behavior and dynamics, societal trends and influences, human migrations, ethnicity, and cultures and their history and origins. **Medicine and Dentistry:** The information and techniques needed to diagnose and treat human injuries, diseases, and deformities. This includes symptoms, treatment alternatives, drug properties and interactions, and preventive healthcare measures. **Education and Training:** Principles and methods for curriculum and training design, teaching and instruction for individuals and groups, and the measurement of training effects. **English Language:** The structure and content of the English language, including the meaning and spelling of words, rules of composition, and grammar. **Computers and Electronics:** Circuit boards; processors; chips; electronic equipment; and computer hardware and software, including applications and programming.

Family and General Practitioners

- Education/Training Required: First professional degree
- Annual Earnings: $140,400
- Growth: 24.0%
- Annual Job Openings: 41,000
- Self-Employed: 11.5%
- Part-Time: 9.6%

The job openings listed here are shared with Anesthesiologists; Internists, General; Obstetricians and Gynecologists; Pediatricians, General; Psychiatrists; and Surgeons.

Diagnose, treat, and help prevent diseases and injuries that commonly occur in the general population. Prescribe or administer treatment, therapy, medication, vaccination, and other specialized medical care to treat or prevent illness, disease, or injury. Order, perform, and interpret tests and analyze records, reports, and examination information to diagnose patients' condition. Monitor the patients' conditions and progress and re-evaluate treatments as necessary. Explain procedures and discuss test results or prescribed treatments with patients. Collect, record, and maintain patient information, such as medical history, reports, and examination results. Advise patients and community members concerning diet, activity, hygiene, and disease prevention. Refer patients to medical specialists or other practitioners when necessary. Direct and coordinate activities of nurses, students, assistants, specialists, therapists, and other medical staff. Coordinate work with nurses, social workers, rehabilitation therapists, pharmacists, psychologists, and other health-care providers. Deliver babies. Operate on patients to remove, repair, or improve functioning of diseased or injured body parts and systems. Plan, implement, or administer health programs or standards in hospital, business, or community for information, prevention, or treatment of injury or illness. Prepare reports for government or management of birth, death, and disease statistics; workforce evaluations; or medical status of individuals. Conduct research to study anatomy and develop or test medications, treatments, or procedures to prevent or control disease or injury.

SKILLS—Most Important: Science Skills; Social Skills; Thought-Processing Skills. **Other Above-Average Skills:** Communication Skills; Management Skills; Quality Control Skills.

GOE—Interest Area: 08. Health Science. **Work Group:** 08.02. Medicine and Surgery. **Other Jobs in This Group:** Anesthesiologists; Internists, General; Medical Assistants; Medical Transcriptionists; Obstetricians and Gynecologists; Pediatricians, General; Pharmacists; Pharmacy Aides; Pharmacy Technicians; Physician Assistants; Psychiatrists; Registered Nurses; Surgeons; Surgical Technologists. **PERSONALITY TYPE:** Investigative. Investigative occupations frequently involve working with ideas and require an extensive amount of thinking. These occupations can involve searching for facts and figuring out problems mentally.

EDUCATION/TRAINING PROGRAM(S)—Medicine (MD); Osteopathic Medicine/Osteopathy (DO); Family Medicine. **RELATED KNOWLEDGE/ COURSES—Medicine and Dentistry:** The information and techniques needed to diagnose and treat human injuries, diseases, and deformities. This includes symptoms, treatment alternatives, drug properties and interactions, and preventive healthcare measures. **Therapy and Counseling:** Principles, methods, and procedures for diagnosis, treatment, and rehabilitation of physical and mental dysfunctions and for career counseling and guidance. **Biology:** Plant and animal organisms and their tissues, cells, functions, interdependencies, and interactions with each other and the environment. **Psychology:** Human behavior and performance; individual differences in ability, personality, and interests; learning and motivation; psychological research methods; and the assessment and treatment of behavioral and affective disorders. **Sociology and Anthropology:** Group behavior and dynamics, societal trends and influences, human migrations, ethnicity, and cultures and their history and origins. **Chemistry:** The chemical composition, structure, and properties of substances and of the chemical processes and transformations that they undergo. This includes uses of chemicals and their danger signs, production techniques, and disposal methods.

Film and Video Editors

- Education/Training Required: Bachelor's degree
- Annual Earnings: $46,930
- Growth: 18.6%
- Annual Job Openings: 3,000
- Self-Employed: 18.2%
- Part-Time: 27.6%

Edit motion picture soundtracks, film, and video. Cut shot sequences to different angles at specific points in scenes, making each individual cut as fluid and seamless as possible. Study scripts to become familiar with production concepts and requirements. Edit films and videotapes to insert music, dialogue, and sound effects; to arrange films into sequences; and to correct errors, using editing equipment. Select and combine the most effective shots of each scene to form a logical and smoothly running story. Mark frames where a particular shot or piece of sound is to begin or end. Determine the specific audio and visual effects and music necessary to complete films. Verify key numbers and time codes on materials. Organize and string together raw footage into a continuous whole according to scripts or the instructions of directors and producers. Review assembled films or edited videotapes on screens or monitors to determine if corrections are necessary. Program computerized graphic effects. Review footage sequence by sequence to become familiar with it before assembling it into a final product. Set up and operate computer editing systems, electronic titling systems, video switching equipment, and digital video effects units to produce a final product. Record needed sounds or obtain them from sound effects libraries. Confer with producers and directors concerning layout or editing approaches needed to increase dramatic or entertainment value of productions. Manipulate plot, score, sound, and graphics to make the parts into a continuous whole, working closely with people in audio, visual, music, optical, or special effects departments. Supervise and coordinate activities of workers engaged in film editing, assembling, and recording activities. Trim film segments to specified lengths and reassemble segments in sequences that present stories with maximum effect. Develop post-production models for films. Piece sounds together to develop film soundtracks. Conduct film screenings for directors and members of production staffs. Collaborate with music editors to select appropriate passages of music and develop production scores. Discuss the sound requirements of pictures with sound effects editors.

SKILLS—Most Important: Equipment/Technology Analysis Skills; Equipment Use/Maintenance Skills. **Other Above-Average Skills:** Thought-Processing Skills; Communication Skills; Social Skills.

GOE—Interest Area: 03. Arts and Communication. **Work Group:** 03.09. Media Technology. **Other Jobs in This Group:** Audio and Video Equipment Technicians; Broadcast Technicians; Camera Operators, Television, Video, and Motion Picture; Multi-Media Artists and Animators; Photographers; Radio Operators; Sound Engineering Technicians. **PERSONALITY TYPE:** Artistic. Artistic occupations frequently involve working with forms, designs, and patterns. They often require self-expression, and the work can be done without following a clear set of rules.

EDUCATION/TRAINING PROGRAM(S)—Photojournalism; Radio and Television; Communications Technology/Technician; Radio and Television Broadcasting Technology/Technician; Audiovisual Communications Technologies/Technicians, Other; Cinematography and Film/Video Production. **RELATED KNOWLEDGE/COURSES—Fine Arts:** The theory and techniques required to compose, produce, and perform works of music, dance, visual arts, drama, and sculpture. **Communications and Media:** Media production, communication, and dissemination techniques and methods. This includes alternative ways to inform and entertain via written, oral, and visual media. **Design:** Design techniques, tools, and principles involved in production of precision technical plans, blueprints, drawings, and models. **Computers and Electronics:** Circuit boards; processors; chips; electronic equipment; and computer hardware and software, including applications and programming. **Education and Training:** Principles and methods for curriculum and training design, teaching and instruction for individuals and groups, and the measurement of training effects. **Telecommunications:** Transmission, broadcasting, switching, control, and operation of telecommunications systems.

Financial Analysts

- ◎ Education/Training Required: Bachelor's degree
- ◎ Annual Earnings: $63,860
- ◎ Growth: 17.3%
- ◎ Annual Job Openings: 28,000
- ◎ Self-Employed: 6.7%
- ◎ Part-Time: 9.8%

Conduct quantitative analyses of information affecting investment programs of public or private institutions. Assemble spreadsheets and draw charts and graphs used to illustrate technical reports, using computer. Analyze financial information to produce forecasts of business, industry, and economic conditions for use in making investment decisions. Maintain knowledge and stay abreast of developments in the fields of industrial technology, business, finance, and economic theory. Interpret data affecting investment programs, such as price, yield, stability, future trends in investment risks, and economic influences. Monitor fundamental economic, industrial, and corporate developments through the analysis of information obtained from financial publications and services, investment banking firms, government agencies, trade publications, company sources, and personal interviews. Recommend investments and investment timing to companies, investment firm staff, or the investing public. Determine the prices at which securities should be syndicated and offered to the public. Prepare plans of action for investment based on financial analyses. Evaluate and compare the relative quality of various securities in a given industry. Present oral and written reports on general economic trends, individual corporations, and entire industries. Contact brokers and purchase investments for companies according to company policy. Collaborate with investment bankers to attract new corporate clients to securities firms.

SKILLS—Most Important: Management Skills; Computer Programming Skills; Mathematics Skills. **Other Above-Average Skills:** Thought-Processing Skills; Communication Skills.

GOE—Interest Area: 06. Finance and Insurance. **Work Group:** 06.02. Finance/Insurance Investigation and Analysis. **Other Jobs in This Group:** Appraisers and Assessors of Real Estate; Appraisers, Real Estate;

Assessors; Claims Adjusters, Examiners, and Investigators; Claims Examiners, Property and Casualty Insurance; Cost Estimators; Credit Analysts; Insurance Adjusters, Examiners, and Investigators; Insurance Appraisers, Auto Damage; Insurance Underwriters; Loan Counselors; Loan Officers; Market Research Analysts; Survey Researchers. **PERSONALITY TYPE:** Investigative. Investigative occupations frequently involve working with ideas and require an extensive amount of thinking. These occupations can involve searching for facts and figuring out problems mentally.

EDUCATION/TRAINING PROGRAM(S)—Accounting and Finance; Accounting and Business/Management; Finance, General. **RELATED KNOWLEDGE/COURSES—Economics and Accounting:** Economic and accounting principles and practices, the financial markets, banking, and the analysis and reporting of financial data. **Mathematics:** Arithmetic, algebra, geometry, calculus, and statistics and their applications. **Law and Government:** Laws, legal codes, court procedures, precedents, government regulations, executive orders, agency rules, and the democratic political process. **Administration and Management:** Business and management principles involved in strategic planning, resource allocation, human resources modeling, leadership technique, production methods, and coordination of people and resources. **English Language:** The structure and content of the English language, including the meaning and spelling of words, rules of composition, and grammar. **Clerical Practices:** Administrative and clerical procedures and systems such as word processing, managing files and records, stenography and transcription, designing forms, and other office procedures and terminology.

Financial Examiners

- Education/Training Required: Bachelor's degree
- Annual Earnings: $63,090
- Growth: 9.5%
- Annual Job Openings: 3,000
- Self-Employed: 0.0%
- Part-Time: No data available

Enforce or ensure compliance with laws and regulations governing financial and securities institutions and financial and real estate transactions. May examine, verify correctness of, or establish authenticity of records. Investigate activities of institutions in order to enforce laws and regulations and to ensure legality of transactions and operations or financial solvency. Review and analyze new, proposed, or revised laws, regulations, policies, and procedures in order to interpret their meaning and determine their impact. Plan, supervise, and review work of assigned subordinates. Recommend actions to ensure compliance with laws and regulations or to protect solvency of institutions. Examine the minutes of meetings of directors, stockholders, and committees in order to investigate the specific authority extended at various levels of management. Prepare reports, exhibits, and other supporting schedules that detail an institution's safety and soundness, compliance with laws and regulations, and recommended solutions to questionable financial conditions. Review balance sheets, operating income and expense accounts, and loan documentation in order to confirm institution assets and liabilities. Review audit reports of internal and external auditors in order to monitor adequacy of scope of reports or to discover specific weaknesses in internal routines. Train other examiners in the financial examination process. Establish guidelines for procedures and policies that comply with new and revised regulations and direct their implementation. Direct and participate in formal and informal meetings with bank directors, trustees, senior management, counsels, outside accountants, and consultants in order to gather information and discuss findings. Verify and inspect cash reserves, assigned collateral, and bank-owned securities in order to check internal control procedures. Review applications for mergers, acquisitions, establishment of new institutions, acceptance in Federal Reserve System, or registration of securities sales in order to determine their public interest value and conformance to regulations and recommend acceptance or rejection. Resolve problems concerning the overall financial integrity of banking institutions, including loan investment portfolios, capital, earnings, and specific or large troubled accounts.

SKILLS—Most Important: Quality Control Skills; Thought-Processing Skills; Communication Skills. **Other Above-Average Skills:** Management Skills; Social Skills.

GOE—**Interest Area:** 07. Government and Public Administration. **Work Group:** 07.03. Regulations Enforcement. **Other Jobs in This Group:** Agricultural Inspectors; Aviation Inspectors; Compliance Officers, Except Agriculture, Construction, Health and Safety, and Transportation; Construction and Building Inspectors; Environmental Compliance Inspectors; Equal Opportunity Representatives and Officers; Fire Inspectors; Fish and Game Wardens; Forest Fire Inspectors and Prevention Specialists; Freight and Cargo Inspectors; Government Property Inspectors and Investigators; Immigration and Customs Inspectors; Licensing Examiners and Inspectors; Nuclear Monitoring Technicians; Occupational Health and Safety Specialists; Occupational Health and Safety Technicians; Tax Examiners, Collectors, and Revenue Agents; Transportation Vehicle, Equipment, and Systems Inspectors, Except Aviation. **PERSONALITY TYPE:** Enterprising. Enterprising occupations frequently involve starting up and carrying out projects. These occupations can involve leading people and making many decisions. They sometimes require risk taking and often deal with business.

EDUCATION/TRAINING PROGRAM(S)—Accounting; Taxation. **RELATED KNOWLEDGE/ COURSES—Economics and Accounting:** Economic and accounting principles and practices, the financial markets, banking, and the analysis and reporting of financial data. **Law and Government:** Laws, legal codes, court procedures, precedents, government regulations, executive orders, agency rules, and the democratic political process. **Clerical Practices:** Administrative and clerical procedures and systems such as word processing, managing files and records, stenography and transcription, designing forms, and other office procedures and terminology. **Mathematics:** Arithmetic, algebra, geometry, calculus, and statistics and their applications. **Administration and Management:** Business and management principles involved in strategic planning, resource allocation, human resources modeling, leadership technique, production methods, and coordination of people and resources. **English Language:** The structure and content of the English language, including the meaning and spelling of words, rules of composition, and grammar.

Financial Managers, Branch or Department

- Education/Training Required: Work experience plus degree
- Annual Earnings: $86,280
- Growth: 14.8%
- Annual Job Openings: 63,000
- Self-Employed: 3.2%
- Part-Time: 4.3%

The job openings listed here are shared with Treasurers and Controllers.

Direct and coordinate financial activities of workers in a branch, office, or department of an establishment, such as branch bank, brokerage firm, risk and insurance department, or credit department. Establish and maintain relationships with individual and business customers and provide assistance with problems these customers may encounter. Examine, evaluate, and process loan applications. Plan, direct, and coordinate the activities of workers in branches, offices, or departments of such establishments as branch banks, brokerage firms, risk and insurance departments, or credit departments. Oversee the flow of cash and financial instruments. Recruit staff members and oversee training programs. Network within communities to find and attract new business. Approve or reject, or coordinate the approval and rejection of, lines of credit and commercial, real estate, and personal loans. Prepare financial and regulatory reports required by laws, regulations, and boards of directors. Establish procedures for custody and control of assets, records, loan collateral, and securities in order to ensure safekeeping. Review collection reports to determine the status of collections and the amounts of outstanding balances. Prepare operational and risk reports for management analysis. Evaluate financial reporting systems, accounting and collection procedures, and investment activities and make recommendations for changes to procedures, operating systems, budgets, and other financial control functions. Plan, direct, and coordinate risk and insurance programs of establishments to control risks and losses. Submit delinquent accounts to attorneys or outside agencies for collection. Communicate with stockholders and other investors to provide information and to raise capital. Evaluate data pertaining to costs in order to plan budgets. Analyze and classify risks and investments to determine their potential impacts on companies. Review reports of securities transactions and price lists in order to analyze market conditions. Develop and analyze information to assess the current and future financial status of firms. Direct insurance negotiations, select insurance brokers and carriers, and place insurance.

SKILLS—Most Important: Management Skills; Social Skills; Thought-Processing Skills. **Other Above-Average Skills:** Communication Skills; Mathematics Skills.

GOE—Interest Area: 06. Finance and Insurance. **Work Group:** 06.01. Managerial Work in Finance and Insurance. **Other Jobs in This Group:** Financial Managers; Treasurers and Controllers. **PERSONALITY TYPE:** Enterprising. Enterprising occupations frequently involve starting up and carrying out projects. These occupations can involve leading people and making many decisions. They sometimes require risk taking and often deal with business.

EDUCATION/TRAINING PROGRAM(S)—Accounting and Finance; Finance, General; International Finance; Public Finance; Credit Management; Finance and Financial Management Services, Other. **RELATED KNOWLEDGE/COURSES—Economics and Accounting:** Economic and accounting principles and practices, the financial markets, banking, and the analysis and reporting of financial data. **Sales and Marketing:** Principles and methods for showing, promoting, and selling products or services. This includes marketing strategy and tactics, product demonstration, sales techniques, and sales control systems. **Customer and Personal Service:** Principles and processes for providing customer and personal services. This includes customer needs assessment, meeting of quality standards for services, and evaluation of customer satisfaction. **Personnel and Human Resources:** Principles and procedures for personnel recruitment, selection, training, compensation and benefits, labor relations and negotiation, and personnel information systems. **Clerical Practices:** Administrative and clerical procedures and systems such as word processing, managing files and records, stenography and transcription, designing forms, and other office procedures and terminology. **Administration and**

Management: Business and management principles involved in strategic planning, resource allocation, human resources modeling, leadership technique, production methods, and coordination of people and resources.

Fire-Prevention and Protection Engineers

- Education/Training Required: Bachelor's degree
- Annual Earnings: $65,210
- Growth: 13.4%
- Annual Job Openings: 2,000
- Self-Employed: 0.5%
- Part-Time: 2.6%

The job openings listed here are shared with Industrial Safety and Health Engineers and Product Safety Engineers.

Research causes of fires, determine fire protection methods, and design or recommend materials or equipment such as structural components or fire-detection equipment to assist organizations in safeguarding life and property against fire, explosion, and related hazards. Design fire detection equipment, alarm systems, and fire extinguishing devices and systems. Inspect buildings or building designs to determine fire protection system requirements and potential problems in areas such as water supplies, exit locations, and construction materials. Advise architects, builders, and other construction personnel on fire prevention equipment and techniques and on fire code and standard interpretation and compliance. Prepare and write reports detailing specific fire prevention and protection issues, such as work performed and proposed review schedules. Determine causes of fires and ways in which they could have been prevented. Direct the purchase, modification, installation, maintenance, and operation of fire protection systems. Consult with authorities to discuss safety regulations and to recommend changes as necessary. Develop plans for the prevention of destruction by fire, wind, and water. Study the relationships between ignition sources and materials to determine how fires start. Attend workshops, seminars, or conferences to present or obtain information regarding fire prevention and protection. Develop training materials and conduct training sessions on fire protection. Evaluate fire department performance and the laws and regulations affecting fire prevention or fire safety. Conduct research on fire retardants and the fire safety of materials and devices.

SKILLS—Most Important: Science Skills; Mathematics Skills; Management Skills. **Other Above-Average Skills:** Equipment/Technology Analysis Skills; Communication Skills; Social Skills.

GOE—Interest Area: 15. Scientific Research, Engineering, and Mathematics. **Work Group:** 15.08. Industrial and Safety Engineering. **Other Jobs in This Group:** Health and Safety Engineers, Except Mining Safety Engineers and Inspectors; Industrial Engineers; Industrial Safety and Health Engineers; Product Safety Engineers. **PERSONALITY TYPE:** Investigative. Investigative occupations frequently involve working with ideas and require an extensive amount of thinking. These occupations can involve searching for facts and figuring out problems mentally.

EDUCATION/TRAINING PROGRAM(S)—Environmental/Environmental Health Engineering. **RELATED KNOWLEDGE/COURSES—Design:** Design techniques, tools, and principles involved in production of precision technical plans, blueprints, drawings, and models. **Engineering and Technology:** The practical application of engineering science and technology. This includes applying principles, techniques, procedures, and equipment to the design and production of various goods and services. **Building and Construction:** The materials, methods, and tools involved in the construction or repair of houses, buildings, or other structures such as highways and roads. **Physics:** Physical principles and laws and their interrelationships and applications to understanding fluid, material, and atmospheric dynamics and mechanical, electrical, atomic, and subatomic structures and processes. **Chemistry:** The chemical composition, structure, and properties of substances and of the chemical processes and transformations that they undergo. This includes uses of chemicals and their danger signs, production techniques, and disposal methods. **Public Safety and Security:** Relevant equipment, policies, procedures, and strategies to promote effective local, state, or national security operations for the protection of people, data, property, and institutions.

First-Line Supervisors/ Managers of Construction Trades and Extraction Workers

- Education/Training Required: Work experience in a related occupation
- Annual Earnings: $51,970
- Growth: 10.9%
- Annual Job Openings: 57,000
- Self-Employed: 24.7%
- Part-Time: 3.8%

Directly supervise and coordinate activities of construction or extraction workers. Examine and inspect work progress, equipment, and construction sites to verify safety and to ensure that specifications are met. Read specifications such as blueprints to determine construction requirements and to plan procedures. Estimate material and worker requirements to complete jobs. Supervise, coordinate, and schedule the activities of construction or extractive workers. Confer with managerial and technical personnel, other departments, and contractors to resolve problems and to coordinate activities. Coordinate work activities with other construction project activities. Locate, measure, and mark site locations and placement of structures and equipment, using measuring and marking equipment. Order or requisition materials and supplies. Record information such as personnel, production, and operational data on specified forms and reports. Assign work to employees based on material and worker requirements of specific jobs. Provide assistance to workers engaged in construction or extraction activities, using hand tools and equipment. Train workers in construction methods, operation of equipment, safety procedures, and company policies. Analyze worker and production problems and recommend solutions, such as improving production methods or implementing motivational plans. Arrange for repairs of equipment and machinery. Suggest or initiate personnel actions such as promotions, transfers, and hires.

SKILLS—**Most Important:** Management Skills; Quality Control Skills; Equipment Use/Maintenance Skills. **Other Above-Average Skills:** None met the criteria.

GOE—**Interest Area:** 01. Agriculture and Natural Resources. **Work Group:** 01.01. Managerial Work in Agriculture and Natural Resources. **Other Jobs in This Group:** Aquacultural Managers; Crop and Livestock Managers; Farm Labor Contractors; Farm, Ranch, and Other Agricultural Managers; Farmers and Ranchers; First-Line Supervisors/Managers of Agricultural Crop and Horticultural Workers; First-Line Supervisors/Managers of Animal Husbandry and Animal Care Workers; First-Line Supervisors/Managers of Aquacultural Workers; First-Line Supervisors/Managers of Farming, Fishing, and Forestry Workers; First-Line Supervisors/Managers of Landscaping, Lawn Service, and Groundskeeping Workers; First-Line Supervisors/Managers of Logging Workers; Nursery and Greenhouse Managers; Park Naturalists; Purchasing Agents and Buyers, Farm Products. **PERSONALITY TYPE:** Enterprising. Enterprising occupations frequently involve starting up and carrying out projects. These occupations can involve leading people and making many decisions. They sometimes require risk taking and often deal with business.

EDUCATION/TRAINING PROGRAM(S)—Blasting/Blaster; Building/Construction Finishing, Management, and Inspection, Other; Building/Construction Site Management/Manager; Building/Construction Trades, Other; Building/Home/Construction Inspection/Inspector; Building/Property Maintenance and Management; Carpentry/Carpenter; Concrete Finishing/Concrete Finisher; Drywall Installation/Drywaller; others. **RELATED KNOWLEDGE/COURSES—Personnel and Human Resources:** Principles and procedures for personnel recruitment, selection, training, compensation and benefits, labor relations and negotiation, and personnel information systems. **Building and Construction:** The materials, methods, and tools involved in the construction or repair of houses, buildings, or other structures such as highways and roads. **Administration and Management:** Business and management principles involved in strategic planning, resource allocation, human resources modeling, leadership technique, production methods, and coordination of people and resources. **Engineering and Technology:** The practical application of engineering science and technology. This includes applying principles, techniques, procedures, and equipment to the design and production of various goods and services. **Mechanical Devices:** Machines and tools, including their designs, uses, repair, and maintenance. **Physics:** Physical principles and laws and their interrelationships and applications to understanding fluid, material, and atmospheric dynamics and mechanical, electrical, atomic, and subatomic structures and processes.

First-Line Supervisors/ Managers of Helpers, Laborers, and Material Movers, Hand

- Education/Training Required: Work experience in a related occupation
- Annual Earnings: $39,000
- Growth: 8.1%
- Annual Job Openings: 15,000
- Self-Employed: 1.3%
- Part-Time: 4.9%

Supervise and coordinate the activities of helpers, laborers, or material movers. Plan work schedules and assign duties to maintain adequate staffing levels, to ensure that activities are performed effectively, and to respond to fluctuating workloads. Collaborate with workers and managers to solve work-related problems. Review work throughout the work process and at completion to ensure that it has been performed properly. Transmit and explain work orders to laborers. Check specifications of materials loaded or unloaded against information contained in work orders. Inform designated employees or departments of items loaded and problems encountered. Examine freight to determine loading sequences. Evaluate employee performance and prepare performance appraisals. Perform the same work duties as those whom they supervise or perform more difficult or skilled tasks or assist in their performance. Prepare and maintain work records and reports that include information such as employee time and wages, daily receipts, and inspection results. Counsel employees in work-related activities, personal growth, and career development. Conduct staff meetings to relay general information or to address specific topics such as safety. Inspect equipment for wear and for conformance to specifications. Resolve personnel problems, complaints, and formal grievances when possible or refer them to higher-level supervisors for resolution. Recommend or initiate personnel actions such as promotions, transfers, and disciplinary measures. Assess training needs of staff; then arrange for or provide appropriate instruction. Schedule times of shipment and modes of transportation for materials. Quote prices to customers. Estimate material, time, and staffing requirements for a given project based on work orders, job specifications, and experience. Provide assistance in balancing books; tracking, monitoring, and projecting a unit's budget needs; and developing unit policies and procedures. Inspect job sites to determine the extent of maintenance or repairs needed. Participate in the hiring process by reviewing credentials, conducting interviews, and making hiring decisions or recommendations.

SKILLS—Most Important: Social Skills; Management Skills; Quality Control Skills. **Other Above-Average Skills:** Thought-Processing Skills; Mathematics Skills.

GOE—Interest Area: 13. Manufacturing. **Work Group:** 13.01. Managerial Work in Manufacturing. **Other Jobs in This Group:** First-Line Supervisors/Managers of Mechanics, Installers, and Repairers; First-Line Supervisors/Managers of Production and Operating Workers; Industrial Production Managers. **PERSONALITY TYPE:** Enterprising. Enterprising occupations frequently involve starting up and carrying out projects. These occupations can involve leading people and making many decisions. They sometimes require risk taking and often deal with business.

EDUCATION/TRAINING PROGRAM(S)—No related CIP programs; this job is learned through work experience in a related occupation. **RELATED KNOWLEDGE/COURSES—Production and Processing:** Raw materials, production processes, quality control, costs, and other techniques for maximizing the effective manufacture and distribution of goods. **Transportation:** Principles and methods for moving people or goods by air, rail, sea, or road, including the relative costs and benefits. **Administration and Management:** Business and management principles involved in strategic planning, resource allocation, human resources modeling, leadership technique, production methods, and coordination of people and resources.

Personnel and Human Resources: Principles and procedures for personnel recruitment, selection, training, compensation and benefits, labor relations and negotiation, and personnel information systems. **Customer and Personal Service:** Principles and processes for providing customer and personal services. This includes customer needs assessment, meeting of quality standards for services, and evaluation of customer satisfaction. **Public Safety and Security:** Relevant equipment, policies, procedures, and strategies to promote effective local, state, or national security operations for the protection of people, data, property, and institutions.

First-Line Supervisors/ Managers of Housekeeping and Janitorial Workers

- Education/Training Required: Work experience in a related occupation
- Annual Earnings: $30,330
- Growth: 19.0%
- Annual Job Openings: 21,000
- Self-Employed: 8.9%
- Part-Time: 14.9%

Supervise work activities of cleaning personnel in hotels, hospitals, offices, and other establishments. Direct activities for stopping the spread of infections in facilities such as hospitals. Inspect work performed to ensure that it meets specifications and established standards. Plan and prepare employee work schedules. Perform or assist with cleaning duties as necessary. Investigate complaints about service and equipment and take corrective action. Coordinate activities with other departments to ensure that services are provided in an efficient and timely manner. Check equipment to ensure that it is in working order. Inspect and evaluate the physical condition of facilities to determine the type of work required. Select the most suitable cleaning materials for different types of linens, furniture, flooring, and surfaces. Instruct staff in work policies and procedures and the use and maintenance of equipment. Issue supplies and equipment to workers. Forecast necessary levels of staffing and stock at different times to facilitate effective scheduling and ordering. Inventory stock to ensure that supplies and equipment are available in adequate amounts. Evaluate employee performance and recommend personnel actions such as promotions, transfers, and dismissals. Confer with staff to resolve performance and personnel problems and to discuss company policies. Establish and implement operational standards and procedures for the departments they supervise. Recommend or arrange for additional services such as painting, repair work, renovations, and the replacement of furnishings and equipment. Select and order or purchase new equipment, supplies, and furnishings. Recommend changes that could improve service and increase operational efficiency. Maintain required records of work hours, budgets, payrolls, and other information. Screen job applicants and hire new employees. Supervise in-house services such as laundries, maintenance and repair, dry cleaning, and valet services. Advise managers, desk clerks, or admitting personnel of rooms ready for occupancy. Perform financial tasks such as estimating costs and preparing and managing budgets. Prepare activity and personnel reports and reports containing information such as occupancy, hours worked, facility usage, work performed, and departmental expenses.

SKILLS—Most Important: Social Skills; Management Skills; Equipment Use/Maintenance Skills. **Other Above-Average Skills:** Science Skills; Communication Skills; Thought-Processing Skills; Mathematics Skills.

GOE—Interest Area: 04. Business and Administration. **Work Group:** 04.02. Managerial Work in Business Detail. **Other Jobs in This Group:** Administrative Services Managers; First-Line Supervisors/Managers of Office and Administrative Support Workers; Meeting and Convention Planners. **PERSONALITY TYPE:** Enterprising. Enterprising occupations frequently involve starting up and carrying out projects. These occupations can involve leading people and making many decisions. They sometimes require risk taking and often deal with business.

EDUCATION/TRAINING PROGRAM(S)—No related CIP programs; this job is learned through work experience in a related occupation. **RELATED KNOWLEDGE/COURSES—Chemistry:** The chemical composition, structure, and properties of substances and of the chemical processes and transformations that they undergo. This includes uses of chemicals and their danger signs, production techniques, and disposal meth-

ods. **Building and Construction:** The materials, methods, and tools involved in the construction or repair of houses, buildings, or other structures such as highways and roads. **Administration and Management:** Business and management principles involved in strategic planning, resource allocation, human resources modeling, leadership technique, production methods, and coordination of people and resources. **Public Safety and Security:** Relevant equipment, policies, procedures, and strategies to promote effective local, state, or national security operations for the protection of people, data, property, and institutions. **Mechanical Devices:** Machines and tools, including their designs, uses, repair, and maintenance. **Physics:** Physical principles and laws and their interrelationships and applications to understanding fluid, material, and atmospheric dynamics and mechanical, electrical, atomic, and subatomic structures and processes.

First-Line Supervisors/ Managers of Mechanics, Installers, and Repairers

- Education/Training Required: Work experience in a related occupation
- Annual Earnings: $51,980
- Growth: 12.4%
- Annual Job Openings: 33,000
- Self-Employed: 0.3%
- Part-Time: 1.0%

Supervise and coordinate the activities of mechanics, installers, and repairers. Determine schedules, sequences, and assignments for work activities based on work priority, quantity of equipment, and skill of personnel. Patrol and monitor work areas and examine tools and equipment to detect unsafe conditions or violations of procedures or safety rules. Monitor employees' work levels and review work performance. Examine objects, systems, or facilities and analyze information to determine needed installations, services, or repairs. Participate in budget preparation and administration, coordinating purchasing and documentation and monitoring departmental expenditures. Counsel employees about work-related issues and assist employees in correcting job-skill deficiencies. Requisition materials and supplies, such as tools, equipment, and replacement parts. Compute estimates and actual costs of factors such as materials, labor, and outside contractors. Conduct or arrange for worker training in safety, repair, and maintenance techniques; operational procedures; or equipment use. Interpret specifications, blueprints, and job orders to construct templates and lay out reference points for workers. Investigate accidents and injuries and prepare reports of findings. Confer with personnel, such as management, engineering, quality control, customer, and union workers' representatives, to coordinate work activities, resolve employee grievances, and identify and review resource needs. Recommend or initiate personnel actions, such as hires, promotions, transfers, discharges, and disciplinary measures. Perform skilled repair and maintenance operations, using equipment such as hand and power tools, hydraulic presses and shears, and welding equipment. Compile operational and personnel records, such as time and production records, inventory data, repair and maintenance statistics, and test results. Develop, implement, and evaluate maintenance policies and procedures. Monitor tool inventories and the condition and maintenance of shops to ensure adequate working conditions. Inspect, test, and measure completed work, using devices such as hand tools and gauges to verify conformance to standards and repair requirements.

SKILLS—Most Important: Management Skills; Equipment Use/Maintenance Skills; Equipment/Technology Analysis Skills. **Other Above-Average Skills:** Quality Control Skills; Social Skills; Science Skills; Communication Skills.

GOE—Interest Area: 13. Manufacturing. **Work Group:** 13.01. Managerial Work in Manufacturing. **Other Jobs in This Group:** First-Line Supervisors/Managers of Helpers, Laborers, and Material Movers, Hand; First-Line Supervisors/Managers of Production and Operating Workers; Industrial Production Managers. **PERSONALITY TYPE:** Enterprising. Enterprising occupations frequently involve starting up and carrying out projects. These occupations can involve leading people and making many decisions. They sometimes require risk taking and often deal with business.

EDUCATION/TRAINING PROGRAM(S)—Operations Management and Supervision. **RELATED**

KNOWLEDGE/COURSES—Mechanical Devices: Machines and tools, including their designs, uses, repair, and maintenance. **Building and Construction:** The materials, methods, and tools involved in the construction or repair of houses, buildings, or other structures such as highways and roads. **Design:** Design techniques, tools, and principles involved in production of precision technical plans, blueprints, drawings, and models. **Personnel and Human Resources:** Principles and procedures for personnel recruitment, selection, training, compensation and benefits, labor relations and negotiation, and personnel information systems. **Engineering and Technology:** The practical application of engineering science and technology. This includes applying principles, techniques, procedures, and equipment to the design and production of various goods and services. **Administration and Management:** Business and management principles involved in strategic planning, resource allocation, human resources modeling, leadership technique, production methods, and coordination of people and resources.

First-Line Supervisors/ Managers of Police and Detectives

- Education/Training Required: Work experience in a related occupation
- Annual Earnings: $65,570
- Growth: 15.5%
- Annual Job Openings: 9,000
- Self-Employed: 0.0%
- Part-Time: 0.9%

Supervise and coordinate activities of members of police force. Explain police operations to subordinates to assist them in performing their job duties. Inform personnel of changes in regulations and policies, implications of new or amended laws, and new techniques of police work. Supervise and coordinate the investigation of criminal cases, offering guidance and expertise to investigators and ensuring that procedures are conducted in accordance with laws and regulations. Investigate and resolve personnel problems within organization and charges of misconduct against staff. Train staff in proper police work procedures. Maintain logs; prepare reports; and direct the preparation, handling, and maintenance of departmental records. Monitor and evaluate the job performance of subordinates and authorize promotions and transfers. Direct collection, preparation, and handling of evidence and personal property of prisoners. Develop, implement, and revise departmental policies and procedures. Conduct raids and order detention of witnesses and suspects for questioning. Prepare work schedules and assign duties to subordinates. Discipline staff for violation of department rules and regulations. Cooperate with court personnel and officials from other law enforcement agencies and testify in court as necessary. Review contents of written orders to ensure adherence to legal requirements. Inspect facilities, supplies, vehicles, and equipment to ensure conformance to standards. Prepare news releases and respond to police correspondence. Requisition and issue equipment and supplies. Meet with civic, educational, and community groups to develop community programs and events and to discuss law enforcement subjects. Direct release or transfer of prisoners. Prepare budgets and manage expenditures of department funds.

SKILLS—Most Important: Social Skills; Management Skills; Thought-Processing Skills. **Other Above-Average Skills:** Communication Skills; Equipment/Technology Analysis Skills.

GOE—Interest Area: 12. Law and Public Safety. **Work Group:** 12.01. Managerial Work in Law and Public Safety. **Other Jobs in This Group:** Emergency Management Specialists; First-Line Supervisors/Managers of Correctional Officers; First-Line Supervisors/Managers of Fire Fighting and Prevention Workers; Forest Fire Fighting and Prevention Supervisors; Municipal Fire Fighting and Prevention Supervisors. **PERSONALITY TYPE:** Enterprising. Enterprising occupations frequently involve starting up and carrying out projects. These occupations can involve leading people and making many decisions. They sometimes require risk taking and often deal with business.

EDUCATION/TRAINING PROGRAM(S)—Corrections; Criminal Justice/Law Enforcement Administration; Criminal Justice/Safety Studies. **RELATED KNOWLEDGE/COURSES—Public Safety and Security:** Relevant equipment, policies, procedures, and strategies to promote effective local, state, or national

security operations for the protection of people, data, property, and institutions. **Psychology:** Human behavior and performance; individual differences in ability, personality, and interests; learning and motivation; psychological research methods; and the assessment and treatment of behavioral and affective disorders. **Law and Government:** Laws, legal codes, court procedures, precedents, government regulations, executive orders, agency rules, and the democratic political process. **Personnel and Human Resources:** Principles and procedures for personnel recruitment, selection, training, compensation and benefits, labor relations and negotiation, and personnel information systems. **Education and Training:** Principles and methods for curriculum and training design, teaching and instruction for individuals and groups, and the measurement of training effects. **Customer and Personal Service:** Principles and processes for providing customer and personal services. This includes customer needs assessment, meeting of quality standards for services, and evaluation of customer satisfaction.

First-Line Supervisors/ Managers of Production and Operating Workers

- ◎ Education/Training Required: Work experience in a related occupation
- ◎ Annual Earnings: $46,140
- ◎ Growth: 2.7%
- ◎ Annual Job Openings: 89,000
- ◎ Self-Employed: 3.9%
- ◎ Part-Time: 2.3%

Supervise and coordinate the activities of production and operating workers, such as inspectors, precision workers, machine setters and operators, assemblers, fabricators, and plant and system operators. Enforce safety and sanitation regulations. Direct and coordinate the activities of employees engaged in the production or processing of goods, such as inspectors, machine setters, and fabricators. Read and analyze charts, work orders, production schedules, and other records and reports to determine production requirements and to evaluate current production estimates and outputs. Confer with other supervisors to coordinate operations and activities within or between departments. Plan and establish work schedules, assignments, and production sequences to meet production goals. Inspect materials, products, or equipment to detect defects or malfunctions. Demonstrate equipment operations and work and safety procedures to new employees or assign employees to experienced workers for training. Observe work and monitor gauges, dials, and other indicators to ensure that operators conform to production or processing standards. Interpret specifications, blueprints, job orders, and company policies and procedures for workers. Confer with management or subordinates to resolve worker problems, complaints, or grievances. Maintain operations data such as time, production, and cost records and prepare management reports of production results. Recommend or implement measures to motivate employees and to improve production methods, equipment performance, product quality, or efficiency. Determine standards, budgets, production goals, and rates based on company policies, equipment and labor availability, and workloads. Requisition materials, supplies, equipment parts, or repair services. Recommend personnel actions such as hirings and promotions. Set up and adjust machines and equipment. Calculate labor and equipment requirements and production specifications, using standard formulas. Plan and develop new products and production processes.

SKILLS—Most Important: Quality Control Skills; Equipment Use/Maintenance Skills; Management Skills. **Other Above-Average Skills:** Equipment/Technology Analysis Skills; Social Skills; Mathematics Skills; Communication Skills.

GOE—Interest Area: 13. Manufacturing. **Work Group:** 13.01. Managerial Work in Manufacturing. **Other Jobs in This Group:** First-Line Supervisors/Managers of Helpers, Laborers, and Material Movers, Hand; First-Line Supervisors/Managers of Mechanics, Installers, and Repairers; Industrial Production Managers. **PERSONALITY TYPE:** Enterprising. Enterprising occupations frequently involve starting up and carrying out projects. These occupations can involve leading people and making many decisions. They sometimes require risk taking and often deal with business.

EDUCATION/TRAINING PROGRAM(S)—Operations Management and Supervision. **RELATED**

KNOWLEDGE/COURSES—Production and Processing: Raw materials, production processes, quality control, costs, and other techniques for maximizing the effective manufacture and distribution of goods. **Personnel and Human Resources:** Principles and procedures for personnel recruitment, selection, training, compensation and benefits, labor relations and negotiation, and personnel information systems. **Mechanical Devices:** Machines and tools, including their designs, uses, repair, and maintenance. **Administration and Management:** Business and management principles involved in strategic planning, resource allocation, human resources modeling, leadership technique, production methods, and coordination of people and resources. **Education and Training:** Principles and methods for curriculum and training design, teaching and instruction for individuals and groups, and the measurement of training effects. **Engineering and Technology:** The practical application of engineering science and technology. This includes applying principles, techniques, procedures, and equipment to the design and production of various goods and services.

First-Line Supervisors/ Managers of Transportation and Material-Moving Machine and Vehicle Operators

- Education/Training Required: Work experience in a related occupation
- Annual Earnings: $47,530
- Growth: 15.3%
- Annual Job Openings: 22,000
- Self-Employed: 1.3%
- Part-Time: 4.9%

Directly supervise and coordinate activities of transportation and material-moving machine and vehicle operators and helpers. Enforce safety rules and regulations. Plan work assignments and equipment allocations to meet transportation, operations, or production goals. Confer with customers, supervisors, contractors, and other personnel to exchange information and to resolve problems. Direct workers in transportation or related services, such as pumping, moving, storing, and loading and unloading of materials or people. Resolve worker problems or collaborate with employees to assist in problem resolution. Review orders, production schedules, blueprints, and shipping and receiving notices to determine work sequences and material shipping dates, types, volumes, and destinations. Monitor fieldwork to ensure that it is being performed properly and that materials are being used as they should be. Recommend and implement measures to improve worker motivation, equipment performance, work methods, and customer services. Maintain or verify records of time, materials, expenditures, and crew activities. Interpret transportation and tariff regulations, shipping orders, safety regulations, and company policies and procedures for workers. Explain and demonstrate work tasks to new workers or assign workers to more experienced workers for further training. Prepare, compile, and submit reports on work activities, operations, production, and work-related accidents. Recommend or implement personnel actions such as employee selection, evaluation, and rewards or disciplinary actions. Requisition needed personnel, supplies, equipment, parts, or repair services. Inspect or test materials, stock, vehicles, equipment, and facilities to ensure that they are safe, are free of defects, and meet specifications. Plan and establish transportation routes. Compute and estimate cash, payroll, transportation, personnel, and storage requirements. Dispatch personnel and vehicles in response to telephone or radio reports of emergencies. Perform or schedule repairs and preventive maintenance of vehicles and other equipment. Examine, measure, and weigh cargo or materials to determine specific handling requirements. Provide workers with assistance in performing tasks such as coupling railroad cars or loading vehicles.

SKILLS—Most Important: Management Skills; Social Skills; Quality Control Skills. **Other Above-Average Skills:** Equipment/Technology Analysis Skills; Thought-Processing Skills.

GOE—Interest Area: 16. Transportation, Distribution, and Logistics. **Work Group:** 16.01. Managerial Work in Transportation. **Other Jobs in This Group:** Aircraft Cargo Handling Supervisors; Postmasters and Mail Superintendents; Railroad Conductors and Yardmasters; Storage and Distribution Managers; Transportation Managers; Transportation, Storage, and Distribution Managers. **PERSONALITY TYPE:** Enterprising. Enterprising occupations frequently involve starting up and carrying out projects. These occupations can involve leading people and making many decisions. They sometimes require risk taking and often deal with business.

EDUCATION/TRAINING PROGRAM(S)—No related CIP programs; this job is learned through work experience in a related occupation. **RELATED KNOWLEDGE/COURSES—Transportation:** Principles and methods for moving people or goods by air, rail, sea, or road, including the relative costs and benefits. **Production and Processing:** Raw materials, production processes, quality control, costs, and other techniques for maximizing the effective manufacture and distribution of goods. **Personnel and Human Resources:** Principles and procedures for personnel recruitment, selection, training, compensation and benefits, labor relations and negotiation, and personnel information systems. **Customer and Personal Service:** Principles and processes for providing customer and personal services. This includes customer needs assessment, meeting of quality standards for services, and evaluation of customer satisfaction. **Administration and Management:** Business and management principles involved in strategic planning, resource allocation, human resources modeling, leadership technique, production methods, and coordination of people and resources. **Public Safety and Security:** Relevant equipment, policies, procedures, and strategies to promote effective local, state, or national security operations for the protection of people, data, property, and institutions.

Fitness Trainers and Aerobics Instructors

- Education/Training Required: Postsecondary vocational training
- Annual Earnings: $25,840
- Growth: 27.1%
- Annual Job Openings: 50,000
- Self-Employed: 6.6%
- Part-Time: 41.3%

Instruct or coach groups or individuals in exercise activities and the fundamentals of sports. Demonstrate techniques and methods of participation. Observe participants and inform them of corrective measures necessary to improve their skills. Explain and enforce safety rules and regulations governing sports, recreational activities, and the use of exercise equipment. Offer alternatives during classes to accommodate different levels of fitness. Plan routines, choose appropriate music, and choose different movements for each set of muscles, depending on participants' capabilities and limitations. Observe participants and inform them of corrective measures necessary for skill improvement. Teach proper breathing techniques used during physical exertion. Teach and demonstrate use of gymnastic and training equipment such as trampolines and weights. Instruct participants in maintaining exertion levels to maximize benefits from exercise routines. Maintain fitness equipment. Conduct therapeutic, recreational, or athletic activities. Monitor participants' progress and adapt programs as needed. Evaluate individuals' abilities, needs, and physical conditions and develop suitable training programs to meet any special requirements. Plan physical education programs to promote development of participants' physical attributes and social skills. Provide students with information and resources regarding nutrition, weight control, and lifestyle issues. Administer emergency first aid, wrap injuries, treat minor chronic disabilities, or refer injured persons to physicians. Advise clients about proper clothing and shoes. Wrap ankles, fingers, wrists, or other body parts with synthetic skin, gauze, or adhesive tape to support muscles and ligaments. Teach individual and team sports to participants through instruction and demonstration, utilizing knowledge of sports techniques and of participants' physical capabilities. Promote health clubs through membership sales and record member information. Organize, lead, and referee indoor and outdoor games such as volleyball, baseball, and basketball. Maintain equipment inventories and select, store, or issue equipment as needed. Organize and conduct competitions and tournaments. Advise participants in use of heat or ultraviolet treatments and hot baths. Massage body parts to relieve soreness, strains, and bruises.

SKILLS—Most Important: Social Skills; Equipment/Technology Analysis Skills; Science Skills. **Other Above-Average Skills:** Thought-Processing Skills; Management Skills.

GOE—Interest Area: 05. Education and Training. **Work Group:** 05.06. Counseling, Health, and Fitness Education. **Other Jobs in This Group:** Educational, Vocational, and School Counselors; Health Educators. **PERSONALITY TYPE:** Social. Social occupations frequently involve working with, communicating with, and teaching people. These occupations often involve helping or providing service to others.

EDUCATION/TRAINING PROGRAM(S)—Physical Education Teaching and Coaching; Health and Physical Education, General; Sport and Fitness Administration/Management. **RELATED KNOWLEDGE/COURSES—Customer and Personal Service:** Principles and processes for providing customer and personal services. This includes customer needs assessment, meeting of quality standards for services, and evaluation of customer satisfaction. **Medicine and Dentistry:** The information and techniques needed to diagnose and treat human injuries, diseases, and deformities. This includes symptoms, treatment alternatives, drug properties and interactions, and preventive healthcare measures. **Psychology:** Human behavior and performance; individual differences in ability, personality, and interests; learning and motivation; psychological research methods; and the assessment and treatment of behavioral and affective disorders. **Sociology and Anthropology:** Group behavior and dynamics, societal trends and influences, human migrations, ethnicity, and cultures and their history and origins. **Sales and Marketing:** Principles and methods for showing, promoting, and selling products or services. This includes marketing strategy and tactics, product demonstration, sales techniques, and sales control systems. **Personnel and Human Resources:** Principles and procedures for personnel recruitment, selection, training, compensation and benefits, labor relations and negotiation, and personnel information systems.

Food Service Managers

- Education/Training Required: Work experience in a related occupation
- Annual Earnings: $41,340
- Growth: 11.5%
- Annual Job Openings: 61,000
- Self-Employed: 40.5%
- Part-Time: 9.3%

Plan, direct, or coordinate activities of an organization or department that serves food and beverages. Test cooked food by tasting and smelling it to ensure palatability and flavor conformity. Investigate and resolve complaints regarding food quality, service, or accommodations. Schedule and receive food and beverage deliveries, checking delivery contents to verify product quality and quantity. Monitor food preparation methods, portion sizes, and garnishing and presentation of food to ensure that food is prepared and presented in an acceptable manner. Monitor budgets and payroll records and review financial transactions to ensure that expenditures are authorized and budgeted. Monitor compliance with health and fire regulations regarding food preparation and serving and building maintenance in lodging and dining facilities. Schedule staff hours and assign duties. Coordinate assignments of cooking personnel to ensure economical use of food and timely preparation. Keep records required by government agencies regarding sanitation and food subsidies when appropriate. Establish standards for personnel performance and customer service. Estimate food, liquor, wine, and other beverage consumption to anticipate amounts to be purchased or requisitioned. Review work procedures and operational problems to determine ways to improve service, performance, or safety. Perform some food preparation or service tasks such as cooking, clearing tables, and serving food and drinks when necessary. Maintain food and equipment inventories and keep inventory records. Organize and direct worker training programs, resolve personnel problems, hire new staff, and evaluate employee performance in dining and lodging facilities. Order and purchase equipment and supplies. Review menus and analyze recipes to determine labor and overhead costs and assign prices to menu items. Record the number, type, and cost of items sold to determine which items may be unpopular or less profitable. Assess staffing needs and recruit staff, using methods such as newspaper advertisements or attendance at job fairs. Arrange for equipment maintenance and repairs and coordinate a variety of services such as waste removal and pest control.

SKILLS—Most Important: Management Skills; Quality Control Skills; Social Skills. **Other Above-Average Skills:** Communication Skills; Thought-Processing Skills.

GOE—Interest Area: 09. Hospitality, Tourism, and Recreation. **Work Group:** 09.01. Managerial Work in Hospitality and Tourism. **Other Jobs in This Group:** First-Line Supervisors/Managers of Food Preparation and Serving Workers; First-Line Supervisors/Managers of Personal Service Workers; Gaming Managers; Gaming Supervisors; Lodging Managers. **PERSONALITY TYPE:** Enterprising. Enterprising occupations frequently involve starting up and carrying out projects. These occupations can involve leading people and making many decisions. They sometimes require risk taking and often deal with business.

EDUCATION/TRAINING PROGRAM(S)—Restaurant, Culinary, and Catering Management/Manager; Hospitality Administration/Management, General; Hotel/Motel Administration/Management; Restaurant/Food Services Management. **RELATED KNOWLEDGE/COURSES—Food Production:** Techniques and equipment for planting, growing, and harvesting food products (both plant and animal) for consumption, including storage/handling techniques. **Sales and Marketing:** Principles and methods for showing, promoting, and selling products or services. This includes marketing strategy and tactics, product demonstration, sales techniques, and sales control systems. **Production and Processing:** Raw materials, production processes, quality control, costs, and other techniques for maximizing the effective manufacture and distribution of goods. **Customer and Personal Service:** Principles and processes for providing customer and personal services. This includes customer needs assessment, meeting of quality standards for services, and evaluation of customer satisfaction. **Administration and Management:**

Business and management principles involved in strategic planning, resource allocation, human resources modeling, leadership technique, production methods, and coordination of people and resources. **Personnel and Human Resources:** Principles and procedures for personnel recruitment, selection, training, compensation and benefits, labor relations and negotiation, and personnel information systems.

Foreign Language and Literature Teachers, Postsecondary

- Education/Training Required: Master's degree
- Annual Earnings: $49,570
- Growth: 32.2%
- Annual Job Openings: 329,000
- Self-Employed: 0.4%
- Part-Time: 27.3%

The job openings listed here are shared with 35 other postsecondary teaching occupations. For a complete list, see the beginning of this section.

Teach courses in foreign (i.e., other than English) languages and literature. Evaluate and grade students' classwork, assignments, and papers. Prepare course materials such as syllabi, homework assignments, and handouts. Initiate, facilitate, and moderate classroom discussions. Maintain student attendance records, grades, and other required records. Compile, administer, and grade examinations or assign this work to others. Plan, evaluate, and revise curricula, course content, and course materials and methods of instruction. Prepare and deliver lectures to undergraduate and graduate students on topics such as how to speak and write a foreign language and the cultural aspects of areas where a particular language is used. Maintain regularly scheduled office hours to advise and assist students. Select and obtain materials and supplies such as textbooks. Keep abreast of developments in their field by reading current literature, talking with colleagues, and participating in professional organizations and activities. Advise students on academic and vocational curricula and on career issues. Conduct research in a particular field of knowledge and publish findings in scholarly journals, books, and/or electronic media. Collaborate with colleagues to address teaching and research issues. Serve on academic or administrative committees that deal with institutional policies, departmental matters, and academic issues. Participate in student recruitment, registration, and placement activities. Compile bibliographies of specialized materials for outside reading assignments. Participate in campus and community events. Act as advisers to student organizations. Perform administrative duties such as serving as department head. Supervise undergraduate and graduate teaching, internship, and research work. Write grant proposals to procure external research funding. Provide professional consulting services to government or industry.

SKILLS—Most Important: Communication Skills; Social Skills; Thought-Processing Skills. **Other Above-Average Skills:** Quality Control Skills; Management Skills.

GOE—Interest Area: 05. Education and Training. **Work Group:** 05.03. Postsecondary and Adult Teaching and Instructing. **Other Jobs in This Group:** Adult Literacy, Remedial Education, and GED Teachers and Instructors; Agricultural Sciences Teachers, Postsecondary; Anthropology and Archeology Teachers, Postsecondary; Architecture Teachers, Postsecondary; Area, Ethnic, and Cultural Studies Teachers, Postsecondary; Art, Drama, and Music Teachers, Postsecondary; Atmospheric, Earth, Marine, and Space Sciences Teachers, Postsecondary; Biological Science Teachers, Postsecondary; Business Teachers, Postsecondary; Chemistry Teachers, Postsecondary; Communications Teachers, Postsecondary; Computer Science Teachers, Postsecondary; Criminal Justice and Law Enforcement Teachers, Postsecondary; Economics Teachers, Postsecondary; Education Teachers, Postsecondary; Engineering Teachers, Postsecondary; English Language and Literature Teachers, Postsecondary; Environmental Science Teachers, Postsecondary; Farm and Home Management Advisors; Forestry and Conservation Science Teachers, Postsecondary; Geography Teachers, Postsecondary; Graduate Teaching Assistants; Health Specialties Teachers, Postsecondary; History Teachers, Postsecondary; Home Economics Teachers, Postsecondary; Law Teachers, Postsecondary; Library Science Teachers, Postsecondary; Mathematical Science Teachers, Postsecondary; Nursing Instructors and Teachers, Postsecondary; Philosophy and Religion

Teachers, Postsecondary; Physics Teachers, Postsecondary; Political Science Teachers, Postsecondary; Psychology Teachers, Postsecondary; Recreation and Fitness Studies Teachers, Postsecondary; Self-Enrichment Education Teachers; Social Work Teachers, Postsecondary; Sociology Teachers, Postsecondary; Vocational Education Teachers, Postsecondary. **PERSONALITY TYPE:** Artistic. Artistic occupations frequently involve working with forms, designs, and patterns. They often require self-expression, and the work can be done without following a clear set of rules.

EDUCATION/TRAINING PROGRAM(S)—Latin Teacher Education; Foreign Languages and Literatures, General; Linguistics; Language Interpretation and Translation; African Languages, Literatures, and Linguistics; East Asian Languages, Literatures, and Linguistics, General; Chinese Language and Literature; Japanese Language and Literature; Korean Language and Literature; Tibetan Language and Literature; others. **RELATED KNOWLEDGE/COURSES**—**Foreign Language:** The structure and content of a foreign (non-English) language, including the meaning and spelling of words, rules of composition and grammar, and pronunciation. **Philosophy and Theology:** Different philosophical systems and religions. This includes their basic principles, values, ethics, ways of thinking, customs, practices, and impact on human culture. **History and Archeology:** Historical events and their causes, indicators, and effects on civilizations and cultures. **Sociology and Anthropology:** Group behavior and dynamics, societal trends and influences, human migrations, ethnicity, and cultures and their history and origins. **English Language:** The structure and content of the English language, including the meaning and spelling of words, rules of composition, and grammar. **Geography:** Principles and methods for describing the features of land, sea, and air masses, including their physical characteristics; locations; interrelationships; and distribution of plant, animal, and human life.

Forensic Science Technicians

- Education/Training Required: Associate degree
- Annual Earnings: $44,590
- Growth: 36.4%
- Annual Job Openings: 2,000
- Self-Employed: 1.5%
- Part-Time: 22.7%

Collect, identify, classify, and analyze physical evidence related to criminal investigations. Perform tests on weapons or substances such as fiber, hair, and tissue to determine significance to investigation. May testify as expert witnesses on evidence or crime laboratory techniques. May serve as specialists in area of expertise, such as ballistics, fingerprinting, handwriting, or biochemistry. Testify in court about investigative and analytical methods and findings. Keep records and prepare reports detailing findings, investigative methods, and laboratory techniques. Interpret laboratory findings and test results to identify and classify substances, materials, and other evidence collected at crime scenes. Operate and maintain laboratory equipment and apparatus. Prepare solutions, reagents, and sample formulations needed for laboratory work. Analyze and classify biological fluids, using DNA typing or serological techniques. Collect evidence from crime scenes, storing it in conditions that preserve its integrity. Identify and quantify drugs and poisons found in biological fluids and tissues, in foods, and at crime scenes. Analyze handwritten and machine-produced textual evidence to decipher altered or obliterated text or to determine authorship, age, or source. Reconstruct crime scenes to determine relationships among pieces of evidence. Examine DNA samples to determine if they match other samples. Collect impressions of dust from surfaces to obtain and identify fingerprints. Analyze gunshot residue and bullet paths to determine how shootings occurred. Visit morgues, examine scenes of crimes, or contact other sources to obtain evidence or information to be used in investigations. Examine physical evidence such as hair, fiber, wood, or soil residues to obtain information about its source and composition. Determine types of bullets used in shooting and whether they were fired from a specific weapon. Examine firearms to determine mechanical condition and legal status, performing restoration work on damaged firearms to obtain information such as serial numbers. Confer with ballistics, fingerprinting, handwriting, document, electronics, medical, chemical, or metallurgical experts concerning evidence and its interpretation. Interpret the pharmacological effects of a drug or a combination of drugs on an individual. Compare objects such as tools with impression marks to determine whether a specific object is responsible for a specific mark.

SKILLS—Most Important: Science Skills; Quality Control Skills; Communication Skills. **Other Above-Average Skills:** Equipment Use/Maintenance Skills; Thought-Processing Skills; Social Skills; Management Skills.

GOE—Interest Area: 12. Law and Public Safety. **Work Group:** 12.04. Law Enforcement and Public Safety. **Other Jobs in This Group:** Bailiffs; Correctional Officers and Jailers; Criminal Investigators and Special Agents; Detectives and Criminal Investigators; Fire Investigators; Parking Enforcement Workers; Police and Sheriff's Patrol Officers; Police Detectives; Police Identification and Records Officers; Police Patrol Officers; Sheriffs and Deputy Sheriffs; Transit and Railroad Police. **PERSONALITY TYPE:** Investigative. Investigative occupations frequently involve working with ideas and require an extensive amount of thinking. These occupations can involve searching for facts and figuring out problems mentally.

EDUCATION/TRAINING PROGRAM(S)—Forensic Science and Technology. **RELATED KNOWLEDGE/COURSES—Chemistry:** The chemical composition, structure, and properties of substances and of the chemical processes and transformations that they undergo. This includes uses of chemicals and their danger signs, production techniques, and disposal methods. **Law and Government:** Laws, legal codes, court procedures, precedents, government regulations, executive orders, agency rules, and the democratic political process. **Biology:** Plant and animal organisms and their tissues, cells, functions, interdependencies, and interactions with each other and the environment. **Public Safety and Security:** Relevant equipment, policies, procedures, and strategies to promote effective local, state, or national security operations for the protection of people, data, property, and institutions. **Customer and**

Personal Service: Principles and processes for providing customer and personal services. This includes customer needs assessment, meeting of quality standards for services, and evaluation of customer satisfaction. **English Language:** The structure and content of the English language, including the meaning and spelling of words, rules of composition, and grammar.

Forest Fire Fighters

- Education/Training Required: Long-term on-the-job training
- Annual Earnings: $39,090
- Growth: 24.3%
- Annual Job Openings: 21,000
- Self-Employed: 0.1%
- Part-Time: 1.5%

The job openings listed here are shared with Municipal Fire Fighters.

Control and suppress fires in forests or vacant public land. Maintain contact with fire dispatchers at all times to notify them of the need for additional firefighters and supplies or to detail any difficulties encountered. Rescue fire victims and administer emergency medical aid. Collaborate with other firefighters as a member of a firefighting crew. Patrol burned areas after fires to locate and eliminate hot spots that may restart fires. Extinguish flames and embers to suppress fires, using shovels or engine- or hand-driven water or chemical pumps. Fell trees, cut and clear brush, and dig trenches to create firelines, using axes, chainsaws, or shovels. Maintain knowledge of current firefighting practices by participating in drills and by attending seminars, conventions, and conferences. Operate pumps connected to high-pressure hoses. Participate in physical training to maintain high levels of physical fitness. Establish water supplies, connect hoses, and direct water onto fires. Maintain fire equipment and firehouse living quarters. Inform and educate the public about fire prevention. Take action to contain any hazardous chemicals that could catch fire, leak, or spill. Organize fire caches, positioning equipment for the most effective response. Transport personnel and cargo to and from fire areas. Participate in fire prevention and inspection programs. Perform forest maintenance and improvement tasks such as cutting brush, planting trees, building trails, and marking timber. Test and maintain tools, equipment, jump gear, and parachutes to ensure readiness for fire-suppression activities. Observe forest areas from fire lookout towers to spot potential problems. Orient self in relation to fire, using compass and map, and collect supplies and equipment dropped by parachute. Serve as fully trained lead helicopter crewmember and as helispot manager. Drop weighted paper streamers from aircraft to determine the speed and direction of the wind at fire sites.

SKILLS—Most Important: Equipment Use/Maintenance Skills; Management Skills; Equipment/Technology Analysis Skills. **Other Above-Average Skills:** Science Skills; Social Skills; Mathematics Skills; Communication Skills.

GOE—Interest Area: 12. Law and Public Safety. **Work Group:** 12.06. Emergency Responding. **Other Jobs in This Group:** Emergency Medical Technicians and Paramedics; Fire Fighters; Municipal Fire Fighters. **PERSONALITY TYPE:** Realistic. Realistic occupations frequently involve work activities that include practical, hands-on problems and solutions. They often deal with plants, animals, and real-world materials like wood, tools, and machinery. Many of the occupations require working outside and do not involve a lot of paperwork or working closely with others.

EDUCATION/TRAINING PROGRAM(S)—Fire Science/Firefighting; Fire Protection, Other. **RELATED KNOWLEDGE/COURSES—Geography:** Principles and methods for describing the features of land, sea, and air masses, including their physical characteristics; locations; interrelationships; and distribution of plant, animal, and human life. **Customer and Personal Service:** Principles and processes for providing customer and personal services. This includes customer needs assessment, meeting of quality standards for services, and evaluation of customer satisfaction. **Mechanical Devices:** Machines and tools, including their designs, uses, repair, and maintenance. **Education and Training:** Principles and methods for curriculum and training design, teaching and instruction for individuals and groups, and the measurement of training effects. **Public Safety and Security:** Relevant equipment, policies, procedures, and strategies to promote effective local, state, or national security operations for the protection of people, data, property, and institutions. **Psychology:**

Human behavior and performance; individual differences in ability, personality, and interests; learning and motivation; psychological research methods; and the assessment and treatment of behavioral and affective disorders.

Forest Fire Fighting and Prevention Supervisors

- Education/Training Required: Work experience in a related occupation
- Annual Earnings: $60,840
- Growth: 21.1%
- Annual Job Openings: 4,000
- Self-Employed: 0.0%
- Part-Time: 0.4%

Supervise fire fighters who control and suppress fires in forests or vacant public land. Communicate fire details to superiors, subordinates, and interagency dispatch centers, using two-way radios. Serve as working leader of an engine, hand, helicopter, or prescribed fire crew of three or more firefighters. Maintain fire suppression equipment in good condition, checking equipment periodically to ensure that it is ready for use. Evaluate size, location, and condition of forest fires in order to request and dispatch crews and position equipment so fires can be contained safely and effectively. Operate wildland fire engines and hoselays. Direct and supervise prescribed burn projects and prepare post-burn reports analyzing burn conditions and results. Monitor prescribed burns to ensure that they are conducted safely and effectively. Identify staff training and development needs to ensure that appropriate training can be arranged. Maintain knowledge of forest fire laws and fire prevention techniques and tactics. Recommend equipment modifications or new equipment purchases. Perform administrative duties such as compiling and maintaining records, completing forms, preparing reports, and composing correspondence. Recruit and hire forest fire-fighting personnel. Train workers in such skills as parachute jumping, fire suppression, aerial observation, and radio communication, both in the classroom and on the job. Review and evaluate employee performance. Observe fires and crews from air to determine fire-fighting force requirements and to note changing conditions that will affect fire-fighting efforts. Inspect all stations, uniforms, equipment, and recreation areas to ensure compliance with safety standards, taking corrective action as necessary. Schedule employee work assignments and set work priorities. Regulate open burning by issuing burning permits, inspecting problem sites, issuing citations for violations of laws and ordinances, and educating the public in proper burning practices. Direct investigations of suspected arsons in wildfires, working closely with other investigating agencies. Monitor fire suppression expenditures to ensure that they are necessary and reasonable.

SKILLS—Most Important: Equipment Use/Maintenance Skills; Science Skills; Management Skills. **Other Above-Average Skills:** Equipment/Technology Analysis Skills; Social Skills; Communication Skills; Mathematics Skills.

GOE—Interest Area: 12. Law and Public Safety. **Work Group:** 12.01. Managerial Work in Law and Public Safety. **Other Jobs in This Group:** Emergency Management Specialists; First-Line Supervisors/Managers of Correctional Officers; First-Line Supervisors/Managers of Fire Fighting and Prevention Workers; First-Line Supervisors/Managers of Police and Detectives; Municipal Fire Fighting and Prevention Supervisors. **PERSONALITY TYPE:** Realistic. Realistic occupations frequently involve work activities that include practical, hands-on problems and solutions. They often deal with plants, animals, and real-world materials like wood, tools, and machinery. Many of the occupations require working outside and do not involve a lot of paperwork or working closely with others.

EDUCATION/TRAINING PROGRAM(S)—Fire Protection and Safety Technology/Technician; Fire Services Administration. **RELATED KNOWLEDGE/COURSES—Public Safety and Security:** Relevant equipment, policies, procedures, and strategies to promote effective local, state, or national security operations for the protection of people, data, property, and institutions. **Customer and Personal Service:** Principles and processes for providing customer and personal services. This includes customer needs assessment, meeting of quality standards for services, and evaluation of customer satisfaction. **Building and Construction:** The materials, methods, and tools involved in the construction or repair of houses, buildings, or other structures such as highways and roads.

Personnel and Human Resources: Principles and procedures for personnel recruitment, selection, training, compensation and benefits, labor relations and negotiation, and personnel information systems. **Mechanical Devices:** Machines and tools, including their designs, uses, repair, and maintenance. **Transportation:** Principles and methods for moving people or goods by air, rail, sea, or road, including the relative costs and benefits.

Foresters

- Education/Training Required: Bachelor's degree
- Annual Earnings: $48,670
- Growth: 6.7%
- Annual Job Openings: 1,000
- Self-Employed: 9.1%
- Part-Time: 6.7%

Manage forested lands for economic, recreational, and conservation purposes. May inventory the type, amount, and location of standing timber; appraise the timber's worth; negotiate the purchase; and draw up contracts for procurement. May determine how to conserve wildlife habitats, creek beds, water quality, and soil stability and how best to comply with environmental regulations. May devise plans for planting and growing new trees, monitor trees for healthy growth, and determine the best time for harvesting. Develop forest management plans for public and privately-owned forested lands. Monitor contract compliance and results of forestry activities to assure adherence to government regulations. Establish short- and long-term plans for management of forest lands and forest resources. Supervise activities of other forestry workers. Choose and prepare sites for new trees, using controlled burning, bulldozers, or herbicides to clear weeds, brush, and logging debris. Plan and supervise forestry projects, such as determining the type, number, and placement of trees to be planted; managing tree nurseries; thinning forest; and monitoring growth of new seedlings. Negotiate terms and conditions of agreements and contracts for forest harvesting, forest management, and leasing of forest lands. Direct and participate in forest-fire suppression. Determine methods of cutting and removing timber with minimum waste and environmental damage. Analyze effect of forest conditions on tree growth rates and tree species prevalence and the yield, duration, seed production, growth viability, and germination of different species. Monitor forest-cleared lands to ensure that they are reclaimed to their most suitable end use. Plan and implement projects for conservation of wildlife habitats and soil and water quality. Plan and direct forest surveys and related studies and prepare reports and recommendations. Perform inspections of forests or forest nurseries. Map forest area soils and vegetation to estimate the amount of standing timber and future value and growth. Conduct public educational programs on forest care and conservation. Procure timber from private landowners. Subcontract with loggers or pulpwood cutters for tree removal and to aid in road layout. Plan cutting programs and manage timber sales from harvested areas, helping companies to achieve production goals. Monitor wildlife populations and assess the impacts of forest operations on population and habitats. Plan and direct construction and maintenance of recreation facilities, fire towers, trails, roads, and bridges, ensuring that they comply with guidelines and regulations set for forested public lands. Contact local forest owners and gain permission to take inventory of the type, amount, and location of all standing timber on the property.

SKILLS—Most Important: Science Skills; Computer Programming Skills; Quality Control Skills. **Other Above-Average Skills:** Mathematics Skills; Management Skills; Thought-Processing Skills; Communication Skills; Equipment Use/Maintenance Skills.

GOE—Interest Area: 01. Agriculture and Natural Resources. **Work Group:** 01.02. Resource Science/Engineering for Plants, Animals, and the Environment. **Other Jobs in This Group:** Agricultural Engineers; Animal Scientists; Conservation Scientists; Environmental Engineers; Mining and Geological Engineers, Including Mining Safety Engineers; Petroleum Engineers; Range Managers; Soil and Plant Scientists; Soil and Water Conservationists; Zoologists and Wildlife Biologists. **PERSONALITY TYPE:** Realistic. Realistic occupations frequently involve work activities that include practical, hands-on problems and solutions. They often deal with plants, animals, and real-world materials like wood, tools, and machinery. Many of the occupations require working outside and do not involve a lot of paperwork or working closely with others.

EDUCATION/TRAINING PROGRAM(S)—Natural Resources/Conservation, General; Natural Resources Management and Policy; Natural Resources Management and Policy, Other; Forestry, General; Forest Sciences and Biology; Forest Management/Forest Resources Management; Urban Forestry; Wood Science and Wood Products/Pulp and Paper Technology; Forest Resources Production and Management; Forestry, Other; Natural Resources and Conservation, Other. **RELATED KNOWLEDGE/COURSES—Biology:** Plant and animal organisms and their tissues, cells, functions, interdependencies, and interactions with each other and the environment. **Geography:** Principles and methods for describing the features of land, sea, and air masses, including their physical characteristics; locations; interrelationships; and distribution of plant, animal, and human life. **Mathematics:** Arithmetic, algebra, geometry, calculus, and statistics and their applications. **Law and Government:** Laws, legal codes, court procedures, precedents, government regulations, executive orders, agency rules, and the democratic political process. **Administration and Management:** Business and management principles involved in strategic planning, resource allocation, human resources modeling, leadership technique, production methods, and coordination of people and resources. **Computers and Electronics:** Circuit boards; processors; chips; electronic equipment; and computer hardware and software, including applications and programming.

Forestry and Conservation Science Teachers, Postsecondary

- Education/Training Required: Master's degree
- Annual Earnings: $64,870
- Growth: 32.2%
- Annual Job Openings: 329,000
- Self-Employed: 0.4%
- Part-Time: 27.3%

The job openings listed here are shared with 35 other postsecondary teaching occupations. For a complete list, see the beginning of this section.

Teach courses in environmental and conservation science. Conduct research in a particular field of knowledge and publish findings in books, professional journals, and/or electronic media. Keep abreast of developments in their field by reading current literature, talking with colleagues, and participating in professional conferences. Prepare and deliver lectures to undergraduate and/or graduate students on topics such as forest resource policy, forest pathology, and mapping. Evaluate and grade students' classwork, assignments, and papers. Write grant proposals to procure external research funding. Supervise undergraduate and/or graduate teaching, internship, and research work. Plan, evaluate, and revise curricula, course content, and course materials and methods of instruction. Prepare course materials such as syllabi, homework assignments, and handouts. Compile, administer, and grade examinations or assign this work to others. Advise students on academic and vocational curricula and on career issues. Initiate, facilitate, and moderate classroom discussions. Supervise students' laboratory work and fieldwork. Maintain student attendance records, grades, and other required records. Collaborate with colleagues to address teaching and research issues. Maintain regularly scheduled office hours in order to advise and assist students. Select and obtain materials and supplies such as textbooks and laboratory equipment. Participate in student recruitment, registration, and placement activities. Serve on academic or administrative committees that deal with institutional policies, departmental matters, and academic issues. Provide professional consulting services to government and/or industry. Perform administrative duties such as serving as department head. Compile bibliographies of specialized materials for outside reading assignments. Act as advisers to student organizations. Participate in campus and community events.

SKILLS—Most Important: Science Skills; Management Skills; Mathematics Skills. **Other Above-Average Skills:** Thought-Processing Skills; Communication Skills; Equipment/Technology Analysis Skills; Quality Control Skills.

GOE—Interest Area: 05. Education and Training. **Work Group:** 05.03. Postsecondary and Adult Teaching and Instructing. **Other Jobs in This Group:** Adult Literacy, Remedial Education, and GED Teachers and Instructors; Agricultural Sciences Teachers, Postsecondary; Anthropology and Archeology Teachers, Postsecondary; Architecture Teachers, Postsecondary; Area, Ethnic, and Cultural Studies Teachers, Postsecondary; Art, Drama, and Music Teachers, Postsecondary; Atmospheric, Earth, Marine, and Space Sciences Teachers, Postsecondary; Biological Science Teachers, Postsecondary; Business Teachers, Postsecondary; Chemistry Teachers, Postsecondary; Communications Teachers, Postsecondary; Computer Science Teachers, Postsecondary; Criminal Justice and Law Enforcement Teachers, Postsecondary; Economics Teachers, Postsecondary; Education Teachers, Postsecondary; Engineering Teachers, Postsecondary; English Language and Literature Teachers, Postsecondary; Environmental Science Teachers, Postsecondary; Farm and Home Management Advisors; Foreign Language and Literature Teachers, Postsecondary; Geography Teachers, Postsecondary; Graduate Teaching Assistants; Health Specialties Teachers, Postsecondary; History Teachers, Postsecondary; Home Economics Teachers, Postsecondary; Law Teachers, Postsecondary; Library Science Teachers, Postsecondary; Mathematical Science Teachers, Postsecondary; Nursing Instructors and Teachers, Postsecondary; Philosophy and Religion Teachers, Postsecondary; Physics Teachers, Postsecondary; Political Science Teachers, Postsecondary; Psychology Teachers, Postsecondary; Recreation and Fitness Studies Teachers, Postsecondary; Self-Enrichment Education Teachers; Social Work Teachers, Postsecondary; Sociology Teachers, Postsecondary; Vocational Education Teachers, Postsecondary. **PERSONALITY TYPE:** Investigative. Investigative occupations frequently involve working with ideas and require an extensive amount of thinking. These occupations can involve searching for facts and figuring out problems mentally.

EDUCATION/TRAINING PROGRAM(S)—Science Teacher Education/General Science Teacher Education. **RELATED KNOWLEDGE/COURSES—Biology:** Plant and animal organisms and their tissues, cells, functions, interdependencies, and interactions with each other and the environment. **Geography:** Principles and methods for describing the features of land, sea, and air masses, including their physical characteristics; locations; interrelationships; and distribution of plant, animal, and human life. **Education and Training:** Principles and methods for curriculum and training design, teaching and instruction for individuals and groups, and the measurement of training effects. **Mathematics:** Arithmetic, algebra, geometry, calculus, and statistics and their applications. **English Language:**

The structure and content of the English language, including the meaning and spelling of words, rules of composition, and grammar. **Chemistry:** The chemical composition, structure, and properties of substances and of the chemical processes and transformations that they undergo. This includes uses of chemicals and their danger signs, production techniques, and disposal methods.

Forging Machine Setters, Operators, and Tenders, Metal and Plastic

- ◎ Education/Training Required: Moderate-term on-the-job training
- ◎ Annual Earnings: $28,970
- ◎ Growth: –4.6%
- ◎ Annual Job Openings: 4,000
- ◎ Self-Employed: 0.7%
- ◎ Part-Time: No data available

Set up, operate, or tend forging machines to taper, shape, or form metal or plastic parts. Measure and inspect machined parts to ensure conformance to product specifications. Read work orders or blueprints to determine specified tolerances and sequences of operations for machine setup. Start machines to produce sample workpieces and observe operations to detect machine malfunctions and to verify that machine setups conform to specifications. Remove dies from machines when production runs are finished. Turn handles or knobs to set pressures and depths of ram strokes and to synchronize machine operations. Confer with other workers about machine setups and operational specifications. Repair, maintain, and replace parts on dies. Set up, operate, or tend presses and forging machines to perform hot or cold forging by flattening, straightening, bending, cutting, piercing, or other operations to taper, shape, or form metal. Position and move metal wires or workpieces through a series of dies that compress and shape stock to form die impressions. Install, adjust, and remove dies, synchronizing cams, forging hammers, and stop guides, by using overhead cranes or other hoisting devices and hand tools. Select, align, and bolt positioning fixtures, stops, and specified dies to rams and anvils, forging rolls, or presses and hammers. Trim and compress finished forgings to specified tolerances. Sharpen cutting tools and drill bits, using bench grinders.

SKILLS—Most Important: Quality Control Skills; Computer Programming Skills; Equipment Use/Maintenance Skills. **Other Above-Average Skills:** Equipment/Technology Analysis Skills; Thought-Processing Skills.

GOE—Interest Area: 13. Manufacturing. **Work Group:** 13.02. Machine Setup and Operation. **Other Jobs in This Group:** Crushing, Grinding, and Polishing Machine Setters, Operators, and Tenders; Cutting, Punching, and Press Machine Setters, Operators, and Tenders, Metal and Plastic; Drilling and Boring Machine Tool Setters, Operators, and Tenders, Metal and Plastic; Extruding and Drawing Machine Setters, Operators, and Tenders, Metal and Plastic; Grinding, Lapping, Polishing, and Buffing Machine Tool Setters, Operators, and Tenders, Metal and Plastic; Lathe and Turning Machine Tool Setters, Operators, and Tenders, Metal and Plastic; Milling and Planing Machine Setters, Operators, and Tenders, Metal and Plastic; Multiple Machine Tool Setters, Operators, and Tenders, Metal and Plastic; Paper Goods Machine Setters, Operators, and Tenders; Rolling Machine Setters, Operators, and Tenders, Metal and Plastic; Textile Cutting Machine Setters, Operators, and Tenders; Textile Knitting and Weaving Machine Setters, Operators, and Tenders; Textile Winding, Twisting, and Drawing Out Machine Setters, Operators, and Tenders. **PERSONALITY TYPE:** Realistic. Realistic occupations frequently involve work activities that include practical, hands-on problems and solutions. They often deal with plants, animals, and real-world materials like wood, tools, and machinery. Many of the occupations require working outside and do not involve a lot of paperwork or working closely with others.

EDUCATION/TRAINING PROGRAM(S)—Machine Tool Technology/Machinist. **RELATED KNOWLEDGE/COURSES—Mechanical Devices:** Machines and tools, including their designs, uses, repair, and maintenance. **Production and Processing:** Raw materials, production processes, quality control, costs, and other techniques for maximizing the effective manufacture and distribution of goods. **Design:** Design techniques, tools, and principles involved in production of precision technical plans, blueprints, drawings, and models. **Mathematics:** Arithmetic, algebra, geometry, calculus, and statistics and their applications. **Public Safety and Security**: Relevant equipment, policies, procedures, and strategies to promote effective local, state, or national security operations for the protection of people, data, property, and institutions.

Gaming Managers

- ◎ Education/Training Required: Work experience in a related occupation
- ◎ Annual Earnings: $59,940
- ◎ Growth: 22.6%
- ◎ Annual Job Openings: 1,000
- ◎ Self-Employed: 4.0%
- ◎ Part-Time: 5.6%

Plan, organize, direct, control, or coordinate gaming operations in a casino. Formulate gaming policies for their area of responsibility. Resolve customer complaints regarding problems such as payout errors. Remove suspected cheaters, such as card counters and other players who may have systems that shift the odds of winning to their favor. Maintain familiarity with all games used at a facility, as well as strategies and tricks employed in those games. Train new workers and evaluate their performance. Circulate among gaming tables to ensure that operations are conducted properly, that dealers follow house rules, and that players are not cheating. Explain and interpret house rules, such as game rules and betting limits. Monitor staffing levels to ensure that games and tables are adequately staffed for each shift, arranging for staff rotations and breaks and locating substitute employees as necessary. Interview and hire workers. Prepare work schedules and station assignments and keep attendance records. Direct the distribution of complimentary hotel rooms, meals, and other discounts or free items given to players based on their length of play and betting totals. Establish policies on issues such as the type of gambling offered and the odds, the extension of credit, and the serving of food and beverages. Track supplies of money to tables and perform any required paperwork. Set and maintain a bank and table limit for each game. Monitor credit extended to players. Review operational expenses, budg-

et estimates, betting accounts, and collection reports for accuracy. Record, collect, and pay off bets, issuing receipts as necessary. Direct workers compiling summary sheets that show wager amounts and payoffs for races and events. Notify board attendants of table vacancies so that waiting patrons can play.

SKILLS—Most Important: Management Skills; Social Skills; Mathematics Skills. **Other Above-Average Skills:** Thought-Processing Skills; Quality Control Skills.

GOE—Interest Area: 09. Hospitality, Tourism, and Recreation. **Work Group:** 09.01. Managerial Work in Hospitality and Tourism. **Other Jobs in This Group:** First-Line Supervisors/Managers of Food Preparation and Serving Workers; First-Line Supervisors/Managers of Personal Service Workers; Food Service Managers; Gaming Supervisors; Lodging Managers. **PERSONALITY TYPE:** Enterprising. Enterprising occupations frequently involve starting up and carrying out projects. These occupations can involve leading people and making many decisions. They sometimes require risk taking and often deal with business.

EDUCATION/TRAINING PROGRAM(S)—Personal and Culinary Services, Other. **RELATED KNOWLEDGE/COURSES—Customer and Personal Service:** Principles and processes for providing customer and personal services. This includes customer needs assessment, meeting of quality standards for services, and evaluation of customer satisfaction. **Sales and Marketing:** Principles and methods for showing, promoting, and selling products or services. This includes marketing strategy and tactics, product demonstration, sales techniques, and sales control systems. **Personnel and Human Resources:** Principles and procedures for personnel recruitment, selection, training, compensation and benefits, labor relations and negotiation, and personnel information systems. **Administration and Management:** Business and management principles involved in strategic planning, resource allocation, human resources modeling, leadership technique, production methods, and coordination of people and resources. **Economics and Accounting:** Economic and accounting principles and practices, the financial markets, banking, and the analysis and reporting of financial data. **Mathematics:** Arithmetic, algebra, geometry, calculus, and statistics and their applications.

Gaming Supervisors

- Education/Training Required: Work experience in a related occupation
- Annual Earnings: $40,300
- Growth: 16.3%
- Annual Job Openings: 8,000
- Self-Employed: 29.6%
- Part-Time: 15.0%

Supervise gaming operations and personnel in an assigned area. Circulate among tables and observe operations. Ensure that stations and games are covered for each shift. May explain and interpret operating rules of house to patrons. May plan and organize activities and create friendly atmosphere for guests in hotels/casinos. May adjust service complaints. Monitor game operations to ensure that house rules are followed, that tribal, state, and federal regulations are adhered to, and that employees provide prompt and courteous service. Observe gamblers' behavior for signs of cheating such as marking, switching, or counting cards; notify security staff of suspected cheating. Maintain familiarity with the games at a facility and with strategies and tricks used by cheaters at such games. Perform paperwork required for monetary transactions. Resolve customer and employee complaints. Greet customers and ask about the quality of service they are receiving. Establish and maintain banks and table limits for each game. Report customer-related incidents occurring in gaming areas to supervisors. Monitor stations and games and move dealers from game to game to ensure adequate staffing. Explain and interpret house rules, such as game rules and betting limits, for patrons. Supervise the distribution of complimentary meals, hotel rooms, discounts, and other items given to players based on length of play and amount bet. Evaluate workers' performance and prepare written performance evaluations. Monitor patrons for signs of compulsive gambling, offering assistance if necessary. Record, issue receipts for, and pay off bets. Monitor and verify the counting, wrapping, weighing, and distribution of currency and coins. Direct workers compiling summary sheets for each race or event to record amounts wagered and amounts to be paid to winners. Determine how many gaming tables to open each day and schedule staff accordingly. Establish policies on types of gambling offered, odds, and extension of credit. Interview, hire, and train workers. Provide fire protection and first-aid assistance when necessary. Review operational expenses, budget estimates, betting accounts, and collection reports for accuracy.

SKILLS—Most Important: Social Skills; Mathematics Skills; Thought-Processing Skills. **Other Above-Average Skills:** Management Skills; Communication Skills.

GOE—Interest Area: 09. Hospitality, Tourism, and Recreation. **Work Group:** 09.01. Managerial Work in Hospitality and Tourism. **Other Jobs in This Group:** First-Line Supervisors/Managers of Food Preparation and Serving Workers; First-Line Supervisors/Managers of Personal Service Workers; Food Service Managers; Gaming Managers; Lodging Managers. **PERSONALITY TYPE:** Enterprising. Enterprising occupations frequently involve starting up and carrying out projects. These occupations can involve leading people and making many decisions. They sometimes require risk taking and often deal with business.

EDUCATION/TRAINING PROGRAM(S)—Personal and Culinary Services, Other. **RELATED KNOWLEDGE/COURSES—Customer and Personal Service:** Principles and processes for providing customer and personal services. This includes customer needs assessment, meeting of quality standards for services, and evaluation of customer satisfaction. **Psychology:** Human behavior and performance; individual differences in ability, personality, and interests; learning and motivation; psychological research methods; and the assessment and treatment of behavioral and affective disorders. **Education and Training:** Principles and methods for curriculum and training design, teaching and instruction for individuals and groups, and the measurement of training effects. **Sales and Marketing:** Principles and methods for showing, promoting, and selling products or services. This includes marketing strategy and tactics, product demonstration, sales techniques, and sales control systems. **Personnel and Human Resources:** Principles and procedures for personnel recruitment, selection, training, compensation and benefits, labor relations and negotiation, and personnel information systems. **Mathematics:** Arithmetic, algebra, geometry, calculus, and statistics and their applications.

General and Operations Managers

- Education/Training Required: Work experience plus degree
- Annual Earnings: $81,480
- Growth: 17.0%
- Annual Job Openings: 208,000
- Self-Employed: 0.6%
- Part-Time: 3.4%

Plan, direct, or coordinate the operations of companies or public and private sector organizations. Duties and responsibilities include formulating policies, managing daily operations, and planning the use of materials and human resources, but are too diverse and general in nature to be classified in any one functional area of management or administration, such as personnel, purchasing, or administrative services. Includes owners and managers who head small business establishments whose duties are primarily managerial. Direct and coordinate activities of businesses or departments concerned with the production, pricing, sales, or distribution of products. Manage staff, preparing work schedules and assigning specific duties. Review financial statements, sales and activity reports, and other performance data to measure productivity and goal achievement and to determine areas needing cost reduction and program improvement. Establish and implement departmental policies, goals, objectives, and procedures, conferring with board members, organization officials, and staff members as necessary. Determine staffing requirements and interview, hire, and train new employees or oversee those personnel processes. Monitor businesses and agencies to ensure that they efficiently and effectively provide needed services while staying within budgetary limits. Oversee activities directly related to making products or providing services. Direct and coordinate organization's financial and budget activities to fund operations, maximize investments, and increase efficiency. Determine goods and services to be sold and set prices and credit terms based on forecasts of customer demand. Manage the movement of goods into and out of production facilities. Locate, select, and procure merchandise for resale, representing management in purchase negotiations.

Perform sales floor work such as greeting and assisting customers, stocking shelves, and taking inventory. Develop and implement product marketing strategies including advertising campaigns and sales promotions. Plan and direct activities such as sales promotions, coordinating with other department heads as required. Direct non-merchandising departments of businesses, such as advertising and purchasing. Recommend locations for new facilities or oversee the remodeling of current facilities. Plan store layouts and design displays.

SKILLS—Most Important: Management Skills; Social Skills; Thought-Processing Skills. **Other Above-Average Skills:** Communication Skills; Mathematics Skills.

GOE—Interest Area: 04. Business and Administration. **Work Group:** 04.01. Managerial Work in General Business. **Other Jobs in This Group:** Chief Executives; Compensation and Benefits Managers; Human Resources Managers; Training and Development Managers. **PERSONALITY TYPE:** No data available.

EDUCATION/TRAINING PROGRAM(S)—Public Administration; Business/Commerce, General; Business Administration and Management, General; Entrepreneurship/Entrepreneurial Studies; International Business/Trade/Commerce. **RELATED KNOWLEDGE/ COURSES—Sales and Marketing:** Principles and methods for showing, promoting, and selling products or services. This includes marketing strategy and tactics, product demonstration, sales techniques, and sales control systems. **Administration and Management:** Business and management principles involved in strategic planning, resource allocation, human resources modeling, leadership technique, production methods, and coordination of people and resources. **Personnel and Human Resources:** Principles and procedures for personnel recruitment, selection, training, compensation and benefits, labor relations and negotiation, and personnel information systems. **Customer and Personal Service:** Principles and processes for providing customer and personal services. This includes customer needs assessment, meeting of quality standards for services, and evaluation of customer satisfaction. **Economics and Accounting:** Economic and accounting principles and practices, the financial markets, banking, and the analysis and reporting of financial data. **Law and Government:** Laws, legal codes, court procedures, precedents, government regulations, executive orders, agency rules, and the democratic political process.

Geographers

- Education/Training Required: Master's degree
- Annual Earnings: $63,550
- Growth: 6.8%
- Annual Job Openings: Fewer than 500
- Self-Employed: 4.2%
- Part-Time: 14.8%

Study nature and use of areas of earth's surface, relating and interpreting interactions of physical and cultural phenomena. Conduct research on physical aspects of a region, including land forms, climates, soils, plants, and animals, and conduct research on the spatial implications of human activities within a given area, including social characteristics, economic activities, and political organization, as well as researching interdependence between regions at scales ranging from local to global. Create and modify maps, graphs, or diagrams, using geographical information software and related equipment and principles of cartography such as coordinate systems, longitude, latitude, elevation, topography, and map scales. Write and present reports of research findings. Develop, operate, and maintain geographical information (GIS) computer systems, including hardware, software, plotters, digitizers, printers, and video cameras. Locate and obtain existing geographic information databases. Analyze geographic distributions of physical and cultural phenomena on local, regional, continental, or global scales. Teach geography. Gather and compile geographic data from sources including censuses, field observations, satellite imagery, aerial photographs, and existing maps. Conduct fieldwork at outdoor sites. Study the economic, political, and cultural characteristics of a specific region's population. Provide consulting services in fields including resource development and management, business location and market area analysis, environmental hazards, regional cultural history, and urban social planning. Collect data on physical characteristics of specified areas, such as geological formations, climates, and vegetation, using surveying or meteorological equipment. Provide geographical information systems support to the private and public sectors.

SKILLS—Most Important: Computer Programming Skills; Science Skills; Mathematics Skills. **Other Above-Average Skills:** Communication Skills; Thought-Processing Skills; Equipment/Technology Analysis Skills; Quality Control Skills.

GOE—Interest Area: 15. Scientific Research, Engineering, and Mathematics. **Work Group:** 15.02. Physical Sciences. **Other Jobs in This Group:** Astronomers; Atmospheric and Space Scientists; Chemists; Geoscientists, Except Hydrologists and Geographers; Hydrologists; Materials Scientists; Physicists. **PERSONALITY TYPE:** Investigative. Investigative occupations frequently involve working with ideas and require an extensive amount of thinking. These occupations can involve searching for facts and figuring out problems mentally.

EDUCATION/TRAINING PROGRAM(S)—Geography. **RELATED KNOWLEDGE/COURSES—Geography:** Principles and methods for describing the features of land, sea, and air masses, including their physical characteristics; locations; interrelationships; and distribution of plant, animal, and human life. **Sociology and Anthropology:** Group behavior and dynamics, societal trends and influences, human migrations, ethnicity, and cultures and their history and origins. **History and Archeology:** Historical events and their causes, indicators, and effects on civilizations and cultures. **Biology:** Plant and animal organisms and their tissues, cells, functions, interdependencies, and interactions with each other and the environment. **Education and Training:** Principles and methods for curriculum and training design, teaching and instruction for individuals and groups, and the measurement of training effects. **Philosophy and Theology:** Different philosophical systems and religions. This includes their basic principles, values, ethics, ways of thinking, customs, practices, and impact on human culture.

Geography Teachers, Postsecondary

- Education/Training Required: Master's degree
- Annual Earnings: $57,870
- Growth: 32.2%
- Annual Job Openings: 329,000
- Self-Employed: 0.4%
- Part-Time: 27.3%

The job openings listed here are shared with 35 other postsecondary teaching occupations. For a complete list, see the beginning of this section.

Teach courses in geography. Prepare and deliver lectures to undergraduate and/or graduate students on topics such as urbanization, environmental systems, and cultural geography. Evaluate and grade students' classwork, assignments, and papers. Compile, administer, and grade examinations or assign this work to others. Initiate, facilitate, and moderate classroom discussions. Maintain student attendance records, grades, and other required records. Prepare course materials such as syllabi, homework assignments, and handouts. Keep abreast of developments in their field by reading current literature, talking with colleagues, and participating in professional conferences. Supervise undergraduate and/or graduate teaching, internship, and research work. Plan, evaluate, and revise curricula, course content, and course materials and methods of instruction. Maintain regularly scheduled office hours to advise and assist students. Supervise students' laboratory work and fieldwork. Conduct research in a particular field of knowledge and publish findings in professional journals, books, and electronic media. Collaborate with colleagues to address teaching and research issues. Select and obtain materials and supplies such as textbooks. Advise students on academic and vocational curricula and on career issues. Serve on academic or administrative committees that deal with institutional policies, departmental matters, and academic issues. Participate in student recruitment, registration, and placement activities. Participate in campus and community events. Compile bibliographies of specialized materials for outside reading assignments. Perform administrative duties such as serving as department head. Write grant proposals to procure external research funding. Maintain geographic information systems laboratories, performing duties such as updating software. Perform spatial analysis and modeling, using geographic information system techniques. Act as advisers to student organizations. Provide professional consulting services to government and industry.

SKILLS—Most Important: Science Skills; Communication Skills; Thought-Processing Skills. **Other Above-Average Skills:** Social Skills; Mathematics Skills.

GOE—Interest Area: 05. Education and Training. **Work Group:** 05.03. Postsecondary and Adult Teaching and Instructing. **Other Jobs in This Group:** Adult Literacy, Remedial Education, and GED Teachers and Instructors; Agricultural Sciences Teachers, Postsecondary; Anthropology and Archeology Teachers, Postsecondary; Architecture Teachers, Postsecondary; Area, Ethnic, and Cultural Studies Teachers, Postsecondary; Art, Drama, and Music Teachers, Postsecondary; Atmospheric, Earth, Marine, and Space Sciences Teachers, Postsecondary; Biological Science Teachers, Postsecondary; Business Teachers, Postsecondary; Chemistry Teachers, Postsecondary; Communications Teachers, Postsecondary; Computer Science Teachers, Postsecondary; Criminal Justice and Law Enforcement Teachers, Postsecondary; Economics Teachers, Postsecondary; Education Teachers, Postsecondary; Engineering Teachers, Postsecondary; English Language and Literature Teachers, Postsecondary; Environmental Science Teachers, Postsecondary; Farm and Home Management Advisors; Foreign Language and Literature Teachers, Postsecondary; Forestry and Conservation Science Teachers, Postsecondary; Graduate Teaching Assistants; Health Specialties Teachers, Postsecondary; History Teachers, Postsecondary; Home Economics Teachers, Postsecondary; Law Teachers, Postsecondary; Library Science Teachers, Postsecondary; Mathematical Science Teachers, Postsecondary; Nursing Instructors and Teachers, Postsecondary; Philosophy and Religion Teachers, Postsecondary; Physics Teachers, Postsecondary; Political Science Teachers, Postsecondary; Psychology Teachers, Postsecondary; Recreation and Fitness Studies Teachers, Postsecondary; Self-Enrichment Education Teachers; Social Work Teachers, Postsecondary; Sociology Teachers, Postsecondary; Vocational Education Teachers, Postsecondary. **PERSONALITY TYPE:** No data available.

EDUCATION/TRAINING PROGRAM(S)—Geography Teacher Education; Geography. **RELATED KNOWLEDGE/COURSES—Geography:** Principles and methods for describing the features of land, sea, and air masses, including their physical characteristics; locations; interrelationships; and distribution of plant, animal, and human life. **Sociology and Anthropology:** Group behavior and dynamics, societal trends and influences, human migrations, ethnicity, and cultures and their history and origins. **History and Archeology:** Historical events and their causes, indicators, and effects on civilizations and cultures. **Philosophy and Theology:** Different philosophical systems and religions. This includes their basic principles, values, ethics, ways of thinking, customs, practices, and impact on human culture. **Education and Training:** Principles and methods for curriculum and training design, teaching and instruction for individuals and groups, and the measurement of training effects. **English Language:** The structure and content of the English language, including the meaning and spelling of words, rules of composition, and grammar.

Graduate Teaching Assistants

- Education/Training Required: Master's degree
- Annual Earnings: $27,340
- Growth: 32.2%
- Annual Job Openings: 329,000
- Self-Employed: 0.4%
- Part-Time: 27.3%

The job openings listed here are shared with 35 other postsecondary teaching occupations. For a complete list, see the beginning of this section.

Assist department chairperson, faculty members, or other professional staff members in college or university by performing teaching or teaching-related duties, such as teaching lower-level courses, developing teaching materials, preparing and giving examinations, and grading examinations or papers. Graduate assistants must be enrolled in a graduate school program. Graduate assistants who primarily perform non-teaching duties, such as laboratory research, should be reported in the occupational category related to the work performed. Lead discussion sections, tutorials, and laboratory sections. Evaluate and grade examinations, assignments, and papers and record grades. Return assignments to students in accordance with established deadlines. Schedule and maintain regular office hours to meet with students. Inform students of the procedures for completing and submitting class work such as lab reports. Prepare and proctor examinations. Notify instructors of errors or problems with assignments. Meet with supervisors to discuss students' grades and to complete required grade-related paperwork. Copy and distribute classroom materials. Demonstrate use of laboratory equipment and enforce laboratory rules. Teach undergraduate-level courses. Complete laboratory projects prior to assigning them to students so that any needed modifications can be made. Develop teaching materials such as syllabi, visual aids, answer keys, supplementary notes, and course Web sites. Provide assistance to faculty members or staff with laboratory or field research. Arrange for supervisors to conduct teaching observations; meet with supervisors to receive feedback about teaching performance. Attend lectures given by the instructor whom they are assisting. Order or obtain materials needed for classes. Provide instructors with assistance in the use of audiovisual equipment. Assist faculty members or staff with student conferences.

SKILLS—Most Important: Science Skills; Communication Skills; Mathematics Skills. **Other Above-Average Skills:** Thought-Processing Skills.

GOE—Interest Area: 05. Education and Training. **Work Group:** 05.03. Postsecondary and Adult Teaching and Instructing. **Other Jobs in This Group:** Adult Literacy, Remedial Education, and GED Teachers and Instructors; Agricultural Sciences Teachers, Postsecondary; Anthropology and Archeology Teachers, Postsecondary; Architecture Teachers, Postsecondary; Area, Ethnic, and Cultural Studies Teachers, Postsecondary; Art, Drama, and Music Teachers, Postsecondary; Atmospheric, Earth, Marine, and Space Sciences Teachers, Postsecondary; Biological Science Teachers, Postsecondary; Business Teachers, Postsecondary; Chemistry Teachers, Postsecondary; Communications Teachers, Postsecondary; Computer Science Teachers, Postsecondary; Criminal Justice and Law Enforcement Teachers, Postsecondary; Economics Teachers, Postsecondary; Education Teachers, Postsecondary; Engineering Teachers, Postsecondary; English Language and Literature Teachers, Postsecondary; Environmental Science Teachers, Postsecondary; Farm and Home Management Advisors; Foreign Language and Literature Teachers, Postsecondary; Forestry and Conservation Science Teachers, Postsecondary; Geography Teachers, Postsecondary; Health Specialties Teachers, Postsecondary; History Teachers, Postsecondary; Home Economics Teachers, Postsecondary; Law Teachers, Postsecondary; Library Science Teachers, Postsecondary; Mathematical Science Teachers, Postsecondary; Nursing Instructors and Teachers, Postsecondary; Philosophy and Religion Teachers, Postsecondary; Physics Teachers, Postsecondary; Political Science

Teachers, Postsecondary; Psychology Teachers, Postsecondary; Recreation and Fitness Studies Teachers, Postsecondary; Self-Enrichment Education Teachers; Social Work Teachers, Postsecondary; Sociology Teachers, Postsecondary; Vocational Education Teachers, Postsecondary. **PERSONALITY TYPE:** Social. Social occupations frequently involve working with, communicating with, and teaching people. These occupations often involve helping or providing service to others.

EDUCATION/TRAINING PROGRAM(S)—Education, General. **RELATED KNOWLEDGE/COURSES—Education and Training:** Principles and methods for curriculum and training design, teaching and instruction for individuals and groups, and the measurement of training effects. **English Language:** The structure and content of the English language, including the meaning and spelling of words, rules of composition, and grammar. **Clerical Practices:** Administrative and clerical procedures and systems such as word processing, managing files and records, stenography and transcription, designing forms, and other office procedures and terminology. **Mathematics:** Arithmetic, algebra, geometry, calculus, and statistics and their applications.

Graphic Designers

- Education/Training Required: Bachelor's degree
- Annual Earnings: $38,390
- Growth: 15.2%
- Annual Job Openings: 35,000
- Self-Employed: 25.6%
- Part-Time: 21.3%

Design or create graphics to meet specific commercial or promotional needs, such as packaging, displays, or logos. May use a variety of media to achieve artistic or decorative effects. Create designs, concepts, and sample layouts based on knowledge of layout principles and esthetic design concepts. Determine size and arrangement of illustrative material and copy and select style and size of type. Use computer software to generate new images. Mark up, paste, and assemble final layouts to prepare layouts for printer. Draw and print charts,

graphs, illustrations, and other artwork, using computer. Review final layouts and suggest improvements as needed. Confer with clients to discuss and determine layout design. Develop graphics and layouts for product illustrations, company logos, and Internet Web sites. Key information into computer equipment to create layouts for client or supervisor. Prepare illustrations or rough sketches of material, discussing them with clients or supervisors and making necessary changes. Study illustrations and photographs to plan presentation of materials, products, or services. Prepare notes and instructions for workers who assemble and prepare final layouts for printing. Develop negatives and prints to produce layout photographs, using negative and print developing equipment and tools. Photograph layouts, using camera, to make layout prints for supervisors or clients. Produce still and animated graphics for on-air and taped portions of television news broadcasts, using electronic video equipment.

SKILLS—Most Important: Equipment/Technology Analysis Skills; Social Skills; Quality Control Skills. **Other Above-Average Skills:** Thought-Processing Skills; Communication Skills.

GOE—Interest Area: 03. Arts and Communication. **Work Group:** 03.05. Design. **Other Jobs in This Group:** Commercial and Industrial Designers; Fashion Design-ers; Floral Designers; Interior Designers; Merchandise Displayers and Window Trimmers; Set and Exhibit Designers. **PERSONALITY TYPE:** Artistic. Artistic occupations frequently involve working with forms, designs, and patterns. They often require self-expression, and the work can be done without following a clear set of rules.

EDUCATION/TRAINING PROGRAM(S)—Agricultural Communication/Journalism; Web Page, Digital/Multimedia, and Information Resources Design; Computer Graphics; Design and Visual Communications, General; Commercial and Advertising Art; Industrial Design; Graphic Design. **RELATED KNOWLEDGE/COURSES—Fine Arts:** The theory and techniques required to compose, produce, and perform works of music, dance, visual arts, drama, and sculpture. **Design:** Design techniques, tools, and principles involved in production of precision technical plans, blueprints, drawings, and models. **Communications and Media:** Media production, communication, and dissemination techniques and methods. This includes alternative ways to inform and entertain via written, oral, and visual media. **Sales and Marketing:** Principles and methods for showing, promoting, and selling products or services. This includes marketing strategy and tactics, product demonstration, sales techniques, and sales control systems. **Computers and Electronics:** Circuit boards; processors; chips; electronic equipment; and computer hardware and software, including applications and programming. **Clerical Practices:** Administrative and clerical procedures and systems such as word processing, managing files and records, stenography and transcription, designing forms, and other office procedures and terminology.

Health Specialties Teachers, Postsecondary

- ◉ Education/Training Required: Master's degree
- ◉ Annual Earnings: $70,890
- ◉ Growth: 32.2%
- ◉ Annual Job Openings: 329,000
- ◉ Self-Employed: 0.4%
- ◉ Part-Time: 27.3%

The job openings listed here are shared with 35 other postsecondary teaching occupations. For a complete list, see the beginning of this section.

Teach courses in health specialties, such as veterinary medicine, dentistry, pharmacy, therapy, laboratory technology, and public health. Initiate, facilitate, and moderate classroom discussions. Keep abreast of developments in their field by reading current literature, talking with colleagues, and participating in professional conferences. Compile, administer, and grade examinations or assign this work to others. Evaluate and grade students' classwork, assignments, and papers. Prepare course materials such as syllabi, homework assignments, and handouts. Prepare and deliver lectures to undergraduate or graduate students on topics such as public health, stress management, and worksite health promotion. Plan, evaluate, and revise curricula, course content, and course materials and methods of instruction. Supervise undergraduate or graduate teaching, internship, and research work. Conduct research in a particular field of knowledge and publish findings in

professional journals, books, or electronic media. Collaborate with colleagues to address teaching and research issues. Supervise laboratory sessions. Maintain student attendance records, grades, and other required records. Maintain regularly scheduled office hours in order to advise and assist students. Advise students on academic and vocational curricula and on career issues. Participate in student recruitment, registration, and placement activities. Write grant proposals to procure external research funding. Serve on academic or administrative committees that deal with institutional policies, departmental matters, and academic issues. Select and obtain materials and supplies such as textbooks and laboratory equipment. Act as advisers to student organizations. Perform administrative duties such as serving as department head. Compile bibliographies of specialized materials for outside reading assignments. Provide professional consulting services to government and industry. Participate in campus and community events.

SKILLS—Most Important: Science Skills; Communication Skills; Thought-Processing Skills. **Other Above-Average Skills:** Social Skills; Management Skills; Equipment/Technology Analysis Skills.

GOE—Interest Area: 05. Education and Training. **Work Group:** 05.03. Postsecondary and Adult Teaching and Instructing. **Other Jobs in This Group:** Adult Literacy, Remedial Education, and GED Teachers and Instructors; Agricultural Sciences Teachers, Postsecondary; Anthropology and Archeology Teachers, Postsecondary; Architecture Teachers, Postsecondary; Area, Ethnic, and Cultural Studies Teachers, Postsecondary; Art, Drama, and Music Teachers, Postsecondary; Atmospheric, Earth, Marine, and Space Sciences Teachers, Postsecondary; Biological Science Teachers, Postsecondary; Business Teachers, Postsecondary; Chemistry Teachers, Postsecondary; Communications Teachers, Postsecondary; Computer Science Teachers, Postsecondary; Criminal Justice and Law Enforcement Teachers, Postsecondary; Economics Teachers, Postsecondary; Education Teachers, Postsecondary; Engineering Teachers, Postsecondary; English Language and Literature Teachers, Postsecondary; Environmental Science Teachers, Postsecondary; Farm and Home Management Advisors; Foreign Language and Literature Teachers, Postsecondary; Forestry and Conservation Science Teachers, Postsecondary; Geography Teachers, Postsecondary; Graduate Teaching Assistants; History Teachers, Postsecondary; Home Economics Teachers,

Postsecondary; Law Teachers, Postsecondary; Library Science Teachers, Postsecondary; Mathematical Science Teachers, Postsecondary; Nursing Instructors and Teachers, Postsecondary; Philosophy and Religion Teachers, Postsecondary; Physics Teachers, Postsecondary; Political Science Teachers, Postsecondary; Psychology Teachers, Postsecondary; Recreation and Fitness Studies Teachers, Postsecondary; Self-Enrichment Education Teachers; Social Work Teachers, Postsecondary; Sociology Teachers, Postsecondary; Vocational Education Teachers, Postsecondary. **PERSONALITY TYPE:** Investigative. Investigative occupations frequently involve working with ideas and require an extensive amount of thinking. These occupations can involve searching for facts and figuring out problems mentally.

EDUCATION/TRAINING PROGRAM(S)—Health Occupations Teacher Education; Biostatistics; Epidemiology; Chiropractic (DC); Communication Disorders, General; Audiology/Audiologist and Hearing Sciences; Speech-Language Pathology/Pathologist; Audiology/Audiologist and Speech-Language Pathology/Pathologist; Dentistry (DDS, DMD); Dental Clinical Sciences, General (MS, PhD); Dental Assisting/Assistant; Dental Hygiene/Hygienist; others. **RELATED KNOWLEDGE/COURSES—Biology:** Plant and animal organisms and their tissues, cells, functions, interdependencies, and interactions with each other and the environment. **Medicine and Dentistry:** The information and techniques needed to diagnose and treat human injuries, diseases, and deformities. This includes symptoms, treatment alternatives, drug properties and interactions, and preventive healthcare measures. **Education and Training:** Principles and methods for curriculum and training design, teaching and instruction for individuals and groups, and the measurement of training effects. **Therapy and Counseling:** Principles, methods, and procedures for diagnosis, treatment, and rehabilitation of physical and mental dysfunctions and for career counseling and guidance. **Sociology and Anthropology:** Group behavior and dynamics, societal trends and influences, human migrations, ethnicity, and cultures and their history and origins. **Psychology:** Human behavior and performance; individual differences in ability, personality, and interests; learning and motivation; psychological research methods; and the assessment and treatment of behavioral and affective disorders.

Heating and Air Conditioning Mechanics and Installers

- Education/Training Required: Long-term on-the-job training
- Annual Earnings: $37,040
- Growth: 19.0%
- Annual Job Openings: 33,000
- Self-Employed: 13.1%
- Part-Time: 3.6%

The job openings listed here are shared with Refrigeration Mechanics and Installers.

Install, service, and repair heating and air conditioning systems in residences and commercial establishments. Obtain and maintain required certifications. Comply with all applicable standards, policies, and procedures, including safety procedures and the maintenance of a clean work area. Repair or replace defective equipment, components, or wiring. Test electrical circuits and components for continuity, using electrical test equipment. Reassemble and test equipment following repairs. Inspect and test system to verify system compliance with plans and specifications and to detect and locate malfunctions. Discuss heating-cooling system malfunctions with users to isolate problems or to verify that malfunctions have been corrected. Test pipe or tubing joints and connections for leaks, using pressure gauge or soap-and-water solution. Record and report all faults, deficiencies, and other unusual occurrences, as well as the time and materials expended on work orders. Adjust system controls to setting recommended by manufacturer to balance system, using hand tools. Recommend, develop, and perform preventive and general maintenance procedures such as cleaning, power-washing, and vacuuming equipment; oiling parts; and changing filters. Lay out and connect electrical wiring between controls and equipment according to wiring diagram, using electrician's hand tools. Install auxiliary components to heating-cooling equipment, such as expansion and discharge valves, air ducts, pipes, blowers, dampers, flues, and stokers, following blueprints. Assist with other work in coordination with repair and maintenance teams.

Install, connect, and adjust thermostats, humidistats, and timers, using hand tools. Generate work orders that address deficiencies in need of correction. Join pipes or tubing to equipment and to fuel, water, or refrigerant source to form complete circuit. Assemble, position, and mount heating or cooling equipment, following blueprints. Study blueprints, design specifications, and manufacturers' recommendations to ascertain the configuration of heating or cooling equipment components and to ensure the proper installation of components. Cut and drill holes in floors, walls, and roof to install equipment, using power saws and drills.

SKILLS—Most Important: Equipment Use/Maintenance Skills; Science Skills; Mathematics Skills. Other Above-Average Skills: Social Skills; Equipment/Technology Analysis Skills; Management Skills.

GOE—Interest Area: 02. Architecture and Construction. Work Group: 02.05. Systems and Equipment Installation, Maintenance, and Repair. Other Jobs in This Group: Electrical and Electronics Repairers, Powerhouse, Substation, and Relay; Electrical Power-Line Installers and Repairers; Elevator Installers and Repairers; Maintenance and Repair Workers, General; Refrigeration Mechanics and Installers; Telecommunications Equipment Installers and Repairers, Except Line Installers; Telecommunications Line Installers and Repairers. PERSONALITY TYPE: Realistic. Realistic occupations frequently involve work activities that include practical, hands-on problems and solutions. They often deal with plants, animals, and real-world materials like wood, tools, and machinery. Many of the occupations require working outside and do not involve a lot of paperwork or working closely with others.

EDUCATION/TRAINING PROGRAM(S)—Heating, Air Conditioning, and Refrigeration Technology/Technician (ACH/ACR/ACHR/HRAC/HVAC); Solar Energy Technology/Technician; Heating, Air Conditioning, Ventilation, and Refrigeration Maintenance Technology/Technician. RELATED KNOWLEDGE/COURSES—Mechanical Devices: Machines and tools, including their designs, uses, repair, and maintenance. Building and Construction: The materials, methods, and tools involved in the construction or repair of houses, buildings, or other structures such as highways and roads. Design: Design techniques, tools, and principles involved in production of precision technical plans, blueprints, drawings, and models. Physics:

Physical principles and laws and their interrelationships and applications to understanding fluid, material, and atmospheric dynamics and mechanical, electrical, atomic, and subatomic structures and processes. Engineering and Technology: The practical application of engineering science and technology. This includes applying principles, techniques, procedures, and equipment to the design and production of various goods and services. Sales and Marketing: Principles and methods for showing, promoting, and selling products or services. This includes marketing strategy and tactics, product demonstration, sales techniques, and sales control systems.

Highway Maintenance Workers

- Education/Training Required: Moderate-term on-the-job training
- Annual Earnings: $30,250
- Growth: 23.3%
- Annual Job Openings: 27,000
- Self-Employed: 1.2%
- Part-Time: 6.3%

Maintain highways, municipal and rural roads, airport runways, and rights-of-way. Duties include patching broken or eroded pavement and repairing guardrails, highway markers, and snow fences. May also mow or clear brush from along road or plow snow from roadway. Flag motorists to warn them of obstacles or repair work ahead. Set out signs and cones around work areas to divert traffic. Drive trucks or tractors with adjustable attachments to sweep debris from paved surfaces, mow grass and weeds, and remove snow and ice. Dump, spread, and tamp asphalt, using pneumatic tampers, to repair joints and patch broken pavement. Drive trucks to transport crews and equipment to worksites. Inspect, clean, and repair drainage systems, bridges, tunnels, and other structures. Haul and spread sand, gravel, and clay to fill washouts and repair road shoulders. Erect, install, or repair guardrails, road shoulders, berms, highway markers, warning signals, and highway lighting, using hand tools and power tools. Remove litter and debris from roadways, including debris from rock slides and mudslides. Clean and clear debris from culverts, catch basins, drop inlets, ditches, and other drain structures.

Perform roadside landscaping work, such as clearing weeds and brush and planting and trimming trees. Paint traffic control lines and place pavement traffic messages by hand or using machines. Inspect markers to verify accurate installation. Apply poisons along roadsides and in animal burrows to eliminate unwanted roadside vegetation and rodents. Measure and mark locations for installation of markers, using tape, string, or chalk. Apply oil to road surfaces, using sprayers. Blend compounds to form adhesive mixtures used for marker installation. Place and remove snow fences used to prevent the accumulation of drifting snow on highways.

SKILLS—Most Important: Equipment Use/Maintenance Skills. Other Above-Average Skills: Equipment/Technology Analysis Skills; Management Skills; Mathematics Skills; Social Skills.

GOE—Interest Area: 02. Architecture and Construction. Work Group: 02.06. Construction Support/Labor. Other Jobs in This Group: Construction Laborers; Helpers—Brickmasons, Blockmasons, Stonemasons, and Tile and Marble Setters; Helpers—Carpenters; Helpers—Electricians; Helpers—Installation, Maintenance, and Repair Workers; Helpers—Painters, Paperhangers, Plasterers, and Stucco Masons; Helpers—Pipelayers, Plumbers, Pipefitters, and Steamfitters; Helpers—Roofers; Septic Tank Servicers and Sewer Pipe Cleaners. PERSONALITY TYPE: Realistic. Realistic occupations frequently involve work activities that include practical, hands-on problems and solutions. They often deal with plants, animals, and real-world materials like wood, tools, and machinery. Many of the occupations require working outside and do not involve a lot of paperwork or working closely with others.

EDUCATION/TRAINING PROGRAM(S)—Construction/Heavy Equipment/Earthmoving Equipment Operation. RELATED KNOWLEDGE/COURSES—Building and Construction: The materials, methods, and tools involved in the construction or repair of houses, buildings, or other structures such as highways and roads. Transportation: Principles and methods for moving people or goods by air, rail, sea, or road, including the relative costs and benefits. Mechanical Devices: Machines and tools, including their designs, uses, repair, and maintenance. Public Safety and Security: Relevant equipment, policies, procedures, and strategies to promote effective local, state, or national security operations for the protection of people, data, property, and institutions. Customer and Personal Service: Principles

and processes for providing customer and personal services. This includes customer needs assessment, meeting of quality standards for services, and evaluation of customer satisfaction. Geography: Principles and methods for describing the features of land, sea, and air masses, including their physical characteristics; locations; interrelationships; and distribution of plant, animal, and human life.

History Teachers, Postsecondary

- Education/Training Required: Master's degree
- Annual Earnings: $54,780
- Growth: 32.2%
- Annual Job Openings: 329,000
- Self-Employed: 0.4%
- Part-Time: 27.3%

The job openings listed here are shared with 35 other postsecondary teaching occupations. For a complete list, see the beginning of this section.

Teach courses in human history and historiography. Prepare and deliver lectures to undergraduate and/or graduate students on topics such as ancient history, postwar civilizations, and the history of third-world countries. Evaluate and grade students' classwork, assignments, and papers. Prepare course materials such as syllabi, homework assignments, and handouts. Compile, administer, and grade examinations or assign this work to others. Initiate, facilitate, and moderate classroom discussions. Keep abreast of developments in their field by reading current literature, talking with colleagues, and participating in professional conferences. Plan, evaluate, and revise curricula, course content, and course materials and methods of instruction. Maintain student attendance records, grades, and other required records. Maintain regularly scheduled office hours to advise and assist students. Conduct research in a particular field of knowledge and publish findings in professional journals, books, or electronic media. Select and obtain materials and supplies such as textbooks. Advise students on academic and vocational curricula and on career issues. Collaborate with colleagues to address teaching and research issues. Serve on academic or administrative committees that deal with institutional policies, departmental matters, and academic issues. Participate in campus and community events. Act as advisers to student organizations. Participate in student recruitment, registration, and placement activities. Compile bibliographies of specialized materials for outside reading assignments. Supervise undergraduate and graduate teaching, internship, and research work. Perform administrative duties such as serving as department head. Write grant proposals to procure external research funding. Provide professional consulting services to government, educational institutions, and industry.

SKILLS—Most Important: Communication Skills; Social Skills; Thought-Processing Skills. **Other Above-Average Skills:** Management Skills.

GOE—Interest Area: 05. Education and Training. **Work Group:** 05.03. Postsecondary and Adult Teaching and Instructing. **Other Jobs in This Group:** Adult Literacy, Remedial Education, and GED Teachers and Instructors; Agricultural Sciences Teachers, Postsecondary; Anthropology and Archeology Teachers, Postsecondary; Architecture Teachers, Postsecondary; Area, Ethnic, and Cultural Studies Teachers, Postsecondary; Art, Drama, and Music Teachers, Postsecondary; Atmospheric, Earth, Marine, and Space Sciences Teachers, Postsecondary; Biological Science Teachers, Postsecondary; Business Teachers, Postsecondary; Chemistry Teachers, Postsecondary; Communications Teachers, Postsecondary; Computer Science Teachers, Postsecondary; Criminal Justice and Law Enforcement Teachers, Postsecondary; Economics Teachers, Postsecondary; Education Teachers, Postsecondary; Engineering Teachers, Postsecondary; English Language and Literature Teachers, Postsecondary; Environmental Science Teachers, Postsecondary; Farm and Home Management Advisors; Foreign Language and Literature Teachers, Postsecondary; Forestry and Conservation Science Teachers, Postsecondary; Geography Teachers, Postsecondary; Graduate Teaching Assistants; Health Specialties Teachers, Postsecondary; Home Economics Teachers, Postsecondary; Law Teachers, Postsecondary; Library Science Teachers, Postsecondary; Mathematical Science Teachers, Postsecondary; Nursing Instructors and Teachers, Postsecondary; Philosophy and Religion Teachers, Postsecondary; Physics Teachers, Postsecondary; Political Science Teachers, Postsecondary; Psychology Teachers, Postsecondary; Recreation and Fit-

ness Studies Teachers, Postsecondary; Self-Enrichment Education Teachers; Social Work Teachers, Postsecondary; Sociology Teachers, Postsecondary; Vocational Education Teachers, Postsecondary. **PERSONALITY TYPE:** Social. Social occupations frequently involve working with, communicating with, and teaching people. These occupations often involve helping or providing service to others.

EDUCATION/TRAINING PROGRAM(S)—History, General; American History (United States); European History; History and Philosophy of Science and Technology; Public/Applied History and Archival Administration; Asian History; Canadian History; History, Other. **RELATED KNOWLEDGE/COURSES—History and Archeology:** Historical events and their causes, indicators, and effects on civilizations and cultures. **Philosophy and Theology:** Different philosophical systems and religions. This includes their basic principles, values, ethics, ways of thinking, customs, practices, and impact on human culture. **Geography:** Principles and methods for describing the features of land, sea, and air masses, including their physical characteristics; locations; interrelationships; and distribution of plant, animal, and human life. **Sociology and Anthropology:** Group behavior and dynamics, societal trends and influences, human migrations, ethnicity, and cultures and their history and origins. **Education and Training:** Principles and methods for curriculum and training design, teaching and instruction for individuals and groups, and the measurement of training effects. **English Language:** The structure and content of the English language, including the meaning and spelling of words, rules of composition, and grammar.

Home Economics Teachers, Postsecondary

- Education/Training Required: Master's degree
- Annual Earnings: $48,720
- Growth: 32.2%
- Annual Job Openings: 329,000
- Self-Employed: 0.4%
- Part-Time: 27.3%

The job openings listed here are shared with 35 other postsecondary teaching occupations. For a complete list, see the beginning of this section.

Teach courses in child care, family relations, finance, nutrition, and related subjects as pertaining to home management. Evaluate and grade students' classwork, laboratory work, projects, assignments, and papers. Initiate, facilitate, and moderate classroom discussions. Prepare and deliver lectures to undergraduate or graduate students on topics such as food science, nutrition, and child care. Prepare course materials such as syllabi, homework assignments, and handouts. Keep abreast of developments in their field by reading current literature, talking with colleagues, and participating in professional conferences. Maintain student attendance records, grades, and other required records. Plan, evaluate, and revise curricula, course content, and course materials and methods of instruction. Compile, administer, and grade examinations or assign this work to others. Advise students on academic and vocational curricula and on career issues. Maintain regularly scheduled office hours to advise and assist students. Supervise undergraduate or graduate teaching, internship, and research work. Select and obtain materials and supplies such as textbooks. Conduct research in a particular field of knowledge and publish findings in professional journals, books, and/or electronic media. Collaborate with colleagues to address teaching and research issues. Act as advisers to student organizations. Participate in student recruitment, registration, and placement activities. Serve on academic or administrative committees that deal with institutional policies, departmental matters, and academic issues. Participate in campus and community events. Compile bibliographies of specialized materials for outside reading assignments. Perform administrative duties such as serving as department head. Write grant proposals to procure external research funding. Provide professional consulting services to government and industry.

SKILLS—Most Important: Social Skills; Thought-Processing Skills; Communication Skills. **Other Above-Average Skills:** Management Skills; Science Skills; Quality Control Skills.

GOE—Interest Area: 05. Education and Training. **Work Group:** 05.03. Postsecondary and Adult Teaching and Instructing. **Other Jobs in This Group:** Adult Literacy, Remedial Education, and GED Teachers and Instructors; Agricultural Sciences Teachers, Postsecondary; Anthropology and Archeology Teachers, Postsecondary; Architecture Teachers, Postsecondary; Area, Ethnic, and Cultural Studies Teachers, Postsecondary; Art, Drama, and Music Teachers, Postsecondary; Atmospheric, Earth, Marine, and Space Sciences Teachers, Postsecondary; Biological Science Teachers, Postsecondary; Business Teachers, Postsecondary; Chemistry Teachers, Postsecondary; Communications Teachers, Postsecondary; Computer Science Teachers, Postsecondary; Criminal Justice and Law Enforcement Teachers, Postsecondary; Economics Teachers, Postsecondary; Education Teachers, Postsecondary; Engineering Teachers, Postsecondary; English Language and Literature Teachers, Postsecondary; Environmental Science Teachers, Postsecondary; Farm and Home Management Advisors; Foreign Language and Literature Teachers, Postsecondary; Forestry and Conservation Science Teachers, Postsecondary; Geography Teachers, Postsecondary; Graduate Teaching Assistants; Health Specialties Teachers, Postsecondary; History Teachers, Postsecondary; Law Teachers, Postsecondary; Library Science Teachers, Postsecondary; Mathematical Science Teachers, Postsecondary; Nursing Instructors and Teachers, Postsecondary; Philosophy and Religion Teachers, Postsecondary; Physics Teachers, Postsecondary; Political Science Teachers, Postsecondary; Psychology Teachers, Postsecondary; Recreation and Fitness Studies Teachers, Postsecondary; Self-Enrichment Education Teachers; Social Work Teachers, Postsecondary; Sociology Teachers, Postsecondary; Vocational Education Teachers, Postsecondary. **PERSONALITY TYPE:** No data available.

EDUCATION/TRAINING PROGRAM(S)—Family and Consumer Sciences/Human Sciences, General; Business Family and Consumer Sciences/Human Sciences; Foodservice Systems Administration/Management; Human Development and Family Studies, General; Child Care and Support Services Management. **RELATED KNOWLEDGE/COURSES—Education and Training:** Principles and methods for curriculum and training design, teaching and instruction for individuals and groups, and the measurement of training effects. **Sociology and Anthropology:** Group behavior and dynamics, societal trends and influences, human migrations, ethnicity, and cultures and their history and origins. **Philosophy and Theology:** Different philosophical systems and religions. This includes their basic principles, values, ethics, ways of thinking, customs, practices, and impact on human culture. **Therapy and Counseling:** Principles, methods, and procedures for diagnosis, treatment, and rehabilitation of physical and mental dysfunctions and for career counseling and guidance. **Psychology:** Human behavior and performance; individual differences in ability, personality, and interests; learning and motivation; psychological research methods; and the assessment and treatment of behavioral and affective disorders. **English Language:** The structure and content of the English language, including the meaning and spelling of words, rules of composition, and grammar.

Human Resources Assistants, Except Payroll and Timekeeping

- Education/Training Required: Short-term on-the-job training
- Annual Earnings: $32,730
- Growth: 16.7%
- Annual Job Openings: 28,000
- Self-Employed: 0.1%
- Part-Time: 6.1%

Compile and keep personnel records. Record data for each employee, such as address, weekly earnings, absences, amount of sales or production, supervisory reports on ability, and date of and reason for termination. Compile and type reports from employment records. File employment records. Search employee files and furnish information to authorized persons. Explain company personnel policies, benefits, and procedures to employees or job applicants. Process, verify, and maintain documentation relating to personnel activities such as staffing, recruitment, training, grievances, performance evaluations, and classifications. Record data for each employee, including such information as addresses, weekly earnings, absences, amount of sales or production, supervisory reports on performance, and dates of and reasons for terminations. Process and review employment applications to evaluate qualifications or eligibility of applicants. Answer questions regarding examinations, eligibility, salaries, benefits, and other pertinent information. Examine employee files to answer inquiries and provide information for personnel

actions. Gather personnel records from other departments or employees. Search employee files to obtain information for authorized persons and organizations such as credit bureaus and finance companies. Interview job applicants to obtain and verify information used to screen and evaluate them. Request information from law enforcement officials, previous employers, and other references to determine applicants' employment acceptability. Compile and prepare reports and documents pertaining to personnel activities. Inform job applicants of their acceptance or rejection of employment. Select applicants meeting specified job requirements and refer them to hiring personnel. Arrange for in-house and external training activities. Arrange for advertising or posting of job vacancies and notify eligible workers of position availability. Provide assistance in administering employee benefit programs and worker's compensation plans. Prepare badges, passes, and identification cards and perform other security-related duties. Administer and score applicant and employee aptitude, personality, and interest assessment instruments.

SKILLS—Most Important: Communication Skills; Mathematics Skills; Management Skills. **Other Above-Average Skills:** None met the criteria.

GOE—Interest Area: 04. Business and Administration. **Work Group:** 04.07. Records and Materials Processing. **Other Jobs in This Group:** Correspondence Clerks; File Clerks; Marking Clerks; Meter Readers, Utilities; Office Clerks, General; Order Fillers, Wholesale and Retail Sales; Postal Service Clerks; Postal Service Mail Sorters, Processors, and Processing Machine Operators; Procurement Clerks; Production, Planning, and Expediting Clerks; Shipping, Receiving, and Traffic Clerks; Stock Clerks and Order Fillers; Stock Clerks, Sales Floor; Stock Clerks—Stockroom, Warehouse, or Storage Yard; Weighers, Measurers, Checkers, and Samplers, Recordkeeping. **PERSONALITY TYPE:** Conventional. Conventional occupations frequently involve following set procedures and routines. These occupations can include working with data and details more than with ideas. Usually there is a clear line of authority to follow.

EDUCATION/TRAINING PROGRAM(S)—General Office Occupations and Clerical Services. **RELATED KNOWLEDGE/COURSES—Clerical Practices:** Administrative and clerical procedures and systems such as word processing, managing files and records, stenography and transcription, designing forms, and other office procedures and terminology. **Personnel and Human Resources:** Principles and procedures for personnel recruitment, selection, training, compensation and benefits, labor relations and negotiation, and personnel information systems. **Customer and Personal Service:** Principles and processes for providing customer and personal services. This includes customer needs assessment, meeting of quality standards for services, and evaluation of customer satisfaction. **Computers and Electronics:** Circuit boards; processors; chips; electronic equipment; and computer hardware and software, including applications and programming. **Education and Training:** Principles and methods for curriculum and training design, teaching and instruction for individuals and groups, and the measurement of training effects. **English Language:** The structure and content of the English language, including the meaning and spelling of words, rules of composition, and grammar.

Hydrologists

- Education/Training Required: Master's degree
- Annual Earnings: $63,820
- Growth: 31.6%
- Annual Job Openings: 1,000
- Self-Employed: 4.3%
- Part-Time: 5.7%

Research the distribution, circulation, and physical properties of underground and surface waters; study the form and intensity of precipitation, its rate of infiltration into the soil, its movement through the earth, and its return to the ocean and atmosphere. Study and document quantities, distribution, disposition, and development of underground and surface waters. Draft final reports describing research results, including illustrations, appendices, maps, and other attachments. Coordinate and supervise the work of professional and technical staff, including research assistants, technologists, and technicians. Prepare hydrogeologic evaluations of known or suspected hazardous waste sites and land treatment and feedlot facilities. Design and conduct scientific hydrogeological investigations to ensure that accurate and appropriate information is available for use in water resource management decisions. Study public water supply issues, including flood and drought risks, water quality, wastewater, and impacts on wetland habitats. Collect and analyze water samples as part of field investigations and/or to validate data from automatic monitors. Apply research findings to help minimize the environmental impacts of pollution, water-borne diseases, erosion, and sedimentation. Measure and graph phenomena such as lake levels, stream flows, and changes in water volumes. Investigate complaints or conflicts related to the alteration of public waters, gathering information, recommending alternatives, informing participants of progress, and preparing draft orders. Develop or modify methods of conducting hydrologic studies. Answer questions and provide technical assistance and information to contractors and/or the public regarding issues such as well drilling, code requirements, hydrology, and geology. Install, maintain, and calibrate instruments such as those that monitor water levels, rainfall, and sediments. Evaluate data and provide recommendations regarding the feasibility of municipal projects such as hydroelectric power plants, irrigation systems, flood warning systems, and waste treatment facilities. Conduct short-term and long-term climate assessments and study storm occurrences. Study and analyze the physical aspects of the Earth in terms of the hydrological components, including atmosphere, hydrosphere, and interior structure. Conduct research and communicate information to promote the conservation and preservation of water resources.

SKILLS—Most Important: Science Skills; Computer Programming Skills; Mathematics Skills. **Other Above-Average Skills:** Management Skills; Equipment/Technology Analysis Skills; Quality Control Skills; Social Skills; Equipment Use/Maintenance Skills.

GOE—Interest Area: 15. Scientific Research, Engineering, and Mathematics. **Work Group:** 15.02. Physical Sciences. **Other Jobs in This Group:** Astronomers; Atmospheric and Space Scientists; Chemists; Geographers; Geoscientists, Except Hydrologists and Geographers; Materials Scientists; Physicists. **PERSONALITY TYPE:** Investigative. Investigative occupations frequently involve working with ideas and require an extensive amount of thinking. These occupations can involve searching for facts and figuring out problems mentally.

EDUCATION/TRAINING PROGRAM(S)—Geology/Earth Science, General; Hydrology and Water Resources Science; Oceanography, Chemical and

Physical. **RELATED KNOWLEDGE/COURSES—Geography:** Principles and methods for describing the features of land, sea, and air masses, including their physical characteristics; locations; interrelationships; and distribution of plant, animal, and human life. **Physics:** Physical principles and laws and their interrelationships and applications to understanding fluid, material, and atmospheric dynamics and mechanical, electrical, atomic, and subatomic structures and processes. **Engineering and Technology:** The practical application of engineering science and technology. This includes applying principles, techniques, procedures, and equipment to the design and production of various goods and services. **Chemistry:** The chemical composition, structure, and properties of substances and of the chemical processes and transformations that they undergo. This includes uses of chemicals and their danger signs, production techniques, and disposal methods. **Biology:** Plant and animal organisms and their tissues, cells, functions, interdependencies, and interactions with each other and the environment. **Mathematics:** Arithmetic, algebra, geometry, calculus, and statistics and their applications.

Immigration and Customs Inspectors

- Education/Training Required: Work experience in a related occupation
- Annual Earnings: $55,790
- Growth: 16.3%
- Annual Job Openings: 9,000
- Self-Employed: 0.0%
- Part-Time: 2.5%

The job openings listed here are shared with Criminal Investigators and Special Agents; Police Detectives; and Police Identification and Records Officers.

Investigate and inspect persons, common carriers, goods, and merchandise arriving in or departing from the United States or moving between states to detect violations of immigration and customs laws and regulations. Examine immigration applications, visas, and passports and interview persons to determine eligibility for admission, residence, and travel in U.S. Detain persons found to be in violation of customs or immigration laws and arrange for legal action such as deportation. Locate and seize contraband or undeclared merchandise and vehicles, aircraft, or boats that contain such merchandise. Interpret and explain laws and regulations to travelers, prospective immigrants, shippers, and manufacturers. Inspect cargo, baggage, and personal articles entering or leaving U.S. for compliance with revenue laws and U.S. Customs Service regulations. Record and report job-related activities, findings, transactions, violations, discrepancies, and decisions. Institute civil and criminal prosecutions and cooperate with other law enforcement agencies in the investigation and prosecution of those in violation of immigration or customs laws. Testify regarding decisions at immigration appeals or in federal court. Determine duty and taxes to be paid on goods. Collect samples of merchandise for examination, appraisal, or testing. Investigate applications for duty refunds and petition for remission or mitigation of penalties when warranted.

SKILLS—Most Important: Social Skills; Communication Skills; Equipment/Technology Analysis Skills. **Other Above-Average Skills:** Thought-Processing Skills; Management Skills; Quality Control Skills.

GOE—Interest Area: 07. Government and Public Administration. **Work Group:** 07.03. Regulations Enforcement. **Other Jobs in This Group:** Agricultural Inspectors; Aviation Inspectors; Compliance Officers, Except Agriculture, Construction, Health and Safety, and Transportation; Construction and Building Inspectors; Environmental Compliance Inspectors; Equal Opportunity Representatives and Officers; Financial Examiners; Fire Inspectors; Fish and Game Wardens; Forest Fire Inspectors and Prevention Specialists; Freight and Cargo Inspectors; Government Property Inspectors and Investigators; Licensing Examiners and Inspectors; Nuclear Monitoring Technicians; Occupational Health and Safety Specialists; Occupational Health and Safety Technicians; Tax Examiners, Collectors, and Revenue Agents; Transportation Vehicle, Equipment, and Systems Inspectors, Except Aviation. **PERSONALITY TYPE:** Conventional. Conventional occupations frequently involve following set procedures and routines. These occupations can include working with data and details more than with ideas. Usually there is a clear line of authority to follow.

EDUCATION/TRAINING PROGRAM(S)—Criminal Justice/Police Science; Criminalistics and Criminal Science. **RELATED KNOWLEDGE/COURSES—Public Safety and Security:** Relevant equipment, policies, procedures, and strategies to promote effective local, state, or national security operations for the protection of people, data, property, and institutions. **Law and Government:** Laws, legal codes, court procedures, precedents, government regulations, executive orders, agency rules, and the democratic political process. **Foreign Language:** The structure and content of a foreign (non-English) language, including the meaning and spelling of words, rules of composition and grammar, and pronunciation. **Customer and Personal Service:** Principles and processes for providing customer and personal services. This includes customer needs assessment, meeting of quality standards for services, and evaluation of customer satisfaction. **Geography:** Principles and methods for describing the features of land, sea, and air masses, including their physical characteristics; locations; interrelationships; and distribution of plant, animal, and human life. **Philosophy and Theology:** Different philosophical systems and religions. This includes their basic principles, values, ethics, ways of thinking, customs, practices, and impact on human culture.

Industrial Engineering Technicians

- Education/Training Required: Associate degree
- Annual Earnings: $45,280
- Growth: 10.5%
- Annual Job Openings: 7,000
- Self-Employed: 0.3%
- Part-Time: 6.7%

Apply engineering theory and principles to problems of industrial layout or manufacturing production, usually under the direction of engineering staff. May study and record time, motion, method, and speed involved in performance of production, maintenance, clerical, and other worker operations for such purposes as establishing standard production rates or improving efficiency. Recommend revision to methods of operation, material handling, equipment layout, or other changes to increase production or improve standards. Study time, motion, methods, and speed involved in maintenance, production, and other operations to establish standard production rate and improve efficiency. Interpret engineering drawings, schematic diagrams, or formulas and confer with management or engineering staff to determine quality and reliability standards. Recommend modifications to existing quality or production standards to achieve optimum quality within limits of equipment capability. Aid in planning work assignments in accordance with worker performance, machine capacity, production schedules, and anticipated delays. Observe workers using equipment to verify that equipment is being operated and maintained according to quality assurance standards. Observe workers operating equipment or performing tasks to determine time involved and fatigue rate, using timing devices. Prepare charts, graphs, and diagrams to illustrate workflow, routing, floor layouts, material handling, and machine utilization. Evaluate data and write reports to validate or indicate deviations from existing standards. Read worker logs, product processing sheets, and specification sheets to verify that records adhere to quality assurance specifications. Prepare graphs or charts of data or enter data into computer for analysis. Record test data, applying statistical quality control procedures. Select products for tests at specified stages in production process and test products for performance characteristics and adherence to specifications. Compile and evaluate statistical data to determine and maintain quality and reliability of products.

SKILLS—Most Important: Equipment/Technology Analysis Skills; Equipment Use/Maintenance Skills; Quality Control Skills. **Other Above-Average Skills:** Mathematics Skills; Social Skills; Science Skills; Communication Skills.

GOE—Interest Area: 04. Business and Administration. **Work Group:** 04.05. Accounting, Auditing, and Analytical Support. **Other Jobs in This Group:** Accountants; Accountants and Auditors; Auditors; Budget Analysts; Logisticians; Management Analysts; Operations Research Analysts. **PERSONALITY TYPE:** Investigative. Investigative occupations frequently involve working with ideas and require an extensive amount of thinking. These occupations can involve searching for facts and figuring out problems mentally.

EDUCATION/TRAINING PROGRAM(S)—Industrial Technology/Technician; Manufacturing Technology/Technician; Industrial Production Technologies/Technicians, Other; Engineering/Industrial Management. **RELATED KNOWLEDGE/COURSES—Production and Processing:** Raw materials, production processes, quality control, costs, and other techniques for maximizing the effective manufacture and distribution of goods. **Engineering and Technology:** The practical application of engineering science and technology. This includes applying principles, techniques, procedures, and equipment to the design and production of various goods and services. **Design:** Design techniques, tools, and principles involved in production of precision technical plans, blueprints, drawings, and models. **Clerical Practices:** Administrative and clerical procedures and systems such as word processing, managing files and records, stenography and transcription, designing forms, and other office procedures and terminology. **Mathematics:** Arithmetic, algebra, geometry, calculus, and statistics and their applications. **Mechanical Devices:** Machines and tools, including their designs, uses, repair, and maintenance.

Industrial Engineers

- Education/Training Required: Bachelor's degree
- Annual Earnings: $66,670
- Growth: 16.0%
- Annual Job Openings: 13,000
- Self-Employed: 0.4%
- Part-Time: 2.6%

Design, develop, test, and evaluate integrated systems for managing industrial production processes, including human work factors, quality control, inventory control, logistics and material flow, cost analysis, and production coordination. Analyze statistical data and product specifications to determine standards and establish quality and reliability objectives of finished product. Develop manufacturing methods, labor utilization standards, and cost analysis systems to promote efficient staff and facility utilization. Recommend methods for improving utilization of personnel, material, and utilities. Plan and establish sequence of operations to fabri-

cate and assemble parts or products and to promote efficient utilization. Apply statistical methods and perform mathematical calculations to determine manufacturing processes, staff requirements, and production standards. Coordinate quality control objectives and activities to resolve production problems, maximize product reliability, and minimize cost. Confer with vendors, staff, and management personnel regarding purchases, procedures, product specifications, manufacturing capabilities, and project status. Draft and design layout of equipment, materials, and workspace to illustrate maximum efficiency, using drafting tools and computer. Review production schedules, engineering specifications, orders, and related information to obtain knowledge of manufacturing methods, procedures, and activities. Communicate with management and user personnel to develop production and design standards. Estimate production cost and effect of product design changes for management review, action, and control. Formulate sampling procedures and designs and develop forms and instructions for recording, evaluating, and reporting quality and reliability data. Record or oversee recording of information to ensure currency of engineering drawings and documentation of production problems. Study operations sequence, material flow, functional statements, organization charts, and project information to determine worker functions and responsibilities. Direct workers engaged in product measurement, inspection, and testing activities to ensure quality control and reliability. Implement methods and procedures for disposition of discrepant material and defective or damaged parts and assess cost and responsibility.

SKILLS—Most Important: Equipment/Technology Analysis Skills; Mathematics Skills; Communication Skills. **Other Above-Average Skills:** Management Skills; Thought-Processing Skills; Science Skills.

GOE—Interest Area: 15. Scientific Research, Engineering, and Mathematics. **Work Group:** 15.08. Industrial and Safety Engineering. **Other Jobs in This Group:** Fire-Prevention and Protection Engineers; Health and Safety Engineers, Except Mining Safety Engineers and Inspectors; Industrial Safety and Health Engineers; Product Safety Engineers. **PERSONALITY TYPE:** Enterprising. Enterprising occupations frequently involve starting up and carrying out projects. These occupations can involve leading people and making many decisions. They sometimes require risk taking and often deal with business.

EDUCATION/TRAINING PROGRAM(S)—Industrial Engineering. **RELATED KNOWLEDGE/ COURSES—Design:** Design techniques, tools, and principles involved in production of precision technical plans, blueprints, drawings, and models. **Engineering and Technology:** The practical application of engineering science and technology. This includes applying principles, techniques, procedures, and equipment to the design and production of various goods and services. **Production and Processing:** Raw materials, production processes, quality control, costs, and other techniques for maximizing the effective manufacture and distribution of goods. **Mechanical Devices:** Machines and tools, including their designs, uses, repair, and maintenance. **Physics:** Physical principles and laws and their interrelationships and applications to understanding fluid, material, and atmospheric dynamics and mechanical, electrical, atomic, and subatomic structures and processes. **Mathematics:** Arithmetic, algebra, geometry, calculus, and statistics and their applications.

Industrial Production Managers

- ◎ Education/Training Required: Work experience in a related occupation
- ◎ Annual Earnings: $75,580
- ◎ Growth: 0.8%
- ◎ Annual Job Openings: 13,000
- ◎ Self-Employed: 1.7%
- ◎ Part-Time: 2.3%

Plan, direct, or coordinate the work activities and resources necessary for manufacturing products in accordance with cost, quality, and quantity specifications. Direct and coordinate production, processing, distribution, and marketing activities of industrial organization. Develop budgets and approve expenditures for supplies, materials, and human resources, ensuring that materials, labor, and equipment are used efficiently to meet production targets. Review processing schedules and production orders to make decisions concerning inventory requirements, staffing requirements, work procedures, and duty assignments, considering budgetary limitations and time constraints.

Review operations and confer with technical or administrative staff to resolve production or processing problems. Hire, train, evaluate, and discharge staff and resolve personnel grievances. Initiate and coordinate inventory and cost control programs. Prepare and maintain production reports and personnel records. Set and monitor product standards, examining samples of raw products or directing testing during processing to ensure finished products are of prescribed quality. Develop and implement production tracking and quality control systems, analyzing production, quality control, maintenance, and other operational reports to detect production problems. Review plans and confer with research and support staff to develop new products and processes. Institute employee suggestion or involvement programs. Coordinate and recommend procedures for facility and equipment maintenance or modification, including the replacement of machines. Maintain current knowledge of the quality control field, relying on current literature pertaining to materials use, technological advances, and statistical studies. Negotiate materials prices with suppliers.

SKILLS—Most Important: Management Skills; Quality Control Skills; Equipment/Technology Analysis Skills. **Other Above-Average Skills:** Social Skills; Thought-Processing Skills; Science Skills; Equipment Use/Maintenance Skills.

GOE—Interest Area: 13. Manufacturing. **Work Group:** 13.01. Managerial Work in Manufacturing. **Other Jobs in This Group:** First-Line Supervisors/ Managers of Helpers, Laborers, and Material Movers, Hand; First-Line Supervisors/Managers of Mechanics, Installers, and Repairers; First-Line Supervisors/ Managers of Production and Operating Workers. **PERSONALITY TYPE:** Enterprising. Enterprising occupations frequently involve starting up and carrying out projects. These occupations can involve leading people and making many decisions. They sometimes require risk taking and often deal with business.

EDUCATION/TRAINING PROGRAM(S)—Business/Commerce, General; Business Administration and Management, General; Operations Management and Supervision. **RELATED KNOWLEDGE/ COURSES—Production and Processing:** Raw materials, production processes, quality control, costs, and other techniques for maximizing the effective manufacture and distribution of goods. **Personnel and Human**

Resources: Principles and procedures for personnel recruitment, selection, training, compensation and benefits, labor relations and negotiation, and personnel information systems. **Education and Training:** Principles and methods for curriculum and training design, teaching and instruction for individuals and groups, and the measurement of training effects. **Mechanical Devices:** Machines and tools, including their designs, uses, repair, and maintenance. **Design:** Design techniques, tools, and principles involved in production of precision technical plans, blueprints, drawings, and models. **Engineering and Technology:** The practical application of engineering science and technology. This includes applying principles, techniques, procedures, and equipment to the design and production of various goods and services.

Industrial-Organizational Psychologists

- Education/Training Required: Master's degree
- Annual Earnings: $84,690
- Growth: 20.4%
- Annual Job Openings: Fewer than 500
- Self-Employed: 37.6%
- Part-Time: 22.8%

Apply principles of psychology to personnel, administration, management, sales, and marketing problems. Activities may include policy planning; employee screening, training, and development; and organizational development and analysis. May work with management to reorganize the work setting to improve worker productivity. Develop and implement employee selection and placement programs. Analyze job requirements and content in order to establish criteria for classification, selection, training, and other related personnel functions. Observe and interview workers in order to obtain information about the physical, mental, and educational requirements of jobs as well as information about aspects such as job satisfaction. Write reports on research findings and implications in order to contribute to general knowledge and to suggest potential changes in organizational functioning. Advise management concerning personnel, managerial, and marketing policies and practices and their potential effects on organizational effectiveness and efficiency. Identify training and development needs. Conduct research studies of physical work environments, organizational structures, communication systems, group interactions, morale, and motivation in order to assess organizational functioning. Formulate and implement training programs, applying principles of learning and individual differences. Develop interview techniques, rating scales, and psychological tests used to assess skills, abilities, and interests for the purpose of employee selection, placement, and promotion. Assess employee performance. Study organizational effectiveness, productivity, and efficiency, including the nature of workplace supervision and leadership. Facilitate organizational development and change. Analyze data, using statistical methods and applications, to evaluate the outcomes and effectiveness of workplace programs. Counsel workers about job and career-related issues. Study consumers' reactions to new products and package designs and to advertising efforts, using surveys and tests. Participate in mediation and dispute resolution.

SKILLS—Most Important: Science Skills; Thought-Processing Skills; Social Skills. **Other Above-Average Skills:** Communication Skills; Mathematics Skills.

GOE—Interest Area: 15. Scientific Research, Engineering, and Mathematics. **Work Group:** 15.04. Social Sciences. **Other Jobs in This Group:** Anthropologists; Anthropologists and Archeologists; Archeologists; Economists; Historians; Political Scientists; School Psychologists; Sociologists. **PERSONALITY TYPE:** Investigative. Investigative occupations frequently involve working with ideas and require an extensive amount of thinking. These occupations can involve searching for facts and figuring out problems mentally.

EDUCATION/TRAINING PROGRAM(S)—Psychology, General; Industrial and Organizational Psychology. **RELATED KNOWLEDGE/COURSES—Personnel and Human Resources:** Principles and procedures for personnel recruitment, selection, training, compensation and benefits, labor relations and negotiation, and personnel information systems. **Psychology:** Human behavior and performance; individual differences in ability, personality, and interests; learning and motivation; psychological research methods; and the assessment and treatment of behavioral and affective disorders. **Education and Training:** Principles and methods for curriculum and training design, teaching and instruction for individuals and groups, and the measurement of training effects. **Sales and Marketing:** Principles and methods for showing, promoting, and selling products or services. This includes marketing strategy and tactics, product demonstration, sales techniques, and sales control systems. **Sociology and Anthropology:** Group behavior and dynamics, societal trends and influences, human migrations, ethnicity, and cultures and their history and origins. **Customer and Personal Service:** Principles and processes for providing customer and personal services. This includes customer needs assessment, meeting of quality standards for services, and evaluation of customer satisfaction.

Instructional Coordinators

- ⑥ Education/Training Required: Master's degree
- ⑥ Annual Earnings: $50,430
- ⑥ Growth: 27.5%
- ⑥ Annual Job Openings: 15,000
- ⑥ Self-Employed: 3.1%
- ⑥ Part-Time: 23.4%

Develop instructional material, coordinate educational content, and incorporate current technology in specialized fields that provide guidelines to educators and instructors for developing curricula and conducting courses. Conduct or participate in workshops, committees, and conferences designed to promote the intellectual, social, and physical welfare of students. Plan and conduct teacher training programs and conferences dealing with new classroom procedures, instructional materials and equipment, and teaching aids. Advise teaching and administrative staff in curriculum development, use of materials and equipment, and implementation of state and federal programs and procedures. Recommend, order, or authorize purchase of instructional materials, supplies, equipment, and visual aids designed to meet student educational needs and district standards. Interpret and enforce provisions of state education codes and rules and regulations of state education boards. Confer with members of educational committees and advisory groups to obtain knowledge of subject areas and to relate curriculum materials to specific subjects, individual student needs, and occupational areas. Organize production and design of curriculum materials. Research, evaluate, and prepare recommendations on curricula, instructional methods, and materials for school systems. Observe work of teaching staff to evaluate performance and to recommend changes that could strengthen teaching skills. Develop instructional materials to be used by educators and instructors. Prepare grant proposals, budgets, and program policies and goals or assist in their preparation. Develop tests, questionnaires, and procedures that measure the effectiveness of curricula and use these tools to determine whether program objectives are being met. Update the content of educational programs to ensure that students are being trained with equipment and processes that are technologically current. Address public audiences to explain program objectives and to elicit support. Advise and teach students. Prepare or approve manuals, guidelines, and reports on state educational policies and practices for distribution to school districts. Develop classroom-based and distance-learning training courses, using needs assessments and skill level analyses. Inspect instructional equipment to determine if repairs are needed and authorize necessary repairs.

SKILLS—Most Important: Management Skills; Social Skills; Thought-Processing Skills. **Other Above-Average Skills:** Communication Skills; Equipment/Technology Analysis Skills; Quality Control Skills.

GOE—Interest Area: 05. Education and Training. **Work Group:** 05.01. Managerial Work in Education. **Other Jobs in This Group:** Education Administrators, Elementary and Secondary School; Education Administrators, Postsecondary; Education Administrators, Preschool and Child Care Center/Program. **PERSONALITY TYPE:** Social. Social occupations frequently involve working with, communicating with, and teaching people. These occupations often involve helping or providing service to others.

EDUCATION/TRAINING PROGRAM(S)—Curriculum and Instruction; Educational/Instructional Media Design; International and Comparative Education. **RELATED KNOWLEDGE/COURSES—Education and Training:** Principles and methods for curriculum and training design, teaching and instruction for individuals and groups, and the measurement of training effects. **Personnel and Human Resources:** Principles and procedures for personnel recruitment, selection, training, compensation and benefits, labor relations and negotiation, and personnel information systems. **English Language:** The structure and content of the English language, including the meaning and spelling of words, rules of composition, and grammar. **Sociology and Anthropology:** Group behavior and dynamics, societal trends and influences, human migrations, ethnicity, and cultures and their history and origins. **Customer and Personal Service:** Principles and processes for providing customer and personal services. This includes customer needs assessment, meeting of quality standards for services, and evaluation of customer satisfaction. **Communications and Media:** Media production, communication, and dissemination techniques and methods. This includes alternative ways to inform and entertain via written, oral, and visual media.

Interior Designers

- ◎ Education/Training Required: Associate degree
- ◎ Annual Earnings: $41,350
- ◎ Growth: 15.5%
- ◎ Annual Job Openings: 10,000
- ◎ Self-Employed: 25.3%
- ◎ Part-Time: 21.3%

Plan, design, and furnish interiors of residential, commercial, or industrial buildings. Formulate design that is practical, aesthetic, and conducive to intended purposes, such as raising productivity, selling merchandise, or improving lifestyle. May specialize in a particular field, style, or phase of interior design. Estimate material requirements and costs and present design to client for approval. Confer with client to determine factors affecting planning interior environments, such as budget, architectural preferences, and purpose and function. Advise client on interior design factors such as space planning, layout, and utilization of furnishings or equipment and color coordination. Select or design and purchase furnishings, artwork, and accessories. Formulate environmental plan to be practical, esthetic, and conducive to intended purposes such as raising productivity or selling merchandise. Subcontract fabrication, installation, and arrangement of carpeting, fixtures, accessories, draperies, paint and wall coverings, artwork, furniture, and related items. Render design ideas in form of paste-ups or drawings. Plan and design

interior environments for boats, planes, buses, trains, and other enclosed spaces.

SKILLS—Most Important: Mathematics Skills; Social Skills; Equipment/Technology Analysis Skills. **Other Above-Average Skills:** Communication Skills; Thought-Processing Skills.

GOE—Interest Area: 03. Arts and Communication. **Work Group:** 03.05. Design. **Other Jobs in This Group:** Commercial and Industrial Designers; Fashion Designers; Floral Designers; Graphic Designers; Merchandise Displayers and Window Trimmers; Set and Exhibit Designers. **PERSONALITY TYPE:** Artistic. Artistic occupations frequently involve working with forms, designs, and patterns. They often require self-expression, and the work can be done without following a clear set of rules.

EDUCATION/TRAINING PROGRAM(S)—Interior Architecture; Facilities Planning and Management; Textile Science; Interior Design. **RELATED KNOWLEDGE/COURSES—Design:** Design techniques, tools, and principles involved in production of precision technical plans, blueprints, drawings, and models. **Sales and Marketing:** Principles and methods for showing, promoting, and selling products or services. This includes marketing strategy and tactics, product demonstration, sales techniques, and sales control systems. **Administration and Management:** Business and management principles involved in strategic planning, resource allocation, human resources modeling, leadership technique, production methods, and coordination of people and resources. **Building and Construction:** The materials, methods, and tools involved in the construction or repair of houses, buildings, or other structures such as highways and roads. **Clerical Practices:** Administrative and clerical procedures and systems such as word processing, managing files and records, stenography and transcription, designing forms, and other office procedures and terminology. **Customer and Personal Service:** Principles and processes for providing customer and personal services. This includes customer needs assessment, meeting of quality standards for services, and evaluation of customer satisfaction.

Internists, General

- Education/Training Required: First professional degree
- Annual Earnings: More than $145,600
- Growth: 24.0%
- Annual Job Openings: 41,000
- Self-Employed: 11.5%
- Part-Time: 9.6%

The job openings listed here are shared with Anesthesiologists; Family and General Practitioners; Obstetricians and Gynecologists; Pediatricians, General; Psychiatrists; and Surgeons.

Diagnose and provide non-surgical treatment of diseases and injuries of internal organ systems. Provide care mainly for adults who have a wide range of problems associated with the internal organs. Treat internal disorders, such as hypertension; heart disease; diabetes; and problems of the lung, brain, kidney, and gastrointestinal tract. Analyze records, reports, test results, or examination information to diagnose medical condition of patient. Prescribe or administer medication, therapy, and other specialized medical care to treat or prevent illness, disease, or injury. Provide and manage long-term, comprehensive medical care, including diagnosis and non-surgical treatment of diseases, for adult patients in an office or hospital. Manage and treat common health problems, such as infections, influenza and pneumonia, as well as serious, chronic, and complex illnesses, in adolescents, adults, and the elderly. Monitor patients' conditions and progress and re-evaluate treatments as necessary. Collect, record, and maintain patient information, such as medical history, reports, and examination results. Make diagnoses when different illnesses occur together or in situations where the diagnosis may be obscure. Explain procedures and discuss test results or prescribed treatments with patients. Advise patients and community members concerning diet, activity, hygiene, and disease prevention. Refer patient to medical specialist or other practitioner when necessary. Immunize patients to protect them from preventable diseases. Advise surgeon of a patient's risk status and recommend appropriate intervention to minimize risk. Direct and coordinate activities of nurses, students, assistants, specialists, therapists, and other medical staff.

Provide consulting services to other doctors caring for patients with special or difficult problems. Operate on patients to remove, repair, or improve functioning of diseased or injured body parts and systems. Plan, implement, or administer health programs in hospitals, businesses, or communities for prevention and treatment of injuries or illnesses. Conduct research to develop or test medications, treatments, or procedures to prevent or control disease or injury. Prepare government or organizational reports on birth, death, and disease statistics; workforce evaluations; or the medical status of individuals.

SKILLS—Most Important: Science Skills; Thought-Processing Skills; Social Skills. **Other Above-Average Skills:** Management Skills; Communication Skills; Mathematics Skills; Equipment Use/Maintenance Skills.

GOE—Interest Area: 08. Health Science. **Work Group:** 08.02. Medicine and Surgery. **Other Jobs in This Group:** Anesthesiologists; Family and General Practitioners; Medical Assistants; Medical Transcriptionists; Obstetricians and Gynecologists; Pediatricians, General; Pharmacists; Pharmacy Aides; Pharmacy Technicians; Physician Assistants; Psychiatrists; Registered Nurses; Surgeons; Surgical Technologists. **PERSONALITY TYPE:** Investigative. Investigative occupations frequently involve working with ideas and require an extensive amount of thinking. These occupations can involve searching for facts and figuring out problems mentally.

EDUCATION/TRAINING PROGRAM(S)—Cardiology; Critical Care Medicine; Endocrinology and Metabolism; Gastroenterology; Geriatric Medicine; Hematology; Infectious Disease; Internal Medicine; Nephrology; Neurology; Nuclear Medicine; Oncology; Pulmonary Disease; Rheumatology. **RELATED KNOWLEDGE/COURSES—Medicine and Dentistry:** The information and techniques needed to diagnose and treat human injuries, diseases, and deformities. This includes symptoms, treatment alternatives, drug properties and interactions, and preventive healthcare measures. **Biology:** Plant and animal organisms and their tissues, cells, functions, interdependencies, and interactions with each other and the environment. **Therapy and Counseling:** Principles, methods, and procedures for diagnosis, treatment, and rehabilitation of physical and mental dysfunctions and for career counseling and guidance. **Psychology:** Human behavior and performance; individual differences in ability, personality, and interests; learning and motivation; psychological research methods; and the assessment and treatment of behavioral and affective disorders. **Chemistry:** The chemical composition, structure, and properties of substances and of the chemical processes and transformations that they undergo. This includes uses of chemicals and their danger signs, production techniques, and disposal methods. **Education and Training:** Principles and methods for curriculum and training design, teaching and instruction for individuals and groups, and the measurement of training effects.

Kindergarten Teachers, Except Special Education

- ⌬ Education/Training Required: Bachelor's degree
- ⌬ Annual Earnings: $42,230
- ⌬ Growth: 22.4%
- ⌬ Annual Job Openings: 28,000
- ⌬ Self-Employed: 1.5%
- ⌬ Part-Time: 25.1%

Teach elemental natural and social science, personal hygiene, music, art, and literature to children from 4 to 6 years old. Promote physical, mental, and social development. May be required to hold state certification. Teach basic skills such as color, shape, number, and letter recognition; personal hygiene; and social skills. Establish and enforce rules for behavior and policies and procedures to maintain order among students. Observe and evaluate children's performance, behavior, social development, and physical health. Instruct students individually and in groups, adapting teaching methods to meet students' varying needs and interests. Read books to entire classes or to small groups. Demonstrate activities to children. Provide a variety of materials and resources for children to explore, manipulate, and use, both in learning activities and in imaginative play. Plan and conduct activities for a balanced program of instruction, demonstration, and work time that provides students with opportunities to observe, question,

and investigate. Confer with parents or guardians, other teachers, counselors, and administrators to resolve students' behavioral and academic problems. Prepare children for later grades by encouraging them to explore learning opportunities and to persevere with challenging tasks. Establish clear objectives for all lessons, units, and projects and communicate those objectives to children. Prepare and implement remedial programs for students requiring extra help. Meet with parents and guardians to discuss their children's progress and to determine their priorities for their children and their resource needs. Prepare objectives and outlines for courses of study, following curriculum guidelines or requirements of states and schools. Organize and lead activities designed to promote physical, mental, and social development such as games, arts and crafts, music, and storytelling. Guide and counsel students with adjustment or academic problems or special academic interests. Identify children showing signs of emotional, developmental, or health-related problems and discuss them with supervisors, parents or guardians, and child development specialists. Instruct and monitor students in the use and care of equipment and materials to prevent injuries and damage. Assimilate arriving children to the school environment by greeting them, helping them remove outerwear, and selecting activities of interest to them.

SKILLS—Most Important: Social Skills; Communication Skills; Thought-Processing Skills. **Other Above-Average Skills:** Management Skills; Science Skills.

GOE—Interest Area: 05. Education and Training. **Work Group:** 05.02. Preschool, Elementary, and Secondary Teaching and Instructing. **Other Jobs in This Group:** Elementary School Teachers, Except Special Education; Middle School Teachers, Except Special and Vocational Education; Preschool Teachers, Except Special Education; Secondary School Teachers, Except Special and Vocational Education; Special Education Teachers, Middle School; Special Education Teachers, Preschool, Kindergarten, and Elementary School; Special Education Teachers, Secondary School; Teacher Assistants; Vocational Education Teachers, Middle School; Vocational Education Teachers, Secondary School. **PERSONALITY TYPE:** Social. Social occupations frequently involve working with, communicating with, and teaching people. These occupations often involve helping or providing service to others.

EDUCATION/TRAINING PROGRAM(S)—Montessori Teacher Education; Waldorf/Steiner Teacher Education; Kindergarten/Preschool Education and Teaching; Early Childhood Education and Teaching. **RELATED KNOWLEDGE/COURSES**—**History and Archeology:** Historical events and their causes, indicators, and effects on civilizations and cultures. **Education and Training:** Principles and methods for curriculum and training design, teaching and instruction for individuals and groups, and the measurement of training effects. **Geography:** Principles and methods for describing the features of land, sea, and air masses, including their physical characteristics; locations; interrelationships; and distribution of plant, animal, and human life. **Sociology and Anthropology:** Group behavior and dynamics, societal trends and influences, human migrations, ethnicity, and cultures and their history and origins. **Philosophy and Theology:** Different philosophical systems and religions. This includes their basic principles, values, ethics, ways of thinking, customs, practices, and impact on human culture. **Psychology:** Human behavior and performance; individual differences in ability, personality, and interests; learning and motivation; psychological research methods; and the assessment and treatment of behavioral and affective disorders.

Landscape Architects

- Education/Training Required: Bachelor's degree
- Annual Earnings: $54,220
- Growth: 19.4%
- Annual Job Openings: 1,000
- Self-Employed: 23.7%
- Part-Time: No data available

Plan and design land areas for such projects as parks and other recreational facilities; airports; highways; hospitals; schools; land subdivisions; and commercial, industrial, and residential sites. Prepare site plans, specifications, and cost estimates for land development, coordinating arrangement of existing and proposed land features and structures. Confer with clients, engineering personnel, and architects on overall program. Compile and analyze data on conditions such as location, drainage, and location of structures for environmental reports and landscaping plans. Inspect landscape work to ensure compliance with specifications, approve quality of materials and work, and advise client and construction personnel.

SKILLS—**Most Important:** Mathematics Skills; Equipment/Technology Analysis Skills; Management Skills. **Other Above-Average Skills:** Social Skills; Thought-Processing Skills; Quality Control Skills.

GOE—**Interest Area:** 02. Architecture and Construction. **Work Group:** 02.02. Architectural Design. **Other Jobs in This Group:** Architects, Except Landscape and Naval. **PERSONALITY TYPE:** Artistic. Artistic occupations frequently involve working with forms, designs, and patterns. They often require self-expression, and the work can be done without following a clear set of rules.

EDUCATION/TRAINING PROGRAM(S)—Environmental Design/Architecture; Landscape Architecture (BS, BSLA, BLA, MSLA, MLA, PhD). **RELATED KNOWLEDGE/COURSES**—**Design:** Design techniques, tools, and principles involved in production of precision technical plans, blueprints, drawings, and models. **Building and Construction:** The materials, methods, and tools involved in the construction or repair of houses, buildings, or other structures such as highways and roads. **Geography:** Principles and methods for describing the features of land, sea, and air masses, including their physical characteristics; locations; interrelationships; and distribution of plant, animal, and human life. **Engineering and Technology:** The practical application of engineering science and technology. This includes applying principles, techniques, procedures, and equipment to the design and production of various goods and services. **Biology:** Plant and animal organisms and their tissues, cells, functions, interdependencies, and interactions with each other and the environment. **Fine Arts:** The theory and techniques required to compose, produce, and perform works of music, dance, visual arts, drama, and sculpture.

Law Teachers, Postsecondary

- Education/Training Required: First professional degree
- Annual Earnings: $89,790
- Growth: 32.2%
- Annual Job Openings: 329,000
- Self-Employed: 0.4%
- Part-Time: 27.3%

The job openings listed here are shared with 35 other postsecondary teaching occupations. For a complete list, see the beginning of this section.

Teach courses in law. Evaluate and grade students' classwork, assignments, papers, and oral presentations. Compile, administer, and grade examinations or assign this work to others. Prepare and deliver lectures to undergraduate or graduate students on topics such as civil procedure, contracts, and torts. Initiate, facilitate, and moderate classroom discussions. Prepare course materials such as syllabi, homework assignments, and handouts. Keep abreast of developments in their field by reading current literature, talking with colleagues, and participating in professional conferences. Plan, evaluate, and revise curricula, course content, and course materials and methods of instruction. Maintain regularly scheduled office hours to advise and assist students. Conduct research in a particular field of knowledge and publish findings in professional journals, books, or electronic media. Advise students on academic and vocational curricula and on career issues. Supervise undergraduate and/or graduate teaching, internship, and research work. Select and obtain materials and supplies such as textbooks. Maintain student attendance records, grades, and other required records. Serve on academic or administrative committees that deal with institutional policies, departmental matters, and academic issues. Perform administrative duties such as serving as department head. Collaborate with colleagues to address teaching and research issues. Participate in student recruitment, registration, and placement activities. Compile bibliographies of specialized materials for outside reading assignments. Participate in campus and community events. Act as advisers to student organiza-

tions. Assign cases for students to hear and try. Provide professional consulting services to government or industry. Write grant proposals to procure external research funding.

SKILLS—Most Important: Communication Skills; Thought-Processing Skills; Social Skills. **Other Above-Average Skills:** None met the criteria.

GOE—Interest Area: 05. Education and Training. **Work Group:** 05.03. Postsecondary and Adult Teaching and Instructing. **Other Jobs in This Group:** Adult Literacy, Remedial Education, and GED Teachers and Instructors; Agricultural Sciences Teachers, Postsecondary; Anthropology and Archeology Teachers, Postsecondary; Architecture Teachers, Postsecondary; Area, Ethnic, and Cultural Studies Teachers, Postsecondary; Art, Drama, and Music Teachers, Postsecondary; Atmospheric, Earth, Marine, and Space Sciences Teachers, Postsecondary; Biological Science Teachers, Postsecondary; Business Teachers, Postsecondary; Chemistry Teachers, Postsecondary; Communications Teachers, Postsecondary; Computer Science Teachers, Postsecondary; Criminal Justice and Law Enforcement Teachers, Postsecondary; Economics Teachers, Postsecondary; Education Teachers, Postsecondary; Engineering Teachers, Postsecondary; English Language and Literature Teachers, Postsecondary; Environmental Science Teachers, Postsecondary; Farm and Home Management Advisors; Foreign Language and Literature Teachers, Postsecondary; Forestry and Conservation Science Teachers, Postsecondary; Geography Teachers, Postsecondary; Graduate Teaching Assistants; Health Specialties Teachers, Postsecondary; History Teachers, Postsecondary; Home Economics Teachers, Postsecondary; Library Science Teachers, Postsecondary; Mathematical Science Teachers, Postsecondary; Nursing Instructors and Teachers, Postsecondary; Philosophy and Religion Teachers, Postsecondary; Physics Teachers, Postsecondary; Political Science Teachers, Postsecondary; Psychology Teachers, Postsecondary; Recreation and Fitness Studies Teachers, Postsecondary; Self-Enrichment Education Teachers; Social Work Teachers, Postsecondary; Sociology Teachers, Postsecondary; Vocational Education Teachers, Postsecondary. **PERSONALITY TYPE:** No data available.

EDUCATION/TRAINING PROGRAM(S)—Legal Studies, General; Law (LL.B., J.D.). **RELATED KNOWLEDGE/COURSES—Law and Government:** Laws, legal codes, court procedures, precedents, government regulations, executive orders, agency rules, and the democratic political process. **English Language:** The structure and content of the English language, including the meaning and spelling of words, rules of composition, and grammar. **Education and Training:** Principles and methods for curriculum and training design, teaching and instruction for individuals and groups, and the measurement of training effects. **History and Archeology:** Historical events and their causes, indicators, and effects on civilizations and cultures. **Philosophy and Theology:** Different philosophical systems and religions. This includes their basic principles, values, ethics, ways of thinking, customs, practices, and impact on human culture. **Communications and Media:** Media production, communication, and dissemination techniques and methods. This includes alternative ways to inform and entertain via written, oral, and visual media.

Lawyers

- ◎ Education/Training Required: First professional degree
- ◎ Annual Earnings: $98,930
- ◎ Growth: 15.0%
- ◎ Annual Job Openings: 40,000
- ◎ Self-Employed: 24.1%
- ◎ Part-Time: 6.8%

Represent clients in criminal and civil litigation and other legal proceedings, draw up legal documents, and manage or advise clients on legal transactions. May specialize in a single area or may practice broadly in many areas of law. Advise clients concerning business transactions, claim liability, advisability of prosecuting or defending lawsuits, or legal rights and obligations. Interpret laws, rulings, and regulations for individuals and businesses. Analyze the probable outcomes of cases, using knowledge of legal precedents. Present and summarize cases to judges and juries. Gather evidence to formulate defense or to initiate legal actions by such means as interviewing clients and witnesses to ascertain the facts of a case. Evaluate findings and develop strategies and arguments in preparation for presentation of cases. Represent clients in court or before government agencies. Examine legal data to determine advisability of defending or prosecuting lawsuit. Select jurors, argue

motions, meet with judges, and question witnesses during the course of a trial. Present evidence to defend clients or prosecute defendants in criminal or civil litigation. Study Constitution, statutes, decisions, regulations, and ordinances of quasi-judicial bodies to determine ramifications for cases. Prepare and draft legal documents, such as wills, deeds, patent applications, mortgages, leases, and contracts. Prepare legal briefs and opinions and file appeals in state and federal courts of appeal. Negotiate settlements of civil disputes. Confer with colleagues with specialties in appropriate areas of legal issue to establish and verify bases for legal proceedings. Search for and examine public and other legal records to write opinions or establish ownership. Supervise legal assistants. Perform administrative and management functions related to the practice of law. Act as agent, trustee, guardian, or executor for businesses or individuals. Probate wills and represent and advise executors and administrators of estates. Help develop federal and state programs, draft and interpret laws and legislation, and establish enforcement procedures. Work in environmental law, representing public interest groups, waste disposal companies, or construction firms in their dealings with state and federal agencies.

SKILLS—Most Important: Communication Skills; Social Skills; Thought-Processing Skills. **Other Above-Average Skills:** Management Skills; Mathematics Skills.

GOE—Interest Area: 12. Law and Public Safety. **Work Group:** 12.02. Legal Practice and Justice Administration. **Other Jobs in This Group:** Administrative Law Judges, Adjudicators, and Hearing Officers; Arbitrators, Mediators, and Conciliators; Judges, Magistrate Judges, and Magistrates. **PERSONALITY TYPE:** Enterprising. Enterprising occupations frequently involve starting up and carrying out projects. These occupations can involve leading people and making many decisions. They sometimes require risk taking and often deal with business.

EDUCATION/TRAINING PROGRAM(S)—Law (LL.B., J.D.); Advanced Legal Research/Studies, General (LL.M., M.C.L., M.L.I., M.S.L., J.S.D./S.J.D.); Programs for Foreign Lawyers (LL.M., M.C.L.); American/U.S. Law/Legal Studies/Jurisprudence (LL.M., M.C.J., J.S.D./S.J.D.); Canadian Law/Legal Studies/ Jurisprudence (LL.M., M.C.J., J.S.D./S.J.D.); Banking, Corporate, Finance, and Securities Law (LL.M., J.S.D./S.J.D.); Comparative Law (LL.M., M.C.L.,

J.S.D./S.J.D.); others. **RELATED KNOWLEDGE/ COURSES—Law and Government:** Laws, legal codes, court procedures, precedents, government regulations, executive orders, agency rules, and the democratic political process. **English Language:** The structure and content of the English language, including the meaning and spelling of words, rules of composition, and grammar. **Personnel and Human Resources:** Principles and procedures for personnel recruitment, selection, training, compensation and benefits, labor relations and negotiation, and personnel information systems. **Economics and Accounting:** Economic and accounting principles and practices, the financial markets, banking, and the analysis and reporting of financial data. **Administration and Management:** Business and management principles involved in strategic planning, resource allocation, human resources modeling, leadership technique, production methods, and coordination of people and resources. **Customer and Personal Service:** Principles and processes for providing customer and personal services. This includes customer needs assessment, meeting of quality standards for services, and evaluation of customer satisfaction.

Legal Secretaries

- Education/Training Required: Postsecondary vocational training
- Annual Earnings: $37,750
- Growth: 17.4%
- Annual Job Openings: 41,000
- Self-Employed: 1.2%
- Part-Time: 20.3%

Perform secretarial duties, utilizing legal terminology, procedures, and documents. Prepare legal papers and correspondence, such as summonses, complaints, motions, and subpoenas. May also assist with legal research. Prepare and process legal documents and papers, such as summonses, subpoenas, complaints, appeals, motions, and pretrial agreements. Mail, fax, or arrange for delivery of legal correspondence to clients, witnesses, and court officials. Receive and place telephone calls. Schedule and make appointments. Make photocopies of correspondence, documents, and other printed matter. Organize and maintain law libraries,

documents, and case files. Assist attorneys in collecting information such as employment, medical, and other records. Attend legal meetings, such as client interviews, hearings, or depositions, and take notes. Draft and type office memos. Review legal publications and perform database searches to identify laws and court decisions relevant to pending cases. Submit articles and information from searches to attorneys for review and approval for use. Complete various forms such as accident reports, trial and courtroom requests, and applications for clients.

SKILLS—Most Important: Communication Skills; Social Skills; Thought-Processing Skills. **Other Above-Average Skills:** Management Skills.

GOE—Interest Area: 04. Business and Administration. **Work Group:** 04.04. Secretarial Support. **Other Jobs in This Group:** Executive Secretaries and Administrative Assistants; Medical Secretaries; Secretaries, Except Legal, Medical, and Executive. **PERSONALITY TYPE:** Conventional. Conventional occupations frequently involve following set procedures and routines. These occupations can include working with data and details more than with ideas. Usually there is a clear line of authority to follow.

EDUCATION/TRAINING PROGRAM(S)—Legal Administrative Assistant/Secretary. **RELATED KNOWLEDGE/COURSES—Clerical Practices:** Administrative and clerical procedures and systems such as word processing, managing files and records, stenography and transcription, designing forms, and other office procedures and terminology. **Law and Government:** Laws, legal codes, court procedures, precedents, government regulations, executive orders, agency rules, and the democratic political process. **Economics and Accounting:** Economic and accounting principles and practices, the financial markets, banking, and the analysis and reporting of financial data. **Customer and Personal Service:** Principles and processes for providing customer and personal services. This includes customer needs assessment, meeting of quality standards for services, and evaluation of customer satisfaction. **Computers and Electronics:** Circuit boards; processors; chips; electronic equipment; and computer hardware and software, including applications and programming. **English Language:** The structure and content of the English language, including the meaning and spelling of words, rules of composition, and grammar.

Library Science Teachers, Postsecondary

- Education/Training Required: Master's degree
- Annual Earnings: $53,810
- Growth: 32.2%
- Annual Job Openings: 329,000
- Self-Employed: 0.4%
- Part-Time: 27.3%

The job openings listed here are shared with 35 other postsecondary teaching occupations. For a complete list, see the beginning of this section.

Teach courses in library science. Prepare course materials such as syllabi, homework assignments, and handouts. Prepare and deliver lectures to undergraduate or graduate students on topics such as collection development, archival methods, and indexing and abstracting. Evaluate and grade students' classwork, assignments, and papers. Keep abreast of developments in their field by reading current literature, talking with colleagues, and participating in professional conferences. Initiate, facilitate, and moderate classroom discussions. Plan, evaluate, and revise curricula, course content, and course materials and methods of instruction. Conduct research in a particular field of knowledge and publish findings in professional journals, books, and/or electronic media. Maintain student attendance records, grades, and other required records. Collaborate with colleagues to address teaching and research issues. Advise students on academic and vocational curricula and on career issues. Compile, administer, and grade examinations or assign this work to others. Supervise undergraduate or graduate teaching, internship, and research work. Maintain regularly scheduled office hours in order to advise and assist students. Write grant proposals to procure external research funding. Select and obtain materials and supplies such as textbooks. Serve on academic or administrative committees that deal with institutional policies, departmental matters, and academic issues. Compile bibliographies of specialized materials for outside reading assignments. Participate in student recruitment, registration, and placement activities. Perform administrative duties such as serving as department head. Participate in campus and community events. Act as advisers to student organizations. Provide professional consulting services to government and/or industry.

SKILLS—Most Important: Communication Skills; Thought-Processing Skills; Social Skills. **Other Above-Average Skills:** Equipment/Technology Analysis Skills; Science Skills; Management Skills.

GOE—Interest Area: 05. Education and Training. **Work Group:** 05.03. Postsecondary and Adult Teaching and Instructing. **Other Jobs in This Group:** Adult Literacy, Remedial Education, and GED Teachers and Instructors; Agricultural Sciences Teachers, Postsecondary; Anthropology and Archeology Teachers, Postsecondary; Architecture Teachers, Postsecondary; Area, Ethnic, and Cultural Studies Teachers, Postsecondary; Art, Drama, and Music Teachers, Postsecondary; Atmospheric, Earth, Marine, and Space Sciences Teachers, Postsecondary; Biological Science Teachers, Postsecondary; Business Teachers, Postsecondary; Chemistry Teachers, Postsecondary; Communications Teachers, Postsecondary; Computer Science Teachers, Postsecondary; Criminal Justice and Law Enforcement Teachers, Postsecondary; Economics Teachers, Postsecondary; Education Teachers, Postsecondary; Engineering Teachers, Postsecondary; English Language and Literature Teachers, Postsecondary; Environmental Science Teachers, Postsecondary; Farm and Home Management Advisors; Foreign Language and Literature Teachers, Postsecondary; Forestry and Conservation Science Teachers, Postsecondary; Geography Teachers, Postsecondary; Graduate Teaching Assistants; Health Specialties Teachers, Postsecondary; History Teachers, Postsecondary; Home Economics Teachers, Postsecondary; Law Teachers, Postsecondary; Mathematical Science Teachers, Postsecondary; Nursing Instructors and Teachers, Postsecondary; Philosophy and Religion Teachers, Postsecondary; Physics Teachers, Postsecondary; Political Science Teachers, Postsecondary; Psychology Teachers, Postsecondary; Recreation and Fitness Studies Teachers, Postsecondary; Self-Enrichment Education Teachers; Social Work Teachers, Postsecondary; Sociology Teachers, Postsecondary; Vocational Education Teachers, Postsecondary. **PERSONALITY TYPE:** No data available.

EDUCATION/TRAINING PROGRAM(S)—Teacher Education and Professional Development, Specific Subject Areas, Other; Library Science/Librarianship.

RELATED KNOWLEDGE/COURSES—Education and Training: Principles and methods for curriculum and training design, teaching and instruction for individuals and groups, and the measurement of training effects. **Sociology and Anthropology:** Group behavior and dynamics, societal trends and influences, human migrations, ethnicity, and cultures and their history and origins. **English Language:** The structure and content of the English language, including the meaning and spelling of words, rules of composition, and grammar. **Communications and Media:** Media production, communication, and dissemination techniques and methods. This includes alternative ways to inform and entertain via written, oral, and visual media. **History and Archeology:** Historical events and their causes, indicators, and effects on civilizations and cultures. **Philosophy and Theology:** Different philosophical systems and religions. This includes their basic principles, values, ethics, ways of thinking, customs, practices, and impact on human culture.

Licensed Practical and Licensed Vocational Nurses

- ◎ Education/Training Required: Postsecondary vocational training
- ◎ Annual Earnings: $35,230
- ◎ Growth: 17.1%
- ◎ Annual Job Openings: 84,000
- ◎ Self-Employed: 0.6%
- ◎ Part-Time: 21.9%

Care for ill, injured, convalescent, or disabled persons in hospitals, nursing homes, clinics, private homes, group homes, and similar institutions. May work under the supervision of a registered nurse. Licensing required. Observe patients, charting and reporting changes in patients' conditions, such as adverse reactions to medication or treatment, and taking any necessary action. Administer prescribed medications or start intravenous fluids and note times and amounts on patients' charts. Answer patients' calls and determine how to assist them. Measure and record patients' vital signs,

such as height, weight, temperature, blood pressure, pulse, and respiration. Provide basic patient care and treatments, such as taking temperatures or blood pressures, dressing wounds, treating bedsores, giving enemas or douches, rubbing with alcohol, massaging, or performing catheterizations. Help patients with bathing, dressing, maintaining personal hygiene, moving in bed, or standing and walking. Supervise nurses' aides and assistants. Work as part of a health-care team to assess patient needs, plan and modify care, and implement interventions. Record food and fluid intake and output. Evaluate nursing intervention outcomes, conferring with other health-care team members as necessary. Assemble and use equipment such as catheters, tracheotomy tubes, and oxygen suppliers. Collect samples such as blood, urine, and sputum from patients and perform routine laboratory tests on samples. Prepare patients for examinations, tests, or treatments and explain procedures. Prepare food trays and examine them for conformance to prescribed diet. Apply compresses, ice bags, and hot water bottles. Clean rooms and make beds. Inventory and requisition supplies and instruments. Provide medical treatment and personal care to patients in private home settings, such as cooking, keeping rooms orderly, seeing that patients are comfortable and in good spirits, and instructing family members in simple nursing tasks. Sterilize equipment and supplies, using germicides, sterilizer, or autoclave. Assist in delivery, care, and feeding of infants. Wash and dress bodies of deceased persons. Make appointments, keep records, and perform other clerical duties in doctors' offices and clinics. Set up equipment and prepare medical treatment rooms.

SKILLS—Most Important: Science Skills; Equipment Use/Maintenance Skills; Communication Skills. **Other Above-Average Skills:** Thought-Processing Skills; Social Skills; Quality Control Skills; Mathematics Skills.

GOE—Interest Area: 08. Health Science. **Work Group:** 08.08. Patient Care and Assistance. **Other Jobs in This Group:** Home Health Aides; Nursing Aides, Orderlies, and Attendants; Psychiatric Aides; Psychiatric Technicians. **PERSONALITY TYPE:** Social. Social occupations frequently involve working with, communicating with, and teaching people. These occupations often involve helping or providing service to others.

EDUCATION/TRAINING PROGRAM(S)—Licensed Practical/Vocational Nurse Training (LPN, LVN,

Cert, Dipl, AAS). **RELATED KNOWLEDGE/ COURSES—Psychology:** Human behavior and performance; individual differences in ability, personality, and interests; learning and motivation; psychological research methods; and the assessment and treatment of behavioral and affective disorders. **Therapy and Counseling:** Principles, methods, and procedures for diagnosis, treatment, and rehabilitation of physical and mental dysfunctions and for career counseling and guidance. **Medicine and Dentistry:** The information and techniques needed to diagnose and treat human injuries, diseases, and deformities. This includes symptoms, treatment alternatives, drug properties and interactions, and preventive healthcare measures. **Customer and Personal Service:** Principles and processes for providing customer and personal services. This includes customer needs assessment, meeting of quality standards for services, and evaluation of customer satisfaction. **Philosophy and Theology:** Different philosophical systems and religions. This includes their basic principles, values, ethics, ways of thinking, customs, practices, and impact on human culture. **Sociology and Anthropology:** Group behavior and dynamics, societal trends and influences, human migrations, ethnicity, and cultures and their history and origins.

Machinists

- Education/Training Required: Long-term on-the-job training
- Annual Earnings: $34,350
- Growth: 4.3%
- Annual Job Openings: 33,000
- Self-Employed: 1.0%
- Part-Time: 1.8%

Set up and operate a variety of machine tools to produce precision parts and instruments. Includes precision instrument makers who fabricate, modify, or repair mechanical instruments. May also fabricate and modify parts to make or repair machine tools or maintain industrial machines, applying knowledge of mechanics, shop mathematics, metal properties, layout, and machining procedures. Calculate dimensions and tolerances, using knowledge of mathematics and instruments such as micrometers and vernier calipers.

Machine parts to specifications, using machine tools such as lathes, milling machines, shapers, or grinders. Measure, examine, and test completed units to detect defects and ensure conformance to specifications, using precision instruments such as micrometers. Set up, adjust, and operate all of the basic machine tools and many specialized or advanced variation tools to perform precision machining operations. Align and secure holding fixtures, cutting tools, attachments, accessories, and materials onto machines. Monitor the feed and speed of machines during the machining process. Study sample parts, blueprints, drawings, and engineering information to determine methods and sequences of operations needed to fabricate products and determine product dimensions and tolerances. Select the appropriate tools, machines, and materials to be used in preparation of machinery work. Lay out, measure, and mark metal stock to display placement of cuts. Observe and listen to operating machines or equipment to diagnose machine malfunctions and to determine need for adjustments or repairs. Check workpieces to ensure that they are properly lubricated and cooled. Maintain industrial machines, applying knowledge of mechanics, shop mathematics, metal properties, layout, and machining procedures. Position and fasten workpieces. Operate equipment to verify operational efficiency. Install repaired parts into equipment or install new equipment. Clean and lubricate machines, tools, and equipment to remove grease, rust, stains, and foreign matter. Advise clients about the materials being used for finished products. Program computers and electronic instruments such as numerically controlled machine tools. Set controls to regulate machining or enter commands to retrieve, input, or edit computerized machine control media. Confer with engineering, supervisory, and manufacturing personnel to exchange technical information. Dismantle machines or equipment, using hand tools and power tools, to examine parts for defects and replace defective parts where needed.

SKILLS—Most Important: Equipment Use/Maintenance Skills; Quality Control Skills; Computer Programming Skills. **Other Above-Average Skills:** Equipment/Technology Analysis Skills; Mathematics Skills.

GOE—Interest Area: 13. Manufacturing. **Work Group:** 13.05. Production Machining Technology. **Other Jobs in This Group:** Computer-Controlled Machine Tool Operators, Metal and Plastic; Foundry

Mold and Coremakers; Lay-Out Workers, Metal and Plastic; Model Makers, Metal and Plastic; Numerical Tool and Process Control Programmers; Patternmakers, Metal and Plastic; Tool and Die Makers; Tool Grinders, Filers, and Sharpeners. **PERSONALITY TYPE:** Realistic. Realistic occupations frequently involve work activities that include practical, hands-on problems and solutions. They often deal with plants, animals, and real-world materials like wood, tools, and machinery. Many of the occupations require working outside and do not involve a lot of paperwork or working closely with others.

EDUCATION/TRAINING PROGRAM(S)—Machine Tool Technology/Machinist; Machine Shop Technology/Assistant. **RELATED KNOWLEDGE/ COURSES—Mechanical Devices:** Machines and tools, including their designs, uses, repair, and maintenance. **Mathematics:** Arithmetic, algebra, geometry, calculus, and statistics and their applications. **Engineering and Technology:** The practical application of engineering science and technology. This includes applying principles, techniques, procedures, and equipment to the design and production of various goods and services. **Design:** Design techniques, tools, and principles involved in production of precision technical plans, blueprints, drawings, and models. **Production and Processing:** Raw materials, production processes, quality control, costs, and other techniques for maximizing the effective manufacture and distribution of goods. **Computers and Electronics:** Circuit boards; processors; chips; electronic equipment; and computer hardware and software, including applications and programming.

Maintenance and Repair Workers, General

- Education/Training Required: Moderate-term on-the-job training
- Annual Earnings: $31,210
- Growth: 15.2%
- Annual Job Openings: 154,000
- Self-Employed: 0.6%
- Part-Time: 6.0%

Perform work involving the skills of two or more maintenance or craft occupations to keep machines, mechanical equipment, or the structure of an establishment in repair. Duties may involve pipe fitting; boiler making; insulating; welding; machining; carpentry; repairing electrical or mechanical equipment; installing, aligning, and balancing new equipment; and repairing buildings, floors, or stairs. Repair or replace defective equipment parts, using hand tools and power tools, and reassemble equipment. Perform routine preventive maintenance to ensure that machines continue to run smoothly, building systems operate efficiently, and the physical condition of buildings does not deteriorate. Inspect drives, motors, and belts; check fluid levels; replace filters; and perform other maintenance actions, following checklists. Use tools ranging from common hand and power tools, such as hammers, hoists, saws, drills, and wrenches, to precision measuring instruments and electrical and electronic testing devices. Assemble, install, or repair wiring, electrical and electronic components, pipe systems and plumbing, machinery, and equipment. Diagnose mechanical problems and determine how to correct them, checking blueprints, repair manuals, and parts catalogs as necessary. Inspect, operate, and test machinery and equipment to diagnose machine malfunctions. Record maintenance and repair work performed and the costs of the work. Clean and lubricate shafts, bearings, gears, and other parts of machinery. Dismantle devices to gain access to and remove defective parts, using hoists, cranes, hand tools, and power tools. Plan and lay out repair work, using diagrams, drawings, blueprints, maintenance manuals, and schematic diagrams. Adjust functional parts of devices and control instruments, using hand tools, levels, plumb bobs, and straightedges. Order parts, supplies, and equipment from catalogs and suppliers or obtain them from storerooms. Paint and repair roofs, windows, doors, floors, woodwork, plaster, drywall, and other parts of building structures. Operate cutting torches or welding equipment to cut or join metal parts. Align and balance new equipment after installation. Inspect used parts to determine changes in dimensional requirements, using rules, calipers, micrometers, and other measuring instruments. Set up and operate machine tools to repair or fabricate machine parts, jigs and fixtures, and tools. Maintain and repair specialized equipment and machinery found in cafeterias, laundries, hospitals, stores, offices, and factories.

SKILLS—**Most Important:** Equipment Use/Maintenance Skills. **Other Above-Average Skills:** Equipment/Technology Analysis Skills; Quality Control Skills; Thought-Processing Skills.

GOE—**Interest Area:** 02. Architecture and Construction. **Work Group:** 02.05. Systems and Equipment Installation, Maintenance, and Repair. **Other Jobs in This Group:** Electrical and Electronics Repairers, Powerhouse, Substation, and Relay; Electrical Power-Line Installers and Repairers; Elevator Installers and Repairers; Heating and Air Conditioning Mechanics and Installers; Refrigeration Mechanics and Installers; Telecommunications Equipment Installers and Repairers, Except Line Installers; Telecommunications Line Installers and Repairers. **PERSONALITY TYPE:** Realistic. Realistic occupations frequently involve work activities that include practical, hands-on problems and solutions. They often deal with plants, animals, and real-world materials like wood, tools, and machinery. Many of the occupations require working outside and do not involve a lot of paperwork or working closely with others.

EDUCATION/TRAINING PROGRAM(S)—Building/Construction Site Management/Manager. **RELATED KNOWLEDGE/COURSES—Building and Construction:** The materials, methods, and tools involved in the construction or repair of houses, buildings, or other structures such as highways and roads. **Mechanical Devices:** Machines and tools, including their designs, uses, repair, and maintenance. **Design:** Design techniques, tools, and principles involved in production of precision technical plans, blueprints, drawings, and models. **Physics:** Physical principles and laws and their interrelationships and applications to understanding fluid, material, and atmospheric dynamics and mechanical, electrical, atomic, and subatomic structures and processes. **Engineering and Technology:** The practical application of engineering science and technology. This includes applying principles, techniques, procedures, and equipment to the design and production of various goods and services. **Public Safety and Security:** Relevant equipment, policies, procedures, and strategies to promote effective local, state, or national security operations for the protection of people, data, property, and institutions.

Management Analysts

- Education/Training Required: Work experience plus degree
- Annual Earnings: $66,380
- Growth: 20.1%
- Annual Job Openings: 82,000
- Self-Employed: 24.7%
- Part-Time: 18.4%

Conduct organizational studies and evaluations, design systems and procedures, conduct work simplifications and measurement studies, and prepare operations and procedures manuals to assist management in operating more efficiently and effectively. Includes program analysts and management consultants. Gather and organize information on problems or procedures. Analyze data gathered and develop solutions or alternative methods of proceeding. Confer with personnel concerned to ensure successful functioning of newly implemented systems or procedures. Develop and implement records management program for filing, protection, and retrieval of records and assure compliance with program. Review forms and reports and confer with management and users about format, distribution, and purpose and to identify problems and improvements. Document findings of study and prepare recommendations for implementation of new systems, procedures, or organizational changes. Interview personnel and conduct on-site observation to ascertain unit functions; work performed; and methods, equipment, and personnel used. Prepare manuals and train workers in use of new forms, reports, procedures, or equipment according to organizational policy. Design, evaluate, recommend, and approve changes of forms and reports. Plan study of work problems and procedures, such as organizational change, communications, information flow, integrated production methods, inventory control, or cost analysis. Recommend purchase of storage equipment and design area layout to locate equipment in space available.

SKILLS—**Most Important:** Quality Control Skills; Management Skills; Equipment Use/Maintenance Skills. **Other Above-Average Skills:** Computer Programming Skills; Social Skills; Science Skills; Communication Skills; Mathematics Skills.

GOE—**Interest Area:** 04. Business and Administration. **Work Group:** 04.05. Accounting, Auditing, and Analytical Support. **Other Jobs in This Group:** Accountants; Accountants and Auditors; Auditors; Budget Analysts; Industrial Engineering Technicians; Logisticians; Operations Research Analysts. **PERSONALITY TYPE:** Enterprising. Enterprising occupations frequently involve starting up and carrying out projects. These occupations can involve leading people and making many decisions. They sometimes require risk taking and often deal with business.

EDUCATION/TRAINING PROGRAM(S)—Business/Commerce, General; Business Administration and Management, General. **RELATED KNOWLEDGE/ COURSES—Personnel and Human Resources:** Principles and procedures for personnel recruitment, selection, training, compensation and benefits, labor relations and negotiation, and personnel information systems. **Customer and Personal Service:** Principles and processes for providing customer and personal services. This includes customer needs assessment, meeting of quality standards for services, and evaluation of customer satisfaction. **Sales and Marketing:** Principles and methods for showing, promoting, and selling products or services. This includes marketing strategy and tactics, product demonstration, sales techniques, and sales control systems. **Clerical Practices:** Administrative and clerical procedures and systems such as word processing, managing files and records, stenography and transcription, designing forms, and other office procedures and terminology. **Administration and Management:** Business and management principles involved in strategic planning, resource allocation, human resources modeling, leadership technique, production methods, and coordination of people and resources. **Economics and Accounting:** Economic and accounting principles and practices, the financial markets, banking, and the analysis and reporting of financial data.

Mapping Technicians

- Education/Training Required: Moderate-term on-the-job training
- Annual Earnings: $31,290
- Growth: 9.6%
- Annual Job Openings: 9,000
- Self-Employed: 4.3%
- Part-Time: 4.3%

The job openings listed here are shared with Surveying Technicians.

Calculate mapmaking information from field notes and draw and verify accuracy of topographical maps. Check all layers of maps to ensure accuracy, identifying and marking errors and making corrections. Determine scales, line sizes, and colors to be used for hard copies of computerized maps, using plotters. Monitor mapping work and the updating of maps to ensure accuracy, the inclusion of new and/or changed information, and compliance with rules and regulations. Identify and compile database information to create maps in response to requests. Produce and update overlay maps to show information boundaries, water locations, and topographic features on various base maps and at different scales. Trace contours and topographic details to generate maps that denote specific land and property locations and geographic attributes. Lay out and match aerial photographs in sequences in which they were taken and identify any areas missing from photographs. Compare topographical features and contour lines with images from aerial photographs, old maps, and other reference materials to verify the accuracy of their identification. Compute and measure scaled distances between reference points to establish relative positions of adjoining prints and enable the creation of photographic mosaics. Research resources such as survey maps and legal descriptions to verify property lines and to obtain information needed for mapping. Form three-dimensional images of aerial photographs taken from different locations, using mathematical techniques and plotting instruments. Enter GPS data, legal deeds, field notes, and land survey reports into GIS workstations so that information can be transformed into graphic land descriptions such as maps and drawings. Analyze aerial photographs to detect and interpret significant military, industrial, resource, or topographical data. Redraw and correct maps, such as revising parcel maps to reflect tax code area changes, using information from official records and surveys. Train staff members in duties such as tax mapping, the use of computerized mapping equipment, and the interpretation of source documents.

SKILLS—Most Important: Computer Programming Skills; Quality Control Skills; Mathematics Skills. **Other Above-Average Skills:** Equipment/Technology Analysis Skills; Science Skills; Communication Skills; Management Skills.

GOE—Interest Area: 15. Scientific Research, Engineering, and Mathematics. **Work Group:** 15.09. Engineering Technology. **Other Jobs in This Group:** Aerospace Engineering and Operations Technicians; Cartographers and Photogrammetrists; Civil Engineering Technicians; Electrical and Electronic Engineering Technicians; Electrical and Electronics Drafters; Electrical Drafters; Electrical Engineering Technicians; Electro-Mechanical Technicians; Electronic Drafters; Electronics Engineering Technicians; Environmental Engineering Technicians; Mechanical Drafters; Mechanical Engineering Technicians; Surveying and Mapping Technicians; Surveying Technicians. **PERSONALITY TYPE:** Conventional. Conventional occupations frequently involve following set procedures and routines. These occupations can include working with data and details more than with ideas. Usually there is a clear line of authority to follow.

EDUCATION/TRAINING PROGRAM(S)—Surveying Technology/Surveying; Cartography. **RELATED KNOWLEDGE/COURSES—Geography:** Principles and methods for describing the features of land, sea, and air masses, including their physical characteristics; locations; interrelationships; and distribution of plant, animal, and human life. **Design:** Design techniques, tools, and principles involved in production of precision technical plans, blueprints, drawings, and models. **Computers and Electronics:** Circuit boards; processors; chips; electronic equipment; and computer hardware and software, including applications and programming. **Engineering and Technology:** The practical application of engineering science and technology. This includes applying principles, techniques, procedures, and equipment to the design and production of various goods and services. **Mathematics:** Arithmetic, algebra, geometry, calculus, and statistics and their applications. **Sales and Marketing:** Principles and methods for showing, promoting, and selling products or services. This includes marketing strategy and tactics, product demonstration, sales techniques, and sales control systems.

Market Research Analysts

- Education/Training Required: Bachelor's degree
- Annual Earnings: $57,300
- Growth: 19.6%
- Annual Job Openings: 20,000
- Self-Employed: 7.2%
- Part-Time: 13.8%

Research market conditions in local, regional, or national areas to determine potential sales of a product or service. May gather information on competitors, prices, sales, and methods of marketing and distribution. May use survey results to create a marketing campaign based on regional preferences and buying habits. Collect and analyze data on customer demographics, preferences, needs, and buying habits to identify potential markets and factors affecting product demand. Prepare reports of findings, illustrating data graphically and translating complex findings into written text. Measure and assess customer and employee satisfaction. Forecast and track marketing and sales trends, analyzing collected data. Seek and provide information to help companies determine their position in the marketplace. Measure the effectiveness of marketing, advertising, and communications programs and strategies. Conduct research on consumer opinions and marketing strategies, collaborating with marketing professionals, statisticians, pollsters, and other professionals. Attend staff conferences to provide management with information and proposals concerning the promotion, distribution, design, and pricing of company products or services. Gather data on competitors and analyze their prices, sales, and method of marketing and distribution. Monitor industry statistics and follow trends in trade literature. Devise and evaluate methods and procedures for collecting data, such as surveys, opinion polls, or questionnaires, or arrange to obtain existing data. Develop and implement procedures for identifying advertising needs. Direct trained survey interviewers.

SKILLS—**Most Important:** Communication Skills; Social Skills; Thought-Processing Skills. **Other Above-Average Skills:** Management Skills; Equipment/Technology Analysis Skills.

GOE—Interest Area: 06. Finance and Insurance. **Work Group:** 06.02. Finance/Insurance Investigation and Analysis. **Other Jobs in This Group:** Appraisers and Assessors of Real Estate; Appraisers, Real Estate; Assessors; Claims Adjusters, Examiners, and Investigators; Claims Examiners, Property and Casualty Insurance; Cost Estimators; Credit Analysts; Financial Analysts; Insurance Adjusters, Examiners, and Investigators; Insurance Appraisers, Auto Damage; Insurance Underwriters; Loan Counselors; Loan Officers; Survey Researchers. **PERSONALITY TYPE:** Investigative. Investigative occupations frequently involve working with ideas and require an extensive amount of thinking. These occupations can involve searching for facts and figuring out problems mentally.

EDUCATION/TRAINING PROGRAM(S)—Economics, General; Applied Economics; Econometrics and Quantitative Economics; International Economics; Business/Managerial Economics; Marketing Research. **RELATED KNOWLEDGE/COURSES—Sales and Marketing:** Principles and methods for showing, promoting, and selling products or services. This includes marketing strategy and tactics, product demonstration, sales techniques, and sales control systems. **Administration and Management:** Business and management principles involved in strategic planning, resource allocation, human resources modeling, leadership technique, production methods, and coordination of people and resources. **Communications and Media:** Media production, communication, and dissemination techniques and methods. This includes alternative ways to inform and entertain via written, oral, and visual media. **Economics and Accounting:** Economic and accounting principles and practices, the financial markets, banking, and the analysis and reporting of financial data. **Customer and Personal Service:** Principles and processes for providing customer and personal services. This includes customer needs assessment, meeting of quality standards for services, and evaluation of customer satisfaction. **Clerical Practices:** Administrative and clerical procedures and systems such as word processing, managing files and records, stenography and transcription, designing forms, and other office procedures and terminology.

Marketing Managers

- Education/Training Required: Work experience plus degree
- Annual Earnings: $92,680
- Growth: 20.8%
- Annual Job Openings: 23,000
- Self-Employed: 3.6%
- Part-Time: 4.5%

Determine the demand for products and services offered by a firm and its competitors and identify potential customers. Develop pricing strategies with the goal of maximizing the firm's profits or share of the market while ensuring that the firm's customers are satisfied. Oversee product development or monitor trends that indicate the need for new products and services. Develop pricing strategies, balancing firm objectives and customer satisfaction. Identify, develop, and evaluate marketing strategy, based on knowledge of establishment objectives, market characteristics, and cost and markup factors. Evaluate the financial aspects of product development, such as budgets, expenditures, research and development appropriations, and return-on-investment and profit-loss projections. Formulate, direct, and coordinate marketing activities and policies to promote products and services, working with advertising and promotion managers. Direct the hiring, training, and performance evaluations of marketing and sales staff and oversee their daily activities. Negotiate contracts with vendors and distributors to manage product distribution, establishing distribution networks and developing distribution strategies. Consult with product development personnel on product specifications such as design, color, and packaging. Compile lists describing product or service offerings. Use sales forecasting and strategic planning to ensure the sale and profitability of products, lines, or services, analyzing business developments and monitoring market trends. Select products and accessories to be displayed at trade or special production shows. Confer with legal staff to resolve problems such as copyright infringement and royalty sharing with outside producers and distributors. Coordinate and participate in promotional activities and trade shows, working with developers, advertisers, and production managers to market products and services. Advise business and other groups on local, national, and international factors affecting the buying and selling of products and services. Initiate market research studies and analyze their findings. Consult with buying personnel to gain advice regarding the types of products or services expected to be in demand. Conduct economic and commercial surveys to identify potential markets for products and services.

SKILLS—Most Important: Management Skills; Social Skills; Science Skills. **Other Above-Average Skills:** Thought-Processing Skills; Computer Programming Skills; Mathematics Skills; Equipment/Technology Analysis Skills; Equipment Use/Maintenance Skills.

GOE—Interest Area: 14. Retail and Wholesale Sales and Service. **Work Group:** 14.01. Managerial Work in Retail/Wholesale Sales and Service. **Other Jobs in This Group:** Advertising and Promotions Managers; First-Line Supervisors/Managers of Non-Retail Sales Workers; First-Line Supervisors/Managers of Retail Sales Workers; Funeral Directors; Property, Real Estate, and Community Association Managers; Purchasing Managers; Sales Managers. **PERSONALITY TYPE:** Enterprising. Enterprising occupations frequently involve starting up and carrying out projects. These occupations can involve leading people and making many decisions. They sometimes require risk taking and often deal with business.

EDUCATION/TRAINING PROGRAM(S)—Consumer Merchandising/Retailing Management; Apparel and Textile Marketing Management; Marketing/Marketing Management, General; Marketing Research; International Marketing; Marketing, Other. **RELATED KNOWLEDGE/COURSES—Sales and Marketing:** Principles and methods for showing, promoting, and selling products or services. This includes marketing strategy and tactics, product demonstration, sales techniques, and sales control systems. **Customer and Personal Service:** Principles and processes for providing customer and personal services. This includes customer needs assessment, meeting of quality standards for services, and evaluation of customer satisfaction. **Administration and Management:** Business and management principles involved in strategic planning, resource allocation, human resources modeling, leadership technique, production methods, and coordination of people and resources. **Personnel and Human Resources:** Principles and procedures for personnel recruitment, selection, training, compensation and benefits, labor relations and negotiation, and personnel

information systems. **Communications and Media:** Media production, communication, and dissemination techniques and methods. This includes alternative ways to inform and entertain via written, oral, and visual media. **Education and Training:** Principles and methods for curriculum and training design, teaching and instruction for individuals and groups, and the measurement of training effects.

Materials Engineers

- Education/Training Required: Bachelor's degree
- Annual Earnings: $69,660
- Growth: 12.2%
- Annual Job Openings: 2,000
- Self-Employed: 0.0%
- Part-Time: 2.4%

Evaluate materials and develop machinery and processes to manufacture materials for use in products that must meet specialized design and performance specifications. Develop new uses for known materials. Includes those working with composite materials or specializing in one type of material, such as graphite, metal and metal alloys, ceramics and glass, plastics and polymers, and naturally occurring materials. Analyze product failure data and laboratory test results in order to determine causes of problems and develop solutions. Monitor material performance and evaluate material deterioration. Supervise the work of technologists, technicians, and other engineers and scientists. Design and direct the testing and/or control of processing procedures. Evaluate technical specifications and economic factors relating to process or product design objectives. Conduct or supervise tests on raw materials or finished products in order to ensure their quality. Perform managerial functions such as preparing proposals and budgets, analyzing labor costs, and writing reports. Solve problems in a number of engineering fields, such as mechanical, chemical, electrical, civil, nuclear, and aerospace. Plan and evaluate new projects, consulting with other engineers and corporate executives as necessary. Review new product plans and make recommendations for material selection based on design objectives, such as strength, weight, heat resistance, electrical conductivity, and cost. Design processing plants and equipment. Modify properties of metal alloys, using thermal and mechanical treatments. Guide technical staff engaged in developing materials for specific uses in projected products or devices. Plan and implement laboratory operations for the purpose of developing material and fabrication procedures that meet cost, product specification, and performance standards. Determine appropriate methods for fabricating and joining materials. Conduct training sessions on new material products, applications, or manufacturing methods for customers and their employees. Supervise production and testing processes in industrial settings such as metal refining facilities, smelting or foundry operations, or non-metallic materials production operations. Write for technical magazines, journals, and trade association publications. Replicate the characteristics of materials and their components with computers. Teach in colleges and universities.

SKILLS—Most Important: Science Skills; Mathematics Skills; Quality Control Skills. **Other Above-Average Skills:** Equipment/Technology Analysis Skills; Communication Skills; Social Skills; Equipment Use/Maintenance Skills.

GOE—Interest Area: 15. Scientific Research, Engineering, and Mathematics. **Work Group:** 15.07. Research and Design Engineering. **Other Jobs in This Group:** Aerospace Engineers; Biomedical Engineers; Chemical Engineers; Civil Engineers; Computer Hardware Engineers; Electrical Engineers; Electronics Engineers, Except Computer; Marine Architects; Marine Engineers; Marine Engineers and Naval Architects; Mechanical Engineers; Nuclear Engineers. **PERSONALITY TYPE:** Investigative. Investigative occupations frequently involve working with ideas and require an extensive amount of thinking. These occupations can involve searching for facts and figuring out problems mentally.

EDUCATION/TRAINING PROGRAM(S)—Ceramic Sciences and Engineering; Materials Engineering; Metallurgical Engineering. **RELATED KNOWLEDGE/COURSES—Engineering and Technology:** The practical application of engineering science and technology. This includes applying principles, techniques, procedures, and equipment to the design and production of various goods and services. **Chemistry:** The chemical composition, structure, and properties of

substances and of the chemical processes and transformations that they undergo. This includes uses of chemicals and their danger signs, production techniques, and disposal methods. **Physics:** Physical principles and laws and their interrelationships and applications to understanding fluid, material, and atmospheric dynamics and mechanical, electrical, atomic, and subatomic structures and processes. **Design:** Design techniques, tools, and principles involved in production of precision technical plans, blueprints, drawings, and models. **Mathematics:** Arithmetic, algebra, geometry, calculus, and statistics and their applications. **Mechanical Devices:** Machines and tools, including their designs, uses, repair, and maintenance.

Materials Scientists

- Education/Training Required: Bachelor's degree
- Annual Earnings: $71,450
- Growth: 8.0%
- Annual Job Openings: Fewer than 500
- Self-Employed: 0.4%
- Part-Time: 6.6%

Research and study the structures and chemical properties of various natural and manmade materials, including metals, alloys, rubber, ceramics, semiconductors, polymers, and glass. Determine ways to strengthen or combine materials or develop new materials with new or specific properties for use in a variety of products and applications. Plan laboratory experiments to confirm feasibility of processes and techniques used in the production of materials having special characteristics. Confer with customers in order to determine how materials can be tailored to suit their needs. Conduct research into the structures and properties of materials such as metals, alloys, polymers, and ceramics to obtain information that could be used to develop new products or enhance existing ones. Prepare reports of materials study findings for the use of other scientists and requestors. Devise testing methods to evaluate the effects of various conditions on particular materials. Determine ways to strengthen or combine materials or develop new materials with new or specific properties for use in a variety of products and applications.

Recommend materials for reliable performance in various environments. Test individual parts and products to ensure that manufacturer and governmental quality and safety standards are met. Visit suppliers of materials or users of products to gather specific information. Research methods of processing, forming, and firing materials to develop such products as ceramic fillings for teeth, unbreakable dinner plates, and telescope lenses. Study the nature, structure, and physical properties of metals and their alloys and their responses to applied forces. Monitor production processes to ensure that equipment is used efficiently and that projects are completed within appropriate time frames and budgets. Test material samples for tolerance under tension, compression, and shear to determine the cause of metal failures. Test metals to determine whether they meet specifications of mechanical strength; strength-weight ratio; ductility; magnetic and electrical properties; and resistance to abrasion, corrosion, heat, and cold. Teach in colleges and universities.

SKILLS—Most Important: Science Skills; Computer Programming Skills; Quality Control Skills. **Other Above-Average Skills:** Mathematics Skills; Equipment/ Technology Analysis Skills; Communication Skills; Social Skills; Management Skills.

GOE—Interest Area: 15. Scientific Research, Engineering, and Mathematics. **Work Group:** 15.02. Physical Sciences. **Other Jobs in This Group:** Astronomers; Atmospheric and Space Scientists; Chemists; Geographers; Geoscientists, Except Hydrologists and Geographers; Hydrologists; Physicists. **PERSONALITY TYPE:** Investigative. Investigative occupations frequently involve working with ideas and require an extensive amount of thinking. These occupations can involve searching for facts and figuring out problems mentally.

EDUCATION/TRAINING PROGRAM(S)—Materials Science. **RELATED KNOWLEDGE/COURSES—Chemistry:** The chemical composition, structure, and properties of substances and of the chemical processes and transformations that they undergo. This includes uses of chemicals and their danger signs, production techniques, and disposal methods. **Engineering and Technology:** The practical application of engineering science and technology. This includes applying principles, techniques, procedures, and equipment to the design and production of various goods and services.

Mathematics: Arithmetic, algebra, geometry, calculus, and statistics and their applications. **Production and Processing:** Raw materials, production processes, quality control, costs, and other techniques for maximizing the effective manufacture and distribution of goods. **Physics:** Physical principles and laws and their interrelationships and applications to understanding fluid, material, and atmospheric dynamics and mechanical, electrical, atomic, and subatomic structures and processes. **Administration and Management:** Business and management principles involved in strategic planning, resource allocation, human resources modeling, leadership technique, production methods, and coordination of people and resources.

Mathematical Science Teachers, Postsecondary

- Education/Training Required: Master's degree
- Annual Earnings: $53,820
- Growth: 32.2%
- Annual Job Openings: 329,000
- Self-Employed: 0.4%
- Part-Time: 27.3%

The job openings listed here are shared with 35 other postsecondary teaching occupations. For a complete list, see the beginning of this section.

Teach courses pertaining to mathematical concepts, statistics, and actuarial science and to the application of original and standardized mathematical techniques in solving specific problems and situations. Evaluate and grade students' classwork, assignments, and papers. Compile, administer, and grade examinations or assign this work to others. Prepare and deliver lectures to undergraduate and/or graduate students on topics such as linear algebra, differential equations, and discrete mathematics. Prepare course materials such as syllabi, homework assignments, and handouts. Maintain student attendance records, grades, and other required records. Maintain regularly scheduled office hours to advise and assist students. Plan, evaluate, and revise curricula, course content, and course materials and methods of instruction. Initiate, facilitate, and moderate classroom discussions. Select and obtain materials and supplies such as textbooks. Keep abreast of developments in their field by reading current literature, talking with colleagues, and participating in professional conferences. Advise students on academic and vocational curricula and on career issues. Collaborate with colleagues to address teaching and research issues. Serve on academic or administrative committees that deal with institutional policies, departmental matters, and academic issues. Participate in student recruitment, registration, and placement activities. Perform administrative duties such as serving as department head. Conduct research in a particular field of knowledge and publish findings in books, professional journals, and/or electronic media. Supervise undergraduate and/or graduate teaching, internship, and research work. Act as advisers to student organizations. Participate in campus and community events. Write grant proposals to procure external research funding. Compile bibliographies of specialized materials for outside reading assignments. Provide professional consulting services to government and/or industry.

SKILLS—Most Important: Mathematics Skills; Science Skills; Thought-Processing Skills. **Other Above-Average Skills:** Communication Skills; Social Skills.

GOE—Interest Area: 05. Education and Training. **Work Group:** 05.03. Postsecondary and Adult Teaching and Instructing. **Other Jobs in This Group:** Adult Literacy, Remedial Education, and GED Teachers and Instructors; Agricultural Sciences Teachers, Postsecondary; Anthropology and Archeology Teachers, Postsecondary; Architecture Teachers, Postsecondary; Area, Ethnic, and Cultural Studies Teachers, Postsecondary; Art, Drama, and Music Teachers, Postsecondary; Atmospheric, Earth, Marine, and Space Sciences Teachers, Postsecondary; Biological Science Teachers, Postsecondary; Business Teachers, Postsecondary; Chemistry Teachers, Postsecondary; Communications Teachers, Postsecondary; Computer Science Teachers, Postsecondary; Criminal Justice and Law Enforcement Teachers, Postsecondary; Economics Teachers, Postsecondary; Education Teachers, Postsecondary; Engineering Teachers, Postsecondary; English Language and Literature Teachers, Postsecondary; Environmental Science Teachers, Postsecondary; Farm and Home Management Advisors; Foreign Language and Literature Teachers, Postsecondary; Forestry and Conservation Science Teachers, Postsecondary; Geo-graphy Teachers, Postsecondary; Graduate Teaching Assistants; Health Specialties Teachers, Postsecondary; History Teachers, Postsecondary; Home Economics Teachers, Postsecondary; Law Teachers, Postsecondary; Library Science Teachers, Postsecondary; Nursing Instructors and Teachers, Postsecondary; Philosophy and Religion Teachers, Postsecondary; Physics Teachers, Postsecondary; Political Science Teachers, Postsecondary; Psychology Teachers, Postsecondary; Recreation and Fitness Studies Teachers, Postsecondary; Self-Enrichment Education Teachers; Social Work Teachers, Postsecondary; Sociology Teachers, Postsecondary; Vocational Education Teachers, Postsecondary. **PERSONALITY TYPE:** Investigative. Investigative occupations frequently involve working with ideas and require an extensive amount of thinking. These occupations can involve searching for facts and figuring out problems mentally.

EDUCATION/TRAINING PROGRAM(S)—Mathematics, General; Algebra and Number Theory; Analysis and Functional Analysis; Geometry/Geometric Analysis; Topology and Foundations; Mathematics, Other; Applied Mathematics; Statistics, General; Mathematical Statistics and Probability; Mathematics and Statistics, Other; Logic; Business Statistics. **RELATED KNOWLEDGE/COURSES—Mathematics:** Arithmetic, algebra, geometry, calculus, and statistics and their applications. **Education and Training:** Principles and methods for curriculum and training design, teaching and instruction for individuals and groups, and the measurement of training effects. **Physics:** Physical principles and laws and their interrelationships and applications to understanding fluid, material, and atmospheric dynamics and mechanical, electrical, atomic, and subatomic structures and processes. **Computers and Electronics:** Circuit boards; processors; chips; electronic equipment; and computer hardware and software, including applications and programming. **English Language:** The structure and content of the English language, including the meaning and spelling of words, rules of composition, and grammar. **Psychology:** Human behavior and performance; individual differences in ability, personality, and interests; learning and motivation; psychological research methods; and the assessment and treatment of behavioral and affective disorders.

Mechanical Engineers

- Education/Training Required: Bachelor's degree
- Annual Earnings: $67,590
- Growth: 11.1%
- Annual Job Openings: 11,000
- Self-Employed: 2.5%
- Part-Time: 2.1%

Perform engineering duties in planning and designing tools, engines, machines, and other mechanically functioning equipment. Oversee installation, operation, maintenance, and repair of such equipment as centralized heat, gas, water, and steam systems. Read and interpret blueprints, technical drawings, schematics, and computer-generated reports. Confer with engineers and other personnel to implement operating procedures, resolve system malfunctions, and provide technical information. Research and analyze customer design proposals, specifications, manuals, and other data to evaluate the feasibility, cost, and maintenance requirements of designs or applications. Specify system components or direct modification of products to ensure conformance with engineering design and performance specifications. Research, design, evaluate, install, operate, and maintain mechanical products, equipment, systems, and processes to meet requirements, applying knowledge of engineering principles. Investigate equipment failures and difficulties to diagnose faulty operation and to make recommendations to maintenance crew. Assist drafters in developing the structural design of products, using drafting tools or computer-assisted design (CAD) or drafting equipment and software. Provide feedback to design engineers on customer problems and needs. Oversee installation, operation, maintenance, and repair to ensure that machines and equipment are installed and functioning according to specifications. Conduct research that tests and analyzes the feasibility, design, operation, and performance of equipment, components, and systems. Recommend design modifications to eliminate machine or system malfunctions. Develop and test models of alternate designs and processing methods to assess feasibility, operating condition effects, possible new applications, and necessity of modification. Develop, coordinate, and monitor all aspects of production, including selection of manufacturing methods, fabrication, and operation of product designs. Estimate costs and submit bids for engineering, construction, or extraction projects and prepare contract documents. Perform personnel functions such as supervision of production workers, technicians, technologists, and other engineers or design of evaluation programs. Solicit new business and provide technical customer service. Establish and coordinate the maintenance and safety procedures, service schedule, and supply of materials required to maintain machines and equipment in the prescribed condition.

SKILLS—Most Important: Science Skills; Mathematics Skills; Equipment/Technology Analysis Skills. **Other Above-Average Skills:** Thought-Processing Skills; Communication Skills; Quality Control Skills.

GOE—Interest Area: 15. Scientific Research, Engineering, and Mathematics. **Work Group:** 15.07. Research and Design Engineering. **Other Jobs in This Group:** Aerospace Engineers; Biomedical Engineers; Chemical Engineers; Civil Engineers; Computer Hardware Engineers; Electrical Engineers; Electronics Engineers, Except Computer; Marine Architects; Marine Engineers; Marine Engineers and Naval Architects; Materials Engineers; Nuclear Engineers. **PERSONALITY TYPE:** Realistic. Realistic occupations frequently involve work activities that include practical, hands-on problems and solutions. They often deal with plants, animals, and real-world materials like wood, tools, and machinery. Many of the occupations require working outside and do not involve a lot of paperwork or working closely with others.

EDUCATION/TRAINING PROGRAM(S)—Mechanical Engineering. **RELATED KNOWLEDGE/ COURSES—Design:** Design techniques, tools, and principles involved in production of precision technical plans, blueprints, drawings, and models. **Engineering and Technology:** The practical application of engineering science and technology. This includes applying principles, techniques, procedures, and equipment to the design and production of various goods and services. **Mechanical Devices:** Machines and tools, including their designs, uses, repair, and maintenance. **Production and Processing:** Raw materials, production processes, quality control, costs, and other techniques for maximizing the effective manufacture and distribution of goods. **Physics:** Physical principles and laws and their interrelationships and applications to understanding fluid, material, and atmospheric dynamics and mechanical, electrical, atomic, and subatomic structures and processes. **Administration and Management:** Business and management principles involved in strategic planning, resource allocation, human resources modeling, leadership technique, production methods, and coordination of people and resources.

Medical and Clinical Laboratory Technicians

- Education/Training Required: Associate degree
- Annual Earnings: $31,700
- Growth: 25.0%
- Annual Job Openings: 14,000
- Self-Employed: 0.1%
- Part-Time: 17.3%

Perform routine medical laboratory tests for the diagnosis, treatment, and prevention of disease. May work under the supervision of a medical technologist. Conduct chemical analyses of body fluids, such as blood and urine, using microscope or automatic analyzer to detect abnormalities or diseases, and enter findings into computer. Set up, adjust, maintain, and clean medical laboratory equipment. Analyze the results of tests and experiments to ensure conformity to specifications, using special mechanical and electrical devices. Analyze and record test data to issue reports that use charts, graphs and narratives. Conduct blood tests for transfusion purposes and perform blood counts. Perform medical research to further control and cure disease. Obtain specimens, cultivating, isolating, and identifying microorganisms for analysis. Examine cells stained with dye to locate abnormalities. Collect blood or tissue samples from patients, observing principles of asepsis to obtain blood sample. Consult with a pathologist to determine a final diagnosis when abnormal cells are found. Inoculate fertilized eggs, broths, or other bacteriological media with organisms. Cut, stain, and mount tissue samples for examination by pathologists. Supervise and instruct other technicians and laboratory assistants. Prepare standard volumetric solutions and reagents to be combined with samples, following standardized formulas or experimental procedures. Prepare vaccines and serums by standard laboratory methods, testing for virus inactivity and sterility. Test raw materials, processes, and finished products to determine quality and quantity of materials or characteristics of a substance.

SKILLS—Most Important: Science Skills; Equipment Use/Maintenance Skills; Quality Control Skills. **Other Above-Average Skills:** Communication Skills; Thought-Processing Skills; Equipment/Technology Analysis Skills; Management Skills.

GOE—Interest Area: 08. Health Science. **Work Group:** 08.06. Medical Technology. **Other Jobs in This Group:** Biological Technicians; Cardiovascular Technologists and Technicians; Diagnostic Medical Sonographers; Medical and Clinical Laboratory Technologists; Medical Equipment Preparers; Medical Records and Health Information Technicians; Nuclear Medicine Technologists; Opticians, Dispensing; Orthotists and Prosthetists; Radiologic Technicians; Radiologic Technologists; Radiologic Technologists and Technicians. **PERSONALITY TYPE:** Realistic. Realistic occupations frequently involve work activities that include practical, hands-on problems and solutions. They often deal with plants, animals, and real-world materials like wood, tools, and machinery. Many of the occupations require working outside and do not involve a lot of paperwork or working closely with others.

EDUCATION/TRAINING PROGRAM(S)—Clinical/Medical Laboratory Assistant; Blood Bank Technology Specialist; Hematology Technology/Technician; Clinical/Medical Laboratory Technician; Histologic Technician. **RELATED KNOWLEDGE/COURSES—Medicine and Dentistry:** The information and techniques needed to diagnose and treat human injuries, diseases, and deformities. This includes symptoms, treatment alternatives, drug properties and interactions, and preventive healthcare measures. **Therapy and Counseling:** Principles, methods, and procedures for diagnosis, treatment, and rehabilitation of physical and mental dysfunctions and for career counseling and guidance. **Biology:** Plant and animal organisms and their tissues, cells, functions, interdependencies, and interactions with each other and the environment. **Clerical Practices:** Administrative and clerical procedures and systems such as word processing, managing files and records, stenography and transcription, designing forms, and other office procedures and terminology. **Education and Training:** Principles and methods for curriculum and training design, teaching and instruction for individuals and groups, and the measurement of training effects.

Medical and Clinical Laboratory Technologists

- Education/Training Required: Bachelor's degree
- Annual Earnings: $47,710
- Growth: 20.5%
- Annual Job Openings: 14,000
- Self-Employed: 0.1%
- Part-Time: 17.3%

Perform complex medical laboratory tests for diagnosis, treatment, and prevention of disease. May train or supervise staff. Analyze laboratory findings to check the accuracy of the results. Conduct chemical analysis of body fluids, including blood, urine, and spinal fluid, to determine presence of normal and abnormal components. Operate, calibrate, and maintain equipment used in quantitative and qualitative analysis, such as spectrophotometers, calorimeters, flame photometers, and computer-controlled analyzers. Enter data from analysis of medical tests and clinical results into computer for storage. Analyze samples of biological material for chemical content or reaction. Establish and monitor programs to ensure the accuracy of laboratory results. Set up, clean, and maintain laboratory equipment. Provide technical information about test results to physicians, family members, and researchers. Supervise, train, and direct lab assistants, medical and clinical laboratory technicians and technologists, and other medical laboratory workers engaged in laboratory testing. Develop, standardize, evaluate, and modify procedures, techniques, and tests used in the analysis of specimens and in medical laboratory experiments. Cultivate, isolate, and assist in identifying microbial organisms and perform various tests on these microorganisms. Study blood samples to determine the number of cells and their morphology, as well as the blood group, type, and compatibility for transfusion purposes, using microscopic technique. Obtain, cut, stain, and mount biolog-

ical material on slides for microscopic study and diagnosis, following standard laboratory procedures. Select and prepare specimen and media for cell culture, using aseptic technique and knowledge of medium components and cell requirements. Conduct medical research under direction of microbiologist or biochemist. Harvest cell cultures at optimum time based on knowledge of cell cycle differences and culture conditions.

SKILLS—Most Important: Quality Control Skills; Science Skills; Equipment Use/Maintenance Skills. **Other Above-Average Skills:** Thought-Processing Skills; Mathematics Skills; Social Skills.

GOE—Interest Area: 08. Health Science. **Work Group:** 08.06. Medical Technology. **Other Jobs in This Group:** Biological Technicians; Cardiovascular Technologists and Technicians; Diagnostic Medical Sonographers; Medical and Clinical Laboratory Technicians; Medical Equipment Preparers; Medical Records and Health Information Technicians; Nuclear Medicine Technologists; Opticians, Dispensing; Orthotists and Prosthetists; Radiologic Technicians; Radiologic Technologists; Radiologic Technologists and Technicians. **PERSONALITY TYPE:** Investigative. Investigative occupations frequently involve working with ideas and require an extensive amount of thinking. These occupations can involve searching for facts and figuring out problems mentally.

EDUCATION/TRAINING PROGRAM(S)—Cytotechnology/Cytotechnologist; Clinical Laboratory Science/Medical Technology/Technologist; Histologic Technology/Histotechnologist; Cytogenetics/Genetics/Clinical Genetics Technology/Technologist; Renal/Dialysis Technologist/Technician; Clinical/Medical Laboratory Science and Allied Professions, Other. **RELATED KNOWLEDGE/COURSES—Biology:** Plant and animal organisms and their tissues, cells, functions, interdependencies, and interactions with each other and the environment. **Chemistry:** The chemical composition, structure, and properties of substances and of the chemical processes and transformations that they undergo. This includes uses of chemicals and their danger signs, production techniques, and disposal methods. **Public Safety and Security:** Relevant equipment, policies, procedures, and strategies to promote effective local, state, or national security operations for the protection of people, data, property, and institutions. **Mechanical Devices:** Machines and tools, including their designs, uses, repair, and maintenance. **Computers**

and **Electronics:** Circuit boards; processors; chips; electronic equipment; and computer hardware and software, including applications and programming. **Mathematics:** Arithmetic, algebra, geometry, calculus, and statistics and their applications.

Medical and Health Services Managers

- ◎ Education/Training Required: Work experience plus degree
- ◎ Annual Earnings: $69,700
- ◎ Growth: 22.8%
- ◎ Annual Job Openings: 33,000
- ◎ Self-Employed: 5.7%
- ◎ Part-Time: 5.7%

Plan, direct, or coordinate medicine and health services in hospitals, clinics, managed care organizations, public health agencies, or similar organizations. Direct, supervise, and evaluate work activities of medical, nursing, technical, clerical, service, maintenance, and other personnel. Establish objectives and evaluative or operational criteria for units they manage. Direct or conduct recruitment, hiring, and training of personnel. Develop and maintain computerized record management systems to store and process data such as personnel activities and information and to produce reports. Develop and implement organizational policies and procedures for the facility or medical unit. Conduct and administer fiscal operations, including accounting, planning budgets, authorizing expenditures, establishing rates for services, and coordinating financial reporting. Establish work schedules and assignments for staff according to workload, space, and equipment availability. Maintain communication between governing boards, medical staff, and department heads by attending board meetings and coordinating interdepartmental functioning. Monitor the use of diagnostic services, inpatient beds, facilities, and staff to ensure effective use of resources and assess the need for additional staff, equipment, and services. Maintain awareness of advances in medicine, computerized diagnostic and treatment equipment, data processing technology, government regulations, health insurance changes, and financing options. Manage change in integrated health-care delivery systems, such as work restructuring, technological innovations, and shifts in the focus of care. Prepare activity reports to inform management of the status and implementation plans of programs, services, and quality initiatives. Plan, implement, and administer programs and services in a health-care or medical facility, including personnel administration, training, and coordination of medical, nursing, and physical plant staff. Consult with medical, business, and community groups to discuss service problems, respond to community needs, enhance public relations, coordinate activities and plans, and promote health programs. Inspect facilities and recommend building or equipment modifications to ensure emergency readiness and compliance to access, safety, and sanitation regulations.

SKILLS—Most Important: Management Skills; Quality Control Skills; Social Skills. **Other Above-Average Skills:** Thought-Processing Skills; Science Skills; Equipment/Technology Analysis Skills; Mathematics Skills; Equipment Use/Maintenance Skills.

GOE—Interest Area: 08. Health Science. **Work Group:** 08.01. Managerial Work in Medical and Health Services. **Other Jobs in This Group:** Coroners. **PERSONALITY TYPE:** Enterprising. Enterprising occupations frequently involve starting up and carrying out projects. These occupations can involve leading people and making many decisions. They sometimes require risk taking and often deal with business.

EDUCATION/TRAINING PROGRAM(S)—Health/Health Care Administration/Management; Hospital and Health Care Facilities Administration/Management; Health Unit Manager/Ward Supervisor; Health Information/Medical Records Administration/Administrator; Medical Staff Services Technology/Technician; Health and Medical Administrative Services, Other; Nursing Administration (MSN, MS, PhD); Public Health, General (MPH, DPH); Community Health and Preventive Medicine; others. **RELATED KNOWLEDGE/COURSES—Therapy and Counseling:** Principles, methods, and procedures for diagnosis, treatment, and rehabilitation of physical and mental dysfunctions and for career counseling and guidance. **Medicine and Dentistry:** The information and techniques needed to diagnose and treat human injuries, diseases, and deformities. This includes symptoms, treatment alternatives, drug properties and inter-actions, and preventive healthcare measures. **Philosophy and Theology:** Different philosophical systems and religions. This includes their basic principles, values, ethics, ways of thinking, customs, practices, and impact on human culture. **Personnel and Human Resources:** Principles and procedures for personnel recruitment, selection, training, compensation and benefits, labor relations and negotiation, and personnel information systems. **Psychology:** Human behavior and performance; individual differences in ability, personality, and interests; learning and motivation; psychological research methods; and the assessment and treatment of behavioral and affective disorders. **Sociology and Anthropology:** Group behavior and dynamics, societal trends and influences, human migrations, ethnicity, and cultures and their history and origins.

Medical and Public Health Social Workers

- Education/Training Required: Bachelor's degree
- Annual Earnings: $41,120
- Growth: 25.9%
- Annual Job Openings: 14,000
- Self-Employed: 3.0%
- Part-Time: 11.5%

Provide persons, families, or vulnerable populations with the psychosocial support needed to cope with chronic, acute, or terminal illnesses, such as Alzheimer's, cancer, or AIDS. Services include advising family caregivers, providing patient education and counseling, and making necessary referrals for other social services. Collaborate with other professionals to evaluate patients' medical or physical condition and to assess client needs. Investigate child abuse or neglect cases and take authorized protective action when necessary. Refer patient, client, or family to community resources to assist in recovery from mental or physical illness and to provide access to services such as financial assistance, legal aid, housing, job placement, or education. Counsel clients and patients in individual and group sessions to help them overcome dependencies, recover from illness, and adjust to life. Organize support groups or counsel family members to assist them in understanding, dealing with, and supporting the client or patient. Advocate for clients or patients to resolve crises. Identify environmental impediments to client or patient progress through interviews and review of patient records. Utilize consultation data and social work experience to plan and coordinate client or patient care and rehabilitation, following through to ensure service efficacy. Modify treatment plans to comply with changes in clients' status. Monitor, evaluate, and record client progress according to measurable goals described in treatment and care plan. Supervise and direct other workers providing services to clients or patients. Develop or advise on social policy and assist in community development. Oversee Medicaid- and Medicare-related paperwork and recordkeeping in hospitals. Conduct social research to advance knowledge in the social work field. Plan and conduct programs to combat social problems, prevent substance abuse, or improve community health and counseling services.

SKILLS—Most Important: Social Skills; Communication Skills; Thought-Processing Skills. **Other Above-Average Skills:** None met the criteria.

GOE—Interest Area: 10. Human Service. **Work Group:** 10.01. Counseling and Social Work. **Other Jobs in This Group:** Child, Family, and School Social Workers; Clinical Psychologists; Clinical, Counseling, and School Psychologists; Counseling Psychologists; Marriage and Family Therapists; Mental Health and Substance Abuse Social Workers; Mental Health Counselors; Probation Officers and Correctional Treatment Specialists; Rehabilitation Counselors; Residential Advisors; Social and Human Service Assistants; Substance Abuse and Behavioral Disorder Counselors. **PERSONALITY TYPE:** Social. Social occupations frequently involve working with, communicating with, and teaching people. These occupations often involve helping or providing service to others.

EDUCATION/TRAINING PROGRAM(S)—Clinical/Medical Social Work. **RELATED KNOWLEDGE/COURSES—Psychology:** Human behavior and performance; individual differences in ability, personality, and interests; learning and motivation; psychological research methods; and the assessment and treatment of behavioral and affective disorders. **Therapy and Counseling:** Principles, methods, and procedures for diagnosis, treatment, and rehabilitation of physical and mental dysfunctions and for career counseling and guidance. **Philosophy and Theology:** Different philosophical systems and religions. This includes their basic principles, values, ethics, ways of thinking, customs, practices, and impact on human culture. **Sociology and Anthropology:** Group behavior and dynamics, societal trends and influences, human migrations, ethnicity, and cultures and their history and origins. **Medicine and Dentistry:** The information and techniques needed to diagnose and treat human injuries, diseases, and deformities. This includes symptoms, treatment alternatives, drug properties and interactions, and preventive health-care measures. **Customer and Personal Service:** Principles and processes for providing customer and personal services. This includes customer needs assessment, meeting of quality standards for services, and evaluation of customer satisfaction.

Medical Assistants

- Education/Training Required: Moderate-term on-the-job training
- Annual Earnings: $25,350
- Growth: 52.1%
- Annual Job Openings: 93,000
- Self-Employed: 0.0%
- Part-Time: 27.5%

Perform administrative and certain clinical duties under the direction of physician. Administrative duties may include scheduling appointments, maintaining medical records, billing, and coding for insurance purposes. Clinical duties may include taking and recording vital signs and medical histories, preparing patients for examination, drawing blood, and administering medications as directed by physician. Interview patients to obtain medical information and measure their vital signs, weight, and height. Show patients to examination rooms and prepare them for the physician. Record patients' medical history, vital statistics, and information such as test results in medical records. Prepare and administer medications as directed by a physician. Collect blood, tissue, or other laboratory specimens; log the specimens; and prepare them for testing. Explain treatment procedures, medications, diets,

and physicians' instructions to patients. Help physicians examine and treat patients, handing them instruments and materials or performing such tasks as giving injections or removing sutures. Authorize drug refills and provide prescription information to pharmacies. Prepare treatment rooms for patient examinations, keeping the rooms neat and clean. Clean and sterilize instruments and dispose of contaminated supplies. Schedule appointments for patients. Change dressings on wounds. Greet and log in patients arriving at office or clinic. Contact medical facilities or departments to schedule patients for tests or admission. Perform general office duties such as answering telephones, taking dictation, or completing insurance forms. Inventory and order medical, lab, or office supplies and equipment. Perform routine laboratory tests and sample analyses. Set up medical laboratory equipment. Keep financial records and perform other bookkeeping duties, such as handling credit and collections and mailing monthly statements to patients. Operate X-ray, electrocardiogram (EKG), and other equipment to administer routine diagnostic tests. Give physiotherapy treatments such as diathermy, galvanics, and hydrotherapy.

SKILLS—Most Important: Social Skills; Mathematics Skills; Communication Skills. **Other Above-Average Skills:** Science Skills; Equipment Use/Maintenance Skills.

GOE—Interest Area: 08. Health Science. **Work Group:** 08.02. Medicine and Surgery. **Other Jobs in This Group:** Anesthesiologists; Family and General Practitioners; Internists, General; Medical Transcriptionists; Obstetricians and Gynecologists; Pediatricians, General; Pharmacists; Pharmacy Aides; Pharmacy Technicians; Physician Assistants; Psychiatrists; Registered Nurses; Surgeons; Surgical Technologists. **PERSONALITY TYPE:** Social. Social occupations frequently involve working with, communicating with, and teaching people. These occupations often involve helping or providing service to others.

EDUCATION/TRAINING PROGRAM(S)—Medical Office Management/Administration; Medical Office Assistant/Specialist; Medical Reception/Receptionist; Medical Insurance Coding Specialist/Coder; Medical Administrative/Executive Assistant and Medical Secretary; Medical/Clinical Assistant; Anesthesiologist Assistant; Chiropractic Assistant/Technician; Allied Health and Medical Assisting

Services, Other; Optomeric Technician/Assistant; others. **RELATED KNOWLEDGE/COURSES— Medicine and Dentistry:** The information and techniques needed to diagnose and treat human injuries, diseases, and deformities. This includes symptoms, treatment alternatives, drug properties and interactions, and preventive healthcare measures. **Therapy and Counseling:** Principles, methods, and procedures for diagnosis, treatment, and rehabilitation of physical and mental dysfunctions and for career counseling and guidance. **Customer and Personal Service:** Principles and processes for providing customer and personal services. This includes customer needs assessment, meeting of quality standards for services, and evaluation of customer satisfaction. **Clerical Practices:** Administrative and clerical procedures and systems such as word processing, managing files and records, stenography and transcription, designing forms, and other office procedures and terminology. **Psychology:** Human behavior and performance; individual differences in ability, personality, and interests; learning and motivation; psychological research methods; and the assessment and treatment of behavioral and affective disorders. **English Language:** The structure and content of the English language, including the meaning and spelling of words, rules of composition, and grammar.

Medical Equipment Repairers

- Education/Training Required: Associate degree
- Annual Earnings: $39,570
- Growth: 14.8%
- Annual Job Openings: 4,000
- Self-Employed: 16.2%
- Part-Time: 12.1%

Test, adjust, or repair biomedical or electromedical equipment. Inspect and test malfunctioning medical and related equipment following manufacturers' specifications, using test and analysis instruments. Examine medical equipment and facility's structural environment and check for proper use of equipment to protect patients and staff from electrical or mechanical hazards and to ensure compliance with safety regulations. Disassemble malfunctioning equipment and remove, repair, and replace defective parts such as motors, clutches, or transformers. Keep records of maintenance, repair, and required updates of equipment. Perform preventive maintenance or service such as cleaning, lubricating, and adjusting equipment. Test and calibrate components and equipment, following manufacturers' manuals and troubleshooting techniques and using hand tools, power tools, and measuring devices. Explain and demonstrate correct operation and preventive maintenance of medical equipment to personnel. Study technical manuals and attend training sessions provided by equipment manufacturers to maintain current knowledge. Plan and carry out work assignments, using blueprints, schematic drawings, technical manuals, wiring diagrams, and liquid and air flow sheets, following prescribed regulations, directives, and other instructions as required. Solder loose connections, using soldering iron. Test, evaluate, and classify excess or in-use medical equipment and determine serviceability, condition, and disposition in accordance with regulations. Research catalogs and repair part lists to locate sources for repair parts, requisitioning parts and recording their receipt. Evaluate technical specifications to identify equipment and systems best suited for intended use and possible purchase based on specifications, user needs, and technical requirements. Contribute expertise to develop medical maintenance standard operating procedures. Compute power and space requirements for installing medical, dental, or related equipment and install units to manufacturers' specifications. Supervise and advise subordinate personnel. Repair shop equipment, metal furniture, and hospital equipment, including welding broken parts and replacing missing parts, or bring item into local shop for major repairs.

SKILLS—Most Important: Equipment Use/Maintenance Skills; Quality Control Skills; Science Skills. **Other Above-Average Skills:** Equipment/Technology Analysis Skills; Social Skills; Management Skills; Communication Skills.

GOE—Interest Area: 13. Manufacturing. **Work Group:** 13.15. Medical and Technical Equipment Repair. **Other Jobs in This Group:** Camera and Photographic Equipment Repairers; Watch Repairers. **PERSONALITY TYPE:** Realistic. Realistic occupations frequently involve work activities that include practical, hands-on problems and solutions. They often deal with plants, animals, and real-world materials like wood, tools, and machinery. Many of the occupations require working outside and do not involve a lot of paperwork or working closely with others.

EDUCATION/TRAINING PROGRAM(S)—Biomedical Technology/Technician. **RELATED KNOWLEDGE/COURSES**—**Mechanical Devices:** Machines and tools, including their designs, uses, repair, and maintenance. **Computers and Electronics:** Circuit boards; processors; chips; electronic equipment; and computer hardware and software, including applications and programming. **Engineering and Technology:** The practical application of engineering science and technology. This includes applying principles, techniques, procedures, and equipment to the design and production of various goods and services. **Physics:** Physical principles and laws and their interrelationships and applications to understanding fluid, material, and atmospheric dynamics and mechanical, electrical, atomic, and subatomic structures and processes. **Customer and Personal Service:** Principles and processes for providing customer and personal services. This includes customer needs assessment, meeting of quality standards for services, and evaluation of customer satisfaction. **Telecommunications:** Transmission, broadcasting, switching, control, and operation of telecommunications systems.

Medical Scientists, Except Epidemiologists

- Education/Training Required: Doctoral degree
- Annual Earnings: $61,730
- Growth: 34.1%
- Annual Job Openings: 15,000
- Self-Employed: 0.4%
- Part-Time: 5.5%

Conduct research dealing with the understanding of human diseases and the improvement of human health. Engage in clinical investigation or other research, production, technical writing, or related activities. Conduct research to develop methodologies, instrumentation, and procedures for medical applica-

tion, analyzing data and presenting findings. Plan and direct studies to investigate human or animal disease, preventive methods, and treatments for disease. Follow strict safety procedures when handling toxic materials to avoid contamination. Evaluate effects of drugs, gases, pesticides, parasites, and microorganisms at various levels. Teach principles of medicine and medical and laboratory procedures to physicians, residents, students, and technicians. Prepare and analyze organ, tissue, and cell samples to identify toxicity, bacteria, or microorganisms or to study cell structure. Standardize drug dosages, methods of immunization, and procedures for manufacture of drugs and medicinal compounds. Investigate cause, progress, life cycle, or mode of transmission of diseases or parasites. Confer with health department, industry personnel, physicians, and others to develop health safety standards and public health improvement programs. Study animal and human health and physiological processes. Consult with and advise physicians, educators, researchers, and others regarding medical applications of physics, biology, and chemistry. Use equipment such as atomic absorption spectrometers, electron microscopes, flow cytometers, and chromatography systems.

SKILLS—**Most Important:** Science Skills; Communication Skills; Management Skills. **Other Above-Average Skills:** Thought-Processing Skills; Computer Programming Skills; Quality Control Skills; Equipment/Technology Analysis Skills.

GOE—**Interest Area:** 15. Scientific Research, Engineering, and Mathematics. **Work Group:** 15.03. Life Sciences. **Other Jobs in This Group:** Biochemists and Biophysicists; Biologists; Environmental Scientists and Specialists, Including Health; Epidemiologists; Microbiologists. **PERSONALITY TYPE:** Investigative. Investigative occupations frequently involve working with ideas and require an extensive amount of thinking. These occupations can involve searching for facts and figuring out problems mentally.

EDUCATION/TRAINING PROGRAM(S)—Biomedical Sciences, General; Biochemistry; Biophysics; Molecular Biology; Cell/Cellular Biology and Histology; Anatomy; Medical Microbiology and Bacteriology; Immunology; Human/Medical Genetics; Physiology, General; Molecular Physiology; Cell Physiology; Endocrinology; Reproductive Biology; Neurobiology and Neurophysiology; Cardiovascular Science; others. **RELATED KNOWLEDGE/COURSES—Biology:** Plant and animal organisms and their tissues, cells, functions, interdependencies, and interactions with each other and the environment. **Medicine and Dentistry:** The information and techniques needed to diagnose and treat human injuries, diseases, and deformities. This includes symptoms, treatment alternatives, drug properties and interactions, and preventive healthcare measures. **Chemistry:** The chemical composition, structure, and properties of substances and of the chemical processes and transformations that they undergo. This includes uses of chemicals and their danger signs, production techniques, and disposal methods. **Communications and Media:** Media production, communication, and dissemination techniques and methods. This includes alternative ways to inform and entertain via written, oral, and visual media. **Personnel and Human Resources:** Principles and procedures for personnel recruitment, selection, training, compensation and benefits, labor relations and negotiation, and personnel information systems. **Mathematics:** Arithmetic, algebra, geometry, calculus, and statistics and their applications.

Mental Health and Substance Abuse Social Workers

- Education/Training Required: Master's degree
- Annual Earnings: $34,410
- Growth: 26.7%
- Annual Job Openings: 15,000
- Self-Employed: 2.5%
- Part-Time: 11.5%

Assess and treat individuals with mental, emotional, or substance abuse problems, including abuse of alcohol, tobacco, and/or other drugs. Activities may include individual and group therapy, crisis intervention, case management, client advocacy, prevention, and education. Counsel clients in individual and group sessions to assist them in dealing with substance abuse, mental and physical illness, poverty, unemployment, or physical abuse. Interview clients, review records, and confer with other professionals to evaluate mental or physical condition of client or patient. Collaborate with counselors, physicians, and nurses to plan and coordinate treatment, drawing on social work experience and patient needs. Monitor, evaluate, and record client progress with respect to treatment goals. Refer patient, client, or family to community resources for housing or treatment to assist in recovery from mental or physical illness, following through to ensure service efficacy. Counsel and aid family members to assist them in understanding, dealing with, and supporting the client or patient. Modify treatment plans according to changes in client status. Plan and conduct programs to prevent substance abuse, to combat social problems, or to improve health and counseling services in community. Supervise and direct other workers who provide services to clients or patients. Develop or advise on social policy and assist in community development. Conduct social research to advance knowledge in the social work field.

SKILLS—Most Important: Social Skills; Thought-Processing Skills; Communication Skills. **Other Above-Average Skills:** Management Skills; Quality Control Skills.

GOE—Interest Area: 10. Human Service. **Work Group:** 10.01. Counseling and Social Work. **Other Jobs in This Group:** Child, Family, and School Social Workers; Clinical Psychologists; Clinical, Counseling, and School Psychologists; Counseling Psychologists; Marriage and Family Therapists; Medical and Public Health Social Workers; Mental Health Counselors; Probation Officers and Correctional Treatment Specialists; Rehabilitation Counselors; Residential Advisors; Social and Human Service Assistants; Substance Abuse and Behavioral Disorder Counselors. **PERSONALITY TYPE:** Social. Social occupations frequently involve working with, communicating with, and teaching people. These occupations often involve helping or providing service to others.

EDUCATION/TRAINING PROGRAM(S)—Clinical/Medical Social Work. **RELATED KNOWLEDGE/COURSES—Psychology:** Human behavior and performance; individual differences in ability, personality, and interests; learning and motivation; psychological research methods; and the assessment and treatment of behavioral and affective disorders. **Therapy and Counseling:** Principles, methods, and procedures for diagnosis, treatment, and rehabilitation of physical and mental dysfunctions and for career counseling and guidance. **Customer and Personal Service:** Principles and processes for providing customer and personal services. This includes customer needs assessment, meeting of quality standards for services, and evaluation of customer satisfaction. **Sociology and Anthropology:** Group behavior and dynamics, societal trends and influences, human migrations, ethnicity, and cultures and their history and origins.

Mental Health Counselors

- Education/Training Required: Master's degree
- Annual Earnings: $34,010
- Growth: 27.2%
- Annual Job Openings: 14,000
- Self-Employed: 5.0%
- Part-Time: 16.7%

Counsel with emphasis on prevention. Work with individuals and groups to promote optimum mental health. May help individuals deal with addictions and substance abuse; family, parenting, and marital problems; suicide; stress management; problems with self-esteem; and issues associated with aging and mental and emotional health. Maintain confidentiality of records relating to clients' treatment. Guide clients in the development of skills and strategies for dealing with their problems. Encourage clients to express their feelings and discuss what is happening in their lives and help them to develop insight into themselves and their relationships. Prepare and maintain all required treatment records and reports. Counsel clients and patients, individually and in group sessions, to assist in overcoming dependencies, adjusting to life, and making changes. Collect information about clients through interviews, observation, and tests. Act as client advocates to coordinate required services or to resolve emergency problems in crisis situations. Develop and implement treatment plans based on clinical experience and knowledge. Collaborate with other staff members to perform clinical assessments and develop treatment plans. Evaluate clients' physical or mental condition based on review of client information. Meet with families, probation officers, police, and other interested parties to exchange necessary information during the treatment process. Refer patients, clients, or family members to communi-

ty resources or to specialists as necessary. Evaluate the effectiveness of counseling programs and clients' progress in resolving identified problems and moving towards defined objectives. Counsel family members to assist them in understanding, dealing with, and supporting clients or patients. Plan, organize, and lead structured programs of counseling, work, study, recreation, and social activities for clients. Modify treatment activities and approaches as needed to comply with changes in clients' status. Learn about new developments in their field by reading professional literature, attending courses and seminars, and establishing and maintaining contact with other social service agencies. Discuss with individual patients their plans for life after leaving therapy. Gather information about community mental health needs and resources that could be used in conjunction with therapy. Monitor clients' use of medications. Supervise other counselors, social service staff, and assistants.

SKILLS—Most Important: Social Skills; Thought-Processing Skills; Communication Skills. **Other Above-Average Skills:** None met the criteria.

GOE—Interest Area: 10. Human Service. **Work Group:** 10.01. Counseling and Social Work. **Other Jobs in This Group:** Child, Family, and School Social Workers; Clinical Psychologists; Clinical, Counseling, and School Psychologists; Counseling Psychologists; Marriage and Family Therapists; Medical and Public Health Social Workers; Mental Health and Substance Abuse Social Workers; Probation Officers and Correctional Treatment Specialists; Rehabilitation Counselors; Residential Advisors; Social and Human Service Assistants; Substance Abuse and Behavioral Disorder Counselors. **PERSONALITY TYPE:** Social. Social occupations frequently involve working with, communicating with, and teaching people. These occupations often involve helping or providing service to others.

EDUCATION/TRAINING PROGRAM(S)—Substance Abuse/Addiction Counseling; Clinical/Medical Social Work; Mental Health Counseling/Counselor; Mental and Social Health Services and Allied Professions, Other. **RELATED KNOWLEDGE/COURSES—Therapy and Counseling:** Principles, methods, and procedures for diagnosis, treatment, and rehabilitation of physical and mental dysfunctions and for career counseling and guidance. **Psychology:** Human behavior and performance; individual differences in ability, personality, and interests; learning and motivation; psychological research methods; and the assessment and treatment of behavioral and affective disorders. **Sociology and Anthropology:** Group behavior and dynamics, societal trends and influences, human migrations, ethnicity, and cultures and their history and origins. **Philosophy and Theology:** Different philosophical systems and religions. This includes their basic principles, values, ethics, ways of thinking, customs, practices, and impact on human culture. **Medicine and Dentistry:** The information and techniques needed to diagnose and treat human injuries, diseases, and deformities. This includes symptoms, treatment alternatives, drug properties and interactions, and preventive healthcare measures. **Education and Training:** Principles and methods for curriculum and training design, teaching and instruction for individuals and groups, and the measurement of training effects.

Microbiologists

- Education/Training Required: Doctoral degree
- Annual Earnings: $56,870
- Growth: 17.2%
- Annual Job Openings: 1,000
- Self-Employed: 2.9%
- Part-Time: 8.2%

Investigate the growth, structure, development, and other characteristics of microscopic organisms, such as bacteria, algae, or fungi. Includes medical microbiologists who study the relationship between organisms and disease or the effects of antibiotics on microorganisms. Isolate and make cultures of bacteria or other microorganisms in prescribed media, controlling moisture, aeration, temperature, and nutrition. Perform tests on water, food, and the environment to detect harmful microorganisms and to obtain information about sources of pollution and contamination. Examine physiological, morphological, and cultural characteristics, using microscope, to identify and classify microorganisms in human, water, and food specimens. Provide laboratory services for health departments, for community environmental health programs, and for physicians needing information for diagnosis and treatment. Observe action of microorganisms upon living tissues of plants, higher animals, and other microorganisms and

on dead organic matter. Investigate the relationship between organisms and disease, including the control of epidemics and the effects of antibiotics on microorganisms. Supervise biological technologists and technicians and other scientists. Study growth, structure, development, and general characteristics of bacteria and other microorganisms to understand their relationship to human, plant, and animal health. Prepare technical reports and recommendations based upon research outcomes. Study the structure and function of human, animal, and plant tissues, cells, pathogens, and toxins. Use a variety of specialized equipment such as electron microscopes, gas chromatographs and high-pressure liquid chromatographs, electrophoresis units, thermocyclers, fluorescence-activated cell sorters, and phosphoimagers. Conduct chemical analyses of substances such as acids, alcohols, and enzymes. Research use of bacteria and microorganisms to develop vitamins, antibiotics, amino acids, grain alcohol, sugars, and polymers.

SKILLS—Most Important: Science Skills; Quality Control Skills; Equipment Use/Maintenance Skills. **Other Above-Average Skills:** Equipment/Technology Analysis Skills; Mathematics Skills; Thought-Processing Skills; Social Skills.

GOE—Interest Area: 15. Scientific Research, Engineering, and Mathematics. **Work Group:** 15.03. Life Sciences. **Other Jobs in This Group:** Biochemists and Biophysicists; Biologists; Environmental Scientists and Specialists, Including Health; Epidemiologists; Medical Scientists, Except Epidemiologists. **PERSONALITY TYPE:** Investigative. Investigative occupations frequently involve working with ideas and require an extensive amount of thinking. These occupations can involve searching for facts and figuring out problems mentally.

EDUCATION/TRAINING PROGRAM(S)—Soil Microbiology; Structural Biology; Biochemistry/Biophysics and Molecular Biology; Neuroanatomy; Cell/Cellular Biology and Anatomical Sciences, Other; Microbiology, General. RELATED KNOWLEDGE/COURSES—Biology: Plant and animal organisms and their tissues, cells, functions, interdependencies, and interactions with each other and the environment. **Chemistry:** The chemical composition, structure, and properties of substances and of the chemical processes and transformations that they undergo. This includes uses of chemicals and their danger signs, production techniques, and disposal methods. **Clerical Practices:** Administrative and clerical procedures and systems such as word processing, managing files and records, stenography and transcription, designing forms, and other office procedures and terminology. **English Language:** The structure and content of the English language, including the meaning and spelling of words, rules of composition, and grammar. **Computers and Electronics:** Circuit boards; processors; chips; electronic equipment; and computer hardware and software, including applications and programming. **Administration and Management:** Business and management principles involved in strategic planning, resource allocation, human resources modeling, leadership technique, production methods, and coordination of people and resources.

Middle School Teachers, Except Special and Vocational Education

- Education/Training Required: Bachelor's degree
- Annual Earnings: $44,640
- Growth: 13.7%
- Annual Job Openings: 83,000
- Self-Employed: 0.0%
- Part-Time: 12.6%

Teach students in public or private schools in one or more subjects at the middle, intermediate, or junior high level, which falls between elementary and senior high school as defined by applicable state laws and regulations. Establish and enforce rules for behavior and procedures for maintaining order among the students for whom they are responsible. Adapt teaching methods and instructional materials to meet students' varying needs and interests. Instruct through lectures, discussions, and demonstrations in one or more subjects such as English, mathematics, or social studies. Prepare, administer, and grade tests and assignments to evaluate students' progress. Establish clear objectives for all lessons, units, and projects and communicate these objectives to students. Plan and conduct activities for a balanced program of instruction, demonstration, and

work time that provides students with opportunities to observe, question, and investigate. Maintain accurate, complete, and correct student records as required by laws, district policies, and administrative regulations. Observe and evaluate students' performance, behavior, social development, and physical health. Assign lessons and correct homework. Prepare materials and classrooms for class activities. Enforce all administration policies and rules governing students. Confer with parents or guardians, other teachers, counselors, and administrators to resolve students' behavioral and academic problems. Prepare students for later grades by encouraging them to explore learning opportunities and to persevere with challenging tasks. Prepare objectives and outlines for courses of study, following curriculum guidelines or requirements of states and schools. Guide and counsel students with adjustment or academic problems or special academic interests. Meet with parents and guardians to discuss their children's progress and to determine their priorities for their children and their resource needs. Meet with other professionals to discuss individual students' needs and progress. Prepare and implement remedial programs for students requiring extra help. Prepare for assigned classes and show written evidence of preparation upon request of immediate supervisors. Instruct and monitor students in the use and care of equipment and materials to prevent injury and damage.

SKILLS—Most Important: Social Skills; Thought-Processing Skills; Communication Skills. **Other Above-Average Skills:** Management Skills; Mathematics Skills.

GOE—Interest Area: 05. Education and Training. **Work Group:** 05.02. Preschool, Elementary, and Secondary Teaching and Instructing. **Other Jobs in This Group:** Elementary School Teachers, Except Special Education; Kindergarten Teachers, Except Special Education; Preschool Teachers, Except Special Education; Secondary School Teachers, Except Special and Vocational Education; Special Education Teachers, Middle School; Special Education Teachers, Preschool, Kindergarten, and Elementary School; Special Education Teachers, Secondary School; Teacher Assistants; Vocational Education Teachers, Middle School; Vocational Education Teachers, Secondary School. **PERSONALITY TYPE:** Social. Social occupations frequently involve working with, communicating with, and teaching people. These occupations often involve helping or providing service to others.

EDUCATION/TRAINING PROGRAM(S)—Junior High/Intermediate/Middle School Education and Teaching; Montessori Teacher Education; Waldorf/Steiner Teacher Education; Art Teacher Education; English/Language Arts Teacher Education; Foreign Language Teacher Education; Health Teacher Education; Family and Consumer Sciences/Home Economics Teacher Education; Technology Teacher Education/Industrial Arts Teacher Education; Mathematics Teacher Education; others. **RELATED KNOWLEDGE/COURSES—Education and Training:** Principles and methods for curriculum and training design, teaching and instruction for individuals and groups, and the measurement of training effects. **Sociology and Anthropology:** Group behavior and dynamics, societal trends and influences, human migrations, ethnicity, and cultures and their history and origins. **History and Archeology:** Historical events and their causes, indicators, and effects on civilizations and cultures. **Philosophy and Theology:** Different philosophical systems and religions. This includes their basic principles, values, ethics, ways of thinking, customs, practices, and impact on human culture. **Geography:** Principles and methods for describing the features of land, sea, and air masses, including their physical characteristics; locations; interrelationships; and distribution of plant, animal, and human life. **Therapy and Counseling:** Principles, methods, and procedures for diagnosis, treatment, and rehabilitation of physical and mental dysfunctions and for career counseling and guidance.

Mobile Heavy Equipment Mechanics, Except Engines

- Education/Training Required: Postsecondary vocational training
- Annual Earnings: $39,410
- Growth: 8.8%
- Annual Job Openings: 14,000
- Self-Employed: 2.9%
- Part-Time: 3.0%

Diagnose, adjust, repair, or overhaul mobile mechanical, hydraulic, and pneumatic equipment, such as cranes, bulldozers, graders, and conveyors, used in construction, logging, and surface mining. Test mechanical products and equipment after repair or assembly to ensure proper performance and compliance with manufacturers' specifications. Repair and replace damaged or worn parts. Diagnose faults or malfunctions to determine required repairs, using engine diagnostic equipment such as computerized test equipment and calibration devices. Operate and inspect machines or heavy equipment to diagnose defects. Dismantle and reassemble heavy equipment, using hoists and hand tools. Clean, lubricate, and perform other routine maintenance work on equipment and vehicles. Examine parts for damage or excessive wear, using micrometers and gauges. Read and understand operating manuals, blueprints, and technical drawings. Schedule maintenance for industrial machines and equipment and keep equipment service records. Overhaul and test machines or equipment to ensure operating efficiency. Assemble gear systems and align frames and gears. Fit bearings to adjust, repair, or overhaul mobile mechanical, hydraulic, and pneumatic equipment. Weld or solder broken parts and structural members, using electric or gas welders and soldering tools. Clean parts by spraying them with grease solvent or immersing them in tanks of solvent. Adjust, maintain, and repair or replace subassemblies, such as transmissions and crawler heads, using hand tools, jacks, and cranes. Adjust and maintain industrial machinery, using control and regulating devices. Fabricate needed parts or items from sheet metal. Direct workers who are assembling or disassembling equipment or cleaning parts.

SKILLS—Most Important: Equipment Use/Maintenance Skills. **Other Above-Average Skills:** Equipment/Technology Analysis Skills; Quality Control Skills; Science Skills; Social Skills.

GOE—Interest Area: 13. Manufacturing. **Work Group:** 13.14. Vehicle and Facility Mechanical Work. **Other Jobs in This Group:** Aircraft Mechanics and Service Technicians; Aircraft Structure, Surfaces, Rigging, and Systems Assemblers; Automotive Body and Related Repairers; Automotive Glass Installers and Repairers; Automotive Master Mechanics; Automotive Service Technicians and Mechanics; Automotive Specialty Technicians; Bus and Truck Mechanics and Diesel Engine Specialists; Farm Equipment Mechanics;

Fiberglass Laminators and Fabricators; Motorboat Mechanics; Motorcycle Mechanics; Outdoor Power Equipment and Other Small Engine Mechanics; Rail Car Repairers; Recreational Vehicle Service Technicians; Tire Repairers and Changers. **PERSONALITY TYPE:** Realistic. Realistic occupations frequently involve work activities that include practical, hands-on problems and solutions. They often deal with plants, animals, and real-world materials like wood, tools, and machinery. Many of the occupations require working outside and do not involve a lot of paperwork or working closely with others.

EDUCATION/TRAINING PROGRAM(S)—Agricultural Mechanics and Equipment/Machine Technology; Heavy Equipment Maintenance Technology/Technician. **RELATED KNOWLEDGE/COURSES—Mechanical Devices:** Machines and tools, including their designs, uses, repair, and maintenance. **Engineering and Technology:** The practical application of engineering science and technology. This includes applying principles, techniques, procedures, and equipment to the design and production of various goods and services. **Physics:** Physical principles and laws and their interrelationships and applications to understanding fluid, material, and atmospheric dynamics and mechanical, electrical, atomic, and subatomic structures and processes. **Customer and Personal Service:** Principles and processes for providing customer and personal services. This includes customer needs assessment, meeting of quality standards for services, and evaluation of customer satisfaction. **Production and Processing:** Raw materials, production processes, quality control, costs, and other techniques for maximizing the effective manufacture and distribution of goods.

Motorboat Mechanics

- Education/Training Required: Long-term on-the-job training
- Annual Earnings: $32,780
- Growth: 15.1%
- Annual Job Openings: 7,000
- Self-Employed: 18.9%
- Part-Time: 13.2%

Repairs and adjusts electrical and mechanical equipment of gasoline or diesel-powered inboard or inboard-outboard boat engines. Replace parts such as gears, magneto points, piston rings, and spark plugs and reassemble engines. Adjust generators and replace faulty wiring, using hand tools and soldering irons. Mount motors to boats and operate boats at various speeds on waterways to conduct operational tests. Document inspection and test results and work performed or to be performed. Start motors and monitor performance for signs of malfunctioning such as smoke, excessive vibration, and misfiring. Set starter locks and align and repair steering or throttle controls, using gauges, screwdrivers, and wrenches. Repair engine mechanical equipment such as power tilts, bilge pumps, or power take-offs. Inspect and repair or adjust propellers and propeller shafts. Disassemble and inspect motors to locate defective parts, using mechanic's hand tools and gauges. Adjust carburetor mixtures, electrical point settings, and timing while motors are running in water-filled test tanks. Repair or rework parts, using machine tools such as lathes, mills, drills, and grinders. Idle motors and observe thermometers to determine the effectiveness of cooling systems.

SKILLS—Most Important: Quality Control Skills; Equipment Use/Maintenance Skills. **Other Above-Average Skills:** None met the criteria.

GOE—Interest Area: 13. Manufacturing. **Work Group:** 13.14. Vehicle and Facility Mechanical Work. **Other Jobs in This Group:** Aircraft Mechanics and Service Technicians; Aircraft Structure, Surfaces, Rigging, and Systems Assemblers; Automotive Body and Related Repairers; Automotive Glass Installers and Repairers; Automotive Master Mechanics; Automotive Service Technicians and Mechanics; Automotive Specialty Technicians; Bus and Truck Mechanics and Diesel Engine Specialists; Farm Equipment Mechanics; Fiberglass Laminators and Fabricators; Mobile Heavy Equipment Mechanics, Except Engines; Motorcycle Mechanics; Outdoor Power Equipment and Other Small Engine Mechanics; Rail Car Repairers; Recreational Vehicle Service Technicians; Tire Repairers and Changers. **PERSONALITY TYPE:** Realistic. Realistic occupations frequently involve work activities that include practical, hands-on problems and solutions. They often deal with plants, animals, and real-world materials like wood, tools, and machinery. Many of the occupations require working outside and do not involve a lot of paperwork or working closely with others.

EDUCATION/TRAINING PROGRAM(S)—Small Engine Mechanics and Repair Technology/Technician; Marine Maintenance/Fitter and Ship Repair Technology/Technician. **RELATED KNOWLEDGE/ COURSES—Mechanical Devices:** Machines and tools, including their designs, uses, repair, and maintenance. **Engineering and Technology:** The practical application of engineering science and technology. This includes applying principles, techniques, procedures, and equipment to the design and production of various goods and services.

Multi-Media Artists and Animators

- Education/Training Required: Bachelor's degree
- Annual Earnings: $50,290
- Growth: 14.1%
- Annual Job Openings: 14,000
- Self-Employed: 60.8%
- Part-Time: 30.9%

Create special effects, animation, or other visual images, using film, video, computers, or other electronic tools and media, for use in products or creations such as computer games, movies, music videos, and commercials. Design complex graphics and animation, using independent judgment, creativity, and computer equipment. Create two-dimensional and three-dimensional images depicting objects in motion or illustrating a process, using computer animation or modeling programs. Make objects or characters appear lifelike by manipulating light, color, texture, shadow, and transparency or manipulating static images to give the illusion of motion. Apply story development, directing, cinematography, and editing to animation to create storyboards that show the flow of the animation and map out key scenes and characters. Assemble, typeset, scan, and produce digital camera-ready art or film negatives and printer's proofs. Script, plan, and create animated narrative sequences under tight deadlines, using computer software and hand-drawing techniques. Create basic designs, drawings, and illustrations for product labels, cartons, direct mail, or television. Create pen-and-paper images to be scanned, edited, colored, textured, or animated by computer. Develop briefings, brochures, multimedia presentations, Web pages, promotional products, technical illustrations, and computer artwork for use in products, technical manuals, literature, newsletters, and slide shows. Use models to simulate the behavior of animated objects in the finished sequence. Create and install special effects as required by the script, mixing chemicals and fabricating needed parts from wood, metal, plaster, and clay. Participate in design and production of multimedia campaigns, handling budgeting and scheduling and assisting with such responsibilities as production coordination, background design, and progress tracking. Convert real objects to animated objects through modeling, using techniques such as optical scanning. Implement and maintain configuration control systems.

SKILLS—Most Important: Equipment/Technology Analysis Skills; Computer Programming Skills; Science Skills. **Other Above-Average Skills:** Mathematics Skills; Communication Skills; Management Skills; Social Skills.

GOE—Interest Area: 03. Arts and Communication. **Work Group:** 03.09. Media Technology. **Other Jobs in This Group:** Audio and Video Equipment Technicians; Broadcast Technicians; Camera Operators, Television, Video, and Motion Picture; Film and Video Editors; Photographers; Radio Operators; Sound Engineering Technicians. **PERSONALITY TYPE:** No data available.

EDUCATION/TRAINING PROGRAM(S)—Animation, Interactive Technology, Video Graphics, and Special Effects; Web Page, Digital/Multimedia, and Information Resources Design; Graphic Design; Drawing; Intermedia/Multimedia; Painting; Printmaking. **RELATED KNOWLEDGE/COURSES—Fine Arts:** The theory and techniques required to compose, produce, and perform works of music, dance, visual arts, drama, and sculpture. **Design:** Design techniques, tools, and principles involved in production of precision technical plans, blueprints, drawings, and models. **Computers and Electronics:** Circuit boards; processors; chips; electronic equipment; and computer hardware and software, including applications and programming. **Communications and Media:** Media production, communication, and dissemination techniques and methods. This includes alternative ways to inform and entertain via written, oral, and visual media. **English Language:** The structure and content of the English language, including the meaning and spelling of words, rules of composition, and grammar. **Administration and Management:** Business and management principles involved in strategic planning, resource allocation, human resources modeling, leadership technique, production methods, and coordination of people and resources.

Municipal Fire Fighters

- Education/Training Required: Long-term on-the-job training
- Annual Earnings: $39,090
- Growth: 24.3%
- Annual Job Openings: 21,000
- Self-Employed: 0.1%
- Part-Time: 1.5%

The job openings listed here are shared with Forest Fire Fighters.

Control and extinguish municipal fires, protect life and property, and conduct rescue efforts. Administer first aid and cardiopulmonary resuscitation to injured persons. Rescue victims from burning buildings and accident sites. Search burning buildings to locate fire victims. Drive and operate fire fighting vehicles and equipment. Move toward the source of a fire, using knowledge of types of fires, construction design, building materials, and physical layout of properties. Dress with equipment such as fire-resistant clothing and breathing apparatus. Position and climb ladders to gain access to upper levels of buildings or to rescue individuals from burning structures. Take action to contain hazardous chemicals that might catch fire, leak, or spill. Assess fires and situations and report conditions to superiors to receive instructions, using two-way radios. Respond to fire alarms and other calls for assistance, such as automobile and industrial accidents. Operate pumps connected to high-pressure hoses. Select and attach hose nozzles, depending on fire type, and direct streams of water or chemicals onto fires. Create openings in buildings for ventilation or entrance, using axes, chisels, crowbars, electric saws, or core cutters. Inspect fire sites after flames have been extinguished to ensure that there is no further danger. Lay hose lines and connect them to water supplies. Protect property from water and smoke, using waterproof salvage covers, smoke ejectors, and deodorants. Participate in physical training activities to maintain a high level of physical fitness. Salvage property by removing broken glass, pumping out water, and ventilating buildings to remove smoke. Participate in fire drills and demonstrations of fire fighting techniques. Clean and maintain fire stations and fire fighting equipment and apparatus. Collaborate with police to respond to accidents, disasters, and arson investigation calls. Establish firelines to prevent unauthorized persons from entering areas near fires. Inform and educate the public on fire prevention. Inspect buildings for fire hazards and compliance with fire prevention ordinances, testing and checking smoke alarms and fire suppression equipment as necessary.

SKILLS—Most Important: Equipment Use/Maintenance Skills; Science Skills; Equipment/Technology Analysis Skills. **Other Above-Average Skills:** Social Skills; Thought-Processing Skills.

GOE—Interest Area: 12. Law and Public Safety. **Work Group:** 12.06. Emergency Responding. **Other Jobs in This Group:** Emergency Medical Technicians and Paramedics; Fire Fighters; Forest Fire Fighters. **PERSONALITY TYPE:** Realistic. Realistic occupations frequently involve work activities that include practical, hands-on problems and solutions. They often deal with plants, animals, and real-world materials like wood, tools, and machinery. Many of the occupations require working outside and do not involve a lot of paperwork or working closely with others.

EDUCATION/TRAINING PROGRAM(S)—Fire Science/Firefighting; Fire Protection, Other. **RELATED KNOWLEDGE/COURSES—Customer and Personal Service:** Principles and processes for providing customer and personal services. This includes customer needs assessment, meeting of quality standards for services, and evaluation of customer satisfaction. **Medicine and Dentistry:** The information and techniques needed to diagnose and treat human injuries, diseases, and deformities. This includes symptoms, treatment alternatives, drug properties and interactions, and preventive healthcare measures. **Physics:** Physical principles and laws and their interrelationships and applications to understanding fluid, material, and atmospheric dynamics and mechanical, electrical, atomic, and subatomic structures and processes. **Building and Construction:** The materials, methods, and tools involved in the construction or repair of houses, buildings, or other structures such as highways and roads. **Chemistry:** The chemical composition, structure, and properties of substances and of the chemical processes and transformations that they undergo. This includes uses of chemicals and their danger signs, production techniques, and disposal methods. **Public Safety and Security:** Relevant equipment, policies, procedures, and strategies to promote effective local, state, or national security operations for the protection of people, data, property, and institutions.

Municipal Fire Fighting and Prevention Supervisors

- Education/Training Required: Work experience in a related occupation
- Annual Earnings: $60,840
- Growth: 21.1%
- Annual Job Openings: 4,000
- Self-Employed: 0.0%
- Part-Time: 0.4%

Supervise fire fighters who control and extinguish municipal fires, protect life and property, and conduct rescue efforts. Assign firefighters to jobs at strategic locations to facilitate rescue of persons and maximize application of extinguishing agents. Provide emergency medical services as required and perform light to heavy rescue functions at emergencies. Assess nature and extent of fire, condition of building, danger to adjacent buildings, and water supply status to determine crew or company requirements. Instruct and drill fire department personnel in assigned duties, including firefighting, medical care, hazardous materials response, fire prevention, and related subjects. Evaluate the performance of assigned firefighting personnel. Direct the training of firefighters, assigning of instructors to training classes, and providing of supervisors with reports on training progress and status. Prepare activity reports listing fire call locations, actions taken, fire types and probable causes, damage estimates, and situation dispositions. Maintain required maps and records.

Attend in-service training classes to remain current in knowledge of codes, laws, ordinances, and regulations. Evaluate fire station procedures to ensure efficiency and enforcement of departmental regulations. Direct firefighters in station maintenance duties and participate in these duties. Compile and maintain equipment and personnel records, including accident reports. Direct investigation of cases of suspected arson, hazards, and false alarms and submit reports outlining findings. Recommend personnel actions related to disciplinary procedures, performance, leaves of absence, and grievances. Supervise and participate in the inspection of properties to ensure that they are in compliance with applicable fire codes, ordinances, laws, regulations, and standards. Write and submit proposals for repair, modification, or replacement of firefighting equipment. Coordinate the distribution of fire prevention promotional materials. Identify corrective actions needed to bring properties into compliance with applicable fire codes and ordinances and conduct follow-up inspections to see if corrective actions have been taken. Participate in creating fire safety guidelines and evacuation schemes for non-residential buildings.

SKILLS—Most Important: Equipment Use/Maintenance Skills; Management Skills; Social Skills. **Other Above-Average Skills:** Equipment/Technology Analysis Skills; Thought-Processing Skills; Communication Skills; Quality Control Skills.

GOE—Interest Area: 12. Law and Public Safety. **Work Group:** 12.01. Managerial Work in Law and Public Safety. **Other Jobs in This Group:** Emergency Management Specialists; First-Line Supervisors/Managers of Correctional Officers; First-Line Supervisors/Managers of Fire Fighting and Prevention Workers; First-Line Supervisors/Managers of Police and Detectives; Forest Fire Fighting and Prevention Supervisors. **PERSONALITY TYPE:** Realistic. Realistic occupations frequently involve work activities that include practical, hands-on problems and solutions. They often deal with plants, animals, and real-world materials like wood, tools, and machinery. Many of the occupations require working outside and do not involve a lot of paperwork or working closely with others.

EDUCATION/TRAINING PROGRAM(S)—Fire Protection and Safety Technology/Technician; Fire Services Administration. **RELATED KNOWLEDGE/COURSES—Public Safety and Security:** Relevant equipment, policies, procedures, and strategies to promote effective local, state, or national security operations for the protection of people, data, property, and institutions. **Building and Construction:** The materials, methods, and tools involved in the construction or repair of houses, buildings, or other structures such as highways and roads. **Medicine and Dentistry:** The information and techniques needed to diagnose and treat human injuries, diseases, and deformities. This includes symptoms, treatment alternatives, drug properties and interactions, and preventive healthcare measures. **Education and Training:** Principles and methods for curriculum and training design, teaching and instruction for individuals and groups, and the measurement of training effects. **Customer and Personal Service:** Principles and processes for providing customer and personal services. This includes customer needs assessment, meeting of quality standards for services, and evaluation of customer satisfaction. **Mechanical Devices:** Machines and tools, including their designs, uses, repair, and maintenance.

Natural Sciences Managers

- Education/Training Required: Work experience plus degree
- Annual Earnings: $93,090
- Growth: 13.6%
- Annual Job Openings: 5,000
- Self-Employed: 0.0%
- Part-Time: 2.8%

Plan, direct, or coordinate activities in such fields as life sciences, physical sciences, mathematics, and statistics and research and development in these fields. Confer with scientists, engineers, regulators, and others to plan and review projects and to provide technical assistance. Develop client relationships and communicate with clients to explain proposals, present research findings, establish specifications, or discuss project status. Plan and direct research, development, and production activities. Prepare project proposals. Design and coordinate successive phases of problem analysis, solution proposals, and testing. Review project activities and prepare and review research, testing, and operational reports. Hire, supervise, and evaluate engineers, techni-

cians, researchers, and other staff. Determine scientific and technical goals within broad outlines provided by top management and make detailed plans to accomplish these goals. Develop and implement policies, standards, and procedures for the architectural, scientific, and technical work performed to ensure regulatory compliance and operations enhancement. Develop innovative technology and train staff for its implementation. Provide for stewardship of plant and animal resources and habitats, studying land use; monitoring animal populations; and providing shelter, resources, and medical treatment for animals. Conduct own research in field of expertise. Recruit personnel and oversee the development and maintenance of staff competence. Advise and assist in obtaining patents or meeting other legal requirements. Prepare and administer budget, approve and review expenditures, and prepare financial reports. Make presentations at professional meetings to further knowledge in the field.

SKILLS—Most Important: Science Skills; Mathematics Skills; Management Skills. **Other Above-Average Skills:** Communication Skills; Thought-Processing Skills; Social Skills; Equipment Use/Maintenance Skills.

GOE—Interest Area: 15. Scientific Research, Engineering, and Mathematics. **Work Group:** 15.01. Managerial Work in Scientific Research, Engineering, and Mathematics. **Other Jobs in This Group:** Engineering Managers. **PERSONALITY TYPE:** Investigative. Investigative occupations frequently involve working with ideas and require an extensive amount of thinking. These occupations can involve searching for facts and figuring out problems mentally.

EDUCATION/TRAINING PROGRAM(S)—Operations Research; Biology/Biological Sciences, General; Biochemistry; Biophysics; Molecular Biology; Radiation Biology/Radiobiology; Botany/Plant Biology; Plant Pathology/Phytopathology; Plant Physiology; Botany/Plant Biology, Other; Cell/Cellular Biology and Histology; Anatomy; Cell/Cellular Biology and Anatomical Sciences, Other; Microbiology, General; others. **RELATED KNOWLEDGE/COURSES—Biology:** Plant and animal organisms and their tissues, cells, functions, interdependencies, and interactions with each other and the environment. **Chemistry:** The chemical composition, structure, and properties of substances and of the chemical processes and transformations that they undergo. This includes uses of chemicals and their danger signs, production techniques, and disposal methods.

Engineering and Technology: The practical application of engineering science and technology. This includes applying principles, techniques, procedures, and equipment to the design and production of various goods and services. **Law and Government:** Laws, legal codes, court procedures, precedents, government regulations, executive orders, agency rules, and the democratic political process. **Administration and Management:** Business and management principles involved in strategic planning, resource allocation, human resources modeling, leadership technique, production methods, and coordination of people and resources. **Production and Processing:** Raw materials, production processes, quality control, costs, and other techniques for maximizing the effective manufacture and distribution of goods.

Network and Computer Systems Administrators

- Education/Training Required: Bachelor's degree
- Annual Earnings: $59,930
- Growth: 38.4%
- Annual Job Openings: 34,000
- Self-Employed: 0.6%
- Part-Time: 4.2%

The job openings listed here are shared with Computer Security Specialists.

Install, configure, and support an organization's local area network (LAN), wide area network (WAN), and Internet system or a segment of a network system. Maintain network hardware and software. Monitor network to ensure network availability to all system users and perform necessary maintenance to support network availability. May supervise other network support and client server specialists and plan, coordinate, and implement network security measures. Diagnose hardware and software problems and replace defective components. Perform data backups and disaster recovery operations. Maintain and administer computer networks and related computing environments, including computer hardware, systems software, applications software, and all configurations. Plan, coordinate, and implement network security measures to protect data, software, and hardware. Operate master consoles to monitor the performance of computer systems and networks and to coordinate computer network access and use. Perform routine network startup and shutdown procedures and maintain control records. Design, configure, and test computer hardware, networking software, and operating system software. Recommend changes to improve systems and network configurations and determine hardware or software requirements related to such changes. Confer with network users about how to solve existing system problems. Monitor network performance to determine whether adjustments need to be made and to determine where changes will need to be made in the future. Train people in computer system use. Load computer tapes and disks and install software and printer paper or forms. Gather data pertaining to customer needs and use the information to identify, predict, interpret, and evaluate system and network requirements. Analyze equipment performance records to determine the need for repair or replacement. Maintain logs related to network functions as well as maintenance and repair records. Research new technology and implement it or recommend its implementation. Maintain an inventory of parts for emergency repairs. Coordinate with vendors and with company personnel to facilitate purchases.

SKILLS—Most Important: Computer Programming Skills; Equipment Use/Maintenance Skills; Equipment/Technology Analysis Skills. **Other Above-Average Skills:** Thought-Processing Skills; Social Skills; Mathematics Skills; Management Skills; Science Skills.

GOE—Interest Area: 11. Information Technology. **Work Group:** 11.01. Managerial Work in Information Technology. **Other Jobs in This Group:** Computer and Information Systems Managers. **PERSONALITY TYPE:** No data available.

EDUCATION/TRAINING PROGRAM(S)—Computer and Information Sciences and Support Services, Other; Computer and Information Sciences, General; Computer and Information Systems Security; Computer Systems Analysis/Analyst; Computer Systems Networking and Telecommunications; Information Science/Studies; System Administration/Administrator; System, Networking, and LAN/WAN Management/Manager. **RELATED KNOWLEDGE/COURSES—Computers and Electronics:** Circuit boards; processors; chips; electronic equipment; and computer hardware and software, including applications and programming.

Telecommunications: Transmission, broadcasting, switching, control, and operation of telecommunications systems. **Customer and Personal Service:** Principles and processes for providing customer and personal services. This includes customer needs assessment, meeting of quality standards for services, and evaluation of customer satisfaction. **Engineering and Technology:** The practical application of engineering science and technology. This includes applying principles, techniques, procedures, and equipment to the design and production of various goods and services. **Education and Training:** Principles and methods for curriculum and training design, teaching and instruction for individuals and groups, and the measurement of training effects. **Design:** Design techniques, tools, and principles involved in production of precision technical plans, blueprints, drawings, and models.

Network Systems and Data Communications Analysts

- Education/Training Required: Bachelor's degree
- Annual Earnings: $61,750
- Growth: 54.6%
- Annual Job Openings: 43,000
- Self-Employed: 19.9%
- Part-Time: 10.0%

Analyze, design, test, and evaluate network systems, such as local area networks (LAN); wide area networks (WAN); and Internet, intranet, and other data communications systems. Perform network modeling, analysis, and planning. Research and recommend network and data communications hardware and software. Includes telecommunications specialists who deal with the interfacing of computer and communications equipment. May supervise computer programmers. Maintain needed files by adding and deleting files on the network server and backing up files to guarantee their safety in the event of problems with the network. Monitor system performance and provide security measures, troubleshooting, and maintenance as needed. Assist users to diagnose and solve data communication problems. Set up user accounts, regulating and monitoring file access to ensure confidentiality and proper use. Design and implement systems, network configurations, and network architecture, including hardware and software technology, site locations, and integration of technologies. Maintain the peripherals, such as printers, that are connected to the network. Identify areas of operation that need upgraded equipment such as modems, fiber-optic cables, and telephone wires. Train users in use of equipment. Develop and write procedures for installation, use, and troubleshooting of communications hardware and software. Adapt and modify existing software to meet specific needs. Work with other engineers, systems analysts, programmers, technicians, scientists, and top-level managers in the design, testing, and evaluation of systems. Test and evaluate hardware and software to determine efficiency, reliability, and compatibility with existing system and make purchase recommendations. Read technical manuals and brochures to determine which equipment meets establishment requirements. Consult customers, visit workplaces, or conduct surveys to determine present and future user needs. Visit vendors, attend conferences or training, and study technical journals to keep up with changes in technology.

SKILLS—Most Important: Computer Programming Skills; Equipment/Technology Analysis Skills; Equipment Use/Maintenance Skills. **Other Above-Average Skills:** Quality Control Skills; Management Skills; Communication Skills; Mathematics Skills.

GOE—Interest Area: 11. Information Technology. **Work Group:** 11.02. Information Technology Specialties. **Other Jobs in This Group:** Computer and Information Scientists, Research; Computer Operators; Computer Programmers; Computer Security Specialists; Computer Software Engineers, Applications; Computer Software Engineers, Systems Software; Computer Support Specialists; Computer Systems Analysts; Computer Systems Engineers/Architects; Database Administrators; Network Designers; Software Quality Assurance Engineers and Testers; Web Administrators; Web Developers. **PERSONALITY TYPE:** Investigative. Investigative occupations frequently involve working with ideas and require an extensive amount of thinking. These occupations can involve searching for facts and figuring out problems mentally.

EDUCATION/TRAINING PROGRAM(S)—Computer and Information Sciences, General; Information Technology; Computer Systems Analysis/Analyst;

Computer Systems Networking and Telecommunications; System, Networking, and LAN/WAN Management/Manager; Computer and Information Systems Security. **RELATED KNOWLEDGE/COURSES— Telecommunications:** Transmission, broadcasting, switching, control, and operation of telecommunications systems. **Computers and Electronics:** Circuit boards; processors; chips; electronic equipment; and computer hardware and software, including applications and programming. **Customer and Personal Service:** Principles and processes for providing customer and personal services. This includes customer needs assessment, meeting of quality standards for services, and evaluation of customer satisfaction. **Engineering and Technology:** The practical application of engineering science and technology. This includes applying principles, techniques, procedures, and equipment to the design and production of various goods and services. **Education and Training:** Principles and methods for curriculum and training design, teaching and instruction for individuals and groups, and the measurement of training effects. **Design:** Design techniques, tools, and principles involved in production of precision technical plans, blueprints, drawings, and models.

Nuclear Medicine Technologists

- Education/Training Required: Associate degree
- Annual Earnings: $59,670
- Growth: 21.5%
- Annual Job Openings: 2,000
- Self-Employed: 0.5%
- Part-Time: 17.2%

Prepare, administer, and measure radioactive isotopes in therapeutic, diagnostic, and tracer studies, utilizing a variety of radioisotope equipment. Prepare stock solutions of radioactive materials and calculate doses to be administered by radiologists. Subject patients to radiation. Execute blood volume, red cell survival, and fat absorption studies, following standard laboratory techniques. Calculate, measure, and record radiation dosage or radiopharmaceuticals received, used, and disposed, using computer and following physician's pre-

scription. Detect and map radiopharmaceuticals in patients' bodies, using a camera to produce photographic or computer images. Explain test procedures and safety precautions to patients and provide them with assistance during test procedures. Administer radiopharmaceuticals or radiation to patients to detect or treat diseases, using radioisotope equipment, under direction of physician. Produce a computer-generated or film image for interpretation by a physician. Process cardiac function studies, using computer. Dispose of radioactive materials and store radiopharmaceuticals, following radiation safety procedures. Record and process results of procedures. Prepare stock radiopharmaceuticals, adhering to safety standards that minimize radiation exposure to workers and patients. Maintain and calibrate radioisotope and laboratory equipment. Gather information on patients' illnesses and medical history to guide the choice of diagnostic procedures for therapy. Measure glandular activity, blood volume, red cell survival, and radioactivity of patient, using scanners, Geiger counters, scintillometers, and other laboratory equipment. Train and supervise student or subordinate nuclear medicine technologists. Position radiation fields, radiation beams, and patient to allow for most effective treatment of patient's disease, using computer. Add radioactive substances to biological specimens, such as blood, urine, and feces, to determine therapeutic drug or hormone levels. Develop treatment procedures for nuclear medicine treatment programs.

SKILLS—Most Important: Science Skills; Quality Control Skills; Equipment Use/Maintenance Skills. **Other Above-Average Skills:** Social Skills; Mathematics Skills; Thought-Processing Skills; Management Skills.

GOE—Interest Area: 08. Health Science. **Work Group:** 08.06. Medical Technology. **Other Jobs in This Group:** Biological Technicians; Cardiovascular Technologists and Technicians; Diagnostic Medical Sonographers; Medical and Clinical Laboratory Technicians; Medical and Clinical Laboratory Technologists; Medical Equipment Preparers; Medical Records and Health Information Technicians; Opticians, Dispensing; Orthotists and Prosthetists; Radiologic Technicians; Radiologic Technologists; Radiologic Technologists and Technicians. **PERSONALITY TYPE:** Investigative. Investigative occupations frequently involve working with ideas and require an extensive amount of thinking. These occupations can involve searching for facts and figuring out problems mentally.

EDUCATION/TRAINING PROGRAM(S)—Nuclear Medical Technology/Technologist; Radiation Protection/Health Physics Technician. **RELATED KNOWLEDGE/COURSES—Medicine and Dentistry:** The information and techniques needed to diagnose and treat human injuries, diseases, and deformities. This includes symptoms, treatment alternatives, drug properties and interactions, and preventive healthcare measures. **Biology:** Plant and animal organisms and their tissues, cells, functions, interdependencies, and interactions with each other and the environment. **Physics:** Physical principles and laws and their interrelationships and applications to understanding fluid, material, and atmospheric dynamics and mechanical, electrical, atomic, and subatomic structures and processes. **Chemistry:** The chemical composition, structure, and properties of substances and of the chemical processes and transformations that they undergo. This includes uses of chemicals and their danger signs, production techniques, and disposal methods. **Customer and Personal Service:** Principles and processes for providing customer and personal services. This includes customer needs assessment, meeting of quality standards for services, and evaluation of customer satisfaction. **Computers and Electronics:** Circuit boards; processors; chips; electronic equipment; and computer hardware and software, including applications and programming.

Numerical Tool and Process Control Programmers

- ⑥ Education/Training Required: Long-term on-the-job training
- ⑥ Annual Earnings: $41,830
- ⑥ Growth: –1.1%
- ⑥ Annual Job Openings: 2,000
- ⑥ Self-Employed: 0.0%
- ⑥ Part-Time: 0.3%

Develop programs to control machining or processing of parts by automatic machine tools, equipment, or systems. Determine the sequence of machine operations and select the proper cutting tools needed to machine workpieces into the desired shapes. Revise programs or tapes to eliminate errors and retest programs to check that problems have been solved. Analyze job orders, drawings, blueprints, specifications, printed circuit board pattern films, and design data to calculate dimensions, tool selection, machine speeds, and feed rates. Determine reference points, machine cutting paths, or hole locations and compute angular and linear dimensions, radii, and curvatures. Observe machines on trial runs or conduct computer simulations to ensure that programs and machinery will function properly and produce items that meet specifications. Compare encoded tapes or computer printouts with original part specifications and blueprints to verify accuracy of instructions. Enter coordinates of hole locations into program memories by depressing pedals or buttons of programmers. Write programs in the language of a machine's controller and store programs on media such as punch tapes, magnetic tapes, or disks. Modify existing programs to enhance efficiency. Enter computer commands to store or retrieve parts patterns, graphic displays, or programs that transfer data to other media. Prepare geometric layouts from graphic displays, using computer-assisted drafting software or drafting instruments and graph paper. Write instruction sheets and cutter lists for a machine's controller to guide setup and encode numerical control tapes. Sort shop orders into groups to maximize materials utilization and minimize machine setup time. Draw machine tool paths on pattern film, using colored markers and following guidelines for tool speed and efficiency. Align and secure pattern film on reference tables of optical programmers and observe enlarger scope views of printed circuit boards.

SKILLS—Most Important: Computer Programming Skills; Mathematics Skills; Quality Control Skills. **Other Above-Average Skills:** Equipment/Technology Analysis Skills; Equipment Use/Maintenance Skills.

GOE—Interest Area: 13. Manufacturing. **Work Group:** 13.05. Production Machining Technology. **Other Jobs in This Group:** Computer-Controlled Machine Tool Operators, Metal and Plastic; Foundry Mold and Coremakers; Lay-Out Workers, Metal and Plastic; Machinists; Model Makers, Metal and Plastic; Patternmakers, Metal and Plastic; Tool and Die Makers; Tool Grinders, Filers, and Sharpeners. **PERSONALITY TYPE:** Realistic. Realistic occupations frequently involve work activities that include practical, hands-on problems and solutions. They often deal with plants, animals, and real-world materials like wood, tools, and machinery. Many of the occupations require working outside and do not involve a lot of paperwork or working closely with others.

EDUCATION/TRAINING PROGRAM(S)—Computer Programming/Programmer, General; Data Processing and Data Processing Technology/Technician. **RELATED KNOWLEDGE/COURSES—Design:** Design techniques, tools, and principles involved in production of precision technical plans, blueprints, drawings, and models. **Computers and Electronics:** Circuit boards; processors; chips; electronic equipment; and computer hardware and software, including applications and programming. **Mathematics:** Arithmetic, algebra, geometry, calculus, and statistics and their applications. **Production and Processing:** Raw materials, production processes, quality control, costs, and other techniques for maximizing the effective manufacture and distribution of goods. **Engineering and Technology:** The practical application of engineering science and technology. This includes applying principles, techniques, procedures, and equipment to the design and production of various goods and services.

Nursing Aides, Orderlies, and Attendants

- ◎ Education/Training Required: Postsecondary vocational training
- ◎ Annual Earnings: $21,440
- ◎ Growth: 22.3%
- ◎ Annual Job Openings: 307,000
- ◎ Self-Employed: 1.9%
- ◎ Part-Time: 28.0%

Provide basic patient care under direction of nursing staff. Perform duties such as feeding, bathing, dressing, grooming, or moving patients or changing linens. Turn and reposition bedridden patients, alone or with assistance, to prevent bedsores. Answer patients' call signals. Feed patients who are unable to feed themselves. Observe patients' conditions, measuring and recording food and liquid intake and output and vital signs, and report changes to professional staff. Provide patient care

by supplying and emptying bedpans, applying dressings, and supervising exercise routines. Provide patients with help walking, exercising, and moving in and out of bed. Bathe, groom, shave, dress, or drape patients to prepare them for surgery, treatment, or examination. Collect specimens such as urine, feces, or sputum. Prepare, serve, and collect food trays. Clean rooms and change linens. Transport patients to treatment units, using a wheelchair or stretcher. Deliver messages, documents, and specimens. Answer phones and direct visitors. Administer medications and treatments, such as catheterizations, suppositories, irrigations, enemas, massages, and douches, as directed by a physician or nurse. Restrain patients if necessary. Maintain inventory by storing, preparing, sterilizing, and issuing supplies such as dressing packs and treatment trays. Explain medical instructions to patients and family members. Perform clerical duties such as processing documents and scheduling appointments. Work as part of a medical team that examines and treats clinic outpatients. Set up equipment such as oxygen tents, portable X-ray machines, and overhead irrigation bottles.

SKILLS—Most Important: Social Skills; Management Skills; Science Skills. **Other Above-Average Skills:** Thought-Processing Skills.

GOE—Interest Area: 08. Health Science. **Work Group:** 08.08. Patient Care and Assistance. **Other Jobs in This Group:** Home Health Aides; Licensed Practical and Licensed Vocational Nurses; Psychiatric Aides; Psychiatric Technicians. **PERSONALITY TYPE:** Social. Social occupations frequently involve working with, communicating with, and teaching people. These occupations often involve helping or providing service to others.

EDUCATION/TRAINING PROGRAM(S)—Nurse/Nursing Assistant/Aide and Patient Care Assistant; Health Aide. **RELATED KNOWLEDGE/COURSES—Psychology:** Human behavior and performance; individual differences in ability, personality, and interests; learning and motivation; psychological research methods; and the assessment and treatment of behavioral and affective disorders. **Medicine and Dentistry:** The information and techniques needed to diagnose and treat human injuries, diseases, and deformities. This includes symptoms, treatment alternatives, drug properties and interactions, and preventive health-care measures. **Customer and Personal Service:** Principles and processes for providing customer and personal services. This includes customer needs assessment, meeting of quality standards for services, and evaluation of customer satisfaction. **Chemistry:** The chemical composition, structure, and properties of substances and of the chemical processes and transformations that they undergo. This includes uses of chemicals and their danger signs, production techniques, and disposal methods. **Education and Training:** Principles and methods for curriculum and training design, teaching and instruction for individuals and groups, and the measurement of training effects. **English Language:** The structure and content of the English language, including the meaning and spelling of words, rules of composition, and grammar.

Nursing Instructors and Teachers, Postsecondary

- Education/Training Required: Master's degree
- Annual Earnings: $53,160
- Growth: 32.2%
- Annual Job Openings: 329,000
- Self-Employed: 0.4%
- Part-Time: 27.3%

The job openings listed here are shared with 35 other postsecondary teaching occupations. For a complete list, see the beginning of this section.

Demonstrate and teach patient care in classroom and clinical units to nursing students. Includes both teachers primarily engaged in teaching and those who do a combination of both teaching and research. Initiate, facilitate, and moderate classroom discussions. Prepare and deliver lectures to undergraduate or graduate students on topics such as pharmacology, mental health nursing, and community health-care practices. Keep abreast of developments in their field by reading current literature, talking with colleagues, and participating in professional conferences. Prepare course materials such as syllabi, homework assignments, and handouts. Supervise students' laboratory and clinical work. Evaluate and grade students' classwork, laboratory and clinic work, assignments, and papers. Collaborate with colleagues to address teaching and research issues. Plan,

evaluate, and revise curricula, course content, and course materials and methods of instruction. Assess clinical education needs and patient and client teaching needs, utilizing a variety of methods. Compile, administer, and grade examinations or assign this work to others. Advise students on academic and vocational curricula and on career issues. Maintain student attendance records, grades, and other required records. Maintain regularly scheduled office hours to advise and assist students. Supervise undergraduate or graduate teaching, internship, and research work. Conduct research in a particular field of knowledge and publish findings in professional journals, books, and/or electronic media. Participate in student recruitment, registration, and placement activities. Serve on academic or administrative committees that deal with institutional policies, departmental matters, and academic issues. Coordinate training programs with area universities, clinics, hospitals, health agencies, and/or vocational schools. Compile bibliographies of specialized materials for outside reading assignments. Select and obtain materials and supplies such as textbooks and laboratory equipment. Participate in campus and community events. Write grant proposals to procure external research funding. Act as advisers to student organizations. Demonstrate patient care in clinical units of hospitals. Perform administrative duties such as serving as department head.

SKILLS—Most Important: Science Skills; Social Skills; Thought-Processing Skills. **Other Above-Average Skills:** Communication Skills; Management Skills; Equipment/Technology Analysis Skills.

GOE—Interest Area: 05. Education and Training. **Work Group:** 05.03. Postsecondary and Adult Teaching and Instructing. **Other Jobs in This Group:** Adult Literacy, Remedial Education, and GED Teachers and Instructors; Agricultural Sciences Teachers, Postsecondary; Anthropology and Archeology Teachers, Postsecondary; Architecture Teachers, Postsecondary; Area, Ethnic, and Cultural Studies Teachers, Postsecondary; Art, Drama, and Music Teachers, Postsecondary; Atmospheric, Earth, Marine, and Space Sciences Teachers, Postsecondary; Biological Science Teachers, Postsecondary; Business Teachers, Postsecondary; Chemistry Teachers, Postsecondary; Communications Teachers, Postsecondary; Computer Science Teachers, Postsecondary; Criminal Justice and Law Enforcement Teachers, Postsecondary; Economics

Teachers, Postsecondary; Education Teachers, Postsecondary; Engineering Teachers, Postsecondary; English Language and Literature Teachers, Postsecondary; Environmental Science Teachers, Postsecondary; Farm and Home Management Advisors; Foreign Language and Literature Teachers, Postsecondary; Forestry and Conservation Science Teachers, Postsecondary; Geography Teachers, Postsecondary; Graduate Teaching Assistants; Health Specialties Teachers, Postsecondary; History Teachers, Postsecondary; Home Economics Teachers, Postsecondary; Law Teachers, Postsecondary; Library Science Teachers, Postsecondary; Mathematical Science Teachers, Postsecondary; Philosophy and Religion Teachers, Postsecondary; Physics Teachers, Postsecondary; Political Science Teachers, Postsecondary; Psychology Teachers, Postsecondary; Recreation and Fitness Studies Teachers, Postsecondary; Self-Enrichment Education Teachers; Social Work Teachers, Postsecondary; Sociology Teachers, Postsecondary; Vocational Education Teachers, Postsecondary. **PERSONALITY TYPE:** Social. Social occupations frequently involve working with, communicating with, and teaching people. These occupations often involve helping or providing service to others.

EDUCATION/TRAINING PROGRAM(S)—Pre-Nursing Studies; Nursing—Registered Nurse Training (RN, ASN, BSN, MSN); Adult Health Nurse/Nursing; Nurse Anesthetist; Family Practice Nurse/Nurse Practitioner; Maternal/Child Health and Neonatal Nurse/Nursing; Nurse Midwife/Nursing Midwifery; Nursing Science (MS, PhD); Pediatric Nurse/Nursing; Psychiatric/Mental Health Nurse/Nursing; Public Health/Community Nurse/Nursing; others. **RELATED KNOWLEDGE/COURSES—Therapy and Counseling:** Principles, methods, and procedures for diagnosis, treatment, and rehabilitation of physical and mental dysfunctions and for career counseling and guidance. **Sociology and Anthropology:** Group behavior and dynamics, societal trends and influences, human migrations, ethnicity, and cultures and their history and origins. **Biology:** Plant and animal organisms and their tissues, cells, functions, interdependencies, and interactions with each other and the environment. **Medicine and Dentistry:** The information and techniques needed to diagnose and treat human injuries, diseases, and deformities. This includes symptoms, treatment alternatives, drug properties and interactions, and preventive healthcare measures. **Education and Training:** Principles and methods for curriculum and training

design, teaching and instruction for individuals and groups, and the measurement of training effects. **Philosophy and Theology:** Different philosophical systems and religions. This includes their basic principles, values, ethics, ways of thinking, customs, practices, and impact on human culture.

Obstetricians and Gynecologists

- Education/Training Required: First professional degree
- Annual Earnings: More than $145,600
- Growth: 24.0%
- Annual Job Openings: 41,000
- Self-Employed: 11.5%
- Part-Time: 9.6%

The job openings listed here are shared with Anesthesiologists; Family and General Practitioners; Internists, General; Pediatricians, General; Psychiatrists; and Surgeons.

Diagnose, treat, and help prevent diseases of women, especially those affecting the reproductive system and the process of childbirth. Care for and treat women during prenatal, natal, and post-natal periods. Explain procedures and discuss test results or prescribed treatments with patients. Treat diseases of female organs. Monitor patients' condition and progress and re-evaluate treatments as necessary. Perform cesarean sections or other surgical procedures as needed to preserve patients' health and deliver babies safely. Prescribe or administer therapy, medication, and other specialized medical care to treat or prevent illness, disease, or injury. Analyze records, reports, test results, or examination information to diagnose medical condition of patient. Collect, record, and maintain patient information, such as medical histories, reports, and examination results. Advise patients and community members concerning diet, activity, hygiene, and disease prevention. Refer patient to medical specialist or other practitioner when necessary. Consult with, or provide consulting services to, other physicians. Direct and coordinate activities of nurses, students, assistants, specialists, therapists, and other medical staff. Plan, implement, or administer health programs in hospitals, businesses, or communities for prevention and treatment of injuries or illnesses. Prepare government and organizational reports on birth, death, and disease statistics; workforce evaluations; or the medical status of individuals. Conduct research to develop or test medications, treatments, or procedures to prevent or control disease or injury.

SKILLS—Most Important: Science Skills; Thought-Processing Skills; Social Skills. **Other Above-Average Skills:** Communication Skills; Quality Control Skills; Mathematics Skills.

GOE—Interest Area: 08. Health Science. **Work Group:** 08.02. Medicine and Surgery. **Other Jobs in This Group:** Anesthesiologists; Family and General Practitioners; Internists, General; Medical Assistants; Medical Transcriptionists; Pediatricians, General; Pharmacists; Pharmacy Aides; Pharmacy Technicians; Physician Assistants; Psychiatrists; Registered Nurses; Surgeons; Surgical Technologists. **PERSONALITY TYPE:** Investigative. Investigative occupations frequently involve working with ideas and require an extensive amount of thinking. These occupations can involve searching for facts and figuring out problems mentally.

EDUCATION/TRAINING PROGRAM(S)—Neonatal-Perinatal Medicine; Obstetrics and Gynecology. **RELATED KNOWLEDGE/COURSES—Medicine and Dentistry:** The information and techniques needed to diagnose and treat human injuries, diseases, and deformities. This includes symptoms, treatment alternatives, drug properties and interactions, and preventive healthcare measures. **Therapy and Counseling:** Principles, methods, and procedures for diagnosis, treatment, and rehabilitation of physical and mental dysfunctions and for career counseling and guidance. **Biology:** Plant and animal organisms and their tissues, cells, functions, interdependencies, and interactions with each other and the environment. **Psychology:** Human behavior and performance; individual differences in ability, personality, and interests; learning and motivation; psychological research methods; and the assessment and treatment of behavioral and affective disorders. **Sociology and Anthropology:** Group behavior and dynamics, societal trends and influences, human migrations, ethnicity, and cultures and their history and origins. **Chemistry:** The chemical composition, structure, and properties of substances and of the chemical processes and transformations that they undergo. This includes uses of chemicals and their danger signs, production techniques, and disposal methods.

Occupational Therapist Assistants

- Education/Training Required: Associate degree
- Annual Earnings: $39,750
- Growth: 34.1%
- Annual Job Openings: 2,000
- Self-Employed: 0.0%
- Part-Time: 18.6%

Assist occupational therapists in providing occupational therapy treatments and procedures. May, in accordance with state laws, assist in development of treatment plans, carry out routine functions, direct activity programs, and document the progress of treatments. Generally requires formal training. Observe and record patients' progress, attitudes, and behavior and maintain this information in client records. Maintain and promote a positive attitude toward clients and their treatment programs. Monitor patients' performance in therapy activities, providing encouragement. Select therapy activities to fit patients' needs and capabilities. Instruct, or assist in instructing, patients and families in home programs, basic living skills, and the care and use of adaptive equipment. Evaluate the daily living skills and capacities of physically, developmentally, or emotionally disabled clients. Aid patients in dressing and grooming themselves. Implement, or assist occupational therapists with implementing, treatment plans designed to help clients function independently. Report to supervisors, verbally or in writing, on patients' progress, attitudes, and behavior. Alter treatment programs to obtain better results if treatment is not having the intended effect. Work under the direction of occupational therapists to plan, implement, and administer educational, vocational, and recreational programs that restore and enhance performance in individuals with functional impairments. Design, fabricate, and repair assistive devices and make adaptive changes to equipment and environments. Assemble, clean, and maintain equipment and materials for patient use. Teach patients how to deal constructively with their emotions. Perform clerical duties such as scheduling appointments, collecting data, and documenting health insurance billings. Transport patients to and from the occupational therapy work area. Demonstrate therapy techniques such as manual and creative arts or games. Order any needed educational or treatment supplies. Assist educational specialists or clinical psychologists in administering situational or diagnostic tests to measure client's abilities or progress.

SKILLS—Most Important: Social Skills; Thought-Processing Skills; Equipment/Technology Analysis Skills. **Other Above-Average Skills:** Communication Skills; Science Skills.

GOE—Interest Area: 08. Health Science. **Work Group:** 08.07. Medical Therapy. **Other Jobs in This Group:** Audiologists; Massage Therapists; Occupational Therapist Aides; Occupational Therapists; Physical Therapist Aides; Physical Therapist Assistants; Physical Therapists; Radiation Therapists; Recreational Therapists; Respiratory Therapists; Respiratory Therapy Technicians; Speech-Language Pathologists. **PERSONALITY TYPE:** Social. Social occupations frequently involve working with, communicating with, and teaching people. These occupations often involve helping or providing service to others.

EDUCATION/TRAINING PROGRAM(S)—Occupational Therapist Assistant. **RELATED KNOWLEDGE/COURSES—Therapy and Counseling:** Principles, methods, and procedures for diagnosis, treatment, and rehabilitation of physical and mental dysfunctions and for career counseling and guidance. **Psychology:** Human behavior and performance; individual differences in ability, personality, and interests; learning and motivation; psychological research methods; and the assessment and treatment of behavioral and affective disorders. **Sociology and Anthropology:** Group behavior and dynamics, societal trends and influences, human migrations, ethnicity, and cultures and their history and origins. **Philosophy and Theology:** Different philosophical systems and religions. This includes their basic principles, values, ethics, ways of thinking, customs, practices, and impact on human culture. **Medicine and Dentistry:** The information and techniques needed to diagnose and treat human injuries, diseases, and deformities. This includes symptoms, treatment alternatives, drug properties and interactions, and preventive healthcare measures. **Biology:** Plant and

animal organisms and their tissues, cells, functions, interdependencies, and interactions with each other and the environment.

Occupational Therapists

- Education/Training Required: Master's degree
- Annual Earnings: $56,860
- Growth: 33.6%
- Annual Job Openings: 7,000
- Self-Employed: 6.0%
- Part-Time: 29.4%

Assess, plan, organize, and participate in rehabilitative programs that help restore vocational, homemaking, and daily living skills, as well as general independence, to disabled persons. Complete and maintain necessary records. Evaluate patients' progress and prepare reports that detail progress. Test and evaluate patients' physical and mental abilities and analyze medical data to determine realistic rehabilitation goals for patients. Select activities that will help individuals learn work and life-management skills within limits of their mental and physical capabilities. Plan, organize, and conduct occupational therapy programs in hospital, institutional, or community settings to help rehabilitate those impaired because of illness, injury or psychological or developmental problems. Recommend changes in patients' work or living environments consistent with their needs and capabilities. Consult with rehabilitation team to select activity programs and coordinate occupational therapy with other therapeutic activities. Help clients improve decisionmaking, abstract reasoning, memory, sequencing, coordination, and perceptual skills, using computer programs. Develop and participate in health promotion programs, group activities, or discussions to promote client health, facilitate social adjustment, alleviate stress, and prevent physical or mental disability. Provide training and supervision in therapy techniques and objectives for students and nurses and other medical staff. Design and create, or requisition, special supplies and equipment, such as splints, braces, and computer-aided adaptive equipment. Plan and implement programs and social activities to help patients learn work and school skills and adjust to handicaps. Lay out materials such as puzzles, scissors, and eating utensils for use in therapy; clean and repair these tools after therapy sessions. Advise on health risks in the workplace and on health-related transition to retirement. Conduct research in occupational therapy. Provide patients with assistance in locating and holding jobs.

SKILLS—Most Important: Science Skills; Social Skills; Communication Skills. **Other Above-Average Skills:** Thought-Processing Skills; Equipment/Technology Analysis Skills.

GOE—Interest Area: 08. Health Science. **Work Group:** 08.07. Medical Therapy. **Other Jobs in This Group:** Audiologists; Massage Therapists; Occupational Therapist Aides; Occupational Therapist Assistants; Physical Therapist Aides; Physical Therapist Assistants; Physical Therapists; Radiation Therapists; Recreational Therapists; Respiratory Therapists; Respiratory Therapy Technicians; Speech-Language Pathologists. **PERSONALITY TYPE:** Social. Social occupations frequently involve working with, communicating with, and teaching people. These occupations often involve helping or providing service to others.

EDUCATION/TRAINING PROGRAM(S)—Occupational Therapy/Therapist. **RELATED KNOWLEDGE/COURSES—Therapy and Counseling:** Principles, methods, and procedures for diagnosis, treatment, and rehabilitation of physical and mental dysfunctions and for career counseling and guidance. **Psychology:** Human behavior and performance; individual differences in ability, personality, and interests; learning and motivation; psychological research methods; and the assessment and treatment of behavioral and affective disorders. **Medicine and Dentistry:** The information and techniques needed to diagnose and treat human injuries, diseases, and deformities. This includes symptoms, treatment alternatives, drug properties and interactions, and preventive healthcare measures. **Customer and Personal Service:** Principles and processes for providing customer and personal services. This includes customer needs assessment, meeting of quality standards for services, and evaluation of customer satisfaction. **Biology:** Plant and animal organisms and their tissues, cells, functions, interdependencies, and interactions with each other and the environment. **Sociology and Anthropology:** Group behavior and dynamics, societal trends and influences, human migrations, ethnicity, and cultures and their history and origins.

Operating Engineers and Other Construction Equipment Operators

- Education/Training Required: Moderate-term on-the-job training
- Annual Earnings: $35,830
- Growth: 11.6%
- Annual Job Openings: 37,000
- Self-Employed: 5.4%
- Part-Time: 2.9%

Operate one or several types of power construction equipment, such as motor graders, bulldozers, scrapers, compressors, pumps, derricks, shovels, tractors, or front-end loaders, to excavate, move, and grade earth; erect structures; or pour concrete or other hard-surface pavement. May repair and maintain equipment in addition to other duties. Learn and follow safety regulations. Take actions to avoid potential hazards and obstructions such as utility lines, other equipment, other workers, and falling objects. Adjust handwheels and depress pedals to control attachments such as blades, buckets, scrapers, and swing booms. Start engines; move throttles, switches, and levers; and depress pedals to operate machines such as bulldozers, trench excavators, road graders, and backhoes. Locate underground services, such as pipes and wires, prior to beginning work. Monitor operations to ensure that health and safety standards are met. Align machines, cutterheads, or depth gauge makers with reference stakes and guidelines or ground or position equipment by following hand signals of other workers. Load and move dirt, rocks, equipment, and materials, using trucks, crawler tractors, power cranes, shovels, graders, and related equipment. Drive and maneuver equipment equipped with blades in successive passes over working areas to remove topsoil, vegetation, and rocks and to distribute and level earth or terrain. Coordinate machine actions with other activities, positioning or moving loads in response to hand or audio signals from crew members. Operate tractors and bulldozers to perform such tasks as clearing land, mixing sludge, trimming backfills, and building roadways and parking lots. Repair and maintain equipment, making emergency adjustments or assisting with major repairs as necessary.

Check fuel supplies at sites to ensure adequate availability. Connect hydraulic hoses, belts, mechanical linkages, or power takeoff shafts to tractors. Operate loaders to pull out stumps, rip asphalt or concrete, rough-grade properties, bury refuse, or perform general cleanup. Select and fasten bulldozer blades or other attachments to tractors, using hitches. Test atmosphere for adequate oxygen and explosive conditions when working in confined spaces. Operate compactors, scrapers, and rollers to level, compact, and cover refuse at disposal grounds. Talk to clients and study instructions, plans, and diagrams to establish work requirements.

SKILLS—Most Important: Equipment Use/Maintenance Skills; Management Skills; Science Skills. **Other Above-Average Skills:** Mathematics Skills; Quality Control Skills.

GOE—Interest Area: 02. Architecture and Construction. **Work Group:** 02.04. Construction Crafts. **Other Jobs in This Group:** Boilermakers; Brickmasons and Blockmasons; Carpet Installers; Cement Masons and Concrete Finishers; Commercial Divers; Construction Carpenters; Crane and Tower Operators; Drywall and Ceiling Tile Installers; Electricians; Fence Erectors; Floor Layers, Except Carpet, Wood, and Hard Tiles; Floor Sanders and Finishers; Glaziers; Hazardous Materials Removal Workers; Insulation Workers, Floor, Ceiling, and Wall; Insulation Workers, Mechanical; Manufactured Building and Mobile Home Installers; Painters, Construction and Maintenance; Paperhangers; Paving, Surfacing, and Tamping Equipment Operators; Pile-Driver Operators; Pipe Fitters and Steamfitters; Pipelayers; Plasterers and Stucco Masons; Plumbers; Plumbers, Pipefitters, and Steamfitters; Rail-Track Laying and Maintenance Equipment Operators; Refractory Materials Repairers, Except Brickmasons; Reinforcing Iron and Rebar Workers; Riggers; Roofers; Rough Carpenters; Security and Fire Alarm Systems Installers; Segmental Pavers; Sheet Metal Workers; Stone Cutters and Carvers, Manufacturing; Stonemasons; Structural Iron and Steel Workers; Tapers; Terrazzo Workers and Finishers; Tile and Marble Setters. **PERSONALITY TYPE:** Realistic. Realistic occupations frequently involve work activities that include practical, hands-on problems and solutions. They often deal with plants, animals, and real-world materials like wood, tools, and machinery. Many of the occupations require working outside and do not involve a lot of paperwork or working closely with others.

EDUCATION/TRAINING PROGRAM(S)—Construction/Heavy Equipment/Earthmoving Equipment Operation; Mobile Crane Operation/Operator. **RELATED KNOWLEDGE/COURSES—Building and Construction:** The materials, methods, and tools involved in the construction or repair of houses, buildings, or other structures such as highways and roads. **Mechanical Devices:** Machines and tools, including their designs, uses, repair, and maintenance. **Engineering and Technology:** The practical application of engineering science and technology. This includes applying principles, techniques, procedures, and equipment to the design and production of various goods and services. **Design:** Design techniques, tools, and principles involved in production of precision technical plans, blueprints, drawings, and models. **Production and Processing:** Raw materials, production processes, quality control, costs, and other techniques for maximizing the effective manufacture and distribution of goods. **Public Safety and Security:** Relevant equipment, policies, procedures, and strategies to promote effective local, state, or national security operations for the protection of people, data, property, and institutions.

Operations Research Analysts

- Education/Training Required: Master's degree
- Annual Earnings: $62,180
- Growth: 8.4%
- Annual Job Openings: 7,000
- Self-Employed: 1.2%
- Part-Time: 5.4%

Formulate and apply mathematical modeling and other optimizing methods, using a computer to develop and interpret information that assists management with decision making, policy formulation, or other managerial functions. May develop related software, service, or products. Frequently concentrates on collecting and analyzing data and developing decision support software. May develop and supply optimal time, cost, or logistics networks for program evaluation, review, or implementation. Formulate mathematical or simulation models of problems, relating constants and variables, restrictions, alternatives, and conflicting objectives and their numerical parameters. Collaborate with others in the organization to ensure successful implementation of chosen problem solutions. Analyze information obtained from management in order to conceptualize and define operational problems. Perform validation and testing of models to ensure adequacy; reformulate models as necessary. Collaborate with senior managers and decision-makers to identify and solve a variety of problems and to clarify management objectives. Define data requirements; then gather and validate information, applying judgment and statistical tests. Study and analyze information about alternative courses of action in order to determine which plan will offer the best outcomes. Prepare management reports defining and evaluating problems and recommending solutions. Break systems into their component parts, assign numerical values to each component, and examine the mathematical relationships between them. Specify manipulative or computational methods to be applied to models. Observe the current system in operation and gather and analyze information about each of the parts of component problems, using a variety of sources. Design, conduct, and evaluate experimental operational models in cases where models cannot be developed from existing data. Develop and apply time and cost networks in order to plan, control, and review large projects. Develop business methods and procedures, including accounting systems, file systems, office systems, logistics systems, and production schedules.

SKILLS—Most Important: Computer Programming Skills; Mathematics Skills; Science Skills. **Other Above-Average Skills:** Equipment/Technology Analysis Skills; Quality Control Skills; Management Skills; Social Skills.

GOE—Interest Area: 04. Business and Administration. **Work Group:** 04.05. Accounting, Auditing, and Analytical Support. **Other Jobs in This Group:** Accountants; Accountants and Auditors; Auditors; Budget Analysts; Industrial Engineering Technicians; Logisticians; Management Analysts. **PERSONALITY TYPE:** Investigative. Investigative occupations frequently involve working with ideas and require an extensive amount of thinking. These occupations can involve searching for facts and figuring out problems mentally.

EDUCATION/TRAINING PROGRAM(S)—Educational Evaluation and Research; Educational Statistics and Research Methods; Operations Research; Management Science, General; Management Sciences and Quantitative Methods, Other. **RELATED KNOWLEDGE/COURSES—Mathematics:** Arithmetic, algebra, geometry, calculus, and statistics and their applications. **Engineering and Technology:** The practical application of engineering science and technology. This includes applying principles, techniques, procedures, and equipment to the design and production of various goods and services. **Computers and Electronics:** Circuit boards; processors; chips; electronic equipment; and computer hardware and software, including applications and programming. **Production and Processing:** Raw materials, production processes, quality control, costs, and other techniques for maximizing the effective manufacture and distribution of goods. **Economics and Accounting:** Economic and accounting principles and practices, the financial markets, banking, and the analysis and reporting of financial data. **Administration and Management:** Business and management principles involved in strategic planning, resource allocation, human resources modeling, leadership technique, production methods, and coordination of people and resources.

Optometrists

- Education/Training Required: First professional degree
- Annual Earnings: $88,040
- Growth: 19.7%
- Annual Job Openings: 2,000
- Self-Employed: 27.4%
- Part-Time: 16.5%

Diagnose, manage, and treat conditions and diseases of the human eye and visual system. Examine eyes and visual system, diagnose problems or impairments, prescribe corrective lenses, and provide treatment. May prescribe therapeutic drugs to treat specific eye conditions. Examine eyes, using observation, instruments, and pharmaceutical agents, to determine visual acuity and perception, focus, and coordination and to diagnose diseases and other abnormalities such as glaucoma or color-blindness. Analyze test results and develop a treatment plan. Prescribe, supply, fit, and adjust eyeglasses, contact lenses, and other vision aids. Prescribe medications to treat eye diseases if state laws permit. Educate and counsel patients on contact lens care, visual hygiene, lighting arrangements, and safety factors. Consult with and refer patients to ophthalmologist or other health-care practitioner if additional medical treatment is determined necessary. Remove foreign bodies from the eye. Provide patients undergoing eye surgeries, such as cataract and laser vision correction, with pre- and post-operative care. Prescribe therapeutic procedures to correct or conserve vision. Provide vision therapy and low vision rehabilitation.

SKILLS—Most Important: Science Skills; Thought-Processing Skills; Management Skills. **Other Above-Average Skills:** Communication Skills; Social Skills; Quality Control Skills; Equipment Use/Maintenance Skills.

GOE—Interest Area: 08. Health Science. **Work Group:** 08.04. Health Specialties. **Other Jobs in This Group:** Chiropractors; Podiatrists. **PERSONALITY TYPE:** Investigative. Investigative occupations frequently involve working with ideas and require an extensive amount of thinking. These occupations can involve searching for facts and figuring out problems mentally.

EDUCATION/TRAINING PROGRAM(S)—Optometry (OD). **RELATED KNOWLEDGE/COURSES—Medicine and Dentistry:** The information and techniques needed to diagnose and treat human injuries, diseases, and deformities. This includes symptoms, treatment alternatives, drug properties and interactions, and preventive healthcare measures. **Biology:** Plant and animal organisms and their tissues, cells, functions, interdependencies, and interactions with each other and the environment. **Psychology:** Human behavior and performance; individual differences in ability, personality, and interests; learning and motivation; psychological research methods; and the assessment and treatment of behavioral and affective disorders. **Sales and Marketing:** Principles and methods for showing, promoting, and selling products or services. This includes marketing strategy and tactics, product demonstration, sales techniques, and sales control systems. **Personnel and Human Resources:** Principles and procedures for personnel recruitment, selection, training, compensation and benefits, labor relations and negotiation, and personnel information systems. **Economics and Accounting:** Economic and accounting principles and practices, the financial markets, banking, and the analysis and reporting of financial data.

Paralegals and Legal Assistants

- Education/Training Required: Associate degree
- Annual Earnings: $41,170
- Growth: 29.7%
- Annual Job Openings: 28,000
- Self-Employed: 4.2%
- Part-Time: 11.1%

Assist lawyers by researching legal precedent, investigating facts, or preparing legal documents. Conduct research to support a legal proceeding, to formulate a defense, or to initiate legal action. Prepare legal documents, including briefs, pleadings, appeals, wills, contracts, and real estate closing statements. Prepare affidavits or other documents, maintain document file, and file pleadings with court clerk. Gather and analyze research data, such as statutes; decisions; and legal articles, codes, and documents. Investigate facts and law of cases to determine causes of action and to prepare cases. Call upon witnesses to testify at hearing. Direct and coordinate law office activity, including delivery of subpoenas. Arbitrate disputes between parties and assist in real estate closing process. Keep and monitor legal volumes to ensure that law library is up to date. Appraise and inventory real and personal property for estate planning.

SKILLS—Most Important: Communication Skills. **Other Above-Average Skills:** None met the criteria.

GOE—Interest Area: 12. Law and Public Safety. **Work Group:** 12.03. Legal Support. **Other Jobs in This Group:** Law Clerks; Title Examiners, Abstractors, and Searchers. **PERSONALITY TYPE:** Enterprising. Enterprising occupations frequently involve starting up and carrying out projects. These occupations can involve leading people and making many decisions. They sometimes require risk taking and often deal with business.

EDUCATION/TRAINING PROGRAM(S)—Legal Assistant/Paralegal. **RELATED KNOWLEDGE/COURSES—Clerical Practices:** Administrative and clerical procedures and systems such as word processing, managing files and records, stenography and transcrip-

P

tion, designing forms, and other office procedures and terminology. **Law and Government:** Laws, legal codes, court procedures, precedents, government regulations, executive orders, agency rules, and the democratic political process. **Computers and Electronics:** Circuit boards; processors; chips; electronic equipment; and computer hardware and software, including applications and programming. **Personnel and Human Resources:** Principles and procedures for personnel recruitment, selection, training, compensation and benefits, labor relations and negotiation, and personnel information systems. **Customer and Personal Service:** Principles and processes for providing customer and personal services. This includes customer needs assessment, meeting of quality standards for services, and evaluation of customer satisfaction. **English Language:** The structure and content of the English language, including the meaning and spelling of words, rules of composition, and grammar.

Payroll and Timekeeping Clerks

- ⦿ Education/Training Required: Moderate-term on-the-job training
- ⦿ Annual Earnings: $31,360
- ⦿ Growth: 17.3%
- ⦿ Annual Job Openings: 36,000
- ⦿ Self-Employed: 1.1%
- ⦿ Part-Time: 14.7%

Compile and post employee time and payroll data. May compute employees' time worked, production, and commission. May compute and post wages and deductions. May prepare paychecks. Process and issue employee paychecks and statements of earnings and deductions. Compute wages and deductions and enter data into computers. Compile employee time, production, and payroll data from time sheets and other records. Review time sheets, work charts, wage computation, and other information to detect and reconcile payroll discrepancies. Verify attendance, hours worked, and pay adjustments and post information onto designated records. Record employee information, such as exemptions, transfers, and resignations, to maintain and update payroll records. Keep informed about changes in tax and deduction laws that apply to the payroll process. Issue and record adjustments to pay related to previous errors or retroactive increases. Provide information to employees and managers on payroll matters, tax issues, benefit plans, and collective agreement provisions. Complete time sheets showing employees' arrival and departure times. Post relevant work hours to client files to bill clients properly. Distribute and collect timecards each pay period. Complete, verify, and process forms and documentation for administration of benefits such as pension plans and unemployment and medical insurance. Prepare and balance period-end reports and reconcile issued payrolls to bank statements. Compile statistical reports, statements, and summaries related to pay and benefits accounts and submit them to appropriate departments. Coordinate special programs, such as United Way campaigns, that involve payroll deductions.

SKILLS—Most Important: Mathematics Skills; Communication Skills; Thought-Processing Skills. **Other Above-Average Skills:** Social Skills; Management Skills.

GOE—Interest Area: 04. Business and Administration. **Work Group:** 04.06. Mathematical Clerical Support. **Other Jobs in This Group:** Billing and Posting Clerks and Machine Operators; Billing, Cost, and Rate Clerks; Bookkeeping, Accounting, and Auditing Clerks; Brokerage Clerks; Statement Clerks; Tax Preparers. **PERSONALITY TYPE:** Conventional. Conventional occupations frequently involve following set procedures and routines. These occupations can include working with data and details more than with ideas. Usually there is a clear line of authority to follow.

EDUCATION/TRAINING PROGRAM(S)—Accounting Technology/Technician and Bookkeeping. **RELATED KNOWLEDGE/COURSES—Clerical Practices:** Administrative and clerical procedures and systems such as word processing, managing files and records, stenography and transcription, designing forms, and other office procedures and terminology. **Economics and Accounting:** Economic and accounting principles and practices, the financial markets, banking, and the analysis and reporting of financial data. **Administration and Management:** Business and management principles involved in strategic planning, resource allocation, human resources modeling, leadership technique, production methods, and coordination of people and resources. **Customer and Personal Service:** Principles and processes for providing customer and personal services. This includes customer needs assessment, meeting of quality standards for services, and evaluation of customer satisfaction. **Personnel and Human Resources:** Principles and procedures for personnel recruitment, selection, training, compensation and benefits, labor relations and negotiation, and personnel information systems. **Mathematics:** Arithmetic, algebra, geometry, calculus, and statistics and their applications.

Pediatricians, General

- Education/Training Required: First professional degree
- Annual Earnings: $136,600
- Growth: 24.0%
- Annual Job Openings: 41,000
- Self-Employed: 11.5%
- Part-Time: 9.6%

The job openings listed here are shared with Anesthesiologists; Family and General Practitioners; Internists, General; Obstetricians and Gynecologists; Psychiatrists; and Surgeons.

Diagnose, treat, and help prevent children's diseases and injuries. Examine patients or order, perform, and interpret diagnostic tests to obtain information on medical condition and determine diagnosis. Examine children regularly to assess their growth and development. Prescribe or administer treatment, therapy, medication, vaccination, and other specialized medical care to treat or prevent illness, disease, or injury in infants and children. Collect, record, and maintain patient information, such as medical history, reports, and examination results. Advise patients, parents or guardians, and community members concerning diet, activity, hygiene, and disease prevention. Treat children who have minor illnesses, acute and chronic health problems, and growth and development concerns. Explain procedures and discuss test results or prescribed treatments with patients and parents or guardians. Monitor patients' condition and progress and re-evaluate treatments as necessary.

Plan and execute medical care programs to aid in the mental and physical growth and development of children and adolescents. Refer patient to medical specialist or other practitioner when necessary. Direct and coordinate activities of nurses, students, assistants, specialists, therapists, and other medical staff. Provide consulting services to other physicians. Plan, implement, or administer health programs or standards in hospital, business, or community for information, prevention, or treatment of injury or illness. Operate on patients to remove, repair, or improve functioning of diseased or injured body parts and systems. Conduct research to study anatomy and develop or test medications, treatments, or procedures to prevent or control disease or injury. Prepare reports for government or management of birth, death, and disease statistics; workforce evaluations; or medical status of individuals.

SKILLS—Most Important: Science Skills; Social Skills; Thought-Processing Skills. **Other Above-Average Skills:** Communication Skills; Management Skills.

GOE—Interest Area: 08. Health Science. **Work Group:** 08.02. Medicine and Surgery. **Other Jobs in This Group:** Anesthesiologists; Family and General Practitioners; Internists, General; Medical Assistants; Medical Transcriptionists; Obstetricians and Gynecologists; Pharmacists; Pharmacy Aides; Pharmacy Technicians; Physician Assistants; Psychiatrists; Registered Nurses; Surgeons; Surgical Technologists. **PERSONALITY TYPE:** Investigative. Investigative occupations frequently involve working with ideas and require an extensive amount of thinking. These occupations can involve searching for facts and figuring out problems mentally.

EDUCATION/TRAINING PROGRAM(S)—Child/Pediatric Neurology; Family Medicine; Neonatal-Perinatal Medicine; Pediatric Cardiology; Pediatric Endocrinology; Pediatric Hemato-Oncology; Pediatric Nephrology; Pediatric Orthopedics; Pediatric Surgery; Pediatrics. **RELATED KNOWLEDGE/COURSES—Medicine and Dentistry:** The information and techniques needed to diagnose and treat human injuries, diseases, and deformities. This includes symptoms, treatment alternatives, drug properties and interactions, and preventive healthcare measures. **Therapy and Counseling:** Principles, methods, and procedures for diagnosis, treatment, and rehabilitation of physical and mental dysfunctions and for career counseling and guidance. **Biology:** Plant and animal organisms and their tissues, cells, functions, interdependencies, and interactions with each other and the environment. **Psychology:** Human behavior and performance; individual differences in ability, personality, and interests; learning and motivation; psychological research methods; and the assessment and treatment of behavioral and affective disorders. **Chemistry:** The chemical composition, structure, and properties of substances and of the chemical processes and transformations that they undergo. This includes uses of chemicals and their danger signs, production techniques, and disposal methods. **Sociology and Anthropology:** Group behavior and dynamics, societal trends and influences, human migrations, ethnicity, and cultures and their history and origins.

Personal and Home Care Aides

- ◎ Education/Training Required: Short-term on-the-job training
- ◎ Annual Earnings: $17,340
- ◎ Growth: 41.0%
- ◎ Annual Job Openings: 230,000
- ◎ Self-Employed: 4.5%
- ◎ Part-Time: 36.6%

Assist elderly or disabled adults with daily living activities at the person's home or in a daytime non-residential facility. Duties performed at a place of residence may include keeping house (making beds, doing laundry, washing dishes) and preparing meals. May provide meals and supervised activities at non-residential care facilities. May advise families, the elderly, and disabled on such things as nutrition, cleanliness, and household utilities. Perform health-care–related tasks, such as monitoring vital signs and medication, under the direction of registered nurses and physiotherapists. Administer bedside and personal care, such as ambulation and personal hygiene assistance. Prepare and maintain records of client progress and services performed, reporting changes in client condition to manager or supervisor. Perform housekeeping duties, such as cooking, cleaning, washing clothes and dishes, and running errands. Care for individuals and families during periods of incapacitation, family disruption, or convalescence, providing companionship, personal care, and help in adjusting to new lifestyles. Instruct and advise clients on issues such as household cleanliness, utilities, hygiene, nutrition, and infant care. Plan, shop for, and prepare nutritious meals or assist families in planning, shopping for, and preparing nutritious meals. Participate in case reviews, consulting with the team caring for the client, to evaluate the client's needs and plan for continuing services. Transport clients to locations outside the home, such as to physicians' offices or on outings, using a motor vehicle. Train family members to provide bedside care. Provide clients with communication assistance, typing their correspondence and obtaining information for them.

SKILLS—Most Important: Social Skills; Communication Skills; Thought-Processing Skills. **Other Above-Average Skills:** None met the criteria.

GOE—Interest Area: 10. Human Service. **Work Group:** 10.03. Child/Personal Care and Services. **Other Jobs in This Group:** Child Care Workers; Funeral Attendants; Nannies. **PERSONALITY TYPE:** Social. Social occupations frequently involve working with, communicating with, and teaching people. These occupations often involve helping or providing service to others.

EDUCATION/TRAINING PROGRAM(S)—Home Health Aide/Home Attendant. **RELATED KNOWLEDGE/COURSES—Medicine and Dentistry:** The information and techniques needed to diagnose and treat human injuries, diseases, and deformities. This includes symptoms, treatment alternatives, drug properties and interactions, and preventive healthcare measures. **Customer and Personal Service:** Principles and processes for providing customer and personal services. This includes customer needs assessment, meeting of quality standards for services, and evaluation of customer satisfaction.

Personal Financial Advisors

- ◉ Education/Training Required: Bachelor's degree
- ◉ Annual Earnings: $63,500
- ◉ Growth: 25.9%
- ◉ Annual Job Openings: 17,000
- ◉ Self-Employed: 38.9%
- ◉ Part-Time: 8.5%

Advise clients on financial plans, utilizing knowledge of tax and investment strategies, securities, insurance, pension plans, and real estate. Duties include assessing clients' assets, liabilities, cash flow, insurance coverage, tax status, and financial objectives to establish investment strategies. Open accounts for clients and disburse funds from account to creditors as agents for clients. Research and investigate available investment opportunities to determine whether they fit into financial plans. Recommend strategies clients can use to achieve their financial goals and objectives, including specific recommendations in such areas as cash management, insurance coverage, and investment planning. Sell financial products such as stocks, bonds, mutual funds, and insurance if licensed to do so. Collect information from students to determine their eligibility for specific financial aid programs. Conduct seminars and workshops on financial planning topics such as retirement planning, estate planning, and the evaluation of severance packages. Contact clients' creditors to arrange for payment adjustments so that payments are feasible for clients and agreeable to creditors. Meet with clients' other advisors, including attorneys, accountants, trust officers, and investment bankers, to fully understand clients' financial goals and circumstances. Authorize release of financial aid funds to students. Participate in the selection of candidates for specific financial aid awards. Determine amounts of aid to be granted to students, considering such factors as funds available, extent of demand, and financial needs. Build and maintain client bases, keeping current client plans up to date and recruiting new clients on an ongoing basis. Review clients' accounts and plans regularly to determine whether life changes, economic changes, or financial performance indicate a need for plan reassessment. Prepare and interpret information for clients such as investment performance reports, financial document summaries, and income projections. Answer clients' questions about the purposes and details of financial plans and strategies. Contact clients periodically to determine if there have been changes in their financial status. Devise debt liquidation plans that include payoff priorities and timelines. Explain and document for clients the types of services that are to be provided and the responsibilities to be taken by the personal financial advisor.

SKILLS—Most Important: Mathematics Skills; Communication Skills. **Other Above-Average Skills:** None met the criteria.

GOE—Interest Area: 06. Finance and Insurance. **Work Group:** 06.05. Finance/Insurance Sales and Support. **Other Jobs in This Group:** Advertising Sales Agents; Insurance Sales Agents; Sales Agents, Financial Services; Sales Agents, Securities and Commodities; Securities, Commodities, and Financial Services Sales Agents. **PERSONALITY TYPE:** Social. Social occupations frequently involve working with, communicating with, and teaching people. These occupations often involve helping or providing service to others.

EDUCATION/TRAINING PROGRAM(S)—Finance, General; Financial Planning and Services. **RELATED KNOWLEDGE/COURSES—Economics and Accounting:** Economic and accounting principles and practices, the financial markets, banking, and the analysis and reporting of financial data. **Mathematics:** Arithmetic, algebra, geometry, calculus, and statistics and their applications. **Administration and Management:** Business and management principles involved in strategic planning, resource allocation, human resources modeling, leadership technique, production methods, and coordination of people and resources.

Personnel Recruiters

- ◉ Education/Training Required: Bachelor's degree
- ◉ Annual Earnings: $41,780
- ◉ Growth: 30.5%
- ◉ Annual Job Openings: 30,000
- ◉ Self-Employed: 2.5%
- ◉ Part-Time: 7.7%

P

The job openings listed here are shared with Employment Interviewers.

Seek out, interview, and screen applicants to fill existing and future job openings and promote career opportunities within an organization. Establish and maintain relationships with hiring managers to stay abreast of current and future hiring and business needs. Interview applicants to obtain information on work history, training, education, and job skills. Maintain current knowledge of Equal Employment Opportunity (EEO) and affirmative action guidelines and laws, such as the Americans with Disabilities Act (ADA). Perform searches for qualified candidates according to relevant job criteria, using computer databases, networking, Internet recruiting resources, cold calls, media, recruiting firms, and employee referrals. Prepare and maintain employment records. Contact applicants to inform them of employment possibilities, consideration, and selection. Inform potential applicants about facilities, operations, benefits, and job or career opportunities in organizations. Screen and refer applicants to hiring personnel in the organization, making hiring recommendations when appropriate. Arrange for interviews and provide travel arrangements as necessary. Advise managers and employees on staffing policies and procedures. Review and evaluate applicant qualifications or eligibility for specified licensing according to established guidelines and designated licensing codes. Hire applicants and authorize paperwork assigning them to positions. Conduct reference and background checks on applicants. Evaluate recruitment and selection criteria to ensure conformance to professional, statistical, and testing standards, recommending revision as needed. Recruit applicants for open positions, arranging job fairs with college campus representatives. Advise management on organizing, preparing, and implementing recruiting and retention programs. Supervise personnel clerks performing filing, typing, and recordkeeping duties. Project yearly recruitment expenditures for budgetary consideration and control. Serve on selection and examination boards to evaluate applicants according to test scores, contacting promising candidates for interviews. Address civic and social groups and attend conferences to disseminate information concerning possible job openings and career opportunities.

SKILLS—Most Important: Management Skills; Social Skills; Thought-Processing Skills. **Other Above-Average Skills:** Communication Skills; Equipment/Technology Analysis Skills.

GOE—Interest Area: 04. Business and Administration. **Work Group:** 04.03. Human Resources Support. **Other Jobs in This Group:** Compensation, Benefits, and Job Analysis Specialists; Employment Interviewers; Employment, Recruitment, and Placement Specialists; Training and Development Specialists. **PERSONALITY TYPE:** Enterprising. Enterprising occupations frequently involve starting up and carrying out projects. These occupations can involve leading people and making many decisions. They sometimes require risk taking and often deal with business.

EDUCATION/TRAINING PROGRAM(S)—Human Resources Management/Personnel Administration, General; Labor and Industrial Relations. **RELATED KNOWLEDGE/COURSES—Personnel and Human Resources:** Principles and procedures for personnel recruitment, selection, training, compensation and benefits, labor relations and negotiation, and personnel information systems. **Clerical Practices:** Administrative and clerical procedures and systems such as word processing, managing files and records, stenography and transcription, designing forms, and other office procedures and terminology. **Sales and Marketing:** Principles and methods for showing, promoting, and selling products or services. This includes marketing strategy and tactics, product demonstration, sales techniques, and sales control systems. **Education and Training:** Principles and methods for curriculum and training design, teaching and instruction for individuals and groups, and the measurement of training effects. **Administration and Management:** Business and management principles involved in strategic planning, resource allocation, human resources modeling, leadership technique, production methods, and coordination of people and resources. **Computers and Electronics:** Circuit boards; processors; chips; electronic equipment; and computer hardware and software, including applications and programming.

Pharmacists

- Education/Training Required: First professional degree
- Annual Earnings: $89,820
- Growth: 24.6%
- Annual Job Openings: 16,000
- Self-Employed: 1.7%
- Part-Time: 21.1%

Compound and dispense medications, following prescriptions issued by physicians, dentists, or other authorized medical practitioners. Review prescriptions to assure accuracy, to ascertain the needed ingredients, and to evaluate their suitability. Provide information and advice regarding drug interactions, side effects, dosage and proper medication storage. Analyze prescribing trends to monitor patient compliance and to prevent excessive usage or harmful interactions. Order and purchase pharmaceutical supplies, medical supplies, and drugs, maintaining stock and storing and handling it properly. Maintain records, such as pharmacy files; patient profiles; charge system files; inventories; control records for radioactive nuclei; and registries of poisons, narcotics, and controlled drugs. Provide specialized services to help patients manage conditions such as diabetes, asthma, smoking cessation, or high blood pressure. Advise customers on the selection of medication brands, medical equipment, and health-care supplies. Collaborate with other health-care professionals to plan, monitor, review, and evaluate the quality and effectiveness of drugs and drug regimens, providing advice on drug applications and characteristics. Compound and dispense medications as prescribed by doctors and dentists by calculating, weighing, measuring, and mixing ingredients or oversee these activities. Offer health promotion and prevention activities, for example, training people to use devices such as blood pressure or diabetes monitors. Refer patients to other health professionals and agencies when appropriate. Prepare sterile solutions and infusions for use in surgical procedures, emergency rooms, or patients' homes. Plan, implement, and maintain procedures for mixing, packaging, and labeling pharmaceuticals according to policy and legal requirements to ensure quality, security, and proper disposal. Assay radiopharmaceuticals, verify rates of disintegration, and calculate the volume required to produce the desired results to ensure proper dosages. Manage pharmacy operations, hiring and supervising staff, performing administrative duties, and buying and selling non-pharmaceutical merchandise. Work in hospitals, clinics, or for Health Management Organizations (HMOs), dispensing prescriptions, serving as a medical team consultant, or specializing in specific drug therapy areas such as oncology or nuclear pharmacotherapy.

SKILLS—Most Important: Science Skills; Communication Skills; Mathematics Skills. **Other Above-Average Skills:** Social Skills; Thought-Processing Skills.

GOE—Interest Area: 08. Health Science. **Work Group:** 08.02. Medicine and Surgery. **Other Jobs in This Group:** Anesthesiologists; Family and General Practitioners; Internists, General; Medical Assistants; Medical Transcriptionists; Obstetricians and Gynecologists; Pediatricians, General; Pharmacy Aides; Pharmacy Technicians; Physician Assistants; Psychiatrists; Registered Nurses; Surgeons; Surgical Technologists. **PERSONALITY TYPE:** Investigative. Investigative occupations frequently involve working with ideas and require an extensive amount of thinking. These occupations can involve searching for facts and figuring out problems mentally.

EDUCATION/TRAINING PROGRAM(S)—Pharmacy (PharmD [USA] PharmD, BS/BPharm [Canada]); Pharmacy Administration and Pharmacy Policy and Regulatory Affairs (MS, PhD); Pharmaceutics and Drug Design (MS, PhD); Medicinal and Pharmaceutical Chemistry (MS, PhD); Natural Products Chemistry and Pharmacognosy (MS, PhD); Clinical and Industrial Drug Development (MS, PhD); Pharmacoeconomics/Pharmaceutical Economics (MS, PhD); Clinical, Hospital, and Managed Care Pharmacy (MS, PhD); others. **RELATED KNOWLEDGE/ COURSES—Medicine and Dentistry:** The information and techniques needed to diagnose and treat human injuries, diseases, and deformities. This includes symptoms, treatment alternatives, drug properties and interactions, and preventive healthcare measures. **Chemistry:** The chemical composition, structure, and properties of substances and of the chemical processes and transformations that they undergo. This includes uses of chemicals and their danger signs, production techniques, and disposal methods. **Therapy and Counseling:** Principles, methods, and procedures for diagnosis, treatment, and rehabilitation of physical and mental dysfunctions and for career counseling and guid-

P

ance. **Biology:** Plant and animal organisms and their tissues, cells, functions, interdependencies, and interactions with each other and the environment. **Psychology:** Human behavior and performance; individual differences in ability, personality, and interests; learning and motivation; psychological research methods; and the assessment and treatment of behavioral and affective disorders. **Customer and Personal Service:** Principles and processes for providing customer and personal services. This includes customer needs assessment, meeting of quality standards for services, and evaluation of customer satisfaction.

Pharmacy Technicians

- Education/Training Required: Moderate-term on-the-job training
- Annual Earnings: $24,390
- Growth: 28.6%
- Annual Job Openings: 35,000
- Self-Employed: 0.3%
- Part-Time: 23.2%

Prepare medications under the direction of a pharmacist. May measure, mix, count out, label, and record amounts and dosages of medications. Receive written prescription or refill requests and verify that information is complete and accurate. Maintain proper storage and security conditions for drugs. Answer telephones, responding to questions or requests. Fill bottles with prescribed medications and type and affix labels. Assist customers by answering simple questions, locating items, or referring them to the pharmacist for medication information. Price and file prescriptions that have been filled. Clean and help maintain equipment and work areas and sterilize glassware according to prescribed methods. Establish and maintain patient profiles, including lists of medications taken by individual patients. Order, label, and count stock of medications, chemicals, and supplies and enter inventory data into computer. Receive and store incoming supplies, verify quantities against invoices, and inform supervisors of stock needs and shortages. Transfer medication from vials to the appropriate number of sterile disposable syringes, using aseptic techniques. Under pharmacist supervision, add measured drugs or nutrients to intra-venous solutions under sterile conditions to prepare intravenous (IV) packs. Supply and monitor robotic machines that dispense medicine into containers and label the containers. Prepare and process medical insurance claim forms and records. Mix pharmaceutical preparations according to written prescriptions. Operate cash registers to accept payment from customers. Compute charges for medication and equipment dispensed to hospital patients and enter data in computer. Deliver medications and pharmaceutical supplies to patients, nursing stations, or surgery. Price stock and mark items for sale. Maintain and merchandise home health-care products and services.

SKILLS—Most Important: Mathematics Skills; Communication Skills. **Other Above-Average Skills:** Thought-Processing Skills; Social Skills.

GOE—Interest Area: 08. Health Science. **Work Group:** 08.02. Medicine and Surgery. **Other Jobs in This Group:** Anesthesiologists; Family and General Practitioners; Internists, General; Medical Assistants; Medical Transcriptionists; Obstetricians and Gynecologists; Pediatricians, General; Pharmacists; Pharmacy Aides; Physician Assistants; Psychiatrists; Registered Nurses; Surgeons; Surgical Technologists. **PERSONALITY TYPE:** Conventional. Conventional occupations frequently involve following set procedures and routines. These occupations can include working with data and details more than with ideas. Usually there is a clear line of authority to follow.

EDUCATION/TRAINING PROGRAM(S)—Pharmacy Technician/Assistant. **RELATED KNOWLEDGE/COURSES—Medicine and Dentistry:** The information and techniques needed to diagnose and treat human injuries, diseases, and deformities. This includes symptoms, treatment alternatives, drug properties and interactions, and preventive healthcare measures. **Chemistry:** The chemical composition, structure, and properties of substances and of the chemical processes and transformations that they undergo. This includes uses of chemicals and their danger signs, production techniques, and disposal methods. **Customer and Personal Service:** Principles and processes for providing customer and personal services. This includes customer needs assessment, meeting of quality standards for services, and evaluation of customer satisfaction. **Mathematics:** Arithmetic, algebra, geometry, calculus, and statistics and their applications. **Clerical Practices:** Administrative and clerical procedures and systems such as word processing, managing files and records, stenography and transcription, designing forms, and other office procedures and terminology. **Education and Training:** Principles and methods for curriculum and training design, teaching and instruction for individuals and groups, and the measurement of training effects.

Philosophy and Religion Teachers, Postsecondary

- ⚙ Education/Training Required: Master's degree
- ⚙ Annual Earnings: $53,210
- ⚙ Growth: 32.2%
- ⚙ Annual Job Openings: 329,000
- ⚙ Self-Employed: 0.4%
- ⚙ Part-Time: 27.3%

The job openings listed here are shared with 35 other postsecondary teaching occupations. For a complete list, see the beginning of this section.

Teach courses in philosophy, religion, and theology. Evaluate and grade students' classwork, assignments, and papers. Initiate, facilitate, and moderate classroom discussions. Prepare and deliver lectures to undergraduate and graduate students on topics such as ethics, logic, and contemporary religious thought. Prepare course materials such as syllabi, homework assignments, and handouts. Compile, administer, and grade examinations or assign this work to others. Keep abreast of developments in their field by reading current literature, talking with colleagues, and participating in professional conferences. Maintain student attendance records, grades, and other required records. Plan, evaluate, and revise curricula, course content, and course materials and methods of instruction. Maintain regularly scheduled office hours to advise and assist students. Select and obtain materials and supplies such as textbooks. Advise students on academic and vocational curricula and on career issues. Conduct research in a particular field of knowledge and publish findings in professional journals, books, or electronic media. Perform administrative duties such as serving as department head. Serve on academic or administrative committees that deal with institutional policies, departmental matters, and academic

issues. Collaborate with colleagues to address teaching and research issues. Participate in campus and community events. Participate in student recruitment, registration, and placement activities. Compile bibliographies of specialized materials for outside reading assignments. Supervise undergraduate and graduate teaching, internship, and research work. Act as advisers to student organizations. Write grant proposals to procure external research funding. Provide professional consulting services to government or industry.

SKILLS—Most Important: Communication Skills; Social Skills; Thought-Processing Skills. **Other Above-Average Skills:** Management Skills; Science Skills.

GOE—Interest Area: 05. Education and Training. **Work Group:** 05.03. Postsecondary and Adult Teaching and Instructing. **Other Jobs in This Group:** Adult Literacy, Remedial Education, and GED Teachers and Instructors; Agricultural Sciences Teachers, Postsecondary; Anthropology and Archeology Teachers, Postsecondary; Architecture Teachers, Postsecondary; Area, Ethnic, and Cultural Studies Teachers, Postsecondary; Art, Drama, and Music Teachers, Postsecondary; Atmospheric, Earth, Marine, and Space Sciences Teachers, Postsecondary; Biological Science Teachers, Postsecondary; Business Teachers, Postsecondary; Chemistry Teachers, Postsecondary; Communications Teachers, Postsecondary; Computer Science Teachers, Postsecondary; Criminal Justice and Law Enforcement Teachers, Postsecondary; Economics Teachers, Postsecondary; Education Teachers, Postsecondary; Engineering Teachers, Postsecondary; English Language and Literature Teachers, Postsecondary; Environmental Science Teachers, Postsecondary; Farm and Home Management Advisors; Foreign Language and Literature Teachers, Postsecondary; Forestry and Conservation Science Teachers, Postsecondary; Geography Teachers, Postsecondary; Graduate Teaching Assistants; Health Specialties Teachers, Postsecondary; History Teachers, Postsecondary; Home Economics Teachers, Postsecondary; Law Teachers, Postsecondary; Library Science Teachers, Postsecondary; Mathematical Science Teachers, Postsecondary; Nursing Instructors and Teachers, Postsecondary; Physics Teachers, Postsecondary; Political Science Teachers, Postsecondary; Psychology Teachers, Postsecondary; Recreation and Fitness Studies Teachers, Postsecondary; Self-Enrichment Education Teachers; Social Work Teachers, Postsecondary; Sociology Teachers, Postsecondary;

Vocational Education Teachers, Postsecondary. **PER-SONALITY TYPE:** No data available.

EDUCATION/TRAINING PROGRAM(S)—Philosophy; Ethics; Philosophy, Other; Religion/Religious Studies; Buddhist Studies; Christian Studies; Hindu Studies; Philosophy and Religious Studies, Other; Bible/Biblical Studies; Missions/Missionary Studies and Missiology; Religious Education; Religious/Sacred Music; Theology/Theological Studies; Divinity/Ministry (BD, MDiv.); Pre-Theology/Pre-Ministerial Studies; others. **RELATED KNOWL-EDGE/COURSES—Philosophy and Theology:** Different philosophical systems and religions. This includes their basic principles, values, ethics, ways of thinking, customs, practices, and impact on human culture. **History and Archeology:** Historical events and their causes, indicators, and effects on civilizations and cultures. **Education and Training:** Principles and methods for curriculum and training design, teaching and instruction for individuals and groups, and the measurement of training effects. **Sociology and Anthropology:** Group behavior and dynamics, societal trends and influences, human migrations, ethnicity, and cultures and their history and origins. **English Language:** The structure and content of the English language, including the meaning and spelling of words, rules of composition, and grammar. **Foreign Language:** The structure and content of a foreign (non-English) language, including the meaning and spelling of words, rules of composition and grammar, and pronunciation.

Physical Therapist Assistants

- ◎ Education/Training Required: Associate degree
- ◎ Annual Earnings: $39,490
- ◎ Growth: 44.2%
- ◎ Annual Job Openings: 7,000
- ◎ Self-Employed: 0.2%
- ◎ Part-Time: 28.6%

Assist physical therapists in providing physical therapy treatments and procedures. May, in accordance with state laws, assist in the development of treatment plans, carry out routine functions, document the progress of treatment, and modify specific treatments in accordance with patient status and within the scope of treatment plans established by a physical therapist. Generally requires formal training. Instruct, motivate, safeguard, and assist patients as they practice exercises and functional activities. Confer with physical therapy staff or others to discuss and evaluate patient information for planning, modifying, and coordinating treatment. Administer active and passive manual therapeutic exercises; therapeutic massage; and heat, light, sound, water, and electrical modality treatments such as ultrasound. Observe patients during treatments to compile and evaluate data on patients' responses and progress and report to physical therapist. Measure patients' range of joint motion, body parts, and vital signs to determine effects of treatments or for patient evaluations. Secure patients into or onto therapy equipment. Fit patients for orthopedic braces, prostheses, and supportive devices such as crutches. Train patients in the use of orthopedic braces, prostheses, or supportive devices. Transport patients to and from treatment areas, lifting and transferring them according to positioning requirements. Monitor operation of equipment and record use of equipment and administration of treatment. Clean work area and check and store equipment after treatment. Assist patients to dress; undress; or put on and remove supportive devices such as braces, splints, and slings. Administer traction to relieve neck and back pain, using intermittent and static traction equipment. Perform clerical duties, such as taking inventory, ordering supplies, answering telephone, taking messages, and filling out forms. Prepare treatment areas and electrotherapy equipment for use by physiotherapists. Perform postural drainage, percussions, and vibrations and teach deep breathing exercises to treat respiratory conditions.

SKILLS—Most Important: Science Skills; Communication Skills; Social Skills. **Other Above-Average Skills:** Thought-Processing Skills; Equipment/Technology Analysis Skills.

GOE—Interest Area: 08. Health Science. **Work Group:** 08.07. Medical Therapy. **Other Jobs in This Group:** Audiologists; Massage Therapists; Occupational Therapist Aides; Occupational Therapist Assistants; Occupational Therapists; Physical Therapist Aides; Physical Therapists; Radiation Therapists; Recreational Therapists; Respiratory Therapists; Respiratory Therapy

Technicians; Speech-Language Pathologists. **PERSON-ALITY TYPE:** Social. Social occupations frequently involve working with, communicating with, and teaching people. These occupations often involve helping or providing service to others.

EDUCATION/TRAINING PROGRAM(S)—Physical Therapist Assistant. **RELATED KNOWLEDGE/ COURSES**—**Psychology:** Human behavior and performance; individual differences in ability, personality, and interests; learning and motivation; psychological research methods; and the assessment and treatment of behavioral and affective disorders. **Therapy and Counseling:** Principles, methods, and procedures for diagnosis, treatment, and rehabilitation of physical and mental dysfunctions and for career counseling and guidance. **Medicine and Dentistry:** The information and techniques needed to diagnose and treat human injuries, diseases, and deformities. This includes symptoms, treatment alternatives, drug properties and interactions, and preventive healthcare measures. **Education and Training:** Principles and methods for curriculum and training design, teaching and instruction for individuals and groups, and the measurement of training effects. **Sociology and Anthropology:** Group behavior and dynamics, societal trends and influences, human migrations, ethnicity, and cultures and their history and origins. **Biology:** Plant and animal organisms and their tissues, cells, functions, interdependencies, and interactions with each other and the environment.

Physical Therapists

- ⊚ Education/Training Required: Master's degree
- ⊚ Annual Earnings: $63,080
- ⊚ Growth: 36.7%
- ⊚ Annual Job Openings: 13,000
- ⊚ Self-Employed: 4.5%
- ⊚ Part-Time: 24.7%

Assess, plan, organize, and participate in rehabilitative programs that improve mobility, relieve pain, increase strength, and decrease or prevent deformity of patients suffering from disease or injury. Plan, prepare, and carry out individually designed programs of physical treatment to maintain, improve, or restore physical functioning; alleviate pain; and prevent physical dysfunction in patients. Perform and document an initial exam, evaluating data to identify problems and determine a diagnosis prior to intervention. Evaluate effects of treatment at various stages and adjust treatments to achieve maximum benefit. Administer manual exercises, massage, or traction to help relieve pain, increase patient strength, or decrease or prevent deformity or crippling. Instruct patient and family in treatment procedures to be continued at home. Confer with the patient, medical practitioners, and appropriate others to plan, implement, and assess the intervention program. Review physician's referral and patient's medical records to help determine diagnosis and physical therapy treatment required. Obtain patients' informed consent to proposed interventions. Record prognosis, treatment, response, and progress in patient's chart or enter information into computer. Discharge patient from physical therapy when goals or projected outcomes have been attained and provide for appropriate follow-up care or referrals. Test and measure patient's strength, motor development and function, sensory perception, functional capacity, and respiratory and circulatory efficiency and record data. Identify and document goals, anticipated progress, and plans for reevaluation. Provide information to the patient about the proposed intervention, its material risks and expected benefits, and any reasonable alternatives. Inform patients when diagnosis reveals findings outside physical therapy and refer to appropriate practitioners. Direct, supervise, assess, and communicate with supportive personnel. Administer treatment involving application of physical agents, using equipment, moist packs, ultraviolet and infrared lamps, and ultrasound machines. Teach physical therapy students as well as those in other health professions. Evaluate, fit, and adjust prosthetic and orthotic devices and recommend modification to orthotist. Provide educational information about physical therapy and physical therapists, injury prevention, ergonomics, and ways to promote health.

SKILLS—Most Important: Science Skills; Social Skills; Communication Skills. **Other Above-Average Skills:** Thought-Processing Skills; Equipment/Technology Analysis Skills.

GOE—Interest Area: 08. Health Science. **Work Group:** 08.07. Medical Therapy. **Other Jobs in This Group:** Audiologists; Massage Therapists; Occupational Therapist Aides; Occupational Therapist Assistants; Occupational Therapists; Physical Therapist Aides;

Physical Therapist Assistants; Radiation Therapists; Recreational Therapists; Respiratory Therapists; Respiratory Therapy Technicians; Speech-Language Pathologists. **PERSONALITY TYPE:** Social. Social occupations frequently involve working with, communicating with, and teaching people. These occupations often involve helping or providing service to others.

EDUCATION/TRAINING PROGRAM(S)—Physical Therapy/Therapist; Kinesiotherapy/Kinesiotherapist. **RELATED KNOWLEDGE/COURSES—Therapy and Counseling:** Principles, methods, and procedures for diagnosis, treatment, and rehabilitation of physical and mental dysfunctions and for career counseling and guidance. **Psychology:** Human behavior and performance; individual differences in ability, personality, and interests; learning and motivation; psychological research methods; and the assessment and treatment of behavioral and affective disorders. **Medicine and Dentistry:** The information and techniques needed to diagnose and treat human injuries, diseases, and deformities. This includes symptoms, treatment alternatives, drug properties and interactions, and preventive healthcare measures. **Biology:** Plant and animal organisms and their tissues, cells, functions, interdependencies, and interactions with each other and the environment. **Customer and Personal Service:** Principles and processes for providing customer and personal services. This includes customer needs assessment, meeting of quality standards for services, and evaluation of customer satisfaction. **Sociology and Anthropology:** Group behavior and dynamics, societal trends and influences, human migrations, ethnicity, and cultures and their history and origins.

Physician Assistants

- Education/Training Required: Bachelor's degree
- Annual Earnings: $72,030
- Growth: 49.6%
- Annual Job Openings: 10,000
- Self-Employed: 1.3%
- Part-Time: 16.7%

Under the supervision of a physician, provide healthcare services typically performed by a physician.
Conduct complete physicals, provide treatment, and counsel patients. May, in some cases, prescribe medication. Must graduate from an accredited educational program for physician assistants. Examine patients to obtain information about their physical condition. Make tentative diagnoses and decisions about management and treatment of patients. Interpret diagnostic test results for deviations from normal. Obtain, compile, and record patient medical data, including health history, progress notes, and results of physical examination. Administer or order diagnostic tests, such as X-ray, electrocardiogram, and laboratory tests. Prescribe therapy or medication with physician approval. Perform therapeutic procedures, such as injections, immunizations, suturing and wound care, and infection management. Instruct and counsel patients about prescribed therapeutic regimens, normal growth and development, family planning, emotional problems of daily living, and health maintenance. Provide physicians with assistance during surgery or complicated medical procedures. Supervise and coordinate activities of technicians and technical assistants. Visit and observe patients on hospital rounds or house calls, updating charts, ordering therapy, and reporting back to physician. Order medical and laboratory supplies and equipment.

SKILLS—Most Important: Science Skills; Communication Skills; Thought-Processing Skills. **Other Above-Average Skills:** Social Skills; Mathematics Skills.

GOE—Interest Area: 08. Health Science. **Work Group:** 08.02. Medicine and Surgery. **Other Jobs in This Group:** Anesthesiologists; Family and General Practitioners; Internists, General; Medical Assistants; Medical Transcriptionists; Obstetricians and Gynecologists; Pediatricians, General; Pharmacists; Pharmacy Aides; Pharmacy Technicians; Psychiatrists; Registered Nurses; Surgeons; Surgical Technologists. **PERSONALITY TYPE:** Investigative. Investigative occupations frequently involve working with ideas and require an extensive amount of thinking. These occupations can involve searching for facts and figuring out problems mentally.

EDUCATION/TRAINING PROGRAM(S)—Physician Assistant. **RELATED KNOWLEDGE/COURSES—Medicine and Dentistry:** The information and techniques needed to diagnose and treat human injuries, diseases, and deformities. This includes symptoms, treatment alternatives, drug properties and interactions, and preventive healthcare measures. **Biology:** Plant and animal organisms and their tissues, cells, functions, interdependencies, and interactions with each other and the environment. **Therapy and Counseling:** Principles, methods, and procedures for diagnosis, treatment, and rehabilitation of physical and mental dysfunctions and for career counseling and guidance. **Psychology:** Human behavior and performance; individual differences in ability, personality, and interests; learning and motivation; psychological research methods; and the assessment and treatment of behavioral and affective disorders. **Chemistry:** The chemical composition, structure, and properties of substances and of the chemical processes and transformations that they undergo. This includes uses of chemicals and their danger signs, production techniques, and disposal methods. **Customer and Personal Service:** Principles and processes for providing customer and personal services. This includes customer needs assessment, meeting of quality standards for services, and evaluation of customer satisfaction.

Physics Teachers, Postsecondary

- Education/Training Required: Master's degree
- Annual Earnings: $65,880
- Growth: 32.2%
- Annual Job Openings: 329,000
- Self-Employed: 0.4%
- Part-Time: 27.3%

The job openings listed here are shared with 35 other postsecondary teaching occupations. For a complete list, see the beginning of this section.

Teach courses pertaining to the laws of matter and energy. Includes both teachers primarily engaged in teaching and those who do a combination of both teaching and research. Evaluate and grade students' classwork, laboratory work, assignments, and papers. Prepare and deliver lectures to undergraduate and/or graduate students on topics such as quantum mechanics, particle physics, and optics. Compile, administer, and grade examinations or assign this work to others. Maintain student attendance records, grades, and other required records. Supervise students' laboratory work.

Prepare course materials such as syllabi, homework assignments, and handouts. Maintain regularly scheduled office hours to advise and assist students. Supervise undergraduate and/or graduate teaching, internship, and research work. Keep abreast of developments in their field by reading current literature, talking with colleagues, and participating in professional conferences. Plan, evaluate, and revise curricula, course content, and course materials and methods of instruction. Initiate, facilitate, and moderate classroom discussions. Conduct research in a particular field of knowledge and publish findings in professional journals, books, and/or electronic media. Advise students on academic and vocational curricula and on career issues. Select and obtain materials and supplies such as textbooks and laboratory equipment. Collaborate with colleagues to address teaching and research issues. Participate in student recruitment, registration, and placement activities. Serve on academic or administrative committees that deal with institutional policies, departmental matters, and academic issues. Write grant proposals to procure external research funding. Perform administrative duties such as serving as department head. Act as advisers to student organizations. Provide professional consulting services to government and/or industry. Compile bibliographies of specialized materials for outside reading assignments. Participate in campus and community events.

SKILLS—Most Important: Science Skills; Computer Programming Skills; Mathematics Skills. **Other Above-Average Skills:** Communication Skills; Thought-Processing Skills; Management Skills; Equipment Use/Maintenance Skills.

GOE—Interest Area: 05. Education and Training. **Work Group:** 05.03. Postsecondary and Adult Teaching and Instructing. **Other Jobs in This Group:** Adult Literacy, Remedial Education, and GED Teachers and Instructors; Agricultural Sciences Teachers, Postsecondary; Anthropology and Archeology Teachers, Postsecondary; Architecture Teachers, Postsecondary; Area, Ethnic, and Cultural Studies Teachers, Postsecondary; Art, Drama, and Music Teachers, Postsecondary; Atmospheric, Earth, Marine, and Space Sciences Teachers, Postsecondary; Biological Science Teachers, Postsecondary; Business Teachers, Postsecondary; Chemistry Teachers, Postsecondary; Communications Teachers, Postsecondary; Computer Science Teachers, Postsecondary; Criminal Justice and Law Enforcement Teachers, Postsecondary; Economics

P

Teachers, Postsecondary; Education Teachers, Postsecondary; Engineering Teachers, Postsecondary; English Language and Literature Teachers, Postsecondary; Environmental Science Teachers, Postsecondary; Farm and Home Management Advisors; Foreign Language and Literature Teachers, Postsecondary; Forestry and Conservation Science Teachers, Postsecondary; Geography Teachers, Postsecondary; Graduate Teaching Assistants; Health Specialties Teachers, Postsecondary; History Teachers, Postsecondary; Home Economics Teachers, Postsecondary; Law Teachers, Postsecondary; Library Science Teachers, Postsecondary; Mathematical Science Teachers, Postsecondary; Nursing Instructors and Teachers, Postsecondary; Philosophy and Religion Teachers, Postsecondary; Political Science Teachers, Postsecondary; Psychology Teachers, Postsecondary; Recreation and Fitness Studies Teachers, Postsecondary; Self-Enrichment Education Teachers; Social Work Teachers, Postsecondary; Sociology Teachers, Postsecondary; Vocational Education Teachers, Postsecondary. **PERSONALITY TYPE:** Investigative. Investigative occupations frequently involve working with ideas and require an extensive amount of thinking. These occupations can involve searching for facts and figuring out problems mentally.

EDUCATION/TRAINING PROGRAM(S)—Physics, General; Atomic/Molecular Physics; Elementary Particle Physics; Plasma and High-Temperature Physics; Nuclear Physics; Optics/Optical Sciences; Solid State and Low-Temperature Physics; Acoustics; Theoretical and Mathematical Physics; Physics, Other. **RELATED KNOWLEDGE/COURSES—Physics:** Physical principles and laws and their interrelationships and applications to understanding fluid, material, and atmospheric dynamics and mechanical, electrical, atomic, and subatomic structures and processes. **Mathematics:** Arithmetic, algebra, geometry, calculus, and statistics and their applications. **Education and Training:** Principles and methods for curriculum and training design, teaching and instruction for individuals and groups, and the measurement of training effects. **Chemistry:** The chemical composition, structure, and properties of substances and of the chemical processes and transformations that they undergo. This includes uses of chemicals and their danger signs, production techniques, and disposal methods. **Engineering and Technology:** The practical application of engineering science and technology. This includes applying principles, techniques, procedures, and equipment to the design and production of various goods and services. **Computers and Electronics:** Circuit boards; processors; chips; electronic equipment; and computer hardware and software, including applications and programming.

Pipe Fitters and Steamfitters

- Education/Training Required: Long-term on-the-job training
- Annual Earnings: $42,160
- Growth: 15.7%
- Annual Job Openings: 61,000
- Self-Employed: 13.3%
- Part-Time: 3.6%

The job openings listed here are shared with Plumbers.

Lay out, assemble, install, and maintain pipe systems, pipe supports, and related hydraulic and pneumatic equipment for steam, hot water, heating, cooling, lubricating, sprinkling, and industrial production and processing systems. Cut, thread, and hammer pipe to specifications, using tools such as saws, cutting torches, and pipe threaders and benders. Assemble and secure pipes, tubes, fittings, and related equipment according to specifications by welding, brazing, cementing, soldering, and threading joints. Attach pipes to walls, structures, and fixtures, such as radiators or tanks, using brackets, clamps, tools, or welding equipment. Inspect, examine, and test installed systems and pipelines, using pressure gauge, hydrostatic testing, observation, or other methods. Measure and mark pipes for cutting and threading. Lay out full scale drawings of pipe systems, supports, and related equipment, following blueprints. Plan pipe system layout, installation, or repair according to specifications. Select pipe sizes and types and related materials, such as supports, hangers, and hydraulic cylinders, according to specifications. Cut and bore holes in structures such as bulkheads, decks, walls, and mains prior to pipe installation, using hand and power tools. Modify, clean, and maintain pipe systems, units, fittings, and related machines and equipment, following specifications and using hand and power tools. Install automatic controls used to regulate pipe systems. Turn valves to shut off steam, water, or other gases or liquids from pipe sections, using valve keys or wrenches. Remove and replace worn components. Prepare cost estimates for clients. Inspect work sites for obstructions and to ensure that holes will not cause structural weakness. Operate motorized pumps to remove water from flooded manholes, basements, or facility floors. Dip nonferrous piping materials in a mixture of molten tin and lead to obtain a coating that prevents erosion or galvanic and electrolytic action.

SKILLS—Most Important: Equipment Use/Maintenance Skills; Equipment/Technology Analysis Skills; Quality Control Skills. **Other Above-Average Skills:** Social Skills; Mathematics Skills; Science Skills.

GOE—Interest Area: 02. Architecture and Construction. **Work Group:** 02.04. Construction Crafts. **Other Jobs in This Group:** Boilermakers; Brickmasons and Blockmasons; Carpet Installers; Cement Masons and Concrete Finishers; Commercial Divers; Construction Carpenters; Crane and Tower Operators; Drywall and Ceiling Tile Installers; Electricians; Fence Erectors; Floor Layers, Except Carpet, Wood, and Hard Tiles; Floor Sanders and Finishers; Glaziers; Hazardous Materials Removal Workers; Insulation Workers, Floor, Ceiling, and Wall; Insulation Workers, Mechanical; Manufactured Building and Mobile Home Installers; Operating Engineers and Other Construction Equipment Operators; Painters, Construction and Maintenance; Paperhangers; Paving, Surfacing, and Tamping Equipment Operators; Pile-Driver Operators; Pipelayers; Plasterers and Stucco Masons; Plumbers; Plumbers, Pipefitters, and Steamfitters; Rail-Track Laying and Maintenance Equipment Operators; Refractory Materials Repairers, Except Brickmasons; Reinforcing Iron and Rebar Workers; Riggers; Roofers; Rough Carpenters; Security and Fire Alarm Systems Installers; Segmental Pavers; Sheet Metal Workers; Stone Cutters and Carvers, Manufacturing; Stonemasons; Structural Iron and Steel Workers; Tapers; Terrazzo Workers and Finishers; Tile and Marble Setters. **PERSONALITY TYPE:** Realistic. Realistic occupations frequently involve work activities that include practical, hands-on problems and solutions. They often deal with plants, animals, and real-world materials like wood, tools, and machinery. Many of the occupations require working outside and do not involve a lot of paperwork or working closely with others.

EDUCATION/TRAINING PROGRAM(S)—Pipefitting/Pipefitter and Sprinkler Fitter. **RELATED KNOWLEDGE/COURSES—Building and Construction:** The materials, methods, and tools involved in the construction or repair of houses, buildings, or other structures such as highways and roads. **Design:** Design techniques, tools, and principles involved in production of precision technical plans, blueprints, drawings, and models. **Mechanical Devices:** Machines and tools, including their designs, uses, repair, and maintenance. **Engineering and Technology:** The practical application of engineering science and technology. This includes applying principles, techniques, procedures, and equipment to the design and production of various goods and services. **Economics and Accounting:** Economic and accounting principles and practices, the financial markets, banking, and the analysis and reporting of financial data. **Transportation:** Principles and methods for moving people or goods by air, rail, sea, or road, including the relative costs and benefits.

Plumbers

- ◎ Education/Training Required: Long-term on-the-job training
- ◎ Annual Earnings: $42,160
- ◎ Growth: 15.7%
- ◎ Annual Job Openings: 61,000
- ◎ Self-Employed: 13.3%
- ◎ Part-Time: 3.6%

The job openings listed here are shared with Pipe Fitters and Steamfitters.

Assemble, install, and repair pipes, fittings, and fixtures of heating, water, and drainage systems according to specifications and plumbing codes. Assemble pipe sections, tubing, and fittings, using couplings; clamps; screws; bolts; cement; plastic solvent; caulking; or soldering, brazing, and welding equipment. Fill pipes or plumbing fixtures with water or air and observe pressure gauges to detect and locate leaks. Review blueprints and building codes and specifications to determine work details and procedures. Prepare written work cost estimates and negotiate contracts. Study building plans and inspect structures to assess material and equipment needs, to establish the sequence of pipe installations,

P

and to plan installation around obstructions such as electrical wiring. Keep records of assignments and produce detailed work reports. Perform complex calculations and planning for special or very large jobs. Locate and mark the position of pipe installations, connections, passage holes, and fixtures in structures, using measuring instruments such as rulers and levels. Measure, cut, thread, and bend pipe to required angle, using hand and power tools or machines such as pipe cutters, pipe-threading machines, and pipe-bending machines. Cut openings in structures to accommodate pipes and pipe fittings, using hand and power tools. Install pipe assemblies, fittings, valves, appliances such as dishwashers and water heaters, and fixtures such as sinks and toilets, using hand and power tools. Hang steel supports from ceiling joists to hold pipes in place. Repair and maintain plumbing, replacing defective washers, replacing or mending broken pipes, and opening clogged drains. Direct workers engaged in pipe cutting and preassembly and installation of plumbing systems and components. Install underground storm, sanitary, and water piping systems and extend piping to connect fixtures and plumbing to these systems. Clear away debris in a renovation. Install oxygen and medical gas in hospitals. Use specialized techniques, equipment, or materials, such as performing computer-assisted welding of small pipes or working with the special piping used in microchip fabrication.

SKILLS—Most Important: Science Skills; Equipment Use/Maintenance Skills; Equipment/Technology Analysis Skills. **Other Above-Average Skills:** Management Skills; Quality Control Skills; Thought-Processing Skills.

GOE—Interest Area: 02. Architecture and Construction. **Work Group:** 02.04. Construction Crafts. **Other Jobs in This Group:** Boilermakers; Brickmasons and Blockmasons; Carpet Installers; Cement Masons and Concrete Finishers; Commercial Divers; Construction Carpenters; Crane and Tower Operators; Drywall and Ceiling Tile Installers; Electricians; Fence Erectors; Floor Layers, Except Carpet, Wood, and Hard Tiles; Floor Sanders and Finishers; Glaziers; Hazardous Materials Removal Workers; Insulation Workers, Floor, Ceiling, and Wall; Insulation Workers, Mechanical; Manufactured Building and Mobile Home Installers; Operating Engineers and Other Construction Equipment Operators; Painters, Construction and Maintenance; Paperhangers; Paving, Surfacing, and Tamping Equipment Operators; Pile-Driver Operators; Pipe Fitters and Steamfitters; Pipelayers; Plasterers and Stucco Masons; Plumbers, Pipefitters, and Steamfitters; Rail-Track Laying and Maintenance Equipment Operators; Refractory Materials Repairers, Except Brickmasons; Reinforcing Iron and Rebar Workers; Riggers; Roofers; Rough Carpenters; Security and Fire Alarm Systems Installers; Segmental Pavers; Sheet Metal Workers; Stone Cutters and Carvers, Manufacturing; Stonemasons; Structural Iron and Steel Workers; Tapers; Terrazzo Workers and Finishers; Tile and Marble Setters. **PERSONALITY TYPE:** Realistic. Realistic occupations frequently involve work activities that include practical, hands-on problems and solutions. They often deal with plants, animals, and real-world materials like wood, tools, and machinery. Many of the occupations require working outside and do not involve a lot of paperwork or working closely with others.

EDUCATION/TRAINING PROGRAM(S)—Pipefitting/Pipefitter and Sprinkler Fitter; Plumbing Technology/Plumber; Plumbing and Related Water Supply Services, Other. **RELATED KNOWLEDGE/COURSES—Building and Construction:** The materials, methods, and tools involved in the construction or repair of houses, buildings, or other structures such as highways and roads. **Physics:** Physical principles and laws and their interrelationships and applications to understanding fluid, material, and atmospheric dynamics and mechanical, electrical, atomic, and subatomic structures and processes. **Mechanical Devices:** Machines and tools, including their designs, uses, repair, and maintenance. **Chemistry:** The chemical composition, structure, and properties of substances and of the chemical processes and transformations that they undergo. This includes uses of chemicals and their danger signs, production techniques, and disposal methods. **Design:** Design techniques, tools, and principles involved in production of precision technical plans, blueprints, drawings, and models. **Sales and Marketing:** Principles and methods for showing, promoting, and selling products or services. This includes marketing strategy and tactics, product demonstration, sales techniques, and sales control systems.

Police Patrol Officers

- Education/Training Required: Long-term on-the-job training
- Annual Earnings: $46,290
- Growth: 15.5%
- Annual Job Openings: 47,000
- Self-Employed: 0.0%
- Part-Time: 1.4%

The job openings listed here are shared with Sheriffs and Deputy Sheriffs.

Patrol assigned area to enforce laws and ordinances, regulate traffic, control crowds, prevent crime, and arrest violators. Provide for public safety by maintaining order, responding to emergencies, protecting people and property, enforcing motor vehicle and criminal laws, and promoting good community relations. Identify, pursue, and arrest suspects and perpetrators of criminal acts. Record facts to prepare reports that document incidents and activities. Review facts of incidents to determine if criminal act or statute violations were involved. Render aid to accident victims and other persons requiring first aid for physical injuries. Testify in court to present evidence or act as witness in traffic and criminal cases. Evaluate complaint and emergency-request information to determine response requirements. Patrol specific area on foot, horseback, or motorized conveyance, responding promptly to calls for assistance. Monitor, note, report, and investigate suspicious persons and situations, safety hazards, and unusual or illegal activity in patrol area. Investigate traffic accidents and other accidents to determine causes and to determine if a crime has been committed. Photograph or draw diagrams of crime or accident scenes and interview principals and eyewitnesses. Monitor traffic to ensure that motorists observe traffic regulations and exhibit safe driving procedures. Relay complaint and emergency-request information to appropriate agency dispatchers. Issue citations or warnings to violators of motor vehicle ordinances. Direct traffic flow and reroute traffic in case of emergencies. Inform citizens of community services and recommend options to facilitate longer-term problem resolution. Provide road information to assist motorists. Process prisoners and prepare and maintain records of prisoner bookings and prisoner status during booking and pre-trial process. Inspect public establishments to ensure compliance with rules and regulations. Act as official escorts, such as when leading funeral processions or firefighters.

SKILLS—Most Important: Social Skills; Thought-Processing Skills; Communication Skills. **Other Above-Average Skills:** Equipment/Technology Analysis Skills; Equipment Use/Maintenance Skills.

GOE—Interest Area: 12. Law and Public Safety. **Work Group:** 12.04. Law Enforcement and Public Safety. **Other Jobs in This Group:** Bailiffs; Correctional Officers and Jailers; Criminal Investigators and Special Agents; Detectives and Criminal Investigators; Fire Investigators; Forensic Science Technicians; Parking Enforcement Workers; Police and Sheriff's Patrol Officers; Police Detectives; Police Identification and Records Officers; Sheriffs and Deputy Sheriffs; Transit and Railroad Police. **PERSONALITY TYPE:** Social. Social occupations frequently involve working with, communicating with, and teaching people. These occupations often involve helping or providing service to others.

EDUCATION/TRAINING PROGRAM(S)—Criminal Justice/Police Science; Criminalistics and Criminal Science. **RELATED KNOWLEDGE/COURSES—Public Safety and Security:** Relevant equipment, policies, procedures, and strategies to promote effective local, state, or national security operations for the protection of people, data, property, and institutions. **Law and Government:** Laws, legal codes, court procedures, precedents, government regulations, executive orders, agency rules, and the democratic political process. **Psychology:** Human behavior and performance; individual differences in ability, personality, and interests; learning and motivation; psychological research methods; and the assessment and treatment of behavioral and affective disorders. **Customer and Personal Service:** Principles and processes for providing customer and personal services. This includes customer needs assessment, meeting of quality standards for services, and evaluation of customer satisfaction. **Therapy and Counseling:** Principles, methods, and procedures for diagnosis, treatment, and rehabilitation of physical and mental dysfunctions and for career counseling and guidance. **Telecommunications:** Transmission, broadcasting, switching, control, and operation of telecommunications systems.

P

Political Science Teachers, Postsecondary

- Education/Training Required: Master's degree
- Annual Earnings: $59,850
- Growth: 32.2%
- Annual Job Openings: 329,000
- Self-Employed: 0.4%
- Part-Time: 27.3%

The job openings listed here are shared with 35 other postsecondary teaching occupations. For a complete list, see the beginning of this section.

Teach courses in political science, international affairs, and international relations. Initiate, facilitate, and moderate classroom discussions. Prepare and deliver lectures to undergraduate or graduate students on topics such as classical political thought, international relations, and democracy and citizenship. Evaluate and grade students' classwork, assignments, and papers. Compile, administer, and grade examinations or assign this work to others. Prepare course materials such as syllabi, homework assignments, and handouts. Keep abreast of developments in their field by reading current literature, talking with colleagues, and participating in professional conferences. Plan, evaluate, and revise curricula, course content, and course materials and methods of instruction. Maintain student attendance records, grades, and other required records. Maintain regularly scheduled office hours in order to advise and assist students. Advise students on academic and vocational curricula and on career issues. Select and obtain materials and supplies such as textbooks. Conduct research in a particular field of knowledge and publish findings in professional journals, books, and electronic media. Supervise undergraduate and graduate teaching, internship, and research work. Collaborate with colleagues to address teaching and research issues. Serve on academic or administrative committees that deal with institutional policies, departmental matters, and academic issues. Participate in student recruitment, registration, and placement activities. Participate in campus and community events. Compile bibliographies of specialized materials for outside reading assignments. Act as advisers to student organizations. Perform administrative duties such as serving as department head. Write grant proposals to procure external research funding. Provide professional consulting services to government and industry.

SKILLS—Most Important: Communication Skills; Thought-Processing Skills; Social Skills. **Other Above-Average Skills:** Management Skills; Science Skills.

GOE—Interest Area: 05. Education and Training. **Work Group:** 05.03. Postsecondary and Adult Teaching and Instructing. **Other Jobs in This Group:** Adult Literacy, Remedial Education, and GED Teachers and Instructors; Agricultural Sciences Teachers, Postsecondary; Anthropology and Archeology Teachers, Postsecondary; Architecture Teachers, Postsecondary; Area, Ethnic, and Cultural Studies Teachers, Postsecondary; Art, Drama, and Music Teachers, Postsecondary; Atmospheric, Earth, Marine, and Space Sciences Teachers, Postsecondary; Biological Science Teachers, Postsecondary; Business Teachers, Postsecondary; Chemistry Teachers, Postsecondary; Communications Teachers, Postsecondary; Computer Science Teachers, Postsecondary; Criminal Justice and Law Enforcement Teachers, Postsecondary; Economics Teachers, Postsecondary; Education Teachers, Postsecondary; Engineering Teachers, Postsecondary; English Language and Literature Teachers, Postsecondary; Environmental Science Teachers, Postsecondary; Farm and Home Management Advisors; Foreign Language and Literature Teachers, Postsecondary; Forestry and Conservation Science Teachers, Postsecondary; Geography Teachers, Postsecondary; Graduate Teaching Assistants; Health Specialties Teachers, Postsecondary; History Teachers, Postsecondary; Home Economics Teachers, Postsecondary; Law Teachers, Postsecondary; Library Science Teachers, Postsecondary; Mathematical Science Teachers, Postsecondary; Nursing Instructors and Teachers, Postsecondary; Philosophy and Religion Teachers, Postsecondary; Physics Teachers, Postsecondary; Psychology Teachers, Postsecondary; Recreation and Fitness Studies Teachers, Postsecondary; Self-Enrichment Education Teachers; Social Work Teachers, Postsecondary; Sociology Teachers, Postsecondary; Vocational Education Teachers, Postsecondary. **PERSONALITY TYPE:** Social. Social occupations frequently involve working with, communicating with, and teaching people. These occupations often involve helping or providing service to others.

EDUCATION/TRAINING PROGRAM(S)—Social Science Teacher Education; Political Science and

Government, General; American Government and Politics (United States); Political Science and Government, Other. **RELATED KNOWLEDGE/ COURSES—History and Archeology:** Historical events and their causes, indicators, and effects on civilizations and cultures. **Philosophy and Theology:** Different philosophical systems and religions. This includes their basic principles, values, ethics, ways of thinking, customs, practices, and impact on human culture. **Sociology and Anthropology:** Group behavior and dynamics, societal trends and influences, human migrations, ethnicity, and cultures and their history and origins. **Geography:** Principles and methods for describing the features of land, sea, and air masses, including their physical characteristics; locations; interrelationships; and distribution of plant, animal, and human life. **Law and Government:** Laws, legal codes, court procedures, precedents, government regulations, executive orders, agency rules, and the democratic political process. **Education and Training:** Principles and methods for curriculum and training design, teaching and instruction for individuals and groups, and the measurement of training effects.

Preschool Teachers, Except Special Education

- ⊚ Education/Training Required: Postsecondary vocational training
- ⊚ Annual Earnings: $21,990
- ⊚ Growth: 33.1%
- ⊚ Annual Job Openings: 77,000
- ⊚ Self-Employed: 1.4%
- ⊚ Part-Time: 25.1%

Instruct children (normally up to 5 years of age) in activities designed to promote social, physical, and intellectual growth needed for primary school in preschool, day care center, or other child development facility. May be required to hold state certification. Provide a variety of materials and resources for children to explore, manipulate, and use, both in learning activities and in imaginative play. Attend to children's basic needs by feeding them, dressing them, and changing their diapers. Establish and enforce rules for behavior

and procedures for maintaining order. Read books to entire classes or to small groups. Teach basic skills such as color, shape, number, and letter recognition; personal hygiene; and social skills. Organize and lead activities designed to promote physical, mental, and social development, such as games, arts and crafts, music, storytelling, and field trips. Observe and evaluate children's performance, behavior, social development, and physical health. Meet with parents and guardians to discuss their children's progress and needs, determine their priorities for their children, and suggest ways that they can promote learning and development. Identify children showing signs of emotional, developmental, or health-related problems and discuss them with supervisors, parents or guardians, and child development specialists. Enforce all administration policies and rules governing students. Prepare materials and classrooms for class activities. Serve meals and snacks in accordance with nutritional guidelines. Teach proper eating habits and personal hygiene. Assimilate arriving children to the school environment by greeting them, helping them remove outerwear, and selecting activities of interest to them. Adapt teaching methods and instructional materials to meet students' varying needs and interests. Establish clear objectives for all lessons, units, and projects and communicate those objectives to children. Demonstrate activities to children. Arrange indoor and outdoor space to facilitate creative play, motor-skill activities, and safety. Plan and conduct activities for a balanced program of instruction, demonstration, and work time that provides students with opportunities to observe, question, and investigate. Maintain accurate and complete student records as required by laws, district policies, and administrative regulations.

SKILLS—Most Important: Social Skills; Communication Skills. **Other Above-Average Skills:** None met the criteria.

GOE—Interest Area: 05. Education and Training. **Work Group:** 05.02. Preschool, Elementary, and Secondary Teaching and Instructing. **Other Jobs in This Group:** Elementary School Teachers, Except Special Education; Kindergarten Teachers, Except Special Education; Middle School Teachers, Except Special and Vocational Education; Secondary School Teachers, Except Special and Vocational Education; Special Education Teachers, Middle School; Special Education Teachers, Preschool, Kindergarten, and Elementary School; Special Education Teachers,

Secondary School; Teacher Assistants; Vocational Education Teachers, Middle School; Vocational Education Teachers, Secondary School. **PERSONALITY TYPE:** Social. Social occupations frequently involve working with, communicating with, and teaching people. These occupations often involve helping or providing service to others.

EDUCATION/TRAINING PROGRAM(S)—Montessori Teacher Education; Early Childhood Education and Teaching; Child Care and Support Services Management. **RELATED KNOWLEDGE/COURSES—Philosophy and Theology:** Different philosophical systems and religions. This includes their basic principles, values, ethics, ways of thinking, customs, practices, and impact on human culture. **Customer and Personal Service:** Principles and processes for providing customer and personal services. This includes customer needs assessment, meeting of quality standards for services, and evaluation of customer satisfaction. **Sociology and Anthropology:** Group behavior and dynamics, societal trends and influences, human migrations, ethnicity, and cultures and their history and origins. **Psychology:** Human behavior and performance; individual differences in ability, personality, and interests; learning and motivation; psychological research methods; and the assessment and treatment of behavioral and affective disorders. **Education and Training:** Principles and methods for curriculum and training design, teaching and instruction for individuals and groups, and the measurement of training effects. **Public Safety and Security:** Relevant equipment, policies, procedures, and strategies to promote effective local, state, or national security operations for the protection of people, data, property, and institutions.

Producers

- Education/Training Required: Work experience plus degree
- Annual Earnings: $53,860
- Growth: 16.6%
- Annual Job Openings: 11,000
- Self-Employed: 30.4%
- Part-Time: 8.1%

The job openings listed here are shared with Directors—Stage, Motion Pictures, Television, and Radio, Program Directors, Talent Directors, and Technical Directors/Managers.

Plan and coordinate various aspects of radio, television, stage, or motion picture production, such as selecting script; coordinating writing, directing, and editing; and arranging financing. Coordinate the activities of writers, directors, managers, and other personnel throughout the production process. Monitor post-production processes to ensure accurate completion of all details. Perform management activities such as budgeting, scheduling, planning, and marketing. Determine production size, content, and budget, establishing details such as production schedules and management policies. Compose and edit scripts or provide screenwriters with story outlines from which scripts can be written. Conduct meetings with staff to discuss production progress and to ensure production objectives are attained. Resolve personnel problems that arise during the production process by acting as liaisons between dissenting parties when necessary. Produce shows for special occasions, such as holidays or testimonials. Edit and write news stories from information collected by reporters. Write and submit proposals to bid on contracts for projects. Hire directors, principal cast members, and key production staff members. Arrange financing for productions. Select plays, scripts, books, or ideas to be produced. Review film, recordings, or rehearsals to ensure conformance to production and broadcast standards. Perform administrative duties such as preparing operational reports, distributing rehearsal call sheets and script copies, and arranging for rehearsal quarters. Obtain and distribute costumes, props, music, and studio equipment needed to complete productions. Negotiate contracts with artistic personnel, often in accordance with collective bargaining agreements. Maintain knowledge of minimum wages and working conditions established by unions or associations of actors and technicians. Plan and coordinate the production of musical recordings, selecting music and directing performers. Negotiate with parties, including independent producers and the distributors and broadcasters who will be handling completed productions. Develop marketing plans for finished products, collaborating with sales associates to supervise product distribution. Determine and direct the content of radio programming.

SKILLS—**Most Important:** Management Skills; Communication Skills; Social Skills. **Other Above-Average Skills:** Thought-Processing Skills; Equipment/Technology Analysis Skills.

GOE—**Interest Area:** 03. Arts and Communication. **Work Group:** 03.01. Managerial Work in Arts and Communication. **Other Jobs in This Group:** Agents and Business Managers of Artists, Performers, and Athletes; Art Directors; Producers and Directors; Program Directors; Public Relations Managers; Technical Directors/Managers. **PERSONALITY TYPE:** Artistic. Artistic occupations frequently involve working with forms, designs, and patterns. They often require self-expression, and the work can be done without following a clear set of rules.

EDUCATION/TRAINING PROGRAM(S)—Radio and Television; Drama and Dramatics/Theatre Arts, General; Directing and Theatrical Production; Theatre/Theatre Arts Management; Dramatic/Theatre Arts and Stagecraft, Other; Film/Cinema Studies; Cinematography and Film/Video Production. **RELATED KNOWLEDGE/COURSES—Communications and Media:** Media production, communication, and dissemination techniques and methods. This includes alternative ways to inform and entertain via written, oral, and visual media. **Fine Arts:** The theory and techniques required to compose, produce, and perform works of music, dance, visual arts, drama, and sculpture. **Clerical Practices:** Administrative and clerical procedures and systems such as word processing, managing files and records, stenography and transcription, designing forms, and other office procedures and terminology. **Sales and Marketing:** Principles and methods for showing, promoting, and selling products or services. This includes marketing strategy and tactics, product demonstration, sales techniques, and sales control systems. **Administration and Management:** Business and management principles involved in strategic planning, resource allocation, human resources modeling, leadership technique, production methods, and coordination of people and resources. **Personnel and Human Resources:** Principles and procedures for personnel recruitment, selection, training, compensation and benefits, labor relations and negotiation, and personnel information systems.

Product Safety Engineers

- Education/Training Required: Bachelor's degree
- Annual Earnings: $65,210
- Growth: 13.4%
- Annual Job Openings: 2,000
- Self-Employed: 0.5%
- Part-Time: 2.6%

The job openings listed here are shared with Fire-Prevention and Protection Engineers and Industrial Safety and Health Engineers.

Develop and conduct tests to evaluate product safety levels and recommend measures to reduce or eliminate hazards. Report accident investigation findings. Conduct research to evaluate safety levels for products. Evaluate potential health hazards or damage that could occur from product misuse. Investigate causes of accidents, injuries, or illnesses related to product usage in order to develop solutions to minimize or prevent recurrence. Participate in preparation of product usage and precautionary label instructions. Recommend procedures for detection, prevention, and elimination of physical, chemical, or other product hazards.

SKILLS—**Most Important:** Quality Control Skills; Science Skills; Mathematics Skills. **Other Above-Average Skills:** Equipment/Technology Analysis Skills; Thought-Processing Skills.

GOE—**Interest Area:** 15. Scientific Research, Engineering, and Mathematics. **Work Group:** 15.08. Industrial and Safety Engineering. **Other Jobs in This Group:** Fire-Prevention and Protection Engineers; Health and Safety Engineers, Except Mining Safety Engineers and Inspectors; Industrial Engineers; Industrial Safety and Health Engineers. **PERSONALITY TYPE:** Investigative. Investigative occupations frequently involve working with ideas and require an extensive amount of thinking. These occupations can involve searching for facts and figuring out problems mentally.

EDUCATION/TRAINING PROGRAM(S)—Environmental/Environmental Health Engineering. **RELATED KNOWLEDGE/COURSES—Chemistry:** The

P

chemical composition, structure, and properties of substances and of the chemical processes and transformations that they undergo. This includes uses of chemicals and their danger signs, production techniques, and disposal methods. **Engineering and Technology:** The practical application of engineering science and technology. This includes applying principles, techniques, procedures, and equipment to the design and production of various goods and services. **Physics:** Physical principles and laws and their interrelationships and applications to understanding fluid, material, and atmospheric dynamics and mechanical, electrical, atomic, and subatomic structures and processes. **Biology:** Plant and animal organisms and their tissues, cells, functions, interdependencies, and interactions with each other and the environment. **Public Safety and Security:** Relevant equipment, policies, procedures, and strategies to promote effective local, state, or national security operations for the protection of people, data, property, and institutions. **Production and Processing:** Raw materials, production processes, quality control, costs, and other techniques for maximizing the effective manufacture and distribution of goods.

Program Directors

- Education/Training Required: Work experience plus degree
- Annual Earnings: $53,860
- Growth: 16.6%
- Annual Job Openings: 11,000
- Self-Employed: 30.4%
- Part-Time: 8.1%

The job openings listed here are shared with Directors—Stage, Motion Pictures, Television, and Radio, Producers, Talent Directors, Technical Directors/Managers.

Direct and coordinate activities of personnel engaged in preparation of radio or television station program schedules and programs such as sports or news. Plan and schedule programming and event coverage based on broadcast length; time availability; and other factors such as community needs, ratings data, and viewer demographics. Monitor and review programming to ensure that schedules are met, guidelines are adhered to, and performances are of adequate quality. Direct and coordinate activities of personnel engaged in broadcast news, sports, or programming. Check completed program logs for accuracy and conformance with FCC rules and regulations and resolve program log inaccuracies. Establish work schedules and assign work to staff members. Coordinate activities between departments such as news and programming. Perform personnel duties such as hiring staff and evaluating work performance. Evaluate new and existing programming for suitability and to assess the need for changes, using information such as audience surveys and feedback. Develop budgets for programming and broadcasting activities and monitor expenditures to ensure that they remain within budgetary limits. Confer with directors and production staff to discuss issues such as production and casting problems, budgets, policies, and news coverage. Select, acquire, and maintain programs, music, films, and other needed materials and obtain legal clearances for their use as necessary. Monitor network transmissions for advisories concerning daily program schedules, program content, special feeds, or program changes. Develop promotions for current programs and specials. Prepare copy and edit tape so that material is ready for broadcasting. Develop ideas for programs and features that a station could produce. Participate in the planning and execution of fundraising activities. Review information about programs and schedules to ensure accuracy and provide such information to local media outlets as necessary. Read news, read or record public service and promotional announcements, and otherwise participate as a member of an on-air shift as required. Operate and maintain on-air and production audio equipment. Direct setup of remote facilities and install or cancel programs at remote stations.

SKILLS—Most Important: Management Skills; Social Skills; Thought-Processing Skills. **Other Above-Average Skills:** Communication Skills; Equipment/Technology Analysis Skills.

GOE—Interest Area: 03. Arts and Communication. **Work Group:** 03.01. Managerial Work in Arts and Communication. **Other Jobs in This Group:** Agents and Business Managers of Artists, Performers, and Athletes; Art Directors; Producers; Producers and Directors; Public Relations Managers; Technical Directors/Managers. **PERSONALITY TYPE:** Enterprising. Enterprising occupations frequently involve starting up and carrying out projects. These occupations can involve leading people and making many decisions. They sometimes require risk taking and often deal with business.

EDUCATION/TRAINING PROGRAM(S)—Radio and Television; Drama and Dramatics/Theatre Arts, General; Directing and Theatrical Production; Theatre/Theatre Arts Management; Dramatic/Theatre Arts and Stagecraft, Other; Film/Cinema Studies; Cinematography and Film/Video Production. RELATED KNOWLEDGE/COURSES—Telecommunications: Transmission, broadcasting, switching, control, and operation of telecommunications systems. Communications and Media: Media production, communication, and dissemination techniques and methods. This includes alternative ways to inform and entertain via written, oral, and visual media. Computers and Electronics: Circuit boards; processors; chips; electronic equipment; and computer hardware and software, including applications and programming. Customer and Personal Service: Principles and processes for providing customer and personal services. This includes customer needs assessment, meeting of quality standards for services, and evaluation of customer satisfaction. Personnel and Human Resources: Principles and procedures for personnel recruitment, selection, training, compensation and benefits, labor relations and negotiation, and personnel information systems. Clerical Practices: Administrative and clerical procedures and systems such as word processing, managing files and records, stenography and transcription, designing forms, and other office procedures and terminology.

Property, Real Estate, and Community Association Managers

- Education/Training Required: Bachelor's degree
- Annual Earnings: $41,900
- Growth: 15.3%
- Annual Job Openings: 58,000
- Self-Employed: 48.2%
- Part-Time: 21.9%

Plan, direct, or coordinate selling, buying, leasing, or governance activities of commercial, industrial, or residential real estate properties. Meet with prospective tenants to show properties, explain terms of occupancy, and provide information about local areas. Direct collection of monthly assessments; rental fees; and deposits and payment of insurance premiums, mortgage, taxes, and incurred operating expenses. Inspect grounds, facilities, and equipment routinely to determine necessity of repairs or maintenance. Investigate complaints, disturbances, and violations and resolve problems, following management rules and regulations. Manage and oversee operations, maintenance, administration, and improvement of commercial, industrial, or residential properties. Plan, schedule, and coordinate general maintenance, major repairs, and remodeling or construction projects for commercial or residential properties. Negotiate the sale, lease, or development of property and complete or review appropriate documents and forms. Maintain records of sales, rental or usage activity, special permits issued, maintenance and operating costs, or property availability. Determine and certify the eligibility of prospective tenants, following government regulations. Prepare detailed budgets and financial reports for properties. Direct and coordinate the activities of staff and contract personnel and evaluate their performance. Maintain contact with insurance carriers, fire and police departments, and other agencies to ensure protection and compliance with codes and regulations. Market vacant space to prospective tenants through leasing agents, advertising, or other methods. Solicit and analyze bids from contractors for repairs, renovations, and maintenance. Review rents to ensure that they are in line with rental markets. Prepare and administer contracts for provision of property services such as cleaning, maintenance, and security services. Purchase building and maintenance supplies, equipment, or furniture. Act as liaisons between on-site managers or tenants and owners. Confer regularly with community association members to ensure their needs are being met. Meet with boards of directors and committees to discuss and resolve legal and environmental issues or disputes between neighbors.

SKILLS—Most Important: Management Skills; Mathematics Skills; Social Skills. Other Above-Average Skills: Equipment Use/Maintenance Skills; Communication Skills.

P

GOE—**Interest Area:** 14. Retail and Wholesale Sales and Service. **Work Group:** 14.01. Managerial Work in Retail/Wholesale Sales and Service. **Other Jobs in This Group:** Advertising and Promotions Managers; First-Line Supervisors/Managers of Non-Retail Sales Workers; First-Line Supervisors/Managers of Retail Sales Workers; Funeral Directors; Marketing Managers; Purchasing Managers; Sales Managers. **PERSONALITY TYPE:** Enterprising. Enterprising occupations frequently involve starting up and carrying out projects. These occupations can involve leading people and making many decisions. They sometimes require risk taking and often deal with business.

EDUCATION/TRAINING PROGRAM(S)—Real Estate. **RELATED KNOWLEDGE/COURSES**— **Sales and Marketing:** Principles and methods for showing, promoting, and selling products or services. This includes marketing strategy and tactics, product demonstration, sales techniques, and sales control systems. **Clerical Practices:** Administrative and clerical procedures and systems such as word processing, managing files and records, stenography and transcription, designing forms, and other office procedures and terminology. **Economics and Accounting:** Economic and accounting principles and practices, the financial markets, banking, and the analysis and reporting of financial data. **Customer and Personal Service:** Principles and processes for providing customer and personal services. This includes customer needs assessment, meeting of quality standards for services, and evaluation of customer satisfaction. **Administration and Management:** Business and management principles involved in strategic planning, resource allocation, human resources modeling, leadership technique, production methods, and coordination of people and resources. **Personnel and Human Resources:** Principles and procedures for personnel recruitment, selection, training, compensation and benefits, labor relations and negotiation, and personnel information systems.

Psychiatrists

- Education/Training Required: First professional degree
- Annual Earnings: More than $145,600
- Growth: 24.0%
- Annual Job Openings: 41,000
- Self-Employed: 11.5%
- Part-Time: 9.6%

The job openings listed here are shared with Anesthesiologists; Family and General Practitioners; Internists, General; Obstetricians and Gynecologists; Pediatricians, General; and Surgeons.

Diagnose, treat, and help prevent disorders of the mind. Analyze and evaluate patient data and test findings to diagnose nature and extent of mental disorder. Prescribe, direct, and administer psychotherapeutic treatments or medications to treat mental, emotional, or behavioral disorders. Collaborate with physicians, psychologists, social workers, psychiatric nurses, or other professionals to discuss treatment plans and progress. Gather and maintain patient information and records, including social and medical history obtained from patients, relatives, and other professionals. Counsel outpatients and other patients during office visits. Design individualized care plans, using a variety of treatments. Examine or conduct laboratory or diagnostic tests on patient to provide information on general physical condition and mental disorder. Advise and inform guardians, relatives, and significant others of patients' conditions and treatment. Review and evaluate treatment procedures and outcomes of other psychiatrists and medical professionals. Teach, conduct research, and publish findings to increase understanding of mental, emotional, and behavioral states and disorders. Prepare and submit case reports and summaries to government and mental health agencies. Serve on committees to promote and maintain community mental health services and delivery systems.

SKILLS—Most Important: Science Skills; Social Skills; Thought-Processing Skills. **Other Above-Average Skills:** Communication Skills; Quality Control Skills.

GOE—**Interest Area:** 08. Health Science. **Work Group:** 08.02. Medicine and Surgery. **Other Jobs in This Group:** Anesthesiologists; Family and General Practitioners; Internists, General; Medical Assistants; Medical Transcriptionists; Obstetricians and Gynecologists; Pediatricians, General; Pharmacists; Pharmacy Aides; Pharmacy Technicians; Physician Assistants; Registered Nurses; Surgeons; Surgical Technologists. **PERSONALITY TYPE:** Investigative. Investigative occupations frequently involve working with ideas and require an extensive amount of thinking. These occupations can involve searching for facts and figuring out problems mentally.

EDUCATION/TRAINING PROGRAM(S)—Child Psychiatry; Psychiatry; Physical Medical and Rehabilitation/Psychiatry. **RELATED KNOWLEDGE/ COURSES**—**Therapy and Counseling:** Principles, methods, and procedures for diagnosis, treatment, and rehabilitation of physical and mental dysfunctions and for career counseling and guidance. **Medicine and Dentistry:** The information and techniques needed to diagnose and treat human injuries, diseases, and deformities. This includes symptoms, treatment alternatives, drug properties and interactions, and preventive healthcare measures. **Psychology:** Human behavior and performance; individual differences in ability, personality, and interests; learning and motivation; psychological research methods; and the assessment and treatment of behavioral and affective disorders. **Biology:** Plant and animal organisms and their tissues, cells, functions, interdependencies, and interactions with each other and the environment. **Philosophy and Theology:** Different philosophical systems and religions. This includes their basic principles, values, ethics, ways of thinking, customs, practices, and impact on human culture. **Sociology and Anthropology:** Group behavior and dynamics, societal trends and influences, human migrations, ethnicity, and cultures and their history and origins.

Psychology Teachers, Postsecondary

- Education/Training Required: Master's degree
- Annual Earnings: $56,370
- Growth: 32.2%
- Annual Job Openings: 329,000
- Self-Employed: 0.4%
- Part-Time: 27.3%

The job openings listed here are shared with 35 other postsecondary teaching occupations. For a complete list, see the beginning of this section.

Teach courses in psychology, such as child, clinical, and developmental psychology, and psychological counseling. Prepare and deliver lectures to undergraduate and/or graduate students on topics such as abnormal psychology, cognitive processes, and work motivation. Evaluate and grade students' classwork, laboratory work, assignments, and papers. Initiate, facilitate, and moderate classroom discussions. Compile, administer, and grade examinations or assign this work to others. Keep abreast of developments in their field by reading current literature, talking with colleagues, and participating in professional conferences. Prepare course materials such as syllabi, homework assignments, and handouts. Plan, evaluate, and revise curricula, course content, and course materials and methods of instruction. Maintain student attendance records, grades, and other required records. Supervise undergraduate and/or graduate teaching, internship, and research work. Maintain regularly scheduled office hours to advise and assist students. Conduct research in a particular field of knowledge and publish findings in professional journals, books, and electronic media. Advise students on academic and vocational curricula and on career issues. Select and obtain materials and supplies such as textbooks. Collaborate with colleagues to address teaching and research issues. Serve on academic or administrative committees that deal with institutional policies, departmental matters, and academic issues. Compile bibliographies of specialized materials for outside reading assignments. Participate in student recruitment, registration, and placement activities. Supervise students'

P

laboratory work. Perform administrative duties such as serving as department head. Act as advisers to student organizations. Write grant proposals to procure external research funding. Participate in campus and community events. Provide professional consulting services to government and industry.

SKILLS—Most Important: Science Skills; Communication Skills; Thought-Processing Skills. **Other Above-Average Skills:** Social Skills; Mathematics Skills.

GOE—Interest Area: 05. Education and Training. **Work Group:** 05.03. Postsecondary and Adult Teaching and Instructing. **Other Jobs in This Group:** Adult Literacy, Remedial Education, and GED Teachers and Instructors; Agricultural Sciences Teachers, Postsecondary; Anthropology and Archeology Teachers, Postsecondary; Architecture Teachers, Postsecondary; Area, Ethnic, and Cultural Studies Teachers, Postsecondary; Art, Drama, and Music Teachers, Postsecondary; Atmospheric, Earth, Marine, and Space Sciences Teachers, Postsecondary; Biological Science Teachers, Postsecondary; Business Teachers, Postsecondary; Chemistry Teachers, Postsecondary; Communications Teachers, Postsecondary; Computer Science Teachers, Postsecondary; Criminal Justice and Law Enforcement Teachers, Postsecondary; Economics Teachers, Postsecondary; Education Teachers, Postsecondary; Engineering Teachers, Postsecondary; English Language and Literature Teachers, Postsecondary; Environmental Science Teachers, Postsecondary; Farm and Home Management Advisors; Foreign Language and Literature Teachers, Postsecondary; Forestry and Conservation Science Teachers, Postsecondary; Geography Teachers, Postsecondary; Graduate Teaching Assistants; Health Specialties Teachers, Postsecondary; History Teachers, Postsecondary; Home Economics Teachers, Postsecondary; Law Teachers, Postsecondary; Library Science Teachers, Postsecondary; Mathematical Science Teachers, Postsecondary; Nursing Instructors and Teachers, Postsecondary; Philosophy and Religion Teachers, Postsecondary; Physics Teachers, Postsecondary; Political Science Teachers, Postsecondary; Recreation and Fitness Studies Teachers, Postsecondary; Self-Enrichment Education Teachers; Social Work Teachers, Postsecondary; Sociology Teachers, Postsecondary; Vocational Education Teachers, Postsecondary. **PERSONALITY TYPE:** Social. Social occupations frequently involve working with, communicating with, and teaching people. These occupations often involve helping or providing service to others.

EDUCATION/TRAINING PROGRAM(S)—Social Science Teacher Education; Psychology Teacher Education; Psychology, General; Clinical Psychology; Cognitive Psychology and Psycholinguistics; Community Psychology; Comparative Psychology; Counseling Psychology; Developmental and Child Psychology; Experimental Psychology; Industrial and Organizational Psychology; Personality Psychology; Physiological Psychology/Psychobiology; others. **RELATED KNOWLEDGE/COURSES—Psychology:** Human behavior and performance; individual differences in ability, personality, and interests; learning and motivation; psychological research methods; and the assessment and treatment of behavioral and affective disorders. **Therapy and Counseling:** Principles, methods, and procedures for diagnosis, treatment, and rehabilitation of physical and mental dysfunctions and for career counseling and guidance. **Sociology and Anthropology:** Group behavior and dynamics, societal trends and influences, human migrations, ethnicity, and cultures and their history and origins. **Philosophy and Theology:** Different philosophical systems and religions. This includes their basic principles, values, ethics, ways of thinking, customs, practices, and impact on human culture. **Education and Training:** Principles and methods for curriculum and training design, teaching and instruction for individuals and groups, and the measurement of training effects. **English Language:** The structure and content of the English language, including the meaning and spelling of words, rules of composition, and grammar.

Public Relations Managers

- Education/Training Required: Work experience plus degree
- Annual Earnings: $76,450
- Growth: 21.7%
- Annual Job Openings: 5,000
- Self-Employed: 1.6%
- Part-Time: 8.6%

Plan and direct public relations programs designed to create and maintain a favorable public image for employer or client or, if engaged in fundraising, plan and direct activities to solicit and maintain funds for special projects and nonprofit organizations. Identify main client groups and audiences and determine the best way to communicate publicity information to them. Write interesting and effective press releases, prepare information for media kits, and develop and maintain company Internet or intranet Web pages. Develop and maintain the company's corporate image and identity, which includes the use of logos and signage. Manage communications budgets. Manage special events such as sponsorship of races, parties introducing new products, or other activities the firm supports to gain public attention through the media without advertising directly. Draft speeches for company executives and arrange interviews and other forms of contact for them. Assign, supervise, and review the activities of public relations staff. Evaluate advertising and promotion programs for compatibility with public relations efforts. Establish and maintain effective working relationships with local and municipal government officials and media representatives. Confer with labor relations managers to develop internal communications that keep employees informed of company activities. Direct activities of external agencies, establishments, and departments that develop and implement communication strategies and information programs. Formulate policies and procedures related to public information programs, working with public relations executives. Respond to requests for information about employers' activities or status. Establish goals for soliciting funds, develop policies for collection and safeguarding of contributions, and coordinate disbursement of funds. Facilitate consumer relations or the relationship between parts of the company such as the managers and employees or different branch offices. Maintain company archives. Manage in-house communication courses. Produce films and other video products, regulate their distribution, and operate film library. Observe and report on social, economic, and political trends that might affect employers.

SKILLS—Most Important: Social Skills; Management Skills; Communication Skills. **Other Above-Average Skills:** Thought-Processing Skills; Equipment/Technology Analysis Skills.

GOE—Interest Area: 03. Arts and Communication. **Work Group:** 03.01. Managerial Work in Arts and Communication. **Other Jobs in This Group:** Agents and Business Managers of Artists, Performers, and Athletes; Art Directors; Producers; Producers and Directors; Program Directors; Technical Directors/Managers. **PERSONALITY TYPE:** No data available.

EDUCATION/TRAINING PROGRAM(S)—Public Relations/Image Management. **RELATED KNOWLEDGE/COURSES—Sales and Marketing:** Principles and methods for showing, promoting, and selling products or services. This includes marketing strategy and tactics, product demonstration, sales techniques, and sales control systems. **Economics and Accounting:** Economic and accounting principles and practices, the financial markets, banking, and the analysis and reporting of financial data. **Education and Training:** Principles and methods for curriculum and training design, teaching and instruction for individuals and groups, and the measurement of training effects. **Foreign Language:** The structure and content of a foreign (non-English) language, including the meaning and spelling of words, rules of composition and grammar, and pronunciation. **Law and Government:** Laws, legal codes, court procedures, precedents, government regulations, executive orders, agency rules, and the democratic political process. **Administration and Management:** Business and management principles involved in strategic planning, resource allocation, human resources modeling, leadership technique, production methods, and coordination of people and resources.

Public Relations Specialists

- Education/Training Required: Bachelor's degree
- Annual Earnings: $45,020
- Growth: 22.9%
- Annual Job Openings: 38,000
- Self-Employed: 2.7%
- Part-Time: 11.8%

Engage in promoting or creating good will for individuals, groups, or organizations by writing or selecting favorable publicity material and releasing it through various communications media. May prepare and arrange displays and make speeches. Prepare or edit organizational publications for internal and external audiences, including employee newsletters and stockholders' reports. Respond to requests for information

P

from the media or designate another appropriate spokesperson or information source. Establish and maintain cooperative relationships with representatives of community, consumer, employee, and public interest groups. Plan and direct development and communication of informational programs to maintain favorable public and stockholder perceptions of an organization's accomplishments and agenda. Confer with production and support personnel to produce or coordinate production of advertisements and promotions. Arrange public appearances, lectures, contests, or exhibits for clients to increase product and service awareness and to promote goodwill. Study the objectives, promotional policies, and needs of organizations to develop public relations strategies that will influence public opinion or promote ideas, products, and services. Consult with advertising agencies or staff to arrange promotional campaigns in all types of media for products, organizations, or individuals. Confer with other managers to identify trends and key group interests and concerns or to provide advice on business decisions. Coach client representatives in effective communication with the public and with employees. Prepare and deliver speeches to further public relations objectives. Purchase advertising space and time as required to promote client's product or agenda. Plan and conduct market and public opinion research to test products or determine potential for product success, communicating results to client or management.

SKILLS—Most Important: Social Skills; Thought-Processing Skills; Communication Skills. **Other Above-Average Skills:** Management Skills.

GOE—Interest Area: 03. Arts and Communication. **Work Group:** 03.03. News, Broadcasting, and Public Relations. **Other Jobs in This Group:** Broadcast News Analysts; Interpreters and Translators; Reporters and Correspondents. **PERSONALITY TYPE:** Enterprising. Enterprising occupations frequently involve starting up and carrying out projects. These occupations can involve leading people and making many decisions. They sometimes require risk taking and often deal with business.

EDUCATION/TRAINING PROGRAM(S)—Communication Studies/Speech Communication and Rhetoric; Public Relations/Image Management; Political Communication; Health Communication; Family and Consumer Sciences/Human Sciences Communication. **RELATED KNOWLEDGE/COURSES—Sales and Marketing:** Principles and methods for showing, promoting, and selling products or services. This includes marketing strategy and tactics, product demonstration, sales techniques, and sales control systems. **Communications and Media:** Media production, communication, and dissemination techniques and methods. This includes alternative ways to inform and entertain via written, oral, and visual media. **Customer and Personal Service:** Principles and processes for providing customer and personal services. This includes customer needs assessment, meeting of quality standards for services, and evaluation of customer satisfaction. **Administration and Management:** Business and management principles involved in strategic planning, resource allocation, human resources modeling, leadership technique, production methods, and coordination of people and resources. **Sociology and Anthropology:** Group behavior and dynamics, societal trends and influences, human migrations, ethnicity, and cultures and their history and origins. **Clerical Practices:** Administrative and clerical procedures and systems such as word processing, managing files and records, stenography and transcription, designing forms, and other office procedures and terminology.

Purchasing Agents, Except Wholesale, Retail, and Farm Products

- Education/Training Required: Work experience in a related occupation
- Annual Earnings: $49,030
- Growth: 8.1%
- Annual Job Openings: 19,000
- Self-Employed: 3.5%
- Part-Time: 5.6%

Purchase machinery, equipment, tools, parts, supplies, or services necessary for the operation of an establishment. Purchase raw or semi-finished materials for manufacturing. Purchase the highest-quality merchandise at the lowest possible price and in correct amounts. Prepare purchase orders, solicit bid proposals, and review requisitions for goods and services. Research and evaluate suppliers based on price, quality, selection, service, support, availability, reliability, production and distribution capabilities, and the supplier's reputation and history. Analyze price proposals, financial reports, and other data and information to determine reasonable prices. Monitor and follow applicable laws and regulations. Negotiate, or renegotiate, and administer contracts with suppliers, vendors, and other representatives. Monitor shipments to ensure that goods come in on time and trace shipments and follow up undelivered goods in the event of problems. Confer with staff, users, and vendors to discuss defective or unacceptable goods or services and determine corrective action. Evaluate and monitor contract performance to ensure compliance with contractual obligations and to determine need for changes. Maintain and review computerized or manual records of items purchased, costs, delivery, product performance, and inventories. Review catalogs, industry periodicals, directories, trade journals, and Internet sites and consult with other department personnel to locate necessary goods and services. Study sales records and inventory levels of current stock to develop strategic purchasing programs that facilitate employee access to supplies. Interview vendors and visit suppliers' plants and distribution centers to examine and learn about products, services, and prices. Arrange the payment of duty and freight charges. Hire, train, and/or supervise purchasing clerks, buyers, and expediters. Write and review product specifications, maintaining a working technical knowledge of the goods or services to be purchased. Monitor changes affecting supply and demand, tracking market conditions, price trends, or futures markets. Formulate policies and procedures for bid proposals and procurement of goods and services. Attend meetings, trade shows, conferences, conventions, and seminars to network with people in other purchasing departments.

SKILLS—Most Important: Management Skills; Mathematics Skills; Communication Skills. **Other Above-Average Skills:** Quality Control Skills; Equipment/Technology Analysis Skills.

GOE—Interest Area: 14. Retail and Wholesale Sales and Service. **Work Group:** 14.05. Purchasing. **Other Jobs in This Group:** Wholesale and Retail Buyers, Except Farm Products. **PERSONALITY TYPE:** Enterprising. Enterprising occupations frequently

involve starting up and carrying out projects. These occupations can involve leading people and making many decisions. They sometimes require risk taking and often deal with business.

EDUCATION/TRAINING PROGRAM(S)—Sales, Distribution, and Marketing Operations, General; Merchandising and Buying Operations. **RELATED KNOWLEDGE/COURSES—Clerical Practices:** Administrative and clerical procedures and systems such as word processing, managing files and records, stenography and transcription, designing forms, and other office procedures and terminology. **Economics and Accounting:** Economic and accounting principles and practices, the financial markets, banking, and the analysis and reporting of financial data. **Production and Processing:** Raw materials, production processes, quality control, costs, and other techniques for maximizing the effective manufacture and distribution of goods. **Administration and Management:** Business and management principles involved in strategic planning, resource allocation, human resources modeling, leadership technique, production methods, and coordination of people and resources. **Computers and Electronics:** Circuit boards; processors; chips; electronic equipment; and computer hardware and software, including applications and programming. **Communications and Media:** Media production, communication, and dissemination techniques and methods. This includes alternative ways to inform and entertain via written, oral, and visual media.

Purchasing Managers

- Education/Training Required: Work experience plus degree
- Annual Earnings: $76,270
- Growth: 7.0%
- Annual Job Openings: 8,000
- Self-Employed: 0.3%
- Part-Time: 1.2%

Plan, direct, or coordinate the activities of buyers, purchasing officers, and related workers involved in purchasing materials, products, and services. Maintain records of goods ordered and received. Locate vendors of materials, equipment, or supplies and interview them to determine product availability and terms of sales. Prepare and process requisitions and purchase orders for supplies and equipment. Control purchasing department budgets. Interview and hire staff and oversee staff training. Review purchase order claims and contracts for conformance to company policy. Analyze market and delivery systems to assess present and future material availability. Develop and implement purchasing and contract management instructions, policies, and procedures. Participate in the development of specifications for equipment, products, or substitute materials. Resolve vendor or contractor grievances and claims against suppliers. Represent companies in negotiating contracts and formulating policies with suppliers. Review, evaluate, and approve specifications for issuing and awarding bids. Direct and coordinate activities of personnel engaged in buying, selling, and distributing materials, equipment, machinery, and supplies. Prepare bid awards requiring board approval. Prepare reports regarding market conditions and merchandise costs. Administer online purchasing systems. Arrange for disposal of surplus materials.

SKILLS—Most Important: Management Skills; Mathematics Skills; Social Skills. **Other Above-Average Skills:** Thought-Processing Skills; Quality Control Skills; Equipment Use/Maintenance Skills.

GOE—Interest Area: 14. Retail and Wholesale Sales and Service. **Work Group:** 14.01. Managerial Work in Retail/Wholesale Sales and Service. **Other Jobs in This Group:** Advertising and Promotions Managers; First-Line Supervisors/Managers of Non-Retail Sales Workers; First-Line Supervisors/Managers of Retail Sales Workers; Funeral Directors; Marketing Managers; Property, Real Estate, and Community Association Managers; Sales Managers. **PERSONALITY TYPE:** Enterprising. Enterprising occupations frequently involve starting up and carrying out projects. These occupations can involve leading people and making many decisions. They sometimes require risk taking and often deal with business.

EDUCATION/TRAINING PROGRAM(S)—Purchasing, Procurement/Acquisitions, and Contracts Management. **RELATED KNOWLEDGE/COURSES—Economics and Accounting:** Economic and accounting principles and practices, the financial markets, banking, and the analysis and reporting of financial data. **Personnel and Human Resources:** Principles and procedures for personnel recruitment, selection, training, compensation and benefits, labor relations and negotiation, and personnel information systems. **Production and Processing:** Raw materials, production processes, quality control, costs, and other techniques for maximizing the effective manufacture and distribution of goods. **Administration and Management:** Business and management principles involved in strategic planning, resource allocation, human resources modeling, leadership technique, production methods, and coordination of people and resources. **Education and Training:** Principles and methods for curriculum and training design, teaching and instruction for individuals and groups, and the measurement of training effects. **Mathematics:** Arithmetic, algebra, geometry, calculus, and statistics and their applications.

Radiation Therapists

- Education/Training Required: Associate degree
- Annual Earnings: $62,340
- Growth: 26.3%
- Annual Job Openings: 1,000
- Self-Employed: 0.0%
- Part-Time: 6.0%

Provide radiation therapy to patients as prescribed by a radiologist according to established practices and standards. Duties may include reviewing prescription and diagnosis; acting as liaison with physician and supportive care personnel; preparing equipment, such as immobilization, treatment, and protection devices; and maintaining records, reports, and files. May assist in dosimetry procedures and tumor localization. Administer prescribed doses of radiation to specific body parts, using radiation therapy equipment according to established practices and standards. Position patients for treatment with accuracy according to prescription. Enter data into computer and set controls to operate and adjust equipment and regulate dosage. Follow principles of radiation protection for patient, self, and others. Maintain records, reports and files as required, including such information as radiation dosages, equipment settings, and patients' reactions.

Review prescription, diagnosis, patient chart, and identification. Conduct most treatment sessions independently in accordance with the long-term treatment plan and under the general direction of the patient's physician. Check radiation therapy equipment to ensure proper operation. Observe and reassure patients during treatment and report unusual reactions to physician or turn equipment off if unexpected adverse reactions occur. Check for side effects such as skin irritation, nausea, and hair loss to assess patients' reaction to treatment. Educate, prepare, and reassure patients and their families by answering questions, providing physical assistance, and reinforcing physicians' advice regarding treatment reactions and post-treatment care. Calculate actual treatment dosages delivered during each session. Prepare and construct equipment, such as immobilization, treatment, and protection devices. Photograph treated area of patient and process film. Help physicians, radiation oncologists, and clinical physicists to prepare physical and technical aspects of radiation treatment plans, using information about patient condition and anatomy. Train and supervise student or subordinate radiotherapy technologists. Provide assistance to other health-care personnel during dosimetry procedures and tumor localization. Implement appropriate follow-up care plans. Act as liaison with physicist and supportive care personnel. Store, sterilize, or prepare the special applicators containing the radioactive substance implanted by the physician. Assist in the preparation of sealed radioactive materials, such as cobalt, radium, cesium, and isotopes, for use in radiation treatments.

SKILLS—Most Important: Science Skills; Equipment/Technology Analysis Skills; Equipment Use/Maintenance Skills. **Other Above-Average Skills:** Quality Control Skills; Social Skills; Management Skills; Thought-Processing Skills.

GOE—Interest Area: 08. Health Science. **Work Group:** 08.07. Medical Therapy. **Other Jobs in This Group:** Audiologists; Massage Therapists; Occupational Therapist Aides; Occupational Therapist Assistants; Occupational Therapists; Physical Therapist Aides; Physical Therapist Assistants; Physical Therapists; Recreational Therapists; Respiratory Therapists; Respiratory Therapy Technicians; Speech-Language Pathologists. **PERSONALITY TYPE:** Social. Social occupations frequently involve working with, communicating with, and teaching people. These occupations often involve helping or providing service to others.

EDUCATION/TRAINING PROGRAM(S)—Medical Radiologic Technology/Science—Radiation Therapist. **RELATED KNOWLEDGE/COURSES— Medicine and Dentistry:** The information and techniques needed to diagnose and treat human injuries, diseases, and deformities. This includes symptoms, treatment alternatives, drug properties and interactions, and preventive healthcare measures. **Biology:** Plant and animal organisms and their tissues, cells, functions, interdependencies, and interactions with each other and the environment. **Psychology:** Human behavior and performance; individual differences in ability, personality, and interests; learning and motivation; psychological research methods; and the assessment and treatment of behavioral and affective disorders. **Physics:** Physical principles and laws and their interrelationships and applications to understanding fluid, material, and atmospheric dynamics and mechanical, electrical, atomic, and subatomic structures and processes. **Customer and Personal Service:** Principles and processes for providing customer and personal services. This includes customer needs assessment, meeting of quality standards for services, and evaluation of customer satisfaction. **Therapy and Counseling:** Principles, methods, and procedures for diagnosis, treatment, and rehabilitation of physical and mental dysfunctions and for career counseling and guidance.

Radiologic Technicians

- Education/Training Required: Associate degree
- Annual Earnings: $45,950
- Growth: 23.2%
- Annual Job Openings: 17,000
- Self-Employed: 0.4%
- Part-Time: 17.2%

The job openings listed here are shared with Radiologic Technologists.

Maintain and use equipment and supplies necessary to demonstrate portions of the human body on X-ray film or fluoroscopic screen for diagnostic purposes. Use beam-restrictive devices and patient-shielding techniques to minimize radiation exposure to patient and

R

staff. Position X-ray equipment and adjust controls to set exposure factors, such as time and distance. Position patient on examining table and set up and adjust equipment to obtain optimum view of specific body area as requested by physician. Determine patients' X-ray needs by reading requests or instructions from physicians. Make exposures necessary for the requested procedures, rejecting and repeating work that does not meet established standards. Process exposed radiographs, using film processors or computer-generated methods. Explain procedures to patients to reduce anxieties and obtain cooperation. Perform procedures such as linear tomography; mammography; sonograms; joint and cyst aspirations; routine contrast studies; routine fluoroscopy; and examinations of the head, trunk, and extremities under supervision of physician. Prepare and set up X-ray room for patient. Assure that sterile supplies, contrast materials, catheters, and other required equipment are present and in working order, requisitioning materials as necessary. Maintain records of patients examined, examinations performed, views taken, and technical factors used. Provide assistance to physicians or other technologists in the performance of more complex procedures. Monitor equipment operation and report malfunctioning equipment to supervisor. Provide students and other technologists with suggestions of additional views, alternate positioning, or improved techniques to ensure the images produced are of the highest quality. Coordinate work of other technicians or technologists when procedures require more than one person. Assist with on-the-job training of new employees and students and provide input to supervisors regarding training performance. Maintain a current file of examination protocols. Operate mobile X-ray equipment in operating room, in emergency room, or at patient's bedside. Provide assistance in radiopharmaceutical administration, monitoring patients' vital signs and notifying the radiologist of any relevant changes.

SKILLS—Most Important: Science Skills; Social Skills; Communication Skills. **Other Above-Average Skills:** Equipment/Technology Analysis Skills; Equipment Use/Maintenance Skills.

GOE—Interest Area: 08. Health Science. **Work Group:** 08.06. Medical Technology. **Other Jobs in This Group:** Biological Technicians; Cardiovascular Technologists

and Technicians; Diagnostic Medical Sonographers; Medical and Clinical Laboratory Technicians; Medical and Clinical Laboratory Technologists; Medical Equipment Preparers; Medical Records and Health Information Technicians; Nuclear Medicine Technologists; Opticians, Dispensing; Orthotists and Prosthetists; Radiologic Technologists; Radiologic Technologists and Technicians. **PERSONALITY TYPE:** Realistic. Realistic occupations frequently involve work activities that include practical, hands-on problems and solutions. They often deal with plants, animals, and real-world materials like wood, tools, and machinery. Many of the occupations require working outside and do not involve a lot of paperwork or working closely with others.

EDUCATION/TRAINING PROGRAM(S)—Medical Radiologic Technology/Science—Radiation Therapist; Radiologic Technology/Science—Radiographer; Allied Health Diagnostic, Intervention, and Treatment Professions, Other. **RELATED KNOWLEDGE/ COURSES—Clerical Practices:** Administrative and clerical procedures and systems such as word processing, managing files and records, stenography and transcription, designing forms, and other office procedures and terminology. **Medicine and Dentistry:** The information and techniques needed to diagnose and treat human injuries, diseases, and deformities. This includes symptoms, treatment alternatives, drug properties and interactions, and preventive healthcare measures. **Psychology:** Human behavior and performance; individual differences in ability, personality, and interests; learning and motivation; psychological research methods; and the assessment and treatment of behavioral and affective disorders. **Physics:** Physical principles and laws and their interrelationships and applications to understanding fluid, material, and atmospheric dynamics and mechanical, electrical, atomic, and subatomic structures and processes. **Biology:** Plant and animal organisms and their tissues, cells, functions, interdependencies, and interactions with each other and the environment. **Customer and Personal Service:** Principles and processes for providing customer and personal services. This includes customer needs assessment, meeting of quality standards for services, and evaluation of customer satisfaction.

Radiologic Technologists

- Education/Training Required: Associate degree
- Annual Earnings: $45,950
- Growth: 23.2%
- Annual Job Openings: 17,000
- Self-Employed: 0.4%
- Part-Time: 17.2%

The job openings listed here are shared with Radiologic Technicians.

Take X rays and Computerized Axial Tomography (CAT or CT) scans or administer nonradioactive materials into patient's bloodstream for diagnostic purposes. Includes technologists who specialize in other modalities, such as computed tomography, ultrasound, and magnetic resonance. Review and evaluate developed X rays, videotape, or computer-generated information to determine if images are satisfactory for diagnostic purposes. Use radiation safety measures and protection devices to comply with government regulations and to ensure safety of patients and staff. Explain procedures and observe patients to ensure safety and comfort during scan. Operate or oversee operation of radiologic and magnetic imaging equipment to produce images of the body for diagnostic purposes. Position and immobilize patient on examining table. Position imaging equipment and adjust controls to set exposure time and distance according to specification of examination. Key commands and data into computer to document and specify scan sequences, adjust transmitters and receivers, or photograph certain images. Monitor video display of area being scanned and adjust density or contrast to improve picture quality. Monitor patients' conditions and reactions, reporting abnormal signs to physician. Prepare and administer oral or injected contrast media to patients. Set up examination rooms, ensuring that all necessary equipment is ready. Take thorough and accurate patient medical histories. Remove and process film. Record, process, and maintain patient data and treatment records and prepare reports. Coordinate work with clerical personnel or other technologists. Demonstrate new equipment, procedures, and techniques to staff and provide technical assistance. Provide assistance in dressing or changing seriously ill, injured, or disabled patients. Move ultrasound scanner over patient's body and watch pattern produced on video screen. Measure thickness of section to be radiographed, using instruments similar to measuring tapes. Operate fluoroscope to aid physician to view and guide wire or catheter through blood vessels to area of interest. Assign duties to radiologic staff to maintain patient flows and achieve production goals. Collaborate with other medical team members, such as physicians and nurses, to conduct angiography or special vascular procedures. Perform administrative duties such as developing departmental operating budget, coordinating purchases of supplies and equipment, and preparing work schedules.

SKILLS—Most Important: Communication Skills; Social Skills; Science Skills. **Other Above-Average Skills:** Equipment Use/Maintenance Skills; Quality Control Skills.

GOE—Interest Area: 08. Health Science. **Work Group:** 08.06. Medical Technology. **Other Jobs in This Group:** Biological Technicians; Cardiovascular Technologists and Technicians; Diagnostic Medical Sonographers; Medical and Clinical Laboratory Technicians; Medical and Clinical Laboratory Technologists; Medical Equipment Preparers; Medical Records and Health Information Technicians; Nuclear Medicine Technologists; Opticians, Dispensing; Orthotists and Prosthetists; Radiologic Technicians; Radiologic Technologists and Technicians. **PERSONALITY TYPE:** Realistic. Realistic occupations frequently involve work activities that include practical, hands-on problems and solutions. They often deal with plants, animals, and real-world materials like wood, tools, and machinery. Many of the occupations require working outside and do not involve a lot of paperwork or working closely with others.

EDUCATION/TRAINING PROGRAM(S)—Medical Radiologic Technology/Science—Radiation Therapist; Radiologic Technology/Science—Radiographer; Allied Health Diagnostic, Intervention, and Treatment Professions, Other. **RELATED KNOWLEDGE/ COURSES—Medicine and Dentistry:** The information and techniques needed to diagnose and treat human injuries, diseases, and deformities. This includes symptoms, treatment alternatives, drug properties and interactions, and preventive healthcare measures. **Biology:** Plant and animal organisms and their tissues, cells, functions, interdependencies, and interactions with each other and the environment. **Physics:** Physical principles and laws and their interrelationships and applications to understanding fluid, material, and atmospheric dynamics and mechanical, electrical, atomic, and subatomic structures and processes. **Psychology:** Human behavior and performance; individual differences in ability, personality, and interests; learning and motivation; psychological research methods; and the assessment and treatment of behavioral and affective disorders. **Chemistry:** The chemical composition, structure, and properties of substances and of the chemical processes and transformations that they undergo. This includes uses of chemicals and their danger signs, production techniques, and disposal methods. **Customer and Personal Service:** Principles and processes for providing customer and personal services. This includes customer needs assessment, meeting of quality standards for services, and evaluation of customer satisfaction.

Railroad Conductors and Yardmasters

- Education/Training Required: Moderate-term on-the-job training
- Annual Earnings: $54,040
- Growth: 20.3%
- Annual Job Openings: 3,000
- Self-Employed: 0.0%
- Part-Time: 0.6%

Conductors coordinate activities of train crew on passenger or freight train. Coordinate activities of switch-engine crew within yard of railroad, industrial plant, or similar location. Yardmasters coordinate activities of workers engaged in railroad traffic operations, such as the makeup or breakup of trains; yard switching; and review train schedules and switching orders. Signal engineers to begin train runs, stop trains, or change speed, using telecommunications equipment or hand signals. Receive information regarding train or rail problems from dispatchers or from electronic monitoring devices. Direct and instruct workers engaged in yard activities, such as switching tracks, coupling and uncoupling cars, and routing inbound and outbound traffic. Keep records of the contents and destination of each

train car and make sure that cars are added or removed at proper points on routes. Operate controls to activate track switches and traffic signals. Instruct workers to set warning signals in front and at rear of trains during emergency stops. Direct engineers to move cars to fit planned train configurations, combining or separating cars to make up or break up trains. Receive instructions from dispatchers regarding trains' routes, timetables, and cargoes. Review schedules, switching orders, way bills, and shipping records to obtain cargo loading and unloading information and to plan work. Confer with engineers regarding train routes, timetables, and cargoes and to discuss alternative routes when there are rail defects or obstructions. Arrange for the removal of defective cars from trains at stations or stops. Inspect each car periodically during runs. Observe yard traffic to determine tracks available to accommodate inbound and outbound traffic. Document and prepare reports of accidents, unscheduled stops, or delays. Confirm routes and destination information for freight cars. Supervise and coordinate crew activities to transport freight and passengers and to provide boarding, porter, maid, and meal services to passengers. Supervise workers in the inspection and maintenance of mechanical equipment to ensure efficient and safe train operation. Record departure and arrival times, messages, tickets and revenue collected, and passenger accommodations and destinations. Inspect freight cars for compliance with sealing procedures and record car numbers and seal numbers. Collect tickets, fares, or passes from passengers. Verify accuracy of timekeeping instruments with engineers to ensure that trains depart on time.

SKILLS—Most Important: Equipment Use/Maintenance Skills. **Other Above-Average Skills:** Communication Skills.

GOE—Interest Area: 16. Transportation, Distribution, and Logistics. **Work Group:** 16.01. Managerial Work in Transportation. **Other Jobs in This Group:** Aircraft Cargo Handling Supervisors; First-Line Supervisors/ Managers of Transportation and Material-Moving Machine and Vehicle Operators; Postmasters and Mail Superintendents; Storage and Distribution Managers; Transportation Managers; Transportation, Storage, and Distribution Managers. **PERSONALITY TYPE:** Realistic. Realistic occupations frequently involve work activities that include practical, hands-on problems and solutions. They often deal with plants, animals, and real-world materials like wood, tools, and machinery.

Many of the occupations require working outside and do not involve a lot of paperwork or working closely with others.

EDUCATION/TRAINING PROGRAM(S)—Truck and Bus Driver/Commercial Vehicle Operation. **RELATED KNOWLEDGE/COURSES**—**Transportation:** Principles and methods for moving people or goods by air, rail, sea, or road, including the relative costs and benefits. **Public Safety and Security:** Relevant equipment, policies, procedures, and strategies to promote effective local, state, or national security operations for the protection of people, data, property, and institutions. **Mechanical Devices:** Machines and tools, including their designs, uses, repair, and maintenance. **Clerical Practices:** Administrative and clerical procedures and systems such as word processing, managing files and records, stenography and transcription, designing forms, and other office procedures and terminology. **Law and Government:** Laws, legal codes, court procedures, precedents, government regulations, executive orders, agency rules, and the democratic political process.

Real Estate Brokers

- ◎ Education/Training Required: Work experience in a related occupation
- ◎ Annual Earnings: $57,190
- ◎ Growth: 7.8%
- ◎ Annual Job Openings: 12,000
- ◎ Self-Employed: 59.9%
- ◎ Part-Time: 18.6%

Operate real estate office or work for commercial real estate firm, overseeing real estate transactions. Other duties usually include selling real estate or renting properties and arranging loans. Sell, for a fee, real estate owned by others. Obtain agreements from property owners to place properties for sale with real estate firms. Monitor fulfillment of purchase contract terms to ensure that they are handled in a timely manner. Compare a property with similar properties that have recently sold to determine its competitive market price. Act as an intermediary in negotiations between buyers and sellers over property prices and settlement details

and during the closing of sales. Generate lists of properties for sale, their locations and descriptions, and available financing options, using computers. Maintain knowledge of real estate law; local economies; fair housing laws; and types of available mortgages, financing options, and government programs. Check work completed by loan officers, attorneys, and other professionals to ensure that it is performed properly. Arrange for financing of property purchases. Appraise property values, assessing income potential when relevant. Maintain awareness of current income tax regulations, local zoning, building and tax laws, and growth possibilities of the area where a property is located. Manage and operate real estate offices, handling associated business details. Supervise agents who handle real estate transactions. Rent properties or manage rental properties. Arrange for title searches of properties being sold. Give buyers virtual tours of properties in which they are interested, using computers. Review property details to ensure that environmental regulations are met. Develop, sell, or lease property used for industry or manufacturing. Maintain working knowledge of various factors that determine a farm's capacity to produce, including agricultural variables and proximity to market centers and transportation facilities.

SKILLS—**Most Important:** Management Skills; Mathematics Skills; Social Skills. **Other Above-Average Skills:** Communication Skills; Thought-Processing Skills.

GOE—**Interest Area:** 14. Retail and Wholesale Sales and Service. **Work Group:** 14.03. General Sales. **Other Jobs in This Group:** Parts Salespersons; Real Estate Sales Agents; Retail Salespersons; Sales Representatives, Wholesale and Manufacturing, Except Technical and Scientific Products; Service Station Attendants. **PERSONALITY TYPE:** No data available.

EDUCATION/TRAINING PROGRAM(S)—Real Estate. **RELATED KNOWLEDGE/COURSES**—**Sales and Marketing:** Principles and methods for showing, promoting, and selling products or services. This includes marketing strategy and tactics, product demonstration, sales techniques, and sales control systems. **Customer and Personal Service:** Principles and processes for providing customer and personal services. This includes customer needs assessment, meeting of quality standards for services, and evaluation of customer satisfaction. **Law and Government:** Laws, legal codes, court procedures, precedents, government regulations, executive orders, agency rules, and the democratic political process. **Building and Construction:** The materials, methods, and tools involved in the construction or repair of houses, buildings, or other structures such as highways and roads. **Personnel and Human Resources:** Principles and procedures for personnel recruitment, selection, training, compensation and benefits, labor relations and negotiation, and personnel information systems. **Administration and Management:** Business and management principles involved in strategic planning, resource allocation, human resources modeling, leadership technique, production methods, and coordination of people and resources.

Real Estate Sales Agents

- Education/Training Required: Postsecondary vocational training
- Annual Earnings: $39,240
- Growth: 14.7%
- Annual Job Openings: 41,000
- Self-Employed: 59.8%
- Part-Time: 18.6%

Rent, buy, or sell property for clients. Perform duties such as studying property listings, interviewing prospective clients, accompanying clients to property site, discussing conditions of sale, and drawing up real estate contracts. Includes agents who represent buyer. Present purchase offers to sellers for consideration. Confer with escrow companies, lenders, home inspectors, and pest control operators to ensure that terms and conditions of purchase agreements are met before closing dates. Interview clients to determine what kinds of properties they are seeking. Prepare documents such as representation contracts, purchase agreements, closing statements, deeds, and leases. Coordinate property closings, overseeing signing of documents and disbursement of funds. Act as an intermediary in negotiations between buyers and sellers, generally representing one or the other. Promote sales of properties through advertisements, open houses, and participation in multiple listing services. Compare a property with similar properties that have recently sold to determine its competitive market price. Coordinate appointments to show homes to

prospective buyers. Generate lists of properties that are compatible with buyers' needs and financial resources. Display commercial, industrial, agricultural, and residential properties to clients and explain their features. Arrange for title searches to determine whether clients have clear property titles. Review plans for new construction with clients, enumerating and recommending available options and features. Answer clients' questions regarding construction work, financing, maintenance, repairs, and appraisals. Accompany buyers during visits to and inspections of property, advising them on the suitability and value of the homes they are visiting. Inspect condition of premises and arrange for necessary maintenance or notify owners of maintenance needs. Advise sellers on how to make homes more appealing to potential buyers. Arrange meetings between buyers and sellers when details of transactions need to be negotiated. Advise clients on market conditions, prices, mortgages, legal requirements, and related matters. Evaluate mortgage options to help clients obtain financing at the best prevailing rates and terms. Review property listings, trade journals, and relevant literature and attend conventions, seminars, and staff and association meetings to remain knowledgeable about real estate markets.

SKILLS—Most Important: Social Skills; Communication Skills; Mathematics Skills. **Other Above-Average Skills:** Thought-Processing Skills.

GOE—Interest Area: 14. Retail and Wholesale Sales and Service. **Work Group:** 14.03. General Sales. **Other Jobs in This Group:** Parts Salespersons; Real Estate Brokers; Retail Salespersons; Sales Representatives, Wholesale and Manufacturing, Except Technical and Scientific Products; Service Station Attendants. **PERSONALITY TYPE:** Enterprising. Enterprising occupations frequently involve starting up and carrying out projects. These occupations can involve leading people and making many decisions. They sometimes require risk taking and often deal with business.

EDUCATION/TRAINING PROGRAM(S)—Real Estate. **RELATED KNOWLEDGE/COURSES— Sales and Marketing:** Principles and methods for showing, promoting, and selling products or services. This includes marketing strategy and tactics, product demonstration, sales techniques, and sales control systems. **Customer and Personal Service:** Principles and processes for providing customer and personal services. This includes customer needs assessment, meeting of quality standards for services, and evaluation of customer satisfaction. **Clerical Practices:** Administrative and clerical procedures and systems such as word processing, managing files and records, stenography and transcription, designing forms, and other office procedures and terminology. **Law and Government:** Laws, legal codes, court procedures, precedents, government regulations, executive orders, agency rules, and the democratic political process. **Economics and Accounting:** Economic and accounting principles and practices, the financial markets, banking, and the analysis and reporting of financial data. **Building and Construction:** The materials, methods, and tools involved in the construction or repair of houses, buildings, or other structures such as highways and roads.

Recreation and Fitness Studies Teachers, Postsecondary

- ⚙ Education/Training Required: Master's degree
- ⚙ Annual Earnings: $45,890
- ⚙ Growth: 32.2%
- ⚙ Annual Job Openings: 329,000
- ⚙ Self-Employed: 0.4%
- ⚙ Part-Time: 27.3%

The job openings listed here are shared with 35 other postsecondary teaching occupations. For a complete list, see the beginning of this section.

Teach courses pertaining to recreation, leisure, and fitness studies, including exercise physiology and facilities management. Evaluate and grade students' classwork, assignments, and papers. Maintain student attendance records, grades, and other required records. Prepare and deliver lectures to undergraduate and graduate students on topics such as anatomy, therapeutic recreation, and conditioning theory. Prepare course materials such as syllabi, homework assignments, and handouts. Maintain regularly scheduled office hours to advise and assist students. Compile, administer, and grade examinations or assign this work to others. Plan, evaluate, and revise curricula, course content, and course materials and methods of instruction. Initiate,

facilitate, and moderate classroom discussions. Keep abreast of developments in their field by reading current literature, talking with colleagues, and participating in professional conferences. Advise students on academic and vocational curricula and on career issues. Participate in student recruitment, registration, and placement activities. Collaborate with colleagues to address teaching and research issues. Select and obtain materials and supplies such as textbooks. Participate in campus and community events. Serve on academic or administrative committees that deal with institutional policies, departmental matters, and academic issues. Compile bibliographies of specialized materials for outside reading assignments. Supervise undergraduate or graduate teaching, internship, and research work. Perform administrative duties such as serving as department heads. Prepare students to act as sports coaches. Conduct research in a particular field of knowledge and publish findings in professional journals, books, or electronic media. Act as advisers to student organizations. Write grant proposals to procure external research funding. Provide professional consulting services to government or industry.

SKILLS—Most Important: Science Skills; Social Skills; Management Skills. **Other Above-Average Skills:** Thought-Processing Skills; Communication Skills.

GOE—Interest Area: 05. Education and Training. **Work Group:** 05.03. Postsecondary and Adult Teaching and Instructing. **Other Jobs in This Group:** Adult Literacy, Remedial Education, and GED Teachers and Instructors; Agricultural Sciences Teachers, Postsecondary; Anthropology and Archeology Teachers, Postsecondary; Architecture Teachers, Postsecondary; Area, Ethnic, and Cultural Studies Teachers, Postsecondary; Art, Drama, and Music Teachers, Postsecondary; Atmospheric, Earth, Marine, and Space Sciences Teachers, Postsecondary; Biological Science Teachers, Postsecondary; Business Teachers, Postsecondary; Chemistry Teachers, Postsecondary; Communications Teachers, Postsecondary; Computer Science Teachers, Postsecondary; Criminal Justice and Law Enforcement Teachers, Postsecondary; Economics Teachers, Postsecondary; Education Teachers, Postsecondary; Engineering Teachers, Postsecondary; English Language and Literature Teachers, Postsecondary; Environmental Science Teachers, Postsecondary; Farm and Home Management Advisors; Foreign Language and Literature Teachers, Postsecondary; Forestry and

Conservation Science Teachers, Postsecondary; Geography Teachers, Postsecondary; Graduate Teaching Assistants; Health Specialties Teachers, Postsecondary; History Teachers, Postsecondary; Home Economics Teachers, Postsecondary; Law Teachers, Postsecondary; Library Science Teachers, Postsecondary; Mathematical Science Teachers, Postsecondary; Nursing Instructors and Teachers, Postsecondary; Philosophy and Religion Teachers, Postsecondary; Physics Teachers, Postsecondary; Political Science Teachers, Postsecondary; Psychology Teachers, Postsecondary; Self-Enrichment Education Teachers; Social Work Teachers, Postsecondary; Sociology Teachers, Postsecondary; Vocational Education Teachers, Postsecondary. **PERSONALITY TYPE:** No data available.

EDUCATION/TRAINING PROGRAM(S)—Parks, Recreation, and Leisure Studies; Health and Physical Education, General; Sport and Fitness Administration/Management. **RELATED KNOWLEDGE/COURSES**—**Education and Training:** Principles and methods for curriculum and training design, teaching and instruction for individuals and groups, and the measurement of training effects. **Psychology:** Human behavior and performance; individual differences in ability, personality, and interests; learning and motivation; psychological research methods; and the assessment and treatment of behavioral and affective disorders. **Philosophy and Theology:** Different philosophical systems and religions. This includes their basic principles, values, ethics, ways of thinking, customs, practices, and impact on human culture. **Therapy and Counseling:** Principles, methods, and procedures for diagnosis, treatment, and rehabilitation of physical and mental dysfunctions and for career counseling and guidance. **Personnel and Human Resources:** Principles and procedures for personnel recruitment, selection, training, compensation and benefits, labor relations and negotiation, and personnel information systems. **Medicine and Dentistry:** The information and techniques needed to diagnose and treat human injuries, diseases, and deformities. This includes symptoms, treatment alternatives, drug properties and interactions, and preventive health-care measures.

Refrigeration Mechanics and Installers

- Education/Training Required: Long-term on-the-job training
- Annual Earnings: $37,040
- Growth: 19.0%
- Annual Job Openings: 33,000
- Self-Employed: 13.1%
- Part-Time: 3.6%

The job openings listed here are shared with Heating and Air Conditioning Mechanics and Installers.

Install and repair industrial and commercial refrigerating systems. Braze or solder parts to repair defective joints and leaks. Observe and test system operation, using gauges and instruments. Test lines, components, and connections for leaks. Dismantle malfunctioning systems and test components, using electrical, mechanical, and pneumatic testing equipment. Adjust or replace worn or defective mechanisms and parts and reassemble repaired systems. Read blueprints to determine location, size, capacity, and type of components needed to build refrigeration system. Supervise and instruct assistants. Perform mechanical overhauls and refrigerant reclaiming. Install wiring to connect components to an electric power source. Cut, bend, thread, and connect pipe to functional components and water, power, or refrigeration system. Adjust valves according to specifications and charge system with proper type of refrigerant by pumping the specified gas or fluid into the system. Estimate, order, pick up, deliver, and install materials and supplies needed to maintain equipment in good working condition. Install expansion and control valves, using acetylene torches and wrenches. Mount compressor, condenser, and other components in specified locations on frames, using hand tools and acetylene welding equipment. Keep records of repairs and replacements made and causes of malfunctions. Schedule work with customers and initiate work orders, house requisitions, and orders from stock. Lay out reference points for installation of structural and functional components, using measuring instruments. Fabricate and assemble structural and functional components of refrigeration system, using hand tools, power tools, and welding equipment. Lift and align components into position, using hoist or block and tackle. Drill holes and install mounting brackets and hangers into floor and walls of building. Insulate shells and cabinets of systems.

SKILLS—Most Important: Equipment Use/Maintenance Skills; Science Skills; Equipment/Technology Analysis Skills. **Other Above-Average Skills:** Mathematics Skills; Social Skills; Communication Skills; Quality Control Skills.

GOE—Interest Area: 02. Architecture and Construction. **Work Group:** 02.05. Systems and Equipment Installation, Maintenance, and Repair. **Other Jobs in This Group:** Electrical and Electronics Repairers, Powerhouse, Substation, and Relay; Electrical Power-Line Installers and Repairers; Elevator Installers and Repairers; Heating and Air Conditioning Mechanics and Installers; Maintenance and Repair Workers, General; Telecommunications Equipment Installers and Repairers, Except Line Installers; Telecommunications Line Installers and Repairers. **PERSONALITY TYPE:** Realistic. Realistic occupations frequently involve work activities that include practical, hands-on problems and solutions. They often deal with plants, animals, and real-world materials like wood, tools, and machinery. Many of the occupations require working outside and do not involve a lot of paperwork or working closely with others.

EDUCATION/TRAINING PROGRAM(S)—Heating, Air Conditioning, and Refrigeration Technology/Technician (ACH/ACR/ACHR/HRAC/HVAC); Solar Energy Technology/Technician; Heating, Air Conditioning, Ventilation, and Refrigeration Maintenance Technology/Technician. **RELATED KNOWLEDGE/COURSES—Building and Construction:** The materials, methods, and tools involved in the construction or repair of houses, buildings, or other structures such as highways and roads. **Mechanical Devices:** Machines and tools, including their designs, uses, repair, and maintenance. **Engineering and Technology:** The practical application of engineering science and technology. This includes applying principles, techniques, procedures, and equipment to the design and production of various goods and services. **Physics:** Physical principles and laws and their interrelationships and applications to understanding fluid, material, and atmospheric dynam-

ics and mechanical, electrical, atomic, and subatomic structures and processes. **Design:** Design techniques, tools, and principles involved in production of precision technical plans, blueprints, drawings, and models. **Chemistry:** The chemical composition, structure, and properties of substances and of the chemical processes and transformations that they undergo. This includes uses of chemicals and their danger signs, production techniques, and disposal methods.

Registered Nurses

- Education/Training Required: Associate degree
- Annual Earnings: $54,670
- Growth: 29.4%
- Annual Job Openings: 229,000
- Self-Employed: 0.7%
- Part-Time: 24.1%

Assess patient health problems and needs, develop and implement nursing care plans, and maintain medical records. Administer nursing care to ill, injured, convalescent, or disabled patients. May advise patients on health maintenance and disease prevention or provide case management. Licensing or registration required. Includes advance practice nurses, such as nurse practitioners, clinical nurse specialists, certified nurse midwives, and certified registered nurse anesthetists. Advanced practice nursing is practiced by RNs who have specialized formal, post-basic education and who function in highly autonomous and specialized roles. Maintain accurate, detailed reports and records. Monitor, record, and report symptoms and changes in patients' conditions. Record patients' medical information and vital signs. Modify patient treatment plans as indicated by patients' responses and conditions. Consult and coordinate with health-care team members to assess, plan, implement, and evaluate patient care plans. Order, interpret, and evaluate diagnostic tests to identify and assess patient's condition. Monitor all aspects of patient care, including diet and physical activity. Direct and supervise less-skilled nursing or health-care personnel or supervise a particular unit. Prepare patients for, and assist with, examinations and treatments. Observe nurses and visit patients to ensure proper nursing care. Assess

R

the needs of individuals, families, or communities, including assessment of individuals' home or work environments, to identify potential health or safety problems. Instruct individuals, families, and other groups on topics such as health education, disease prevention, and childbirth; develop health improvement programs. Prepare rooms, sterile instruments, equipment, and supplies and ensure that stock of supplies is maintained. Inform physician of patient's condition during anesthesia. Deliver infants and provide prenatal and postpartum care and treatment under obstetrician's supervision. Administer local, inhalation, intravenous, and other anesthetics. Provide health care, first aid, immunizations, and assistance in convalescence and rehabilitation in locations such as schools, hospitals, and industry. Conduct specified laboratory tests. Perform physical examinations, make tentative diagnoses, and treat patients en route to hospitals or at disaster site triage centers. Hand items to surgeons during operations. Prescribe or recommend drugs; medical devices; or other forms of treatment, such as physical therapy, inhalation therapy, or related therapeutic procedures. Direct and coordinate infection control programs, advising and consulting with specified personnel about necessary precautions. Perform administrative and managerial functions, such as taking responsibility for a unit's staff, budget, planning, and long-range goals.

SKILLS—Most Important: Science Skills; Social Skills; Thought-Processing Skills. **Other Above-Average Skills:** Communication Skills; Mathematics Skills.

GOE—Interest Area: 08. Health Science. **Work Group:** 08.02. Medicine and Surgery. **Other Jobs in This Group:** Anesthesiologists; Family and General Practitioners; Internists, General; Medical Assistants; Medical Transcriptionists; Obstetricians and Gynecologists; Pediatricians, General; Pharmacists; Pharmacy Aides; Pharmacy Technicians; Physician Assistants; Psychiatrists; Surgeons; Surgical Technologists. **PERSONALITY TYPE:** Social. Social occupations frequently involve working with, communicating with, and teaching people. These occupations often involve helping or providing service to others.

EDUCATION/TRAINING PROGRAM(S)— Nursing—Registered Nurse Training (RN, ASN, BSN, MSN); Adult Health Nurse/Nursing; Nurse Anesthetist; Family Practice Nurse/Nurse Practitioner;

Maternal/Child Health and Neonatal Nurse/Nursing; Nurse Midwife/Nursing Midwifery; Nursing Science (MS, PhD); Pediatric Nurse/Nursing; Psychiatric/Mental Health Nurse/Nursing; Public Health/Community Nurse/Nursing; others. **RELATED KNOWLEDGE/COURSES—Medicine and Dentistry:** The information and techniques needed to diagnose and treat human injuries, diseases, and deformities. This includes symptoms, treatment alternatives, drug properties and interactions, and preventive healthcare measures. **Psychology:** Human behavior and performance; individual differences in ability, personality, and interests; learning and motivation; psychological research methods; and the assessment and treatment of behavioral and affective disorders. **Therapy and Counseling:** Principles, methods, and procedures for diagnosis, treatment, and rehabilitation of physical and mental dysfunctions and for career counseling and guidance. **Biology:** Plant and animal organisms and their tissues, cells, functions, interdependencies, and interactions with each other and the environment. **Customer and Personal Service:** Principles and processes for providing customer and personal services. This includes customer needs assessment, meeting of quality standards for services, and evaluation of customer satisfaction. **Sociology and Anthropology:** Group behavior and dynamics, societal trends and influences, human migrations, ethnicity, and cultures and their history and origins.

Respiratory Therapists

- ◎ Education/Training Required: Associate degree
- ◎ Annual Earnings: $45,140
- ◎ Growth: 28.4%
- ◎ Annual Job Openings: 7,000
- ◎ Self-Employed: 0.4%
- ◎ Part-Time: 15.9%

Assess, treat, and care for patients with breathing disorders. Assume primary responsibility for all respiratory care modalities, including the supervision of respiratory therapy technicians. Initiate and conduct therapeutic procedures; maintain patient records; and

select, assemble, check, and operate equipment. Set up and operate devices such as mechanical ventilators, therapeutic gas administration apparatus, environmental control systems, and aerosol generators, following specified parameters of treatment. Provide emergency care, including artificial respiration, external cardiac massage, and assistance with cardiopulmonary resuscitation. Determine requirements for treatment, such as type, method, and duration of therapy; precautions to be taken; and medication and dosages, compatible with physicians' orders. Monitor patient's physiological responses to therapy, such as vital signs, arterial blood gases, and blood chemistry changes, and consult with physician if adverse reactions occur. Read prescription, measure arterial blood gases, and review patient information to assess patient condition. Work as part of a team of physicians, nurses, and other health-care professionals to manage patient care. Enforce safety rules and ensure careful adherence to physicians' orders. Maintain charts that contain patients' pertinent identification and therapy information. Inspect, clean, test, and maintain respiratory therapy equipment to ensure equipment is functioning safely and efficiently, ordering repairs when necessary. Educate patients and their families about their conditions and teach appropriate disease management techniques, such as breathing exercises and the use of medications and respiratory equipment. Explain treatment procedures to patients to gain cooperation and allay fears. Relay blood analysis results to a physician. Perform pulmonary function and adjust equipment to obtain optimum results in therapy. Perform bronchopulmonary drainage and assist or instruct patients in performance of breathing exercises. Demonstrate respiratory care procedures to trainees and other health-care personnel. Teach, train, supervise, and utilize the assistance of students, respiratory therapy technicians, and assistants. Make emergency visits to resolve equipment problems. Use a variety of testing techniques to assist doctors in cardiac and pulmonary research and to diagnose disorders. Conduct tests, such as electrocardiograms (EKGs), stress testing, and lung capacity tests, to evaluate patients' cardiopulmonary functions.

SKILLS—Most Important: Science Skills; Mathematics Skills; Communication Skills. **Other Above-Average Skills:** Social Skills; Thought-Processing Skills.

GOE—Interest Area: 08. Health Science. **Work Group:** 08.07. Medical Therapy. **Other Jobs in This Group:** Audiologists; Massage Therapists; Occupational Therapist Aides; Occupational Therapist Assistants; Occupational Therapists; Physical Therapist Aides; Physical Therapist Assistants; Physical Therapists; Radiation Therapists; Recreational Therapists; Respiratory Therapy Technicians; Speech-Language Pathologists. **PERSONALITY TYPE:** Investigative. Investigative occupations frequently involve working with ideas and require an extensive amount of thinking. These occupations can involve searching for facts and figuring out problems mentally.

EDUCATION/TRAINING PROGRAM(S)—Respiratory Care Therapy/Therapist. **RELATED KNOWLEDGE/COURSES—Medicine and Dentistry:** The information and techniques needed to diagnose and treat human injuries, diseases, and deformities. This includes symptoms, treatment alternatives, drug properties and interactions, and preventive healthcare measures. **Psychology:** Human behavior and performance; individual differences in ability, personality, and interests; learning and motivation; psychological research methods; and the assessment and treatment of behavioral and affective disorders. **Biology:** Plant and animal organisms and their tissues, cells, functions, interdependencies, and interactions with each other and the environment. **Customer and Personal Service:** Principles and processes for providing customer and personal services. This includes customer needs assessment, meeting of quality standards for services, and evaluation of customer satisfaction. **Therapy and Counseling:** Principles, methods, and procedures for diagnosis, treatment, and rehabilitation of physical and mental dysfunctions and for career counseling and guidance. **Chemistry:** The chemical composition, structure, and properties of substances and of the chemical processes and transformations that they undergo. This includes uses of chemicals and their danger signs, production techniques, and disposal methods.

Rough Carpenters

- Education/Training Required: Long-term on-the-job training
- Annual Earnings: $35,580
- Growth: 13.8%
- Annual Job Openings: 210,000
- Self-Employed: 32.4%
- Part-Time: 8.2%

The job openings listed here are shared with Construction Carpenters.

Build rough wooden structures, such as concrete forms, scaffolds, tunnel, bridge, or sewer supports, billboard signs, and temporary frame shelters, according to sketches, blueprints, or oral instructions. Study blueprints and diagrams to determine dimensions of structure or form to be constructed. Measure materials or distances, using square, measuring tape, or rule to lay out work. Cut or saw boards, timbers, or plywood to required size, using handsaw, power saw, or woodworking machine. Assemble and fasten material together to construct wood or metal framework of structure, using bolts, nails, or screws. Anchor and brace forms and other structures in place, using nails, bolts, anchor rods, steel cables, planks, wedges, and timbers. Mark cutting lines on materials, using pencil and scriber. Erect forms, framework, scaffolds, hoists, roof supports, or chutes, using hand tools, plumb rule, and level. Install rough door and window frames, subflooring, fixtures, or temporary supports in structures undergoing construction or repair. Examine structural timbers and supports to detect decay and replace timbers as required, using hand tools, nuts, and bolts. Bore boltholes in timber, masonry, or concrete walls, using power drill. Fabricate parts, using woodworking and metalworking machines. Dig or direct digging of post holes and set poles to support structures. Build sleds from logs and timbers for use in hauling camp buildings and machinery through wooded areas. Build chutes for pouring concrete.

SKILLS—Most Important: Mathematics Skills; Equipment/Technology Analysis Skills; Equipment Use/Maintenance Skills. **Other Above-Average Skills:** Management Skills.

GOE—Interest Area: 02. Architecture and Construction. **Work Group:** 02.04. Construction

Crafts. **Other Jobs in This Group:** Boilermakers; Brickmasons and Blockmasons; Carpet Installers; Cement Masons and Concrete Finishers; Commercial Divers; Construction Carpenters; Crane and Tower Operators; Drywall and Ceiling Tile Installers; Electricians; Fence Erectors; Floor Layers, Except Carpet, Wood, and Hard Tiles; Floor Sanders and Finishers; Glaziers; Hazardous Materials Removal Workers; Insulation Workers, Floor, Ceiling, and Wall; Insulation Workers, Mechanical; Manufactured Building and Mobile Home Installers; Operating Engineers and Other Construction Equipment Operators; Painters, Construction and Maintenance; Paperhangers; Paving, Surfacing, and Tamping Equipment Operators; Pile-Driver Operators; Pipe Fitters and Steamfitters; Pipelayers; Plasterers and Stucco Masons; Plumbers; Plumbers, Pipefitters, and Steamfitters; Rail-Track Laying and Maintenance Equipment Operators; Refractory Materials Repairers, Except Brickmasons; Reinforcing Iron and Rebar Workers; Riggers; Roofers; Security and Fire Alarm Systems Installers; Segmental Pavers; Sheet Metal Workers; Stone Cutters and Carvers, Manufacturing; Stonemasons; Structural Iron and Steel Workers; Tapers; Terrazzo Workers and Finishers; Tile and Marble Setters. **PERSONALITY TYPE:** Realistic. Realistic occupations frequently involve work activities that include practical, hands-on problems and solutions. They often deal with plants, animals, and real-world materials like wood, tools, and machinery. Many of the occupations require working outside and do not involve a lot of paperwork or working closely with others.

EDUCATION/TRAINING PROGRAM(S)—Carpentry/Carpenter. **RELATED KNOWLEDGE/COURSES—Building and Construction:** The materials, methods, and tools involved in the construction or repair of houses, buildings, or other structures such as highways and roads. **Design:** Design techniques, tools, and principles involved in production of precision technical plans, blueprints, drawings, and models. **Engineering and Technology:** The practical application of engineering science and technology. This includes applying principles, techniques, procedures, and equipment to the design and production of various goods and services. **Mechanical Devices:** Machines and tools, including their designs, uses, repair, and maintenance. **Production and Processing:** Raw materials, production processes, quality control, costs, and other techniques for maximizing the effective manufacture and distribution of goods. **Public Safety and Security:** Relevant equipment, policies, procedures, and strategies to promote effective local, state, or national security operations for the protection of people, data, property, and institutions.

Sales Agents, Financial Services

- Education/Training Required: Bachelor's degree
- Annual Earnings: $67,130
- Growth: 11.5%
- Annual Job Openings: 37,000
- Self-Employed: 12.5%
- Part-Time: 8.4%

The job openings listed here are shared with Sales Agents, Securities and Commodities.

Sell financial services such as loan, tax, and securities counseling to customers of financial institutions and business establishments. Determine customers' financial services needs and prepare proposals to sell services that address these needs. Contact prospective customers to present information and explain available services. Sell services and equipment, such as trusts, investments, and check processing services. Prepare forms or agreements to complete sales. Develop prospects from current commercial customers, referral leads, and sales and trade meetings. Review business trends in order to advise customers regarding expected fluctuations. Make presentations on financial services to groups to attract new clients. Evaluate costs and revenue of agreements to determine continued profitability.

SKILLS—Most Important: Social Skills; Communication Skills; Mathematics Skills. **Other Above-Average Skills:** Thought-Processing Skills; Management Skills.

GOE—Interest Area: 06. Finance and Insurance. **Work Group:** 06.05. Finance/Insurance Sales and Support. **Other Jobs in This Group:** Advertising Sales Agents; Insurance Sales Agents; Personal Financial Advisors; Sales Agents, Securities and Commodities; Securities, Commodities, and Financial Services Sales Agents.

PERSONALITY TYPE: Enterprising. Enterprising occupations frequently involve starting up and carrying out projects. These occupations can involve leading people and making many decisions. They sometimes require risk taking and often deal with business.

EDUCATION/TRAINING PROGRAM(S)—Financial Planning and Services; Investments and Securities; Business and Personal/Financial Services Marketing Operations. **RELATED KNOWLEDGE/COURSES—Sales and Marketing:** Principles and methods for showing, promoting, and selling products or services. This includes marketing strategy and tactics, product demonstration, sales techniques, and sales control systems. **Economics and Accounting:** Economic and accounting principles and practices, the financial markets, banking, and the analysis and reporting of financial data. **Customer and Personal Service:** Principles and processes for providing customer and personal services. This includes customer needs assessment, meeting of quality standards for services, and evaluation of customer satisfaction. **Mathematics:** Arithmetic, algebra, geometry, calculus, and statistics and their applications. **Law and Government:** Laws, legal codes, court procedures, precedents, government regulations, executive orders, agency rules, and the democratic political process. **Personnel and Human Resources:** Principles and procedures for personnel recruitment, selection, training, compensation and benefits, labor relations and negotiation, and personnel information systems.

Sales Agents, Securities and Commodities

- Education/Training Required: Bachelor's degree
- Annual Earnings: $67,130
- Growth: 11.5%
- Annual Job Openings: 37,000
- Self-Employed: 12.5%
- Part-Time: 8.4%

The job openings listed here are shared with Sales Agents, Financial Services.

Buy and sell securities in investment and trading firms and develop and implement financial plans for individuals, businesses, and organizations. Complete sales order tickets and submit for processing of client requested transactions. Interview clients to determine clients' assets, liabilities, cash flow, insurance coverage, tax status, and financial objectives. Record transactions accurately and keep clients informed about transactions. Develop financial plans based on analysis of clients' financial status and discuss financial options with clients. Review all securities transactions to ensure accuracy of information and ensure that trades conform to regulations of governing agencies. Offer advice on the purchase or sale of particular securities. Relay buy or sell orders to securities exchanges or to firm trading departments. Identify potential clients, using advertising campaigns, mailing lists, and personal contacts. Review financial periodicals, stock and bond reports, business publications, and other material to identify potential investments for clients and to keep abreast of trends affecting market conditions. Contact prospective customers to determine customer needs, present information, and explain available services. Prepare documents needed to implement plans selected by clients. Analyze market conditions to determine optimum times to execute securities transactions. Explain stock market terms and trading practices to clients. Inform and advise concerned parties regarding fluctuations and securities transactions affecting plans or accounts. Calculate costs for billings and commissions purposes. Supply the latest price quotes on any security, as well as information on the activities and financial positions of the corporations issuing these securities. Prepare financial reports to monitor client or corporate finances. Read corporate reports and calculate ratios to determine best prospects for profit on stock purchases and to monitor client accounts.

SKILLS—Most Important: Social Skills; Thought-Processing Skills; Mathematics Skills. **Other Above-Average Skills:** Communication Skills; Management Skills.

GOE—Interest Area: 06. Finance and Insurance. **Work Group:** 06.05. Finance/Insurance Sales and Support. **Other Jobs in This Group:** Advertising Sales Agents; Insurance Sales Agents; Personal Financial Advisors; Sales Agents, Financial Services; Securities, Commodities, and Financial Services Sales Agents. **PERSONALITY TYPE:** Enterprising. Enterprising occupations frequently involve starting up and carrying out projects.

These occupations can involve leading people and making many decisions. They sometimes require risk taking and often deal with business.

EDUCATION/TRAINING PROGRAM(S)—Financial Planning and Services; Investments and Securities. **RELATED KNOWLEDGE/COURSES—Customer and Personal Service:** Principles and processes for providing customer and personal services. This includes customer needs assessment, meeting of quality standards for services, and evaluation of customer satisfaction. **Economics and Accounting:** Economic and accounting principles and practices, the financial markets, banking, and the analysis and reporting of financial data. **Sales and Marketing:** Principles and methods for showing, promoting, and selling products or services. This includes marketing strategy and tactics, product demonstration, sales techniques, and sales control systems. **Clerical Practices:** Administrative and clerical procedures and systems such as word processing, managing files and records, stenography and transcription, designing forms, and other office procedures and terminology. **Law and Government:** Laws, legal codes, court procedures, precedents, government regulations, executive orders, agency rules, and the democratic political process. **Mathematics:** Arithmetic, algebra, geometry, calculus, and statistics and their applications.

Sales Engineers

- Education/Training Required: Bachelor's degree
- Annual Earnings: $74,200
- Growth: 14.0%
- Annual Job Openings: 8,000
- Self-Employed: 0.7%
- Part-Time: 1.8%

Sell business goods or services, the selling of which requires a technical background equivalent to a baccalaureate degree in engineering. Plan and modify product configurations to meet customer needs. Confer with customers and engineers to assess equipment needs and to determine system requirements. Collaborate with sales teams to understand customer requirements, to promote the sale of company products, and to provide sales support. Secure and renew orders and arrange delivery. Develop, present, or respond to proposals for specific customer requirements, including request for proposal responses and industry-specific solutions. Sell products requiring extensive technical expertise and support for installation and use, such as material handling equipment, numerical-control machinery, and computer systems. Diagnose problems with installed equipment. Prepare and deliver technical presentations that explain products or services to customers and prospective customers. Recommend improved materials or machinery to customers, documenting how such changes will lower costs or increase production. Provide technical and non-technical support and services to clients or other staff members regarding the use, operation, and maintenance of equipment. Research and identify potential customers for products or services. Visit prospective buyers at commercial, industrial, or other establishments to show samples or catalogs and to inform them about product pricing, availability, and advantages. Create sales or service contracts for products or services. Arrange for demonstrations or trial installations of equipment. Keep informed on industry news and trends; products; services; competitors; relevant information about legacy, existing, and emerging technologies; and the latest product-line developments. Attend company training seminars to become familiar with product lines. Provide information needed for the development of custom-made machinery. Develop sales plans to introduce products in new markets. Write technical documentation for products. Identify resale opportunities and support them to achieve sales plans. Document account activities, generate reports, and keep records of business transactions with customers and suppliers.

SKILLS—Most Important: Science Skills; Computer Programming Skills; Equipment/Technology Analysis Skills. **Other Above-Average Skills:** Mathematics Skills; Management Skills; Equipment Use/Maintenance Skills; Thought-Processing Skills; Communication Skills.

GOE—Interest Area: 14. Retail and Wholesale Sales and Service. **Work Group:** 14.02. Technical Sales. **Other Jobs in This Group:** Sales Representatives, Wholesale and Manufacturing, Technical and Scientific Products. **PERSONALITY TYPE:** Enterprising. Enterprising occupations frequently involve starting up and carrying out projects. These occupations can involve leading people and making many decisions. They sometimes require risk taking and often deal with business.

EDUCATION/TRAINING PROGRAM(S)—Selling Skills and Sales Operations. **RELATED KNOWLEDGE/COURSES—Sales and Marketing:** Principles and methods for showing, promoting, and selling products or services. This includes marketing strategy and tactics, product demonstration, sales techniques, and sales control systems. **Engineering and Technology:** The practical application of engineering science and technology. This includes applying principles, techniques, procedures, and equipment to the design and production of various goods and services. **Design:** Design techniques, tools, and principles involved in production of precision technical plans, blueprints, drawings, and models. **Computers and Electronics:** Circuit boards; processors; chips; electronic equipment; and computer hardware and software, including applications and programming. **Customer and Personal Service:** Principles and processes for providing customer and personal services. This includes customer needs assessment, meeting of quality standards for services, and evaluation of customer satisfaction. **Physics:** Physical principles and laws and their interrelationships and applications to understanding fluid, material, and atmospheric dynamics and mechanical, electrical, atomic, and subatomic structures and processes.

Sales Managers

- Education/Training Required: Work experience plus degree
- Annual Earnings: $87,580
- Growth: 19.7%
- Annual Job Openings: 40,000
- Self-Employed: 3.5%
- Part-Time: 4.5%

Direct the actual distribution or movement of a product or service to the customer. Coordinate sales distribution by establishing sales territories, quotas, and goals and establish training programs for sales representatives. Analyze sales statistics gathered by staff to determine sales potential and inventory requirements and monitor the preferences of customers. Resolve customer complaints regarding sales and service. Monitor customer preferences to determine focus of sales efforts. Direct and coordinate activities involving sales of manufactured products, services, commodities, real estate, or other subjects of sale. Determine price schedules and discount rates. Review operational records and reports to project sales and determine profitability. Direct, coordinate, and review activities in sales and service accounting and recordkeeping and in receiving and shipping operations. Confer or consult with department heads to plan advertising services and to secure information on equipment and customer specifications. Advise dealers and distributors on policies and operating procedures to ensure functional effectiveness of business. Prepare budgets and approve budget expenditures. Represent company at trade association meetings to promote products. Plan and direct staffing, training, and performance evaluations to develop and control sales and service programs. Visit franchised dealers to stimulate interest in establishment or expansion of leasing programs. Confer with potential customers regarding equipment needs and advise customers on types of equipment to purchase. Oversee regional and local sales managers and their staffs. Direct clerical staff to keep records of export correspondence, bid requests, and credit collections and to maintain current information on tariffs, licenses, and restrictions. Direct foreign sales and service outlets of an organization. Assess marketing potential of new and existing store locations, considering statistics and expenditures.

SKILLS—Most Important: Social Skills; Management Skills; Thought-Processing Skills. **Other Above-Average Skills:** Communication Skills; Mathematics Skills.

GOE—Interest Area: 14. Retail and Wholesale Sales and Service. **Work Group:** 14.01. Managerial Work in Retail/Wholesale Sales and Service. **Other Jobs in This Group:** Advertising and Promotions Managers; First-Line Supervisors/Managers of Non-Retail Sales Workers; First-Line Supervisors/Managers of Retail Sales Workers; Funeral Directors; Marketing Managers; Property, Real Estate, and Community Association Managers; Purchasing Managers. **PERSONALITY TYPE:** Enterprising. Enterprising occupations frequently involve starting up and carrying out projects. These occupations can involve leading people and making many decisions. They sometimes require risk taking and often deal with business.

EDUCATION/TRAINING PROGRAM(S)—Consumer Merchandising/Retailing Management; Business/Commerce, General; Business Administration and Management, General; Marketing/Marketing Management, General; Marketing, Other. **RELATED**

KNOWLEDGE/COURSES—Sales and Marketing: Principles and methods for showing, promoting, and selling products or services. This includes marketing strategy and tactics, product demonstration, sales techniques, and sales control systems. **Computers and Electronics:** Circuit boards; processors; chips; electronic equipment; and computer hardware and software, including applications and programming. **Mathematics:** Arithmetic, algebra, geometry, calculus, and statistics and their applications. **Administration and Manage-ment:** Business and management principles involved in strategic planning, resource allocation, human resources modeling, leadership technique, production methods, and coordination of people and resources. **Law and Government:** Laws, legal codes, court procedures, precedents, government regulations, executive orders, agency rules, and the democratic political process. **Customer and Personal Service:** Principles and processes for providing customer and personal services. This includes customer needs assessment, meeting of quality standards for services, and evaluation of customer satisfaction.

Sales Representatives, Wholesale and Manufacturing, Except Technical and Scientific Products

- Education/Training Required: Moderate-term on-the-job training
- Annual Earnings: $47,380
- Growth: 12.9%
- Annual Job Openings: 169,000
- Self-Employed: 3.5%
- Part-Time: 7.3%

Sell goods for wholesalers or manufacturers to businesses or groups of individuals. Work requires substantial knowledge of items sold. Answer customers' questions about products, prices, availability, product uses, and credit terms. Recommend products to customers based on customers' needs and interests. Contact regular and prospective customers to demonstrate products, explain product features, and solicit orders. Estimate or quote prices, credit or contract terms, warranties, and delivery dates. Consult with clients after sales or contract signings to resolve problems and to provide ongoing support. Prepare drawings, estimates, and bids that meet specific customer needs. Provide customers with product samples and catalogs. Identify prospective customers by using business directories, following leads from existing clients, participating in organizations and clubs, and attending trade shows and conferences. Arrange and direct delivery and installation of products and equipment. Monitor market conditions; product innovations; and competitors' products, prices, and sales. Negotiate details of contracts and payments and prepare sales contracts and order forms. Perform administrative duties, such as preparing sales budgets and reports, keeping sales records, and filing expense account reports. Obtain credit information about prospective customers. Forward orders to manufacturers. Check stock levels and reorder merchandise as necessary. Plan, assemble, and stock product displays in retail stores or make recommendations to retailers regarding product displays, promotional programs, and advertising. Negotiate with retail merchants to improve product exposure such as shelf positioning and advertising. Train customers' employees to operate and maintain new equipment. Buy products from manufacturers or brokerage firms and distribute them to wholesale and retail clients.

SKILLS—Most Important: Social Skills; Management Skills; Communication Skills. **Other Above-Average Skills:** Thought-Processing Skills; Mathematics Skills.

GOE—Interest Area: 14. Retail and Wholesale Sales and Service. **Work Group:** 14.03. General Sales. **Other Jobs in This Group:** Parts Salespersons; Real Estate Brokers; Real Estate Sales Agents; Retail Salespersons; Service Station Attendants. **PERSONALITY TYPE:** Enterprising. Enterprising occupations frequently involve starting up and carrying out projects. These occupations can involve leading people and making many decisions. They sometimes require risk taking and often deal with business.

EDUCATION/TRAINING PROGRAM(S)—Insurance; Sales, Distribution, and Marketing Operations, General; General Merchandising, Sales, and Related Marketing Operations, Other; Fashion Merchandising; Apparel and Accessories Marketing Operations; Special Products Marketing Operations; Specialized Merchandising, Sales, and Related Marketing Operations, Other; Business, Management, Marketing, and Related Support Services, Other. **RELATED KNOWLEDGE/COURSES—Sales and Marketing:** Principles and methods for showing, promoting, and selling products or services. This includes marketing strategy and tactics, product demonstration, sales techniques, and sales control systems. **Customer and Personal Service:** Principles and processes for providing customer and personal services. This includes customer needs assessment, meeting of quality standards for services, and evaluation of customer satisfaction. **Economics and Accounting:** Economic and accounting principles and practices, the financial markets, banking, and the analysis and reporting of financial data. **Administration and Management:** Business and management principles involved in strategic planning, resource allocation, human resources modeling, leadership technique, production methods, and coordination of people and resources. **Transportation:** Principles and methods for moving people or goods by air, rail, sea, or road, including the relative costs and benefits. **Mathematics:** Arithmetic, algebra, geometry, calculus, and statistics and their applications.

School Psychologists

- Education/Training Required: Doctoral degree
- Annual Earnings: $57,170
- Growth: 19.1%
- Annual Job Openings: 10,000
- Self-Employed: 38.2%
- Part-Time: 22.8%

The job openings listed here are shared with Clinical Psychologists and Counseling Psychologists.

Investigate processes of learning and teaching and develop psychological principles and techniques applicable to educational problems. Compile and interpret students' test results, along with information from teachers and parents, to diagnose conditions and to help assess eligibility for special services. Report any pertinent information to the proper authorities in cases of child endangerment, neglect, or abuse. Assess an individual child's needs, limitations, and potential, using observation, review of school records, and consultation with parents and school personnel. Select, administer, and score psychological tests. Provide consultation to parents, teachers, administrators, and others on topics such as learning styles and behavior modification techniques. Promote an understanding of child development and its relationship to learning and behavior. Collaborate with other educational professionals to develop teaching strategies and school programs. Counsel children and families to help solve conflicts and problems in learning and adjustment. Develop individualized educational plans in collaboration with teachers and other staff members. Maintain student records, including special education reports, confidential records, records of services provided, and behavioral data. Serve as a resource to help families and schools deal with crises, such as separation and loss. Attend workshops, seminars, or professional meetings to remain informed of new developments in school psychology. Design classes and programs to meet the needs of special students. Refer students and their families to appropriate community agencies for medical, vocational, or social services. Initiate and direct efforts to foster tolerance, understanding, and appreciation of diversity in school communities. Collect and analyze data to evaluate the effectiveness of academic programs and other services, such as behavioral management systems. Provide educational programs on topics such as classroom management, teaching strategies, or parenting skills. Conduct research to generate new knowledge that can be used to address learning and behavior issues.

SKILLS—Most Important: Social Skills; Communication Skills; Thought-Processing Skills. Other Above-Average Skills: Science Skills; Mathematics Skills.

GOE—Interest Area: 15. Scientific Research, Engineering, and Mathematics. Work Group: 15.04. Social Sciences. Other Jobs in This Group: Anthropologists; Anthropologists and Archeologists; Archeologists; Economists; Historians; Industrial-Organizational Psychologists; Political Scientists; Sociologists. PERSONALITY TYPE: Investigative. Investigative occupations frequently involve working with ideas and require an extensive amount of thinking. These occupations can involve searching for facts and figuring out problems mentally.

EDUCATION/TRAINING PROGRAM(S)—Educational Assessment, Testing, and Measurement; Psychology, General; Clinical Psychology; Counseling Psychology; Developmental and Child Psychology; School Psychology; Psychoanalysis and Psychotherapy. RELATED KNOWLEDGE/COURSES—Therapy and Counseling: Principles, methods, and procedures for diagnosis, treatment, and rehabilitation of physical and mental dysfunctions and for career counseling and guidance. Psychology: Human behavior and performance; individual differences in ability, personality, and interests; learning and motivation; psychological research methods; and the assessment and treatment of behavioral and affective disorders. Sociology and Anthropology: Group behavior and dynamics, societal trends and influences, human migrations, ethnicity, and cultures and their history and origins. Philosophy and Theology: Different philosophical systems and religions. This includes their basic principles, values, ethics, ways of thinking, customs, practices, and impact on human culture. Education and Training: Principles and methods for curriculum and training design, teaching and instruction for individuals and groups, and the measurement of training effects. Customer and Personal Service: Principles and processes for providing customer and personal services. This includes customer needs assessment, meeting of quality standards for services, and evaluation of customer satisfaction.

Secondary School Teachers, Except Special and Vocational Education

- ◎ Education/Training Required: Bachelor's degree
- ◎ Annual Earnings: $46,060
- ◎ Growth: 14.4%
- ◎ Annual Job Openings: 107,000
- ◎ Self-Employed: 0.0%
- ◎ Part-Time: 9.2%

Instruct students in secondary public or private schools in one or more subjects at the secondary level, such as English, mathematics, or social studies. May be designated according to subject matter specialty, such as typing instructors, commercial teachers, or English teachers. Establish and enforce rules for behavior and procedures for maintaining order among the students for whom they are responsible. Instruct through lectures, discussions, and demonstrations in one or more subjects such as English, mathematics, or social studies. Establish clear objectives for all lessons, units, and projects and communicate those objectives to students. Prepare, administer, and grade tests and assignments to evaluate students' progress. Prepare materials and classrooms for class activities. Adapt teaching methods and instructional materials to meet students' varying needs and interests. Assign and grade classwork and homework. Maintain accurate and complete student records as required by laws, district policies, and administrative regulations. Enforce all administration policies and rules governing students. Observe and evaluate students' performance, behavior, social development, and physical health. Plan and conduct activities for a balanced program of instruction, demonstration, and work time that provides students with opportunities to observe, question, and investigate. Prepare students for later grades by encouraging them to explore learning opportunities and to persevere with challenging tasks. Guide and counsel students with adjustment and/or academic problems or special academic interests. Instruct and monitor students in the use and care of equipment and materials to prevent injuries and damage. Prepare for assigned classes and show written evidence of preparation upon request of immediate supervisors. Meet with parents and guardians to discuss their children's progress and to determine their priorities for their children and their resource needs. Confer with parents or guardians, other teachers, counselors, and administrators in order to resolve students' behavioral and academic problems. Use computers, audiovisual aids, and other equipment and materials to supplement presentations. Prepare objectives and outlines for courses of study, following curriculum guidelines or requirements of states and schools. Meet with other professionals to discuss individual students' needs and progress.

SKILLS—Most Important: Social Skills; Thought-Processing Skills; Communication Skills. **Other Above-Average Skills:** Management Skills; Equipment/Technology Analysis Skills.

GOE—Interest Area: 05. Education and Training. **Work Group:** 05.02. Preschool, Elementary, and Secondary Teaching and Instructing. **Other Jobs in This Group:** Elementary School Teachers, Except Special Education; Kindergarten Teachers, Except Special Education; Middle School Teachers, Except Special and Vocational Education; Preschool Teachers, Except Special Education; Special Education Teachers, Middle School; Special Education Teachers, Preschool, Kindergarten, and Elementary School; Special Education Teachers, Secondary School; Teacher Assistants; Vocational Education Teachers, Middle School; Vocational Education Teachers, Secondary School. **PERSONALITY TYPE:** Social. Social occupations frequently involve working with, communicating with, and teaching people. These occupations often involve helping or providing service to others.

EDUCATION/TRAINING PROGRAM(S)—Junior High/Intermediate/Middle School Education and Teaching; Secondary Education and Teaching; Teacher Education, Multiple Levels; Waldorf/Steiner Teacher Education; Agricultural Teacher Education; Art Teacher Education; Business Teacher Education; Driver and Safety Teacher Education; English/Language Arts Teacher Education; Foreign Language Teacher Education; Health Teacher Education; others. **RELATED KNOWLEDGE/COURSES—Education and Training:** Principles and methods for curriculum and training design, teaching and instruction for individuals and groups, and the measurement of training effects. **History and Archeology:** Historical events and their causes, indicators, and effects on civilizations and cultures. **Philosophy and Theology:** Different philosophical systems and religions. This includes their basic principles, values, ethics, ways of thinking, customs, practices, and impact on human culture. **Sociology and Anthropology:** Group behavior and dynamics, societal trends and influences, human migrations, ethnicity, and cultures and their history and origins. **Geography:** Principles and methods for describing the features of land, sea, and air masses, including their physical characteristics; locations; interrelationships; and distribution of plant, animal, and human life. **Therapy and Counseling:** Principles, methods, and procedures for diagnosis, treatment, and rehabilitation of physical and mental dysfunctions and for career counseling and guidance.

Self-Enrichment Education Teachers

- Education/Training Required: Work experience in a related occupation
- Annual Earnings: $32,360
- Growth: 25.3%
- Annual Job Openings: 74,000
- Self-Employed: 31.1%
- Part-Time: 45.6%

Teach or instruct courses other than those that normally lead to an occupational objective or degree. Courses may include self-improvement, nonvocational, and nonacademic subjects. Teaching may or may not take place in a traditional educational institution. Adapt teaching methods and instructional materials to meet students' varying needs and interests. Conduct classes, workshops, and demonstrations and provide individual instruction to teach topics and skills such as cooking, dancing, writing, physical fitness, photography, personal finance, and flying. Monitor students' performance to make suggestions for improvement and to ensure that they satisfy course standards, training requirements, and objectives. Observe students to determine qualifications, limitations, abilities, interests, and other individual characteristics. Instruct students individually and in groups, using various teaching methods such as lectures, discussions, and demonstrations. Establish clear objectives for all lessons, units, and projects and communicate those objectives to students. Instruct and monitor students in use and care of equipment and materials to prevent injury and damage. Prepare students for further development by encouraging them to explore learning opportunities and to persevere with challenging tasks. Prepare materials and classrooms for class activities. Enforce policies and rules governing students. Plan and conduct activities for a balanced program of instruction, demonstration, and work time that provides students with opportunities to observe, question, and investigate. Prepare instructional program objectives, outlines, and lesson plans. Maintain accurate and complete student records as required by administrative policy. Participate in publicity planning and student recruitment. Plan and supervise class projects, field trips, visits by guest speakers, contests, or other experiential activities and guide students in learning from those activities. Attend professional meetings, conferences, and workshops in order to maintain and improve professional competence. Meet with other instructors to discuss individual students and their progress. Confer with other teachers and professionals to plan and schedule lessons promoting learning and development. Attend staff meetings and serve on committees as required. Prepare and administer written, oral, and performance tests and issue grades in accordance with performance.

SKILLS—Most Important: Social Skills; Thought-Processing Skills; Communication Skills. **Other Above-Average Skills:** None met the criteria.

GOE—Interest Area: 05. Education and Training. **Work Group:** 05.03. Postsecondary and Adult Teaching and Instructing. **Other Jobs in This Group:** Adult Literacy, Remedial Education, and GED Teachers and Instructors; Agricultural Sciences Teachers, Postsecondary; Anthropology and Archeology Teachers, Postsecondary; Architecture Teachers, Postsecondary; Area, Ethnic, and Cultural Studies Teachers, Postsecondary; Art, Drama, and Music Teachers, Postsecondary; Atmospheric, Earth, Marine, and Space Sciences Teachers, Postsecondary; Biological Science Teachers, Postsecondary; Business Teachers, Postsecondary; Chemistry Teachers, Postsecondary; Communications Teachers, Postsecondary; Computer Science Teachers, Postsecondary; Criminal Justice and Law Enforcement Teachers, Postsecondary; Economics Teachers, Postsecondary; Education Teachers, Postsecondary; Engineering Teachers, Postsecondary; English Language and Literature Teachers, Postsecondary; Environmental Science Teachers, Postsecondary; Farm and Home Management Advisors; Foreign Language and Literature Teachers, Postsecondary; Forestry and Conservation Science Teachers, Postsecondary; Geography Teachers, Postsecondary; Graduate Teaching Assistants; Health Specialties Teachers, Postsecondary; History Teachers, Postsecondary; Home Economics Teachers, Postsecondary; Law Teachers, Postsecondary; Library Science Teachers, Postsecondary; Mathematical Science Teachers, Postsecondary; Nursing Instructors and Teachers, Postsecondary; Philosophy and Religion Teachers, Postsecondary; Physics Teachers, Postsecondary; Political Science Teachers, Postsecondary; Psychology Teachers, Postsecondary; Recreation and Fitness Studies Teachers, Postsecondary; Social Work Teachers,

Postsecondary; Sociology Teachers, Postsecondary; Vocational Education Teachers, Postsecondary. **PERSONALITY TYPE:** Social. Social occupations frequently involve working with, communicating with, and teaching people. These occupations often involve helping or providing service to others.

EDUCATION/TRAINING PROGRAM(S)—Adult and Continuing Education and Teaching. **RELATED KNOWLEDGE/COURSES**—**Fine Arts:** The theory and techniques required to compose, produce, and perform works of music, dance, visual arts, drama, and sculpture. **Education and Training:** Principles and methods for curriculum and training design, teaching and instruction for individuals and groups, and the measurement of training effects. **Psychology:** Human behavior and performance; individual differences in ability, personality, and interests; learning and motivation; psychological research methods; and the assessment and treatment of behavioral and affective disorders. **Customer and Personal Service:** Principles and processes for providing customer and personal services. This includes customer needs assessment, meeting of quality standards for services, and evaluation of customer satisfaction. **Sales and Marketing:** Principles and methods for showing, promoting, and selling products or services. This includes marketing strategy and tactics, product demonstration, sales techniques, and sales control systems. **Administration and Management:** Business and management principles involved in strategic planning, resource allocation, human resources modeling, leadership technique, production methods, and coordination of people and resources.

Sheet Metal Workers

- Education/Training Required: Long-term on-the-job training
- Annual Earnings: $36,390
- Growth: 12.2%
- Annual Job Openings: 50,000
- Self-Employed: 4.9%
- Part-Time: 5.7%

Fabricate, assemble, install, and repair sheet metal products and equipment, such as ducts, control boxes, drainpipes, and furnace casings. Work may involve any of the following: setting up and operating fabricating machines to cut, bend, and straighten sheet metal; shaping metal over anvils, blocks, or forms, using hammer; operating soldering and welding equipment to join sheet metal parts; and inspecting, assembling, and smoothing seams and joints of burred surfaces. Determine project requirements, including scope, assembly sequences, and required methods and materials, according to blueprints, drawings, and written or verbal instructions. Lay out, measure, and mark dimensions and reference lines on material such as roofing panels according to drawings or templates, using calculators, scribes, dividers, squares, and rulers. Maneuver completed units into position for installation and anchor the units. Convert blueprints into shop drawings to be followed in the construction and assembly of sheet metal products. Install assemblies such as flashing, pipes, tubes, heating and air conditioning ducts, furnace casings, rain gutters, and downspouts in supportive frameworks. Select gauges and types of sheet metal or non-metallic material according to product specifications. Drill and punch holes in metal for screws, bolts, and rivets. Fasten seams and joints together with welds, bolts, cement, rivets, solder, caulks, metal drive clips, and bonds to assemble components into products or to repair sheet metal items. Fabricate or alter parts at construction sites, using shears, hammers, punches, and drills. Finish parts, using hacksaws and hand, rotary, or squaring shears. Trim, file, grind, deburr, buff, and smooth surfaces, seams, and joints of assembled parts, using hand tools and portable power tools. Maintain equipment, making repairs and modifications when necessary. Shape metal material over anvils, blocks, or other forms, using hand tools. Transport prefabricated parts to construction sites for assembly and installation. Develop and lay out patterns that use materials most efficiently, using computerized metalworking equipment to experiment with different layouts. Inspect individual parts, assemblies, and installations for conformance to specifications and building codes, using measuring instruments such as calipers, scales, and micrometers. Secure metal roof panels in place and interlock and fasten grooved panel edges. Fasten roof panel edges and machine-made molding to structures, nailing or welding pieces into place.

SKILLS—Most Important: Mathematics Skills; Equipment Use/Maintenance Skills; Social Skills. **Other**

Above-Average Skills: Equipment/Technology Analysis Skills; Thought-Processing Skills.

GOE—Interest Area: 02. Architecture and Construction. **Work Group:** 02.04. Construction Crafts. **Other Jobs in This Group:** Boilermakers; Brickmasons and Blockmasons; Carpet Installers; Cement Masons and Concrete Finishers; Commercial Divers; Construction Carpenters; Crane and Tower Operators; Drywall and Ceiling Tile Installers; Electricians; Fence Erectors; Floor Layers, Except Carpet, Wood, and Hard Tiles; Floor Sanders and Finishers; Glaziers; Hazardous Materials Removal Workers; Insulation Workers, Floor, Ceiling, and Wall; Insulation Workers, Mechanical; Manufactured Building and Mobile Home Installers; Operating Engineers and Other Construction Equipment Operators; Painters, Construction and Maintenance; Paperhangers; Paving, Surfacing, and Tamping Equipment Operators; Pile-Driver Operators; Pipe Fitters and Steamfitters; Pipelayers; Plasterers and Stucco Masons; Plumbers; Plumbers, Pipefitters, and Steamfitters; Rail-Track Laying and Maintenance Equipment Operators; Refractory Materials Repairers, Except Brickmasons; Reinforcing Iron and Rebar Workers; Riggers; Roofers; Rough Carpenters; Security and Fire Alarm Systems Installers; Segmental Pavers; Stone Cutters and Carvers, Manufacturing; Stonemasons; Structural Iron and Steel Workers; Tapers; Terrazzo Workers and Finishers; Tile and Marble Setters. **PERSONALITY TYPE:** Realistic. Realistic occupations frequently involve work activities that include practical, hands-on problems and solutions. They often deal with plants, animals, and real-world materials like wood, tools, and machinery. Many of the occupations require working outside and do not involve a lot of paperwork or working closely with others.

EDUCATION/TRAINING PROGRAM(S)—Sheet Metal Technology/Sheetworking. **RELATED KNOWLEDGE/COURSES—Building and Con-struction:** The materials, methods, and tools involved in the construction or repair of houses, buildings, or other structures such as highways and roads. **Mechanical Devices:** Machines and tools, including their designs, uses, repair, and maintenance. **Design:** Design techniques, tools, and principles involved in production of precision technical plans, blueprints, drawings, and models. **Physics:** Physical principles and laws and their interrelationships and applications to understanding fluid, material, and atmospheric dynamics and mechanical, electrical, atom-ic, and subatomic structures and processes. **Production and Processing:** Raw materials, production processes, quality control, costs, and other techniques for maximizing the effective manufacture and distribution of goods. **Mathematics:** Arithmetic, algebra, geometry, calculus, and statistics and their applications.

Sheriffs and Deputy Sheriffs

- Education/Training Required: Long-term on-the-job training
- Annual Earnings: $46,290
- Growth: 15.5%
- Annual Job Openings: 47,000
- Self-Employed: 0.0%
- Part-Time: 1.4%

The job openings listed here are shared with Police Patrol Officers.

Enforce law and order in rural or unincorporated districts or serve legal processes of courts. May patrol courthouse, guard court or grand jury, or escort defendants. Drive vehicles or patrol specific areas to detect law violators, issue citations, and make arrests. Investigate illegal or suspicious activities. Verify that the proper legal charges have been made against law offenders. Execute arrest warrants, locating and taking persons into custody. Record daily activities and submit logs and other related reports and paperwork to appropriate authorities. Patrol and guard courthouses, grand jury rooms, or assigned areas to provide security, enforce laws, maintain order, and arrest violators. Notify patrol units to take violators into custody or to provide needed assistance or medical aid. Place people in protective custody. Serve statements of claims, subpoenas, summonses, jury summonses, orders to pay alimony, and other court orders. Take control of accident scenes to maintain traffic flow, to assist accident victims, and to investigate causes. Question individuals entering secured areas to determine their business, directing and rerouting individuals as necessary. Transport or escort prisoners and defendants en route to courtrooms, prisons or jails, attorneys' offices, or medical facilities.

Locate and confiscate real or personal property, as directed by court order. Manage jail operations and tend to jail inmates.

SKILLS—Most Important: Social Skills; Thought-Processing Skills; Communication Skills. **Other Above-Average Skills:** Science Skills; Equipment/Technology Analysis Skills; Mathematics Skills.

GOE—Interest Area: 12. Law and Public Safety. **Work Group:** 12.04. Law Enforcement and Public Safety. **Other Jobs in This Group:** Bailiffs; Correctional Officers and Jailers; Criminal Investigators and Special Agents; Detectives and Criminal Investigators; Fire Investigators; Forensic Science Technicians; Parking Enforcement Workers; Police and Sheriff's Patrol Officers; Police Detectives; Police Identification and Records Officers; Police Patrol Officers; Transit and Railroad Police. **PERSONALITY TYPE:** Social. Social occupations frequently involve working with, communicating with, and teaching people. These occupations often involve helping or providing service to others.

EDUCATION/TRAINING PROGRAM(S)—Criminal Justice/Police Science; Criminalistics and Criminal Science. **RELATED KNOWLEDGE/COURSES—Public Safety and Security:** Relevant equipment, policies, procedures, and strategies to promote effective local, state, or national security operations for the protection of people, data, property, and institutions. **Law and Government:** Laws, legal codes, court procedures, precedents, government regulations, executive orders, agency rules, and the democratic political process. **Telecommunications:** Transmission, broadcasting, switching, control, and operation of telecommunications systems. **Psychology:** Human behavior and performance; individual differences in ability, personality, and interests; learning and motivation; psychological research methods; and the assessment and treatment of behavioral and affective disorders. **Customer and Personal Service:** Principles and processes for providing customer and personal services. This includes customer needs assessment, meeting of quality standards for services, and evaluation of customer satisfaction. **Therapy and Counseling:** Principles, methods, and procedures for diagnosis, treatment, and rehabilitation of physical and mental dysfunctions and for career counseling and guidance.

Social and Community Service Managers

- Education/Training Required: Bachelor's degree
- Annual Earnings: $49,500
- Growth: 25.5%
- Annual Job Openings: 17,000
- Self-Employed: 2.2%
- Part-Time: 12.5%

Plan, organize, or coordinate the activities of a social service program or community outreach organization. Oversee the program or organization's budget and policies regarding participant involvement, program requirements, and benefits. Work may involve directing social workers, counselors, or probation officers. Establish and maintain relationships with other agencies and organizations in community to meet community needs and to ensure that services are not duplicated. Prepare and maintain records and reports, such as budgets, personnel records, or training manuals. Direct activities of professional and technical staff members and volunteers. Evaluate the work of staff and volunteers to ensure that programs are of appropriate quality and that resources are used effectively. Establish and oversee administrative procedures to meet objectives set by boards of directors or senior management. Participate in the determination of organizational policies regarding such issues as participant eligibility, program requirements, and program benefits. Research and analyze member or community needs to determine program directions and goals. Speak to community groups to explain and interpret agency purposes, programs, and policies. Recruit, interview, and hire or sign up volunteers and staff. Represent organizations in relations with governmental and media institutions. Plan and administer budgets for programs, equipment, and support services. Analyze proposed legislation, regulations, or rule changes to determine how agency services could be impacted. Act as consultants to agency staff and other community programs regarding the interpretation of program-related federal, state, and county regulations and policies. Implement and evaluate staff training programs. Direct fundraising activities and the preparation of public relations materials.

SKILLS—Most Important: Social Skills; Management Skills; Communication Skills. **Other Above-Average Skills:** Thought-Processing Skills; Quality Control Skills.

GOE—Interest Area: 07. Government and Public Administration. **Work Group:** 07.01. Managerial Work in Government and Public Administration. **Other Jobs in This Group:** No other jobs in this group. **PERSONALITY TYPE:** Social. Social occupations frequently involve working with, communicating with, and teaching people. These occupations often involve helping or providing service to others.

EDUCATION/TRAINING PROGRAM(S)—Human Services, General; Community Organization and Advocacy; Public Administration; Business/Commerce, General; Business Administration and Management, General; Non-Profit/Public/Organizational Management; Entrepreneurship/Entrepreneurial Studies; Business, Management, Marketing, and Related Support Services, Other. **RELATED KNOWLEDGE/COURSES—Sociology and Anthropology:** Group behavior and dynamics, societal trends and influences, human migrations, ethnicity, and cultures and their history and origins. **Therapy and Counseling:** Principles, methods, and procedures for diagnosis, treatment, and rehabilitation of physical and mental dysfunctions and for career counseling and guidance. **Psychology:** Human behavior and performance; individual differences in ability, personality, and interests; learning and motivation; psychological research methods; and the assessment and treatment of behavioral and affective disorders. **Education and Training:** Principles and methods for curriculum and training design, teaching and instruction for individuals and groups, and the measurement of training effects. **Customer and Personal Service:** Principles and processes for providing customer and personal services. This includes customer needs assessment, meeting of quality standards for services, and evaluation of customer satisfaction. **Philosophy and Theology:** Different philosophical systems and religions. This includes their basic principles, values, ethics, ways of thinking, customs, practices, and impact on human culture.

Social and Human Service Assistants

- Education/Training Required: Moderate-term on-the-job training
- Annual Earnings: $25,030
- Growth: 29.7%
- Annual Job Openings: 61,000
- Self-Employed: 0.1%
- Part-Time: 16.0%

Assist professionals from a wide variety of fields, such as psychology, rehabilitation, or social work, to provide client services, as well as support for families. May assist clients in identifying available benefits and social and community services and help clients obtain them. May assist social workers with developing, organizing, and conducting programs to prevent and resolve problems relevant to substance abuse, human relationships, rehabilitation, or adult daycare. Provide information and refer individuals to public or private agencies or community services for assistance. Keep records and prepare reports for owner or management concerning visits with clients. Visit individuals in homes or attend group meetings to provide information on agency services, requirements, and procedures. Advise clients regarding food stamps, child care, food, money management, sanitation, or housekeeping. Submit reports and review reports or problems with superior. Oversee day-to-day group activities of residents in institution. Interview individuals and family members to compile information on social, educational, criminal, institutional, or drug history. Meet with youth groups to acquaint them with consequences of delinquent acts. Transport and accompany clients to shopping areas or to appointments, using automobile. Explain rules established by owner or management, such as sanitation and maintenance requirements and parking regulations. Observe and discuss meal preparation and suggest alternate methods of food preparation. Demonstrate use and care of equipment for tenant use. Consult with supervisor concerning programs for individual families. Monitor free, supplementary meal program to ensure cleanliness of facility and that eligibility guidelines are met for persons receiving meals. Observe clients' food selections and recommend alternate economical and nutritional food choices. Inform tenants of facilities such as laundries and playgrounds. Care for children in client's home during client's appointments. Assist in locating housing for displaced individuals. Assist clients with preparation of forms, such as tax or rent forms. Assist in planning of food budget, using charts and sample budgets.

SKILLS—Most Important: Social Skills; Communication Skills; Management Skills. **Other Above-Average Skills:** Thought-Processing Skills.

GOE—Interest Area: 10. Human Service. **Work Group:** 10.01. Counseling and Social Work. **Other Jobs in This Group:** Child, Family, and School Social Workers; Clinical Psychologists; Clinical, Counseling, and School Psychologists; Counseling Psychologists; Marriage and Family Therapists; Medical and Public Health Social Workers; Mental Health and Substance Abuse Social Workers; Mental Health Counselors; Probation Officers and Correctional Treatment Specialists; Rehabilitation Counselors; Residential Advisors; Substance Abuse and Behavioral Disorder Counselors. **PERSONALITY TYPE:** Social. Social occupations frequently involve working with, communicating with, and teaching people. These occupations often involve helping or providing service to others.

EDUCATION/TRAINING PROGRAM(S)—Mental and Social Health Services and Allied Professions, Other. **RELATED KNOWLEDGE/COURSES— Therapy and Counseling:** Principles, methods, and procedures for diagnosis, treatment, and rehabilitation of physical and mental dysfunctions and for career counseling and guidance. **Psychology:** Human behavior and performance; individual differences in ability, personality, and interests; learning and motivation; psychological research methods; and the assessment and treatment of behavioral and affective disorders. **Philosophy and Theology:** Different philosophical systems and religions. This includes their basic principles, values, ethics, ways of thinking, customs, practices, and impact on human culture. **Sociology and Anthropology:** Group behavior and dynamics, societal trends and influences, human migrations, ethnicity, and cultures and their history and origins. **Clerical Practices:** Administrative and clerical procedures and systems such as word processing, managing files and records, stenography and transcription, designing forms, and other office procedures and terminology. **Customer and Personal Service:** Principles and processes for providing customer and personal services. This includes customer needs assessment, meeting of quality standards for services, and evaluation of customer satisfaction.

Social Work Teachers, Postsecondary

- Education/Training Required: Master's degree
- Annual Earnings: $52,660
- Growth: 32.2%
- Annual Job Openings: 329,000
- Self-Employed: 0.4%
- Part-Time: 27.3%

The job openings listed here are shared with 35 other postsecondary teaching occupations. For a complete list, see the beginning of this section.

Teach courses in social work. Initiate, facilitate, and moderate classroom discussions. Evaluate and grade students' classwork, assignments, and papers. Prepare and deliver lectures to undergraduate or graduate students on topics such as family behavior, child and adolescent mental health, and social intervention evaluation. Keep abreast of developments in their field by reading current literature, talking with colleagues, and participating in professional conferences. Supervise students' laboratory work and fieldwork. Conduct research in a particular field of knowledge and publish findings in professional journals, books, or electronic media. Prepare course materials such as syllabi, homework assignments, and handouts. Maintain regularly scheduled office hours to advise and assist students. Supervise undergraduate or graduate teaching, internship, and research work. Plan, evaluate, and revise curricula, course content, and course materials and methods of instruction. Collaborate with colleagues and with community agencies to address teaching and research issues. Compile, administer, and grade examinations or assign this work to others. Advise students on academic and vocational curricula and on career issues. Maintain student attendance records, grades, and other required records. Write grant proposals to procure external research funding. Serve on academic or administrative committees that deal with institutional policies, departmental matters, and academic issues. Perform administrative duties such as serving as department head. Compile bibliographies of specialized materials for outside reading assignments. Select and obtain materials and supplies such as textbooks and laboratory equipment. Participate in student recruitment, registration, and placement activities. Participate in campus and community events. Provide professional consulting services to government and industry. Act as advisers to student organizations.

SKILLS—Most Important: Social Skills; Thought-Processing Skills; Communication Skills. **Other Above-Average Skills:** Science Skills; Management Skills; Equipment/Technology Analysis Skills.

GOE—Interest Area: 05. Education and Training. **Work Group:** 05.03. Postsecondary and Adult Teaching and Instructing. **Other Jobs in This Group:** Adult Literacy, Remedial Education, and GED Teachers and Instructors; Agricultural Sciences Teachers, Postsecondary; Anthropology and Archeology Teachers, Postsecondary; Architecture Teachers, Postsecondary; Area, Ethnic, and Cultural Studies Teachers, Postsecondary; Art, Drama, and Music Teachers, Postsecondary; Atmospheric, Earth, Marine, and Space Sciences Teachers, Postsecondary; Biological Science Teachers, Postsecondary; Business Teachers, Postsecondary; Chemistry Teachers, Postsecondary; Communications Teachers, Postsecondary; Computer Science Teachers, Postsecondary; Criminal Justice and Law Enforcement Teachers, Postsecondary; Economics Teachers, Postsecondary; Education Teachers, Postsecondary; Engineering Teachers, Postsecondary; English Language and Literature Teachers, Postsecondary; Environmental Science Teachers, Postsecondary; Farm and Home Management Advisors; Foreign Language and Literature Teachers, Postsecondary; Forestry and Conservation Science Teachers, Postsecondary; Geography Teachers, Postsecondary; Graduate Teaching Assistants; Health Specialties Teachers, Postsecondary; History Teachers, Postsecondary; Home Economics Teachers, Postsecondary; Law Teachers, Postsecondary; Library Science Teachers, Postsecondary; Mathematical Science Teachers, Postsecondary; Nursing Instructors and Teachers, Postsecondary; Philosophy and Religion Teachers, Postsecondary; Physics Teachers, Postsecondary; Political Science Teachers, Postsecondary; Psychology Teachers, Postsecondary; Recreation and Fitness Studies Teachers, Postsecondary; Self-Enrichment Education Teachers; Sociology Teachers, Postsecondary;

Vocational Education Teachers, Postsecondary. **PERSONALITY TYPE:** No data available.

EDUCATION/TRAINING PROGRAM(S)—Teacher Education and Professional Development, Specific Subject Areas, Other; Social Work; Clinical/Medical Social Work. **RELATED KNOWLEDGE/COURSES—Therapy and Counseling:** Principles, methods, and procedures for diagnosis, treatment, and rehabilitation of physical and mental dysfunctions and for career counseling and guidance. **Sociology and Anthropology:** Group behavior and dynamics, societal trends and influences, human migrations, ethnicity, and cultures and their history and origins. **Psychology:** Human behavior and performance; individual differences in ability, personality, and interests; learning and motivation; psychological research methods; and the assessment and treatment of behavioral and affective disorders. **Education and Training:** Principles and methods for curriculum and training design, teaching and instruction for individuals and groups, and the measurement of training effects. **Philosophy and Theology:** Different philosophical systems and religions. This includes their basic principles, values, ethics, ways of thinking, customs, practices, and impact on human culture. **English Language:** The structure and content of the English language, including the meaning and spelling of words, rules of composition, and grammar.

Sociology Teachers, Postsecondary

- Education/Training Required: Master's degree
- Annual Earnings: $54,320
- Growth: 32.2%
- Annual Job Openings: 329,000
- Self-Employed: 0.4%
- Part-Time: 27.3%

The job openings listed here are shared with 35 other postsecondary teaching occupations. For a complete list, see the beginning of this section.

Teach courses in sociology. Evaluate and grade students' classwork, assignments, and papers. Prepare and deliver lectures to undergraduate and graduate students on topics such as race and ethnic relations, measurement and data collection, and workplace social relations. Initiate, facilitate, and moderate classroom discussions. Prepare course materials such as syllabi, homework assignments, and handouts. Compile, administer, and grade examinations or assign this work to others. Keep abreast of developments in their field by reading current literature, talking with colleagues, and participating in professional conferences. Maintain student attendance records, grades, and other required records. Maintain regularly scheduled office hours in order to advise and assist students. Plan, evaluate, and revise curricula, course content, and course materials and methods of instruction. Advise students on academic and vocational curricula and on career issues. Collaborate with colleagues to address teaching and research issues. Conduct research in a particular field of knowledge and publish findings in professional journals, books, or electronic media. Select and obtain materials and supplies such as textbooks and laboratory equipment. Supervise undergraduate and graduate teaching, internship, and research work. Serve on academic or administrative committees that deal with institutional policies, departmental matters, and academic issues. Participate in student recruitment, registration, and placement activities. Perform administrative duties such as serving as department head. Supervise students' laboratory work and fieldwork. Write grant proposals to procure external research funding. Act as advisers to student organizations. Compile bibliographies of specialized materials for outside reading assignments. Participate in campus and community events. Provide professional consulting services to government and industry.

SKILLS—Most Important: Science Skills; Communication Skills; Social Skills. **Other Above-Average Skills:** Thought-Processing Skills; Mathematics Skills.

GOE—Interest Area: 05. Education and Training. **Work Group:** 05.03. Postsecondary and Adult Teaching and Instructing. **Other Jobs in This Group:** Adult Literacy, Remedial Education, and GED Teachers and Instructors; Agricultural Sciences Teachers, Postsecondary; Anthropology and Archeology Teachers, Postsecondary; Architecture Teachers, Postsecondary; Area, Ethnic, and Cultural Studies Teachers, Postsecondary; Art, Drama, and Music Teachers, Postsecondary; Atmospheric, Earth, Marine, and Space Sciences Teachers, Postsecondary; Biological Science Teachers, Postsecondary; Business Teachers, Postsecondary; Chemistry Teachers, Postsecondary; Communications Teachers, Postsecondary; Computer Science Teachers, Postsecondary; Criminal Justice and Law Enforcement Teachers, Postsecondary; Economics Teachers, Postsecondary; Education Teachers, Postsecondary; Engineering Teachers, Postsecondary; English Language and Literature Teachers, Postsecondary; Environmental Science Teachers, Postsecondary; Farm and Home Management Advisors; Foreign Language and Literature Teachers, Postsecondary; Forestry and Conservation Science Teachers, Postsecondary; Geography Teachers, Postsecondary; Graduate Teaching Assistants; Health Specialties Teachers, Postsecondary; History Teachers, Postsecondary; Home Economics Teachers, Postsecondary; Law Teachers, Postsecondary; Library Science Teachers, Postsecondary; Mathematical Science Teachers, Postsecondary; Nursing Instructors and Teachers, Postsecondary; Philosophy and Religion Teachers, Postsecondary; Physics Teachers, Postsecondary; Political Science Teachers, Postsecondary; Psychology Teachers, Postsecondary; Recreation and Fitness Studies Teachers, Postsecondary; Self-Enrichment Education Teachers; Social Work Teachers, Postsecondary; Vocational Education Teachers, Postsecondary. **PERSONALITY TYPE:** Social. Social occupations frequently involve working with, communicating with, and teaching people. These occupations often involve helping or providing service to others.

EDUCATION/TRAINING PROGRAM(S)—Social Science Teacher Education; Sociology. **RELATED KNOWLEDGE/COURSES—Sociology and Anthropology:** Group behavior and dynamics, societal trends and influences, human migrations, ethnicity, and cultures and their history and origins. **Philosophy and Theology:** Different philosophical systems and religions. This includes their basic principles, values, ethics, ways of thinking, customs, practices, and impact on human culture. **History and Archeology:** Historical events and their causes, indicators, and effects on civilizations and cultures. **Education and Training:** Principles and methods for curriculum and training design, teaching and instruction for individuals and groups, and the measurement of training effects. **English Language:** The structure and content of the English language, including the meaning and spelling of words, rules of composition, and grammar. **Psychology:**

Human behavior and performance; individual differences in ability, personality, and interests; learning and motivation; psychological research methods; and the assessment and treatment of behavioral and affective disorders.

Sound Engineering Technicians

◉ Education/Training Required: Postsecondary vocational training

◉ Annual Earnings: $38,390

◉ Growth: 18.4%

◉ Annual Job Openings: 2,000

◉ Self-Employed: 6.5%

◉ Part-Time: 18.3%

Operate machines and equipment to record, synchronize, mix, or reproduce music, voices, or sound effects in sporting arenas, theater productions, recording studios, or movie and video productions. Confer with producers, performers, and others in order to determine and achieve the desired sound for a production such as a musical recording or a film. Set up, test, and adjust recording equipment for recording sessions and live performances; tear down equipment after event completion. Regulate volume level and sound quality during recording sessions, using control consoles. Prepare for recording sessions by performing activities such as selecting and setting up microphones. Report equipment problems and ensure that required repairs are made. Mix and edit voices, music, and taped sound effects for live performances and for prerecorded events, using sound mixing boards. Synchronize and equalize prerecorded dialogue, music, and sound effects with visual action of motion pictures or television productions, using control consoles. Record speech, music, and other sounds on recording media, using recording equipment. Reproduce and duplicate sound recordings from original recording media, using sound editing and duplication equipment. Separate instruments, vocals, and other sounds; then combine sounds later during the mixing or post-production stage. Keep logs of record-

ings. Create musical instrument digital interface programs for music projects, commercials, or film post-production.

SKILLS—Most Important: Equipment Use/Maintenance Skills; Equipment/Technology Analysis Skills; Quality Control Skills. **Other Above-Average Skills:** Management Skills; Social Skills.

GOE—Interest Area: 03. Arts and Communication. **Work Group:** 03.09. Media Technology. **Other Jobs in This Group:** Audio and Video Equipment Technicians; Broadcast Technicians; Camera Operators, Television, Video, and Motion Picture; Film and Video Editors; Multi-Media Artists and Animators; Photographers; Radio Operators. **PERSONALITY TYPE:** Realistic. Realistic occupations frequently involve work activities that include practical, hands-on problems and solutions. They often deal with plants, animals, and real-world materials like wood, tools, and machinery. Many of the occupations require working outside and do not involve a lot of paperwork or working closely with others.

EDUCATION/TRAINING PROGRAM(S)—Communications Technology/Technician; Recording Arts Technology/Technician. **RELATED KNOWLEDGE/ COURSES—Fine Arts:** The theory and techniques required to compose, produce, and perform works of music, dance, visual arts, drama, and sculpture. **Communications and Media:** Media production, communication, and dissemination techniques and methods. This includes alternative ways to inform and entertain via written, oral, and visual media. **Telecommunications:** Transmission, broadcasting, switching, control, and operation of telecommunications systems. **Computers and Electronics:** Circuit boards; processors; chips; electronic equipment; and computer hardware and software, including applications and programming. **Customer and Personal Service:** Principles and processes for providing customer and personal services. This includes customer needs assessment, meeting of quality standards for services, and evaluation of customer satisfaction. **Production and Processing:** Raw materials, production processes, quality control, costs, and other techniques for maximizing the effective manufacture and distribution of goods.

Special Education Teachers, Preschool, Kindergarten, and Elementary School

- Education/Training Required: Bachelor's degree
- Annual Earnings: $44,630
- Growth: 23.3%
- Annual Job Openings: 18,000
- Self-Employed: 0.5%
- Part-Time: 10.5%

Teach elementary and preschool school subjects to educationally and physically handicapped students. Includes teachers who specialize and work with audibly and visually handicapped students and those who teach basic academic and life processes skills to the mentally impaired. Instruct students in academic subjects, using a variety of techniques such as phonetics, multisensory learning, and repetition to reinforce learning and to meet students' varying needs and interests. Employ special educational strategies and techniques during instruction to improve the development of sensory- and perceptual-motor skills, language, cognition, and memory. Teach socially acceptable behavior, employing techniques such as behavior modification and positive reinforcement. Modify the general education curriculum for special-needs students based upon a variety of instructional techniques and technologies. Meet with parents and guardians to discuss their children's progress and to determine their priorities for their children and their resource needs. Plan and conduct activities for a balanced program of instruction, demonstration, and work time that provides students with opportunities to observe, question, and investigate. Establish and enforce rules for behavior and policies and procedures to maintain order among the students for whom they are responsible. Confer with parents, administrators, testing specialists, social workers, and professionals to develop individual educational plans designed to promote students' educational, physical, and social development. Maintain accurate and complete student records and prepare reports on children

and activities as required by laws, district policies, and administrative regulations. Establish clear objectives for all lessons, units, and projects and communicate those objectives to students. Develop and implement strategies to meet the needs of students with a variety of handicapping conditions. Prepare classrooms for class activities and provide a variety of materials and resources for children to explore, manipulate, and use, both in learning activities and imaginative play. Confer with parents or guardians, teachers, counselors, and administrators to resolve students' behavioral and academic problems. Observe and evaluate students' performance, behavior, social development, and physical health. Teach students personal development skills such as goal setting, independence, and self-advocacy.

SKILLS—Most Important: Social Skills; Communication Skills; Thought-Processing Skills. **Other Above-Average Skills:** Management Skills; Mathematics Skills.

GOE—Interest Area: 05. Education and Training. **Work Group:** 05.02. Preschool, Elementary, and Secondary Teaching and Instructing. **Other Jobs in This Group:** Elementary School Teachers, Except Special Education; Kindergarten Teachers, Except Special Education; Middle School Teachers, Except Special and Vocational Education; Preschool Teachers, Except Special Education; Secondary School Teachers, Except Special and Vocational Education; Special Education Teachers, Middle School; Special Education Teachers, Secondary School; Teacher Assistants; Vocational Education Teachers, Middle School; Vocational Education Teachers, Secondary School. **PERSONALITY TYPE:** Social. Social occupations frequently involve working with, communicating with, and teaching people. These occupations often involve helping or providing service to others.

EDUCATION/TRAINING PROGRAM(S)—Special Education and Teaching, General; Education/Teaching of Individuals with Hearing Impairments, Including Deafness; Education/Teaching of the Gifted and Talented; Education/Teaching of Individuals with Emotional Disturbances; Education/Teaching of Individuals with Mental Retardation; Education/Teaching of Individuals with Multiple Disabilities; Education/Teaching of Individuals with Orthopedic and Other Physical Health Impairments; others. **RELATED KNOWLEDGE/COURSES—Psychology:** Human behavior and performance; individual differences in ability, personality, and interests; learning and motivation; psychological research methods; and the assessment and treatment of behavioral and affective disorders. **History and Archeology:** Historical events and their causes, indicators, and effects on civilizations and cultures. **Therapy and Counseling:** Principles, methods, and procedures for diagnosis, treatment, and rehabilitation of physical and mental dysfunctions and for career counseling and guidance. **Geography:** Principles and methods for describing the features of land, sea, and air masses, including their physical characteristics; locations; interrelationships; and distribution of plant, animal, and human life. **Philosophy and Theology:** Different philosophical systems and religions. This includes their basic principles, values, ethics, ways of thinking, customs, practices, and impact on human culture. **Education and Training:** Principles and methods for curriculum and training design, teaching and instruction for individuals and groups, and the measurement of training effects.

Statistical Assistants

- ⊚ Education/Training Required: Moderate-term on-the-job training
- ⊚ Annual Earnings: $28,950
- ⊚ Growth: 5.7%
- ⊚ Annual Job Openings: 1,000
- ⊚ Self-Employed: 0.0%
- ⊚ Part-Time: 11.8%

Compile and compute data according to statistical formulas for use in statistical studies. May perform actuarial computations and compile charts and graphs for use by actuaries. Includes actuarial clerks. Compute and analyze data, using statistical formulas and computers or calculators. Enter data into computers for use in analyses and reports. Compile statistics from source materials, such as production and sales records, quality-control and test records, time sheets, and survey sheets. Compile reports, charts, and graphs that describe and interpret findings of analyses. Check source data to verify its completeness and accuracy. Participate in the publication of data and information. Discuss data presentation requirements with clients. File data and related information and maintain and update databases.

Select statistical tests for analyzing data. Organize paperwork such as survey forms and reports for distribution and for analysis. Code data as necessary prior to computer entry, using lists of codes. Check survey responses for errors such as the use of pens instead of pencils and set aside response forms that cannot be used. Interview people and keep track of their responses. Send out surveys.

SKILLS—Most Important: Mathematics Skills; Quality Control Skills; Computer Programming Skills. **Other Above-Average Skills:** Thought-Processing Skills; Communication Skills; Science Skills.

GOE—Interest Area: 15. Scientific Research, Engineering, and Mathematics. **Work Group:** 15.06. Mathematics and Data Analysis. **Other Jobs in This Group:** Actuaries; Mathematical Technicians; Mathematicians; Social Science Research Assistants; Statisticians. **PERSONALITY TYPE:** Conventional. Conventional occupations frequently involve following set procedures and routines. These occupations can include working with data and details more than with ideas. Usually there is a clear line of authority to follow.

EDUCATION/TRAINING PROGRAM(S)—Accounting Technology/Technician and Bookkeeping. **RELATED KNOWLEDGE/COURSES—Mathematics:** Arithmetic, algebra, geometry, calculus, and statistics and their applications. **Clerical Practices:** Administrative and clerical procedures and systems such as word processing, managing files and records, stenography and transcription, designing forms, and other office procedures and terminology. **Computers and Electronics:** Circuit boards; processors; chips; electronic equipment; and computer hardware and software, including applications and programming. **Customer and Personal Service:** Principles and processes for providing customer and personal services. This includes customer needs assessment, meeting of quality standards for services, and evaluation of customer satisfaction. **Administration and Management:** Business and management principles involved in strategic planning, resource allocation, human resources modeling, leadership technique, production methods, and coordination of people and resources. **Communications and Media:** Media production, communication, and dissemination techniques and methods. This includes alternative ways to inform and entertain via written, oral, and visual media.

Statisticians

- Education/Training Required: Master's degree
- Annual Earnings: $62,450
- Growth: 4.6%
- Annual Job Openings: 2,000
- Self-Employed: 3.6%
- Part-Time: 10.9%

Engage in the development of mathematical theory or apply statistical theory and methods to collect, organize, interpret, and summarize numerical data to provide usable information. May specialize in fields such as bio-statistics, agricultural statistics, business statistics, economic statistics, or other fields. Report results of statistical analyses, including information in the form of graphs, charts, and tables. Process large amounts of data for statistical modeling and graphic analysis, using computers. Identify relationships and trends in data, as well as any factors that could affect the results of research. Analyze and interpret statistical data in order to identify significant differences in relationships among sources of information. Prepare data for processing by organizing information, checking for any inaccuracies, and adjusting and weighting the raw data. Evaluate the statistical methods and procedures used to obtain data in order to ensure validity, applicability, efficiency, and accuracy. Evaluate sources of information in order to determine any limitations in terms of reliability or usability. Plan data collection methods for specific projects and determine the types and sizes of sample groups to be used. Design research projects that apply valid scientific techniques and utilize information obtained from baselines or historical data in order to structure uncompromised and efficient analyses. Develop an understanding of fields to which statistical methods are to be applied in order to determine whether methods and results are appropriate. Supervise and provide instructions for workers collecting and tabulating data. Apply sampling techniques or utilize complete enumeration bases in order to determine and define groups to be surveyed. Adapt statistical methods in order to solve specific problems in many fields, such as economics, biology, and engineering. Develop and test experimental designs, sampling techniques, and analytical methods. Examine theories, such as those of probability and inference, in order to discover mathematical bases for new or improved methods of obtaining and evaluating numerical data.

SKILLS—Most Important: Computer Programming Skills; Science Skills; Mathematics Skills. **Other Above-Average Skills:** Thought-Processing Skills; Communication Skills; Management Skills; Equipment/Technology Analysis Skills.

GOE—Interest Area: 15. Scientific Research, Engineering, and Mathematics. **Work Group:** 15.06. Mathematics and Data Analysis. **Other Jobs in This Group:** Actuaries; Mathematical Technicians; Mathematicians; Social Science Research Assistants; Statistical Assistants. **PERSONALITY TYPE:** Investigative. Investigative occupations frequently involve working with ideas and require an extensive amount of thinking. These occupations can involve searching for facts and figuring out problems mentally.

EDUCATION/TRAINING PROGRAM(S)—Biostatistics; Mathematics, General; Applied Mathematics; Statistics, General; Mathematical Statistics and Probability; Statistics, Other; Business Statistics. **RELATED KNOWLEDGE/COURSES—Mathematics:** Arithmetic, algebra, geometry, calculus, and statistics and their applications. **Computers and Electronics:** Circuit boards; processors; chips; electronic equipment; and computer hardware and software, including applications and programming. **English Language:** The structure and content of the English language, including the meaning and spelling of words, rules of composition, and grammar. **Education and Training:** Principles and methods for curriculum and training design, teaching and instruction for individuals and groups, and the measurement of training effects. **Law and Government:** Laws, legal codes, court procedures, precedents, government regulations, executive orders, agency rules, and the democratic political process. **Administration and Management:** Business and management principles involved in strategic planning, resource allocation, human resources modeling, leadership technique, production methods, and coordination of people and resources.

Storage and Distribution Managers

- ◎ Education/Training Required: Work experience in a related occupation
- ◎ Annual Earnings: $69,120
- ◎ Growth: 12.7%
- ◎ Annual Job Openings: 15,000
- ◎ Self-Employed: 2.8%
- ◎ Part-Time: 4.0%

The job openings listed here are shared with Transportation Managers.

Plan, direct, and coordinate the storage and distribution operations within an organization or the activities of organizations that are engaged in storing and distributing materials and products. Supervise the activities of workers engaged in receiving, storing, testing, and shipping products or materials. Plan, develop, and implement warehouse safety and security programs and activities. Review invoices, work orders, consumption reports, and demand forecasts to estimate peak delivery periods and to issue work assignments. Schedule and monitor air or surface pickup, delivery, or distribution of products or materials. Interview, select, and train warehouse and supervisory personnel. Confer with department heads to coordinate warehouse activities, such as production, sales, records control, and purchasing. Respond to customers' or shippers' questions and complaints regarding storage and distribution services. Inspect physical conditions of warehouses, vehicle fleets, and equipment and order testing, maintenance, repair, or replacement as necessary. Develop and document standard and emergency operating procedures for receiving, handling, storing, shipping, or salvaging products or materials. Examine products or materials to estimate quantities or weight and type of container required for storage or transport. Negotiate with carriers, warehouse operators, and insurance company representatives for services and preferential rates. Issue shipping instructions and provide routing information to ensure that delivery times and locations are coordinated. Examine invoices and shipping manifests for conformity to tariff and customs regulations. Prepare and manage departmental budgets. Prepare or direct preparation of correspondence; reports; and operations, maintenance, and safety manuals. Arrange for necessary shipping documentation and contact customs officials to effect release of shipments. Advise sales and billing departments of transportation charges for customers' accounts. Evaluate freight costs and the inventory costs associated with transit times to ensure that costs are appropriate. Participate in setting transportation and service rates. Track and trace goods while they are en route to their destinations, expediting orders when necessary. Arrange for storage facilities when required.

SKILLS—Most Important: Management Skills; Equipment/Technology Analysis Skills; Social Skills. **Other Above-Average Skills:** Thought-Processing Skills; Quality Control Skills.

GOE—Interest Area: 16. Transportation, Distribution, and Logistics. **Work Group:** 16.01. Managerial Work in Transportation. **Other Jobs in This Group:** Aircraft Cargo Handling Supervisors; First-Line Supervisors/Managers of Transportation and Material-Moving Machine and Vehicle Operators; Postmasters and Mail Superintendents; Railroad Conductors and Yardmasters; Transportation Managers; Transportation, Storage, and Distribution Managers. **PERSONALITY TYPE:** Enterprising. Enterprising occupations frequently involve starting up and carrying out projects. These occupations can involve leading people and making many decisions. They sometimes require risk taking and often deal with business.

EDUCATION/TRAINING PROGRAM(S)—Public Administration; Aeronautics/Aviation/Aerospace Science and Technology, General; Aviation/Airway Management and Operations; Business Administration and Management, General; Logistics and Materials Management; Transportation/Transportation Management. **RELATED KNOWLEDGE/COURSES—Sales and Marketing:** Principles and methods for showing, promoting, and selling products or services. This includes marketing strategy and tactics, product demonstration, sales techniques, and sales control systems. **Customer and Personal Service:** Principles and processes for providing customer and personal services. This includes customer needs assessment, meeting of quality standards for services, and evaluation of customer satisfaction. **Administration and Management:** Business and management principles involved in strategic planning, resource allocation, human resources modeling, leadership technique, production methods, and coordination of people and resources. **Personnel and Human Resources:** Principles and procedures for personnel recruitment, selection, training, compensation and benefits, labor relations and negotiation, and personnel information systems. **Production and Processing:** Raw materials, production processes, quality control, costs, and other techniques for maximizing the effective manufacture and distribution of goods. **Education and Training:** Principles and methods for curriculum and training design, teaching and instruction for individuals and groups, and the measurement of training effects.

Surgeons

- Education/Training Required: First professional degree
- Annual Earnings: More than $145,600
- Growth: 24.0%
- Annual Job Openings: 41,000
- Self-Employed: 11.5%
- Part-Time: 9.6%

The job openings listed here are shared with Anesthesiologists; Family and General Practitioners; Internists, General; Obstetricians and Gynecologists; Pediatricians, General; and Psychiatrists.

Treat diseases, injuries, and deformities by invasive methods, such as manual manipulation, or by using instruments and appliances. Analyze patient's medical history, medication allergies, physical condition, and examination results to verify operation's necessity and to determine best procedure. Operate on patients to correct deformities, repair injuries, prevent and treat diseases, or improve or restore patients' functions. Follow established surgical techniques during the operation. Prescribe preoperative and postoperative treatments and procedures, such as sedatives, diets, antibiotics, and preparation and treatment of the patient's operative area. Examine patient to provide information on medical condition and surgical risk. Diagnose bodily disorders and orthopedic conditions and provide treatments, such as medicines and surgeries, in clinics, hospital wards, and operating rooms. Direct and coordinate activities of nurses, assistants, specialists, residents, and other medical staff. Provide consultation and surgical

assistance to other physicians and surgeons. Refer patient to medical specialist or other practitioners when necessary. Examine instruments, equipment, and operating room to ensure sterility. Prepare case histories. Manage surgery services, including planning, scheduling and coordination, determination of procedures, and procurement of supplies and equipment. Conduct research to develop and test surgical techniques that can improve operating procedures and outcomes.

SKILLS—Most Important: Science Skills; Thought-Processing Skills; Communication Skills. **Other Above-Average Skills:** Equipment/Technology Analysis Skills; Social Skills; Mathematics Skills; Equipment Use/Maintenance Skills.

GOE—Interest Area: 08. Health Science. **Work Group:** 08.02. Medicine and Surgery. **Other Jobs in This Group:** Anesthesiologists; Family and General Practitioners; Internists, General; Medical Assistants; Medical Transcriptionists; Obstetricians and Gynecologists; Pediatricians, General; Pharmacists; Pharmacy Aides; Pharmacy Technicians; Physician Assistants; Psychiatrists; Registered Nurses; Surgical Technologists. **PERSONALITY TYPE:** Investigative. Investigative occupations frequently involve working with ideas and require an extensive amount of thinking. These occupations can involve searching for facts and figuring out problems mentally.

EDUCATION/TRAINING PROGRAM(S)—Colon and Rectal Surgery; Critical Care Surgery; General Surgery; Hand Surgery; Neurological Surgery/Neurosurgery; Orthopedics/Orthopedic Surgery; Otolaryngology; Pediatric Orthopedics; Pediatric Surgery; Plastic Surgery; Sports Medicine; Thoracic Surgery; Urology; Vascular Surgery; Adult Reconstructive Orthopedics (Orthopedic Surgery); Orthopedic Surgery of the Spine. **RELATED KNOWLEDGE/COURSES—Medicine and Dentistry:** The information and techniques needed to diagnose and treat human injuries, diseases, and deformities. This includes symptoms, treatment alternatives, drug properties and interactions, and preventive healthcare measures. **Biology:** Plant and animal organisms and their tissues, cells, functions, interdependencies, and interactions with each other and the environment. **Therapy and Counseling:** Principles, methods, and procedures for diagnosis, treatment, and rehabilitation of physical and mental dysfunctions and for career counseling and guidance. **Psychology:** Human behavior and performance;

individual differences in ability, personality, and interests; learning and motivation; psychological research methods; and the assessment and treatment of behavioral and affective disorders. **Customer and Personal Service:** Principles and processes for providing customer and personal services. This includes customer needs assessment, meeting of quality standards for services, and evaluation of customer satisfaction. **Chemistry:** The chemical composition, structure, and properties of substances and of the chemical processes and transformations that they undergo. This includes uses of chemicals and their danger signs, production techniques, and disposal methods.

Surgical Technologists

- Education/Training Required: Postsecondary vocational training
- Annual Earnings: $34,830
- Growth: 29.5%
- Annual Job Openings: 12,000
- Self-Employed: 0.3%
- Part-Time: 23.2%

Assist in operations under the supervision of surgeons, registered nurses, or other surgical personnel. May help set up operating room; prepare and transport patients for surgery; adjust lights and equipment; pass instruments and other supplies to surgeons and surgeon's assistants; hold retractors; cut sutures; and help count sponges, needles, supplies, and instruments. Count sponges, needles, and instruments before and after operation. Hand instruments and supplies to surgeons and surgeons' assistants, hold retractors and cut sutures, and perform other tasks as directed by surgeon during operation. Scrub arms and hands and assist the surgical team in scrubbing and putting on gloves, masks, and surgical clothing. Position patients on the operating table and cover them with sterile surgical drapes to prevent exposure. Provide technical assistance to surgeons, surgical nurses, and anesthesiologists. Wash and sterilize equipment, using germicides and sterilizers. Prepare, care for, and dispose of tissue specimens taken for laboratory analysis. Clean and restock the operating room, placing equipment and supplies and arranging instruments according to instruction. Prepare dressings or bandages and apply or assist with their application

following surgery. Operate, assemble, adjust, or monitor sterilizers, lights, suction machines, and diagnostic equipment to ensure proper operation. Monitor and continually assess operating room conditions, including patient and surgical team needs. Observe patients' vital signs to assess physical condition. Maintain supply of fluids, such as plasma, saline, blood, and glucose, for use during operations. Maintain files and records of surgical procedures.

SKILLS—Most Important: Science Skills; Equipment/Technology Analysis Skills; Social Skills. **Other Above-Average Skills:** Equipment Use/Maintenance Skills; Quality Control Skills; Mathematics Skills.

GOE—Interest Area: 08. Health Science. **Work Group:** 08.02. Medicine and Surgery. **Other Jobs in This Group:** Anesthesiologists; Family and General Practitioners; Internists, General; Medical Assistants; Medical Transcriptionists; Obstetricians and Gynecologists; Pediatricians, General; Pharmacists; Pharmacy Aides; Pharmacy Technicians; Physician Assistants; Psychiatrists; Registered Nurses; Surgeons. **PERSONALITY TYPE:** Realistic. Realistic occupations frequently involve work activities that include practical, hands-on problems and solutions. They often deal with plants, animals, and real-world materials like wood, tools, and machinery. Many of the occupations require working outside and do not involve a lot of paperwork or working closely with others.

EDUCATION/TRAINING PROGRAM(S)—Pathology/Pathologist Assistant; Surgical Technology/Technologist. **RELATED KNOWLEDGE/COURSES—Medicine and Dentistry:** The information and techniques needed to diagnose and treat human injuries, diseases, and deformities. This includes symptoms, treatment alternatives, drug properties and interactions, and preventive healthcare measures. **Chemistry:** The chemical composition, structure, and properties of substances and of the chemical processes and transformations that they undergo. This includes uses of chemicals and their danger signs, production techniques, and disposal methods. **Customer and Personal Service:** Principles and processes for providing customer and personal services. This includes customer needs assessment, meeting of quality standards for services, and evaluation of customer satisfaction. **Psychology:** Human behavior and performance; individual differences in ability, personality, and interests; learning and motivation; psychological research methods; and the assessment and treatment of behavioral and affective disorders. **Philosophy and Theology:** Different philosophical systems and religions. This includes their basic principles, values, ethics, ways of thinking, customs, practices, and impact on human culture. **Therapy and Counseling:** Principles, methods, and procedures for diagnosis, treatment, and rehabilitation of physical and mental dysfunctions and for career counseling and guidance.

Technical Directors/Managers

- Education/Training Required: Long-term on-the-job training
- Annual Earnings: $53,860
- Growth: 16.6%
- Annual Job Openings: 11,000
- Self-Employed: 30.4%
- Part-Time: 8.1%

The job openings listed here are shared with Directors—Stage, Motion Pictures, Television, and Radio, Producers, Program Directors, and Talent Directors.

Coordinate activities of technical departments, such as taping, editing, engineering, and maintenance, to produce radio or television programs. Direct technical aspects of newscasts and other productions, checking and switching between video sources and taking responsibility for the on-air product, including camera shots and graphics. Test equipment to ensure proper operation. Monitor broadcasts to ensure that programs conform to station or network policies and regulations. Observe pictures through monitors and direct camera and video staff concerning shading and composition. Act as liaisons between engineering and production departments. Supervise and assign duties to workers engaged in technical control and production of radio and television programs. Schedule use of studio and editing facilities for producers and engineering and maintenance staff. Confer with operations directors to formulate and maintain fair and attainable technical policies for programs. Operate equipment to produce programs or broadcast live programs from remote loca-

tions. Train workers in use of equipment such as switchers, cameras, monitors, microphones, and lights. Switch between video sources in a studio or on multi-camera remotes, using equipment such as switchers, video slide projectors, and video effects generators. Set up and execute video transitions and special effects such as fades, dissolves, cuts, keys, and supers, using computers to manipulate pictures as necessary. Collaborate with promotions directors to produce on-air station promotions. Discuss filter options, lens choices, and the visual effects of objects being filmed with photography directors and video operators. Follow instructions from production managers and directors during productions, such as commands for camera cuts, effects, graphics, and takes.

SKILLS—Most Important: Equipment Use/ Maintenance Skills; Equipment/Technology Analysis Skills; Management Skills. **Other Above-Average Skills:** Thought-Processing Skills; Social Skills.

GOE—Interest Area: 03. Arts and Communication. **Work Group:** 03.01. Managerial Work in Arts and Communication. **Other Jobs in This Group:** Agents and Business Managers of Artists, Performers, and Athletes; Art Directors; Producers; Producers and Directors; Program Directors; Public Relations Managers. **PERSONALITY TYPE:** Realistic. Realistic occupations frequently involve work activities that include practical, hands-on problems and solutions. They often deal with plants, animals, and real-world materials like wood, tools, and machinery. Many of the occupations require working outside and do not involve a lot of paperwork or working closely with others.

EDUCATION/TRAINING PROGRAM(S)—Radio and Television; Drama and Dramatics/Theatre Arts, General; Directing and Theatrical Production; Theatre/Theatre Arts Management; Dramatic/Theatre Arts and Stagecraft, Other; Film/Cinema Studies; Cinematography and Film/Video Production. **RELATED KNOWLEDGE/COURSES—Communications and Media:** Media production, communication, and dissemination techniques and methods. This includes alternative ways to inform and entertain via written, oral, and visual media. **Telecommunications:** Transmission, broadcasting, switching, control, and operation of telecommunications systems. **Computers and Electronics:** Circuit boards; processors; chips; electronic equipment; and computer hardware and software, including applications and programming. **Philosophy and Theology:** Different philosophical systems and religions. This includes their basic principles, values, ethics, ways of thinking, customs, practices, and impact on human culture. **Sales and Marketing:** Principles and methods for showing, promoting, and selling products or services. This includes marketing strategy and tactics, product demonstration, sales techniques, and sales control systems. **Engineering and Technology:** The practical application of engineering science and technology. This includes applying principles, techniques, procedures, and equipment to the design and production of various goods and services.

Technical Writers

- Education/Training Required: Bachelor's degree
- Annual Earnings: $55,160
- Growth: 23.2%
- Annual Job Openings: 5,000
- Self-Employed: 7.3%
- Part-Time: 7.3%

Write technical materials, such as equipment manuals, appendices, or operating and maintenance instructions. May assist in layout work. Organize material and complete writing assignment according to set standards regarding order, clarity, conciseness, style, and terminology. Maintain records and files of work and revisions. Edit, standardize, or make changes to material prepared by other writers or establishment personnel. Confer with customer representatives, vendors, plant executives, or publisher to establish technical specifications and to determine subject material to be developed for publication. Review published materials and recommend revisions or changes in scope, format, content, and methods of reproduction and binding. Select photographs, drawings, sketches, diagrams, and charts to illustrate material. Study drawings, specifications, mockups, and product samples to integrate and delineate technology, operating procedure, and production sequence and detail. Interview production and engineering personnel and read journals and other material to become familiar with product technologies and production methods. Observe production, developmental, and experimental activities to determine operating procedure and detail. Arrange for typing, duplication, and distribution of material. Assist in laying out material for publication. Analyze developments in specific field to determine need for revisions in previously published materials and development of new material. Review manufacturer's and trade catalogs, drawings, and other data relative to operation, maintenance, and service of equipment. Draw sketches to illustrate specified materials or assembly sequence.

SKILLS—Most Important: Communication Skills; Quality Control Skills; Equipment/Technology Analysis Skills. **Other Above-Average Skills:** Thought-Processing Skills; Social Skills.

GOE—Interest Area: 03. Arts and Communication. **Work Group:** 03.02. Writing and Editing. **Other Jobs in This Group:** Copy Writers; Editors; Poets, Lyricists and Creative Writers; Writers and Authors. **PERSONALITY TYPE:** Artistic. Artistic occupations frequently involve working with forms, designs, and patterns. They often require self-expression, and the work can be done without following a clear set of rules.

EDUCATION/TRAINING PROGRAM(S)—Communication Studies/Speech Communication and Rhetoric; Technical and Business Writing; Business/Corporate Communications. **RELATED KNOWLEDGE/COURSES—Communications and Media:** Media production, communication, and dissemination techniques and methods. This includes alternative ways to inform and entertain via written, oral, and visual media. **Clerical Practices:** Administrative and clerical procedures and systems such as word processing, managing files and records, stenography and transcription, designing forms, and other office procedures and terminology. **English Language:** The structure and content of the English language, including the meaning and spelling of words, rules of composition, and grammar. **Computers and Electronics:** Circuit boards; processors; chips; electronic equipment; and computer hardware and software, including applications and programming. **Education and Training:** Principles and methods for curriculum and training design, teaching and instruction for individuals and groups, and the measurement of training effects. **Engineering and Technology:** The practical application of engineering science and technology. This includes applying principles, techniques, procedures, and equipment to the design and production of various goods and services.

Telecommunications Equipment Installers and Repairers, Except Line Installers

- ☺ Education/Training Required: Long-term on-the-job training
- ☺ Annual Earnings: $50,620
- ☺ Growth: –4.9%
- ☺ Annual Job Openings: 21,000
- ☺ Self-Employed: 6.6%
- ☺ Part-Time: 4.9%

Set up, rearrange, or remove switching and dialing equipment used in central offices. Service or repair telephones and other communication equipment on customers' property. May install equipment in new locations or install wiring and telephone jacks in buildings under construction. Note differences in wire and cable colors so that work can be performed correctly. Test circuits and components of malfunctioning telecommunications equipment to isolate sources of malfunctions, using test meters, circuit diagrams, polarity probes, and other hand tools. Test repaired, newly installed, or updated equipment to ensure that it functions properly and conforms to specifications, using test equipment and observation. Drive crew trucks to and from work areas. Inspect equipment on a regular basis to ensure proper functioning. Repair or replace faulty equipment such as defective and damaged telephones, wires, switching system components, and associated equipment. Remove and remake connections to change circuit layouts, following work orders or diagrams. Demonstrate equipment to customers, explain how it is to be used, and respond to any inquiries or complaints. Analyze test readings, computer printouts, and trouble reports to determine equipment repair needs and required repair methods. Adjust or modify equipment to enhance equipment performance or to respond to customer requests. Remove loose wires and other debris after work is completed. Request support from technical service centers when on-site procedures fail to solve installation or maintenance problems. Assemble and install communication equipment such as data and telephone communication lines, wiring, switching equip-ment, wiring frames, power apparatus, computer systems, and networks. Communicate with bases, using telephones or two-way radios to receive instructions or technical advice or to report equipment status. Collaborate with other workers to locate and correct malfunctions. Review manufacturer's instructions, manuals, technical specifications, building permits, and ordinances to determine communication equipment requirements and procedures. Test connections to ensure that power supplies are adequate and that communications links function. Refer to manufacturers' manuals to obtain maintenance instructions pertaining to specific malfunctions. Climb poles and ladders, use truck-mounted booms, and enter areas such as man-holes and cable vaults to install, maintain, or inspect equipment.

SKILLS—Most Important: Quality Control Skills; Equipment Use/Maintenance Skills. **Other Above-Average Skills:** None met the criteria.

GOE—Interest Area: 02. Architecture and Construction. **Work Group:** 02.05. Systems and Equipment Installation, Maintenance, and Repair. **Other Jobs in This Group:** Electrical and Electronics Repairers, Powerhouse, Substation, and Relay; Electrical Power-Line Installers and Repairers; Elevator Installers and Repairers; Heating and Air Conditioning Mechanics and Installers; Maintenance and Repair Workers, General; Refrigeration Mechanics and Installers; Telecommunications Line Installers and Repairers. **PERSONALITY TYPE:** Realistic. Realistic occupations frequently involve work activities that include practical, hands-on problems and solutions. They often deal with plants, animals, and real-world materials like wood, tools, and machinery. Many of the occupations require working outside and do not involve a lot of paperwork or working closely with others.

EDUCATION/TRAINING PROGRAM(S)—Communications Systems Installation and Repair Technology. **RELATED KNOWLEDGE/COURSES—Telecommunications:** Transmission, broadcasting, switching, control, and operation of telecommunications systems. **Computers and Electronics:** Circuit boards; processors; chips; electronic equipment; and computer hardware and software, including applications and programming. **Design:** Design techniques, tools, and principles involved in production of precision technical plans, blueprints, drawings, and models. **Mechanical Devices:** Machines and tools, including their designs, uses, repair, and maintenance. **Engineering and Technology:** The practical application of engineering science and technology. This includes applying principles, techniques, procedures, and equipment to the design and production of various goods and services.

Telecommunications Line Installers and Repairers

- ◎ Education/Training Required: Long-term on-the-job training
- ◎ Annual Earnings: $42,410
- ◎ Growth: 10.8%
- ◎ Annual Job Openings: 23,000
- ◎ Self-Employed: 1.5%
- ◎ Part-Time: 2.5%

String and repair telephone and television cable, including fiber optics and other equipment for transmitting messages or television programming. Travel to customers' premises to install, maintain, and repair audio and visual electronic reception equipment and accessories. Inspect and test lines and cables, recording and analyzing test results, to assess transmission characteristics and locate faults and malfunctions. Splice cables, using hand tools, epoxy, or mechanical equipment. Measure signal strength at utility poles, using electronic test equipment. Set up service for customers, installing, connecting, testing, and adjusting equipment. Place insulation over conductors and seal splices with moisture-proof covering. Access specific areas to string lines and install terminal boxes, auxiliary equipment, and appliances, using bucket trucks or by climbing poles and ladders or entering tunnels, trenches, or crawl spaces. String cables between structures and lines from poles, towers, or trenches and pull lines to proper tension. Install equipment such as amplifiers and repeaters to maintain the strength of communications transmissions. Lay underground cable directly in trenches or string it through conduits running through trenches. Pull up cable by hand from large reels mounted on trucks; then pull lines through ducts by hand or with winches. Clean and maintain tools and test equip-

ment. Explain cable service to subscribers after installation and collect any installation fees that are due. Compute impedance of wires from poles to houses to determine additional resistance needed for reducing signals to desired levels. Use a variety of construction equipment to complete installations, including digger derricks, trenchers, and cable plows. Dig trenches for underground wires and cables. Dig holes for power poles, using power augers or shovels; set poles in place with cranes; and hoist poles upright, using winches. Fill and tamp holes, using cement, earth, and tamping devices. Participate in the construction and removal of telecommunication towers and associated support structures.

SKILLS—Most Important: Equipment Use/Maintenance Skills. **Other Above-Average Skills:** None met the criteria.

GOE—Interest Area: 02. Architecture and Construction. **Work Group:** 02.05. Systems and Equipment Installation, Maintenance, and Repair. **Other Jobs in This Group:** Electrical and Electronics Repairers, Powerhouse, Substation, and Relay; Electrical Power-Line Installers and Repairers; Elevator Installers and Repairers; Heating and Air Conditioning Mechanics and Installers; Maintenance and Repair Workers, General; Refrigeration Mechanics and Installers; Telecommunications Equipment Installers and Repairers, Except Line Installers. **PERSONALITY TYPE:** Realistic. Realistic occupations frequently involve work activities that include practical, hands-on problems and solutions. They often deal with plants, animals, and real-world materials like wood, tools, and machinery. Many of the occupations require working outside and do not involve a lot of paperwork or working closely with others.

EDUCATION/TRAINING PROGRAM(S)—Communications Systems Installation and Repair Technology. **RELATED KNOWLEDGE/COURSES—Telecommunications:** Transmission, broadcasting, switching, control, and operation of telecommunications systems. **Mechanical Devices:** Machines and tools, including their designs, uses, repair, and maintenance. **Computers and Electronics:** Circuit boards; processors; chips; electronic equipment; and computer hardware and software, including applications and programming.

Tile and Marble Setters

- Education/Training Required: Long-term on-the-job training
- Annual Earnings: $36,530
- Growth: 22.9%
- Annual Job Openings: 9,000
- Self-Employed: 24.4%
- Part-Time: 12.3%

Apply hard tile, marble, and wood tile to walls, floors, ceilings, and roof decks. Align and straighten tile, using levels, squares, and straightedges. Determine and implement the best layout to achieve a desired pattern. Cut and shape tile to fit around obstacles and into odd spaces and corners, using hand- and power-cutting tools. Finish and dress the joints and wipe excess grout from between tiles, using damp sponge. Apply mortar to tile back, position the tile, and press or tap with trowel handle to affix tile to base. Mix, apply, and spread plaster, concrete, mortar, cement, mastic, glue, or other adhesives to form a bed for the tiles, using brush, trowel, and screed. Prepare cost and labor estimates based on calculations of time and materials needed for project. Measure and mark surfaces to be tiled, following blueprints. Level concrete and allow to dry. Build underbeds and install anchor bolts, wires, and brackets. Prepare surfaces for tiling by attaching lath or waterproof paper or by applying a cement mortar coat onto a metal screen. Study blueprints and examine surface to be covered to determine amount of material needed. Cut, surface, polish, and install marble and granite or install pre-cast terrazzo, granite, or marble units. Install and anchor fixtures in designated positions, using hand tools. Cut tile backing to required size, using shears. Remove any old tile, grout, and adhesive, using chisels and scrapers, and clean the surface carefully. Lay and set mosaic tiles to create decorative wall, mural, and floor designs. Assist customers in selection of tile and grout. Remove and replace cracked or damaged tile. Measure and cut metal lath to size for walls and ceilings, using tin snips. Select and order tile and other items to be installed, such as bathroom accessories, walls, panels, and cabinets, according to specifications. Mix and apply mortar or cement to edges and ends of drain tiles to seal halves and joints. Spread mastic or other adhesive base on roof deck to form base for promenade tile, using ser-rated spreader. Apply a sealer to make grout stain- and water-resistant. Brush glue onto manila paper on which design has been drawn and position tiles, finished side down, onto paper.

SKILLS—Most Important: Mathematics Skills; Management Skills; Equipment/Technology Analysis Skills. **Other Above-Average Skills:** Social Skills; Thought-Processing Skills.

GOE—Interest Area: 02. Architecture and Construction. **Work Group:** 02.04. Construction Crafts. **Other Jobs in This Group:** Boilermakers; Brickmasons and Blockmasons; Carpet Installers; Cement Masons and Concrete Finishers; Commercial Divers; Construc-tion Carpenters; Crane and Tower Operators; Drywall and Ceiling Tile Installers; Electricians; Fence Erectors; Floor Layers, Except Carpet, Wood, and Hard Tiles; Floor Sanders and Finishers; Glaziers; Hazardous Materials Removal Workers; Insulation Workers, Floor, Ceiling, and Wall; Insulation Workers, Mechanical; Manufactured Building and Mobile Home Installers; Operating Engineers and Other Construction Equipment Operators; Painters, Construction and Maintenance; Paperhangers; Paving, Surfacing, and Tamping Equipment Operators; Pile-Driver Operators; Pipe Fitters and Steamfitters; Pipelayers; Plasterers and Stucco Masons; Plumbers; Plumbers, Pipefitters, and Steamfitters; Rail-Track Laying and Maintenance Equipment Operators; Refractory Materials Repairers, Except Brickmasons; Reinforcing Iron and Rebar Workers; Riggers; Roofers; Rough Carpenters; Security and Fire Alarm Systems Installers; Segmental Pavers; Sheet Metal Workers; Stone Cutters and Carvers, Manufacturing; Stonemasons; Structural Iron and Steel Workers; Tapers; Terrazzo Workers and Finishers. **PERSONALITY TYPE:** Realistic. Realistic occupations frequently involve work activities that include practical, hands-on problems and solutions. They often deal with plants, animals, and real-world materials like wood, tools, and machinery. Many of the occupations require working outside and do not involve a lot of paperwork or working closely with others.

EDUCATION/TRAINING PROGRAM(S)—Mason/Masonry. RELATED KNOWLEDGE/COURSES—Building and Construction: The materials, methods, and tools involved in the construction or repair of houses, buildings, or other structures such as highways and roads. **Design:** Design techniques, tools, and principles involved in production of precision technical plans, blueprints, drawings, and models. **Production and Processing:** Raw materials, production processes, quality control, costs, and other techniques for maximizing the effective manufacture and distribution of goods. **Economics and Accounting:** Economic and accounting principles and practices, the financial markets, banking, and the analysis and reporting of financial data. **Administration and Management:** Business and management principles involved in strategic planning, resource allocation, human resources modeling, leadership technique, production methods, and coordination of people and resources. **Transportation:** Principles and methods for moving people or goods by air, rail, sea, or road, including the relative costs and benefits.

Training and Development Managers

- Education/Training Required: Work experience plus degree
- Annual Earnings: $74,180
- Growth: 25.9%
- Annual Job Openings: 3,000
- Self-Employed: 1.3%
- Part-Time: 3.5%

Plan, direct, or coordinate the training and development activities and staff of an organization. Conduct orientation sessions and arrange on-the-job training for new hires. Evaluate instructor performance and the effectiveness of training programs, providing recommendations for improvement. Develop testing and evaluation procedures. Conduct or arrange for ongoing technical training and personal development classes for staff members. Confer with management and conduct surveys to identify training needs based on projected production processes, changes, and other factors. Develop and organize training manuals, multimedia visual aids, and other educational materials. Plan, develop, and provide training and staff development programs, using knowledge of the effectiveness of methods such as classroom training, demonstrations, on-the-job training, meetings, conferences, and workshops. Analyze training needs to develop new training pro-

grams or modify and improve existing programs. Review and evaluate training and apprenticeship programs for compliance with government standards. Train instructors and supervisors in techniques and skills for training and dealing with employees. Coordinate established courses with technical and professional courses provided by community schools and designate training procedures. Prepare training budget for department or organization.

SKILLS—Most Important: Management Skills; Social Skills; Thought-Processing Skills. **Other Above-Average Skills:** Communication Skills; Mathematics Skills.

GOE—Interest Area: 04. Business and Administration. **Work Group:** 04.01. Managerial Work in General Business. **Other Jobs in This Group:** Chief Executives; Compensation and Benefits Managers; General and Operations Managers; Human Resources Managers. **PERSONALITY TYPE:** Enterprising. Enterprising occupations frequently involve starting up and carrying out projects. These occupations can involve leading people and making many decisions. They sometimes require risk taking and often deal with business.

EDUCATION/TRAINING PROGRAM(S)—Human Resources Management/Personnel Administration, General; Human Resources Development. **RELATED KNOWLEDGE/COURSES—Personnel and Human Resources:** Principles and procedures for personnel recruitment, selection, training, compensation and benefits, labor relations and negotiation, and personnel information systems. **Clerical Practices:** Administrative and clerical procedures and systems such as word processing, managing files and records, stenography and transcription, designing forms, and other office procedures and terminology. **Administration and Management:** Business and management principles involved in strategic planning, resource allocation, human resources modeling, leadership technique, production methods, and coordination of people and resources. **Education and Training:** Principles and methods for curriculum and training design, teaching and instruction for individuals and groups, and the measurement of training effects. **Psychology:** Human behavior and performance; individual differences in ability, personality, and interests; learning and motivation; psychological research methods; and the assessment and treatment of behavioral and affective disorders. **Computers and Electronics:** Circuit boards;

processors; chips; electronic equipment; and computer hardware and software, including applications and programming.

Training and Development Specialists

- Education/Training Required: Bachelor's degree
- Annual Earnings: $45,870
- Growth: 20.8%
- Annual Job Openings: 32,000
- Self-Employed: 2.8%
- Part-Time: 7.7%

Conduct training and development programs for employees. Keep up with developments in area of expertise by reading current journals, books, and magazine articles. Present information, using a variety of instructional techniques and formats such as role playing, simulations, team exercises, group discussions, videos, and lectures. Schedule classes based on availability of classrooms, equipment, and instructors. Organize and develop, or obtain, training procedure manuals and guides and course materials such as handouts and visual materials. Offer specific training programs to help workers maintain or improve job skills. Monitor, evaluate, and record training activities and program effectiveness. Attend meetings and seminars to obtain information for use in training programs or to inform management of training program status. Coordinate recruitment and placement of training program participants. Evaluate training materials prepared by instructors, such as outlines, text, and handouts. Develop alternative training methods if expected improvements are not seen. Assess training needs through surveys; interviews with employees; focus groups; or consultation with managers, instructors, or customer representatives. Screen, hire, and assign workers to positions based on qualifications. Select and assign instructors to conduct training. Devise programs to develop executive potential among employees in lower-level positions. Design, plan, organize, and direct orientation and training for employees or customers of industrial or commercial establishment. Negotiate contracts with clients, including desired training outcomes, fees, and expenses. Supervise instructors,

evaluate instructor performance, and refer instructors to classes for skill development. Monitor training costs to ensure budget is not exceeded and prepare budget reports to justify expenditures. Refer trainees to employer relations representatives, to locations offering job placement assistance, or to appropriate social services agencies if warranted.

SKILLS—Most Important: Communication Skills; Social Skills; Thought-Processing Skills. **Other Above-Average Skills:** Mathematics Skills; Quality Control Skills.

GOE—Interest Area: 04. Business and Administration. **Work Group:** 04.03. Human Resources Support. **Other Jobs in This Group:** Compensation, Benefits, and Job Analysis Specialists; Employment Interviewers; Employment, Recruitment, and Placement Specialists; Personnel Recruiters. **PERSONALITY TYPE:** Social. Social occupations frequently involve working with, communicating with, and teaching people. These occupations often involve helping or providing service to others.

EDUCATION/TRAINING PROGRAM(S)—Human Resources Management/Personnel Administration, General; Organizational Behavior Studies. **RELATED KNOWLEDGE/COURSES—Psychology:** Human behavior and performance; individual differences in ability, personality, and interests; learning and motivation; psychological research methods; and the assessment and treatment of behavioral and affective disorders. **Sociology and Anthropology:** Group behavior and dynamics, societal trends and influences, human migrations, ethnicity, and cultures and their history and origins. **Customer and Personal Service:** Principles and processes for providing customer and personal services. This includes customer needs assessment, meeting of quality standards for services, and evaluation of customer satisfaction. **Personnel and Human Resources:** Principles and procedures for personnel recruitment, selection, training, compensation and benefits, labor relations and negotiation, and personnel information systems. **Therapy and Counseling:** Principles, methods, and procedures for diagnosis, treatment, and rehabilitation of physical and mental dysfunctions and for career counseling and guidance. **Education and Training:** Principles and methods for curriculum and training design, teaching and instruction for individuals and groups, and the measurement of training effects.

Transportation Managers

- ◉ Education/Training Required: Work experience in a related occupation
- ◉ Annual Earnings: $69,120
- ◉ Growth: 12.7%
- ◉ Annual Job Openings: 15,000
- ◉ Self-Employed: 2.8%
- ◉ Part-Time: 4.0%

The job openings listed here are shared with Storage and Distribution Managers.

Plan, direct, and coordinate the transportation operations within an organization or the activities of organizations that provide transportation services. Direct activities related to dispatching, routing, and tracking transportation vehicles such as aircraft and railroad cars. Plan, organize, and manage the work of subordinate staff to ensure that the work is accomplished in a manner consistent with organizational requirements. Direct investigations to verify and resolve customer or shipper complaints. Serve as contact persons for all workers within assigned territories. Implement schedule and policy changes. Collaborate with other managers and staff members to formulate and implement policies, procedures, goals, and objectives. Monitor operations to ensure that staff members comply with administrative policies and procedures, safety rules, union contracts, and government regulations. Promote safe work activities by conducting safety audits, attending company safety meetings, and meeting with individual staff members. Develop criteria, application instructions, procedural manuals, and contracts for federal and state public transportation programs. Monitor spending to ensure that expenses are consistent with approved budgets. Direct and coordinate, through subordinates, activities of operations department to obtain use of equipment, facilities, and human resources. Direct activities of staff performing repairs and maintenance to equipment, vehicles, and facilities. Conduct investigations in cooperation with government agencies to determine causes of transportation accidents and to improve safety procedures. Analyze expenditures and other financial information to develop plans, policies, and budgets for increasing profits and improving services. Negotiate and authorize contracts with equipment and materials suppliers and monitor contract fulfillment. Supervise workers assigning tariff classifications and preparing billing. Set operations policies and standards, including determination of safety procedures for the handling of dangerous goods. Recommend or authorize capital expenditures for acquisition of new equipment or property to increase efficiency and services of operations department. Prepare management recommendations, such as proposed fee and tariff increases or schedule changes.

SKILLS—Most Important: Management Skills; Mathematics Skills; Social Skills. **Other Above-Average Skills:** Thought-Processing Skills; Communication Skills.

GOE—Interest Area: 16. Transportation, Distribution, and Logistics. **Work Group:** 16.01. Managerial Work in Transportation. **Other Jobs in This Group:** Aircraft Cargo Handling Supervisors; First-Line Supervisors/Managers of Transportation and Material-Moving Machine and Vehicle Operators; Postmasters and Mail Superintendents; Railroad Conductors and Yardmasters; Storage and Distribution Managers; Transportation, Storage, and Distribution Managers. **PERSONALITY TYPE:** Enterprising. Enterprising occupations frequently involve starting up and carrying out projects. These occupations can involve leading people and making many decisions. They sometimes require risk taking and often deal with business.

EDUCATION/TRAINING PROGRAM(S)—Public Administration; Aeronautics/Aviation/Aerospace Science and Technology, General; Aviation/Airway Management and Operations; Business Administration and Management, General; Logistics and Materials Management; Transportation/Transportation Management. **RELATED KNOWLEDGE/COURSES—Transportation:** Principles and methods for moving people or goods by air, rail, sea, or road, including the relative costs and benefits. **Customer and Personal Service:** Principles and processes for providing customer and personal services. This includes customer needs assessment, meeting of quality standards for services, and evaluation of customer satisfaction. **Clerical Practices:** Administrative and clerical procedures and systems such as word processing, managing files and records, stenography and transcription, designing forms, and other office procedures and terminology. **Sales and Marketing:** Principles and methods for showing, promoting, and selling products or services. This includes marketing strategy and tactics, product demonstration, sales techniques, and sales control systems. **Administration and Management:** Business and management principles involved in strategic planning, resource allocation, human resources modeling, leadership technique, production methods, and coordination of people and resources. **Production and Processing:** Raw materials, production processes, quality control, costs, and other techniques for maximizing the effective manufacture and distribution of goods.

Transportation Vehicle, Equipment, and Systems Inspectors, Except Aviation

- Education/Training Required: Work experience in a related occupation
- Annual Earnings: $49,490
- Growth: 11.4%
- Annual Job Openings: 2,000
- Self-Employed: 1.9%
- Part-Time: 2.3%

The job openings listed here are shared with Aviation Inspectors and with Freight and Cargo Inspectors.

Inspect and monitor transportation equipment, vehicles, or systems to ensure compliance with regulations and safety standards. Investigate and make recommendations on carrier requests for waiver of federal standards. Prepare reports on investigations or inspections and actions taken. Examine carrier operating rules, employee qualification guidelines, and carrier training and testing programs for compliance with regulations or safety standards. Examine transportation vehicles, equipment, or systems to detect damage, wear, or malfunction. Inspect repairs to transportation vehicles and equipment to ensure that repair work was performed properly. Inspect vehicles or equipment to ensure compliance with rules, standards, or regulations. Investigate complaints regarding safety violations. Investigate inci-

dents or violations, such as delays, accidents, and equipment failures. Issue notices and recommend corrective actions when infractions or problems are found. Inspect vehicles and other equipment for evidence of abuse, damage, or mechanical malfunction. Conduct vehicle or transportation equipment tests, using diagnostic equipment.

SKILLS—Most Important: Quality Control Skills; Equipment Use/Maintenance Skills. **Other Above-Average Skills:** None met the criteria.

GOE—Interest Area: 07. Government and Public Administration. **Work Group:** 07.03. Regulations Enforcement. **Other Jobs in This Group:** Agricultural Inspectors; Aviation Inspectors; Compliance Officers, Except Agriculture, Construction, Health and Safety, and Transportation; Construction and Building Inspectors; Environmental Compliance Inspectors; Equal Opportunity Representatives and Officers; Financial Examiners; Fire Inspectors; Fish and Game Wardens; Forest Fire Inspectors and Prevention Specialists; Freight and Cargo Inspectors; Government Property Inspectors and Investigators; Immigration and Customs Inspectors; Licensing Examiners and Inspectors; Nuclear Monitoring Technicians; Occupational Health and Safety Specialists; Occupational Health and Safety Technicians; Tax Examiners, Collectors, and Revenue Agents. **PERSONALITY TYPE:** Realistic. Realistic occupations frequently involve work activities that include practical, hands-on problems and solutions. They often deal with plants, animals, and real-world materials like wood, tools, and machinery. Many of the occupations require working outside and do not involve a lot of paperwork or working closely with others.

EDUCATION/TRAINING PROGRAM(S)—No related CIP programs; this job is learned through work experience in a related occupation. **RELATED KNOWLEDGE/COURSES—Transportation:** Principles and methods for moving people or goods by air, rail, sea, or road, including the relative costs and benefits. **Public Safety and Security:** Relevant equipment, policies, procedures, and strategies to promote effective local, state, or national security operations for the protection of people, data, property, and institutions. **Mechanical Devices:** Machines and tools, including their designs, uses, repair, and maintenance.

Treasurers and Controllers

- Education/Training Required: Work experience plus degree
- Annual Earnings: $86,280
- Growth: 14.8%
- Annual Job Openings: 63,000
- Self-Employed: 3.2%
- Part-Time: 4.3%

The job openings listed here are shared with Financial Managers, Branch or Department.

Direct financial activities, such as planning, procurement, and investments, for all or part of an organization. Prepare and file annual tax returns or prepare financial information so that outside accountants can complete tax returns. Prepare or direct preparation of financial statements, business activity reports, financial position forecasts, annual budgets, and/or reports required by regulatory agencies. Supervise employees performing financial reporting, accounting, billing, collections, payroll, and budgeting duties. Delegate authority for the receipt, disbursement, banking, protection, and custody of funds, securities, and financial instruments. Maintain current knowledge of organizational policies and procedures, federal and state policies and directives, and current accounting standards. Conduct or coordinate audits of company accounts and financial transactions to ensure compliance with state and federal requirements and statutes. Receive and record requests for disbursements; authorize disbursements in accordance with policies and procedures. Monitor financial activities and details such as reserve levels to ensure that all legal and regulatory requirements are met. Monitor and evaluate the performance of accounting and other financial staff; recommend and implement personnel actions such as promotions and dismissals. Develop and maintain relationships with banking, insurance, and non-organizational accounting personnel in order to facilitate financial activities. Coordinate and direct the financial planning, budgeting, procurement, or investment activities of all or part of an organization. Develop internal control policies, guidelines, and procedures for activities such as budget administration, cash and credit management, and accounting. Analyze the financial details of past, present, and expected operations in order to identify development opportunities and areas where improvement is needed. Advise management on short-term and long-term financial objectives, policies, and actions. Provide direction and assistance to other organizational units regarding accounting and budgeting policies and procedures and efficient control and utilization of financial resources. Evaluate needs for procurement of funds and investment of surpluses and make appropriate recommendations.

SKILLS—Most Important: Management Skills; Mathematics Skills; Thought-Processing Skills. **Other Above-Average Skills:** Communication Skills; Social Skills.

GOE—Interest Area: 06. Finance and Insurance. **Work Group:** 06.01. Managerial Work in Finance and Insurance. **Other Jobs in This Group:** Financial Managers; Financial Managers, Branch or Department. **PERSONALITY TYPE:** Enterprising. Enterprising occupations frequently involve starting up and carrying out projects. These occupations can involve leading people and making many decisions. They sometimes require risk taking and often deal with business.

EDUCATION/TRAINING PROGRAM(S)—Accounting and Finance; Accounting and Business/Management; Finance, General; International Finance; Public Finance; Credit Management; Finance and Financial Management Services, Other. **RELATED KNOWLEDGE/COURSES—Economics and Accounting:** Economic and accounting principles and practices, the financial markets, banking, and the analysis and reporting of financial data. **Administration and Management:** Business and management principles involved in strategic planning, resource allocation, human resources modeling, leadership technique, production methods, and coordination of people and resources. **Personnel and Human Resources:** Principles and procedures for personnel recruitment, selection, training, compensation and benefits, labor relations and negotiation, and personnel information systems. **Law and Government:** Laws, legal codes, court procedures, precedents, government regulations, executive orders, agency rules, and the democratic political process. **English Language:** The structure and content of the English language, including the meaning and spelling of words, rules of composition, and grammar. **Mathematics:** Arithmetic, algebra, geometry, calculus, and statistics and their applications.

Truck Drivers, Heavy and Tractor-Trailer

- ◎ Education/Training Required: Moderate-term on-the-job training
- ◎ Annual Earnings: $34,280
- ◎ Growth: 12.9%
- ◎ Annual Job Openings: 274,000
- ◎ Self-Employed: 9.3%
- ◎ Part-Time: 9.1%

Drive a tractor-trailer combination or a truck with a capacity of at least 26,000 GVW to transport and deliver goods, livestock, or materials in liquid, loose, or packaged form. May be required to unload truck. May require use of automated routing equipment. Requires commercial drivers' license. Follow appropriate safety procedures when transporting dangerous goods. Check vehicles before driving them to ensure that mechanical, safety, and emergency equipment is in good working order. Maintain logs of working hours and of vehicle service and repair status, following applicable state and federal regulations. Obtain receipts or signatures when loads are delivered and collect payment for services when required. Check all load-related documentation to ensure that it is complete and accurate. Maneuver trucks into loading or unloading positions, following signals from loading crew as needed; check that vehicle position is correct and any special loading equipment is properly positioned. Drive trucks with capacities greater than 3 tons, including tractor-trailer combinations, to transport and deliver products, livestock, or other materials. Secure cargo for transport, using ropes, blocks, chain, binders, or covers. Read bills of lading to determine assignment details. Report vehicle defects, accidents, traffic violations, or damage to the vehicles. Read and interpret maps to determine vehicle routes. Couple and uncouple trailers by changing trailer jack positions, connecting or disconnecting air and electrical lines, and manipulating fifth-wheel locks. Collect delivery instructions from appropriate sources, verifying instructions and routes. Drive trucks to weigh stations before and after loading and along routes to document weights and to comply with state regulations. Operate equipment such as truck cab computers, CB radios, and telephones to exchange necessary information with bases, supervisors, or other drivers. Check conditions of trailers after contents have been unloaded to ensure that there has been no damage. Crank trailer landing gear up and down to safely secure vehicles. Wrap goods, using pads, packing paper, and containers, and secure loads to trailer walls, using straps. Perform basic vehicle maintenance tasks such as adding oil, fuel, and radiator fluid or performing minor repairs. Load and unload trucks or help others with loading and unloading, operating any special loading-related equipment on vehicles and using other equipment as necessary.

SKILLS—Most Important: Equipment Use/Maintenance Skills. **Other Above-Average Skills:** Mathematics Skills.

GOE—Interest Area: 16. Transportation, Distribution, and Logistics. **Work Group:** 16.03. Truck Driving. **Other Jobs in This Group:** Truck Drivers, Light or Delivery Services. **PERSONALITY TYPE:** Realistic. Realistic occupations frequently involve work activities that include practical, hands-on problems and solutions. They often deal with plants, animals, and real-world materials like wood, tools, and machinery. Many of the occupations require working outside and do not involve a lot of paperwork or working closely with others.

EDUCATION/TRAINING PROGRAM(S)—Truck and Bus Driver/Commercial Vehicle Operation. **RELATED KNOWLEDGE/COURSES—Transportation:** Principles and methods for moving people or goods by air, rail, sea, or road, including the relative costs and benefits. **Geography:** Principles and methods for describing the features of land, sea, and air masses, including their physical characteristics; locations; interrelationships; and distribution of plant, animal, and human life. **Public Safety and Security:** Relevant equipment, policies, procedures, and strategies to promote effective local, state, or national security operations for the protection of people, data, property, and institutions. **Law and Government:** Laws, legal codes, court procedures, precedents, government regulations, executive orders, agency rules, and the democratic political process. **Mechanical Devices:** Machines and tools, including their designs, uses, repair, and maintenance.

Veterinarians

- ◎ Education/Training Required: First professional degree
- ◎ Annual Earnings: $68,910
- ◎ Growth: 17.4%
- ◎ Annual Job Openings: 8,000
- ◎ Self-Employed: 20.7%
- ◎ Part-Time: 10.8%

Diagnose and treat diseases and dysfunctions of animals. May engage in a particular function, such as research and development, consultation, administration, technical writing, sale or production of commercial products, or rendering of technical services to commercial firms or other organizations. Includes veterinarians who inspect livestock. Examine animals to detect and determine the nature of diseases or injuries. Treat sick or injured animals by prescribing medication, setting bones, dressing wounds, or performing surgery. Inoculate animals against various diseases such as rabies and distemper. Collect body tissue, feces, blood, urine, or other body fluids for examination and analysis. Operate diagnostic equipment such as radiographic and ultrasound equipment and interpret the resulting images. Advise animal owners regarding sanitary measures, feeding, and general care necessary to promote health of animals. Educate the public about diseases that can be spread from animals to humans. Train and supervise workers who handle and care for animals. Provide care to a wide range of animals or specialize in a particular species, such as horses or exotic birds. Euthanize animals. Establish and conduct quarantine and testing procedures that prevent the spread of diseases to other animals or to humans and that comply with applicable government regulations. Conduct postmortem studies and analyses to determine the causes of animals' deaths. Perform administrative duties such as scheduling appointments, accepting payments from clients, and maintaining business records. Drive mobile clinic vans to farms so that health problems can be treated or prevented. Direct the overall operations of animal hospitals, clinics, or mobile services to farms. Specialize in a particular type of treatment such as dentistry, pathology, nutrition, surgery, microbiology, or internal medicine. Inspect and test horses, sheep, poultry, and other animals to detect the presence of communicable diseases.

Research diseases to which animals could be susceptible. Plan and execute animal nutrition and reproduction programs. Inspect animal housing facilities to determine their cleanliness and adequacy. Determine the effects of drug therapies, antibiotics, or new surgical techniques by testing them on animals.

SKILLS—Most Important: Science Skills; Management Skills; Thought-Processing Skills. **Other Above-Average Skills:** Social Skills; Communication Skills; Equipment Use/Maintenance Skills; Quality Control Skills.

GOE—Interest Area: 08. Health Science. **Work Group:** 08.05. Animal Care. **Other Jobs in This Group:** Animal Breeders; Animal Trainers; Nonfarm Animal Caretakers; Veterinary Assistants and Laboratory Animal Caretakers; Veterinary Technologists and Technicians. **PERSONALITY TYPE:** Investigative. Investigative occupations frequently involve working with ideas and require an extensive amount of thinking. These occupations can involve searching for facts and figuring out problems mentally.

EDUCATION/TRAINING PROGRAM(S)—Veterinary Medicine (DVM); Veterinary Sciences/Veterinary Clinical Sciences, General (Cert, MS, PhD); Veterinary Anatomy (Cert, MS, PhD); Veterinary Physiology (Cert, MS, PhD); Veterinary Microbiology and Immunobiology (Cert, MS, PhD); Veterinary Pathology and Pathobiology (Cert, MS, PhD); Veterinary Toxicology and Pharmacology (Cert, MS, PhD); Large Animal/Food Animal and Equine Surgery & Medicine (Cert, MS, PhD); others. **RELATED KNOWLEDGE/COURSES—Biology:** Plant and animal organisms and their tissues, cells, functions, interdependencies, and interactions with each other and the environment. **Medicine and Dentistry:** The information and techniques needed to diagnose and treat human injuries, diseases, and deformities. This includes symptoms, treatment alternatives, drug properties and interactions, and preventive healthcare measures. **Chemistry:** The chemical composition, structure, and properties of substances and of the chemical processes and transformations that they undergo. This includes uses of chemicals and their danger signs, production techniques, and disposal methods. **Therapy and Counseling:** Principles, methods, and procedures for diagnosis, treatment, and rehabilitation of physical and mental dysfunctions and for career counseling and guidance. **Customer and Personal Service:** Principles and processes for providing customer and personal services. This includes customer needs assessment, meeting of quality standards for services, and evaluation of customer satisfaction. **Sales and Marketing:** Principles and methods for showing, promoting, and selling products or services. This includes marketing strategy and tactics, product demonstration, sales techniques, and sales control systems.

Vocational Education Teachers, Postsecondary

- Education/Training Required: Work experience in a related occupation
- Annual Earnings: $41,750
- Growth: 32.2%
- Annual Job Openings: 329,000
- Self-Employed: 0.4%
- Part-Time: 27.3%

The job openings listed here are shared with 35 other postsecondary teaching occupations. For a complete list, see the beginning of this section.

Teach or instruct vocational or occupational subjects at the postsecondary level (but at less than the baccalaureate) to students who have graduated or left high school. Includes correspondence school instructors; industrial, commercial, and government training instructors; and adult education teachers and instructors who prepare persons to operate industrial machinery and equipment and transportation and communications equipment. Teaching may take place in public or private schools whose primary business is education or in a school associated with an organization whose primary business is other than education. Supervise and monitor students' use of tools and equipment. Observe and evaluate students' work to determine progress, provide feedback, and make suggestions for improvement. Present lectures and conduct discussions to increase students' knowledge and competence, using visual aids such as graphs, charts, videotapes, and slides. Administer oral, written, or performance tests to measure progress and to evaluate training effectiveness. Prepare reports and maintain records such as student grades, attendance rolls, and training activity details.

Supervise independent or group projects, field placements, laboratory work, or other training. Determine training needs of students or workers. Provide individualized instruction and tutorial or remedial instruction. Conduct on-the-job training, classes, or training sessions to teach and demonstrate principles, techniques, procedures, and methods of designated subjects. Develop curricula and plan course content and methods of instruction. Prepare outlines of instructional programs and training schedules and establish course goals. Integrate academic and vocational curricula so that students can obtain a variety of skills. Develop teaching aids such as instructional software, multimedia visual aids, or study materials. Select and assemble books, materials, supplies, and equipment for training, courses, or projects. Advise students on course selection, career decisions, and other academic and vocational concerns. Participate in conferences, seminars, and training sessions to keep abreast of developments in the field and integrate relevant information into training programs. Serve on faculty and school committees concerned with budgeting, curriculum revision, and course and diploma requirements. Review enrollment applications and correspond with applicants to obtain additional information. Arrange for lectures by experts in designated fields.

SKILLS—Most Important: Social Skills; Thought-Processing Skills; Communication Skills. **Other Above-Average Skills:** Management Skills; Science Skills; Equipment Use/Maintenance Skills; Quality Control Skills.

GOE—Interest Area: 05. Education and Training. **Work Group:** 05.03. Postsecondary and Adult Teaching and Instructing. **Other Jobs in This Group:** Adult Literacy, Remedial Education, and GED Teachers and Instructors; Agricultural Sciences Teachers, Postsecondary; Anthropology and Archeology Teachers, Postsecondary; Architecture Teachers, Postsecondary; Area, Ethnic, and Cultural Studies Teachers, Postsecondary; Art, Drama, and Music Teachers, Postsecondary; Atmospheric, Earth, Marine, and Space Sciences Teachers, Postsecondary; Biological Science Teachers, Postsecondary; Business Teachers, Postsecondary; Chemistry Teachers, Postsecondary; Communications Teachers, Postsecondary; Computer Science Teachers, Postsecondary; Criminal Justice and Law Enforcement Teachers, Postsecondary; Economics Teachers, Postsecondary; Education Teachers, Postsecondary; Engineering Teachers, Postsecondary; English

Language and Literature Teachers, Postsecondary; Environmental Science Teachers, Postsecondary; Farm and Home Management Advisors; Foreign Language and Literature Teachers, Postsecondary; Forestry and Conservation Science Teachers, Postsecondary; Geography Teachers, Postsecondary; Graduate Teaching Assistants; Health Specialties Teachers, Postsecondary; History Teachers, Postsecondary; Home Economics Teachers, Postsecondary; Law Teachers, Postsecondary; Library Science Teachers, Postsecondary; Mathematical Science Teachers, Postsecondary; Nursing Instructors and Teachers, Postsecondary; Philosophy and Religion Teachers, Postsecondary; Physics Teachers, Postsecondary; Political Science Teachers, Postsecondary; Psychology Teachers, Postsecondary; Recreation and Fitness Studies Teachers, Postsecondary; Self-Enrichment Education Teachers; Social Work Teachers, Postsecondary; Sociology Teachers, Postsecondary. **PERSONALITY TYPE:** Social. Social occupations frequently involve working with, communicating with, and teaching people. These occupations often involve helping or providing service to others.

EDUCATION/TRAINING PROGRAM(S)—Agricultural Teacher Education; Business Teacher Education; Technology Teacher Education/Industrial Arts Teacher Education; Sales and Marketing Operations/Marketing and Distribution Teacher Education; Technical Teacher Education; Trade and Industrial Teacher Education; Health Occupations Teacher Education; Teacher Education and Professional Development, Specific Subject Areas, Other. **RELATED KNOWLEDGE/COURSES—Education and Training:** Principles and methods for curriculum and training design, teaching and instruction for individuals and groups, and the measurement of training effects. **Psychology:** Human behavior and performance; individual differences in ability, personality, and interests; learning and motivation; psychological research methods; and the assessment and treatment of behavioral and affective disorders. **Therapy and Counseling:** Principles, methods, and procedures for diagnosis, treatment, and rehabilitation of physical and mental dysfunctions and for career counseling and guidance. **Computers and Electronics:** Circuit boards; processors; chips; electronic equipment; and computer hardware and software, including applications and programming. **Sales and Marketing:** Principles and methods for showing, promoting, and selling products or services. This includes marketing strategy and tactics, product demon-

stration, sales techniques, and sales control systems. **Design:** Design techniques, tools, and principles involved in production of precision technical plans, blueprints, drawings, and models.

Wholesale and Retail Buyers, Except Farm Products

- ◎ Education/Training Required: Work experience in a related occupation
- ◎ Annual Earnings: $42,870
- ◎ Growth: 8.4%
- ◎ Annual Job Openings: 20,000
- ◎ Self-Employed: 10.9%
- ◎ Part-Time: 18.4%

Buy merchandise or commodities, other than farm products, for resale to consumers at the wholesale or retail level, including both durable and nondurable goods. Analyze past buying trends, sales records, price, and quality of merchandise to determine value and yield. Select, order, and authorize payment for merchandise according to contractual agreements. May conduct meetings with sales personnel and introduce new products. Examine, select, order, and purchase at the most favorable price merchandise consistent with quality, quantity, specification requirements, and other factors. Negotiate prices, discount terms, and transportation arrangements for merchandise. Analyze and monitor sales records, trends, and economic conditions to anticipate consumer buying patterns and determine what the company will sell and how much inventory is needed. Interview and work closely with vendors to obtain and develop desired products. Authorize payment of invoices or return of merchandise. Inspect merchandise or products to determine value or yield. Set or recommend markup rates, markdown rates, and selling prices for merchandise. Confer with sales and purchasing personnel to obtain information about customer needs and preferences. Consult with store or merchandise managers about budget and goods to be purchased. Conduct staff meetings with sales personnel to introduce new merchandise. Manage the department for which they buy. Use computers to organize and locate inventory and operate spreadsheet and word processing software. Provide clerks with information to print on price tags, such as price, markups or markdowns, manufacturer number, season code, and style number. Train and supervise sales and clerical staff. Determine which products should be featured in advertising, the advertising medium to be used, and when the ads should be run. Monitor competitors' sales activities by following their advertisements in newspapers and other media.

SKILLS—Most Important: Management Skills; Quality Control Skills; Mathematics Skills. **Other Above-Average Skills:** Social Skills; Equipment/Technology Analysis Skills.

GOE—Interest Area: 14. Retail and Wholesale Sales and Service. **Work Group:** 14.05. Purchasing. **Other Jobs in This Group:** Purchasing Agents, Except Wholesale, Retail, and Farm Products. **PERSONALITY TYPE:** Enterprising. Enterprising occupations frequently involve starting up and carrying out projects. These occupations can involve leading people and making many decisions. They sometimes require risk taking and often deal with business.

EDUCATION/TRAINING PROGRAM(S)—Apparel and Textile Marketing Management; Sales, Distribution, and Marketing Operations, General; Merchandising and Buying Operations; Fashion Merchandising; Apparel and Accessories Marketing Operations. **RELATED KNOWLEDGE/COURSES—Sales and Marketing:** Principles and methods for showing, promoting, and selling products or services. This includes marketing strategy and tactics, product demonstration, sales techniques, and sales control systems. **Economics and Accounting:** Economic and accounting principles and practices, the financial markets, banking, and the analysis and reporting of financial data. **Clerical Practices:** Administrative and clerical procedures and systems such as word processing, managing files and records, stenography and transcription, designing forms, and other office procedures and terminology. **Customer and Personal Service:** Principles and processes for providing customer and personal services. This includes customer needs assessment, meeting of quality standards for services, and evaluation of customer satisfaction. **Administration and Management:** Business and management principles involved in strategic planning, resource allocation, human resources modeling, leadership technique, production methods, and coordination of people and resources. **Transportation:** Principles and methods for moving people or goods by air, rail, sea, or road, including the relative costs and benefits.

APPENDIX A

Resources for Further Exploration

The facts and pointers in this book provide a good beginning to the subject of jobs that make use of your top skills. If you want additional details, we suggest you consult some of the resources listed here.

Facts About Careers

The *Occupational Outlook Handbook* (or the *OOH*) (JIST): Updated every two years by the U.S. Department of Labor, this book provides descriptions for almost 270 major jobs covering more than 85 percent of the workforce.

The *Enhanced Occupational Outlook Handbook* (JIST): Includes all descriptions in the *OOH* plus descriptions of more than 6,300 more-specialized jobs related to them.

The *O*NET Dictionary of Occupational Titles* (JIST): The only printed source of the nearly 950 jobs described in the U.S. Department of Labor's Occupational Information Network database. It covers all the jobs in the book you're now reading, but it offers more topics than we were able to fit here.

The *New Guide for Occupational Exploration* (JIST): An important career reference that allows you to explore all major O*NET jobs based on your interests.

Career Decision Making and Planning

Overnight Career Choice, by Michael Farr, America's Career Expert (JIST): This book can help you choose a career goal based on a variety of criteria, including skills, interests, and values. It is part of the *Help in a Hurry* series, so it is designed to produce quick results.

50 Best Jobs for Your Personality, by Michael Farr, America's Career Expert, and Laurence Shatkin, Ph.D. (JIST): Built around the six Holland personality types, this book includes an assessment to help you identify your dominant and secondary personality types, plus lists and descriptions of high-paying and high-growth civilian jobs linked to those personality types.

Job Hunting

Same-Day Resume, by Michael Farr, America's Career Expert (JIST): Learn how to write an effective resume in an hour. This book includes dozens of sample resumes from professional writers and even offers advice on cover letters, online resumes, and more.

Seven-Step Job Search, by Michael Farr, America's Career Expert (JIST): In seven easy steps, learn what it takes to land the right job fast. Quick worksheets will help you identify your skills, define your ideal job, use the most effective job search methods, write a superior resume, organize your time to get two interviews a day, dramatically improve your interviewing skills, and follow up on all job leads effectively.

Job Banks by Occupation. This is a set of links offered by America's Career InfoNet. At www.acinet.org, find the Career Tools box, click Career Resource Library, and then click Job & Resume Banks. The Job Banks by Occupation link leads you to groups of jobs such as "Healthcare Practitioners and Technical Occupations" and "Legal Occupations," which in turn lead you to more specific job titles and occupation-specific job-listing sites maintained by various organizations.

APPENDIX B

The GOE Interest Areas and Work Groups

A s Part I explains, the GOE is a way of organizing the world of work into large interest areas and more-specific work groups containing jobs that have a lot in common. Part III defines the 16 GOE interest areas, but Part IV also lists the work groups for each job described. We thought you would want to see the complete GOE taxonomy so you would understand how any job that interests you fits into this structure.

Interest areas have two-digit code numbers; work groups have four-digit code numbers beginning with the code number for the interest area in which they are classified. These are the 16 GOE interest areas and work groups:

01 Agriculture and Natural Resources

>01.01 Managerial Work in Agriculture and Natural Resources

>01.02 Resource Science/Engineering for Plants, Animals, and the Environment

>01.03 Resource Technologies for Plants, Animals, and the Environment

>01.04 General Farming

>01.05 Nursery, Groundskeeping, and Pest Control

>01.06 Forestry and Logging

>01.07 Hunting and Fishing

>01.08 Mining and Drilling

02 Architecture and Construction

>02.01 Managerial Work in Architecture and Construction

>02.02 Architectural Design

>02.03 Architecture/Construction Engineering Technologies

>02.04 Construction Crafts

>02.05 Systems and Equipment Installation, Maintenance, and Repair

>02.06 Construction Support/Labor

03 Arts and Communication

    03.01 Managerial Work in Arts and Communication

    03.02 Writing and Editing

    03.03 News, Broadcasting, and Public Relations

    03.04 Studio Art

    03.05 Design

    03.06 Drama

    03.07 Music

    03.08 Dance

    03.09 Media Technology

    03.10 Communications Technology

    03.11 Musical Instrument Repair

04 Business and Administration

    04.01 Managerial Work in General Business

    04.02 Managerial Work in Business Detail

    04.03 Human Resources Support

    04.04 Secretarial Support

    04.05 Accounting, Auditing, and Analytical Support

    04.06 Mathematical Clerical Support

    04.07 Records and Materials Processing

    04.08 Clerical Machine Operation

05 Education and Training

    05.01 Managerial Work in Education

    05.02 Preschool, Elementary, and Secondary Teaching and Instructing

    05.03 Postsecondary and Adult Teaching and Instructing

    05.04 Library Services

    05.05 Archival and Museum Services

    05.06 Counseling, Health, and Fitness Education

06 Finance and Insurance

    06.01 Managerial Work in Finance and Insurance

    06.02 Finance/Insurance Investigation and Analysis

    06.03 Finance/Insurance Records Processing

    06.04 Finance/Insurance Customer Service

    06.05 Finance/Insurance Sales and Support

07 Government and Public Administration

   07.01 Managerial Work in Government and Public Administration

   07.02 Public Planning

   07.03 Regulations Enforcement

   07.04 Public Administration Clerical Support

08 Health Science

   08.01 Managerial Work in Medical and Health Services

   08.02 Medicine and Surgery

   08.03 Dentistry

   08.04 Health Specialties

   08.05 Animal Care

   08.06 Medical Technology

   08.07 Medical Therapy

   08.08 Patient Care and Assistance

   08.09 Health Protection and Promotion

09 Hospitality, Tourism, and Recreation

   09.01 Managerial Work in Hospitality and Tourism

   09.02 Recreational Services

   09.03 Hospitality and Travel Services

   09.04 Food and Beverage Preparation

   09.05 Food and Beverage Service

   09.06 Sports

   09.07 Barber and Beauty Services

10 Human Service

   10.01 Counseling and Social Work

   10.02 Religious Work

   10.03 Child/Personal Care and Services

   10.04 Client Interviewing

11 Information Technology

   11.01 Managerial Work in Information Technology

   11.02 Information Technology Specialties

   11.03 Digital Equipment Repair

12 Law and Public Safety

  12.01 Managerial Work in Law and Public Safety

  12.02 Legal Practice and Justice Administration

  12.03 Legal Support

  12.04 Law Enforcement and Public Safety

  12.05 Safety and Security

  12.06 Emergency Responding

  12.07 Military

13 Manufacturing

  13.01 Managerial Work in Manufacturing

  13.02 Machine Setup and Operation

  13.03 Production Work, Assorted Materials Processing

  13.04 Welding, Brazing, and Soldering

  13.05 Production Machining Technology

  13.06 Production Precision Work

  13.07 Production Quality Control

  13.08 Graphic Arts Production

  13.09 Hands-On Work, Assorted Materials

  13.10 Woodworking Technology

  13.11 Apparel, Shoes, Leather, and Fabric Care

  13.12 Electrical and Electronic Repair

  13.13 Machinery Repair

  13.14 Vehicle and Facility Mechanical Work

  13.15 Medical and Technical Equipment Repair

  13.16 Utility Operation and Energy Distribution

  13.17 Loading, Moving, Hoisting, and Conveying

14 Retail and Wholesale Sales and Service

  14.01 Managerial Work in Retail/Wholesale Sales and Service

  14.02 Technical Sales

  14.03 General Sales

  14.04 Personal Soliciting

  14.05 Purchasing

  14.06 Customer Service

Index

T